FITCHBURG PUBLIC LIBRARY
P9-CDX-882

Reference Sources *for* Small *and* Medium-sized Libraries

WITHDRAWN

SIXTH EDITION

Scott E. Kennedy
Editor

COMPILED BY
Reference Sources for Small and Medium-sized
Libraries Editorial Committee
Collection Development and Evaluation Section
Reference and User Services Association

American Library Association
Chicago and London 1999

Ref.
025.5
R332rf6

While extensive effort has gone into ensuring the reliability of information appearing in this book, the publisher makes no warranty, express or implied, on the accuracy or reliability of the information, and does not assume and hereby disclaims any liability to any person for any loss or damage caused by errors or omissions in this publication.

Project editor, Eloise L. Kinney

Text and cover design by Dianne M. Rooney

Composition by the dotted i in Berkeley and Fenice, using QuarkXPress 3.32 on a Macintosh G3

Printed on 50-pound white offset, a pH-neutral stock, and bound in 10-point coated cover stock by Data Reproductions

The paper used in this publication meets the minimum requirements of American National Standard for Information Sciences—Permanence of Paper for Printed Library Materials, ANSI Z39.48-1992. ♾

Library of Congress Cataloging-in-Publication Data

Reference sources for small and medium-sized libraries / Scott E. Kennedy, editor. — 6th ed. / compiled by Reference Sources for Small and Medium-sized Libraries Editorial Committee, Collection Development and Evaluation Section, Reference and User Services Association.
p. cm.
Includes index.
ISBN 0-8389-3468-4
1. Reference books—Bibliography. 2. Small libraries—United States—Book lists. I. Kennedy, Scott, 1952– II. Reference and User Services Association. Reference Sources for Small and Medium-sized Libraries Editorial Committee.
Z1035.1.A47 1999
011′.02—dc21 98-52880
Rev.

Copyright © 1999 by the American Library Association. All rights reserved except those which may be granted by Sections 107 and 108 of the Copyright Revision Act of 1976.

Printed in the United States of America.

03 02 01 00 99 5 4 3 2 1

Bro 2/00 $60.

The sixth edition of *Reference Sources for Small and Medium-sized Libraries* was compiled by the Reference Sources for Small and Medium-sized Libraries Editorial Committee under the direction of the American Library Association's Reference and User Services Association (RUSA).

Committee Members

Scott E. Kennedy, Chair
Head, Research and Information Services
University of Connecticut Libraries
Storrs, Connecticut

Susan C. Awe
Assistant Director for Business and Economics
Parish Memorial Library, University of New Mexico
Albuquerque, New Mexico

Barbara M. Bibel
Reference Librarian
Science–Social Science–Documents Department, Oakland Public Library
Oakland, California

Carole Dyal
Library Conservator
University of Connecticut Libraries
Storrs, Connecticut

Betsy Hoagg
Reference Librarian
University of Connecticut Libraries
Storrs, Connecticut

Donald W. Maxwell
Reference Librarian
Indiana Cooperative Library Services Authority
Bloomington, Indiana

Carolyn M. Mulac
Assistant Unit Head, Information Center
Harold Washington Library Center, Chicago Public Library
Chicago, Illinois

Jack O'Gorman
Electronic Reference Services Librarian
Steely Library, Northern Kentucky University
Highland Heights, Kentucky

Deborah L. Thomas
Head of Circulation Services
University of Tennessee
Knoxville, Tennessee

This work benefited from the expert advice of Marlene R. Chamberlain of ALA Editions and David Epstein, formerly with ALA Editions; from the guidance and kind support of RUSA's former Deputy Executive Director, Michael Dowling; and, most especially, from the tireless and boundless enthusiasm of our publication Project Editor, Eloise L. Kinney.

CONTENTS

PREFACE xvii

1 Selection Aids for Reference Materials 1

Books 1
Periodicals 5

2 Bibliographies and General Sources 7

Bibliographies and Guides 7
- Selection Aids for Various Reader Groups 7
- In-print Sources 9
- National Bibliographies (United States) 11
- Serials and Periodicals 12

Directories 13
- Guides 13
- Persons and Organizations: Phones, Faxes, and Zip Codes 13
- Libraries 15
- Publishers and Booksellers 15
- Serials and Periodicals 16

Fact Books and Almanacs 17
Indexes and Abstracts 18
- General 18
- Newspapers 19
- Periodicals 19
- Reviews 20

Government Publications 21

3 Encyclopedias 24

Guides 24
Encyclopedias 25

4 Philosophy, Religion, and Ethics 28
Philosophy 28
Bibliographies and Guides 28
Indexes and Abstracts 28
Dictionaries and Encyclopedias 29
Biographical Sources 30
Religion 30
General 30
Bibliographies and Guides 30
Indexes and Abstracts 30
Dictionaries and Encyclopedias 30
Bible 31
Indexes and Abstracts 31
Atlases 31
Commentaries 32
Concordances 32
Dictionaries and Encyclopedias 32
Handbooks 33
Religion in the United States 33
Dictionaries and Encyclopedias 33
Directories 34
Statistical Sources 34
Biographical Sources 34
Christianity 35
Dictionaries and Encyclopedias 35
Directories, Yearbooks, and Almanacs 36
Biographical Sources 37
Judaism 37
Other Living Religions 39
Mythology, Folklore, Witchcraft, and Superstition 41
Ethics 43
Bibliographies and Guides 43
Dictionaries and Encyclopedias 43

5 Psychology, Psychiatry, and Occult Sciences 44
Psychology and Psychiatry 44
Bibliographies and Guides 44
Indexes and Abstracts 44
Dictionaries and Encyclopedias 44
Handbooks 46
Testing and Measurement 46
Occult Sciences 47

6 Social Sciences (General), Sociology, and Anthropology 49

Social Sciences (General) 49
- Indexes and Abstracts 49
- Dictionaries and Encyclopedias 50
- Handbooks, Yearbooks, and Almanacs 50

Sociology 51
- Bibliographies and Guides 51
- Dictionaries and Encyclopedias 51
- Aging 52
- Alcoholism and Drug Abuse 53
- Children and Youth 53
- Criminology 54
- Ethnic Studies 55
  - General 55
  - African Americans 56
  - Asian Americans 58
  - Hispanic Americans 58
  - Native Peoples of North America 59
- Social Service and Philanthropy 60
- Statistics and Demography 62
- Urban Affairs 64
- Women's Studies 64

Anthropology and Archaeology 65
- Atlases 65
- Dictionaries and Encyclopedias 66
- Handbooks 67

7 Business and Careers 68

Bibliographies and Guides 68
Indexes and Abstracts 69
Dictionaries and Encyclopedias 70
Directories 71
Handbooks, Yearbooks, and Almanacs 75
- Accounting 77
- Banking and Finance 78
- Insurance 79
- Investments 79
- Management 82
- Marketing and Sales 82
- Real Estate 83
- Secretarial Handbooks 83
- Taxes 83

Biographical Sources 84
Careers and Vocational Guidance 84

8 Political Science and Law 86
Bibliographies and Guides 86
Indexes and Abstracts 87
Dictionaries and Encyclopedias 87
Handbooks, Yearbooks, and Almanacs 90
Directories 92
Biographical Sources 93
Legal and Political Documents 94
Elections and Campaigns 95
Federal Executive Branch Sources 96
Federal Judicial Branch Sources 97
Federal Legislative Branch Sources 98

9 Education 101
Bibliographies and Guides 101
General 101
Media and Curriculum Materials 102
Indexes and Abstracts 103
Dictionaries and Encyclopedias 103
Directories 104
School and College Directories 106
Handbooks, Yearbooks, and Almanacs 111
Statistical Sources 111
Biographical Sources 112

10 Words and Language 113
General 113
Bibliographies and Guides 113
Encyclopedias, Companions, and Atlases 114
English Language 114
Bibliographies and Guides 114
Encyclopedias and Companions 115
Dictionaries 115
Principal English-Language Dictionaries 115
Desk Dictionaries 116
Abbreviations and Acronyms 116
Crossword Puzzle Dictionaries 117
Etymology and Word and Phrase Origins 117
Foreign Words and Phrases Used in the English Language 118
Idioms and Usage Dictionaries 118

Pronunciation Dictionaries 119
Rhyming Dictionaries 119
Sign Language Dictionaries 119
Similes, Metaphors, and Clichés 120
Slang and Euphemisms 120
Thesauri: Synonyms, Antonyms, and Homonyms 121
Style Manuals 122
Foreign-Language Dictionaries 124
Bibliographies and Guides 124
Chinese 124
French 124
German 125
Greek 126
Hebrew 126
Italian 126
Japanese 126
Latin 127
Russian 127
Spanish 127

11 Science and Technology 129
General 129
Bibliographies and Guides 129
Indexes and Abstracts 130
Dictionaries and Encyclopedias 130
Handbooks, Yearbooks, and Almanacs 132
Biographical Sources 132
History of Science 133
Agriculture 134
Gardening 135
Astronomy 137
Chemistry 138
Bibliographies and Guides 138
Dictionaries and Encyclopedias 138
Handbooks, Yearbooks, and Almanacs 139
Biographical Sources 140
Computer Science 141
Indexes and Abstracts 141
Dictionaries and Encyclopedias 141
Directories 142
Internet 143
Earth Sciences 143
Geology 144
Meteorology 144
Oceanography 145

Energy 145
Engineering 146
Aerospace and Aeronautics 146
Electronics and Electrical Engineering 147
Mechanical and Civil Engineering 149
Environment 149
Life Sciences 152
Biology 152
Botany 153
Paleontology—Dinosaurs 153
Zoology 154
Manufacturing 155
Mathematics 156
Physics 157
Transportation 158
Vehicular Maintenance and Repair 158
Weapons and Warfare 159

12 Health and Medicine 160

General 160
Bibliographies and Guides 160
Indexes and Abstracts 161
Dictionaries and Encyclopedias 161
Directories 163
Handbooks, Statistics, and Diagnosis 164
AIDS 166
Alternative Health Care 167
Anatomy and Physiology 168
Cancer 168
Children's Health 169
Drugs 169
Nutrition and Diet 170
Physical Impairments 171
Women's Health 171

13 Household 173

Beverages, Cooking, and Foods 173
Beverages 173
Cooking 174
Foods 176
Calendars, Festivals, and Holidays 176
Calendars 176
Festivals and Holidays 177

Consumer Affairs 177
Etiquette 178
Home Maintenance 179
Construction 179
Home Improvement 180
Housekeeping 180
Interior Decoration 181
Maintenance and Repair 181
Tools 182
Parenting 183
Pets 184
Birds 184
Cats 184
Dogs 185
Fish 185
Horses 186
Reptiles and Amphibians 186
Unusual Pets 186

14 Visual Arts 188
Bibliographies and Guides 188
Indexes and Abstracts 189
Indexes to Reproductions and Illustrations 189
Dictionaries and Encyclopedias 190
Directories 193
Handbooks 194
Biographical Sources 194
Architecture 194
Ceramics 196
Costume 196
Decorative Arts and Design 197
Photography 199

15 Performing Arts 201
General Sources 201
Bibliographies and Guides 201
Indexes and Abstracts 201
Directories 202
Biographical Sources 202
Awards 202
Dance 203
Film and Video 204
Indexes 204

Dictionaries and Encyclopedias 204
Directories 206
Handbooks 207
Biographical Sources 208
Television, Radio, and Telecommunications 208
Dictionaries and Encyclopedias 208
Directories 209
Handbooks 210
Theater 210
Bibliographies and Guides 210
Indexes 210
Dictionaries and Encyclopedias 212
Handbooks 213

16 Music 214
General Sources 214
Bibliographies and Discographies 214
Indexes 215
Dictionaries and Encyclopedias 215
Directories 217
Handbooks 217
Biographical Sources 218
Classical Music 218
Discographies 218
Indexes 218
Dictionaries and Encyclopedias 219
Handbooks 219
Biographical Sources 220
Nonclassical Music 220
Bibliographies and Discographies 220
Dictionaries and Encyclopedias 221
Biographical Sources 221
Songs 221
Blues 223
Country and Folk 224
Jazz 224
Rock 225

17 Crafts and Hobbies 226
Indexes 226
Handbooks 227
Crafts 227
Beading 227

Embroidery 227
Knitting 228
Quilts 228
Sewing 229
Woodworking 230
Hobbies 230
Antiques and Collectibles 230
Coins and Paper Money 231
Stamps 232

18 Games and Sports 234

Guides 234
Indexes 234
Encyclopedias 235
History 235
Rules 235
Sports Science 235
Directories 236
Handbooks and Almanacs 236
Atlases 237
Biographical Sources 237
Video Guides 238
Backpacking 238
Baseball 238
Basketball 240
Bicycling 241
Billiards and Pool 241
Card Games 241
Chess 242
Exercise 242
Fishing 242
Football 243
Gambling 243
Golf 243
Hiking 244
Hockey 244
Martial Arts 245
Olympics 245
Recreational Games 245
Rock Climbing and Mountaineering 246
Running 246
Sailing 247
Soccer 247
Swimming 247

Tennis 247
Wilderness Training 248

19 Literature 249

General Works 249
Bibliographies and Guides 249
Indexes and Abstracts 250
Encyclopedias 250
Handbooks 251
Digests 251
Literary Characters 252
Literary Prizes 252
Quotations 252
Proverbs 253
Multivolume Criticism 254
Biography 254
Special Interest 256
Black American Literature 256
Gay and Lesbian Literature 257
Women's Literature 257
Specific Genres 258
Children's Literature 258
Prizes and Awards 260
Drama 261
Fiction 261
Novel 262
Mystery 262
Romance 263
Science Fiction, Fantasy, and the Gothic 263
Short Story 264
Poetry 265
Speech and Rhetoric 266
National and Regional Literatures 267
American 267
Arabic 269
British 269
Shakespeare 270
Classical 271
Latin American 272
African 273
Australian 273
Canadian 273
Chinese 273
French 273

German 274
Irish 274
Italian 274
Japanese 274
Russian 275
Spanish 275

20 History 276
Bibliographies and Guides 276
Indexes and Abstracts 277
Chronologies 277
Dictionaries and Encyclopedias 278
Directories 283
Handbooks, Yearbooks, and Almanacs 283
Primary Sources 284
Historical Atlases 285
Biographical Sources 286

21 Geography, Area Studies, and Travel 287
Dictionaries, Encyclopedias, and Gazetteers 287
Handbooks, Yearbooks, and Almanacs 290
Atlases 291
Bibliographies and Guides 291
World 292
Regional 292
United States 293
Travel Guides 294

22 Biography, Genealogy, and Names 296
Biographical Sources 296
Indexes 296
Collective Biography 297
Genealogy 299
Bibliographies and Guides 299
Indexes and Abstracts 301
Directories 301
Handbooks, Yearbooks, and Almanacs 302
Heraldry 303
Names 303

Index 307

PREFACE

The sixth edition of *Reference Sources for Small and Medium-sized Libraries* is the latest version of a work that first appeared in 1969 under the title *Reference Books for Small and Medium-sized Public Libraries.* Its purpose was and is to serve as "an authoritative buying guide for the purchase of reference collections for newly established libraries and for improving and expanding existing collections." Each subsequent edition, 1973, 1979, 1984, and 1992, has attempted to define a basic collection of sources for the general reference library, but each has used a slightly different set of criteria for inclusion. The second edition dropped the word *Public* from the title, allowing that the guide had applicability to college as well as public library collections; the third edition firmly established the academic library as a coequal player and modified the selection profile accordingly; the fourth edition changed the focus from *Books* to *Sources,* officially recognizing alternative formats; the fourth edition also began to record the disappearance of standard titles, titles regarded as vital to the general collection but no longer in print; the fifth edition focused on recording the appearance of important newer works and included, for the first time, reference works aimed at children and young adults; as a result, the number of new titles presented in the fifth edition approached 75 percent of the total. The present work has attempted to steer a middle course, reverting, for the sake of depth, to the classic profile of the third edition yet retaining, for the sake of modernity, the contemporary focus of the fifth.

Scope of the Sixth Edition

The sixth edition of *Reference Sources for Small and Medium-sized Libraries* aims to serve two functions: (1) to present a descriptive guide to standard time-tested reference sources that can be used to build or augment a basic general reference collection and (2) to highlight the very best of the new reference sources that have appeared over the past five or so years. The intention is to produce a list of significant reference titles that almost any public or academic library would want to consider for the reference collection. Excluded from consideration are pamphlets, reference works of purely local scope, highly specialized works, foreign-language publications, and works created specifically for children or young adults.

The State of Reference Publishing

To those engaged in collection building, there is no doubt that we are in the midst of a remarkably creative period in the world of reference publishing. Though it has proven to be a volatile age for the printed page in general, the past decade has spawned an unprecedented number of scholarly, yet approachable and truly captivating, reference titles. Although this renaissance in reference publishing is clearly traceable to the raw energy unleashed by computer technologies, real credit must also be given to those in the reference publishing world who have elected to work closely with librarians and other information professionals to explore new regions of intellectual culture, develop new standards of excellence, and formulate ever higher expectations for the works they bring into existence.

Ten years ago, were one to select a single reference tool to bring away to a desert island, it would likely have been a standard multivolume encyclopedia such as the *Encyclopaedia Britannica;* five years ago, one might have chosen a LEXIS-NEXIS account; today, there is little doubt that the single most valuable tool for the reference librarian is the vast and unpredictable arena of the Internet. Given this context, it will perhaps seem ironic that the editors of this latest edition of fundamental reference sources chose to include not a single Internet site among the entries. There were two basic reasons for this editorial decision: the guide is meant to identify items that can be acquired and retained; and the guide is meant to identify items that remain stable over time. The Internet, for all its splendor, is neither stable nor consistent—nor would one wish it to be. However, there are strong indications that large, internally consistent mega-reference sites will soon be emerging. Gale's proposed *Literature Resource Center*—combining biography, bibliography, secondary criticism, plot summary and analysis, commentary, primary research material, related works, and dynamic Internet hyperlinks for hundreds of standard literary works—embodies the image of one such mega-reference site; the federal government's *GPO Access,* another. At the time of this writing, however, both the *Literature Resource Center* and *GPO Access* are still in the early stages of development.

Selecting the Sources for Inclusion

Responsibility for surveying the specific content areas described in this work was assigned to the individual chapter editors in 1994. Editors were selected based upon their expertise in reference sources and their individual expertise in specific subject areas. It is the chapter editors who performed the long hours of work required to review the many potential candidates for inclusion and who prepared, for each editorial meeting, focused, yet representative, selections of the best reference sources available on the market. The sources selected were brought forward on a continuous basis by each chapter editor for validation by the editorial team as a whole. The final selection reflects the collective experience of a plurality of public and academic librarians serving culturally diverse and geographically distinct user communities; it reflects a snapshot in time of their joint recommendations on the most pragmatic reference works available for small to medium-sized academic and public libraries. All individual chapter editors had submitted their final selections to the general editor by the end of 1996. However, additional entries continued to be incorporated into all chapters of the text until March 1998, when copy for this edition was closed. The final choice for inclusion and omission, and responsibility for all error, rests with the general editor.

Form and Presentation

With regard to the form and presentation of the selection, the present effort resides comfortably upon the shoulders of our bibliographic predecessors and the experts at ALA Editions; however, certain features—such as Dewey and Library of Congress (LC) call numbers and alternative format icons—are innovations devised by the current editorial team and are included here for the first time. As is the tradition of this work, a number of standard entries have been carried forward from the preceding edition, revised and updated as appropriate. The current editors wish to acknowledge not only their indebtedness to their predecessors, but also to the host of unsung collaborators who regularly publish reference book reviews in such sources as *Booklist, Choice, Library Journal,* and *Reference and User Services Quarterly.* Their collective effort, more than any other single factor, ensures that compilations such as this remain reliable, authoritative, and complete. It should also be noted in this context that the many reference publishers contacted during the preparation of this text were more than generous in supplying review copies upon request; this generosity saved not only time and energy, but also reduced, by at least a score, the number of journeys each chapter editor had to make to various holding libraries far and wide.

Keeping Up-to-Date

Excellent new works have appeared since March 1998, when copy for this edition was closed, and many others will appear in succeeding years until a new edition is brought forth. Those intending to use this work to build or augment their reference collections will want to keep in mind that, in this age of instant digitization, new updated editions of popular works are likely to be released after relatively short intervals. It is also important to remember that paper editions often become available at the same time as, or but a few months after, the hard-cover version appears. As time passes, it is always wise to request the *latest edition* when placing an order, as opposed to the specific edition described in this work. Publishers' web sites and the sites of electronic bookstores such as www.amazon.com and www.barnesandnoble.com will be helpful in identifying the price, ISBN, and format of the most recent editions.

Those wishing to keep up-to-date with the best of the new reference sources are encouraged to adopt some of the methods used by the editors of this work: (1) consult the latest editions of the selection aids for reference materials listed in chapter 1 of this book and, in particular, the periodicals such as *Booklist, Choice, Library Journal,* and *Reference and User Services Quarterly;* all these reviewing periodicals publish annual annotated lists of "best reference sources," which have proven to be both convenient and reliable; (2) visit libraries larger than one's own and review their collection choices; (3) consult reference specialists, either in person or via electronic discussion or distribution lists; (4) attend the regular open review sessions of such groups as the American Library Association's Reference Sources Committee (RUSA CODES), which meets both at the association's annual and midwinter meetings; (5) explore the extensive publishers' exhibits at the American Library Association's annual and midwinter meetings; and (6) regularly request publishers' catalogs from the principal reference publishers and regularly visit their web sites.

Features New to This Edition

In preparing this edition, a survey of active users of the preceding edition was conducted to determine how important and successful certain features of that work were and to receive input on suggested new features that might be incorporated in the current edition. Some suggested improvements validated by the survey group, such as keyword indexing, are still deemed uneconomical in a guide targeted for the widest possible audience; others, such as the recording of root Dewey and LC call numbers for each title, and indicating the existence of all known alternative formats, were actively incorporated. Based on input received in this survey, the extensive cross-referencing and the inclusion of children's and young adult reference sources—significant features of the preceding edition—were not continued.

How to Approach This Guide

Although this guide to basic reference sources includes a complete author-title index, it is, in fact, designed to be approached systematically; that is, the most effective way to access the entries is to first study the extensive contents pages that precede the text so as to identify subject areas of interest and then to proceed to those sections to review the sources listed. The chapter editors have attempted, within the space available to them, to highlight not only the best and most pragmatic sources available on a particular subject, but also to indicate the range of sources available on that subject. One of the intentions of this work is to provide a framework within which to review actual and potential resources. Knowing, for example, that a generic sports almanac exists enables one to speculate that there may be a variety of market choices in this product area and that there may in fact be almanacs devoted to individual sports or groups of sports as well. Armed with this insight, the selector has a broader consciousness from which to investigate the many sources available and to query and probe publishers' representatives.

Order of Presentation

In keeping with tradition, the twenty-two chapters in this work have been arranged to reflect the major divisions of the Dewey decimal classification (DDC). Although no attempt was made to impose a strict DDC ordering, users familiar with that system will recognize a progression from bibliographic generalities to philosophy and psychology, religion, the social sciences, language, the natural sciences, technology and applied sciences, the arts, literature, and finally geography, history, and biography. Within each chapter, subdivisions or layers of subdivisions were developed by the chapter editors to create a pragmatic outline for the resources contained therein. Approaching this work through the contents outline is the most practical way to access the entries as a whole.

Interpreting the Entries

For each title, standard bibliographic elements are listed in the following prescribed order: title, edition, author (or editor or compiler), pagination (or number of volumes), publisher, date of publication, price, and ISBN or ISSN. For serial publications, the initial date of publication and frequency are noted, and the price given is the annual subscription price. For all titles, root Dewey decimal and Library of Congress classification numbers are supplied; for federal government publications, the Superintendent of Documents classification numbers have also been supplied. Paperback pricing is given, when known. Except for a handful of truly significant forthcoming titles, all entries listed in this edition were personally examined by at least one member of the editorial team; and all bibliographic elements were checked in more than one standard source to ensure accuracy, completeness, and availability.

It is our hope that the members of the profession will find the sixth edition of *Reference Sources for Small and Medium-sized Libraries* to be as useful a tool for their needs as its predecessors have been for ours.

SCOTT E. KENNEDY
Editor

1

Selection Aids for Reference Materials

CAROLYN M. MULAC

Sources listed here are useful in the selection and evaluation of current reference materials for small and medium-sized libraries. Most of these works are buying guides focused on reference sources, although a few of the titles included consider some aspects of reference service. Subject-specific selection aids are found in the corresponding chapters. Collection development is treated in chapter 2, Bibliographies and General Sources, under the heading Bibliographies and Guides: Selection Aids for Various Reader Groups.

Additional information on many of the entries in this book can be found in the selection aids listed.

Books

1 **American Library Association guide to information access: a complete research handbook and directory.** Sandy Whiteley, ed. 533p. Random House, 1994. op. Paper $19. ISBN 0-679-75075-4.
025.5 Z711

Intended for a general audience, this handbook will also be of interest to library school students and reference librarians. Introductory chapters provide explanations of types of resources as well as providers of information (e.g., libraries, archives, and government agencies). The bulk of the text consists of topical chapters covering thirty-six popular subjects from agriculture to writing. These chapters cite the most prominent resources for each area represented. This reasonably priced reference will serve as an introduction or refresher and is an essential purchase for all reference collections.

2 **American reference books annual.** Bohdan S. Wynar, ed. Libraries Unlimited, 1970– . Annual. $100. ISSN 0065-9959.

Best reference books 1986–1990: titles of lasting value selected from American reference books annual. Bohdan S. Wynar, ed. 5440p. Libraries Unlimited, 1992. $75. ISBN 0-87287-936-4.

Recommended reference books for small and medium-sized libraries and media centers. Bohdan S. Wynar, ed. Libraries Unlimited, 1981– . Annual. $45. ISSN 0277-5948.
011.02 Z1035.1

ARBA reviews most of the English-language reference books published in the United States and Canada during a single year. The signed, critical reviews (1,651 in the 1998 edition) are two to five paragraphs and longer; they cite reviews from fourteen selected journals and make comparisons to other works. Government publications, pamphlets, and how-to books published for the mass market are generally not reviewed. Each edition of *ARBA* is indexed, and there are five-year cumulative indexes available (*Index to American reference books annual,* 1990–94, Libraries Unlimited, 1994. $65. ISBN 1-56308-272-1). Although *ARBA* is highly recommended, small libraries may prefer the abridged version. *Best reference books 1986–1990* selects some 1,000 titles from the indicated years of *ARBA* and excludes serials, travel guides, and works about individual authors. *Recommended reference books* offers about a third of the reviews (558 in the 1994 edition) for about half the price. Unlike its parent volume, *Recommended reference books* keys reviews to library type—college, public, and school. Both sources offer evaluative coverage of the year's reference output.

3 **Canadian reference sources: an annotated bibliography/Ouvrages de reference canadiens: une bibliographie annotee.** Mary E. Bond and Martine M. Caron, comps. 1150p. Univ. of British Columbia Pr. in association with the National Library of Canada, 1996. $225. ISBN 0-7748-0565-X.
016.971 Z1365

This comprehensive, bilingual work considerably expands the coverage of its predecessor, Dorothy Ryder's *Canadian reference sources: a selective guide* (2d ed., 1981). Reference works published as late as July 1995 are included. Descriptive annotations of sources about Canadian people, institutions, organizations, publications, art, literature, languages, and history as well as general titles and works in history and the humanities. Indexed by author, title, French subject, and English subject. Bilingual publications are entered twice, and unilingual works are cited both in their original language and in a bilingual annotation. The availability of nonprint formats is noted.

4 **Encyclopedias, atlases, and dictionaries.** Marion Sader and Amy Lewis, eds. 495p. Bowker, 1995. $85. ISBN 0-8352-3669-2.
031 AE1

Combining two previous Bowker titles, *Reference books for young readers* and *General reference books for adults,* evaluations of more than 200 general encyclopedias, world atlases, and general dictionaries currently available in the United States are provided. Facsimile pages from each title reviewed are included. Large-print and electronic reference works are covered. Reviews are concise, and each is preceded by a "Facts at a Glance" feature about the title under consideration. Comparative charts track titles by scope, level, and price.

5 **Fundamental reference sources.** 2d ed. Frances Neel Cheney and Wiley J. Williams. 300p. American Library Assn., 1980. Contact publisher to purchase. ISBN 0-8389-0308-8. 3d ed. pending.
011.02 Z1035.1

Discusses sources of bibliographical, biographical, linguistic, statistical, and geographical information. Separate chapter on encyclopedias. Selection of titles based on their importance in general reference collections in American libraries. Limited quantities available from the publisher.

6 **Government reference books 94/96: a guide to U.S. government publications.** John A. Schuler, ed. 250p. Libraries Unlimited. Irreg. (1997. $67.50. ISBN 1-56308-433-3.) ISSN 0072-5188.
015.73 Z1223.27

A descriptive annotated bibliography of U.S. government publications arranged by subject. It includes atlases, bibliographies, catalogs, compendia, dictionaries, directories, guides, handbooks, indexes, and other monographs. Complete bibliographic information, including price, is provided. Updated every two or three years. Indexed.

7 **Guide to reference books.** 11th ed. Robert Balay, ed. 2000p. American Library Assn., 1996. $275. ISBN 0-8389-0669-9.
■ cd
011.2 Z1035.1

Continuing a publishing tradition begun in 1907, the latest edition of this venerable work is the largest and the first to appear also in a nonbook format. The 15,875 titles are cited in five sections: A, General Reference Works; B, Humanities; C,

Social and Behavioral Sciences; D, History and Area Studies; and E, Science, Technology, and Medicine. There is comprehensive coverage of works published through 1993. A few titles published after that year are also included. Printed sources are emphasized, but other formats are acknowledged. A basic element of every reference collection.

8 Guide to reference materials for school library media centers. 5th ed. Barbara Ripp Safford, ed. 463p. Libraries Unlimited, 1998. $45. ISBN 1-56308-545-3.
011.2 Z1037.1

This bibliography of reference books and print, nonprint, and electronic resources, specifically designed for the needs of school media centers, is the only comprehensive reference guide of its type for students and teachers of grades K–12. Its arrangement by topic includes both curricular and extracurricular topics. Evaluative annotations; references to reviews in other sources. Complete access to all entries is achieved through the author-title-subject index. Valuable also for classes in children's materials.

9 Guide to the use of libraries and information sources. 7th ed. Jean Key Gates. 304p. McGraw-Hill, 1994. Paper $20. ISBN 0-07-023000-5.
025.56 Z10

After introductory sections on the history of books and libraries and the arrangement of materials in libraries, the bulk of the work emphasizes how to use information sources through a sampling of the better basic reference materials as reviewed in evaluative bibliographies. It covers not only general reference sources but those in subject fields. Index.

10 The humanities: a selective guide to information sources. 4th ed. Ron Blazek and Elizabeth Aversa. 525p. Libraries Unlimited, 1994. $55. ISBN 1-56308-167-9; paper $42. ISBN 1-56308-168-7.
■ cd
016.016 Z6265

Covers the humanistic disciplines—philosophy, religion, visual arts, performing arts, and language and literature—and features chapters entitled "Assessing Information in . . ." and "Principal Information Sources in . . ." for each. Titles are listed by type within each chapter; entries are annotated. The CD-ROM version contains 250 works not included in the print version.

11 Introduction to reference work. 7th rev. ed. William A. Katz. 2v. McGraw-Hill, 1997. v.1, Basic information sources. $30.25. ISBN 0-07-033638-5; v.2, Reference services and reference processes. $27.50. ISBN 0-07-033639-3.
025.52 Z711

A useful work, frequently used as a text, directed at the beginning or inexperienced reference librarian. Volume 1, which deals with basic information sources, is arranged by form of materials; volume 2 covers reference sources, processes, evaluation, and techniques, including online reference.

12 A micro handbook for small libraries and media centers. 3d ed. Betty Costa and Marie Costa. 443p. Libraries Unlimited, 1991. $32.50. ISBN 0-87287-901-1.
025.00285 Z678.93

A basic guide with practical advice on a wide range of automation topics, from computer-related services for patrons to online database searching to the management of LANs. Suggestions for further reading and lists of library software, organizations, periodicals, and services are included.

13 Reader's adviser. 14th ed. Marion Sader, ed. 6v. Bowker/Reed Reference, 1994. $500/set. ISBN 0-8352-3320-0. v.1, The best in reference works, British literature, and American literature. 1512p. 1994. $110. ISBN 0-8352-3321-9; v.2, The best in world literature. 1162p. 1994. $110. ISBN 0-8352-3322-7; v.3, The best in social sciences, history, and the arts. 1168p. 1994. $110. ISBN 0-8352-3323-5; v.4, The best in philosophy and religion. 1088p. 1994. $110. ISBN 0-8352-3324-3; v.5, The best in science, technology, and medicine. 976p. 1994. $110. ISBN 0-8352-3325-1; v.6, Indexes. 840p. 1994. $110. ISBN 0-8352-3326-X.
016.028 Z1035

Reference works as well as nonreference titles from most fields of knowledge. An authoritative reference tool for background information and reading lists.

14 The reader's catalog: an annotated selection of more than 40,000 of the best books in print in 208 categories. Geoffrey O'Brien. 1382p. Jason Epstein,

1989. $24.95. ISBN 0-924322-00-4.
011.7 Z1035

Provides buying information on a wide range of books in each of the categories listed in the content pages. Indexed by author, biographee, or major subject in the index. Readers are advised that although this source is still in print, some of the titles included in it may no longer be available.

15 Recommended reference books in paperback. 2d ed. Andrew L. March. 263p. Libraries Unlimited, 1992. $47.50. ISBN 1-56308-067-2
011.73 Z1035.1

A selection of price-worthy paperbound reference tools, noted for their quality as well as their economy. Lists some 1,000 titles in broad subject categories with evaluative annotations. A third edition is due out in early 2000.

16 Reference and information services: an introduction. 2d ed. Richard E. Bopp and Linda C. Smith, eds. 626p. Libraries Unlimited, 1995. $47.50. ISBN 1-56308-130-X; paper $35. ISBN 1-56308-129-6
025.52. Z711

Part 1 covers concepts and theory: ethics, library instruction, the reference interview, bibliographic control, and the evaluation and management of reference services. Part 2 offers general principles and sources for the selection and evaluation of reference tools. Sample questions and search strategies are included.

17 Reference books for children. 4th ed. Carolyn Sue Peterson and Ann D. Fenton. 414p. Scarecrow, 1992. $45. ISBN 0-8108-2543-0.
028.162 Z1037.1

Evaluative annotations of approximately 1,000 suitable titles. The introduction defines reference services to children and provides criteria for evaluating reference sources. There is a chapter on general reference sources followed by chapters subdivided by specific topics. Entries are arranged alphabetically within subject groupings. Full annotations with useful comparisons with other works. Titles published after June 1990 are not included.

18 Reference sources for small and medium-sized libraries. 6th ed. Scott E. Kennedy, ed.; comp. by Reference Sources for Small and Medium-sized Libraries Editorial Committee. 368p. American Library Assn., 1999. $60. ISBN 0-8389-3468-4.
011.02 Z1035.1.A47

Expanded coverage and some reorganization of contents are not the only changes in the latest edition of a well-respected source. Dewey and Library of Congress call numbers are provided with each entry; statistical sources have been incorporated into the corresponding subject chapters; a separate chapter focusing on health and medicine has been created; and all chapters follow a standard presentation hierarchy. Emphasis is still on print sources, but alternative formats are indicated when known.

19 Reference sources in library and information services: a guide to the literature. Gary R. Purcell with Gail Ann Schlachter. 359p. ABC-Clio, 1984. op.
011.02 Z666

This unique guide closes the bibliographic gap that exists in our own area of library and information science. Limiting themselves to twentieth-century material of value to English-language users, the authors have annotated the major kinds of publications of library-related sources. Part 1, arranged by type of publication, covers library and information services as a whole; part 2 focuses on more than 100 subject areas, subdivided by format: library-related issues, techniques, processes, developments, or institutions. Valuable for the practicing librarian, researchers, and educators in library and information science, their students, and finally those who build library collections. Many cross-references, especially in part 2, eliminate the need for a subject index. Author, title, and geographic indexes.

20 The social sciences: a cross-disciplinary guide to selected sources. 2d ed. Nancy L. Herron, ed. 323p. Libraries Unlimited, 1996. $43. ISBN 1-56308-309-4; paper $32. ISBN 1-56308-351-5.
016.3 Z7161

This new edition covers the areas of the general social sciences, political science, economics, business, history, law and legal issues, anthropology, sociology, education, psychology, geography, and communication in more than 1,000 annotated citations. Each chapter includes references to electronic resources.

21 303 CD-ROMs to use in your library: descriptions, evaluations, and practical advice. Patrick R. Dewey. 385p. American Library Assn., 1995. Paper $30.

ISBN 0-8389-0666-4.
028.1 Z1040

Concise descriptions of CD-ROM packages and series organized by subject include vendor price, platform and hardware requirements, and availability of network versions. Written in nontechnical language, the evaluations cover content, searching features and capabilities, and the level of user sophistication required. Includes a glossary, bibliography, and a list of vendor addresses and phone numbers. Sources included have been tested by the author.

22 **Topical reference books: authoritative evaluations of recommended resources in specialized areas.** Marion Sader, ed. 892p. Bowker, 1991. $104.95.
ISBN 0-8352-3087-2.
011.02 Z1035.1

Arranged by subject, from "Advertising" to "Zoology," each chapter identifies core titles and provides extensive annotations for them. A chart in each chapter notes which books are appropriate for public, academic, or school libraries. Supplementary titles are also listed with briefer annotations and sources of reviews.

23 **Walford's guide to reference material.** 6th ed. v.1, Science and technology. A. J. Walford, M. Mullay, and P. Schlicke, eds. 943p. Library Assn. Pub. (dist. by UNIPUB), 1993. $195.
ISBN 1-85604-015-1; v.2, Social and historical sciences, philosophy and religion. Allen Day and Joan M. Harvey, eds. 1156p. Library Assn. Pub. (dist. by UNIPUB), 1994. $210.
ISBN 1-85604-044-5.
011.02 Z1035

These two volumes represent two-thirds of the British counterpart to *Guide to reference books*. The third portion, volume 3, *Generalia, language, and literature arts,* is still in the fifth edition. Although the scope is international, the emphasis is on works published in Britain.

Periodicals

24 **Booklist.** v.26– . American Library Assn., 1930– . Twice monthly; once in July and Aug. $65. ISSN 0006-7385.
■ cd
020 Z1035.A1

Mandatory for any public library and very helpful to many college and school libraries. Reference librarians will be most interested in the *Reference books bulletin (RBB)* section. The *RBB* reviews, written by members of the *RBB* Editorial Board, are the most substantial in the literature. They are detailed, comparative, and conclude with a clear recommendation. If one is not sure about purchasing an expensive source, one should wait for the *RBB* review. The reviews are also available on CD-ROM as part of Bowker's *Reviews plus. RBB* also contains excellent bibliographic essays and omnibus reviews on specific types of sources or special topics. A "News and Views" section provides information when a full-length review is not necessary or feasible. The ALA/RASD Reference Sources Committee's list of the year's outstanding reference sources is printed, unannotated, in the May 1 issue of *Booklist. Reference books bulletin, [yr.]* (American Library Assn., ISSN 8755-0962) is an annual, indexed, paperback cumulation of the *RBB* reviews and omnibus articles arranged by subject.

25 **Choice.** v.1– . Assn. of College and Research Libraries, American Library Assn., 1964– . 11/yr. $160. ISSN 0009-4978.
■ cd
028 Z1035

Required for all academic libraries and valuable to medium-sized and larger public libraries. Each issue includes reviews of a sizable number of reference sources (including online databases) appropriate for the undergraduate library. The reviews are brief, critical, comparative, and signed. An annual list (May) points out the "Outstanding Academic Books and Nonbook Materials, [yr.]." Reviews available on CD-ROM and on three-by-five cards.

26 **College and research libraries.** v.1– . Assn. of College and Research Libraries, American Library Assn., 1939– . Bimonthly. $50 to nonmembers.
ISSN 0010-0870.
027.7 Z671

Useful to academic librarians. Of primary interest to reference librarians is the semiannual (January and July) annotated list of reference books prepared by the reference department of Columbia University. The "purpose of the list is to present a selection of recent scholarly and general works of interest to reference workers in university libraries." The article concludes with a roundup of new editions and supplements.

27 **Library journal.** v.1– . Cahners/Bowker, 1876– . Twice monthly; once in Jan.,

Aug., and Dec. $94.50. ISSN 0363-0277.
■ cd
020.5 Z671

A must for even the smallest library. A good part of each issue is devoted to book reviews, reference books included. The reviews are brief, signed, timely, and critical. There is also an annual list of outstanding reference sources (April 15) and of notable government documents (May 15). Online databases are frequently discussed in articles and columns. The book reviews are also available on three-by-five cards and on CD-ROM.

28 **Reference and user services quarterly.** v.1– . Reference and User Services Association, American Library Assn., 1960– . Quarterly. Membership journal. $50 to nonmembers. ISSN 1094-9054.
025.5 Z671

The "Sources" section of *Reference and User Services Quarterly* (formerly *RQ*) contains reviews of databases, reference books, and professional reading. The reviews are critical, comparative, and written by practicing librarians or educators. The "Reference Books" and the "Professional Materials" sections also list books received but not reviewed. One of the best periodicals for the evaluation and selection of reference sources.

29 **Reference services review.** v.1– . Pierian, 1973– . Quarterly. $65. ISSN 0090-7234.
011.02 Z1035.1

A useful acquisition for medium-sized to large reference departments. Rather than isolated reviews of just-published books, *RSR* provides a generous number of review essays, most focusing on a particular subject or type of reference source. Whether the articles are literature surveys, comparative reviews, core collections, or examination of databases, they are highly informative and cover the broad range of issues and sources important to reference service.

30 **School library journal.** v.1– . Cahners/Bowker, 1954– . Monthly except June and July. $79.50. ISSN 0362-8930.
■ cd
027.8 Z675

One of the standard selection tools for libraries serving children and young adults. Approximately half of each issue is devoted to reviews, including audiovisual materials, computer software, and more than 2,800 books each year. Because so few reference sources are published for young people, however, most of these reviews are of circulating books. Of particular interest to reference librarians is the annual "Reference Books Roundup" in the May issue. The reviews are also available on three-by-five cards and on CD-ROM.

31 **Voice of youth advocates.** v.1– . Scarecrow, 1978– . Bimonthly, Apr. through Feb. $38.50. ISSN 0160-4201.
027.62 Z718.5

An essential purchase for libraries serving young adults. Although *VOYA,* as it is commonly called, contains news notes, comments, and features, it is most useful for its reviews and collection development articles. The journal examines a variety of materials, including reference sources. The reviews are usually two to three paragraphs long and evaluate the sources in light of their value and appeal to young adults.

2

Bibliographies and General Sources

CAROLYN M. MULAC

The bibliographies and sources listed in this section offer avenues to primary materials and information about primary materials that are otherwise difficult to obtain. Publishing houses in the United States have developed a variety of sophisticated tools for locating such information, and sometimes it is necessary to use several of them to locate all the needed materials. Subject bibliographies relevant to specific fields will be found in later chapters.

Bibliographies and Guides

Selection Aids for Various Reader Groups

32 **Adventuring with books: a booklist for pre K–grade 6.** 11th ed. Wendy K. Sutton, ed. 401p. National Council of Teachers of English, 1997. Paper $22.95. ISBN 0-8141-0080-5.
011.62 Z1037

An annotated, selective list of some 2,000 recommended titles published between 1988 and 1996 arranged under thirteen broad subject categories. Author, title, illustrator, and subject indexes. Books included are suitable for home as well as classroom and library.

33 **Best books for children: preschool through grade six.** 6th ed. John T. Gillespie and Corinne J. Naden, eds. 1500p. Bowker/Reed Reference, 1998. $65. ISBN 0-8352-4099-1.
011.62 Z1037

A listing of more than 15,000 books for ages three through fourteen grouped in broad subject areas. Fiction titles are divided by type of story. Brief annotations indicate grade level. Dewey decimal classification numbers and ISBNs are provided. Review citations for titles published after 1985 are included. There are separate author, title, illustrator, and subject indexes. An important tool for collection building and reading guidance.

34 **Best books for junior high readers.** John T. Gillespie. 567p. Bowker, 1991. $43. ISBN 0-8352-3020-1.
011.625 Z1037

More than 6,000 books for ages twelve to fifteen are arranged by popular subject classifications and supplemented by an appendix of 750 titles to challenge advanced readers. Brief annotations include Dewey decimal numbers for nonfiction works and review citations for titles published after 1985. Author, title, and subject- or grade-level indexes.

35 Best books for senior high readers. John T. Gillespie. 931p. Bowker, 1991. $48. ISBN 0-8352-3021-X.
011.625 Z1037

A listing of more than 10,000 titles, most of which have received two or three favorable reviews, for ages fifteen to eighteen, arranged by subject. Similar in format to the preceding title for junior high readers, it also uses the same subject classifications.

36 Books for adult new readers: a bibliography developed by Project LEARN. 5th ed. Frances Josephson Pursell. 227p. New Readers Pr., 1993. $15.95. ISBN 0-88336-599-5.
011.6 Z1039

An annotated bibliography of titles appropriate for English-speaking adults who read at the seventh-grade level or below. Gives the usual bibliographic data, print components (e.g., workbooks), and a synopsis. Fiction of several kinds and a variety of nonfiction topics are included.

37 Books for college libraries. 3d ed. 6v. American Library Assn., 1988. $600/set. ISBN 0-8389-3353-X; v.1, Humanities. $125. ISBN 0-8389-3357-2; v.2, Language and literature. op; v.3, History. $125. ISBN 0-8389-3355-6; v.4, Social science. op; v.5, Psychology, Science, Technology, Bibliography. $125. ISBN 0-8389-3358-0; v.6, Index. $125. ISBN 0-8389-3359-9.
025.2 Z1039.C65

Compiled as a core collection for undergraduate libraries, the list includes recommended reference titles throughout. Arranged by LC classification; author, title, and subject indexes.

38 Books for public libraries. 3d ed. Constance Koehn, ed. 374p. American Library Assn., 1982. op. Contact publisher to purchase.
011.7 Z1035

Following trends in collection development as expressed in *The public library mission statement and its imperatives,* this is a representative public library collection that would serve as an alternative book selection tool for new libraries or for assessing existing library collections. Arranged according to the nineteenth edition of *Dewey decimal classification* (1979), each entry states author, title, edition, publisher, date, price, ISBN, and LC catalog card number. Author-title index. Unfortunately, it has not been updated.

39 Books for secondary school libraries. 6th ed. Ad Hoc Library Com. of the National Assn. of Independent Schools: Pauline Anderson et al., comps. 844p. Bowker, 1981. $39.95. ISBN 0-8352-1111-8.
011.62 Z1035

Geared to the needs of college-bound students, this unannotated work presents more than 9,000 nonfiction titles and series, an increase of more than 3,000 titles from the first edition. In spite of the increase, fiction, biography, and nonbook media are not included. Entries are grouped in twelve sections ranging from professional tools and reference works to one section each through the Dewey classes. Complements Wilson's *Senior high school library catalog,* offering titles on a more advanced level than those always found in high school libraries.

40 Children's catalog. 17th ed. 1400p. Wilson, 1996. Base v. and 4 annual supplements 1997–2000. ISBN 0-8242-0893-5. Contact publisher for price and availability.
011 CHI Z1037

A valuable selection tool since 1909. Annotated citations for more than 6,000 books for children from preschool through sixth grade are organized by abridged Dewey decimal classification. There are also author, title, subject, and analytical indexes. A directory of publishers and distributors is another useful feature of this standard work.

41 The elementary school library collection: a guide to books and other media. Phases 1-2-3. 21st ed. Linda L. Homa, ed. 1152p. Brodart, 1998. $139.95. ISBN 0-87272-114-0.
■ cd
011.62 Z1037

Entries include complete cataloging, order information, and descriptive annotations for books, periodicals, and audiovisual and computer materials. This edition presents a core collection of more than 10,000 titles in twelve formats, about a quarter of which are new. Titles are recommended as either "essential for all libraries," "for further development," or "for special interest or regional importance." The CD-ROM version enables the user to create bibliographies quite easily, a boon for library media specialists and teachers.

42 Guide to library collection development. John T. Gillespie and Ralph J. Folcarelli. 441p. Libraries Unlimited, 1994. $49.50. ISBN 1-56308-173-3.
025.2 Z1002

A tool providing descriptions of important collection development titles published between 1986 and 1993. Divided into three main parts: part 1, "Periodicals and Serials"; part 2, "Children's and Young Adult Sources"; and part 3, "Adult Sources." Prices and ISBN numbers are part of each citation. Author-title and subject indexes are included. Because this is a selection aid, titles listed are in print. The intended audience encompasses school and small and medium-sized academic and public libraries.

43 Middle and junior high school library catalog. 7th ed. 1008p. Wilson, 1995. $175/base v. and 4 annual supplements, 1996–99. ISBN 0-8242-0880-3.
011.62 Z1037

Formerly *Junior high school library catalog,* this standard work is an annotated list of more than 4,000 fiction and nonfiction titles for students in grades five through nine. The annual supplements will each list some 600 new titles. Books in part one are arranged according to the abridged *Dewey decimal classification*. Annotations usually include one or more evaluative statements from published reviews. Analytical index is arranged by title, author, and subject.

44 Public library catalog: guide to reference books and adult nonfiction. 10th ed. 1325p. Wilson, 1994. $230/base v. and 4 annual supplements, 1995–98. ISBN 0-8242-0859-5.
025.2 Z1035

Bibliographies and reference books are included in this classified annotated catalog of titles selected primarily for small to medium-sized public libraries. Annotations include quoted evaluations from other sources. Includes some paperbacks. Author, title, subject, and analytical index. A directory of publishers and distributors.

45 Senior high school library catalog. 14th ed. 1464p. Wilson, 1992. $115/base v. and 4 annual supplements, 1983–96. ISBN 0-8242-0831-5.
011.62 Z1037

Fiction and nonfiction titles for grades nine through twelve are presented in a familiar format. A classified catalog consisting of titles arranged by Dewey decimal classification is supported by author, title, subject, and analytical indexes. A directory of publishers and distributors rounds out this standard work.

In-print Sources

46 Alternative publications: a guide to directories, indexes, bibliographies and other sources. Cathy Seitz Whitaker, ed. 96p. McFarland, 1990. Trade paper $21.95. ISBN 0-89950-484-1.
016.6 1033

A bibliographic guide to print and nonprint materials from outside the mainstream. Author and title indexing and full ordering information provided.

47 Books in print. 9v. Bowker, 1948– . Annual. $550. ISSN 0068-0214.
■ micro cd online tape
015.73 Z1215

Lists in-print and forthcoming titles, published or exclusively distributed in the United States. Entries include date of publication, price, publisher, LC card number, and ISBN. Available online through Dialog, CompuServe, and OCLC. The CD-ROM version, entitled *Books in print with book reviews plus,* is now available in a Canadian edition. Quarterly updates are provided by *Books in print supplement,* which is also available in microfiche, CD-ROM, online, and tape editions.

48 Books on-demand author fiche guides. UMI, 1977– . Call publisher at (800) 521-3042, ext. 3781, for further information.
■ micro
016.4 Z1033

This microfiche author listing lists out-of-print books available as xerographic reproductions or on microfilm from University Microfilms International (UMI). Includes order number and price. Minimum price is $25, maximum $180, and library binding is $6 extra. Cost is determined at 28.5 cents per page for paper copies. Subject catalogs are available (on paper), but there is no title guide.

49 CD-ROMs in print: an international guide to CD-ROM, CD-I, 3DO, MMCD, CD32, multimedia and electronic products. 12th ed. Erin E. Holmberg, ed. 1450p. Gale, 1998. $155.

ISBN 0-7876-1445-9.
025 Z699.22

Descriptive listings for more than 13,000 CD-ROM titles are included along with indexing by audience level, multimedia, other electronic formats, and so forth. An activity index provides details on eleven facets of the CD-ROM market (e.g., content development, data preparation, packaging, etc.) and each company's involvement.

50 **Children's books in print.** 2v. Bowker, 1969– . Annual. $165. ISSN 0069-3580.
■ cd online tape
011.62 Z1037.A1

An author, title, and illustrator index to children's books currently available. The index to children's book awards has been a helpful feature since the 1987–88 edition. *Children's reference plus* is a CD-ROM product containing the text of *Children's books in print, EL-HI textbooks and serials in print,* and many other Bowker bibliographies and children's literature reference books.

51 **The complete directory of large print books and serials.** v.1– . Bowker, 1970– . Annual. $189.95. ISSN 0000-1120.
■ micro cd online tape
015.73 Z5348

Fiction, nonfiction, textbooks, children's books, and periodicals available from publishers and associations printing them in large type (14 point or larger). Arranged by subject under three categories, general reading, children's, and textbooks, with full bibliographic data and ordering information. Author index, title index, directory of publishers, and service organizations. Printed in 18 point type.

52 **Forthcoming books.** v.1– . Bowker, 1966– . Bimonthly. Paper $249.95. ISSN 0015-8119.
■ micro cd online tape
015.73 Z1219

A supplement to *Books in print* provides separate author and title indexes to books that are to appear in the next five-month period. Includes access through LC subject headings and gives price, publisher, edition, ISBN, LC numbers, and expected publication date.

53 **GPO sales publications reference file (PRF).** Monthly microfiche. Govt. Print. Off., 1978– . $145/yr.; foreign $181.25/yr. S/N 721-002-00000-4. SuDoc GP 3.22/3: Date (PRF bimonthly cumulation); GP 3.22/3-2: Date (PRF monthly update).

GPO sales publications reference file magnetic tapes. Biweekly magnetic computer tape. $850. S/N 721-004-00000-7.

Out-of-print GPO sales publications reference file. Microfiche. Govt. Print. Off., 1980– . (1996, $20; foreign, $25.) S/N 021-000-00169-4. SuDoc GP3.22/3-3:yr.
■ micro cd online
015 Z1223.A1

Serving as a combination of *Books in print* and *Forthcoming books* for U.S. government publications, this is a microfiche catalog of all publications currently available for sale by the Superintendent of Documents. The bimonthly cumulation is complete; the monthly update is produced in the alternate month. Access points occur in three separate sequences: GPO stock number, Superintendent of Documents classification number, and an alphabetical interfiling of entries by title and subject keywords, personal author names, agency series, and report numbers. Because of its updated format, it provides more current access than the *Monthly catalog* and does not demand a two-step process (from index to entry or abstract number) in locating the Superintendent of Documents classification number. The *Out-of-print GPO sales publications reference file* lists publications that are no longer available. Information about GPO sales products is readily accessible online via *GPO Access.*

54 **Guide to microforms in print.** Microform Review, 1961–81. K. G. Saur, 1982– . Annual. Price varies per yr. Author-title. $430. ISSN 0164-0747; Subject. $430. ISSN 0163-8386; Supplement. $185. ISSN 0164-0739.
086.4 Z1033

An alphabetically arranged guide to micropublications available throughout the world. Does not include theses or dissertations. Essentially a price list with pertinent ordering information.

55 **Information America: sources of print and nonprint materials available from organizations, industry, government agencies, and specialized publishers.** 2d ed. Fran Malin and Richard Stanzi, eds. 900p. Neal-Schuman, 1993. $150. ISBN 1-55570-078-X.
028.70973 Z674.5

Unique in the field of information control, its purpose is to show which nontraditional sources of print and nonprint materials, not indexed in many standard bibliographic aids, are providing information in various subject areas. Directory information, the objective of the organization, information services provided by the group, and representative publications in all forms (e.g., books, pamphlets, periodicals, charts, microforms, cassettes, and multimedia kits) are listed. Covering many types of organizations not in *Encyclopedia of associations,* it also brings together groups with similar interests in specific subjects. Organizationally, the subject approach is used. Its indexes, particularly the subject index, allow one to find topics frequently researched by high school students, college students, or the general public. Title index to periodicals, free and inexpensive materials; a listing of organizations covered; subject index. *See also* Directories in this chapter.

56 Publishers' trade list annual. 2v. Bowker, 1873– . Annually in fall. $335. ISSN 0079-7855.
■ micro cd online
015.73 Z1215

Compilation of publishers' catalogs in alphabetical order. Amount of information supplied by publisher varies.

57 Subject guide to books in print. 7v. Bowker, 1957– . Annually in fall. $369.95. ISSN 0000-0519.
■ micro cd online tape
015.73 Z1215

Arranges the books listed in *Books in print* by Library of Congress subject headings with many cross-references and subheadings. Areas omitted are fiction, literature, poetry, and drama by one author. Quarterly updates are available on microfiche.

58 Subject guide to children's books in print. Bowker, 1971– . $165. ISSN 0000-0167.
■ cd tape
028.52 Z1037

Covers titles appearing in *Children's books in print* with subject headings based primarily on the *Sears list of subject headings* with a few from *Library of Congress subject headings.* Provides bibliographic information, plus grade range, language (if other than English), and binding (if other than cloth). The volume includes instructions for use plus a directory of publishers and distributors.

59 Words on cassette. 2v. 2569p. Bowker, 1999. $159.95. ISBN 0-8352-4095-9.
■ cd
011.38 ML156.2

The equivalent of *Books in print* for this popular format provides detailed listings for more than 68,000 spoken-word recordings. Four indexes (title, author-readers-performers, subject, producer-distributor) offer quick and easy access to a wide variety of material, from lectures and seminars to old radio programs and foreign-language instruction.

National Bibliographies (United States)

60 American book publishing record. v.1– . Bowker, 1960– . Monthly. $275/yr. ISSN 0002-7707. See their catalog for cumulations.
■ tape
015 Z1219

Arranged by Dewey decimal classification, the entries give full Library of Congress cataloging and price. Separate sections for fiction, juvenile fiction, and paperbacks. Author and title indexes and subject guide.

61 Books in series 1876–1949: original, reprinted, in-print, and out-of-print books, published or distributed in the United States in popular, scholarly, and professional series. 3v. Bowker, 1982. $195. ISBN 0-8352-1443-5.

Books in series 1950–1984. 4th ed. 6v. Bowker, 1985. $349. ISBN 0-8352-1938-0.

Books in series 1985–1989. 5th ed. 2v. Bowker, 1989. $199.95. ISBN 0-8352-2679-4.
■ cd online
011.34 Z1215

All the sets consist of an alphabetical listing of series by Library of Congress series title. Titles in series are arranged numerically, or alphabetically when unnumbered. The three-volume set gives retrospective coverage to 1876, listing more than 75,000 titles. The six-volume set gives full bibliographic data on each of the 280,000 titles in about 35,000 series. In the two-volume set some untraced series are added as well as author information. Each set contains the following: the table of contents as a series heading index; author-title index; subject index; and directory of publishers and distributors.

62 Cumulative book index: a world list of books in the English language. Wilson, 1898– . Monthly except Aug. Service basis. ISSN 0011-300X.
■ cd online tape
015 Z1219

Scope widened in 1928 to include books in English issued in the United States and Canada and selected publications from other English-speaking places. Omits government documents and pamphlets. All entries (author, title, and subject) are arranged in a single alphabetical list. Full bibliographic data only in author entries. For cumulations and their prices, consult the Wilson catalog.

63 Publishers weekly. v.1– . Bowker, 1872– . Weekly. $169/yr. ISSN 0000-0019.
070 Z1219

Provides news of the book trade. Section entitled "PW Forecasts" contains reviews of a selection of forthcoming titles. Spring, summer, and fall announcements issues preview upcoming publishing seasons. Regular issues often highlight specific subject areas such as travel, religion, and children's books.

Serials and Periodicals

64 From radical left to extreme right: a bibliography of current periodicals of protest, controversy, advocacy, or dissent, with dispassionate content summaries to guide librarians and other educators. 3d rev. ed. Gail Skidmore and Theodore Jurgen Spahn. 503p. Scarecrow, 1987. $62.50. ISBN 0-8108-1967-8.
016.3224 Z7165

A classified, fully annotated bibliography of more than 280 periodicals of political content about which satisfactory information is often impossible to find elsewhere. In addition to full bibliographic data, address, price, indexing, and format for each periodical, there are contents summaries of editorial positions. A unique feature of this work is that each periodical's editor could comment on the contents summary prepared for the journal. That comment, if forthcoming, appears under the heading "feedback." Geographical, title-editor-publisher, and subject indexes. Cessation list for titles of previous editions.

65 Magazines for children: a guide for parents, teachers and librarians. 2d ed. Selma K. Richardson. 139p. American Library Assn., 1991. Paper $20. ISBN 0-8389-0552-8.
051.083 PN4878

The first edition of this book was published in 1983. An annotated list of periodicals published primarily for children ages two through fourteen, it includes all children's magazines indexed in *Children's magazine guide*. Each entry includes subscription information, frequency, and a descriptive annotation and evaluation. Age and grade levels, circulation figures, additional young adult and adult magazines often found in children's collections, and a subject index are appended.

66 Magazines for libraries. 9th ed. Bill A. Katz and Linda Sternberg Katz. 1402p. Bowker, 1997. $170. ISBN 0-8352-3907-1.
050.25 Z6941

A classified and critically annotated list of magazines designed to display for each title the purpose, audience, scope, and reading level. Bibliographical information is given, as is a statement of where each title is indexed. More recent information can be found in the section "Magazines," a regular feature of *Library journal.*

67 Magazines for young adults: selections for school and public libraries. Selma K. Richardson. 360p. American Library Assn., 1984. op.
011.34 Z6944

Based on Richardson's 1978 title, *Periodicals for school media programs,* this work has been expanded to include some 600 magazines and indexes of value and interest to young people, grades seven through twelve. Critical annotations and a subject index.

68 Serials for libraries: an annotated guide to continuations, annuals, yearbooks, almanacs, transactions, proceedings, directories, services. 2d ed. John V. Ganly and Diane M. Sciattara, eds. 441p. Neal-Schuman, 1985. $85. ISBN 0-918212-85-5.
015.73034 Z1035.1

A reference tool for the selection, acquisition, and control of serials of English-language titles available in the United States. It gives the contents, frequency, audience level, and price of serials for school, college, and public libraries. Divided into five major subject areas with many subdivisions, it also contains title and subject indexes. One section lists serials online; another section tells when to buy which serial.

Directories

Guides

69 Directories in print. 17th ed. 2v. Gale, 1989– . Annual. $489. ISSN 0899-353X.
016.025 Z5771

Describes and indexes nearly 15,500 directories of all kinds, arranged in sixteen broad subject categories. A detailed subject index of more than 3,000 headings and cross-references gives access to entries on a specific topic. Each entry gives title, subtitle, publisher's address, telephone number, description of contents, arrangement, what each entry includes, frequency, usual month of publication, pages, indexes, price, editor's name, ISBN, GPO, or other pertinent number. Subject and title-keyword indexes. Price includes interedition supplement.

70 Guide to American directories. 14th ed. Barry J. Klein. 550p. Todd, 1998. $95. ISBN 0-915344-67-X. ISSN 0533-5248.
016.38 Z5771

Lists under subject more than 8,000 directories published in the United States, with some international coverage. Gives descriptive annotation, publisher, frequency of issue, and price. Title index. May be preferable for smaller libraries when price and frequent updating are not necessary.

Persons and Organizations: Phones, Faxes, and Zip Codes

71 Canada's postal code directory/ Repertoire des codes postaux au Canada. 1872p. National Control Centre, Canada Post Corporation, 1998. $21.95. (Order from National Philatelic Centre, Canada Post Corporation, Station 1, Antigonish, Nova Scotia, Canada B2G 2R8, [800] 565-4362.)
383.145 HE6653

The official source for Canadian postal codes.

72 Congressional yellow book: a directory of members of Congress, includes their committees and key staff aids. Leadership Directories, 1995– . Quarterly. Paper $235. ISSN 0191-1422.
■ cd tape
328.73 JK1083

A quarterly publication schedule keeps this directory as current as possible. Also available as mailing labels.

73 Encyclopedia of associations. 33d ed. Sandra Jaszcak, ed. Gale, 1998. 3v. ISSN 0071-0202. v.1, National organizations of the United States, 3 pts. $470. ISBN 0-7876-1080-1; v.2, Geographic and executive index. $365. ISBN 0-7876-1084-4; v.3, Supplement. $390. ISBN 0-7876-2241-9.
■ cd online tape
060 AS22

Essential information on more than 23,000 national membership organizations representing numerous business, social, educational, religious, fraternal, ethnic, and avocational interests. Convention and meeting dates and locations and titles of organizations' directories and publications are included in the entries. There are also the *Encyclopedia of associations: international organizations* (32d ed., Gale, 1997. 2v. $570. ISBN 0-7876-1382-7) and *Encyclopedia of associations: regional, state and local organizations* (7th ed., Gale, 1997. 5v. $550/set. ISBN 0-7876-1074-7. $130/v.).

74 Federal yellow book: who's who in federal departments and agencies. Leadership Directories, 1995– . Quarterly. $235. ISSN 0145-6202.
353 JK6

Coping with frequent changes in personnel is made easier with this quarterly publication.

75 The foundation directory. Foundation Center, 1960– . Annual. $210; paper $190. ISSN 0071-8092.
■ online
060.2 AS911

Lists nongovernmental, nonprofit organizations having assets of $2 million or more or making annual grants totaling at least $200,000. Data elements covered for each include donor, purpose, assets, expenditures, officers, and grant application information. Arranged by states. Four indexes: by state and city; donors, trustees, and administrators; foundation name; and fields of interest.

76 Information industry directory. 20th ed. 2v. Gale, 1979– . Annual. $605. ISSN 1051-6239.
025.3 Z674.3

Tracks companies that produce and provide electronic systems, services, and products, including online, CD-ROM, and Internet products. Contains a product directory of information products available; a trade directory of the information industry; and a directory of names and numbers arranged in seven sections: information production, information distribution, information retailing, support services and suppliers, associations and government agencies, conferences and courses, and sources of information. Geographic index lists each firm by county and by state in the United States and by country in the rest of the world; names and numbers section provides access to firms, individuals, databases, and print products in the text.

77 Literary agents of North America: the complete guide to U.S. and Canadian literary agencies. 3d ed. Arthur Orrmont and Leonie Rosentiel, eds. 204p. Author Aid Associates (340 E. 52 St., New York, NY 10022), 1988. $19.95. ISBN 0-911085-04-1.
070.5 PN163

Almost every author needs an agent. This guide provides more than 1,000 profiles of agencies with full directory listings, agency policies, manuscript categories, specialties, subject interests, and procedures. After the alphabetical list by agent, the material is classified by the following indexes: subject, policy, size, geographical, and personnel. Useful to writers, editors, publishers, and agents.

78 National directory of addresses and telephone numbers. 19th ed. Omnigraphics, 1997. $80. ISSN 0740-7203.
973 E154.5

A directory of more than 60,000 of the most useful addresses and telephone numbers in the United States. Contains both a classified and an alphabetical section. General categories in the classified section include business and finance; government, politics, and diplomacy; education, foundations, and religious denominations; hospitals; associations and unions; transportation and hotels; communications and media; culture and recreation; and business services. Toll-free numbers for hotels, car and airline services, and discount office supplies.

79 National e-mail and fax directory. Gale, 1989– . Annual. $126. ISSN 1045-9499.
384.14 TK6710

More than 180,000 fax numbers for major U.S. businesses, organizations, and other agencies have been taken from the databases of Gale Research. Fax numbers may be located by an organization's name or through the subject listings. Telephone numbers and mailing and e-mailing addresses are also provided for each listing.

80 National five digit zip code and post office directory. 1974– . Govt. Print. Off. Annual. Available at main post offices. $21. ISSN 0731-9185.
383 HE6361

Comprehensive list of zip code information by state and post office. Instructions for finding proper zip code when address is known. The organization of the codes in the book may be confusing to some patrons. Alphabetical and numerical lists of post offices. When multiple zip codes are necessary in a city, they are listed by streets. Purchase the complete directory, not the smaller ones that exclude such multiple zip codes. APOs and FPOs and current regulations are included, along with mailing information for the mail user and the public in general.

81 Phonefiche: current telephone directories on microfiche. UMI, 1987– . $50 and up. ISSN 0275-8172.
384.6 HE8801.C65

Durable four-by-six-inch negative diazos save 95 percent of the shelf space taken by paper directories. It saves staff time and is flexible because librarians can order those directories they need for their specific area. A wide variety of specialty-priced categories are available. Write for catalog *Discover Phonefiche.*

82 [yr.] TDI national directory of TTY numbers. 431p. Telecommunications for the Deaf, 1968– . Annual. $15.
362.42 HV2510

Fifteen categories, from "Emergency Services" to "Recreational Services" to "Utilities," are used to divide up the TTY listings for each state. Residential as well as office numbers are provided. Listings of e-mail addresses, a last-name index, and a yellow-pages section of advertisers are among the special features of this useful directory.

83 Toll-free phone book USA [yr.]: a directory of toll-free numbers for business and organizations nationwide, [yr.]. Omnigraphics, 1997– . Annual. $110. ISSN 1092-0285.
384.6 HE8811

Lists toll-free numbers for more than 35,000 U.S. companies, associations, educational institutions, travel providers, and government agencies. Listings include mailing address.

84 World of learning. 48th ed. 2v. Europa (dist. by Gale), 1947– . Annual. $495/set. ISSN 0084-2117.
060.25 AS2.W6

The standard international directory for the nations of the world, covering learned societies, research institutes, libraries, museums and art galleries, and universities and colleges. Includes for each institution address, officers, purpose, foundation date, publications, and so forth. Index.

Libraries

85 American library directory. 52d ed. 2v. Bowker, 1923– . Annual. $259.95. ISSN 0065-910X.
■ cd online
027 Z731

Includes U.S. and Canadian public, academic, and special libraries arranged by state or province, city, and institution. Gives personnel and statistical data, subject interests, and special collections. Biennial until 1978.

86 Bowker annual of library and book trade almanac. 44th ed. Bowker, 1956– . Annually in spring. $185. ISSN 0068-0540. (*formerly* **Bowker annual of library and book trade information.**)
■ cd
020.5 Z731

A compendium of statistical and directory information relating to most aspects of librarianship and the book trade. Professional reports from the field; international library news; library legislation; grants; survey articles of developments during the preceding year. Index.

87 The librarian's companion: a handbook of thousands of facts and figures on libraries/librarians, books/newspapers, publishers/booksellers. 2d ed. Vladimir F. Wertsman. 220p. Greenwood, 1996. $65. ISBN 0-313-29975-7.
011.02 Z670

A condensed version of library and publishing information by country. Sections on noted librarians; quotations relevant to librarians, publishers, booksellers; librarians in literature; and Latin phrases useful to librarians. A list of ALA awards and the UNESCO Public Library Manifesto are among the items appended. Index.

88 Subject collections. 7th ed. Lee Ash and William G. Miller, eds. 2v. Bowker, 1993. $275. ISBN 0-8352-3141-0.
026 Z731

This guide to special book collections and subject emphases as reported by university, college, public, and special libraries and museums in the United States and Canada provides the information necessary to locate, evaluate, and use such collections. Arranged alphabetically by subject of collection and alphabetically by state under each heading. Entry includes name and address of library, description of collection, and photocopy and loan restrictions.

Publishers and Booksellers

89 American book trade directory. 44th ed. Bowker staff, ed. Bowker, 1915– . Annual. $249.95. ISSN 0065-759X.
■ cd tape
070.5025 Z475

Includes lists of booksellers, wholesalers, and publishers in the United States, with related information on the book trade in Canada, the United Kingdom, and Ireland. Bookstores are arranged under state and city, with specialty of each noted. Separate lists include exporters, importers, and dealers in foreign books. Index of retailers and wholesalers in the United States and Canada. Academic libraries may need the *International book trade directory* (3d ed. K. G. Saur staff, eds. 1100p. Bowker, 1996. $360. ISBN 3-598-22236-X).

90 AV market place. v.1– . Bowker, 1969– . Annual. $165.95. ISSN 1044-0445. (*formerly* **Audiovisual market place; Audio video market place.**)
371.33 LB1043

A guide to more than 7,500 firms and individuals that produce, supply, or service audiovisual, including video, materials. Covers both software and hardware. Supplementary lists include reference books and directories, periodicals and trade journals, and associations. An alphabetical-by-name company directory. A products and services index cross-referenced to companies; a products, services, and companies index.

91 Editor and publisher international year book, 1921– . Editor and Publisher, 1921– . Annual. 2 pts. Pt. 1, $115. Pt. 2,

$35. ISSN 0424-4923. (*formerly* **International yearbook.**)
070.5025 PN4700

A geographical listing of newspapers, giving circulation and advertising information. Includes information on many foreign newspapers, national newspaper representatives, press associations, award winners, action- and hot-line editors, and aspects of the newspaper industry. Part 2 offers a directory of newspaper industry professionals.

92 Literary market place: the directory of the American book publishing industry. 2v. Bowker, 1940– . Annual. $189.95. ISSN 0000-1155.
■ cd online
070.5 PN161

A directory of American book publishing useful for a variety of data. Includes information on publishers, book manufacturers, book reviewers, literary agents, literary awards and fellowships, and magazine subscription agencies. Contains directory of telephone numbers and addresses for names most used by the American book trade. Helpful to the amateur and professional writer in selecting a publisher. For similar information on an international basis, consult *International literary market place* (Bowker, 1965– . Annual. $189.95. ISSN 0074-6827).

93 Publishers, distributors, and wholesalers. 2v. Bowker, 1978– . Annual. $215. ISSN 0000-0671.
■ cd online
070.5 Z475

Essential contact information on virtually every publisher, distributor, and wholesaler, even small independent and alternative presses, associations, museums, and publishers of all types of publications, including audiovisual materials and software. Lists publishers not in *Books in print.* Indexes: name, geographic, ISBN, toll-free phone numbers, imprint, publishers by field of activity, inactive and out of business, and wholesalers and distributors.

94 Writer's market. Writer's Digest, 1929– . Annual. $49.99. "Electronic edition with CD-ROM." ISSN 0084-2729.
■ cd
808.02 PN161.W83

Information on agents and markets for authors. A subject listing of special-interest markets from astrology to women's magazines. Each listing includes name and address of the publication or company, its editorial needs, and its rate of payment. Additional lists of syndicates, writers' conferences, and writers' clubs are useful for the amateur author.

Serials and Periodicals

95 Gale directory of publications and broadcast media. 132d ed. 5v. Gale, 1987– . Annual. $599. ISSN 0892-1636. (*formerly* **Ayer directory of publications,** 1880–1982; **The IMS [yr.] Ayer directory of publications,** 1983–85; **The 1986 IMS directory of publications; Gale directory of publications,** 1987–89.)
050 Z6951

Geographical list of newspapers and magazines published in the United States, Canada, and Puerto Rico. Size, format, periodicity, subscription price, circulation, editors, publishers, and political sympathies are indicated. Classified lists include agricultural, collegiate, foreign language, Jewish, fraternal, Black, religious, trade, technical publications, and newsletters. Also lists radio and TV stations. Maps. Master alphabetical-keyword index. Index of periodicals by subject and special-interest classifications. Title index.

96 International directory of little magazines and small presses. Len Fulton and Ellen Furber, eds. Dustbooks, 1997– . Annual. $47.95. ISSN 0037-7228.
070.5 Z6944

Alphabetical listings, containing all the important data one expects, with subject and regional indexes; a list of distributors, jobbers, and agents; and a list of organization acronyms.

97 Periodical title abbreviations. 11th ed. 3v. Gale, 1998. v.1, by abbreviation. $224. ISBN 0-7876-1212-X; v.2, by title. $224. ISBN 0-7876-1213-8; v.3, new periodical title abbreviations, 1998. $150. ISBN 0-7876-1512-9.
051.148 Z6945

International coverage in all fields. Volume 1 is a single alphabetical list of abbreviations together with their full titles; volume 2 is the reverse dictionary, with each periodical title given alphabetically. Volume 2 may not be necessary for many libraries. Updated supplements are published annually.

98 The serials directory: an international reference book. 9th ed. 5v. 8751p. EBSCO,

1995. $339/set. ISBN 0-614-04087-6.
ISSN 0886-4179.
■ cd
050.2 Z6941

More than 114,000 titles are listed, including annuals and irregular serials, with MARC record and CONSER file data; DDC, LC, UDC, and NLM classifications; and CODEN designations. Quarterly cumulative updates. Good descriptions, subject headings, cross-references. Volume 3 is a tripart index: alphabetical, ceased titles by alphabet and subject heading, and ISSN.

99 Standard periodical directory [yr.].
21st ed. Oxbridge, 1989– . Annual.
$695. ISSN 0085-6630.
■ cd
016.051 Z6951

A listing of some 90,000 periodicals published in the United States and Canada. Includes publications issued at least once every two years. Many entries are annotated. Easy-to-read print. Telephone numbers an added advantage. Subject arrangement, title index.

100 Ulrich's international periodicals directory. 5v. Bowker, 1932– . Annual.
$459.95. ISSN 0000-0175.
■ micro cd online tape
050 Z6941

A classified list of current domestic and foreign periodicals, including irregular serials and annuals. Provides complete publishing and subscription information and indications of where each title is indexed or abstracted. Also includes a list of serials that have ceased or suspended publication since last edition. New features include indexes of serials available on CD-ROM or online.

101 World press encyclopedia. George Thomas Kurian, ed. 2v. Facts on File, 1982. $145. v.1, ISBN 0-87196-392-2; v.2, ISBN 0-87196-497-X; set, ISBN 0-87196-621-2.
070 PN4735

Covers the international press scene, providing profiles of the world's developed press systems by country, with briefer country-by-country treatment of smaller and developing press systems and minimal and underdeveloped press systems. Various lists provided in appendixes. Index. A definitive survey of the state of the press in 180 countries of the world, the most comprehensive ever attempted.

Fact Books and Almanacs

102 Awards, honors, and prizes.
15th ed. 2v. Gale, 1998. $450/set.
ISBN 0-7876-1500-5. v.1, United States and Canada. $228. ISBN 0-7876-1501-3; v.2, International and foreign. $255.
ISBN 0-7876-1502-1.
001.44 AS8

Arranged alphabetically by sponsoring organizations, volume 1 lists awards recognizing achievements in all fields. Volume 2 provides international awards of interest to Americans. Exclusions are principally scholarships, fellowships, and study awards. Subject, organization, and award indexes.

103 Canadian almanac and directory.
Canadian Almanac and Directory (dist. by Gale), 1847– . Annual. $249.
ISSN 0068-8193.
971.0025 AY414

The standard directory source for Canada, including addresses and officers of associations, institutions, professional and trade organizations, government departments, and so forth. Statistical and factual data. Arranged alphabetically by topic. Detailed subject index.

104 The copyright primer for librarians and educators. 2d ed. Janis H. Bruwelheide. 151p. American Library Assn./ National Education Assn., 1995. Paper $22. ISBN 0-8389-0642-7.
025.5 Z649

Copublished with the National Education Association; a question-and-answer format offers concise explanations of copyright topics. Internet, multimedia, and electronic environment and digital issues are addressed in this timely title.

105 Facts on file: a weekly world news digest with cumulative index. Facts on File, 1940– . Weekly, with bound annual v. $695. ISSN 0014-6641. Library and school discounts available.
■ micro cd
909.82 D410

A weekly digest arranged under broad headings (e.g., world affairs, national affairs). Indexes published twice a month and are cumulated throughout the year. Ten five-year indexes also available: 1946–50; 1951–55; 1956–60; 1961–65; 1966–70; 1971–75; 1976–80; 1981–85; 1986–90; and 1991–95. $110/v. Bound annuals at varying prices.

106 **Famous first facts: a record of first happenings, discoveries, and inventions in the United States.** 5th ed. Joseph Nathan Kane. 1122p. Wilson, 1997. $95. ISBN 0-8242-0930-3.
031.02 AG5

Compilation of first happenings, discoveries, and inventions in America. Several indexes are provided: by years, days of the month, personal names, subject, and geographical location.

107 **Guinness book of records.** Guinness Records, 1990– . Annual. $24.95. ISSN 0300-1679. (*formerly* **Guinness book of world records**, 1955–89.)
032 AG243

A guide to the superlatives of the natural and human worlds: the first, the last, the tallest, the shortest, the most, the least, and so forth. Arranged by broad topics into eleven sections. Larger in format than former editions. Charts, graphs, and diagrams show comparisons. Detailed subject index.

108 **Information please almanac.** Houghton, 1947– . Annual. $24.95; paper $10.95. ISSN 0073-7860.
310 AY64

Many facts assembled for quick reference. Special features include articles on such topics as the environment, religion, and taxes. Needed even if *World almanac* is purchased, because each volume contains some material not found in the other. Index.

109 **Panati's extraordinary origins.** Charles Panati. 480p. HarperPerennial, 1989. $16. ISBN 0-06-096419-7.
031 AG6.P37

Broad in scope, this carefully researched and organized collection of curious beginnings explores the history of more than 500 things, from games, magazines, holidays, and superstitions to household objects such as buttons, graham crackers, wallpaper, and Kleenex. A bibliographic essay, illustrations, and index enhance the volume.

110 **Universal almanac.** John W. Wright, general ed. Andrews & McMeel, 1990– . Annual. $22.95; paper $12.95. ISSN 1045-9020.
051 AY64

A worthy supplement to the *World almanac* and *Information please almanac* offering particularly good coverage of business and economic topics in a user-friendly format.

111 **Whitaker's almanack.** Joseph Whitaker. Whitaker (dist. by Gale), 1869– . Annual. $105. ISSN 0083-9256. (*formerly* **Almanack.**)
032.02 AY754

Similar to *World almanac,* this annual contains an enormous amount of statistical and descriptive information concerning Great Britain, plus brief information for other parts of the world. Detailed index.

112 **World almanac and book of facts.** World Almanac Bks., 1898– . Annual. $27.95; paper $9.95. ISSN 0084-1382.
310 AY67

An essential ready reference tool containing much statistical material for the current and preceding years, important events of the year, associations and societies and their addresses, and many other items. Index.

Indexes and Abstracts

General

113 **Bibliographic index: a subject list of bibliographies in English and foreign languages.** Wilson, 1938– . Three times a yr.: Apr., Aug., with a Dec. permanent bound annual cumulation. Service basis. ISSN 0006-1255. Cumulations available. $250/v.
■ online
016.016 Z1002

A subject list of bibliographies published separately or as parts of books, pamphlets, and periodicals. Includes bibliographies in both English and foreign languages that contain fifty or more citations.

114 **Essay and general literature index, 1900–** . Wilson, 1934– . Semiannual with bound annual. $125/yr. Five-year cumulations. $245/v. ISSN 0014-083X. See their catalog for cumulations.
■ cd online tape
080.16 AI3

Indexes by author and subject essays appearing in collections from 1900 on. *EGLI: works indexed 1900–1969* (437p. 1972. $43. ISBN 0-8242-0503-0) cites 9,917 titles indexed in the first seven cumulations. Each listed under edition, author, title. Cross-references.

115 **Library literature.** Wilson, 1921– . 6/yr. with annual cumulation. Service basis. ISSN 0024-2373.
■ cd online tape
020.5 Z666

An important tool for keeping the library staff apprised of developments in the field.

116 **Vertical file index.** Wilson, 1935– . Monthly except Aug. $50. ISSN 0042-4439.
■ online
025.172 Z1231

A subject index to current pamphlets of interest to the general public. Entries include title, publisher, paging, and price and often a descriptive note. Each issue also features a title index.

Newspapers

Many newspapers and other periodicals are now available through online services such as Data Times, Infotrac, LEXIS-NEXIS, Proquest, America Online, and Dialog. Because no library can afford to subscribe to every publication, these services offer a way to extend the collection beyond the library's walls. Dialog, for example, includes the full text of the *Boston Globe, Chicago Tribune, Christian Science Monitor, Los Angeles Times,* and *San Francisco Chronicle,* to name but a few. Users of America Online have access to *Time, U.S. News and World Report, Macleans,* and other publications. *Business Week,* the *New York Times,* and the *Washington Post* can be searched on NEXIS.

117 **Editorials on file: newspaper editorial reference service with index.** Facts on File, 1970– . Semimonthly. $460. ISSN 0013-0966. Microfiche: 1970–86, $500; 1986–93, $99/yr.
■ micro
070.172 PN477.8

Editorials and editorial cartoons from more than 100 American and Canadian newspapers are printed in full and offer a cross section of opinions on crucial issues of the day. Monthly subject and cumulative quarterly indexes ensure easy access to the needed editorials.

118 **The national newspaper index.** 1979– . Information Access Corp., 1979– . Contact publisher for pricing schedule.
■ cd online

Indexes the *New York Times, Wall Street Journal, Christian Science Monitor, Los Angeles Times,* and *Washington Post.*

119 **New York Times index.** New York Times Co., 1851– . Full service: semimonthly paper indexes, three quarterly cumulations, and hardbound annual cumulation. $1281. Cumulated annual only. $875. ISSN 0147-538X. Cumulated five-year index, 1985–89, $2,210.
■ cd online
071.471 AI21

Summarizes and classifies news alphabetically by subjects, persons, and organizations. Helpful in locating articles not only in the *New York Times,* but also in other papers, as entries establish the date of events. Indexes for earlier volumes may be obtained from UMI. See catalog or call (800) 521-0600. Access to the full text of the *New York Times* online is available through NEXIS or America Online. An online *Historical index to the* New York Times, *1851–1920* has been announced to appear sometime soon.

120 **Newspaper abstracts ondisc, 1988– .** CD-ROM updated monthly. UMI. Contact publisher for pricing.
■ cd

Indexed and abstracted here are the five newspapers in *The national newspaper index.*

Periodicals

121 **Alternative press index.** v.1– . Alternative Pr. Ctr., 1969– . Quarterly. $250. ISSN 0002-662X.
■ online
051.016 AI3

An index to alternative and radical publications—subtitle. Indexes by subject more than 150 periodicals. Includes reviews.

122 **Free magazines for libraries.** 4th ed. Diane Jones Langston and Adeline Mercer Smith. 293p. McFarland, 1994.

Paper $28.50. ISBN 0-89950-947-9.
025.2 Z692

This guide to some 700 house magazines includes full bibliographic data and descriptive annotations. More than sixty broad subject categories are used to organize the contents. Indexing by title, publisher, and subject is included. Appendixes list titles useful for vocational guidance, those outstanding for illustrations, basic titles for small to medium-sized libraries, and those indexed in various sources.

123 **Humanities index.** Wilson, 1974– . Quarterly with annual cumulations. Service basis. ISSN 0095-5981. (*formerly* **International index,** 1907–65; **Social sciences and humanities index,** 1965–74.)
■ cd online tape
016.05 AI3

Author-subject index to some 400 English-language periodicals in the humanities. Book reviews indexed by author in a separate section.

124 **The left index: a quarterly index to periodicals of the left.** v.1– . Joan Nordquist, ed. Reference Research Services (511 Lincoln St., Santa Cruz, CA 95060), 1982– . Quarterly. Institution $55/yr.; individuals $35/yr. ISSN 0733-2998.
016.3 AI3.L4

Journals indexed have a Marxist, radical, or left perspective and contain lengthy, critical, analytical material of a professional and scholarly nature. Newsletters and newspapers are excluded. Topics covered are anthropology, art, literature, economics, history, education, sociology, science, philosophy, psychology, Black studies, women's studies, and political science. Indexing of periodicals published in one quarter is available within two months of the next quarter. Access is by author and subject (standardized subject headings used) in two alphabets. The book review index section is arranged alphabetically by surname of the author or editor. The journal index section is relatively unique, listing the numbers referring to the entries of the author list section. If one remembers an article in a certain journal, this index will lead to it directly, even if the title and author were forgotten. There is some overlap with *Alternative press index,* but the promptness, format, continuously cumulated subject index, scholarly articles, access to foreign journals, book review index, and journal index offer advantages.

125 **The magazine index, 1977– .** Information Access Corp., 1977– . Contact publisher for pricing schedule.
■ cd online

The magazine index, abridged, 1988– . Information Access Corp., 1988– . Contact publisher for pricing schedule.
051 AI3.M34

Contains total indexing of more than 370 popular periodicals by title, authors, and subjects (LC subject headings and some natural-language subjects). Notes reviews, illustrations, and biographic material. Abridged edition indexes more than 100 titles.

126 **Readers' guide to periodical literature.** Wilson, 1900– . Semimonthly (monthly Feb., July, and Aug.), with quarterly and permanent bound annual cumulations. $200. ISSN 0034-0464.
■ cd online tape
051 AI3

The standard author-subject index to more than 240 of the most popular general and nontechnical magazines. Book reviews indexed by author in a separate section. The online and CD-ROM versions can be purchased with abstracts. Retrospective volumes (1900–90) are in print at $200 each. *Nineteenth century readers' guide to periodical literature* (2v. $200. ISBN 0-8242-0584-7) may interest academic libraries. *Abridged readers' guide to periodical literature* ($100. ISSN 0001-334X), published since 1935, indexes eighty-two titles and may be satisfactory for schools and small public libraries.

127 **Social sciences index.** Wilson, 1974– . Quarterly with annual cumulations. Service basis. ISSN 0094-4920. (*formerly* **International index,** 1907–65; **Social sciences and humanities index,** 1965–74.)
■ cd online tape
016.05 AI3

Author-subject index to some 400 periodicals in the social sciences. Specific subject headings and many cross-references aid research. Book reviews indexed by author in a separate section.

Reviews

128 **Book review digest, 1905– .** Wilson, 1906– . Monthly except Feb. and July, with quarterly and annual cumulations. Service basis. ISSN 0006-7326.

■ cd online tape
015.73 Z1219

An index with excerpts and digests of more than 7,000 current reviews each year in more than ninety American, English, and Canadian periodicals. Nonfiction books must be reviewed in at least two sources and fiction books in at least four to be included. Covers children's and young adult literature. Besides bibliographic information, it includes Dewey number and Sears subject headings. Each issue has a title and subject index. Issues for 1905–79 are available at $155 per volume. Annuals (1980–) sold on service basis. *Author/title index 1905–1974* sold separately for $155 per volume and *Author/title index 1975–1984* (1500p. 1987. ISBN 0-8242-0724-7) for $65.

129 Book review index. Gale, 1965– . Bimonthly. Annual cumulation. $260. ISSN 0524-0581. Annual cumulations from 1969 to 1997 are available.

Book review index 1965–1984: a master cumulation. 10v. Gale, 1985. $1315/set. ISBN 0-8103-0577-1.

Book review index 1985–1992: a master cumulation. 6v. Gale, 1993. $1315/set. ISBN 0-8103-9626-2.

Book review index 1993–1998: a master cumulation. 6v. Gale, 1999. $1360/set. ISBN 0-7876-2828-X.
■ cd online tape
015 Z1035.A1

An author index to reviews in more than 500 periodicals. Title index added beginning in 1976. Differs from *Book review digest* in that all reviews from the sources indexed are cited, regardless of the number of reviews for a particular book. No excerpts from reviews are provided.

130 Children's book review index. Gale, 1975– . Annual. $114. ISSN 0147-5681. Cumulation 1985–1997. 4v. $400/set. ISBN 0-8103-5457-8. Contact publisher for availability of previous cumulations.
028.5 Z1037.A1

Based on Gale's *Book review index (BRI)*. Includes all citations for children's books listed in *BRI*. A few periodicals included in *Children's book review index* are not listed in *BRI*. No information is given about the content of the reviews. Indexes of illustrators and titles.

131 Media review digest. Pierian, 1971– . Annual with semiannual supplement. $245. ISSN 0363-7778. (*formerly* **Multimedia reviews index,** 1970–72.)
011 LB1043

Indexes and digests reviews, evaluations, and descriptions of nonbook media (films and filmstrips, records and tapes, and miscellaneous media). Includes cataloging information, subject indexing, and review ratings assigned by the *Digest* staff. Indexed.

Government Publications

As the federal government moves us further in the direction of a digital society, it will become increasingly difficult to find government documents in paper form. One way to stay informed is to follow the work of ALA's Government Documents Round Table (GODORT), which works to increase the availability, use, and bibliographic control of documents. Another is to visit the GPO's home page on the Internet regularly at http://www.access.gpo.gov/su_docs/. It offers GPO Access online databases, GPO Access Federal locator services, on-demand delivery services, and U.S. Government Bookstore and depository library information.

132 Accessing U.S. government information, revised and expanded edition. Jerrold Zwirn, comp. (Bibliographies and indexes in law and political science; no. 24). 200p. Greenwood, 1996. $59.95. ISBN 0-313-29765-7.
015.73 Z1223

Subtitled *Subject guide to jurisdiction of the executive and legislative branches,* this guide is helpful for finding sources of information about government business and policy making.

133 Guide to popular U.S. government publications. 4th ed. Frank W. Hoffmann and Richard J. Ward. 285p. Libraries Unlimited, 1997. $35. ISBN 1-56308-462-7.
015.73 J83

Covers titles through January 1997 and arranges them by subject. Entries include title, author, date, number of pages, price, GPO stock number, and SuDoc classification number. The broad spectrum of subjects covered are geared to the general reader.

134 **A guide to publications of the executive branch.** Frederic J. O'Hara. 287p. Pierian, 1979. $39.50. ISBN 0-87650-072-6; paper $24.50. ISBN 0-87650-088-2.
015.73 Z1223

Describes the various publications of the executive branch to enable the reader to understand the functions and operations of many agencies. May be used as a selection tool, because it cites free but useful publications, indicates how a document fits into a collection, and emphasizes publications that recur or are kept current by new editions and regular revisions. Although this book is still in print, users should be aware that all the titles listed may no longer be available in printed form.

135 **Index to current urban documents, 1972– .** Greenwood, 1972– . Quarterly with annual clothbound cumulated v. $450. ISSN 0046-8908. Back volumes available. $450/v.
016.U5 Z7165

Index of annual reports, audit reports, budgets, community development programs, conference transcripts of proceedings, consultants' reports, demographic profiles, directories, economic studies, environmental impact statements, evaluations and analyses, planning reports, policy statements, surveys and questionnaires, zoning ordinances, and so forth. *Urban documents microfiche collection* can provide the actual documents, available through the same publisher.

136 **Informing the nation: a handbook of government information for librarians.** Frederic J. O'Hara, ed. 560p. Greenwood, 1990. $65. ISBN 0-313-27267-0.
016.0253 Z688.G6

Aimed primarily at nondepository libraries, this book includes substantial portions of four government publications relating to classification and standards. Because of the changing availability of government publications in paper format, some of the advice offered in this handbook may no longer be applicable.

137 **Introduction to United States government information sources.** 5th ed. Joe Morehead and Mary Fetzer. 474p. Libraries Unlimited, 1996. $55. ISBN 1-56308-485-6; paper $40. ISBN 1-56308-460-0.
015.73 Z1223.Z7

Includes chapters dealing with major public documents issued by the several branches of the federal government. Attention given to commercially published reference aids and services, as well as to official catalogs and indexes. GPO micropublishing, microform distribution to depository libraries, bibliographic control of nondepository publications, and the online availability of the *Monthly catalog* are covered.

138 **Monthly catalog of United States government publications.** Govt. Print. Off., 1895– . $245/yr. S/N 721-011-00000-3. SuDoc GP 3.8. ISSN 0362-6830.
■ cd online

Cumulative personal author indexes to the Monthly catalog of U.S. government publications, 1941–1975. Edward Przebienda, ed. 5v. Pierian, 1971–78. $49.50/v.; $225/set. ISBN 0-686-76934-1.

Cumulative subject guide to U.S. government bibliographies, 1924–1973. Edna A. Kanely, comp. 7v. Carrollton Pr., 1976. $765/set. ISBN 0-8408-0150-5.

Cumulative subject index to the Monthly catalog of United States government publications, 1900–1971. 15v. Research Pub., 1975. $1350/set. ISBN 0-8408-0312-5.
015 Z1223

Each issue includes between 1,500 and 3,000 new documents, arranged by Superintendent of Documents classification number. Includes sales information and complete cataloging data. Utilizes Anglo-American cataloging rules and Library of Congress subject headings. Author, title, subject, and series and report index in each issue. Price includes twelve issues, serials supplement, semiannual index, and annual index. To find citations by personal author quickly and efficiently, use *Cumulative personal author indexes,* alphabetically arranged by author, followed by volume and entry number, as in the *Monthly catalog*. For the subject approach, the cumulative subject indexes listed above are useful.

139 **New products from the U.S. government.** U.S. Superintendent of

Documents. Govt. Print. Off., 1994– .
Bimonthly. Free. ISSN 0734-2772.
SuDoc GP 3.17/6:v./no. (*formerly* **New books**, 1982–94.)
015.73 Z1223

Issues list all publications added to the Superintendent of Documents sales inventory since the previous issue. Information is limited to title, date, format or pagination, SuDoc number, GPO stock number, and price. No annotations.

140 State publications and depository libraries: a reference handbook.
Margaret T. Lane. 560p. Greenwood, 1981. $105. ISBN 0-313-22118-9.
027.5 Z688

Part 1 describes state depository library legislation, including guidelines approved by ALA's Government Documents Round Table (GODORT). Part 2 surveys the literature of state publications, followed by a lengthy bibliography of relevant literature with complete bibliographic information; many titles annotated. Part 3 lists alphabetically for the fifty states the legislation governing state depository libraries, followed by a "state comment" and a bibliography. A model law sets norms for improvement. Index of names and subjects. Contact individual state libraries for updated information.

141 State reference publications: a bibliographic guide to state blue books, legislative manuals, and other general reference sources.
Lynn Hellebust, ed. Annual. $40.
Government Research Service, 1991– .
ISSN 1057-0586. (*formerly* **State blue books, legislative manuals, and reference publications: a selected bibliography.**)
016.3539 Z7165.U5

Listings by state of those reference publications dealing with the legislature and general state government; guides and statistical compilations. Includes address, price, and frequency of publication.

142 Subject bibliographies, 1975– .
U.S. Superintendent of Documents.
Govt. Print. Off. Irreg. Free.
S/N 021-310-00305-0. SuDoc GP 3.22.
015.73 Z1223.Z7

More than 270 subject bibliographies listing publications available for sale by the Superintendent of Documents. Many deal with topics of current interest.

143 Tapping the government grapevine: the user-friendly guide to U.S. government information sources. 3d ed. Judith Schiek Robinson. 296p. Oryx, 1998. $43.50. ISBN 1-57356-024-3.
015.73 J83

A practical guide to locating and using government information resources, including the many new agency Internet sites. Provides extensive narrative as well as bibliographic information on the key print, online, and electronic data sources. Includes a helpful, and often amusing, commentary on the remarkable bureaucratic apparatus we have created.

144 Using government information sources: print and electronic. 2d ed. Jean L. Sears and Marilyn K. Moody. 539p. Oryx, 1994. $115.
ISBN 0-89774-670-8.
015.73 Z1223.Z754

Government information is approached from the point of view of the searcher rather than by specific agency. Various search strategies are discussed, and citations include SuDoc and item numbers and ASI numbers when pertinent.

3

Encyclopedias

CAROLYN M. MULAC

Whether used as a destination for a quick check of facts or a launching pad for further journeys into research, an encyclopedia is an integral part of the reference collection. Many collections, in fact, own two or more sets, depending upon the public served. Encyclopedia purchases should be alternated, and sets should be replaced at no greater than five-year intervals. This chapter will not discuss children's encyclopedias, as was done in the previous edition.

In this section in the previous edition, the editor noted that "only the *Academic American encyclopedia* is available online." Today, four major encyclopedias are available online, and almost all resources of this type are available on CD-ROM. Although some factors make nonprint versions attractive, there will always be a need, particularly in public libraries, for print encyclopedias, which are handier than online, portable, and always available.

Guides

145 ARBA guide to subject encyclopedias and dictionaries. 2d ed. Susan C. Awe, ed. 482p. Libraries Unlimited, 1997. $65. ISBN 1-56308-467-8.
016.031 Z5848

This is an excellent collection development tool, providing complete bibliographic data and evaluative reviews of more than 1,000 subject-based encyclopedias and dictionaries that have appeared in the past ten years or so. The reviews are drawn from the 1986–96 editions of *ARBA,* but citations have been updated for new printings and reviews expanded for relevancy and consistency of presentation. Excluded from this collection are general dictionaries and encyclopedias. Includes an author-title index and subject index.

146 Kister's best encyclopedias: a comparative guide to general and specialized encyclopedias. 2d ed. Kenneth F. Kister. 506p. Oryx, 1994. $42.50. ISBN 0-89774-744-5.
031 AE1

Surveys more than 1,000 encyclopedias in both print and electronic formats. General encyclopedias are profiled in chapters grouped by size (large, medium, small) and age level (adults and older students; children and younger students). There are sections on electronic encyclopedias (CD-ROM, online, handheld) and out-of-print encyclopedias, as well as subject encyclopedias (architecture to transportation) and foreign-language encyclopedias (nine languages represented). An annotated bibliography and a directory of encyclopedia publishers and distributors complete this comprehensive reference source.

147 Purchasing an encyclopedia: twelve points to consider. 5th ed. Sandy Whiteley, ed. 43p. American Library Assn., 1996. $7.95. ISBN 0-8389-7823-1.
031 AE1

For the last eleven years, reference librarians have relied on the "Encyclopedia Update" in the September 15 issue of *Booklist/reference books bulletin* for timely, carefully prepared reviews of annually revised multivolume general encyclopedias. Detailed reviews of print and electronic titles conclude with capsule appraisals indicating the most appropriate type of library or audience for the work. This handy booklet reprints the twelfth and latest of these reviews (September 15, 1995) and also provides selection advice and charts comparing features and prices for both print and CD-ROM titles. Public libraries in particular should consider purchasing an extra copy to circulate.

Encyclopedias

148 Academic American encyclopedia. Lawrence T. Lorimer, ed. dir.; K. Anne Ranson, ed. in chief. 21v. Grolier, 1997. $725. ISBN 0-7172-2064-8.
■ cd online
031 AE5

This twenty-one-volume general encyclopedia, geared to the informational needs of students at the high school and college levels and for the inquiring adult, fills the gap between a young people's encyclopedia and a scholarly encyclopedia. First issued in 1980, the latest edition boasts more than 29,000 articles and some 17,000 illustrations, three-quarters of which are in color. It is comprehensive in the coverage of information that the editors consider to be of major concern in American schools and universities. The arts and humanities, science, popular sports, and contemporary events are well covered. There are 110 completely new articles and revisions and partial revisions of nearly 3,000 entries. Many of the articles include bibliographies. An effective system of cross-references allows optimal access to the contents. Quarterly updates (text only) are available on CompuServe, America Online, Delphi, Genie, and Dow Jones News/Retrieval. The CD-ROM version is *The Grolier multimedia encyclopedia,* which may be directly linked to CompuServe via modem for current information.

149 Cambridge encyclopedia. 3d ed. David Crystal, ed. 1344p. Cambridge Univ. Pr., 1997. $54.95. ISBN 0-521-58459-0.
031 AG5

The aim here is "to provide a succinct, systematic, and readable guide to the facts, events, issues, beliefs, and achievements which make up the sum of human knowledge." Thousands of short entries on a myriad of topics are attractively presented in a work appropriate for adult patrons of academic and public libraries.

150 Cambridge paperback encyclopedia. 2d ed. David Crystal, ed. 1100p. Cambridge Univ. Pr., 1995. Paper $19.95. ISBN 0-521-55968-5.
031 AE5

An abridged version of the previous title, convenient for home and desk use.

151 Collier's encyclopedia. Lauren S. Bahr, ed. dir.; Bernard Johnson, ed. in chief. 24v. Collier, 1997. $680. ISBN 0-02-864840-4.
■ cd
031 AE5.C683

Suitable for high school and college students as well as adult readers, this is "a scholarly, systematic, continuously revised summary of the knowledge that is most significant to mankind." Approximately 23,000 articles are arranged alphabetically (letter-by-letter) and indexed in a volume of some 450,000 entries. The arts, humanities, social sciences, and biography are particularly well represented. In recent years more full-color illustrations have been added to the pictorial matter (which accounts for about two-fifths of the pages). The final volume includes a thematically arranged bibliography of approximately 11,500 titles. There are no references to those works from the articles in the main part of the set. Some articles are followed by glossaries of related terms or brief biographies of noteworthy individuals.

152 Columbia encyclopedia. 5th ed. Barbara A. Chernow and George A. Vallasi, eds. 3072p. Columbia Univ. Pr. (dist. by Houghton), 1993. $125. ISBN 0-395-62438-X.
031 AG5

Successor to *The new Columbia encyclopedia* (4th ed., 1975), this is a hefty single-volume encyclopedia for the layperson with scholarly interests. Some 50,000 entries, heavily seasoned with cross-references, offer a smorgasbord of topics for the curious browser. Major articles are accompanied by bibliographies. Pronunciation guidance is provided by the use of diacritical marks. Arrangement is alphabetical, letter-by-letter. Illustrations (maps, charts, chemical diagrams, and drawings) are successfully integrated with the text.

153 Compton's encyclopedia. Dale Good, ed. dir. 26v. Compton's Learning Co., 1996. $395. ISBN 0-944262-03-3.
■ cd online
031 AG5

Recommended for home and school use by young people ages nine through eighteen. The main text, consisting of more than 5,000 articles, is supported by the nearly 30,000 brief articles among the 70,000 entries in the "fact-index." This volume presents brief dictionary entries, biographical sketches, statistics, and capsule treatments of topics not considered in the main text. This edition has been considerably revised, with more than 500 new articles and significant revisions to some 30 articles. Seven articles were added to the main text, and there were revisions and updates of more than 400 main text entries. Illustrations are plentiful in this encyclopedia, with roughly 65 percent in color. Geography, nature study, U.S. history, sports and games, biography, and basic science are handled especially well in *Compton's*. It is sometimes awkward to go from the main text to the "fact-index" in search of information. Online access to *Compton's* (and weekly updates) is available through America Online and Prodigy. The CD-ROM version is entitled *Compton's interactive encyclopedia;* the disc also contains Simon and Schuster's *Webster's new world dictionary and thesaurus*. Audio and video are included, and users with a modem can subscribe to America Online for those current updates.

154 Concise Columbia encyclopedia. 3d ed. Paul G. Lagasse, ed. 973p. Columbia Univ. Pr. (dist. by Houghton), 1994. $49.95. ISBN 0-395-62439-8.
■ cd
031 AG5

Based on the fifth edition of *The Columbia encyclopedia,* this edition boasts 2,000 more entries than its predecessor (2d ed., 1989). Updated in the interval between its publication and that of its parent volume, it is a compact reference especially suitable for home use. It is also available on CD-ROM as part of the Microsoft Bookshelf, where it is directly interfaced with the *Hammond atlas*.

155 Encyclopedia Americana. Lawrence T. Lorimer, ed. dir.; Mark Cummings, ed. 30v. Grolier, 1995. $999. ISBN 0-7172-0126-0.
■ cd online
031 AE5

An encyclopedia suitable for junior and senior high school students as well as adults and college-level students. Cross-references are plentiful throughout the 45,000 articles. The index is comprehensive and analytical. *Americana* contains an exceptionally large number of U.S. place-names and biographies. The sciences, mathematics, American history, and the social sciences are particularly well developed. There are bibliographies at the end of major articles, nearly 400 of which have been updated for this edition. Nearly 40 articles are new or replacements, and there are more than 600 minor revisions and 45 major ones. Although a continuous revision policy is in place, updating is sometimes not as thorough as one would like. The CD-ROM version features more than 4,000 updated articles not found in the print version, but it does not contain some 20,000 maps and photographs from the traditional format.

156 The new encyclopaedia britannica. 15th ed. Robert McHenry, ed. in chief. 32v. Encyclopaedia Britannica, 1995. $1299. ISBN 0-85229-605-3.
■ cd online
031 AE5

This most famous, scholarly, and venerable of English-language encyclopedias is suitable for an adult audience and competent high school and college students. The unique three-part structure is by now familiar: the *Propaedia,* a one-volume outline of recorded knowledge and contents guide to the *Macropaedia's* articles; the *Micropaedia,* a twelve-volume ready reference set; and the *Macropaedia,* a seventeen-volume compilation of longer, scholarly, signed articles with bibliographies. The *Micropaedia* provides cross-references from articles to more extended treatment in the *Macropaedia* or to other related *Micropaedia* coverage. The other two parts of the set also give adequate assistance to the seeker of information in broad topical areas of philosophy, law, history, and religion, with access to specific subjects aided by the two-volume comprehensive analytical index. There are more than 100 new articles in this edition's *Micropaedia*, and nearly 900 articles have been revised. *Britannica* is now available in a CD-ROM version, which contains more than 1,000 articles not in the printed version. *Britannica online*, which is available via the World Wide Web on the Internet, is updated daily and provides numerous links to other Internet resources.

157 **The world book encyclopedia.** Dale W. Jacobs, ed. 22v. World Book, 1997. $644. ISBN 0-7166-0098-5.
■ cd
031 AE5

Appropriate for elementary grades through high school and for general use in the home, *World book* is also a favorite with reference librarians. More than 17,000 signed articles are arranged alphabetically, word-by-word. Numerous cross-references and an exhaustive (more than 150,000 entries) analytical index ensure easy access to the contents of the set. The social sciences, arts and humanities, life and physical sciences, literature, and biography are covered in a clear, lively style. Technical terms are explained as they are introduced, and maps are placed near related text. Illustrations account for about one-third of the layout, and some 80 percent are in color. More than 2,000 of the articles in this edition have been at least partially revised, and there are more than 100 new articles included. The index volume, titled *Research guide and index*, also provides 200 "Reading and Study Guides," offering suggested topics for study along with listings of readings often subdivided by user level. The CD-ROM version is the *World book multimedia encyclopedia*, which contains the complete text of the print version as well as the *World book dictionary*. It also features illustrations, maps, animations, and audio and video clips. The *World book information finder* is a DOS text-only version offering the complete text and *World book dictionary*.

4

Philosophy, Religion, and Ethics

SCOTT E. KENNEDY AND BARBARA M. BIBEL

General reference sources in the areas of philosophy and ethics are few in number, and librarians are ever on the lookout for new works that can help readers understand these complex fields. Sources in the area of religion, however, appear almost daily. Religion is a topic of regular and abiding interest for users of both public and academic libraries. Although most of the sources in this field reflect the prominent Judeo-Christian influences in American culture today, there are now excellent materials on the Eastern and nontraditional religions and movements. Sources on mythology, superstition, and folklore are included in this chapter as they reflect the ancient social traditions that deeply permeate much of modern Western culture.

Philosophy

Bibliographies and Guides

158 Philosophy: a guide to the reference literature. 2d ed. Hans E. Bynagle. 233p. Libraries Unlimited, 1997. $38.50. ISBN 1-56308-376-0.
016.1 B72

The general sources in the guide are arranged by type of reference work (encyclopedia, dictionary, bibliography, etc.). There is also considerable attention devoted to individual philosophers. This authoritative guide belongs in every serious philosophy reference collection.

Indexes and Abstracts

159 Philosopher's index: an international index to philosophical periodicals and books. Bowling Green Univ. Pr., v.1– . 1967– . Quarterly with annual cumulations. $205. ISSN 0031-7993.
■ cd online
105 B1

The principal index in the field; useful also for investigating the philosophy of science and the philosophical underpinnings of academic disciplines such as history and psychology. Electronic versions cover materials published since 1940.

Dictionaries and Encyclopedias

160 Cambridge dictionary of philosophy. Robert Audi, ed. 882p. Cambridge Univ. Pr., 1995. $89.95. ISBN 0-521-40224-7; paper $27.95. ISBN 0-521-48328-X.
103 B41

A comprehensive and scholarly reference work, with clear, thorough definitions. An excellent one-volume handbook, produced by an international team of scholars. Suitable as a reference work for the home or the library. Highly recommended.

161 Dictionary of the history of ideas: studies of selected pivotal ideas. Philip P. Wiener, ed. 5v. Scribner, 1980. Paper boxed set $67.50. ISBN 0-684-16418-3.
909 CB5.D52

Encyclopedic and interdisciplinary in character; sets forth the relationship among intellectual concepts in different disciplines. Treatment is either cross-cultural and chronological, tracing the origin of a thought from ancient times to the present, or analytical, giving the evolution of an idea as it appears in the writings of its proponents. Bibliographies, cross-references, and the excellent fifth-volume index, which includes birth and death dates for historical figures, make this set essential for medium-sized libraries whose clientele ask for interdisciplinary material.

162 Encyclopedia of classical philosophy. Donald J. Zeyl, ed. 614p. Greenwood, 1997. $99.50. ISBN 0-313-28775-9.
180.3 B163.E53

A scholarly, yet eminently readable, work dedicated to the teachings, schools, and philosophers of ancient Greece and Rome.

163 Encyclopedia of philosophy. Paul Edwards, ed. 4v. Free Pr., 1973. $450/set. ISBN 0-02-894950-1.
103 B51

Scholarly work within the understanding of the general reader. For all periods; covers both Oriental and Western philosophers, concepts, and schools of philosophy. Useful also for investigating peripheral fields in the sciences and social sciences. Signed articles; contributors represent subject authority on international level. Good bibliographies follow articles. Full cross-referencing is sometimes lacking, but there is a good index. A major contribution to this field.

164 The encyclopedia of unbelief. Gordon Stein, ed. 2v. Prometheus Books, 1985. $99.95/set. ISBN 0-87975-307-2.
210.321 BL2705

More than 200 signed articles on the forces behind and history of the free thought movements. These include atheism, humanism, and rationalism. More than 100 scholars contributed to this introduction to people and ideas often ignored in many standard philosophical and religious sources. Appendixes and index. Thoroughly cross-referenced.

165 Masterpieces of world philosophy. Frank N. Magill, ed. 684p. HarperCollins, 1990. $40. ISBN 0-06-016430-1.
100 B75.M37

Straightforward essays on major philosophical works from the *Bhagavad Gita* to John Rawls's *Theory of justice.* Each entry provides an account of the principal ideas advanced, pertinent literature, a brief summary of the text, and recommended reading.

166 Routledge encyclopedia of philosophy. Edward Craig, ed. 10v. Routledge, 1998. $2495/set. ISBN 0-415-07310-3.
■ cd
100.21 B51.R68

More than 2,000 entries, including important essays on the philosophy of mind, philosophy of science, and applied ethics; a quarter of the entries are devoted to non-Western philosophy; up-to-date discussions of contemporary theorists, such as Derrida. The *Routledge encyclopedia of philosophy* will most likely replace the thirty-year-old *Encyclopedia of philosophy* as the standard reference work in the field.

167 World philosophy: essay-reviews of 225 major works. Frank N. Magill, ed. 5v. Salem, 1982. $250/set. ISBN 0-89356-325-0.
190 B29

Synopses of basic philosophical works chronologically arranged from ancient to modern times, prefaced by a statement of "principal ideas advanced," with critical comments to identify influences of earlier philosophers. Analyzes secondary works and bibliographies, reviews pertinent literature of the philosopher and his or her work, and concludes with a recommended reading list. Includes indexes and a glossary of philosophical terms.

Biographical Sources

168 **Biographical dictionary of twentieth-century philosophers.** Stuart Brown et al., eds. Routledge, 1996. $150. ISBN 0-415-06043-5.
109.2 B804

With more than 1,000 entries, international in scope, this dictionary provides essential information on twentieth-century philosophers that is otherwise very difficult to obtain. Includes biographical highlights, major publications, secondary literature, and key concepts.

Religion

General

BIBLIOGRAPHIES AND GUIDES

169 **Recent reference books in religion: a guide for students, scholars, researchers, buyers, and readers.** 2d ed. William M. Johnston. 350p. Fitzroy Dearborn, 1998. $40. ISBN 1-57958-035-1.
016.2 BL48

A superb guide to the field of contemporary reference works in the field of religion. Lengthy annotations describe scope, strengths, weaknesses, and competitors of works. Covers the major world religions as well as works on mythology, folklore, and ethics.

170 **Religious information sources: a worldwide guide.** J. Gordon Melton and Michael A. Koszegi. 657p. Garland, 1992. $90. ISBN 0-8240-7102-6.
016.2 BL48

An extensive guide to works on religions of all types and to sources in all media. Author, title, subject, and organization indexes.

INDEXES AND ABSTRACTS

171 **Religion index one.** American Theological Assn., 1977– . $470. ISSN 0419-8428.
■ cd online
016.2 BL1

The principal index for scholarship in the West. Indexes more than 550 periodicals pertaining to religion. Subject index, author-editor index, and scripture index. Supersedes the *Index to religious periodical literature* (1949–76).

DICTIONARIES AND ENCYCLOPEDIAS

172 **Eerdmans' handbook to the world's religions.** Rev. ed. 464p. Eerdmans, 1994. $21.95. ISBN 0-8028-0853-0.
291 BL80.2

This colorful handbook depicts the development and the cultural features of the world's many religions, from neolithic times to the present. It includes graphs, charts, photos, and case studies for each topic.

173 **The encyclopedia of religion.** Mircea Eliade, ed. 16v. Macmillan, 1986. $1100. ISBN 0-02-909480-1.
■ cd
200.3 BL31

This magnificent set is a comprehensive, ecumenical guide to all aspects of religion. It contains accurate information on ancient and living religions, personalities, beliefs, practices, themes, and symbols. The eminence and range of the 1,400 contributors make this a work of impeccable scholarship. Most entries are approximately 300 words, but many are of short book length. The scope and balance of this encyclopedia make it an exciting and essential source. Smaller libraries may wish to purchase the *Macmillan compendium: world religions* (Macmillan, 1997. $125. ISBN 0-02-864918-4), which incorporates the most essential articles from the larger set into a handy one-volume reference work.

174 **The encyclopedia of world faiths: an illustrated survey of the world's living religions.** Peter D. Bishop and Michael Darnton, eds. 352p. Facts on File, 1988. $40. ISBN 0-8160-1860-X.
291 BL80.2

A well-illustrated collection of essays about all the world's major religions, including newly emerging ones. Articles describe rituals, myths, doctrines, ethics, and social features of each faith. Essays include bibliographies and glossaries.

175 **Oxford dictionary of world religions.** John Bowker, ed. 1136p. Oxford Univ. Pr., 1997. $55. ISBN 0-19-213965-7.
200.3 BL31.O84

Provides clear, intelligent information that goes far beyond mere definition. An excellent work that educates as well as informs.

176 Perennnial dictionary of world religions. Keith Crim et al., eds. 830p. Abingdon, 1989. $19.95. ISBN 0-06-061613-X.
291 BL31

Originally published under the title *Abingdon dictionary of living religions,* this work is both authoritative and concise. More than 1,600 signed articles provide a description of all modern religions practiced in the world today. It gives clear, brief descriptions of beliefs, practices, historical developments, major figures, and sacred literature. Arrangement is biographical and topical, with short bibliographies and cross-references.

177 A reader's guide to the great religions. 2d ed. Charles J. Adams, ed. 521p. Free Pr., 1977. $24.95. ISBN 0-02-900240-0.
016.2 BL80.2

Bibliographical essays on the world's great religious traditions including primitive religions and the ancient world as well as Hinduism, Buddhism, Judaism, Christianity, Islam, and so forth. The items recommended in each bibliographical essay are set in the framework of the religion. Each essay can serve as an introduction to the religion and as a stimulus for further reading. The second edition has been considerably revised and brought up-to-date. Author index. Subject index.

178 Who's who of religions. 560p. Penguin, 1996. $14.95. ISBN 0-14-051349-3.
200.922 BL72

Originally published as *Who's who of world religions* by Simon and Schuster, the coverage extends backward in time to the earliest known religious leaders and includes people of all religions and cultures. A solid work with extensive bibliographies.

179 World religions from ancient history to the present. Geoffrey Parrinder, ed. 528p. Facts on File, 1984. $29.95. ISBN 0-87196-129-6; paper $15.95. ISBN 0-8160-1289-X.
291 BL80.2

A smooth revision of the 1971 *Religions of the world* that thoughtfully surveys the impact of religious theory and practice on the peoples and cultures of the world. Includes black-and-white photographs, a bibliography, and a useful index.

Bible

INDEXES AND ABSTRACTS

180 New Testament abstracts. Weston School of Theology, 1956– . (subscriptions to Catholic Biblical Assn., Catholic University, Washington, DC 20064.) 3 issues/yr. $27. ISSN 0028-6877.

Old Testament abstracts. Catholic Biblical Assn. of America, 1978– . 3 issues/yr. $14. ISSN 0364-8591.
220 BS410

Each publication provides abstracts of books and articles from 350 Jewish, Catholic, and Protestant periodicals.

ATLASES

181 Atlas of the Bible. John William Rogerson. 240p. Facts on File, 1984. $45. ISBN 0-8160-1207-5.
220 B2230

A beautifully illustrated guide to the land of the Bible. Covers composition and origins of the Bible as a literary work and describes the history and culture of the Old and New Testaments. Lavish use of color in maps, photographs, and illustrations. Chronological table, bibliography, gazetteer, and index, plus many special features, make this guide useful indeed.

182 Harper atlas of the Bible. James B. Prichard, ed. 256p. HarperCollins, 1987. $49.95. ISBN 0-06-181883-6.
220 B2230

This atlas presents maps relating to the Bible in a chronological order, from prehistory to the second century C.E. It includes materials based upon archaeological evidence using a curved earth format. Text integrates biblical history, geography, and social and cultural life. A chronology, a biographical dictionary, and a place-name index are included.

183 Macmillan Bible atlas. 3d ed. Yohanan Aharoni, ed. 215p. Macmillan, 1993. $35. ISBN 0-02-500605-3.
220 G2230

Recent research and excavations are described in this edition, which contains clear and attractive maps with relevant discussion and illustrations. Chronological outlines of biblical history from 3000 B.C. to A.D. 200. Makes use of an intelligent and ingenious scheme of arrows and symbols.

COMMENTARIES

184 Harper's Bible commentary. James L. Mays, ed. 1326p. HarperCollins, 1988. $40. ISBN 0-06-065541-0.
220.7 BS491

Companion to the *HarperCollins Bible dictionary,* this is a commentary arranged by book and chapter to help the reader understand the Bible.

185 The international Bible commentary. Rev. ed. F. F. Bruce, ed. 1644p. Zondervan, 1986. $29.95. ISBN 0-310-22020-3.
220.77 BS491.2

A careful revision of an evangelical Protestant commentary using the New International Version of the Bible. Literary analysis of the Old and New Testaments by forty-three contributing scholars.

186 New interpreter's Bible. 12v. Abingdon, 1994– . (in progress) $60–$70/v. v.1, ISBN 0-687-27814-7.
■ cd
220.77 BS491.2

One of the most important works currently in progress, the *New interpreter's Bible* provides authoritative exposition and exegesis of the Bible using both the New Revised Standard and the New International Versions as base text.

187 The new Jerome biblical commentary. Raymond E. Brown et al., eds. 1484p. Prentice-Hall, 1990. $69.95. ISBN 0-13-509612-X.
220.7 BS491.2

A one-volume commentary on the Bible by Roman Catholic scholars. In addition to an ample exegetical explanation for the line-by-line commentary on the entire Bible are long and thorough topical articles. The new edition significantly revises the older work and incorporates advances in biblical scholarship as well as in archaeology, hermeneutics, and manuscript discoveries. It is arranged by book and chapter of the Bible. Bibliographic guides.

CONCORDANCES

188 New Strong's exhaustive concordance of the Bible: with main concordance, appendix to the main concordance, Hebrew and Aramaic dictionary of the Old Testament, Greek dictionary of the New Testament. 1920p. Nelson, 1997. $24.99. ISBN 0-7852-1195-0.
220.2 BS425

The classic source since 1894. Based on the King James Bible. New type and readable spacing make this a pleasure to use. Assists the reader with the original Hebrew, Greek, or Chaldee term from which the English is translated. A keyword comparison enables readers to compare selected, controversial words and phrases in five contemporary Bible translations. Indispensable.

DICTIONARIES AND ENCYCLOPEDIAS

189 Anchor Bible dictionary. David Noel Freedman. 6v. Doubleday, 1992. $360/set. ISBN 0-385-42583-X.
220.3 BS440

A comprehensive work in all senses of the word. Nearly 1,000 scholars participated in the preparation of the 6,200 entries. Scholarly, yet jargon free, with useful bibliographies for each article.

190 The dictionary of Bible and religion. William M. Genz, ed. 1152p. Abingdon, 1986. $26.95. ISBN 0-687-10757-1.
203.2 BR95

The authoritative, comprehensive result of the work of twenty-eight scholars. All aspects of the Bible and its times are covered. Jewish and Christian religious traditions receive better coverage than those of Hinduism, Buddhism, or Islam. Careful scholarship makes this a fine dictionary that libraries will really use.

191 HarperCollins Bible dictionary. Rev. ed. Paul Achtemeier, ed. 1256p. HarperCollins, 1996. $45. ISBN 0-06-060037-3.
220.3 BS440

A superb revision of an old favorite. A nonsectarian scholarly work that includes an outline of each book of the Bible. Based on the Revised Standard Version, the writing is objective and precise, the coverage thorough. Includes all important names, places, and topics. Pronunciation is given where appropriate. Major articles explore recent archaeological findings and explain the variety and significance of the many versions of the Bible. Most entries are signed. Many black-and-white photographs and maps are provided. Color map section at back. Well indexed and carefully cross-referenced.

192 The international standard Bible encyclopedia. Rev. ed. Geoffrey W. Bromley, ed. 4v. Eerdmans, 1979–88. $39.50/v. v.1, ISBN 0-8028-8161-0; v.2, ISBN 0-8028-0162-9; v.3,

ISBN 0-8028-8163-7; v.4,
ISBN 0-8028-8164-5.
220.3 BS440

A substantial revision, actually a rewriting, of a standard Bible encyclopedia. Its purpose is to define, identify, and explain terms and topics of interest to both the more advanced student and the average pastor or Bible student. This revision is more scholarly and more conservative than the first edition.

193 Mercer dictionary of the Bible. Watson E. Mills et al., eds. 987p. Mercer Univ. Pr., 1990. $55. ISBN 0-86554-299-6; paper $27.50. ISBN 0-86554-373-9.
220.3 BS440

A balanced dictionary of up-to-date biblical scholarship provides thorough and current Bible information. The 1,450 signed articles, arranged alphabetically, give the user relevant information on a variety of biblical subjects. Consideration of feminist thought is evident in appropriate articles.

194 Zondervan pictorial encyclopedia of the Bible. Merrill C. Tenney and Steven Barabas, eds. 5v. Zondervan, 1974. $149.95/set. ISBN 0-310-33188-9.
220.3 BS440

A conservative critical and theological approach to persons, places, objects, customs, historical events, key themes, and doctrines of the Bible. Pictorial illustrations; the colored illustrations are particularly valuable. Index to maps; signed articles, with bibliographies for longer ones; cross-references by use of outlines preceding longer articles.

HANDBOOKS

195 Abingdon Bible handbook. Rev. ed. Edward P. Blair. 528p. Abingdon, 1982. Paper $23.95. ISBN 0-687-00710-6.
220 BS475

Individual chapters cover the Bible book-by-book, giving various modern scholarly interpretations, including contents and theology, authorship, significance or value, and literary style. Protestant viewpoint.

196 Oxford companion to the Bible. Bruce M. Metzger and Michael D. Coogans, eds. 874p. Oxford Univ. Pr., 1993. $45. ISBN 0-19-504645-5.
220.3 BS440

Criticism and historical background on the full range of questions surrounding the Bible and its content. Includes index, maps, and bibliography.

197 Roget's thesaurus of the Bible. A. Colin Day. 927p. Harper, 1992. $30. ISBN 0-06-061772-1.
220.3 BS570

Useful for locating Bible verses and passages by subject.

198 Who's who in the Bible. Peter Calvocoressi, ed. 304p. Penguin, 1989. Paper $10. ISBN 0-1405-1212-8.
220.92 BS570

Biographical information about biblical figures, broken down by Old and New Testaments.

Religion in the United States

DICTIONARIES AND ENCYCLOPEDIAS

199 Dictionary of Christianity in America: a comprehensive resource on the religious impulse that shaped a continent. Daniel G. Reid. 1306p. InterVarsity, 1990. $39.95. ISBN 0-8308-1776-X.
277 BR515

This convenient source for authoritative information on Christianity in English-speaking North America gives a broad coverage in a historical perspective. Information on movements, denominations, and individuals who left their mark on Christianity are among the 4,000 topics included. Signed articles, many bibliographies, and cross-references are useful features.

200 Encyclopedia of African American religions. Larry G. Murphy, ed. 926p. Garland, 1993. $125. ISBN 0-8153-0500-1.
200.8 BR563

Alphabetical entries, including 777 biographies; provides much cultural background on current practices. Does not, however, attempt to trace these practices back to their African origins as one might expect.

201 The encyclopedia of American religions. 5th ed. J. Gordon Melton. 1150p. Gale, 1996. $195. ISBN 0-8103-7714-4.
200 BL2525

An excellent, massive guide to contemporary religion; the most thorough treatment of many obscure religions. This updated revision covers more than 2,100 North American religious groups. The first section describes the historical development, theology, and lifestyle of major religious families and traditions. The second section includes details and directory information about the smaller bodies in each family. Numerous separate indexes provide easy access for casual readers and scholars alike. Extensive bibliographical references.

202 **Encyclopedia of Native American religions.** Arlene Hirschfleder. 367p. MJF Books, 1996. $12.95. ISBN 1-56731-101-6.
299.7 E98.R3

A sourcebook for the beginning student, this work provides straightforward entries on practices, ceremonies, sacred places, myths, and principal figures; includes missionaries of all periods.

203 **Encyclopedia of the American religious experience.** Charles H. Lippy and Peter W. Williams, eds. 1872p. Scribner, 1988. $225. ISBN 0-684-18062-6.
291 BL2525

This three-volume source presents 105 essays written by religious scholars for the general reader. Topics include all major denominations, indigenous movements, and the interaction of religion with society and politics.

204 **Encyclopedic handbook of cults in America.** Rev. ed. J. Gordon Melton. 407p. Garland, 1992. $26.95. ISBN 0-8153-0502-8.
291 BL2525

A fascinating survey of cults that should provide answers to many questions on cult origins and founders, beliefs and practices, current status, and controversies. The opening chapter surveys the topic of cults as alternative religion and is followed by sections reviewing thirty-seven movements active today. Countercult groups are discussed, and an excellent section on violence and cults ends the book. Well written, thoroughly documented, and indexed.

DIRECTORIES

205 **Directory of African American religious bodies.** 2d ed. Wardell J. Payne, ed. 382p. Howard Univ. Pr., 1995. $49.95. ISBN 0-88258-184-8; paper $29.95. ISBN 0-88258-185-6.
280 BR563

Part handbook, part directory, the entries in this work provide narrative detail and location information on more than 1,000 African American religions and denominations. Includes an extensive bibliography, numerous indexes, and compendia of related information, such as principal colleges and seminaries offering religious studies.

206 **Directory of religious organizations in the United States.** 3d ed. 728p. Gale, 1992. $130. ISBN 0-8103-9890-7.
291.6 BL2530

Contact and descriptive information on approximately 2,500 religious organizations headquartered in the United States. Includes personnel, function, religious affiliation, address, and other directory information for each organization listed.

207 **Handbook of denominations in the United States.** 10th ed. Frank S. Mead. 352p. Abingdon, 1995. $19.95. ISBN 0-687-01478-6.
291 BL2525

Much useful information including history, relevant statistics, and principal doctrines of denominations covered.

208 **Religious bodies in the United States: a directory.** J. Gordon Melton. 313p. Garland, 1992. $20. ISBN 0-8153-0806-X.
200.25 BL2525

This revised, expanded edition provides a comprehensive listing of all religious groups known to be operating in the United States, including a brief description, a contact person, the headquarter's address, a telephone number, and a complete listing of periodicals for each movement.

STATISTICAL SOURCES

209 **Churches and church membership in the United States, 1990: an enumeration by region, state, and county.** Glenmary Research Center, 1992. $36. ISBN 0-914422-22-7.
280 BR526

Sponsored by the Association of Statisticians of American Religious Bodies, provides statistics on 133 major denominations down to the county level. One of the few sources to present detailed statistical information on religious bodies.

BIOGRAPHICAL SOURCES

210 **Biographical dictionary of American cult and sect leaders.** J. Gordon Melton. 534p. Garland, 1986. $39.95.

ISBN 0-8240-9037-3.
291 BL2525

A guide to influential religious leaders who are neglected in many standard sources. Most articles average one to two pages in length and are written for the general reader. Facts about birth and death, career and education, and marriage and divorce are included. A partial list of works about and by each person is added to each entry. Useful appendixes list leaders by birthplace and date and by religious family. The table of contents does not include page numbers. A valuable source of information on several hundred important figures in American religious history.

211 Dictionary of American religious biography. 2d ed. Henry Warner Bowden. 686p. Greenwood, 1993. $75. ISBN 0-313-27825-3.
209.22 BL72

Included are more than 550 American religious figures of significance.

Christianity

DICTIONARIES AND ENCYCLOPEDIAS

212 Atlas of the Christian church. Henry Chadwick and G. R. Evans, eds. 240p. Facts on File, 1987. $40. ISBN 0-8160-1643-7.
912 BR98

This is a beautifully illustrated handbook on the development of Christianity, not a true atlas. The text is elegant, concise, and highlighted with lavish color in photographs, maps, charts, and diagrams. A vast amount of information is packed into this slim volume, which should be useful to all libraries in need of readable introductory material on the history of Christianity.

213 Blackwell encyclopedia of modern Christian thought. Alister McGrath, ed. 701p. Blackwell, 1993. $115.95. ISBN 0-631-16896-6; paper (1995) $31.95. ISBN 0-631-19896-2.
230 BR95

Presents the views of the most authoritative theologians of the eighteenth through the twentieth centuries on the key issues of our time. An intelligent compendium of the best theological thought, surprisingly comprehensible.

214 Dictionary of pentecostal and charismatic movements. Stanley M. Burgess et al., eds. 960p. Zondervan, 1988. $29.95. ISBN 0-310-44100-5.
270 BR1644

A biographical, biblical, theological, and topical dictionary of pentecostal and charismatic movements in North America and Europe. Signed articles with bibliographies provide coverage of pentecostal denominations with more than 2,000 members. Historical and contemporary photographs.

215 Dictionary of the liturgy. Jovian P. Lang. 687p. Catholic Book (dist. by Franciscan Fathers, 10701 S. Military Trail, Boynton Beach, FL 33436), 1989. $14.50. ISBN 0-89942-273-X.
264 BV173

A comprehensive dictionary of the terms involved with Roman Catholic worship: words, gestures, rites, prayers, themes, service books, sacred vessels, vestments, art, music, Bible and liturgy, and so forth. It incorporates Vatican II changes, gives pronunciations, and is interspersed with cross-references.

216 Encyclopedia of early Christianity. 2d ed. Everett Ferguson, ed. 2v. 1213p. Garland, 1997. $150. ISBN 0-8153-1663-1.
270.1 BR162.2

Scholarly and authoritative but not pedantic. The most important reference work on the seminal period of church history.

217 Encyclopedia of Mormonism. Daniel H. Ludlow, ed. 5v. 2480p. Macmillan, 1992. $400. ISBN 0-02-904040-X.
289.3 BX8605.5

More than 1,300 entries are found in this scholarly work, which presents the history and doctrines of Mormonism in meticulous detail. Includes reprints of Joseph Smith's three major texts, *The book of Mormon, The doctrine and the covenants,* and *The pearl of great price,* in the final volume.

218 New Catholic encyclopedia. Prep. by ed. staff, Catholic Univ. of America. 15v. McGraw-Hill, 1967. Reprint: New Catholic Encyclopedia (330 W. Colfax, Palatine, IL 60067), 1981. $750. ISBN 0-07-010235-X. Supplementary v.16, 1974; v.17, 1979; v.18, 1989.
282.03 BX841

Highly objective, modern, and ecumenical in tone, with many non-Catholic contributors. Although its level of scholarship is high, it is generally more readable than its predecessor. Partially replaces and supersedes the *Catholic encyclopedia* (Gilmary Society, 1907–22, 1950–54, 18v. op.), which should be retained for older, more historical points of view. Recent supplementary volumes ($74.50 each) reflect the accelerating tempo of change in the world and in the church. They include biographies of statesmen and religious leaders who have died since the new work appeared, an analysis of the major trends in the church since Vatican II, a survey of biblical scholarship, and many other pertinent issues. Up-to-date bibliographies; cross-references to the 1967 edition.

219 New Westminster dictionary of liturgy and worship. Rev. ed. J. G. Davies, ed. 560p. Westminster, 1986. $29.95. ISBN 0-664-21270-0.
264 BV173

An ecumenical approach to the structures and rationale of liturgical functions. Sects, rites, sacraments, and some subjects (e.g., architecture and vestments) are treated at length, with illustrations and bibliographies. This revised edition includes the changes in the Catholic Church and in the other Christian churches that have made comparable revisions. It relates historical background to contemporary subjects of interest, with fresh ideas on the role of women, liturgical dance and movement-prayer, cremation, children and family worship, the disabled, drama, laity, law and worship, and media worship. Signed articles, cross-references; sources are cited.

220 Oxford dictionary of the Christian church. 3d ed. E. A. Livingstone, ed. 1824p. Oxford Univ. Pr., 1997. $125. ISBN 0-19-211655-X.
203 BR95

The authoritative one-volume dictionary of the Christian church. More than 6,000 entries presented in an alphabetical arrangement provide extensive information on the history, beliefs, practices, people, and traditions of the 2,000-year-old Christian world.

DIRECTORIES, YEARBOOKS, AND ALMANACS

221 Catholic almanac. Our Sunday Visitor, 1904– . Annual. $21.95. ISSN 0069-1254.
282 BX845

Variously titled since 1904, this annual of Catholic facts and current information is comprehensive and authoritative. Besides typical handbook information on a wide variety of Catholic topics, of particular interest is the chronological news summary, "News Events," which describes most important and some minor events occurring in the Vatican, the United States, and the world. Text and résumés of significant documents appear. Well edited and thoroughly indexed.

222 A guide to monastic guest houses. 3d ed. Robert J. Regalbuto. 224p. Morehouse, 1998. Paper $17.95. ISBN 0-8192-1713-1.
647.94 TX907.2

This directory lists information supplied by eighty monastic communities continuing the tradition that monasteries and convents have had since the sixth century of allowing interested persons a refreshing period of rest and reflection. Accommodations described include houses of Christian traditions from southern California to New England, giving details on meals, charges (or donations), history and description of the community, and travel directions. Alphabetically arranged by monasteries under states (alphabetical). Content pages serve as index.

223 Official Catholic directory. National Register staff. Kenedy, 1886– . Annual. $219.95. ISSN 0078-3854. October supplement $28.
282 BX845

Provides for each diocese (arranged alphabetically) information on churches and clergy, schools and teachers, hospitals and other institutions, religious communities, plus statistics. Sections on the hierarchy of the Catholic Church, missions, religious orders, and a chronology. Besides the indispensable place index, an alphabetical list of the clergy.

224 Yearbook of American and Canadian churches. Constant H. Jacquet, ed. Abingdon, 1916– . Annual. Paper $29.95. ISSN 0195-9043.
277 BR513

Directory, statistical, and historical information on many religious and ecumenical organizations and service agencies, accredited seminaries, colleges and universities, and depositories of church history materials. Also a list of religious periodicals.

BIOGRAPHICAL SOURCES

225 Dictionary of saints. John J. Delaney. 648p. Doubleday, 1980. $29.95. ISBN 0-385-13594-7.
270 BX4655.8

A compendium of 5,000 saints, compiled for the general public, provides more details about more saints than similar dictionaries and provides accurate information, indicating when it is legendary. The appendix contains lists of saints as patrons and saints' symbols in art and a chronological chart of popes and world rulers. Byzantine and Roman calendars include saints not in the liturgical calendar who are locally or universally honored on certain days. The alphabetizing of many saints under surnames may prove frustrating. An abridged edition with 1,500 entries of the most popular and appealing saints and *beati* (blesseds) with the appendixes of patrons and symbols appeared in 1983 in paper (528p. $6.95. ISBN 0-385-18274-0).

226 Lives of the saints. Alban Butler. Comp., ed., rev., and suppl. by Herbert Thurston and Donald Attwater. 4v. Christian Classics, 1956. $140/set. ISBN 0-87061-137-2.
270 BX4654

Incorporates most of the saints of the Roman martyrology including those recently canonized. Arranged by date of feast according to the Roman calendar before the 1969 change. The index can be used to circumvent problems caused by the date changes. If local demand is slight and a small paragraph for identification is sufficient, the following is recommended: Donald Attwater, *Penguin dictionary of saints* (Penguin, 1995. Paper $13.95. ISBN 0-14-051312-4).

227 The Oxford dictionary of popes. J. N. D. Kelly. 368p. Oxford Univ. Pr., 1989. Paper $8.95. ISBN 0-19-282085-0.
282 BX995

An excellent source of information, arranged chronologically with an alphabetical index. Includes popes, antipopes, and an appendix on Pope Joan.

228 Oxford dictionary of saints. 3d ed. David Hugh Farmer, ed. 530p. Oxford Univ. Pr., 1993. $13.95. ISBN 0-19-283069-4.
270 BR1710

Alphabetically arranged entries identify more than 1,500 martyrs and saints of the Christian Church. Brief bibliographies are included.

Judaism

229 American Jewish yearbook. American Jewish Committee. 1899– . Annual. $35. ISBN 0-82765-108-9. ISSN 0065-8987.
296 E184

An almanac of Jewish life and culture including population statistics, directories of Jewish organizations and periodicals, a religious calendar, necrology, coverage of international Jewish politics and communities, and periodicals.

230 American synagogue: a historical dictionary and sourcebook. Kerry M. Olitzky. 432p. Greenwood, 1996. $105. ISBN 0-313-28856-9.
296.6 BM205.045

Embraces the assumption that the core institution of the Jewish community is the synagogue. Describes the history of more than 350 synagogues of the four major movements of Judaism: Orthodox, Conservative, Reconstructionist, and Reform, as well as those of independent movements. Serves as a sourcebook for synagogue history and development in the United States and Canada.

231 The complete book of Jewish observance. Leo Trepp. 370p. Behrman House/Summit Books, 1980. $18.45. ISBN 0-6714-1797-5.
296.4 BM50

A one-volume guide to the ceremonies and practices of Judaism written by a rabbi. It includes information on synagogue etiquette, mourning practices, holiday observance, and prayers.

232 Dictionary of Jewish lore and legend. Alan Unterman. 240p. Thames & Hudson, 1991. $35. ISBN 0-500-11022-0.
296.03 BM50

This illustrated volume explains the colorful characters and legends of Jewish folklore and the traditions upon which they are based. Both Ashkenazic and Sephardic lore are included. Information on mystical movements, customs, festivals, and home life is given.

233 Encyclopedia Judaica. 16v. Macmillan/Keter, 1972. Decennial

yearbook, 1973–82. Yearbooks, 1983–85, 1986–89. $895/16v. set. $187/3 yearbook vol. Reprint: Coronet, 1994. $995. ISBN 0-685-36253-1.
■ cd
909.04 DS102.8

A major reference work covering all aspects of Judaism in great detail: history, theology, culture, archaeology, and religious practice. There are black-and-white illustrations. Both scholars and lay readers will find the set useful despite the fact that it has not been updated recently. The new CD-ROM version includes multimedia enhancements.

234 Encyclopedia of the Jewish religion. Rev. ed. R. J. Zwi Werblowsky and Geoffrey Wigoder, eds. 470p. Adama, 1986. $39.95. ISBN 0-915361-53-1.
296.03 BM50

This encyclopedia explains and analyzes the major religious concepts and vocabulary of the Jewish religion. Accurate information about customs, traditions, people, influential movements, and doctrines is provided. The clear explanations are accessible to all users. This should be a standard work in all collections.

235 The essential Kabbalah: the heart of Jewish mysticism. Daniel C. Matt. 221p. HarperCollins, 1995. $18. ISBN 0-06-251164-5.
296.16 BM525

A new anthology in translation of the principal Jewish mystical texts by an authority on the subject.

236 How to run a traditional Jewish household. Blu Greenberg. 536p. Reprint: Aronson, 1997. $40. ISBN 0-87668-882-2; paper $16. Simon & Schuster, 1985. ISBN 0-671-60270-5.
296.7 BM700

A concise guide to Jewish living with clear explanations of dietary laws, family purity laws, traditions, and holidays and how they are integrated into home life.

237 The Jewish book of why. Alfred J. Kolatch. 324p. Jonathan David, 1981. $17.95. ISBN 0-824-60256-0.
296.7 BM700

The second Jewish book of why. Alfred J. Kolatch. 423p. Jonathan David, 1985. $17.95. ISBN 0-842-60305-2.
296.74 BM700

These two books provide basic information about Jewish law, theology, and traditions in question-answer format. The first covers the Sabbath, holidays, synagogue ritual, and life-cycle events. The second deals with complex issues such as birth control, abortion, conversion, who is a Jew, and Jewish-Christian relations.

238 The Jewish holidays, a guide and commentary. Michael Strassfield. HarperCollins, 1985. $20. ISBN 0-685-72282-1.

Seasons of our joy: a handbook of Jewish festivals. Arthur I. Waskow. 243p. Beacon, 1991. $14. ISBN 0-8070-3611-0.
296.43 BM690

These two books explain Jewish festivals and the traditions associated with them. They discuss the theological bases of the holidays and offer appropriate readings. Waskow's book includes recipes for special holiday foods.

239 Jewish literacy: the most important things to know about the Jewish religion, its people, and its history. Joseph Telushkin. 688p. Morrow, 1991. $24.95. ISBN 0-688-08506-7.
296 BM155.2

Jewish wisdom: the essential teachings and how they have shaped the Jewish religion, its people, culture, and history. Joseph Telushkin. 663p. Morrow, 1994. $25. ISBN 0-688-12958-7.
296.3 BM565

These two volumes by Rabbi Telushkin provide a comprehensive overview of Judaism. The first covers essential concepts, trends, and personalities. The second is an anthology of writings from the Bible and the Talmud and commentaries from various historical eras that illustrate Jewish beliefs and ethics.

240 The Jewish way: living the holidays. Irving Greenberg. 463p. Touchstone/ Simon & Schuster, 1993. $13. ISBN 0-671-87303-2.
296.4 BM660

Rabbi Greenberg explains the holidays as the essence of spiritual renewal in Judaism.

241 Jewish women in America: an historical encyclopedia. Paula E. Hyman and Deborah Dash Moore, eds. 2v. 1800p. Routledge, 1997. $250.

ISBN 0-415-91936-3.
920.72 DS115.2

Sponsored by the American Jewish Historical Society, this award-winning work contains authoritative biographical entries on more than 800 women as well as 110 topical entries on organizations, movements, vocations, culture, and so forth. Spanning the years 1654 to the present, these volumes include more than 500 photographs and extensive bibliography. A masterful reference source.

242 **Judaica reference sources: a selective, annotated bibliographic guide.** 2d ed. 224p. Denali Pr., 1993. $35. ISBN 0-938737-31-7.
016.909 Z6366

An annotated guide to resources dealing with all aspects of Judaica. The entries do not contain prices or ISBNs. There are author and title indexes and a detailed table of contents that provides subject access. Sources at all levels are included.

243 **The new standard Jewish encyclopedia.** 7th ed. Geoffrey Wigoder, ed. 1036p. Facts on File, 1992. $59.95. ISBN 0-8160-2690-4.
909.04 DS102.8

The latest edition of a one-volume ready reference source first published in 1959. It is illustrated and offers current, accurate, accessible information for readers at all levels.

244 **Oxford dictionary of the Jewish religion.** R. J. Zwi Werblowsky and Geoffrey Wigoder. 764p. Oxford Univ. Pr., 1997. $125. ISBN 0-19-508605-8.
296.03 BM50.O94

A one-volume work that serves as a reference to the various facets of Jewish religion and its teachings. With its focus on religion, as opposed to culture, it provides an excellent scholarly reference work for the library and for the home. Includes significant bibliographic citations for each entry.

245 **The Talmud, the Steinsaltz edition: a reference guide.** Adin Steinsaltz. 323p. Random House, 1989. $30. ISBN 0-39457-665-9.
296.1 BM499.5

Adin Steinsaltz is one of the greatest living teachers of the Talmud. This volume is an introduction to his critical edition of the Babylonian Talmud and an excellent explanation of the structure and content of Talmudic literature. It contains a glossary and explanations of Rashi and Aramaic script as well as a general index to the Talmud set. The volume can stand alone in small libraries that do not own the set.

246 **Tanakh: a new translation of the Holy Scriptures according to the traditional Hebrew text.** 1624p. Jewish Pub. Society, 1988. $24.95. ISBN 0-8276-0252-9.
221.52 BS896

A new translation of the complete Old Testament according to the tenth-century Hebrew Masoretic text. This version is based on contemporary biblical scholarship.

247 **To pray as a Jew.** Hayim Halevy Donin. 416p. Basic Books, 1991. $25. ISBN 0-465-08640-3; paper $15. ISBN 0-465-08633-0.
296.4 BM675

This book explains the role of prayer in Jewish life, synagogue etiquette and procedure, and the prayer cycle in the synagogue and at home.

248 **The Torah: a modern commentary.** W. Gunther Plaut and Bernard J. Bamberger, eds. 1781p. Union of American Hebrew Congregations, 1981. $40. ISBN 0-807-40055-6.
222 BS1225

The Hebrew text and English translation of the Pentateuch and Haftorot (weekly readings from the prophetic books that accompany the Torah portion). The readings are annotated with commentary. There is an introductory essay at the beginning of each of the five books. Bibliography.

Other Living Religions

249 **The American Muslim, [yr.] resource directory of Islam in America.** American Muslim Support Group, 1992– . Annual. $15. ISSN 1078-8808.
297 BP10

This directory contains a religious calendar and listings of community events, organizations, periodicals, Islamic centers and mosques, student organizations, and books. It also lists business and professional networks.

250 **The Buddhist handbook: a complete guide to Buddhist schools, teaching, practice, and history.** John Snelling. 337p. Inner Traditions

International: American International Distribution Corp., 1991. $14.95. ISBN 0-89281-319-9.
294.3 BQ4012

A good overview of Buddhist history, philosophy, schools, and practices.

251 The concise encyclopedia of Islam. April Glasse. 472p. Harper, 1989. $24.95. ISBN 0-06-063126-0.
297.03 BP40

A one-volume alphabetically arranged encyclopedia providing basic explanations of Islamic beliefs and traditions and biographies of important religious figures. Entries are several paragraphs long.

252 Encyclopedia of the Sikh religion and culture. Ramesh Chander Dogra and Gobind Singh Mansukhani. 511p. Vikas (dist. by South Asia Books), 1995. $44. ISBN 0-7069-8368-8.
294.6 BL2018

This one-volume encyclopedia is the first to cover all major aspects of the Sikh religion. It includes information about customs, castes, festivals, folklore, tribes, culture, and history. There are selections from the Guru Granth Sahib (the Sikh holy book). Entries are alphabetical, ranging in length from one paragraph to four pages. There is a bibliography of books and articles. This work is well prepared and easy to use.

253 The Hindu world: an encyclopedic survey of Hinduism. Benjamin Walker. 2v. Coronet Books, 1983. $125. ISBN 0-685-13687-6.
294.509 BL1105

Alphabetical entries explain the beliefs, deities, practices, and history of the Hindu religion.

254 Holy Qur'an = al-Qur'an al-hakim. 5th U.S. ed. M. H. Shakir, ed. 600p. Tahrike Tarsile Qur'an, 1988. $19.95. ISBN 0-940368-16-1.
297 BP109

Authorized edition of the Muslim holy book; the Arabic text and English translation are arranged in parallel columns with commentary.

255 The illustrated encyclopedia of active new religions, sects, and cults. Benjamin Beit-Hallahmi. 341p. Rosen, 1993. $49.95. ISBN 0-8239-1505-0.
291.903 BL80

This book contains alphabetical entries that offer brief sketches of many diverse religious groups (e.g., Hare Krishna, Nichren Shoshu) active all over the world.

256 The Muslim almanac: a reference work on the history, faith, culture, and peoples of Islam. Azim A. Nanji, ed. 581p. Gale, 1996. $95. ISBN 0-8103-8924-X.
297 BP40

The title is self-explanatory. This book covers the history, religious beliefs, practices, and the various Islamic cultures in the world, including contemporary issues such as women's roles and fundamentalism.

257 New age encyclopedia: a guide to the beliefs, concepts, terms, people, and organizations that make up the new global movement toward spiritual development, health and healing, higher consciousness, and related subjects. J. Gordon Melton et al. 586p. Gale, 1990. $59.50. ISBN 0-8103-7159-6. ISSN 1047-2746.
299 BP605.N48

Beginning with a historical development leading to current patterns and trends, this work describes new age topics and groups. It discusses related elements of the movement. An objective reference source that dispels misunderstanding or skepticism. Biographical information on key people; a chronology identifing dates; a master index, alphabetical and key word, leads the reader to all events, people, terms, and groups in the more than 330 entries.

258 Rastafari roots and ideology. Barry Chevannes. 304p. Syracuse Univ. Pr., 1994. $34.95. ISBN 0-8156-0296-0; paper $17.95. ISBN 0-8156-2368-X.
299.6 BL2532

This book explains the doctrines, history, and splits within the Rastafari religion. The popularity of reggae music and the use of marijuana as a sacrament have sparked interest in this sect.

259 Santeria: the religion, faith, rites, magic. 2d ed. Migene Gonzalez-Wippler. 346p. Llewellyn, 1994. $16.95. ISBN 1-56718-329-8.
299.67 BL2532

Santeria, practiced in Latin American communities, is often misunderstood. This book provides detailed explanations of its origins, rites, traditions, and relation to the Catholic Church.

260 Spiritual community guide. Staff. Spiritual Community (P.O. Box 1550, Pomona, CA 91769), 1972– . Irregular. (1985, $8.95.) ISSN 0160-0354.
200 BP602

For identification and directory information of the newer sects and religious movements included in the "new consciousness," such as environmentalism, whole mind/whole body, spiritual growth, and so forth, this work gives useful information on the organizations, their books, and their beliefs that is difficult to find elsewhere.

261 Voodoo in Haiti. Alfred Metraux, trans. by Hugo Charteris. 400p. Schocken, 1989 (reissue). $16.75. ISBN 0-8052-0894-1.
133.4 BL2490

This classic book explains the origins of voodoo and its rites and traditions.

262 Wicca: a guide for the solitary practitioner. Scott Cunningham. 240p. Llewellyn, 1988. $9.95. ISBN 0-87542-118-0.
299 BF1566

An explanation of the deities, rituals, and uses of herbs associated with Wicca. It also covers spells, crystals, and the construction of altars.

263 The world of Buddhism: Buddhist monks and nuns in society and culture. Heinz Bechert and Richard Francis Gombrich. 308p. Thames & Hudson, 1991. $29.95. ISBN 0-500-27628-5.
294.3 BQ4012

Describes the teachings, sects, and traditions of Buddhism in different countries. It is illustrated and has an index.

Mythology, Folklore, Witchcraft, and Superstition

264 American folklore: an encyclopedia. Jan Harold Brunvand, ed. 794p. Garland, 1996. $95. ISBN 0-8153-0751-9.
398.2 GR101

The 500 articles cover American and Canadian folklore. Illustrations and short bibliographies enhance the text.

265 Dictionary of classical mythology. Pierre Grimal and A. R. Maxwell-Hyslop, trans. 580p. Basil Blackwell, 1985. $50. ISBN 0-631-13209-0.

A concise dictionary of classical mythology. Basil Blackwell, 1990. $34.95. ISBN 0-631-16696-3.
292.13 BL715

The first English translation of a French classic. A superb guide supplemented with thirty-four pages of genealogical tables to clarify relationships. Illustrations, references, and sources provided. The *Concise dictionary* lacks photographs, Latin and Greek texts, and index, but the cross-reference structure is useful.

266 Dictionary of classical mythology: symbols, attributes, and associations. Robert E. Bell. 390p. ABC-Clio, 1982. $49. ISBN 0-87436-305-5.
292.13 BL715

A topical dictionary of Greek and Roman mythology. Under subjects (bear, indigestion, sculpture) various mortal and immortal personae are listed with brief identifications and descriptions of their relationship to the subject.

267 A dictionary of superstitions. Sophie Lasne and Andre Pascal Gaultier. 355p. Prentice-Hall, 1984. $10.95. ISBN 0-13-210873-9.
001.9 BF1775

A fascinating guide to irrational beliefs. Arranged in topical chapters with many illustrations and drawings. Index is adequate, though not perfect.

268 A dictionary of superstitions. Iona Opie and Moira Tatem. 512p. Oxford Univ. Pr., 1990. $30. ISBN 0-19-211597-9.
001.9 BF1775

Predominantly British Isles superstitions arranged alphabetically by central idea. Includes example of superstition and year of oral or written occurrences of its use. Analytical index and cross-references.

269 An encyclopedia of fairies: hobgoblins, brownies, bogies and other supernatural creatures. Katherine M. Briggs. 481p. Pantheon, 1978. Paper $11.95. ISBN 0-394-73467-X.
398.2 GR549

All kinds of fairies in the broadest definition are included, as well as terms with significance in the folklore of fairies. The entries are authoritative, with generous quotes from sources.

270 Encyclopedia of the gods: over 2,500 deities of the world. Michael Jordan. 337p. Facts on File, 1993. $40. ISBN 0-8160-2909-1.
291.2 BL473.J67

Entries are in alphabetical order and include more than 2,500 figures from ancient times to the present. Entries indicate the significance of each deity as well as their cultural, ethnic, and geographic identity.

271 Encyclopedia of witchcraft and demonology. Russell Hope Robbins. 576p. Crown, 1988. Paper $8.98. ISBN 0-517-36245-7.
272 BF1503

Facts, history, and legend from 1450 to 1750. Extensive bibliography. Illustrations.

272 Encyclopedia of witches and witchcraft. Rosemary Ellen Guiley. 432p. Facts on File, 1989. $45. ISBN 0-8160-1793-X; paper $19.95. ISBN 0-8160-2268-2.
133.4 BF1566

More than 400 entries deal with animals, beliefs, legends, myths, people, places, and other aspects of witchcraft from ancient to modern times. Topics are defined in a factual manner that neither affirms nor denies the reality of witchcraft. Related material, such as Satanism, voodoo, and other rituals, is included. Broad, balanced coverage of a controversial topic.

273 Facts on File encyclopedia of world mythology and legend. Anthony S. Mercatante. 807p. Facts on File, 1988. $95. ISBN 0-8160-1049-8.
291 BL303

A comprehensive volume of world myths, legends, fables, hagiography, and folktales, along with their derivative literature, art, and music. It includes 3,200 entries with more than 450 illustrations. General index, cultural and ethnic index, key to variant spellings, and an annotated bibliography conclude the volume.

274 Folklore: an encyclopedia of beliefs, customs, tales, music, and art. Thomas A. Green, ed. 2v. ABC-Clio, 1997. $150. ISBN 0-87436-986-X.
398.03 GR35

This award-winning work offers 200 alphabetically arranged, authoritative essays on such topics as animism, carnival, costume, evil eye, festival, graffiti, lullaby, mask, pilgrimage, and tongue twister. Each entry is followed by a bibliography of essential resources.

275 Folklore and folklife: a guide to English language reference sources. Susan Steinfirst. 2v. 1208p. Garland, 1992. $130. ISBN 0-8153-0068-9.
016.398 Z5981

A comprehensive bibliography aimed at those beginning their study in the area of folklore and folk life. Includes author, title, and subject indexes.

276 Guide to the gods. Marjorie Leach. 995p. ABC-Clio, 1992. $159.50. ISBN 0-87436-591-0.
291.2 BL473.L43

An exhaustive dictionary treating all the many thousand deities that have appeared worldwide. Arranged by form, attribute, and function of deity. Entries are keyed to an extensive scholarly bibliography for further study. Index.

277 The illustrated who's who in mythology. Michael Senior. 233p. Macmillan, 1985. $35. ISBN 0-02-923770-X.
291.1 BL303

This guide to the characters in world mythology has more than 1,200 names identified and placed in the context of culture and belief. The layout includes many photographs of statues, drawings, and artifacts. Sources in world literature are cited at appropriate points. Beautiful color-plate section; many cross-references given in capital letters. An interesting index of themes allows the reader to compare how one people developed an idea or character with the concepts of a different culture.

278 Mythical and fabulous creatures: a sourcebook and research guide. Malcolm South, ed. 393p. Greenwood, 1987. $49.95. ISBN 0-313-24338-7.
398.469 GR825.M87

Focuses on twenty fabulous types, ranging from unicorns and dragons to giants and fairies. Provides a thorough account of each species and includes lengthy bibliography for each.

279 World mythology. Roy Willis, ed. 311p. Henry Holt, 1993. $45. ISBN 0-8050-2701-7.
291.13 BL311.W66

Describes world mythologies by geographic (cultural) region.

Ethics

Bibliographies and Guides

280 Bibliography of bioethics. LeRoy Walters, ed. Gale, 1975– . Annual. $60. ISSN 0363-0161.
■ online
016.174 QH332

Print and nonprint materials are contained in this annual bibliography on the new multidimensional subject of bioethics, relating to the moral, ethical, and legal aspects of the life sciences and healing arts, including such topics as euthanasia, abortion, right to life, genetic intervention, human experimentation, organ transplants, quality of life, death and dying, allocation of scarce resources, behavior modification, and so forth. A bioethics thesaurus of more than 475 terms features cross-references from common synonyms. A subject entry section, list of journals cited, and title and author index are included.

Dictionaries and Encyclopedias

281 Encyclopaedia of religion and ethics. James Hastings et al. 13v. Scribner, 1908–37. Reprint: Books International, 1995–97. $1250/set. ISBN 0-567-09489-8.
203 BL31

Still the standard comprehensive work in English, particularly from the historical point of view. Includes discussions of religions and ethical systems as these relate to other disciplines, such as anthropology, folklore, psychology, and so forth. Full bibliographies.

282 Encyclopedia of applied ethics. Ruth Chadwick, ed. 4v. Academic Pr., 1998. $625/set. ISBN 0-12-227065-7.
170 BJ63.E44

This award-winning work divides the realm of ethics into twelve major subject areas including medical, scientific, legal, business, and media ethics. Within this frame, 281 signed articles of 5,000 to 6,000 words discuss specific topics such as abortion, adoption, advertising, animal research, archaeological ethics, Aristotelian ethics, and auditing practices. Each entry includes a contents outline, a glossary of key terms, a defining statement, and a bibliography. A topical index provides quick access to specific information.

283 Encyclopedia of bioethics. Rev. ed. Warren T. Reich, ed. 5v. 2500p. Macmillan, 1995. $450. ISBN 0-02-897355-0.
■ cd
174.2 QH332

The scientific state-of-the-art and the full range of ethical views and policy options in matters dealing with the life sciences are summarized in 464 signed articles by 437 expert contributors. The articles range in length from brief to comprehensive and include bibliographies. Concrete ethical and legal problems such as abortion, medical malpractice, test-tube fertilization, organ transplantation, and euthanasia are objectively described. Also covered are basic concepts and principles, ethical theories, religious traditions, and historical perspectives.

284 Encyclopedia of ethics. Lawrence C. Becker, ed. 2v. 1462p. Garland, 1992. $150. ISBN 0-8153-0403-X.
170.3 BJ63.E45

Presents 435 signed articles on topics ranging from altruism and atheism to suicide and work. Includes significant entries on the major ethical theorists. Index.

285 Encyclopedia of values and ethics. Joseph P. Hester. 376p. ABC-Clio, 1996. $60. ISBN 0-87436-875-X.
170.3 BJ63.H47

Abortion, adultery, animal rights, ban the bomb, racism, and survival of the fittest are but a few of the "pragmatic" entries found here. Entries identify essential facts, issues, and trends relating to each topic, where appropriate, as well as sources for further consultation. Includes glossary, bibliography, and comprehensive index.

286 Westminster dictionary of Christian ethics. James F. Childress and John Macquarrie, eds. 678p. Westminster, 1986. $37. ISBN 0-664-20940-8.
241.03 BJ1199.W47

Scholars from many different countries and religious backgrounds contributed to this ecumenical work whose 620 entries address ethical questions of relevance to both philosophy and theology.

5

Psychology, Psychiatry, and Occult Sciences

BARBARA M. BIBEL

Psychology has proven to be the most studied social science of the twentieth century. The sources included here will be useful for students engaged in research as well as for lay readers.

Psychology and Psychiatry

Bibliographies and Guides

287 **Psychology: a guide to reference and information sources.** Pam M. Baxter. 219p. Libraries Unlimited, 1993. $36.50. ISBN 0-87287-708-6.
016.150 BF1

This book describes 600 sources published since 1970. Divided into four broad sections—general social sciences, specific resources in social sciences, general psychology, and special topics in psychology—it includes resource guides, bibliographies, indexes, online databases, handbooks, dictionaries, encyclopedias, journals, biographical sources, and organizations.

Indexes and Abstracts

288 **Psychological abstracts.** American Psychological Assn., 1927– . Monthly. $1359 to nonmember or institutions in the United States. $1437 to institutions outside the United States. $680 to members. ISSN 0033-2887.
■ cd online
150.5 BF1

A list of books, articles, reports, and documents with signed abstracts of each work arranged in seventeen categories. Author and subject indexes. Annual cumulations. Separate cumulative author and subject indexes, 1927–80, available from Hall.

Dictionaries and Encyclopedias

289 **American psychiatric glossary.** 7th ed. 274p. American Psychiatric Pr., 1994. $27. ISBN 0-88048-526-4; paper $18.50. ISBN 0-88048-508-6.
616.89 RC437

Provides brief definitions. Incorporates nomenclature of *DSM-III-R* and includes psychological tests, legal terms, and schools of psychiatry.

290 Biographical dictionary of psychology. Noel Sheehy, Anthony J. Chapman, and Wendy Conroy, eds. 704p. Routledge, 1997. $155. ISBN 0-415-09997-8.
150.92 BF109

Provides biographical information and critical analysis of more than 500 individuals who have made significant contributions to the field. Entries are in alphabetical order and follow a consistent presentation: name, date and place of birth and death (if applicable), areas of interest, education, principal appointments and honors, principal publications, sources for further reading, main ideas and contributions, and key terms for indexing. Authoritative.

291 Companion encyclopedia of psychology. Andrew M. Coleman, ed. 2v. Routledge, 1994. $199.95. ISBN 0-415-06446-5.
150.3 BF31

This encyclopedia provides an introduction and historical overview of psychology. There are articles on all the psychological specialties. Articles are by many different authors. All are British. There is a bibliography at the end of each chapter. A glossary and index complete the set.

292 Dictionary of behavioral science. 2d ed. Benjamin B. Wolman, comp. and ed. 478p. Academic Pr., 1989. $65. ISBN 0-12-762455-4.
150.3 BF31

Contains 20,000 brief definitions of terms used in psychology, psychiatry, psychoanalysis, neurology, psychopharmacology, biochemistry, endocrinology, and related subjects. It also contains brief biographies of important contributors to the field, a classification of mental disorders, and ethical standards for psychologists.

293 Dictionary of philosophy and psychology. James M. Baldwin, ed. 3v. Gordon Pr., 1977. $395. ISBN 0-8490-1721-1.
103 B41

The information in this reprint of a 1925 edition is still useful. Volumes 1 and 2 comprise the *Dictionary of philosophical and psychological terms.* They include definitions as well as brief biographies of philosophers, theologians, and other scholars of interest to psychologists. Volume 3 is Benjamin Rand's *Bibliography of philosophy, psychology, and cognate subjects.* Illustrations, plates, and diagrams.

294 The encyclopedia of human behavior. V. S. Ramachandran, ed. 4v. Academic Pr., 1994. $595. ISBN 0-12-226920-9.
150.3 BF31

This encyclopedia contains 250 signed articles with bibliographies. It provides an overview of broad topics within the physiological and psychosocial areas of human behavior. Each article begins with an outline and a glossary of terms. The articles are clearly written and accessible to readers at all levels of sophistication.

295 Encyclopedia of psychology. 2d ed. Raymond J. Corsini, ed. 4v. Wiley, 1994. $475. ISBN 0-471-55819-2.
150.3 BF31

A comprehensive scholarly encyclopedia covering all aspects of psychology. Articles are on subject areas as well as on important contributors to the field. Volume 4 contains an extensive bibliography, biographies, and name and subject indexes. There is also an appendix: the psychologist's code of conduct and ethics and sample contracts.

296 The encyclopedic dictionary of psychology. 4th ed. Terry Pettijohn, ed. 304p. Dushkin, 1991. $14.95. ISBN 0-87967-885-2.
150.3 BF31

This work contains entries for approximately 1,400 terms, people, and concepts in the field, written by subject specialists. Longer entries are signed. There are biographical and subject indexes.

297 International encyclopedia of psychiatry, psychology, psychoanalysis and neurology. Benjamin B. Wolman, ed. 12v. and progress vol. Aesculapius, 1977. $675. ISBN 0-918228-01-8. Progress vol., 1983. $90. ISBN 0-918228-28-X.
616.8 RC334

Despite its age, this set is a respected basic reference tool for the psychological disciplines. The 1,500 authors have written signed articles—with bibliographies on the basic subject areas and major theories—that are accessible to general readers as well as scholars. Extensive cross-references within the text and comprehensive name and subject indexes make this encyclopedia easy to use. It is an excellent starting point for research.

298 The Penguin dictionary of psychology. Arthur S. Reber. 864p. Viking Penguin,

1986. Paper $12. ISBN 0-14-051079-6.
150.3 BF31

A comprehensive dictionary containing 17,000 entries covering psychology and related disciplines. The entries are brief, but they define both technical and colloquial terms. There are extensive cross-references and examples.

299 Psychiatric dictionary. 7th ed. Robert Jean Campbell. 848p. Oxford Univ. Pr., 1996. $159.95. ISBN 0-19-510259-2.
616.89 RC437

A more advanced dictionary, useful as a supplement to medical and general dictionaries. It includes terms from the fields of psychosomatic medicine and adolescent and geriatric psychology. Pronunciations and quotations using the terms are included.

Handbooks

300 Caring for the mind: the comprehensive guide to mental health. Dianne Hales and Robert E. Hales. 880p. Bantam, 1995. $39.95. ISBN 0-553-09146-8.
616.89 RC460

An outstanding, comprehensive work in lay language by a professional writer and her psychiatrist husband. All aspects of diagnosis and treatment of mental disorders are covered. Different types of talking therapy, drugs, electroshock, hypnosis, and self-help are among the topics included. Criteria for diagnoses are from the *DSM-IV.* This is an extremely useful work for both professional and lay readers.

301 Diagnostic and statistical manual of mental disorders: DSM-IV. 4th ed. 886p. American Psychiatric Assn., 1994. $54.95. ISBN 0-890-42061-0.

DSM-IV casebook: A learning companion to the diagnostic and statistical manual of mental disorders, fourth edition. Robert L. Spiter et al. 576p. American Psychiatric Pr., 1994. $45. ISBN 0-88048-674-0.
616.89 RC455.2

These two books form the basis for psychiatric diagnosis and treatment. The *DSM-IV* is the official classification system used by psychiatrists when diagnosing mental conditions. The *DSM-IV Casebook* provides examples of cases that illustrate the diagnostic criteria for each disorder. Both professional and lay readers use these sources.

302 How therapists diagnose: seeing through the psychiatric eye. Bruce Hamstra. 334p. St. Martin's, 1994. $23.95. ISBN 0-312104-76-6.
616.89 RC469

This book explains psychiatric diagnostic techniques in lay language. It also provides sound advice on choosing a therapist and a list of associations for referral.

303 The Oxford companion to the mind. Richard L. Gregory and O. L. Zangwill. 856p. Oxford Univ. Pr., 1987. $49.95. ISBN 0-19-866124-X; paper (reprint ed., 1998) $27.50. ISBN 0-19-860224-3.

The 1,000 entries in this *Companion* cover concepts related to psychology, philosophy, and the physiology of the higher nervous system. The book is enhanced by several hundred illustrations and by bibliographies at the end of many entries.

Testing and Measurement

304 The mental measurements yearbook. Buros Institute of Mental Measurements, Univ. of Nebraska, Lincoln, 1941– . Irregular. (13th ed. 1998, $165.) ISSN 0076-6461.
■ online
016.371 Z5814.P8

The mental measurements yearbook is the premier research tool for investigating mental measurement testing. Each yearbook covers only tests that are new or have been significantly revised since the previous edition; therefore, each edition should be retained. Each entry includes the test title, intended population, author and publisher, acronym, scoring, availability, time to administer, a statement about validity and reliability, a lengthy review, and references. The yearbook provides indexes by title, acronym, subject, publisher, name, and score. The publishers directory is invaluable.

305 Test critiques. Daniel Keyser and Richard Sweetland, eds. 10v. PRO-ED. $590/set. $89/v. v.1, 1985. ISBN 0-9611286-6-6; v.2, 1985. ISBN 0-9611286-7-4; v.3, 1985. ISBN 0-9611286-8-2; v.4, 1986. ISBN 0-9337010-2-0; v.5, 1986. ISBN 0-9337010-4-7; v.6, 1987.

ISBN 0-933701-10-1; v.7, 1988.
ISBN 0-933701-20-9; v.8, 1989.
ISBN 0-89079-254-2; v.9, 1992.
ISBN 0-89079-521-5; v.10, Gale, 1993. ISBN 0-685-59036-4.
150.28 BF176

A good companion to *The mental measurements yearbook*. It contains signed articles several pages in length that offer detailed information about the practical applications and technical aspects of major psychological tests. The critiques and comparisons to other tests are very useful. References are included. Volumes 3 and 4 contain cumulative subject indexes. The table of contents serves as an index in the individual volumes.

306 Tests: a comprehensive reference for assessments in psychology, education, and business. 5th ed. Richard C. Sweetland and Daniel J. Keyser, eds. 1250p. PRO-ED, 1996. $89. ISBN 0-685-58995-1.
150.287 BF176

An excellent ready reference tool written in lay language so that it is accessible to all readers. It provides brief information on thousands of available tests, including their purpose, price, publisher, and a description of the test itself. There are cross-references and five cumulative indexes.

307 Tests in print IV: an index to tests, test reviews, and the literature on specific tests. Linda L. Murphy et al., eds. 2v. Buros Institute of Mental Measurements, Univ. of Nebraska, Lincoln, 1994. $250. ISBN 0-91067-453-1.
016.371 LB3051

Brief information on more than 4,000 tests: descriptions, population, administration, and scoring. It also includes a directory of more than 500 publishers. It serves as an index to the *The mental measurements yearbook*.

Occult Sciences

308 Alternative realities: the paranormal, the mystic, and the transcendent in human experience. Leonard George. 360p. Facts on File, 1995. $35. ISBN 0-8160-2828-1; paper $17.95. ISBN 0-8160-3213-0.
133.8 BF1031

A clinical psychologist explains paranormal experiences and examines scientific research on topics such as extrasensory perception, psychokinesis, unidentified flying objects, and mystical experiences. Entries are alphabetical. There is an extensive bibliography.

309 The Arkana dictionary of astrology. Fred Gettings. 575p. Arkana, 1991. $10.95. ISBN 0-14-019287-5.
133.5 BF1625

A British dictionary containing entries under 3,000 headings with extensive cross-references and black-and-white illustrations. There is a bibliography. The material is easy to understand, but the small print is hard on the eyes. A useful general source on a popular subject.

310 The astrology encyclopedia. James R. Lewis. 503p. Gale, 1994. $42.95. ISBN 0-8103-8900-2; paper $19.95. Visible Ink Pr., 1994. ISBN 0-8103-8900-2.
133.5 BF1625

This is the only encyclopedia of astrology currently in print. It contains more than 780 alphabetical entries on topics such as planets, zodiac signs, and asteroids. There are appendixes explaining birth charting and listing astrology organizations and periodicals. Illustrations, a detailed table of contents, and an index complete the work. A comprehensive, useful source.

311 Divining the future: prognostication from astrology to zoomancy. Eva Shaw. 293p. Facts on File, 1995. $35. ISBN 0-8160-2937-7.
133.3 BF1751

The brief alphabetical entries in this source provide an introduction to both fortune-telling methods and their famous practitioners. All entries contain bibliographies. I Ching, tarot, palmistry, tea leaves, and obscure methods—such as tiromancy and divination by examining and interpreting the holes or mold on or in cheese—are among the techniques included. There are illustrations and an index.

312 Encyclopedia of occultism and parapsychology. 4th ed. Leslie Shepherd, ed. 2v. Gale, 1996. $295. ISBN 0-8103-5487-X.
133.05 BF1407

A revision of the 1991 edition, this work defines *occult* in the broadest sense. It includes people, gods, plants, organizations, writing, and even countries. All types of psychic phenomena, superstitions, and legends appear. Some of the longer entries have bibliographies. Many cross-references, as well as general and subject indexes, make the work easy to use.

313 The encyclopedia of tarot. Stuart R. Kaplan. 2v. U.S. Games Systems. v.1, 1978. $25. ISBN 0-913866-11-3; v.2, 1985. $35. ISBN 0-913866-36-9.
133.3 BF1879

This beautifully illustrated work will interest both students of the occult and art historians. It includes a history of the tarot as well as various interpretations of the cards. There is an extensive bibliography.

314 Encyclopedia of the unexplained: magic, occultism and parapsychology. Richard Cavendish, ed. 304p. Reprint: Penguin, 1990. Paper $20. ISBN 0-14-019190-9.
133.05 BF1411

This work presents brief entries describing terms, organizations, and people associated with the occult, magic, spirituality, psychic research, parapsychology, and divination. It offers information appearing after 1800. There are cross-references, a bibliography, and a detailed index.

315 Harper's encyclopedia of mystical and paranormal experience. Rosemary Ellen Guiley. 688p. Harper San Francisco, 1991. Paper $22. ISBN 0-06-250366-9.
133.03 BF1407

Alphabetical entries range in length from three paragraphs to three pages on assorted topics related to spirituality, mythology, and the new age (e.g., angels, body work, crystals, cabala). Foreword by Marion Zimmer Bradley. HarperCollins has just released a Spanish-language version of this book.

316 Man, myth, and magic: the illustrated encyclopedia of mythology, religion, and the unknown. 3d ed. Richard Cavendish, ed. 21v. Marshall Cavendish, 1994. $549.95. ISBN 1-85435-731-X.
133 BF1411

An interdisciplinary source that covers large areas of mythology, world religions, and the supernatural, emphasizing anthropology, art, and symbolism. It is profusely illustrated and written in a lively style. Articles are individually authored by experts in the field. There is an extensive bibliography as well as a general and a subject index. This edition has seventy-four new articles on subjects such as women's mysteries and African American lore.

317 The occult in the western world: an annotated bibliography. Cosette Kies. 233p. Shoe String Pr., 1986. $29.95. ISBN 0-208-02113-2.
016.0019 BF1411

A fine guide to materials and sources defining and exploring the occult. Topics include witchcraft and Satanism, magic, mysticism, psychical research, ghosts, myths, legends and folklore, UFOs, monsters, prophecy and fortune-telling, and astrology. Provides a brief section on skeptics and debunkers. Useful and well written. Glossary and indexes by name and title.

6

Social Sciences (General), Sociology, and Anthropology

DEBORAH L. THOMAS

Today's social sciences present reference librarians with particularly stimulating challenges. Society's commitment to understanding and correcting its problems grows as enhanced computer capabilities and improving analytical skills markedly increase the store of information concerning social interactions. This has resulted in an almost bewildering array of reference sources.

Selectors should note several principles that underlie our choices for the social sciences. First, the perishability of data and the nature of policy questions make currency essential. Whenever possible, reference collections should offer the latest editions of directories and statistical compendiums. The committee preferred fewer but current titles to a wider variety of out-of-date sources.

Secondly, academic librarians will find relatively few bibliographies. For the most part, the choice of subjects to be covered is somewhat idiosyncratic to the institution. All college libraries will want to offer bibliographies attuned to the curricula they support, although they may prefer to house them in the circulating collection.

Finally, reference collections should also provide local directories of community services as well as information on services and resources at the state level.

Social Sciences (General)

Indexes and Abstracts

318 **Social sciences index.** Wilson, 1974– . Quarterly with annual cumulations. Service basis. ISSN 0094-4920. (*formerly* **International index**, 1907–65; **Social sciences and humanities index**, 1965–74.)
■ cd online tape
016.05 AI3

Author-subject index to some 400 periodicals in the social sciences. Specific subject headings and many cross-references aid research. Book reviews indexed by author in a separate section.

Dictionaries and Encyclopedias

319 A dictionary of the social sciences. Julius Gould and William L. Kolb, eds. 761p. Free Pr., 1964. op.
300.3 H41

Compiled under the auspices of UNESCO, this aging classic defines approximately 1,000 concepts and terms. Alphabetically arranged entries are extensively cross-referenced and signed. Frequent references to major works appear in the text.

320 Encyclopaedia of the social sciences. E. R. A. Seligman, ed. in chief. Alvin Johnson, assoc. ed. 15v. Macmillan, 1930–35. op.
303 H41

The first comprehensive encyclopedia of the social sciences, including not only political science, economics, law, anthropology, sociology, penology, and social work, but also the social aspects of many other disciplines (ethics, education, philosophy, biology, etc.). Long, signed articles by specialists. Many biographical articles stressing contributions to the social sciences rather than purely personal details. A classic complemented, but not superseded, by the *International encyclopedia of the social sciences.*

321 International encyclopedia of population. John A. Ross, ed. 2v. 750p. Macmillan, 1982. $250. ISBN 0-02-927430-3.
304.6 HB849.2

A wide variety of people will be well served by this interdisciplinary work. The *IEP* not only covers the standard topics—fertility and contraception, marriage and divorce, distribution and migration—but also contains articles on the eleven most populous nations, eight geographical regions, professional techniques, and a host of other population-related topics. There are 129 signed articles on substantive topics, as well as a number of "core entries," contributed by the editorial staff, that define important terms and concepts. All of the entries have bibliographies. Use is facilitated by an alphabetically arranged table of contents, a topical outline of the subjects covered, cross-references, and an index.

322 International encyclopedia of the social sciences. David L. Sills, ed. 17v. Free Pr., 1968. op; v.18, Biographical supplement. 1979. op; v.19, Social science quotations. 1991. $110. ISBN 0-02-928751-0. Reprint: 17v. in 8v. 1977. op; v.9, Biographical supplement. 1979. $110. ISBN 0-02-895690-7.
300.3 H40

A classic subject encyclopedia reflecting the development and rapid expansion of all the social sciences into the 1960s. Complements, but does not supersede, the *Encyclopaedia of the social sciences.* The *Biographical supplement* (volume 18 of the original set, volume 9 of the 1977 reprint) includes signed biographical sketches, with bibliographies, of 215 social scientists who were either deceased by 1978 or born no later than 1908. Though dated, the long, signed, authoritative articles still provide excellent entries into the literature of the social sciences.

Handbooks, Yearbooks, and Almanacs

323 American social attitudes data sourcebook: 1947–1978. Philip E. Converse et al. 441p. Harvard Univ. Pr., 1980. Spiral bindg. $37. ISBN 0-674-02880-5.
303.3 HN65

Time series data of the results of sample surveys, standardized to provide comparable longitudinal data. Arranged by broad chapters with a detailed table of contents outlining subdivisions of each topic.

324 Fraternal organizations. Alvin J. Schmidt. (Greenwood encyclopedia of American institutions; 3.) 410p. Greenwood, 1980. $95. ISBN 0-313-21436-0.
366 HS17

An important survey of 450 active and defunct fraternal organizations in the United States and Canada from fraternal orders (Masons, Elks) to religious and ethnic fraternal groups (Knights of Columbus, B'nai B'rith). College fraternities and patriotic and service organizations are excluded. Each alphabetically arranged entry examines an organization's history, primary function, causes supported, rituals, number of members, membership qualifications, and relationships to other organizations, in addition to providing a list of further readings. The five valuable appendixes include listings of organizations by ethnic and religious affiliation and geographical area. Subject index.

325 The Gallup poll: public opinion 1935–1971. George H. Gallup. 3v. Greenwood, 1977. $150. ISBN 0-313-20129-3.

The Gallup poll: public opinion 1972–1977. George H. Gallup. 2v. Scholarly Resources, 1978. $120. ISBN 0-8420-2129-9.

The Gallup poll: public opinion 1978– . George H. Gallup. Scholarly Resources, 1979– . Annual. $70. ISSN 0195-962X.
301.15 HN90.P8

Presents the findings of all U.S. Gallup Poll reports from the founding of the poll in 1935, comprising an easily accessed and valuable record of American public opinion. In addition, provides excellent explanations of survey techniques, sample size and selection, and the analysis of survey results. All volumes in this series should be displayed prominently in all libraries serving the public or students of junior high level and above.

326 Handbook of American popular culture. 2d ed. Thomas M. Inge, ed. 3v. Greenwood, 1989. $185/set. ISBN 0-313-25406-0.
306.4 E169.1

An especially useful introduction to the scholarly study of popular culture, ranging from advertising, the automobile, and computers to comic strips, graffiti, minorities, and television. In each of the forty-six chapters an authority provides a brief history; a critical bibliographic essay covering the most useful bibliographies, histories, critical studies, and journals; a description of research centers and collections of primary and secondary materials; and a bibliography of works cited. Proper name and subject indexes. Reference librarians and researchers should note that the essays on popular literature included in the first edition of the *Handbook* have been revised and published separately as the *Handbook of American popular literature* (Thomas M. Inge, ed. 408p. Greenwood, 1988. $57.95. ISBN 0-313-25405-2).

327 St. James Press gay and lesbian almanac. Neil Schlager, ed. 680p. St. James, 1998. $100. ISBN 1-55862-358-2.
305.9 HQ76.3

The aim of this work is to create an "in-depth reference source that provides substantive surveys of most aspects of gay and lesbian history and culture." The focus is on "gay and lesbian experience in the United States, both historically and in the present." It is divided into twenty-three chapters (e.g., "Politics," "Family," "Sports," and "Labor and Employment") and includes a chronology of significant events, a list of key organizations, and the full or partial text of relevant primary documents. Each chapter contains references for further study, and there is a comprehensive bibliography listing books of interest for gay and lesbian studies at the end.

Sociology

Bibliographies and Guides

328 Sociology: a guide to reference and information sources. 2d ed. Stephen H. Aby. 227p. Libraries Unlimited, 1997. $42. ISBN 1-56308-422-8.
016.301 HM51

Describes 576 major English-language reference sources in sociology and its subdisciplines. Entries include indexes, bibliographies, handbooks, databases, World Wide Web sites, dictionaries, and electronic resources. Has sections on the principal journals in the field, research centers, and organizations. Subject and author-title indexes.

329 The student sociologist's handbook. 4th ed. Pauline Bart and Linda Frankel. 291p. McGraw-Hill, 1986. Paper $17.50. ISBN 0-07-554884-4.
301.07 HM68

Includes useful discussions of social change, the "sociological approach," preparing a sociology paper, and computers in sociological work in addition to chapters on the periodical literature, research guides, government publications, and other sources of data.

Dictionaries and Encyclopedias

330 Collins dictionary of sociology. 2d ed. David Jary and Julia Jary. HarperCollins, 1995. Paper $16. ISBN 0-00-470804-0.
300.3 HM17

Clearly written current definitions and short biographies with a mildly British slant. Works cited in the text appear in a general bibliography at the end of the dictionary.

331 Encyclopedia of homosexuality. Wayne R. Dynes, ed. 2v. Garland, 1990. $150/set. ISBN 0-8240-6544-1.
306.76 HQ76.25

In more than 770 alphabetically arranged, signed articles, some eighty experts address an impressively broad spectrum of topics and biographies (of deceased persons) pertinent to the study of homosexuality. The interdisciplinary and cross-cultural coverage includes both male and female homosexuality, bisexuality, and the effects of homophilia and homophobia on various aspects of society. Editorial policy strove for an absence of partisanship and attempted to alert readers to differing positions, when appropriate. Cross-references within articles, an extensive index, and bibliographies for further reading at the end of most articles enhance this unique encyclopedia. Essential for school, public, and academic libraries.

332 Encyclopedia of sociology. Edgar F. Borgatta, ed. 4v. Macmillan, 1992. $375. ISBN 0-02-897051-9.
301.03 HM17

The only authoritative and comprehensive encyclopedia of sociology. The 370 alphabetically arranged articles range in length from two to about twenty pages. Topics include sociological theories, statistical approaches, contemporary social problems, and national sociologies. Articles, written primarily by U.S. academics, are accessible to the lay reader and conclude with extensive bibliographies. The new standard source in the discipline of sociology and an essential purchase for academic collections.

Aging

333 Consumer's directory of continuing care retirement communities, 1994–1995. 621p. American Assn. of Homes and Services for the Aging, 1994. $19.95. ISBN 0-943774-53-5.
362.6 HQ1063

State-by-state directory of more than 600 retirement communities offering prepaid contracts for long-term care. The description of each facility provides address, phone number, ownership, year opened, stage of development, resident population, independent living units and fees, residential and personal care and fees, nursing care levels and fees, general services, health-related services, and medical insurance requirements. Indexed by metropolitan area, special features, and name.

334 The encyclopedia of aging. 2d ed. George L. Maddox, ed. 1256p. Springer, 1995. $159. ISBN 0-8261-4841-7.
305.26 HQ1061

Brief, signed introductions to key topics and issues in aging as well as to the "infrastructure of legislation and organizations . . . which have evolved as populations have aged." The clearly written, alphabetically arranged entries provide particularly valuable references to both classic and current sources of further information. Detailed index and liberal cross-references.

335 Older Americans almanac. Ronald J. Manheimer, ed. 881p. Gale, 1994. $99.50. ISBN 0-8103-8348-9.
305.26 HQ1064

An attractive source containing thirty-eight chapters on aging issues, including employment and retirement, financial concerns, elder care, health and health problems, and physical, mental, and social processes of aging. Bibliographies are included, as are many photographs, tables, and charts. Keyword index.

336 Retirement places rated. 4th ed. David Savageau. 309p. Macmillan, 1995. Paper $20. ISBN 0-02-860055-X. (*formerly* **Places rated retirement guide.**)
646.7 HQ1063.2

Evaluates and ranks more than 100 places in the United States for characteristics of importance to retirees. Compares each location in considerable detail as to climate, housing, money matters, personal safety, services (including health and transportation), and leisure activities. Similar in organization and a worthy companion to the *Places rated almanac.*

337 Social security, medicare and pensions: the sourcebook for older Americans. 7th ed. Joseph L. Matthews with Dorothy Matthews Berman. 264p. Nolo, 1999. $19.95. ISBN 0-87337-487-8. (*formerly* **Sourcebook for older Americans.**)
344.73 KF3650

Explains in simple, clear language the income and benefit programs for and the laws designed to protect the interests of older Americans. Coverage includes social security retirement, disability, and dependents' and survivors' benefits; medicare, medicaid, and "medi-gap"; supplemental security income (SSI); government employment, railroad worker, and veterans' benefits; private pensions; and age discrimination in employment. Large print and the clean, easy-to-read format aid access for those with fading eyesight. Subject index. A must for public libraries.

338 Statistical record of older Americans. 2d ed. Arsen J. Darnay, ed. 926p. Gale, 1996. $109. ISBN 0-8103-6431-X.
305.26 HQ1064

More than 700 tables present the most recent data available on the status of older Americans. Topics include health, leisure activities, nursing homes, socioeconomic status, and consumer buying. Statistics are drawn from government publications as well as opinion surveys.

Alcoholism and Drug Abuse

339 The encyclopedia of alcoholism. 2d ed. Glen Evans et al. 400p. Facts on File, 1991. $45. ISBN 0-8160-1955-X.
362.29 HV5035.027

A concise compilation of more than 500 alphabetically arranged entries on alcohol, the socioeconomic interrelations that have an impact on alcoholism, and the physical and psychological effects of the disease. The definitions, ranging from one sentence to several pages long, are nontechnical, informative, and cross-referenced. Other features are an extensive bibliography and numerous tables and charts. Forty-three tables in the appendix provide such hard-to-find facts as the age limit for purchase and consumption of alcohol, public revenue from such beverages, and the cost of abuse. Useful for students, laypersons, and professionals. Index. This volume, with its companion *The encyclopedia of drug abuse,* will appeal to libraries wanting a less expensive alternative to the Macmillan *Encyclopedia of drugs and alcohol.*

340 The encyclopedia of drug abuse. 2d ed. Glen Evans et al. 496p. Facts on File, 1992. $45. ISBN 0-8160-1956-8.
362.2 HV5804

More than 1,000 entries varying in length from one-sentence definitions to thousand-word essays reveal the physical effects of drugs, the psychological and legal factors in drug abuse, and how drug abuse is handled in different countries. Appendixes present tabular information concerning the use, treatment, and traffic in drugs. Index and extensive bibliography.

341 Encyclopedia of drugs and alcohol. Jerome H. Jaffe, ed. 4v. Macmillan, 1995. $350. ISBN 0-02-897185-X.
362.29 HV5804

A comprehensive source of information for nonspecialists on all aspects of substance abuse—physical effects of drugs on the body, treatment and prevention of drug abuse, international trafficking and law enforcement, and social policy, to name a few. The alphabetically arranged entries range in length from a paragraph on the "breathalyzer" to a twenty-page overview on the causes of drug dependence. Most articles include references for additional research. Volume 4 contains five directories: a list of poison control centers for drug overdoses, a U.S. and state government drug resources directory, a state-by-state directory of drug abuse and alcoholism treatment and prevention programs, a selection of Bureau of Justice statistics relating to U.S. drug control efforts, and schedules of U.S. controlled substances. Essential for all libraries.

342 National directory of drug abuse and alcoholism treatment and prevention programs. U.S. Department of Health and Human Services, 1982– . Annual. Free from the National Clearinghouse for Alcohol and Drug Information (800-729-6686). SuDoc HE 20.410/3:yr.
362.29 HV5825

Arranged by state, then by city, this directory provides names, addresses, and phone numbers for more than 12,000 federal, state, local, and privately funded agencies responsible for the administration or provision of alcoholism or drug abuse services. Each entry is coded to indicate the facility's orientation (e.g., alcoholism, drug abuse), function (e.g., treatment, prevention), type of care, and specialized programs (e.g., Blacks, elderly, disabled). Also lists state authorities, state prevention contacts, and Veterans Administration medical centers.

Children and Youth

343 The adoption directory. 2d ed. Eileen Paul, ed. 571p. Gale, 1995. $65. ISBN 0-8103-7495-1.
362.7 HV875

A sourcebook of information about adoption agencies, private facilitators, support groups, and adoption laws in all fifty states, the District of Columbia, and seven foreign nations. Entries list contact information, area served, parental requirements, number and description of children placed, fees, and average wait for a child.

344 Childhood information resources. Marda Woodbury. 593p. Information Resources Pr., 1985. $45. ISBN 0-87815-051-X.
016.3052 Z7164

Comprehensive guide to major information sources on all aspects of childhood. Long, helpful annotations describe printed reference works, computerized retrieval sources, child-related organizations, and special subjects such as tests and measurements, statistics, and parenting. Detailed subject and title index.

345 The encyclopedia of child abuse. Robin E. Clark and Judith Clark. 360p. Facts on File, 1989. $45. ISBN 0-8160-1584-8.
362.7 HV6626.5

More than 500 entries treat laws, court cases, classes of abusers, forms of neglect, treatment programs, and organizations involved in protecting children. Charts and tables present statistics. A lengthy bibliography lists sources of further information. Appendixes provide lists of state agencies, state abuse statutes, states' reporting requirements, and texts of model statements on children's rights.

346 National directory of children, youth, and families services [yr.]. Penny Spencer. National Directory of Children, Youth, and Families Services, 1979– . Biennial. $119. ISSN 1072-902X.
362.7 HV741

Broad coverage: child- and youth-oriented social services, health and mental health services, youth advocacy services, and so forth, in state agencies, major cities, and 3,100 counties, plus information on private agencies in some 200 major population centers. Part 2 offers directory information for federal programs, congressional committees, information clearinghouses, runaway youth centers, and more. Part 3 is a buyer's guide to services and products.

347 Statistical record of children. Linda Schmittroth, ed. 983p. Gale, 1994. $105. ISBN 0-8103-9196-1.
305.23 HQ767.8

More than 900 tables collected from U.S. Census Bureau information, government reports, associations, research centers, and other sources. Topical areas include crime, health, education, vital statistics, recreation, and domestic life. Most of the data concern U.S. children, although there is a single chapter of international comparative figures. Each table cites its source.

Criminology

348 Directory: juvenile and adult correctional departments, institutions, agencies and paroling authorities: United States and Canada, 1979– . American Correctional Assn., 1979– . Annual. $80. ISSN 0190-2555.
365.025 HV9463

For each state and territory of the United States and for each Canadian province, this directory describes the organization of corrections and parole and provides directory information for correctional facilities, probation and transition centers, parole offices, and juvenile services. Valuable statistical data are presented in tables and with directory information. The *National jail and adult detention directory* (American Correctional Assn., 1978– . 1996/1998, $70. ISSN 0192-8228) is a state-by-state directory to county correctional facilities.

349 Encyclopedia of crime and justice. Sanford H. Kadish, ed. 4v. Free Pr., 1983. $375/set. ISBN 0-02-918110-0.
364.03 HV6017

In-depth, signed, authoritative articles ranging from 1,000 to 10,000 words draw from all disciplines to explore the nature and causes of criminal behavior, the prevention of crime, punishment and treatment of offenders, the institutions of criminal justice, and the body of law that defines criminal behavior. Extensive cross-references, a clear style, and selective bibliographies for further research make this a valued resource for a wide variety of general users and students. Cumulative indexes for cases, legal documents, subjects, and contributors.

350 Sourcebook of criminal justice statistics. U.S. Department of Justice. Bureau of Justice Statistics. Govt. Print. Off., 1974– . Annual. $53. S/N 027-000-01379-1. ISSN 0360-3431. SuDoc J29.9/6:yr.
364.973 HV7245

The first source for national criminal justice data drawn from government sources, academic and research institutions, and public polling services. Six sections provide information on characteristics of the criminal justice system, public attitudes, the nature and distribution of known offenses, characteristics and distribution of persons arrested, the judicial processing of defendants, and persons under correctional supervision. A rich and essential compendium of graphs, charts, and statistical tables.

351 Uniform crime reports for the United States. U.S. Department of Justice. Federal Bureau of Investigation. Govt. Print. Off., 1930– . Annual. $25. ISSN 0082-7592. SuDoc J1.14/7:yr.
■ cd online
364.1 HV6787

Also known by the title *Crime in the United States,* this essential source of social indicators presents detailed data on U.S. crime as reported to the FBI by nearly 16,000 city, county, and state law enforcement agencies. Data are narrower in scope and from more limited sources than those in the *Sourcebook of criminal justice statistics* but somewhat more current and more detailed. State-level uniform crime-reporting programs in forty-one states cumulate data from individual law enforcement agencies for input into the national program. Where available, libraries should provide reports for their states. A directory of state crime-reporting programs is appended.

Ethnic Studies

GENERAL

352 American immigrant cultures: builders of a nation. David Levinson and Melvin Ember, eds. 2v. 1091p. Macmillan, 1997. $250.75. ISBN 0-02-897208-2.
305.8 E184

Prepared under the auspices of the *Human Relations Area File* at Yale University, this work provides an authoritative historical and descriptive overview of nearly every conceivable ethnic culture present in the United States, from the Amish to the Carpatho-Rusyns and from the Sinhalese to the Zoroastrians. A pragmatic bibliography is provided for each ethnic group described.

353 Gale encyclopedia of multicultural America. Judy Galens et al. 2v. 1477p. Gale, 1995. $129. ISBN 0-8103-9163-5.
305.8 E184

These essays covering 101 ethnic groups focus mainly on immigrant groups, although religious and Native American groups are also represented. The signed articles include a history of migration to the United States and information on traditions, customs, language, religion, politics, and employment. Also included are short biographies and directories of organizations and media serving the group. An up-to-date source particularly recommended for public libraries.

354 Harvard encyclopedia of American ethnic groups. Stephan Thernstrom et al., eds. 1076p. Harvard Univ. Pr., 1980. $115. ISBN 0-674-37512-2.
305.8 E184

Contains 106 substantive essays about ethnic groups from Acadians to Zoroastrians; 29 thematic essays on such topics as assimilation, intermarriage, labor, and politics; eighty-seven maps; and other supplementary tables. The signed articles are scholarly yet readable and are accompanied by bibliographical essays. Many articles are lengthy, such as the fifty-six pages on Native Americans, and many provide information not available elsewhere. A valuable tool for school, public, and academic libraries.

355 Minority organizations: a national directory. 5th ed. Elizabeth H. Oakes, ed. 636p. Ferguson, 1997. $50. ISBN 0-89434-176-6. ISSN 0162-9034.
301.451 E184.A1

Provides names, addresses, phone numbers, and brief descriptions of some 7,700 organizations established by or for the benefit of Alaska natives, Native Americans, Blacks, Hispanics, and Asian Americans and lists 2,800 no longer operating or for which current information could not be found. Entries are arranged alphabetically by the name of the organization and indexed by minority group, type of organization, program, professional and academic fields of membership, and state. A list of other directories and reference sources on minorities is provided.

356 We the people: an atlas of America's ethnic diversity. James Paul Allen and Eugene James Turner. 315p. Macmillan, 1988. $175. ISBN 0-02-901420-4.
305.8 G1201

A beautifully executed snapshot of the ethnic composition of the United States in 1980. Based upon 1980 U.S. census data, chapters devoted to broad geographic areas of ethnic origin (e.g., people of early North American origin, people of African origin) present large, clear maps showing ethnic distribution by county; summary statistics; and text offering historical geographic interpretation. Individual maps and discussions within chapters focus on relatively small groups such as those of Serbian or Basque ancestry. Appendixes provide ethnic population data for states and counties as well as reference maps identifying U.S. counties. Ethnic population and place indexes.

AFRICAN AMERICANS

357 The African-American almanac. 7th ed. Kenneth Estell, ed. 1467p. Gale, 1996. $165. ISBN 0-8103-7867-1. (*formerly* **The Negro almanac.**)
305.8 E185

A basic source for public, secondary school, and undergraduate collections. Twenty-seven chapters cover history, biography, and statistical analysis with particular attention to the current situation of African Americans in society, including civil rights, legal status, employment, capitalism, education, the African American family, and the arts. Extensive use of illustrations, charts, and graphs greatly enhances the work. Includes directories of national African American organizations and print and broadcast media. Selective bibliography. Index.

358 African American historic places. Beth L. Savage, ed. 623p. Preservation Pr., 1994. $29.95. ISBN 0-89133-253-7.
973.0496073 E185

Descriptions of the more than 800 places recognized in the National Register of Historic Places as significant to Black social history, community development, education, women's history, civil rights, military events, or achievements in the arts, literature, science, and medicine. Arranged alphabetically by state, then by county, entries discuss the location, history, and significance of each place. City, occupation, and subject indexes.

359 Afro-American reference: an annotated bibliography of selected sources. Nathaniel Davis, comp. and ed. (Bibliographies and indexes in Afro-American and African studies; 9.) 288p. Greenwood, 1985. $80. ISBN 0-313-24930-X.
016.973 E185

Many of the 642 annotated entries describe reference works (e.g., indexes, dictionaries, handbooks, and bibliographies) focusing on Afro-American studies, apparently limiting its use to specialized research collections. But this useful guide also directs a wide variety of general readers and students to the most important monographs, statistical compendiums, government documents, and other sources for beginning research in this field.

360 Black Americans information directory. 3d ed. Wendy S. Van de Sande, ed. 556p. Gale, 1993. $79. ISBN 0-8103-8082-X.
973 E185.5

Provides current information on more than 5,000 institutions, organizations, programs, and publications pertaining to Black American life and culture.

361 Black firsts. Jessie Carney Smith. 529p. Gale, 1995. $39.95. ISBN 0-8103-8902-9; paper $16.95. ISBN 0-8103-9490-1.
909.0496 E185

Almost 3,000 groundbreaking "firsts" detailing the history and achievements of Black people. Arranged in fifteen subject chapters (such as education, military, business, and arts and entertainment), this source emphasizes the accomplishments of African Americans, although some international entries are included. Chapters are arranged chronologically, and a foldout time line is included. Events are listed separately by month and by year and may also be accessed through a keyword index. This attractive volume includes many black-and-white photographs.

362 Black women in America: an historical encyclopedia. Darlene Clark Hine et al., eds. 2v. Carlson, 1993. $195. ISBN 0-926019-61-9.
920.72 E185

More than 800 signed entries, tracing African American women from Jamestown in 1619 to 1992. Topical essays as well as biography. A chronology, annotated bibliography, and extensive index.

363 Dictionary of American Negro biography. Rayford W. Logan and Michael R. Winston, eds. 680p. Norton, 1982. $65. ISBN 0-393-01513-0.
920 E185.96

Includes persons who died before January 1, 1970. A comprehensive biographical dictionary based on scholarly research. Signed entries range from a column to several pages and cite additional biographical references and primary source materials. A landmark publication.

364 Encyclopedia of African-American culture and history. Jack Salzman, David Lionel Smith, and Cornel West, eds. 5v. Macmillan, 1996. $495. ISBN 0-02-897345-3.
973 E185

This five-volume award-winning encyclopedia covers all aspects of the African American experience from 1619 to the present day. There are more than 2,300 signed articles covering topics ranging from "Abolition" to "Zydeco"; about two-thirds are biographical, and the remainder deal with "events, historical eras, legal cases, areas of cultural achievement (music, architecture, the visual arts), professions, sports, and places." Entries are authoritative and scholarly and include extensive references for further study. The fifth volume includes a listing of the biographical entries by profession as well as a comprehensive index.

365 Encyclopedia of Black America. W. Augustus Low, ed. Virgil A. Clift, assoc. ed. 921p. McGraw-Hill, 1981. $130.95. ISBN 0-07-038834-2.
973 E185

A comprehensive one-volume general encyclopedia on Afro-American life and culture. About 1,700 *A-Z* articles, of which 1,400 are biographical and 125 others are major topical articles (artists, civil disobedience, newspapers, etc.). Bibliographical references append many entries. Black-and-white illustrations; tables and graphs.

366 Historical statistics of Black America. Jessie Carney Smith and Carrell Peterson Horton. 2v. Gale, 1995. $125. ISBN 0-8103-8542-2.
973.0496073 E185

Statistical tables reporting the Black experience in America, beginning with information recorded in the eighteenth century and extending through 1975. Arranged in topical chapters, subjects include agriculture, the family, labor and employment, education, housing, health, media, religion, and vital statistics. Most of the data are drawn from government publications, although a significant amount of material comes from publications by African American institutions and authors. Indexing by subject and by year.

367 Kaiser index to Black resources, 1948–1986: from the Schomburg Center for Research in Black Culture of the New York Public Library. 5v. Carlson, 1992. $995. ISBN 0-926019-60-0.
016.973 E185

The index is a compilation of more than 174,000 citations to articles, reviews, and obituaries from some 150 scholarly and general interest periodicals dealing with the African American experience. The citations are arranged under 15,000 alphabetical subject headings; many are followed by brief annotations and notes. The *Kaiser index* leads to a wealth of information not otherwise easily uncovered, and though one may have to rely on the interlibrary loan service for many items, the result is well worth the wait.

368 The Negro in America: a bibliography. 2d ed. Elizabeth W. Miller. 351p. Harvard Univ. Pr., 1970. Paper $16.50. ISBN 0-674-60702-3.
016.3 E185

Intended for both scholars and nonspecialists, the approximately 6,500 entries (some with brief annotations) for books, parts of books, and articles provide an interdisciplinary overview of African American history. Most references are to materials published in the United States since 1954 or to older, seminal works and appear alphabetically within subject groupings. Author index.

369 Notable Black American men. Jessie Carney Smith, ed. 1365p. Gale, 1998. $90. ISBN 0-7876-0763-0.
920.41 E185.86

Contains 500 alphabetically arranged biographies of notable African American men, past and present. Includes sources for further study, photographs, and addresses for living individuals.

370 Notable Black American women. Jessie Carney Smith, ed. 1334p. Gale, 1992. $80. ISBN 0-8103-4749-0.

Notable Black American women, book II. Jessie Carney Smith, ed. 775p. Gale, 1996. $80. ISBN 0-8103-9177-5.
920.72 E185.96

The original volume presents narrative essays on 500 African American women who have made significant contributions to American culture from the colonial era to the present. Contains almost 200 photographs. Authoritative and entertaining. *Book II* contains essays on an additional 300 women, including Anita Baker, Florence Griffith Joyner, and Whitney Houston.

371 Statistical record of Black America. 4th ed. Jessie Carney Smith and Carrell P. Horton, eds. 1145p. Gale, 1996. $109. ISBN 0-8103-9252-6.
305.8 E185.5

More than 1,000 graphs and tables provide information on a wide range of topics, from social services, health, and education to spending and wealth.

372 Timelines of African-American history: five hundred years of Black achievement. Tom Cowan and Jack Maguire. 368p. Roundtable, 1994. Paper $15. ISBN 0-399-52127-5.
973.049673 E185

Lists the major events in African American history from 1492 through 1993. Events are categorized under topics such as "Politics and Civil Rights," "Literature and Journalism," "Science and Technology," and "Religion and Education." Detailed index. A good value.

373 Who's who among African Americans. Gale. Biennial. (9th ed. 1539p. 1996/1997, $140.) ISSN 1081-1400. (*formerly* **Who's who among Black Americans.**)
920.073 E185.96

Standard "who's who" information for African Americans in all fields.

ASIAN AMERICANS

374 Asian American almanac: a reference work on Asians in the United States. Susan Gall and Irene Natividad, eds. 834p. Gale, 1995. $95. ISBN 0-8103-9193-7.
973 EE184.06

Provides basic reference information on fifteen major Asian American groups. Includes chapters on prominent Asian American figures; reprints notable speeches. Well indexed.

375 The Asian American encyclopedia. Franklin Ng, ed. 6v. Marshall Cavendish, 1995. $449.95. ISBN 1-85435-677-1.
973.0495 E184.06

More than 2,000 entries detail the history and culture of this fast-growing U.S. ethnic minority. The unsigned entries range from a few lines to several pages; longer entries conclude with a short bibliography of additional sources. Subjects covered include immigration policies, community studies (with demographic data from the 1990 census), historical background matter, and many biographical profiles. Includes many black-and-white photographs, a chronology, a filmography, and directories of Asian American organizations, museums, study programs, research centers, and print media.

376 Asian Americans information directory. 2d ed. Charles B. Montney, ed. 480p. Gale, 1994. $75. ISBN 0-8103-8501-5.
973.0495 E184.06

Brief directory information on a variety of organizations, agencies, programs, publications, and services concerned with Asian Americans. Nineteen ethnic groups are covered in more than 5,200 listings. The topics covered include culture, economics, politics, and employment. Although most of the material included is compiled from other Gale publications, libraries with interest in this area will appreciate the convenience of this volume.

377 Dictionary of Asian American history. Hyung-Chan Kim, ed. 642p. Greenwood, 1986. $85. ISBN 0-313-23760-3.
973.0495 E184.06

In the first of two parts, seven essays treat the historical development in the United States of ethnic groups from Asian countries and the Pacific Islands, followed by eight essays on Asian Americans in the American social order. The second part is an alphabetically arranged dictionary of nearly 800 entries covering key facts, events, laws, court cases, and people. Appendixes present a select bibliography of monographs, a chronology, and an extract of 1980 census data. Index.

378 Notable Asian Americans. Helen Zia and Susan B. Gall, eds. 468p. Gale, 1995. $75. ISBN 0-8103-9623-8.
920.0092 E184.06

One- to three-page essays detailing the life and accomplishments of Asian Americans in all fields of endeavor. Most of the people profiled are still living. Essays usually contain a photograph and a brief list of additional sources. Index by occupation and ethnicity.

HISPANIC AMERICANS

379 Dictionary of Mexican American history. Matt S. Meier and Feliciano Rivera. 498p. Greenwood, 1981. $49.95. ISBN 0-313-21203-1.
973 E184

Recognized authorities provide brief commentaries on topics from Chicano history to the contemporary social and political scene. Entries range from one-line definitions to essays several pages long. Extensive cross-references enhance the usefulness of the entire text. Suggestions for further reading accompany longer essays. Students, interested general readers, and specialists will appreciate the appended bibliography of general works, chronology, glossary of Chicano terms, maps, and tables of census, education, employment, and immigration statistics. Index.

380 Handbook of Hispanic cultures in the United States. Nicolas Kanellos and Claudio Esteva-Fabregat, eds. 4v. Arte Publico, 1993. $200/set. ISBN 1-55885-103-8; Anthropology. $60. ISBN 1-55885-102-X; History. $60. ISBN 1-55885-100-3; Literature and art. $60. ISBN 1-55885-074-0; Sociology. $60. ISBN 1-55885-101-1.
973.0468 E184

An attractive and scholarly survey of Hispanic American history, anthropology, sociology, literature, and art. Each volume is a subject encyclopedia on some aspect of Hispanic American culture. The long, signed articles include extensive bibliographies. Many photographs and illustrations. For academic and large public collections.

381 Hispanic-American almanac. 2d ed. Nicolas Kanellos, ed. 884p. Gale, 1996. $110. ISBN 0-8103-8595-3.
973.0468 E184

An overview of Hispanic American life and culture in twenty-five subject chapters. Topics covered include education, art, literature, sports, religion, and family. Includes bibliographies and many photographs and tables.

382 Hispanic Americans information directory. 3d ed. Charles B. Montney, ed. 515p. Gale, 1994. $85. ISBN 0-8103-7849-7.
973 E184

A comprehensive guide to more than 4,500 organizations, institutions, programs, and publications, this lists the top 500 Hispanic companies, radio and TV stations, newspapers, and periodicals.

383 Notable Hispanic American women. Diane Telgen and Jim Kamp, eds. 448p. Gale, 1993. $59.95. ISBN 0-8103-7578-8.

Notable Hispanic American women, book II. 377p. Gale, 1998. $70. ISBN 0-7876-2068-8.
920.72 E184

The original volume presents nearly 300 entries, listed alphabetically by surname, covering women who were born in or who claim origin from Mexico, Puerto Rico, Cuba, Spain, or any of the Spanish-speaking countries of Central and South America. Indexed by occupation, ethnicity, personal name, corporate or institutional affiliation, and "subject," including such concepts as "alienation." *Book II* provides an additional 200 profiles, including Jennifer Lopez, Mariah Carey, and Rebecca Lobo, and features an introduction by Elsa Sanchez.

384 Statistical handbook on U.S. Hispanics. Frank L. Schick and Renee Schick. 255p. Oryx, 1991. $49.50. ISBN 0-89774-554-X.
305.8 E184.5

Almost 300 tables present statistics on population, immigration, education, politics, employment, health, and economic status. Many tables give data on Whites, Blacks, and Asians.

385 Statistical record of Hispanic Americans. 2d ed. 1141p. Gale, 1995. $109. ISBN 0-8103-6422-0.
305.8 E184.5

Provides 921 charts, tables, and graphs that serve to quantify the status of the Hispanic American population. Source information for all data is provided. Includes an annotated bibliography and both subject and keyword indexes.

386 Who's who among Hispanic Americans. 4th ed. Gale, 1999. $100. ISBN 0-8103-9327-1.
920 E184

This title provides basic information about 5,000 Hispanics in a typical "who's who" format. There are indexes by city, by occupation, and by ethnic and cultural heritage (e.g., Cuban, Puerto Rican, Mexican, etc.).

NATIVE PEOPLES OF NORTH AMERICA

387 American Indian literatures: an introduction, bibliographic review, and selected bibliography. A. LaVonne Brown Ruoff. 200p. Modern Language Assn., 1990. $45. ISBN 0-87352-187-0; paper $19.75. ISBN 0-87352-188-9.
897 PM155

Covering both oral and written literature, this book lists anthologies, scholarship, and criticism, as well as works by Native Americans. Whenever a Native American author is mentioned, his or her tribal affiliation is noted in parentheses.

388 Gale encyclopedia of Native American tribes. Sharon Malinowski and Anna Sheets, eds. 4v. Gale, 1998. $349/set.

ISBN 0-7876-1085-2.
973 E77

Arranged in four regional volumes—(1) Northeast and Southeast; (2) Great Basin and Southwest; (3) Arctic, Subarctic, Plateau, and Great Plains; and (4) Pacific Northwest and California—the encyclopedia provides rich and detailed information on more than 400 Native American groups. For each region, there is a lengthy signed overview essay, which sets the context for the tribes in that region; then the tribes are presented in alphabetical order. Each entry describes the history and culture of the tribe, followed by a section on current issues and concluding with a bibliography for further reading. Also included are short biographies of some 200 tribal leaders; more than 655 photos and illustrations; key date boxes that highlight significant events in each tribe's history; a glossary; and both cumulative and volume-specific indexes.

389 Native America in the twentieth century: an encyclopedia. Mary B. Davis, ed. 787p. Garland, 1994. $95. ISBN 0-8240-4846-6; paper $29.95. ISBN 0-8153-2583-5.
970.004 E76.2

The best place to begin research on current Native American issues. Arranged alphabetically, the one- to five-page entries cover important aspects of Native American life and include such topics as "Red Power," land claims, gaming, art, and urbanization. More than half the articles are devoted to contemporary Native American nations. Biographical entries are not included, nor is coverage of Canadian Native affairs. Articles were contributed by 218 scholars (113 of whom are Native Americans) and include brief bibliographies. Unique and authoritative.

390 Native American women: a biographical dictionary. Gretchen M. Bataille, ed. 360p. Garland, 1993. $55. ISBN 0-8240-5267-6.
920 E98

A selection of 240 women, both contemporary and historical figures. Arranged alphabetically, with a listing by areas of specialization, decade and state or province of birth, and tribal affiliation. Bibliographies at the end of each entry.

391 Notable Native Americans. Sharon Malinowski, ed. 492p. Gale, 1995. $65. ISBN 0-8103-9638-6.
920.00297 E89

Two hundred sixty-five biographical essays on Native Americans throughout history and from all fields: politics, law, journalism, science, medicine, religion, the arts, sports, education, and entertainment. About 30 percent of the entries focus on historical figures and 70 percent on contemporary individuals. The signed essays are one to three pages in length and include a short list of additional references. Many entries contain photographs or illustrations. Detailed subject index and tribal group and occupational directories.

392 Reference encyclopedia of the American Indian. 7th ed. Barry T. Klein, ed. 883p. Todd, 1995. $125. ISBN 0-915344-45-9; paper $49.95. ISBN 0-915344-46-7.
970 E76.2

The first section is a directory of U.S. reservations, government agencies, schools, museums, events, casinos, and so forth, relating to Native Americans. The second section is a similar Canadian directory. The third section is a bibliography of 4,500 books about Native Americans. The last section gives brief biographies of prominent Native Americans and non-Indians active in Indian affairs.

393 Statistical record of Native North Americans. 2d ed. Marlita A. Reddy, ed. 1272p. Gale, 1995. $109. ISBN 0-8103-6421-2.
304.6 E98

A convenient repackaging of data, bringing together statistics from 143 different publications on nearly 200 North American tribes. Many U.S. statistics are from the decennial censuses. Canadian figures are from the 1986 census. Arranged in eleven subject chapters; topics covered include demographics, education, health, and business. Most chapters include both current and historic data, and each table cites its source. Detailed keyword index.

Social Service and Philanthropy

394 Catalog of federal domestic assistance. 1995 ed. Executive Office of the President. c1500p. Loose-leaf. Govt. Print. Off., 1986– . (1995, $53/yr. S/N 922-010-00000-6. SuDoc PrEx 2.20:990.)
338.973 HC110

Guide to federal programs, projects, services, and activities providing assistance or benefits to the public. Describes each program, how to apply, and financial resources. Subscription includes the basic loose-leaf volume and periodic updates.

395 Encyclopedia of social work, 1965– . Richard L. Edwards, ed. National Assn. of Social Workers, 1965– . Irreg. (19th ed., 1995. 3v. $150/set. ISBN 0-87101-255-3.) ISSN 0071-0237. (*formerly* **Social work year book, 1929–60.**)
■ cd
361.003 HV35

Well-written and authoritative articles on social work and social welfare activities in the United States selected for their relevance to social work practice (e.g., abortion, case management, foster care, and homelessness). Extensive bibliographies. Biographical section chronicles now-deceased persons who have made significant contributions to social welfare in the United States. Appendixes include a chronology of important dates in social welfare history, a listing of acronyms, and codes of ethics for social work organizations. Essential for academic libraries supporting social work degree programs.

396 The foundation directory. Foundation Center, 1960– . Annual. $210; paper $190. ISSN 0071-8092.
■ online
060.2 AS911

The standard source for information about private and community grant-making foundations in the United States. The 1998 edition includes entries for more than 7,000 foundations with assets of at least $2 million or annual giving of $200,000. Arranged alphabetically by state, entries include contact information, purpose and activities, fields of interest, types of support, limitations on giving, application information, and selected grants awarded previously. Extensive indexing by donors, officers, and trustees; geographic area; subject; and foundation name. Libraries needing more depth in their coverage of foundations may acquire *The foundation directory supplement,* which updates address, staff, policy changes, and other information in the fall of each year; and *The foundation directory. Part 2. A guide to grant programs $50,000–$200,000* (Foundation Center. Annual. $185. ISSN 1058-6210), which provides information about 4,800 foundations with grant programs between $50,000 and $200,000.

397 Public welfare directory, 1940– . American Public Welfare Assn., 1940– . Annual. Paper $80. ISSN 0163-8297.
360.58 HV89

A comprehensive list of federal, state, and local public assistance and public welfare agencies, including officials. Entries include a description of the agency's purpose as well as contact and address information. Includes Canadian as well as U.S. agencies. Material on "where to write" for vital records. Very useful for public and academic libraries.

398 Refugee and immigrant resource directory. 3d ed. Alan Edward Schorr, ed. 256p. Denali Pr., 1994. Paper $47.50. ISBN 0-938737-28-7. (*formerly* **Directory of services for refugees and immigrants.**)
362.8 HV640.4

Provides basic directory information—name, address, phone number, contact person—for 2,270 organizations, agencies, and educational institutions providing services primarily to refugees and immigrants or providing policy analysis about this population. Geographic, organization, and contact person indexes. Appendixes include statistical information and a glossary. A useful adjunct to directories of local social services.

399 Social service organizations. Peter Romanofsky, ed. (Greenwood encyclopedia of American institutions; 2.) 2v. Greenwood, 1978. $150/set. ISBN 0-8371-9829-1.
361.7 HV88

Historical sketches of nearly 200 national and local voluntary social service agencies and their respective contributions to American social work. Bibliographical notes add references to historical source materials. Appendixes list religious affiliated agencies, a chronology by founding dates, agencies by function, and genealogies of mergers and name changes. The concise, readable essays on such groups as the YMCA, Planned Parenthood Federation of America, or the Fresh Air Fund will be valuable to both public and academic libraries.

400 Social service organizations and agencies directory. Anthony T. Kruzas, ed. 548p. Gale, 1982. $140. ISBN 0-8103-0329-9.
361 HV89

The 6,500 entries cover public and private service organizations and agencies on both state and national levels. Arranged in chapters for areas such as the aged, battered women, child abuse, the disabled, and so forth, with a name and keyword index.

401 Social work almanac. 2d ed. Leon H. Ginsberg. 391p. National Assn. of Social Workers, 1995. $34.95.

ISBN 0-87101-248-0.
361.973 HV90

A handy compilation of social services and social welfare statistics. Topics covered include older adults, children, homelessness and housing, mental illness and developmental disabilities, and health. Most material presented comes from data collected by the U.S. government and the National Association of Social Workers. Descriptive text interprets the statistical tables and charts.

402 The social work dictionary. 4th ed. Robert L. Barker. 447p. National Assn. of Social Workers, 1995. Paper $34.95. ISBN 0-87101-298-7.
361.3 HV12

Defines terms used in social work administration, research, policy development, and planning; community organization; human growth and development; health and mental health; and clinical theory and practice. The more than 3,000 definitions were reviewed by a board of experts for consensus and accuracy. Appendixes include a chronology of milestones in the development of social work and social welfare and a directory of state boards regulating social work.

Statistics and Demography

403 Atlas of the 1990 census. Mark T. Mattson. 168p. Macmillan, 1992. $95. ISBN 0-02-897302-X.
304.6 G1201

A graphic representation of many of the most-requested statistics of the 1990 census of population and housing. The atlas contains 200 four-color maps and eighty tables and is arranged in six parts: population, households, housing, race and ethnicity, economy, and education. Each section contains a national map of 1980 census data, a map showing change from 1980 to 1990, and a map of 1990 census results. Attractive and easy to use.

404 County and city data book, 1994. Bureau of the Census. 1104p. Govt. Print. Off., 1994. $40. S/N 003-024-08753-7. SuDoc C3.134/2:C83/2/994.
■ micro cd online
317.3 HA202

Brings together a variety of social and economic data from the U.S. Census Bureau and other sources for states, counties, and cities of 25,000 or more. Tables cover population, age, money, education, births, deaths, poverty, health care, business, and many other topics. A supplement to the *Statistical abstract of the United States.*

405 County and city extra: annual metro, city, and county data book. Bernan, 1992– . Annual. $109. ISSN 1059-9096.
317.3 HA202

The *County and city extra* was created to serve as a convenient update to the *County and city data book,* produced only irregularly by the Bureau of the Census. Its extensive data are presented in a similar format to that of the government publication, but the data are easier to read and understand. The book has useful appendixes and much additional information.

406 Demographic yearbook/Annuaire demographique, 1948– . UN Statistical Office. UN Publications, 1949– . Annual. $125. ISSN 0082-8041.
312.058 HA17

Official compilation of international demographic data in such fields as area and population, natality, mortality, marriage, divorce, and international migration. Each year some aspect of demographic statistics is treated intensively. Cumulative index covers contents of all issues of *Yearbook.*

407 1990 census of population and housing. Bureau of the Census. Govt. Print. Off., 1990– . Price and S/N vary.
■ micro cd online tape
304.6 HA201

The 1990 census reports are organized into three major series. The population census reports (1990 CP series) display results from population questions (for example, age, sex, race, education, employment). The housing census reports (1990 CH series) display results from housing questions (for example, number of rooms, rent, value, plumbing facilities). The 1990 CPH series combine the results of the population and housing census. In each series most reports are organized geographically. Many of these series consist of fifty-four reports—one for each state, the District of Columbia, Puerto Rico, the Virgin Islands, and a U.S. summary. Every library will want those volumes containing the U.S. summary, its state volumes, and perhaps those covering contiguous states. In addition, there are many subject reports issued for the nation as a whole that libraries will want to acquire. Libraries with an interest in the census will want *Bureau of the Census catalog and guide* (Bureau of the Census, Govt. Print. Off., 1946– .

[1997, $19.] ISSN 0007-618X), which describes available reports and files and is available online.

408 Places, towns, and townships. Richard W. Dodge, Deirdre A. Gaquin, and Mark S. Littman. 2d ed. Bernan, 1998. $82.50. ISBN 0-89059-072-9.
317.3 HA203

A complement to the *County and city extra,* this new series provides detailed demographic and economic data for even the very smallest geographic units. The second edition provides considerably more economic data, gathered from numerous sources and compiled together here for convenient access.

409 Population and housing characteristics for congressional districts of the 103rd congress. Bureau of the Census. Govt. Print Off., 1990. S/N and price vary for each state part. (Census of population and housing; 1990, Series PHC 90-4.) SuDoc C3.223/20:90-4- .
304.6 HA201

Statistical information for congressional districts obtained from the 1990 census files for population and housing.

410 State and metropolitan area data book, 1979– . Bureau of the Census. Govt. Print. Off., 1980– . (5th ed. 1997–98, $24.) S/N 003-024-08827-4. SuDoc C3.134/5:yr. ISSN 0276-6566.
■ micro disk online
317.3 HA202

This supplement to the *Statistical abstract of the United States* presents more than 1,500 data tables for states and more than 200 for metropolitan areas. Statistics cover the standard areas of population, education, employment, income, crime, housing, manufacturing, and so forth. The ranking tables are particularly useful. This title should stand beside the *Statistical abstract of the United States* and *County and city data book* as a standard source on the reference shelf of any library.

411 Statistical abstract of the United States. Govt. Print. Off., 1879– . Annual. $51. S/N 003-024- . SuDoc C3.134:yr. ISSN 0081-4741.
■ micro cd online
317.3 HA202

An indispensable collection of social, political, and economic data selected from many statistical publications, both governmental and private. The 1995 edition includes data from selected years from 1790 to 1996, with an emphasis on recent years. A section of international statistics is included for comparative purposes. Each table cites its source and thus also serves as a guide to other statistical publications and sources. Classified arrangement and detailed index. The single most important statistical fact book on American life.

412 Statistical handbook of the American family. Bruce A. Chadwick and Tim B. Heaton, eds. 295p. Oryx, 1995. $59.50. ISBN 0-89774-687-2.
306.85 HQ536

More than 400 tables of data covering many aspects of American life—marriage rates, living arrangements, contraceptive use, family violence, working women, divorce, and child care. Data are drawn from government publications, the census, Gallup polls, professional journals, various public-domain databases, and some unpublished sources. Source documents for the various tables are listed in an appendix.

413 Statistical portrait of the United States: social conditions and trends. Mark S. Littman, ed. 425p. Bernan, 1998. $79. ISBN 0-89059-076-1.
317.3 HA214

Offers twenty-five-year trends and international comparisons on American population; living arrangements; education; health; work; income; poverty and wealth; housing; crimes and victims; leisure, volunteerism, and religion; voting; the environment; and government. Offers data summaries and concise analysis; provides sources for additional information, including web site addresses.

414 Statistical yearbook, 1948– . UN Statistical Office. UN Pubs., 1949– . Annual. Price varies. $115. ISSN 0082-8459.
310.5 HA12.5

A summary volume of international economic and social statistics. Tables arranged in broad subject categories, such as education, science and technology, culture, and mass media. Includes world summary data.

415 Statistics sources: a subject guide to data on industrial, business, social, educational, financial, and other topics for the United States and internationally. 1st ed.– . Jacqueline Wasserman O'Brien and Steven R.

Wasserman, eds. Gale, 1962– .
(21st ed. 2v. 1997, $415/set.
ISBN 0-7876-0162-4.) ISSN 0585-198X.
016.31 Z7551

"A finding guide to statistics." A subject listing of terms and phrases under which are cited both published and unpublished statistical sources. International in coverage. Includes a selected bibliography of key statistical sources.

416 USA counties on CD-ROM. Bureau of the Census. Govt. Print. Off., 1994.
$150. S/N n/a. SuDoc C3.134/6:UN3/yr.
■ cd
317.3 HA729

Lists 2,844 data items by county on a variety of demographic, economic, and governmental subjects. Data files include age, agriculture, ancestry, banking, business, crime, health, households, housing, labor force, income, population, poverty, and vital statistics. Easy to use.

Urban Affairs

417 Encyclopedia of urban planning.
Arnold Whittick, ed. 1218p. McGraw-Hill, 1974. Reprint: Krieger, 1980.
$79.50. ISBN 0-89874-104-1.
309.2 HT166

An international encyclopedia with signed articles that cover planning in forty-eight different countries, as well as articles on various aspects of planning and subjects related to it (e.g., population growth and distribution, economic considerations, landscape architecture). Also includes biographical articles, bibliographies, illustrations, and an index.

Women's Studies

418 Chronology of women's history. Kirstin Olsen. 506p. Greenwood, 1994. $39.95.
ISBN 0-313-28803-8.
305.4 HQ1121.047

Landmarks in international women's history from 20,000 B.C. to 1993. Arrangement is by chronological sections that get progressively smaller; the twentieth century is covered year-by-year. Most sections include events in ten categories: general status and daily life; government, the military, and the law; literature and the visual arts; performing arts and entertainment; athletics actvism; exploration activism; business and industry; science and medicine; education and scholarship; and religion. Appended is an eighty-page selective bibliography and an extensive index.

419 Encyclopedia of feminism. Lisa Tuttle.
399p. Facts on File, 1986. $24.95.
ISBN 0-8160-1424-8.
305.4 HQ1115

More than 1,000 brief yet informative entries treat feminist terms (e.g., *reproductive freedom*), events and persons significant to the feminist movement, books, organizations, and even works of art. Many general terms (e.g., *theater, ecology*) are discussed in a feminist context. Extensive cross-references and a selected bibliography.

420 Statistical handbook on women in America. 2d ed. Cynthia Murray Taeuber, ed. 344p. Oryx, 1996. $64.50.
ISBN 1-57356-005-7.
305.4 HQ1420

More than 400 tables are arranged in chapters covering demographics, employment, health, status, and social conditions. Most data are from 1985 to 1990. Data for foreign countries and some historical figures are given for comparison. Topics include population, fertility, poverty, health, and marriage and divorce.

421 Statistical record of women worldwide. Linda Schmittroth, ed. 1047p.
Gale, 1995. $99. ISBN 0-8103-8872-3.
305.4 HQ1150

Data drawn from a variety of governmental sources, periodical literature, association reports, and organizational and research center studies. Topics include attitudes and opinions, education, vital statistics, domestic life, income and wealth, health and medical care, employment, and public life. Coverage is about half United States and half international. Each table gives source. Subject and geographic index.

422 Who's who of American women. v.1– .
Marquis Who's Who, 1958– . Biennial.
$259. ISSN 0083-9841.
■ cd online
920.73 E176

Includes short biographies in the standard Marquis format of 29,000 American women who are currently prominent in various professions and government.

423 Women in the world: an international atlas. Joni Seager and Ann Olson.
128p. Simon & Schuster, 1986. $19.45.

ISBN 0-671-60297-7; paper $12.95.
ISBN 0-671-63070-9.
305.4 G1046

Brightly colored, clear, and easily understood maps and illustrations depict the status of women throughout the world. Each of forty topics (e.g., birth care, earnings, refugees, military service, rape, channels of change) is introduced by a brief text accompanying maps and graphics. Subject coverage includes marriage, motherhood, work, resources, welfare, authority, body politics, change, and statistical politics. Notes to the maps, bibliography, and index. An excellent companion to *The women's atlas of the United States* for school, public, and academic collections.

424 The women's atlas of the United States. Rev. ed. Timothy H. Fast and Cathy Carroll Fast. 256p. Facts on File, 1995. $75. ISBN 0-8160-2970-9.
305.4 G1201

Dramatic and colorful maps convert demographic and other data concerning women to fascinating graphic presentations accompanied by discussions of general issues. Students and beginning researchers will find choropleth maps, symbol maps, pie chart maps, and cartograms addressing demographics, education, employment, the family, health, crime, and politics. Notes and an index.

425 The women's book of world records and achievements. Lois Decker O'Neill. 798p. Doubleday, 1979. Reprint: Da Capo Pr., 1983. Paper $14.95. ISBN 0-306-80206-6.
920.72 CT3234

An inspiring summary of women's achievements in the late nineteenth and twentieth centuries, this volume in seventeen subject chapters provides information on about 5,000 women's firsts, greats, leaders, and successes in every field of human endeavor. Each chapter begins with an introductory essay written by an authority in that field. The fields include politics, agriculture, sports, home and community, and religion. The brief sketches of women that follow are well written and succinctly outline the achievements of each woman. A detailed subject and personal name index is included.

426 Women's information directory. Shawan Brennan, ed. 795p. Gale, 1993. $75. ISBN 0-8103-8422-1.
362.83 HQ1115

Directory information about 10,000 organizations, agencies, institutions, programs, publications, and services relevant to U.S. women's issues. Arranged in twenty-six subject chapters, most entries contain contact information and a brief description of the program or association. Included are lists of women's studies programs, libraries with special collections of interest to women's studies scholars, women's colleges, and scholarships and loans available to women. Subject and name index.

ANTHROPOLOGY AND ARCHAEOLOGY

Atlases

427 The atlas of early man. Jacquetta Hawkes. 255p. St. Martin's, 1993. Paper $18.95. ISBN 0-312-09746-8.
930 CB311

This book indicates events occurring around the world during eight time steps between 35,000 B.C. and A.D. 500. Identifies for each time step the major events and developments, famous people, and happenings in such fields as religion, technology, and art. Includes summary charts for each time step and an atlas of archaeological site maps. Illustrated. Index.

428 Atlas of world cultures: a geographical guide to ethnographic literature. David H. Price. 156p. Sage (in cooperation with the Human Relations Area File), 1989. $49.95. ISBN 0-8039-3240-5; paper $22.50. ISBN 0-8039-4075-0.
912.1 G1046

An easy-to-use and valuable guide to the physical location of some 3,500 groups, tribes, and peoples worldwide and to classic works of ethnographic literature about them. The main body of the atlas includes forty maps indicating the location of each cultural group. These are followed by the 1,237-item bibliography and the culture index, which direct researchers to as many as two bibliographic citations per culture, a map and location, and, if applicable, the *Human Relations Area File* (HRAF) code and the classification code used in George P. Murdock's *Atlas of world cultures* (Univ. of Pittsburgh Pr., 1981. $49.95. ISBN 0-8229-3432-9). Most appropriate for academic collections, especially those providing access to the *Human Relations Area File*.

429 Past worlds: the Times atlas of archaeology. 320p. Random House, 1995. $34.99. ISBN 0-517-12174-3.
912 G1046

From the introductory chapter on understanding archaeological methods and techniques to the extensive index in the back of the book, this is a beautifully produced reference volume. The atlas covers prehistory, the agriculture revolution, the rise of cities, the development of empires, and the civilizations of the New World. The maps are carefully prepared and with the superior drawings serve to enhance and explain the text. Frequent photographs help bring the past alive for the modern student.

430 **The world atlas of archaeology.** Foreword by Michael Wood. 423p. Hall, 1985. $95. ISBN 0-8161-8747-9.
912 G1046

Nearly 100 essays primarily by European scholars cover the archaeological history of the world by region and by period. Each section, such as "Prehistoric Europe" or "Oceania," begins with a two-page survey of the archaeological background before developing special topics, which vary by region. Profusely illustrated with color maps, drawings, and photographs. Bibliography, glossary, and detailed index.

Dictionaries and Encyclopedias

431 **The Cambridge encyclopedia of archaeology.** Andrew Sherratt, ed. 495p. Cambridge Univ. Pr., 1980. op.
930.1 CC165

A topically arranged encyclopedia prepared by fifty-five contributors (each a specialist) for the educated general reader rather than for the scholar. In three main parts: the development of modern archaeology; various archaeological periods, regions, and empires; and framework: dating and distribution. Excellent illustrations (500, 150 colored); bibliography (by chapter); and analytical index.

432 **Encyclopedia of anthropology.** David E. Hunter and Phillip Whitten, eds. 411p. HarperCollins, 1976. op.
301.2 GN11

Includes some 1,400 entries. Articles range in length from 25 to 3,000 words and cover concepts, theories, terminology, and individuals in the field of anthropology as well as material from the related fields of linguistics, psychology, and sociology. Illustrated.

433 **Encyclopedia of cultural anthropology.** David Levinson and Melvin Ember, eds. 4v. 1486p. Henry Holt, 1996. $395. ISBN 0-8050-2877-3.
305 GN307

Sponsored by the *Human Relations Area File* project at Yale University, this authoritative resource provides detailed information on all aspects of human cultural experience, from cyberculture to poetics. Includes more than 340 articles with bibliographies.

434 **The encyclopedia of the peoples of the world.** Amiram Gonen, ed. 704p. Henry Holt, 1993. $125. ISBN 0-8050-2256-2.
305.8 GN495.4

More than 2,000 brief entries on contemporary nationalities and ethnic groups. Most entries include information on race, religion, location, language, and population. Includes many large black-and-white photographs of representative people and about 250 maps showing the location of selected peoples and ethnic groups. A good choice for high school and public libraries.

435 **Encyclopedia of world cultures.** David Levinson, ed. 10v. Hall, 1991. $1100/set. ISBN 0-8161-1840-X; v.1, North America. $110. ISBN 0-8161-1808-6; v.2, Oceania. $110. ISBN 0-8161-1809-4; v.3, South Asia. $110. ISBN 0-8161-1812-4; v.4, Europe. $110. ISBN 0-8161-1811-6; v.5, East and Southeast Asia. $110. ISBN 0-8161-1814-0; v.6, Russia and Eurasia/China. $110. ISBN 0-8161-1810-8; v.7, South America. $110. ISBN 0-8161-1813-2; v.8, Middle America and the Caribbean. $110. ISBN 0-8161-1816-7; v.9, Africa and the Middle East. $110. ISBN 0-8161-1815-9; v.10, Indexes. $110. ISBN 0-8161-1817-5.
306.097 GN307

A comprehensive and authoritative survey of the cultures of the world based on the *Human Relations Area File*. Volumes 1 through 9 contain introductory essays; cultural summaries, which range in length from a few lines to a few pages; maps detailing the location of cultural groups; a filmography; and a glossary. Volume 10 contains the cumulative list of the cultures, their alternate names, and a subject index. Expensive but essential for academic collections.

436 **Larousse dictionary of world folklore.** Alison Jones. 493p. Larousse, 1995.

$27.50. ISBN 0-7523-0012-1.
398.03 GR35

Brief alphabetical entries about characters, themes, and symbols prominent in folklore. Includes many black-and-white illustrations. Appended are a list of sources for further reading, biographical notes on prominent folklorists, a list of world ethnographical and folklore museums, and a calendar of international festivals and folkloric events.

437 Marriage, family, and relationships: a cross-cultural encyclopedia. Gwen J. Broude. 372p. ABC-Clio, 1994. $49.50. ISBN 0-87436-736-0.
306.8 GN480

A fascinating multicultural survey of societal expectations, customs, and rituals relating to marriage and the family. Topical areas include courtship, monogamy, attractiveness, and the elderly. Arranged alphabetically by topic. Includes bibliographic references.

438 World directory of minorities. Minority Rights Group. 840p. Paul & Co. Pub. Consortium, 1997. $145. ISBN 1-873194-35-6.
305.56 HM201

This subject encyclopedia defines a minority as a group numerically inferior to the rest of a state's population and whose members differ linguistically, ethnically, or religiously from the majority. Minority groups are described in one- to four-page essays arranged in eleven regional groupings. Essays describe the location, language, religion, historical background, and current situation of the minority. Most of the information in the entries comes from Minority Rights Group reports.

Handbooks

439 America's ancient treasures: a guide to archeological sites and museums in the United States and Canada. 4th ed. Franklin Folsom and Mary Elting Folsom. 459p. Univ. of New Mexico Pr., 1993. $39.95. ISBN 0-8263-1424-4; paper $24.95. ISBN 0-8263-1450-3.
970.1 E56

Grouped first by region, then by state, alphabetically arranged entries tell how to get to visitable archaeological sites and museums, hours of operation, cost, and what is to be seen. Glossary, bibliography, and detailed index.

7

Business and Careers

SUSAN C. AWE

Libraries are offered an array of sources—most of which are expensive—to meet the demand for business information. With the development of the global economy, most of these information sources have become international in scope; however, a strong demand for local and regional business data does still exist, and sources have developed to fill that niche as well. The emphasis is definitely on currency—thus, the heavy reliance on nonmonographic sources such as loose-leaf services, data files, annuals with periodic supplements, and newsletters. Accessing business data and business-related topics through the Internet is clearly the way of the future.

Bibliographies and Guides

440 Business information: how to find it, how to use it. 2d ed. Michael R. Lavin. 512p. Oryx, 1992. $49.95. ISBN 0-89774-556-6; paper $38.50. ISBN 0-89774-643-0.
650.072 HF5356

Lavin has a talent for making complex business publications comprehensible to laypersons and librarians. He explains concepts essential for effectively using many of the business sources identified in this title. Buy this for every business collection.

441 Business information sources. 3d ed. Lorna M. Daniells. 725p. Univ. of California Pr., 1993. $35. ISBN 0-520-08180-3.
016.33 HF5351

This new edition guides the practicing businessperson, the business student, and the librarian through the vast and varied sources of business information. Twenty chapters on all aspects of management, insurance, international business, marketing, accounting, investment sources, industry statistics, trends, and so forth give annotated references to the most useful sources. Coverage of electronic sources has been expanded. Included are a detailed index, a basic bibliography, and a special chapter on "time-saving sources."

442 Directory of business periodical special issues. Trip Wyckoff, ed.

162p. Reference Pr., 1995. $49.95.
ISBN 1-878753-60-6.
051.016 Z7164

A definitive up-to-date guide covering the most important business and technology magazines and trade journals, including buying guides, salary surveys, industry forecasts, annual lists of top companies, and other special topics. Each of the entries includes address and phone number, special issue with publication dates, subject classification, and a list of periodical indexes where the magazine is indexed and abstracted.

443 Encyclopedia of business information sources. 12th ed. James Woy, ed. 1118p. Gale, 1998. $308. ISBN 0-7876-1258-8. ISSN 0071-0210.
016.33 HF5353

More than 31,000 entries arranged under more than 1,100 subject headings (*A-Z*). Under each subject, sources are listed by type—bibliographies, encyclopedias and dictionaries, directories, periodicals, online databases, statistics sources, trade associations, and so forth. Many entries provide e-mail addresses and URLs.

444 Guide to special issues and indexes of periodicals. 4th ed. Miriam Uhlan and Doris B. Katz, eds. 240p. Special Libraries Assn., 1994. $56. ISBN 0-87111-400-3.
051.016 Z7164

Arranged alphabetically. More than 1,700 U.S. and Canadian consumer, trade, association, and technical periodicals publishing recurring special issues (features, supplements, and sections appearing on a continuing basis). Indicates in which machine-readable database the periodical is indexed and abstracted. Gives price of special issues, as well as subscription price of periodical. Detailed subject index to special issues. In this update, the addition of a listing of "Online Producers/Vendors" and expanded coverage of regional publications will help researchers and librarians.

445 How to find information about companies. 678p. Washington Researchers, 1993. $395. ISBN 1-56365-021-5.
658.00216 HD2785

This research guide lists federal, state, local, and private organizations that are information sources on public and private companies, domestic and foreign; includes governmental offices, the courts, trade and professional associations, databases, libraries, credit-reporting and bond-rating companies, and so forth.

446 International business information: how to find it, how to use it. 2d ed. Ruth A. Pagell and Michael Halperin. 464p. Oryx, 1997. $100. ISBN 1-57356-050-2
332.1753 HF54.5

Describes a selective list of resources widely available in libraries and emphasizes interpretation of data and sources. Detailed table of contents, title index, and subject index provide three excellent access points. Ten appendixes covering topics such as "The Synthesis of Accounting Standards in Forty-eight Countries" and "Disclosure Requirements of Major Stock Exchanges" are unique aids.

447 Small business sourcebook. 11th ed. Amy Lynn Park, ed. 3556p. Gale, 1998. $305/2v. set. ISBN 0-7876-1121-2.
658.022 HD2346

Provides listings of 24,798 sources designed to facilitate the start-up, development, and growth of small businesses. Categories include primary associations, statistical sources, trade periodicals, trade shows and conventions, and computer databases. Also included are descriptive data on general business information sources such as venture capital firms and state government agencies. The "Master List of Specific Small Business Profiles" is now in both volumes. A boon to the small businessperson.

Indexes and Abstracts

448 ABI/INFORM Global. 1971– . UMI, 1988– . Monthly on CD-ROM. $6500.
■ cd online tape

This index to more than 1,000 business and management journals began as an online database in the 1970s; it has never appeared in printed form. The CD-ROM version includes coverage of the last five years on one disk. Additional disks can be purchased covering back to 1971. Lengthy abstracts of articles make this a very popular source for business students.

449 Business index. Jan. 1979– . Information Access Corp., 1980– . Monthly, each issue cumulative to date; computer-output-microfilm (COM). $3500; school subscription (9 months) $2800. ISSN 0273-3684.
■ cd online tape
050 Z7164

Comprehensive coverage of more than 800 business periodicals and the *Wall Street Journal* (cover-to-cover), selective coverage of the *New York Times*, more than 1,000 general and legal periodicals, and business books and reports from the Library of Congress and Government Printing Office cataloging records.

450 **Business periodicals index.** Wilson, 1958– . Monthly except Aug., with annual cumulation. Service basis. ISSN 0007-6961.
■ cd online tape
016.650 HF5001

A subject index to periodicals in the fields of accounting, advertising, automation, banking, communications, economics, finance and investments, insurance, labor, management, marketing, taxes, and so forth. When the *Industrial arts index* was divided into two separate indexes in 1958, *Business periodicals index* and *Applied science and technology index* were established.

Dictionaries and Encyclopedias

451 **Dictionary of business and management.** 3d ed. Jerry M. Rosenberg. 384p. Wiley, 1992. $39.95. ISBN 0-471-57812-6; paper $14.95. ISBN 0-471-54536-8.
330.03 HF1001

Concisely and clearly defines more than 7,500 words, phrases, acronyms, and symbols from thirty-three fields, including administration, collective bargaining, and personnel. This edition reflects the increasing importance of a global perspective affecting these fields. Appendixes include tables of measurement and simple interest, "Foreign Exchange" list, quotations, and a chronology of major U.S. business and economic events.

452 **International directory of company histories.** St. James, 1988–98. Vols. 1–24 (in progress). $160/v.
338.7 HD2721

This ongoing project is important not for any directory information it supplies, but as an encyclopedia of company histories. The set provides detailed historical information about the world's largest companies. Each volume contains about 250 entries, and each entry runs about three pages. In addition to an informative company history, entries include company logo, legal name, and date incorporated, as well as traditional directory information. A cumulative alphabetical index to companies and persons and a cumulative index to companies by industry are included in the latest volume. A welcome addition to any business collection.

453 **Labor unions.** Gary M. Fink, ed. 544p. Greenwood, 1977. $50.95. ISBN 0-8371-8938-1.
331.880973 HD6508

Historical sketches of more than 200 national unions and labor federations selected for their significance, longevity, and public impact as part of the American labor movement. The work is a handy companion to Fink et al.'s *Biographical dictionary of American labor.* The alphabetically arranged entries are several pages in length. Some are signed, and all include suggestions for further research. Of particular reference value are the five appendixes: a list of all national unions chartered by AFL, CIO, and AFL-CIO; a chronology of American labor; genealogies of the unions; a list of executive leadership for selected unions; and a chart of membership in selected unions in twelve stages from 1897 to 1975. A list of acronyms would have been helpful. A glossary and a detailed index facilitate use.

454 **The McGraw-Hill encyclopedia of economics.** 2d ed. Douglas Greenwald, ed. 1070p. McGraw-Hill, 1994. $99.50. ISBN 0-07-024410-3.
330.3 HB61

This timely and readable work consists of signed articles written by prominent economists on such topics as supply-side economics and the balance of international payments, including definitions of each topic, an explanation of the subject, and opposing viewpoints. Cross-references assist access. There is a chronological listing of economic events, technological developments, financial changes, and economic thought. A relevant purchase for most libraries.

455 **The new Palgrave: a dictionary of economics.** John Eatwell et al., eds. 4v. Stockton Pr., 1987. $750/set. ISBN 0-935859-10-1; paper $225. ISBN 1-56159-197-1.
330.03 HB61

A classic, with more than 1,900 signed, encyclopedia-length articles that thoroughly document technical economic theories. Only fifty classic entries are reprinted from the original and so noted. It includes traditional topics and new areas such as environmental law and game theory; also biographies of 655 important economists and politicians. Equations, diagrams, or graphs accompany some articles. Besides a classified subject guide, an excellent index is included. A related work, *The new Palgrave dictionary of economics and the law* (Peter Newman, ed., 3v. Stockton Pr., 1998. $550. ISBN 1-56159-215-3), provides focused coverage of a growing subdiscipline of economics.

Directories

Reference collections should include the following basic tools, if they exist, for the library's own city, county, and state: alphabetical and classified telephone directories for local and adjacent areas; industrial directory for the city, county, or state; directory of directors of corporations for the local area; and directory of labor unions for the local area. Though not inexpensive, MacRae's directories are available for most states (check *Books in print*).

456 Advertising slogans of America. Harold S. Sharp, comp. 554p. Scarecrow, 1984. $50. ISBN 0-8108-1681-4.
659.113 HF6135

Advertising slogans, extensively used in the United States for more than a century, document a colorful aspect of business history. Sharp has compiled a listing—from a variety of sources—of some 15,000 slogans used by 6,000 businesses and other organizations. Access is by product, slogan, and company or organization.

457 American export register. 1980– . Thomas International, 1980– . Annual. $120/2v. set. ISSN 0272-1163. (*formerly* **American register of exporters and importers**, 1945–79. ISSN 0065-9567.)
382.025 HF3010

List of U.S. firms from which specific products may be purchased by foreign countries, arranged by product with alphabetical listing of exporters, importers, and export agents.

458 Brands and their companies, 1990– . Donna Wood, ed. 3v. Gale, 1990– . (18th ed. 1998, $790/set. ISBN 0-7876-0988-9.) ISSN 1047-6407. (*formerly* **Trade names dictionary.**)
■ online
658.827 HD69

Lists some 365,000 U.S. brands from almost every area of consumer interest. Each entry gives the trade name, a brief description of the product, the company name, and a code referring to one of the more than 100 sources consulted. A "company yellow pages" provides the name, address, phone number, and source code for each of the approximately 80,000 manufacturers, distributors, and importers. Updated by a midyear supplement included in the price. A companion set, *Companies and their brands* (2v. Gale, 1994– . $499/set. ISBN 0-7876-0994-3. ISSN 0277-0369), lists companies with the trade names of their products. International editions for both publications are available.

459 Business organizations, agencies, and publications directory. 9th ed. Jennifer Mast, ed. 1800p. Gale, 1998. $390. ISBN 0-7876-0951-X.
■ online
380.1025 HF3010

A vast compendium of data on business-related organizations arranged in five major groups: national and international organizations, government agencies and programs, facilities and services, research and education, and publication and information services. Basic entries include name, address, contact person, and telephone number; most entries include descriptive annotations as well. Many of the entries were drawn from government publications and other Gale directories.

460 Business rankings annual 1998: lists of companies, products, services, and activities compiled from a variety of published sources. Brooklyn Public Library, Business Library Staff, comps. 800p. Gale, 1998. $185. ISBN 0-7876-1357-6.
338.74016 HG4050

This compilation of published lists and rankings from major business publications is a good source for researchers. Citations are grouped by subject; subjects are arranged alphabetically. Information includes criteria for rankings, number ranked, what firm tops the list, and complete bibliographic details for the source of the ranking. In addition, the volume contains an index to number ones and sources.

461 Compact D/SEC (machine-readable data file). Disclosure (Bethesda, Maryland), 1986– . File size: 12,000 records, updated monthly. Software needed: MS extensions (included in package). Coverage: most recent five years. Cost: Contact Disclosure. Includes CD-ROM reader, software compact disc, and user's manual.

(*formerly* **Compact disclosure.**)
■ micro cd online tape
338 HG4050

An extensive and expensive database of very detailed financial and management information excerpted from reports filed with the Securities and Exchange Commission for more than 12,000 publicly held companies with at least $5 million in assets and 500 shareholders. Patrons can search without librarians' help in either an "Easy Menu" or well-thought-out "Dialog Emulation" mode and can manipulate 256 data elements from the company ratios, balance sheets, and so forth, to create customized reports, with the ability to print or download to spreadsheet or word-processing software. Average record is ten pages in length. Users can locate companies with specified characteristics (such as product type, geographic location, etc.) in common to create helpful, very specific lists. This mode provides easy accessibility, an elegant corporate reference tool, and a godsend for business people, investors, job seekers, and researchers.

462 **Consultants and consulting organizations directory.** 1st ed.– . 1966– . Janice McLean, ed. Gale, 1966– . (18th ed. 1998, $565.) ISSN 0192-091X.
■ online
658.46025 HD69

Information on more than 24,000 organizations and individuals in fourteen general categories, including names, addresses, phone and fax numbers, year founded, staff, and description of services offered. Geographic, consulting activity, personal name, and firm indexes. Interedition supplement: *New consultants* (1973– . ISSN 0192-091X).

463 **Directory of business and financial information services.** 1st ed.– . 1924– . Special Libraries Assn., 1924– . (9th ed. 488p. 1995, $80. ISBN 0-87111-420-8.)
650.025 HG151.7

Describes 1,000-plus print and nonprint sources (many of which are investment oriented). Arranged by title of service. Publishers index; subject index.

464 **Directory of corporate affiliations: who owns whom.** 1967– . 5v. National Register, 1967– . Annual. $1029.95. ISSN 0070-5365.
■ cd online
338.7402 HG4057

Provides information on corporate affiliations for public and private business in the United States and throughout the world. The organization is geographical (by parent company). The 1998 edition lists 14,778 parent companies, 47,366 U.S.-located subcompanies, and 54,432 non-U.S.-located subcompanies. Also includes 27,617 service firms. Volume 1: *Master index* ("Master Company Name Index"; "Master Brand Name Index"; "Master Geographic Index, U.S."; "Master Geographic Index, Non-U.S."). Volume 2: *Master index* ("SIC Index"; "Master Corporate Responsibilities Index"). Volume 3: *U.S. public companies* ("Public Company Name Index"; "Public Company Listings"; "Public SIC Index"). Volume 4: *U.S. private companies* ("Private Company Name Index"; "Private Company Listings"; "Private SIC Index"). Volume 5: *International public and private companies* ("International Company Name Index"; "International Company Listings"; "International SIC Index"). Entries include company name, address, telecommunications data, electronic addresses, ticker symbol and stock exchanges, financial information, number of employees, business description, Standard Industrial Classification (SIC) codes, key personnel, members of the board, name and address, and phone number of outside services firm (e.g., legal firm or auditor). Following the parent company entry are entries for affiliates, divisions, joint ventures, and subsidiaries, with levels of reportage indicated.

465 **Directory of executive recruiters.** Kennedy, 1971– . Annual. $44.95. ISSN 0090-6484.
650.14 HF5549.5

Designed for job seekers, this directory profiles executive recruiting firms (including contingency companies), providing address, telephone number, salary minimum, and key contact personnel. In addition, valuable indexes for management specialties, industries, individual recruiters, and geographic locations are included.

466 **Directory of foreign manufacturers in the United States.** 5th ed. Jeffrey S. Arpan and David Ricks, eds. Virginia M. Mason, comp. 419p. Georgia State Univ. Business Pr., 1993. $195. ISBN 0-88406-255-4.
338.88873 HD9723

Address, type of manufacturer, and parent or foreign office for almost 7,000 firms engaged in manufacturing, mining, and petroleum production in the United States. Access by several indexes including parent companies, state, country, and products by Standard Industrial Classification (SIC).

467 Exporters' encyclopaedia. Dun & Bradstreet, 1904– . Annual. $495. ISSN 8755-013X.
382.6. HF3011

In-depth information on trade regulations and practices for more than 200 markets in specific countries. Shipping services, postal information, currency, banks, embassies, laws, practices, reference data, overseas ports and trade centers, and much more.

468 Fortune's directory of the 500 largest U.S. industrial corporations. Time, 1930– . Annual (in May). $5. Reprint: **The Fortune double 500 directory.** $12. ISSN 0532-2758.
338 HG4057

The Fortune double 500 directory is a listing of 500 service firms published in June. A listing of 500 international companies appears in July but is not included in the reprint.

469 Franchise annual. 1969– . Info Pr., 1969– . Annual. $39.95. ISSN 0318-8752.
658.87 HF5429

The "handbook" portion discusses the franchise method of doing business, sample franchise contract clauses, and so forth. The "directory" portion —organized in forty-seven categories (accounting and tax services, fast food, real estate, etc.)— includes U.S., Canadian, and overseas franchises, giving for each main office address, type of business, telephone number of contact person, number of company-owned and franchisee-owned units, required monthly royalty, and approximate initial and total investment. Subject index.

470 Franchise opportunities handbook. 1972– . Industrial Trade Administration and Minority Business Development Agency of U.S. Dept. of Commerce. Govt. Print. Off., 1972– . Paper. (1994, $21. ISBN 0-89059-033-8.) S/N 003-009– . SuDoc C61.31:yr.
658.87 E1.108

Brief general information on securing and operating franchise businesses is followed by a directory of U.S. franchisors, arranged in some forty-five categories (e.g., automotive products and services; foods—donuts and four other food categories; optical products and services). An entry typically includes name and address of franchising organization, number of franchises, date business was established, equity capital needed, financial assistance available, and managerial assistance available.

471 Hoover's handbook of emerging companies. Patrick J. Spain and James R. Talbot, eds. 416p. Reference Pr., 1990– . Annual. $64.95. ISSN 1069-7519.
■ disk cd online
338.7025 HF3010

Each new edition includes lists of fast-growing newcomers, such as Starbucks, Grow Biz, and Safeskin. Entries similar to other Hoover's products. Indexed by industry, by headquarters' locations, and by people, companies, and brand names.

472 Hoover's handbook of world business. Gary Hoover et al., eds. 1000p. Reference Pr., 1990– . Annual. $79.95. ISSN 1055-7199.
■ disk cd online
338.7025 HF3010

About 220 company profiles, each two pages long, cover five regions of the world, sixty-six countries, and the United Nations. Enterprises of various types, arranged alphabetically, include basic information on the nature and history of each, people involved, products and services, and financial performance. Each profile has eight sections: overview, when, how much, who, where, what, rankings, and competition. The section entitled "A List-Lover's Compendium" lists the largest companies in this title, largest companies in key industries, and so forth. A very useful index includes brands, companies, and people names from the profiles. For inexpensive information on major foreign companies and quality-of-life measures for countries, *Hoover's* is one of the best.

473 Million dollar directory. 1959– . 5v. Dun & Bradstreet, 1959– . Annual. $1250. ISSN 1051-3442.
■ cd
380.1025 HC102

Lists 160,000 U.S. business concerns having a net worth of more than $500,000. Alphabetical by company name, giving addresses and officers, Standard Industrial Classification (SIC) numbers, sales, and number of employees. Geographical and SIC indexes.

474 National trade and professional associations of the United States. (title var.) 1966– . Columbia, 1966– . Annual. Paper $85. ISSN 0734-354X.
061.3 HD2425

Includes nearly 6,500 organizations arranged by subject. Indexed by title, key word, geographical location, size of budget, and executive officers. Particularly valuable for its data on the annual budget as well as such general information as date of establishment, address, headquarters staff, size of membership, publications, and telephone number.

475 Principal international businesses: the world marketing directory. 1974– . Dun & Bradstreet, 1974– . Annual. $695. ISSN 0097-6288.
338.88025 HF54

Arranged alphabetically by country, covers approximately 55,000 major companies in 140 countries. Information for each company includes its name and address, chief executive, lines of business, Standard Industrial Classification (SIC) number, sales, and number of employees. Indexed by SIC and company.

476 Reference book of corporate managements. 4v. Dun & Bradstreet, 1980– . Annual. $785. ISSN 0735-6498.
658.1145 HF5035

Continues *Dun & Bradstreet reference book of corporate managements,* 1967–79. Brief biographical information (date of birth, educational data, professional career data, corporate title, directorships, etc.) on the chief officers and directors of some 12,000 companies.

477 Standard & Poor's register of corporations, directors and executives. Standard & Poor's Corp., 1928– . Annual with three supplements. $625. ISSN 0361-3623.
■ cd online
338.7025 HG4057

Lists executive rosters and annual sales of 45,000 companies in the United States and Canada. Volume 2 gives brief biographical information on approximately 70,000 directors and executives, arranged in alphabetical "who's who" order. Volume 3 indexes corporations by Standard Industrial Classification (SIC), geographical area, new individuals, obituaries, and new companies.

478 Standard directory of advertisers. National Register, 1914– . Annual. Issued in two parts: Business classifications ed. $499.95; Geographic ed. $499.95. ISSN 0081-4229.
338.4025 HF5805

A listing of some 25,000 companies that spend more than $200,000 on national or regional advertising. Provides addresses, business descriptions, Standard Industrial Classification (SIC) codes, statistics, officers (including sales personnel), and kinds of media used. Also notes products and trademarks.

479 Standard directory of advertising agencies. National Register, 1964– . 2/yr. with supplements. $500. ISSN 0085-6614.
338.76165 HF5804

For more than 9,000 U.S. and Canadian advertising agencies, the "Agency Red Book" provides specialization, officers, account executives, names of accounts, approximate annual billings, and percentage by media. Includes geographical and special market indexes.

480 Standard rate and data service directories.
659.1 HF5801

Business publication rates and data. 1951– . Monthly. Paper $528. ISSN 0038-948X.

Community publication rates and data. 1975– . Semiannual. Paper $90. ISSN 0162-8887.

Consumer magazine and agri-media rates and data. 1956– . Monthly. Paper $528. ISSN 0746-2522.

Direct mail list rates and data. 1967– . Bimonthly. Paper $369. ISSN 0419-182X.

Newspaper rates and data. 1952– . Monthly. Paper $509. ISSN 0038-9587.

Spot radio rates and data. 1954– . Monthly. Paper $396. ISSN 0038-9560.

Spot television rates and data. 1954– . Monthly. Paper $369. ISSN 0038-9552.

SRDS directories provide detailed and up-to-date information on advertising rates for a wide spectrum of the media. Information given includes specifications and audience and readership figures as well as rates. Several of the publications include demographic estimates. In addition, because they are current, they serve as excellent directories to magazines, newspapers, and broadcast stations. *Direct mail list rates and data* offers information to marketers on the availability, characteristics, and costs of several thousand mailing lists.

481 Thomas register of American manufacturers and Thomas register catalog file. Thomas, 1905– . Annual. $695/25v. ISSN 0082-4216.
■ cd online
670.216 T12

National purchase guide, supplying names and addresses of manufacturers, producers, importers, and other sources of supply in all lines and in all sections of the United States. Symbols show minimum capital of each firm. Concluding volumes contain manufacturers' catalogs in alphabetical order and are referred to as "THOMCAT"—*Thomas register catalog file.*

482 Ward's business directory of U.S. private and public companies, 1990– . Gale, 1990– . Annual. 8v./$2365. ISSN 1048-8707.
■ disk cd online tape
338.74025 HG4009

Comprehensive guide to some 135,000 public and private companies. The alphabetically arranged entries of volumes 1, 2, and 3 provide company name, address, phone number, sales, employees, company type, immediate parent, ticker symbol and exchange, fiscal year end, year founded, import and export status, business description, and up to five officers' names. Volume 4 is a geographic listing of the companies in volumes 1 through 3. Volume 5 offers briefer profiles of the same companies organized by state and then alphabetically within zip code. Volume 5 also includes ranked lists of largest private companies, largest public companies, and largest employers, and several tables of special analyses. Volumes 6 and 7 rank companies by sales within four-digit Standard Industrial Classification (SIC) code indexed by company name. An alphabetical company-name index with SIC codes and rankings enables independent use of volumes 6 and 7 (sold separately for $890). Volume 8 ranks companies by sales within the six-digit North American Industry Classification System (sold separately for $595).

483 World chamber of commerce directory. Johnson, 1965– . Annual. Paper $35. ISSN 0893-346X. (*formerly* **Worldwide chamber of commerce directory.**)
380.06 HF294

Lists chambers of commerce within and outside the United States (including foreign chambers of commerce with U.S. offices) and foreign embassies and government agencies located in the United States.

Handbooks, Yearbooks, and Almanacs

484 Almanac of business and industrial financial ratios. Leo Troy, ed. Prentice-Hall, 1971– . Annual. $99.95. ISSN 0747-9107.
■ cd
338.09 HF5681

This frequently used source of ratios is based on summary statistics generated by the U.S. Internal Revenue Service (usually data are three years old before available). About 200 Standard Industrial Classification (SIC) codes are covered, but many companies in each line of business are included. Each entry is two pages long, the first presenting composite data for all companies in the industry and the second limited to companies that earned a profit for the year reported. Figures are divided into twelve asset-size categories, plus totals for all companies.

485 Business profitability data. John B. Walton. 185p. Weybridge, 1996. Paper $40. ISBN 0-939356-10-4.
658.0220 HD2346

Using data acquired from the respected Robert Harris Associates, Walton addresses questions as to how profitable a particular business is and how it compares with other types of businesses. In addition, he provides needed information as to risks, potentials, and trends. Arrangement is by type of business—jewelry retailers, stationery wholesalers, fertilizer manufacturers, and so forth. *Profitability* is defined as the funds generated by the business divided by the funds required by the business.

486 Corporate finance sourcebook 1997: the guide to major capital investment sources and related financial services. Editing staff. 2300p. National Register, 1998. $499. ISBN 0-87217-945-1.
■ disk
332 HG4057

This very useful directory of all types of firms that provide corporate financing is arranged in eighteen sections. Sections include banks, pension managers, major private lenders, business insurance brokers, corporate real estate services, and more. Concluding the volume is a list of mergers and acquisitions for the previous year.

487 Craighead's international business, travel, and relocation guide to eighty-one countries, 1998–99. 9th ed. 4v. Gale, 1998. ISBN 0-7876-2697-X.
658 HF5549.5

Provides in-depth information about doing business, living, and traveling in eighty-one foreign countries. Each entry is several pages in length and includes a general country orientation, an economic and political overview, tax and banking information, business protocols, health and safety concerns, and visa and work permit regulations, as well as information on housing, schools, social etiquette, cost of living, and more. Of interest to the general traveler as well as the corporate traveler.

488 The Dartnell direct mail and mail order handbook. 3d ed. Richard S. Hodgson. 1538p. Dartnell, 1980. $49.95. ISBN 0-85013-116-2.
659.133 HF5861

Forty-nine chapters spell out the practical aspects of this highly utilized advertising medium. The straightforward work has long been an industry "classic." Topics covered include direct mail copy, mailing list maintenance, sampling and couponing, and usage of computers.

489 Guide to economic indicators. Norman Frumkin. 242p. Sharpe, 1994. $49.95. ISBN 1-56324-243-5; paper $21.95. ISBN 1-56324-244-3.
330.973 HC103

The many economic indicators reported in the media can be difficult to understand and appreciate. This book clarifies the confusion by explaining more than fifty statistical indicators of the U.S. economy for persons who have no special background in economics. Accuracy and relevance of the indicators are discussed, as are concepts such as index numbers and seasonal adjustment. Of greatest value is the explanation of how to understand the economy better with the indicators.

490 Handbook of United States economic and financial indicators. Frederick M. O'Hara Jr. and Robert Sicignano. 224p. Greenwood, 1985. $42.95. ISBN 0-313-23954-1.
330.973 HC106.8

The authors have brought together 200 measures of economic and financial activity in the United States. Among basic indicators discussed are Dow Jones Composite Average, Standard & Poor's 500 Price-Earning Ratio, Gross National Product, and Barron's Confidence Index. Specialized indicators include the Revenue Passenger Miles (for airlines) and the Parity Ratio (for farm products). For each indicator description, derivation, use, compiler, where and when announced, cumulations, and a bibliography are provided. Arranged alphabetically by indicator and includes appendixes on "Nonquantitative Indicators" (the Misery Index and the Super Bowl Predictor). Most entries contain a short bibliography.

491 Industry norms and key business ratios. Dun & Bradstreet Credit Services, 1982– . Annual. $315. ISSN 8755-2396.
338.0973 HF5681

Similar to the *RMA annual statement studies,* this annual is generated from D&B's unique database of business credit reports. More than 800 industry groups are covered and are arranged by the four-digit Standard Industrial Classification (SIC) code. Fourteen ratios are calculated, although RMA provides sixteen. A "typical" balance sheet and summary income statement are also calculated for each industry. Especially useful features are timeliness and a wide array of industries covered.

492 Irwin business and investment almanac. Irwin Professional, 1977– . Annual. $75. ISSN 1072-6136.
330.905 HF5003

Continues the *Dow Jones–Irwin business almanac* (5v. ISSN 0146-6534) with additional information from *The Dow Jones commodities handbook* (ISSN 0362-0689), *The Dow Jones investor's handbook,* and so forth. A unique compendium of up-to-the-minute information for Americans in business or investing in businesses. An introductory business review and forecast for the year is followed by basic statistics related to all areas of business and economics. Includes data on federal legislation, regulatory agency actions, accounting, taxes, addresses and phone numbers of key agencies, international and national trade exhibitions, custom offices, and economic indicators.

493 McGraw-Hill handbook of business letters. 3d ed. Roy W. Poe. 363p. McGraw-Hill, 1994. $19.95. ISBN 0-07-050451-2.

McGraw-Hill handbook of more business letters. Ann Poe. 416p. McGraw-Hill, 1998. $19.95. ISBN 0-07-050517-9.
808.06665 HF5725

Correspondence is critically important in the business world. The Poes discuss how to write effective letters, demonstrating dos and don'ts, and each provides more than 300 correspondence samples covering a wide variety of letter-writing situations. Among topics included are credit and collection, customer relations, social correspondence, public relations, and personnel.

494 North American industry classification system (NAICS). Office of Management and Budget Staff. National Technical Information Service, U.S. Dept. of Commerce, 1998. $28.50. ISBN 0-89059-097-4.
338 HF1041.5

The NAICS classification system has been jointly developed by the governmental offices of Mexico, Canada, and the United States "to provide a framework for the collection, analysis, and dissemination of industrial statistics used by government analysts, by academics and researchers, by the business community, and by the public." It makes the industrial statistics produced in the three countries comparable and is already supplanting the more familiar SIC code.

495 RMA annual statement studies. Robert Morris Associates, 1964– . Wiley, 1995– . Annual. $119. ISSN 0080-3340.
657.30723 HC14

This classic annual contains composite financial data on manufacturing, wholesaling, retailing, service, and contracting businesses. Financial statements for each industry are shown in a standardized form and are accompanied by the most widely used ratios, used to determine if a business is performing as well as it should or to evaluate areas within a business that need attention.

496 Standard & Poor's statistical service. 1926– . Standard & Poor's Corp., 1926– . Monthly. $640. ISSN 0147-636X.
332.632 HG4921

Divided into twelve sections: current statistics; banking and finance; production and labor; price indexes; income and trade; building; electric power, and fuels; metals; transportation; textiles, chemical, paper; agricultural products; and security price index record. Each section, except current statistics, provides both historical and current data for the indicated categories and industries. Current statistics furnishes data on gross national product, national income, personal income, production, and so forth.

497 Standard industrial classification manual. 705p. Govt. Print. Off., 1987. $29. S/N 041-001-00314-2. SuDoc PrEx2.6/2. In27.987.
338.02012 HA40

The official guide to the Standard Industrial Classification, or SIC, code used in most statistical reference tools. The SIC system, used by federal and state statistical agencies and private organizations, is divided as follows: one digit—broad economic divisions; two digits—major industry groups; three digits—industry groups; and four digits—industries. The manual is divided into eleven major categories (e.g., construction, wholesale trade, public administration). The manual conceptualizes the framework for U.S. industries and is necessary for all business collections.

498 U.S. industrial outlook. 1983– . U.S. Dept. of Commerce, Bureau of Industrial Economics. Govt. Print. Off., 1983– . Annual. $37. ISSN 0733-365X. SuDoc C61.34:yr.
338.5443 HF1041

Arranged by Standard Industrial Classification (SIC) code, information by industry consists of narrative, tables, and graphs that describe the recent performance and project the future level of activity for manufacturing, high technology, and service industries in terms of domestic and overseas markets, five-year industry projections (to 1998), and product data. Index provides access to comments on specific products (e.g., purses, yogurt). Also lists sources for in-depth research.

Accounting

499 Accountants' handbook. 9th ed. D. R. Carmichael, Steven B. Lilien, and Martin Mellman, eds. 1808p. Wiley, 1999. $125. ISBN 0-471-29122-6.
657 HF5621

The standard text in the field of accounting for more than seventy-five years. Its aim is "to provide in a single reference source an answer to all reasonable questions on accounting and financial reporting." Includes chapters on accounting frameworks and standards, FASB, and SEC reporting, as well as methodology, financial statement areas, specialized financial industries, compensation and benefits, special areas of accounting, and auditing and management information systems. This is a work directed at the professional mind.

500 **Kohler's dictionary for accountants.** 6th ed. W. W. Cooper and Yuji Ijiri, eds. 574p. Prentice-Hall, 1983. $69. ISBN 0-13-516658-6.
657.0321 HF5621

A standard work in the field, giving current definitions and information on more than 4,500 terms in everyday language. Charts and forms where applicable.

Banking and Finance

501 **Dictionary of banking.** Jerry M. Rosenberg. 384p. Wiley, 1992. $49.95. ISBN 0-471-57435-X. (*formerly* **Dictionary of banking and financial services.**)
332.103 HG151

This practical dictionary briefly defines about 15,000 terms from banking and finance, foreign trade, savings and loan and securities industries, and so forth. Useful appendixes: state banking laws, holidays, statistics on commercial banks, savings and loan associations, finance and bank holding companies, and more.

502 **Fitzroy Dearborn encyclopedia of banking and finance.** 10th ed. Charles J. Woelfel, ed. 1219p. Fitzroy Dearborn, 1997. $128.25. ISBN 1-884964-07-9.
332.03 HG151

The preeminent publication in its field, serving the banking, financial, and allied vocations with explanations and definitions of banking terms, but it's still not too technical for the student. Alphabetically arranged. Bibliographies. Comprehensive index appears in each volume, providing access to all entries, cross-references, and discussions of topics.

503 **Handbook of corporate finance.** Edward I. Altman, ed. 912p. Wiley, 1986. $115. ISBN 0-471-81957-3.
658.15 HG4026

Handbook of financial markets and institutions. 6th ed. Edward I. Altman, ed. 1216p. Wiley, 1987. $105. ISBN 0-471-81954-9. (*formerly* **Financial handbook.**)
658.15 HG173

Authoritative, comprehensive handbooks covering four major areas: U.S. financial markets and institutions, international markets and institutions, investment theory and practice, and corporate finance. Authors are business executives, financial economists from the academic and business worlds, government authorities, and financial consultants. Appendixes in both volumes address the mathematics of finance and sources of financial information.

504 **International financial statistics.** v.1– . Jan. 1948– . International Monetary Fund, 1948– . Monthly with two supplements and yearbook. $218. ISSN 0020-6725. SuDoc I113.In8:yr.
■ cd
332.45 HG3881

Shows current data needed in the analysis of problems of international payments and of inflation and deflation: exchange rates, international liquidity, money and banking, international trade, prices production, government finance, interest rates, and so forth. Information is presented in country tables and in tables of area and world aggregates. The *Yearbook* (1979–) continues the information formerly found in the May issue of this publication.

505 **Polk's financial institutions directory.** North American ed. Annual. (semiannual and bimonthly supplements available.) R. L. Polk & Co., 1993– . $350. ISSN 1058-0611.
332.1025 HG2431.P6

This geographic list by state provides telephone, cable, fax, and online information as well as officers and directors, out-of-town branches, assets, and liabilities. Supplemental information includes maps for each state, state banking officials, legal holidays, list of bank holding companies, transit numbers, and ranked list of largest institutions. Detailed index provides many access places.

506 **Pratt's guide to venture capital sources, 1997 edition.** 21st ed. Venture Economics Staff, eds. 968p. Securities Data, 1997. $325. ISBN 0-914470-84-1.
658.15 HG65

More than 800 American and foreign venture capital companies are listed here, alphabetical by state for U.S. and by company name for foreign firms. Information provided includes project, geographic, and industry preferences. Beginning chapters discuss venture capital topics and are written by venture capitalists. Indexes provide access by company, name, and industry preferences.

507 The Thorndike encyclopedia of banking and financial tables. David Thorndike, ed. 1792p. Warren, Gorham & Lamont, 1977– . Annual. $175.95; paper $96. ISSN 0196-7762.
332.80212 HG1626

Includes all essential banking, financial, and real estate tables such as mortgage schedules, compound interest and annuity, interest and savings rates, installment loan payments, bond values, and so forth. Each table is preceded by a brief explanation and, when useful, examples. Glossary and index.

Insurance

508 Best's Flitcraft compend. (title var.) 1st ed.– . Best, 1914– . Annual. $55. ISSN 0733-9631.
368.011 HG8881

Gives quick-reference information on policies, rates, values, and dividends of major U.S. life insurance companies and data on selected fraternal organizations, plus business figures and sample rates, values, and settlement options for more than 400 companies.

509 Best's insurance reports, life-health . . . , 1906–07– . (title var.) Best, 1906– . Annual. $600. ISSN 0161-7745.
368.32 HG8943

Comprehensive statistical reports on the financial position, history, and operating results of legal reserve life insurance companies, fraternal benefit societies, and assessment associations operating in the United States and Canada. Update with the monthly *Best's review—life-health insurance edition.* Similar coverage for property-casualty institutions is found in *Best's insurance reports, property-casualty, 1899/1900–* . (title var.) Annual. $600. ISSN 0148-3218. Title is updated with the monthly *Best's review—property-casualty insurance edition.*

510 Best's key rating guide: property-casualty. Best, 1906– . Annual. $95. ISSN 0148-3064. (*formerly* **Best's insurance guide with key ratings** and **Best's key rating guide: property-liability.**)
368 HG9765

Supplies quick-reference key ratings and comprehensive statistics showing the financial condition, general standing, and transactions of various types of insurance companies operating in the United States.

511 Life insurance fact book. American Council of Life Insurance, 1945– . Annual. Biennial, 1986– . Paper, free. ISSN 0075-9406.
368.32 HG8943

A source useful to all U.S. legal reserve life insurance companies, with tables, charts, and interpretive text. Data are taken from annual statements and give statistics, yearly statements, ownership, payments, assets, officials, and so forth. Glossary. Index. Updated by supplement: *Life insurance fact book update.*

512 Social security handbook. 1st ed.– . 1960– . Social Security Administration. Govt. Print. Off., 1960– . Irreg. (1997, $36. S/N 017-070-00479-2.) SuDoc HE3.6/8:yr. ISSN 0361-5200.
368.4 HD7125

Detailed explanation without commentary of the federal retirement, survivors, disability, black lung benefits, supplementary security income, and health insurance programs; who is entitled to benefits; and how such benefits may be obtained.

513 Source book of health insurance data. 1959– . Health Insurance Assn. of America, 1959– . Biennial with updates. $25. ISSN 0073-148X.
368.382 HG9396

A statistical report of the private health insurance business, providing data on major forms of health insurance, medical care costs, morbidity, and the health workforce.

Investments

Information sources relating to investments are a significant component of every business collection. However, because they are expensive, individual libraries will need to determine the number and type of sources required for a given community. Current information about prices and contractual arrangements should be obtained directly from the publishers noted.

To complement the types of sources treated below, librarians may wish to consider—as source material—files of annual reports to stockholders and of annual reports and other documents that publicly traded companies must file with the Securities and Exchange Commission (e.g., 10-K, annual reports, 10-Q, quarterly financial report, proxy statement, prospectus). The Internet will also become a new and wonderful source of investment information.

514 **Commodity year book.** Knight Ridder, formerly Commodity Research Bureau, 1939– . Annual. $75; $95 for Update service including triennial Commodity year book supplement; or all, $150. ISSN 0069-6862.
332.6328 HF1041

Background data and statistical history of more than 100 basic commodities and special commodity studies. A good quick-reference source.

515 **Dun & Bradstreet's guide to your investments.** 1974/75– . HarperCollins, 1974– . Annual. $35. ISSN 0098-2466.
332.678 HG4921

Continues *Your investments: how to increase your capital and income.* A comprehensive handbook for investors and investment counselors that gives basic data on how to make decisions, how to set up a portfolio, and how to develop profit strategies. Sample portfolios, glossary, abbreviations, and bibliography. A good companion volume is the *Dow Jones investor's handbook* (1994, $20), which also explains the principles of investment and describes stock market strategies.

516 **Investment companies.** Wiesenberger Financial Services, 1941– . Annual with monthly and quarterly supplements. $295. ISSN 1068-9958.
332.6 HG4497

The best single source on mutual funds and other investment companies. Provides background information, management policy, and other salient features (such as income and dividend record, price ranges, operating details, etc.) on more than 2,200 U.S. and Canadian companies. Introductory material gives textual description of mutual funds and is followed by a list of companies. Tracks performance of industrial funds over ten-year intervals and back twenty-five years. Glossary and brief bibliography are included.

517 **Investment statistics locator, revised and expanded.** Linda Holman Bentley and Jennifer J. Kiesl. 275p. Oryx, 1995. $69.95. ISBN 0-89774-781-X.
332.60973 HG4910

This update of the 1988 edition includes an increased number of electronic resources and more international statistics for the global economy. More than fifty current, English, widely available sources are indexed. This title is sure to be popular in any business collection.

518 **Moody's handbook of common stocks.** Moody's Investors Service, 1957– . Quarterly. $250. ISSN 0027-0830.
332.67 HG4905

Standard & Poor's stock market encyclopedia. Standard & Poor's Corp., 1961– . Quarterly. $140. ISSN 0882-5467.
332.6322 HG4921

These resources provide quick-and-easy access to financial statistics on almost 1,000 widely held common stocks. Information on earnings, dividends, price history, and more is provided; charts trace the market action of each stock. In addition, basic corporate data are given. The *Standard & Poor's stock market encyclopedia* is updated by *Outlook,* a weekly publication ($219. ISSN 0030-7246).

519 **Moody's manuals.** Moody's Investors Service, 1900– . Annual. Back files available on microfiche from the Service.
■ cd partially online

Moody's bank and finance manual. 3v. $1395. ISSN 0027-0814.
332.67 HG4961

Moody's industrial manual. 2v. $1395. ISSN 0027-0849.
332.67 HG4961

Moody's international manual. 2v. $2495. ISSN 0278-3509.
332.632 HG4963

Moody's municipal and government manual. 2v. $1995. ISSN 0027-0857.
332.632 HG4963

Moody's OTC [over-the-counter] industrial manual. 1v. $1275. ISSN 0027-0865.
338.67 HG4961

Moody's OTC unlisted manual. 1v. $1150. ISSN 0890-5282.
338.474 HG4961

Moody's public utilities manual. 2v. $1250. ISSN 0027-0873.
332.67 HG4961

Moody's transportation manual. 1v. $1150. ISSN 0027-089X.
332.67 HG4961

Each of the eight Moody manuals is published annually with weekly or semiweekly news reports. Except for the government volume, each manual usually provides brief company history, subsidiaries, plants and properties, officers, income statement, balance-sheet data, and selected operating and financial ratios. *Moody's municipal and government manual* provides information on the finances and obligations of federal, state, and municipal governments; school districts; and foreign governments (securities offered, assessed value, tax collections, bond rating, etc.). Moody's offers special collections and prices for public and academic libraries.

520 Morningstar mutual funds. Morningstar, 1991– . Biweekly. $395. ISSN 1059-1443.
■ cd
332.6 HG4930

A very popular mutual fund advisory publication, the Morningstar service includes a biweekly newsletter with single-page reports on individual funds, each of which is updated once per twenty-week cycle. It includes all NASDAQ-listed funds. In addition to listing the top twenty-five securities in its current portfolio, reports describe the fund's investment criteria, narrative analysis of its performance, twelve years of comparative data, and fund ratings. (Also available is an annual edition called *Mutual fund sourcebook* in two volumes.)

521 Standard & Poor's industry surveys. Jan. 1973– . Standard & Poor's Corp., 1973– . (1998, $1800.) ISSN 0196-4666. (*formerly* **Standard & Poor's Corp. industry surveys.**)
338.74 HG4921

Continuous economic and investment analyses of thirty-three leading U.S. industries and approximately 1,000 of their constituent companies. For each industry there is an annual basic survey and three current surveys during a year. A monthly *Trends and projections bulletin* summarizes the state of the economy.

522 Standard & Poor's stock and bond guide. Standard & Poor's Corp., 1933– . Irreg. Annual, 1993– . $22.95. ISSN 0737-4135.

Over-the-counter and regional exchange reports. (1998, $1035.)

Standard ASE stock reports. (1998, $1145.)

Standard & Poor's stock reports. New York Stock Exchange. (1998, $1295.) ISSN 0160-4899.
338.740 HG4921

Its two-page financial data and investment advisory sheets cover about 3,500 companies in three loose-leaf services of four volumes each. The *Over-the-counter and regional exchange reports* are supplemented by *Standard & Poor's OTC profiles,* published three times a year ($65). All three services are available weekly or in quarterly bound volumes at somewhat reduced prices.

523 Standard corporation descriptions. (title, publisher var.) Standard & Poor's Corp., 1915– . 6v. Loose-leaf. Daily News Section available. $1435/6v.; $1061/Daily News Section; $2422/both parts. ISSN 0277-500X.
338.740 HG4501

Coverage in *Corporation records* (title on spine) is similar to that of Moody's manuals except that finance, industrial, public utilities, and transportation companies are all in one set of alphabetical volumes. Back files available on microfiche from the corporation.

524 Value Line investment survey. 1936– . Arnold Bernhard, 1936– . Loose-leaf with weekly additions. $570. ISSN 0042-2401.
■ disk online
332.6 HG4501

This comprehensive advisory service continuously analyzes and reports on some 1,700 stocks in ninety-nine industries (part 3, "Ratings and Reports"). Part 1 is "Summary and Index"; part 2 is "Selection and Opinion," Value Line's comment on the business and economic outlook and the stock market, Value Line averages, and a highlighted stock. Reports on companies are updated quarterly on a weekly rotation.

Management

525 AMA management handbook. 3d ed. John J. Hampton, ed. 1600p. AMACOM, 1994. $110. ISBN 0-8144-0105-8.
658 HD31

A comprehensive one-volume source for concise and practical information on a wide range of management topics. Written as a joint effort by more than 200 experts, the handbook is arranged within sixteen broad subject areas such as finance, entrepreneurship, information systems and technology, international business, and so forth.

526 The Dartnell office administration handbook. 6th ed. Robert S. Minor and Clark W. Fetridge, eds. 1087p. Dartnell, 1983. $49.95. ISBN 0-85013-142-1.
651 HF5547

Extensive treatment on management, personnel, organization of records, physical facilities, and so forth; some consideration of computer and electronic technology. Glossary, sources of information, index.

527 International dictionary of management. 5th ed. Hano Johannsen and G. Terry Page. 359p. Nichols, 1994. $45.95. ISBN 0-89397-438-2.
658 HD30.15

Defines and explains about 6,500 words, abbreviations, institutions, and concepts, taken from a wide variety of subject areas: business, finance, production, personnel, employee relations, data processing, research and development, economics, law, sociology, and statistics.

Marketing and Sales

528 Editor and publisher market guide. 756p. Editor and Publisher, 1924– . Annual. $100. ISSN 1082-0779.
070.03 HF5905

Comprehensive data on more than 1,500 daily newspaper markets, such as a city's population, location, trade areas, banks, climate, principal industries, colleges and universities, and so forth. Arranged by state and city (United States and Canada).

529 Lesly's handbook of public relations and communications. 5th ed. Philip Lesly. 850p. NTC Contemporary, 1997. $100. ISBN 0-8442-3257-2.
659.2 HM263

Comprehensive handbook (fifty-five chapters by forty-eight professionals). Bibliography, glossary.

530 Marketing information: a professional reference guide. 3d ed. Hiram C. Barksdale, ed. 456p. Georgia State Univ. Business Pr., 1994. $149.95. ISBN 0-88406-260-0.
658.80035 HF5415

Part 1 is a directory of marketing organizations—associations, research centers, special libraries, government agencies, advertising agencies, and so forth. Part 2 briefly annotates books, journals, audiovisual materials, and some computer software on such topics as advertising, sales forecasting, and market research—each with subdivisions. Although most titles are nonreference works, reference sources are well selected. Useful for businesspeople and undergraduates; librarians may profitably use this in collection development. Publisher and title indexes.

531 NTC's dictionary of advertising. 2d ed. Jack C. Wiechmann, ed. 222p. National Textbook Co., 1993. $39. ISBN 0-8442-3040-5.
659.103 HF5803

Wiechmann has updated Urdang's work of the first edition of *Dictionary of advertising terms.* More than 4,000 terms used by specialists in advertising and marketing are explained, including ordinary words and phrases used in new ways by advertisers.

532 Rand McNally commercial atlas and marketing guide. Rand McNally, 1876– . Annual. $395. ISSN 0361-9723.
912 G1019

An atlas of the United States with large, clear maps projecting commercial information. Includes statistical tables as well as graphical depictions of population density, businesses, manufacturers, agricultural products, market potentials, and other commercial data.

533 Sales manager's handbook. (title var.: **Dartnell sales manager's handbook.**) 1st ed.– . 1934– . Dartnell, 1934– . Irreg. (14th ed. 1272p. 1994, $49.95.

ISBN 0-85013-162-6.)
658.81 HF5438.4

A classic in the field; each edition adds much new information to assist the manager on sales organization, training, methods of selling, and marketing research. Explanation of trade practices is an important feature.

534 Sales promotion handbook. 1st ed.– . 1950– . Dartnell, 1950– . Irreg. (1994, $69.95. ISBN 0-85013-212-6.)
658.82 HF5415

A companion volume to *Sales manager's handbook*, this title emphasizes sales techniques and promotion ideas.

535 Survey of buying power. S & MM: Sales & Marketing Management, 1929– . Annual. Part 1, $100; part 2, $50. ISSN 0361-1329.
339.410 HF5415.2

Published as two issues of the periodical; part 1 is a definitive survey of population, effective buying income, and retail sales. Additional statistical projections are included in part 2, which covers the United States and Canada.

Real Estate

536 The Arnold encyclopedia of real estate. Alvin L. Arnold and Jack Kusnet. 900p. Wiley, 1993. $120. ISBN 0-471-58102-X.
333.33 HD1365

Informative definitions or explanations of real estate and related banking, tax, and legal terms. Appendix includes charts or statistics on construction, interest rates, mortgage loans, depreciation schedules, and more. Updated by *The Arnold encyclopedia of real estate yearbook, 1980–* . ISSN 0270-921X.

537 The language of real estate. 3d ed. John W. Reilly. 600p. Dearborn Financial, 1993. Paper $28.95. ISBN 0-7931-0583-8.
346.7301 KF568.5

Almost 2,000 of the most frequently encountered real estate terms are defined here. Of particular interest is a forms appendix that features finished examples of common documents used in real estate transactions.

538 McGraw-Hill real estate handbook. 2d ed. Robert Irwin, ed. 641p. McGraw-Hill, 1994. $69.50. ISBN 0-07-032149-3.
333.33 HD1375

This handbook provides answers to some of the most widely asked questions in the ever-changing field of real estate. Thirty-six chapters are organized into seven major areas: financing, investing, taxation, law, exchanges, appraisal, and marketing.

Secretarial Handbooks

539 Complete secretary's handbook. Deluxe ed., rev. Lillian Doris and Besse May Miller. Mary A. De Vries, ed. 664p. Prentice-Hall, 1993. $39.95. ISBN 0-13-159666-7.
651 HF5547.5

First published in 1951. Extensive detail on general secretarial basics, including preparation of minutes, reports, and legal papers; telephone personality; and office etiquette.

540 Webster's new world secretarial handbook. 4th ed. 691p. Prentice-Hall, 1989. $12. ISBN 0-6718-6471-8.
651.3741 HF5547.5

Previously published in 1968, 1974, and 1983, its thirty chapters recognize the arrival of today's professional secretary, so that both the typewriter and word processor are discussed, along with filing cabinets and optical scanners and manual and automated offices. Index.

Taxes

541 All states tax handbook. Prentice-Hall, 1977– . Annual. $30. ISSN 0148-9976.

State tax handbook. Commerce Clearing House, 1964– . Annual. $32. ISSN 0081-4598.
351.724 KF6750

Up-to-date information on types, forms, and rates of taxation operative in the various states. Information, in greatly condensed form, is extracted from each publisher's comprehensive loose-leaf services.

542 H & R Block income tax guide. Macmillan, 1967– . Annual. Paper $12.95. ISSN 0196-1896.
343.73052 HG179

A handy guide to home preparation of tax returns that incorporates examples and sample forms. Index.

543 J. K. Lasser's your income tax. Simon & Schuster, 1937– . Annual. Paper $10.50. ISSN 0084-4314.
343.73052 HG179

Designed to facilitate preparation of income tax returns. Includes sample forms. Indexed.

544 Reproducible federal tax forms for use in libraries, 1982– . U.S. Internal Revenue Service, 1983– . Annual. $42. (Publication 1132.) *See* below.
■ cd
343.7 KF6286

A loose-leaf service providing frequently used forms and instructions for their use.

545 RIA Federal tax handbook. Research Institute of America, 1975– . Annual. $38. ISSN 0749-212X.

U.S. master tax guide. 80th ed. Commerce Clearing House, 1913– . Annual. $32.50; paper $15.50. ISSN 0083-1700.
343.7304 KF6289

Fast, accurate answers to tax questions are found in either of these standard resources. Each reflects federal tax changes, basic rules affecting personal and business taxes, and gives examples based on typical tax situations. References to the Internal Revenue code and regulations are included as well as rate tables, tax calendar, state sales tax deduction guides, and checklists of taxable and nontaxable items and deductible and nondeductible items.

546 A selection of U.S. Internal Revenue Service tax information publications, 1982– . U.S. Internal Revenue Service, 1982– . 4v. (1994, $52.) (Publication 1194.) *See* below.
343.7 KF6286

A set of frequently requested publications in a convenient format.

Order these two publications from [yr.] Tax Forms, Superintendent of Documents, Dept. IRS-[yr.], P.O. Box 360218, Pittsburgh, PA 15250-6218.

Biographical Sources

547 Biographical dictionary of American labor. 2d ed. Gary M. Fink et al., eds. 767p. Greenwood, 1984. Lib. bindg. $95. ISBN 0-313-22865-5.
331.8809 HD8073

Includes more than 725 biographies of persons who have had a substantial impact on the American labor movement: leaders of trade unions, labor-oriented radicals, politicians, editors, staff members, lawyers, reformers, and intellectuals. Six appendixes: union affiliation, religious preference, place of birth, formal education, major public offices, and political preference. Detailed index.

548 Who's who in economics: a biographical dictionary of major economists, 1700–1986. 2d ed. Mark Blaug, ed. 935p. MIT Pr., 1986. $120. ISBN 0-262-02256-7.
330 D720

Brief sketches of more than 1,400 living and deceased economists. Appendixes include an index of principal fields of interest (listing living economists only), an index of country of residence (if not United States), and an index of country of birth (if not United States).

549 Who's who in finance and industry. (title var.) 1st ed.– . 1936– . Marquis Who's Who. Biennial. (1998/99, $279.95. ISBN 0-8379-0332-7.) ISSN 0083-9523.
338.0092 HF3023

Includes more than 25,000 sketches of North American and international business executives: insurance, international banking, commercial and investment, mutual and pension fund management, commercial and consumer credit, international trade, real estate, and other professions closely related to the business and financial worlds. Unfortunately, information is only accessible by name of individual.

Careers and Vocational Guidance

550 American almanac of jobs and salaries. 1997–98 ed. John Wright. 656p. Avon, 1997. Paper $20. ISBN 0-380-78361-4.
331.21 HD8038

Current information on occupations and salaries is often difficult to locate. This comprehensive almanac is written to inform the career minded of the present status, salaries, and outlook of hundreds of jobs. The book covers a large variety of fields, including data on federal employment and the salaries of personalities in industry, the arts, and sports. This title is a worthwhile purchase for any career collection.

551 Dictionary of occupational titles. Rev. 4th ed. U.S. Dept. of Labor. 1445p. Govt. Print. Off., 1991. $50. S/N 029-013-00094-2. SuDoc L37.2:Oc1.

Selected characteristics of occupations defined in the revised Dictionary of occupational titles. U.S. Dept. of Labor. 658p. Govt. Print. Off., 1993. $40. S/N 029-014-00246-1. SuDoc L37.2:Oc1/4.
371.42 HB2595

The standard codification of definitions and classifications of occupational titles in the United States, used both in the federal government and throughout the private sector. The supplement *Selected characteristics of occupations* provides estimates of physical demands, environmental conditions, and training-time ratings for jobs listed in the *Dictionary.*

552 Encyclopedia of careers and vocational guidance. 10th ed. Holli Cosgrove, ed. 4v. 2616p. J. G. Ferguson, 1997. $149.95. ISBN 0-89434-170-7.
■ cd
371.42 HF5381.E52

The first of the four volumes presents profiles of some seventy-five industries, including employment statistics and outlook; the subsequent volumes describe various kinds of careers (more than 540), including professional, technical, trade, clerical, and general. Entries describe duties, salaries, educational requirements, and prospects and suggest key addresses for additional sources of information.

553 Occupational outlook handbook. v.1– . U.S. Bureau of Labor Statistics. Govt. Print. Off., 1949– . Biennial. (1998/99, $42.50. S/N 029-001-03220-0.) SuDoc L2.3/4:yr.
■ cd
371.42 HF5382.5

This handbook contains current and accurate career information about education and training requirements, employment outlook, places of employment, and earnings and working conditions for more than 200 occupations. The index contains an alphabetical list of occupations and industries. A quarterly publication, *Occupational outlook quarterly* (Govt. Print. Off. $6.50/yr. S/N 029-008-00000-1. SuDoc L2.70/4:yr.), updates the handbook between editions.

554 Peterson's internships. Peterson's Guides, 1981– . Annual. $29.95. ISSN 1082-2577.
331.25 L901

Entries are arranged by job categories, listing description of duties, length and season of internship, qualifications required, pay and fringe benefits, availability of college credit, application contacts, procedures, and deadline dates. For beginners or those planning a career change. Indexed by field of interest, geographic location, and employing organization.

8

Political Science and Law

DEBORAH L. THOMAS

Selections for political science and law emphasize the government and politics of the United States at the federal level. Libraries wishing to develop political science reference collections in other directions will find Frederick L. Holler's *Information sources of political science* (4th ed. 417p. ABC-Clio, 1986. $89.50. ISBN 0-87436-375-6) helpful. All libraries should supplement the following titles with information on their own state, such as a state manual or blue book, a state budget or budget summary, and the state code. Libraries will also want to acquire local city publications.

Bibliographies and Guides

555 How to find the law. 9th ed. Morris L. Cohen et al. 716p. West, 1989. Reprint, 1993. $35.50. ISBN 0-314-55318-4.
340.073 KF240.C538

Text designed to assist beginning law students in the daunting task of finding the law. After an introduction devoted to the context of legal research, chapters describe the use and content of types of publications such as court reporters, digests, statutes, loose-leaf services, and encyclopedias. Explanations are liberally supported by reproductions of sample pages, and the discussion of computer-based methods has been integrated throughout. Name, title, and subject indexes.

556 Legal research in a nutshell. 6th ed. Morris L. Cohen and Kent C. Olson. 397p. West, 1996. $19.75. ISBN 0-314-09589-6.
340.072 KF240

A handy guide for those engaging in legal research at any level. Describes print, electronic, online, and Internet resources. Covers the research process, court reports, case research, statutes and constitutions, legislative history, administrative law, international materials, English and Commonwealth law, the civil law system, and secondary sources.

557 Political science: a guide to reference and information sources. Henry E. York. 249p. Libraries Unlimited, 1990.

$38. ISBN 0-87287-794-9.
016.32 JA71

Descriptive annotations for about 800 books, periodicals, databases, organizations, and publishers in the field of political science. Most book entries date from the period 1980–1987. Author-title and subject indexes.

Indexes and Abstracts

558 CIS index to publications of the United States Congress. 1970– . Congressional Information Service, 1970– . Monthly, with quarterly and annual cumulations. Service basis. ISSN 0007-8514.
■ online
348.2 KF49

Indexes and abstracts congressional publications—hearings, committee prints, reports, documents, and special publications. Indexes by subjects, names, titles, and by bill, report, and document numbers. *CIS annual* contains legislative histories. Multiple-year cumulative indexes (but not abstracts) are also compiled. Consult latest CIS *Catalog* and *Price list* for pre-1970 coverage and for availability of pre- and post-1970 publications on microfiche.

559 PAIS international. Public Affairs Information Service, 1991– . ISSN 1051-4015.
■ cd online tape
016.3 Z7163

The *PAIS bulletin* (1915–90) and *PAIS foreign language index* merged to form *PAIS international,* a database continuing a tradition of more than eighty years of bibliographic access to books, pamphlets, government publications, periodicals, and agency reports relating to economic and social conditions, public administration, and international relations. Entries consist of standard bibliographic citations, miniabstracts and assigned subject headings. *PAIS select* is a full-text CD-ROM consisting of English-language articles drawn from *PAIS international.* It is intended for use by students in senior high through college, and *PAIS international* serves a more scholarly and technical audience.

Dictionaries and Encyclopedias

560 The American political dictionary. 9th ed. Jack C. Plano and Milton Greenberg. 672p. Harcourt Brace, 1993. Paper $21.75. ISBN 0-15-500281-3.
320.973 JK9.P55

The vocabulary of governmental institutions, practices, and problems at the federal, state, and local levels. Defines and discusses the significance of more than 1,200 terms, agencies, court cases, and statutes arranged in fourteen subject chapters. Term and subject index.

561 Black's law dictionary. 6th ed. Publisher's editorial staff; contributing authors: Joseph R. Nolan and M. J. Connolly. 1511p. West, 1990. Deluxe ed. $46.50. ISBN 0-8299-2045-5; text ed. $22.95. ISBN 0-8299-2041-2.
■ disc
340.03 KF156.B54

The standard law dictionary for ready reference, comprehensively covering all areas of the law. Appendixes provide abbreviations, time chart of the U.S. Supreme Court, and text of the U.S. Constitution.

562 Dictionary of modern war. Edward Luttwak and Stuart Koehl. 680p. HarperCollins, 1991. $45. ISBN 0-06-270021-9.
355.003 U24.L93

Descriptions and evaluative comments on weapons and weapon systems as well as military concepts, strategy, pacts, and organizations. Discussion of individual weapons includes information on the weapon's size, range, weight, and speed, as well as an analysis of its strategic value. A readable treatment of a complex subject.

563 Encyclopedia of American foreign policy: studies of the principal movements and ideas. Alexander DeConde, ed. 3v. 1201p. Scribner, 1978. $295/set. ISBN 0-684-15503-6.
327.73 JX1407.E53

A unique collection of original essays on the basic concepts and recurring issues of American foreign policy (such as manifest destiny, the cold war, peace movements, etc.). Leading scholars in the field who represent varying ideological viewpoints have contributed substantive and readable essays, supplemented with bibliographies. Abundant cross-references and a detailed index provide increased access. A biographical appendix embellishes this excellent tool, which should be of great use to students of American history and government.

564 Encyclopedia of American political history. Jack P. Greene, ed. 3v. Scribner, 1984. $275/set. ISBN 0-684-17003-5.
320.973 E183.E5

Expert authors penned ninety in-depth, scholarly articles chronicling the tapestry of American political history for a general audience of students and lay readers. The detailed accounts illuminate important events, selected documents such as the Constitution, major issues, institutions, and developments. Selective bibliographies complete each essay. Cumulative index.

565 Encyclopedia of arms control and disarmament. Richard Dean Burns, ed. 3v. 1692p. Scribner, 1993. $295/set. ISBN 0-684-19281-0.
327.1 JX1974.E57

Seventy-six signed scholarly articles discuss armament and disarmament activities from antiquity to the present. Volume 1 contains detailed descriptions of military activities and peace movements in fifteen world regions. Volume 2 covers historical dimensions of the subject, and volume 3 contains chronologically arranged excerpts from 150 treaties, with about 30 modern treaties examined in detail. A useful list of acronyms and a detailed index are included. Most appropriate for academic collections.

566 Encyclopedia of civil rights in America. David Bradley and Shelley Fisher Fishkin. 3v. Sharpe Reference, 1998. $299. ISBN 0-7656-8000-9.
323.1 E185.61

The encyclopedia's 683 articles serve to survey "the history, meaning, and application of civil rights issues in the United States." Suggested readings follow the longer entries. The set includes a comprehensive index, a separate index to the hundreds of relevant court cases discussed in the set, 300 photographs and special appendixes that provide the text of key civil rights documents, a table of civil rights court cases, a chronology of major events, and other reference features.

567 Encyclopedia of democracy. Seymour Martin Lipset, ed. 4v. Congressional Quarterly, 1995. $395. ISBN 0-87187-675-2.
321.8 JC423.E53

A worldwide survey of democracy from antiquity to the present. More than 400 signed articles contributed by an international team of scholars explore democracy's development in more than eighty countries and regions, profile statesmen and leaders, and explain democratic processes, concepts, and philosophies. Each article contains a current bibliography, and good indexing and cross-references make the set easy to use. Appended are twenty-one primary source documents (such as the 1981 "African charter on human and peoples' rights") that are important to democracy's history. A unique and well-done source appropriate for all libraries.

568 Encyclopedia of human rights. 2d ed. Edward Lawson. Taylor & Francis, 1996. 1715p. $340. ISBN 1-56032-362-0.
323.4 JC571.E67

The standard reference work on human rights activities and programs. Includes texts of key documents relating to human rights, essays on individual countries, and many subject entries of relevance. Includes an extensive index and a chronological listing of international instruments concerned with human rights.

569 Encyclopedia of the American constitution. Leonard W. Levy et al., eds. 4v. Macmillan, 1986. $400/set. ISBN 0-02-918610-2. Also available in a reformatted 2v. set. $175/set. ISBN 0-02-918695-1.

Encyclopedia of the American constitution supplement. Leonard W. Levy et al., eds. 668p. Macmillan, 1992. $100. ISBN 0-02-918675-7.
■ cd
342.73 KF4548.E53

Some 260 scholars celebrate the bicentennial of the U.S. Constitution in approximately 2,100 alphabetically arranged, signed articles covering doctrinal concepts of constitutional law (55 percent), people (15 percent), judicial decisions (15 percent), public acts (5 percent), and historical periods (10 percent). Articles range from brief definitions to major treatments as long as 6,000 words. Many articles, including significant Supreme Court decisions, conclude with selective bibliographies for further research. Volume 4 contains the texts of the Articles of Confederation and the Constitution, two chronologies, and detailed case, name, and subject indexes. The supplement covers major decisions and developments in constitutional law since 1985. An important companion to *West's encyclopedia of American law,* with somewhat greater emphasis given to constitutional principles and historical background.

570 Encyclopedia of the American legislative system. Joel H. Silbey, ed. 3v. 1738p. Scribner, 1994. $320/set. ISBN 0-684-19243-8.
328.73 JF501.E53

Scholarly coverage of the workings of federal, state, and local legislatures throughout the course of the nation's history. Long, signed articles are arranged in six topical sections—history of the American legislative system, personnel and elections, legislative processes, behavior, public policy, and the role of the legislature within the political system. Most appropriate for an academic audience.

571 Encyclopedia of the American military. John Jessup and Louise Ketz, eds. 3v. 2255p. Scribner, 1994. $320/set. ISBN 0-684-19255-1.
355.00973 UA23.E56

A sweeping study of the U.S. military in the context of American society. Sixty-nine lengthy articles are arranged topically in six sections—an account of war and American history, a discussion of U.S. government and military policy, a survey of each of the armed forces, a discussion of military arts and science, and one on military practices. An eighty-page chronology compares American military history with current events of the time. Information is current through the Bush administration. Comprehensive index. Appropriate for public, academic, and high school collections.

572 The encyclopedia of the United Nations and international agreements. 2d ed. Edmund Jan Osmanczyk. 1220p. Taylor & Francis, 1990. $295. ISBN 0-85066-833-6.
341.23 JX1977.O8213

An alphabetically arranged treasure trove of information on the United Nations, its specialized agencies, and many intergovernmental and nongovernmental organizations. This especially valuable resource for smaller collections includes the full or partial texts of some 3,000 international agreements, conventions, and treaties as well as definitions of political, economic, military, geographical, and diplomatic terms. Analytical and agreements-conventions-treaties indexes.

573 Great American trials. Edward W. Knappman, ed. 872p. Gale, 1993. $50. ISBN 0-8103-8875-9; paper $17.95. ISBN 0-8103-9134-1.
347.737 KF220.G74

Descriptions of 200 court cases chosen for their historic significance, political controversy, notoriety, or literary significance. Arranged in chronological order, each entry gives the facts of the case, the strategies used to argue it, the verdict, and the case's legal significance and impact. A bibliography cites additional sources for each case. For popular collections.

574 International relations dictionary. 5th ed. Lawrence Ziring et al. 300p. ABC-Clio, 1995. $60. ISBN 0-87436-791-3.
327.03 JX1226.P55

A succinct handbook of current terms arranged in twelve topical chapters with a detailed subject index. Topical arrangement affords a contextual analysis; index provides access to particular terms.

575 Legal problem solver: a quick and easy action guide to the law. 639p. Reader's Digest, 1994. $32.95. ISBN 0-89577-550-6.
■ online
349.73 KF387.L44

A useful family legal guide and a good place to begin finding the answers to common legal questions. Topics are geared to those likely to be experienced by the average person: divorce, buying a home, consumer issues, making a will. The 700 alphabetically arranged entries contain nontechnical language and numerous examples. Sample legal forms are included.

576 Political parties and civic action groups. Edward L. Schapsmeier and Frederick H. Schapsmeier. (Greenwood encyclopedia of American institutions; 4.) 554p. Greenwood, 1981. $105. ISBN 0-313-21442-5.
324.273 JK2260.S36

Covers nearly 300 historical and contemporary political parties or civic action groups with some kind of formal existence or organizational structure, involved in activities with political implications such as lobbying or influencing public opinion, and having some historical significance or relevance to the national political scene. Arranged alphabetically, the encyclopedia provides cross-references within the texts of entries as well as a general index. Appendixes list organizations by primary function and chronologically, and there is a glossary of technical terms and political terminology. Many entries suggest additional sources as well as cite publications produced by the group.

577 **Safire's new political dictionary: the definitive guide to the new language of politics.** William Safire. 930p. Random House, 1993. $35. ISBN 0-679-42068-1.
320.03 JK9.S2

Superior, nonpartisan writing style in a work that records the colorful language of politics, with an emphasis on contemporary American usage. Terms include a definition of a word or phrase and a history of the way it was used politically and by whom. Detailed index.

578 **West's encyclopedia of American law.** 2d ed. 12v. Gale, 1998. $995/set. ISBN 0-3142-2777-9.

[yr.] American law yearbook. Supplement. Gale, 1999– . Annual. $140. ISSN 1521-0901.
348.73 KF154.W47

This encyclopedia replaces the *Guide to American law: everyone's legal encyclopedia,* which was published from 1983 to 1985 by West. A fine multivolume legal encyclopedia for the nonlawyer. Alphabetically arranged entries lucidly explain legal principles and concepts, landmark documents, law, famous trials, and historical movements. Lengthy, signed articles by legal scholars provide in-depth analysis of selected topics. Each volume offers appendixes listing cases cited, popular names of acts mentioned, legal documents and forms appearing in volume 11 that are mentioned in the volume, and a list of special topics in addition to topic, author, illustration, name, and subject indexes. Volume 11 contains legal forms and many texts essential to an understanding of Western legal tradition (e.g., the Ten Commandments, Magna Charta, Universal Declaration of Human Rights, and codes of legal ethics). Volume 12 completes the set with a dictionary of legal terms and detailed cumulative indexes. The *Guide to American law yearbook* updates entries and articles that appeared in the basic encyclopedia and adds new articles, entries, and documents of significance.

HANDBOOKS, YEARBOOKS, AND ALMANACS

579 **Almanac of American politics, 1972– .** Times Books, 1972– . Biennial. $52.95. ISSN 0362-076X.
328.73 JK271.B343

Provides essential data for the assessment of each representative and senator in Congress. Specifics include political background on the state or congressional district, biographies, voting records, group ratings (by such groups as Americans for Democratic Action and Americans for Constitutional Action), and recent election results. Provides information on the governor of each state. Arrranged by state. Congressional district maps. Index.

580 **Almanac of state legislatures.** 2d ed. William Lilley III et al. 333p. Congressional Quarterly, 1998. $135. ISBN 1-56802-434-7.
912.73 G1201.F7

A statistical reference atlas providing geographic, economic, political, and sociological profiles of each of the 6,743 House and Senate districts in all fifty state legislatures. Thirteen characteristics (such as average household income, percentages of minority groups, percentage college educated) are used to provide a district-by-district profile of residents. Base data are drawn from the 1990 census but have been updated to reflect current changes. The comparisons between each district and its state are especially useful. Contains more than 300 full-page, four-color maps of the legislative districts. Unique, attractive, and useful.

581 **Book of the states.** Council of State Governments, 1935– . Biennial. $99. ISSN 0068-0125.
353.9 JK2402.B724

In addition to general articles on various aspects of state government, this source provides many statistical and directory data, the principal state officials, and such information as the nickname, motto, flower, bird, song, and tree of each state. Supplements provide rosters: *State elective officials and the legislatures* (Paper $35. ISSN 0191-9466), *State legislative leadership, committees and staff* (Paper $30. ISSN 0195-6639), and *State administrative officials classified by function* (Paper $30. ISSN 0191-9423).

582 **Congress and the nation: a review of government and politics.** Congressional Quarterly, 1965– . v.1, 1945–64. 1965, op; v.2, 1965–68. 1969. $209. ISBN 0-87187-004-5; v.3, 1969–72. 1973. $209. ISBN 0-87187-055-X; v.4, 1972–76. 1977. $209. ISBN 0-87187-112-2; v.5, 1977–80. 1981. $209. ISBN 0-87187-216-1; v.6, 1981–84. 1985. $209. ISBN 0-87187-334-6; v.7, 1985–88. 1990. $209. ISBN 0-87187-532-2; v.8, 1989–92. 1993. $209. ISBN 0-87187-789-9.
328.73 KF49.C653

Comprehensive surveys of the interactions of national issues in all fields of social concern and politics. Condenses Congressional Quarterly's legislative, presidential, Supreme Court, and political coverage under broad topics such as economic policy, foreign policy, health and human services, energy and the environment, and education policy. Extensive appendixes provide the voting records of members of Congress on key issues, a listing of congressional membership, and the texts of presidential messages and statements. Detailed index.

583 Congressional Quarterly's desk reference on American government. Bruce Wetterau. 349p. Congressional Quarterly, 1995. $39.95. ISBN 0-87187-956-5.
320.473 JK274.W449

A convenient question-and-answer guide to government, the presidency, Congress, campaigns and elections, and the Supreme Court. Topically arranged, with a detailed index that refers users to relevant question numbers. Abbreviations show which of the forty-four reference sources listed in the bibliography was used to answer the question. Although larger libraries will already own many of the sources listed in the bibliography, this is a good choice for smaller collections.

584 Everyone's United Nations. 11th ed. 1979– . United Nations, 1979– . $19.95. ISSN 0071-3244.
341.23 JX1977.A37

Titled *Everyman's United Nations* for first through eighth editions (1948–68). A first purchase for general information about the United Nations.

585 Government agencies. Donald R. Whitnah, ed. 683p. Greenwood, 1983. $125. ISBN 0-313-22017-4.
353.04 JK421 .G65

Each of the more than 100 articles provides a history of an agency of the federal government, stressing the agency's purpose, achievements, failures, administrative structure, and in-house and external conflicts. Sources for additional information conclude each essay, and appendixes provide a chronology of starting years and a genealogy of name changes. An important companion to the *United States government manual.*

586 The military balance, 1963–64– . International Institute for Strategic Studies. Pergamon, 1964– . Publishers vary. Annual. Paper $102. ISSN 0459-7222.
355.03 UA15.L652

Convenient, current, independent, and authoritative quantitative assessment of military power and defense expenditures. For each country, part 1 provides basic economic and demographic data, an overview of the defense budget, the composition of the armed forces, the number of personnel assigned, and the number of weapons by type or system. Part 2 features comparative tables and several analytical essays.

587 Municipal year book, 1934– . International City Management Assn., 1934– . Annual. $79.95. ISSN 0077-2186.
352 JK101.M45

Very complete statistical data on individual cities and counties, combined with articles on contemporary urban management trends and issues. Includes directory of city officials and bibliography for major areas of local government administration. Index.

588 Oxford companion to the politics of the world. Joel Krieger et al. 1056p. $49.95. Oxford Univ. Pr., 1993. ISBN 0-19-505934-4.
320.03 JA61.095

Contains 650 alphabetically arranged articles written by an international group of scholars. Entries cover a wide range of topics, including forms of government, international organizations, historical events, conventions, treaties, and biographies. Users familiar with the popular *Oxford companion* series will recognize this as a good place to begin research on a variety of international political science topics.

589 Political handbook of the world [yr.]. Pub. for the Center for Education and Social Research of the State Univ. of New York at Binghamton and for the Council on Foreign Relations by CSA Publications, 1927– . Annual. $109.95. ISSN 0193-175X.
320.9 JF37.P6

Provides data for each country on chief officials, government and politics, political parties, and news media. Sections devoted to intergovernmental organizations and to issues concerned with particular regions (e.g., Middle East, Latin America). Index to geographical, organizational, and personal names.

590 Public interest profiles, 1977–78– . Foundation for Public Affairs. Congressional Quarterly, 1978– . (1998–99,

$215. ISBN 1-56802-424-X.)
ISSN 1058-627X.
342.2 JK118.P79

Essential information on more than 200 of the most important public interest and public policy organizations in the United States. Profiles of from two to six pages are organized under twelve topical chapters (e.g., environment, consumer, and think tanks) and include a wealth of information such as name, address, and phone number of the organization; budget data and funding sources; board of directors; publications; conferences; and current concerns. Provides considerably more information for profiled groups than the *Encyclopedia of associations* provides. Name and subject indexes.

591 Robert's rules of order. 9th ed. Henry M. Robert III and William J. Evans, eds. HarperCollins, 1991. $27.50. ISBN 0-06-275002-X; paper $15. ISBN 0-06-276051-3.
060.4 JF515.R692

Long the standard compendium of parliamentary law, explaining methods of organizing and conducting the business of societies, conventions, and other assemblies. Includes convenient charts and tables. Subject index.

592 Standard code of parliamentary procedure. 3d ed., new and rev. Alice Sturgis. 275p. McGraw-Hill, 1993. Paper $11.95. ISBN 0-07-062522-0.
060.42 JK515.S88

A somewhat simpler and clearer presentation of the rules of parliamentary procedure, supported by explanations of the underlying purpose of the rules and examples of their use. Revised with the assistance of the Revision Committee, American Institute of Parliamentarians.

593 United States government manual. Govt. Print. Off., 1935– . Annual. $41. S/N 069-000-00076-2. SuDoc AE2.108/2:yr. ISSN 0092-1904.
353 JK421.A3

The official handbook of the federal government provides information on all agencies of the legislative, judicial, and executive branches, as well as on selected organizations in which the United States participates (e.g., Asian Development Bank, Organization of American States), independent establishments and government corporations, and quasi-official agencies. Agency entries include purpose, programs, history, officials (with addresses and phone numbers), regional offices, and sources for further information. Appendixes list abolished and transferred agencies and provide useful organizational charts. Name and subject-agency indexes.

594 World encyclopedia of parliaments and legislatures. George Thomas Kurian, ed. 2v. 878p. Congressional Quarterly, 1998. $401.50. ISBN 0-87187-987-5.
328.03 JF511.W67

In an alphabetical arrangement by country, this set provides a historical overview of the parliament or legislature of 193 countries. Provides essential background data, maps, continent locator points, and a bibliography for each entry. A useful complement to *Constitutions of the world.*

595 Yearbook of the United Nations [yr.]. Martinus Nijhoff (dist. in the U.S. by Kluwer Academic), 1946/47– . Annual. $150. ISSN 0082-8521.
341.13 JX1977.A37

Part 1 summarizes the activities of the United Nations, its constituent bodies, and its specialized agencies. Part 2 reports on the workings of related intergovernmental organizations, such as the World Health Organization and the International Monetary Fund. Appendixes list member nations and U.N. information centers and include the U.N. Charter, the organization's structure, and its agenda for the year covered. Subject, name, and resolution-decision indexes.

Directories

596 Carroll's state directory. Carroll, 1995– . Annual. $150; with 2 updates, $210. ISSN 1082-1929.
■ cd
353.9 JK2482.E94

Organized first by state, provides name, title, address, phone number, and term of office of top state elected officials; the names and phone numbers of state legislators; the chairs of legislative standing committees; and the names, addresses, and phone numbers of administrators categorized by policy or functional areas (e.g., athletics, budget, refugee settlement, women). A second section groups agencies and administrators in all states by functional areas.

597 Directory of U.S. military bases worldwide. 3d ed. William R. Evinger, ed. 456p. Oryx, 1998. $125. ISBN 1-57356-049-9.
355.7 UA26.A2

Basic directory information and a convenient listing of more than 1,000 military bases, recruiting offices, command headquarters, and military camps. Entries also include information on anticipated base closings, when applicable. Although this volume is somewhat expensive, it contains information difficult to locate elsewhere.

598 Federal regulatory directory, 1979/80– . Congressional Quarterly, 1979– . Biennial. $139.95. ISSN 0195-749X.
353.091 KF5406.A15

Part 1 of this companion to *Washington information directory* treats current issues related to regulation. Part 2 profiles in detail the largest, most important agencies (Equal Employment Opportunity Commission, OSHA, SEC, etc.), providing histories, powers and authority, members, organization descriptions, details on public participation, regional offices, and sources for further information. Part 3 covers additional agencies with summaries of responsibilities and lists of telephone contacts, information sources, and regional offices. The appendix includes information on using the *Federal register* and the *Code of federal regulations.* Published every four years, but even an older edition will be quite useful for the economy-minded librarian. Agency-subject and personnel indexes.

599 Martindale-Hubbell law directory, 1931– . Martindale-Hubbell, 1931– . Annual. $695. ISSN 0191-0221.
■ cd
340.025 KF190.M3

Arranged geographically by state, then by city. Contains list of firms and lawyers of the United States and Canada; selected list of foreign lawyers, by country; roster of registered patent attorneys; and a biographical section. Also included are digests of the laws of the states, Canada, and foreign countries; U.S. copyright, patent, and trademark laws; court calendars and uniform and model acts. Has no single alphabetical list of lawyers.

600 Washington information directory, 1975/76– . Congressional Quarterly, 1976– . Annual. $105. ISSN 0887-8064.
975.3 F192.3

An annual subject directory of governmental and nongovernmental agencies and organizations located in Washington, D.C. Gives address, telephone number, name and title of director, and a brief description of work performed by agency or organization. Includes addresses for Washington and local offices of senators and representatives, names of key staff members, and committee assignments. Indexed by subject and by agency or organization. An important adjunct to the *United States government manual* for its more detailed access to executive and congressional offices and for its listing of nongovernmental sources.

Biographical Sources

601 American bench: judges of the nation, 1997–1998. 9th ed. Jeanie J. Clapp and Ruth A. Kennedy, eds. 2500p. Forster-Long, 1997. $340. ISBN 0-931398-37-1.
347.7 KF8700.A19

Combines biographical information on judges from all levels of federal and state courts with jurisdictional and geographical information on the courts they serve. Each biography includes title, court level, and address; many include additional biographical information. For each state the volume describes various types of state courts and methods of judge selection and includes delineations of court districts. Alphabetical name index. Revised biennially.

602 Biographical directory of the governors of the United States, 1789–1978. Robert Sobel and John Raimo, eds. 4v. Meckler, 1978. $375/set. ISBN 0-930466-00-4.

Biographical directory of the governors of the United States, 1978–1983. John W. Raimo, ed. 352p. Meckler, 1985. $75. ISBN 0-930466-62-4.

Biographical directory of the governors of the United States, 1983–1988. Marie Marmo Mullaney. 398p. Meckler, 1989. $75. ISBN 0-88736-177-3.

Biographical directory of the governors of the United States, 1988–1994. Marie Marmo Mullaney. 425p. Greenwood, 1994. $83.50. ISBN 0-313-28312-5.
973.0992 E176

Entries, arranged by state and then chronologically by dates of service, provide information on the life and career of persons who have taken the oath of office as governor of one of the fifty states between 1789 and 1994. Includes portrait and information on birth, death, ancestry and family, political and religious affiliation, and political career. Bibliographical references and locations of the governor's papers complete each entry. Larger collections will want to supplement this set with the *Biographical directory of American colonial and revolutionary gov-*

ernors, 1607–1789 (John W. Raimo. 521p. Meckler, 1980. $125. ISBN 0-930466-07-1) and the *Biographical directory of American territorial governors* (Thomas A. McMullin and David Walker. 353p. Meckler, 1984. $79.50. ISBN 0-930466-11-X).

603 **Heads of states and governments: a world-wide encyclopedia of over 2,300 leaders, 1945 through 1992.** Harris M. Lentz. 912p. McFarland, 1994. $95. ISBN 0-89950-926-6.
920.02 D412.L46

Arranged by country, this source provides biographies of the postwar leaders of 174 countries. Carefully researched entries provide birth and death dates and a respectable summary of political careers. Indexing by name, place, and subject. Although material will go quickly out-of-date, there is no comparable source.

604 **Who's who in American law.** 1977/78– . Marquis Who's Who, 1978– . (1996, $269.95.) ISSN 0162-7880.
■ cd tape
340.092 KF372.W48

Very brief biographical and directory information about U.S. attorneys, key members of bar associations, general counsel to large U.S. corporations, and partners in major law firms; many federal, state, and local judges and deans and prominent professors from leading law schools. Entries include data on career history, education, awards, and areas of professional interest.

605 **Who's who in American politics.** 1967/68– . Bowker, 1967/68– . Biennial. $259. ISSN 0000-0205.
340.092 KF372.W48

Biographical directory of political leaders in Congress, the executive branch of the federal government, state legislatures, state executive branches, mayors of cities with populations over 50,000, national and state party chairs, national party committee members, county chairs, and state supreme court justices. Entries are arranged by state, then alphabetically by name. Indexed by name.

Legal and Political Documents

606 **Budget of the United States government.** U.S. Office of Management and Budget. Govt. Print. Off., 1922– . Annual. Paper. Issued in 7 parts: **Budget of the United States government, fiscal year [yr.].** $27. S/N 041-001-00495-5. **Budget of the United States government, fiscal year [yr.]—Appendix.** $62. S/N 041-001-00496-3. **Analytical perspectives, fiscal year [yr.].** $42. S/N 041-001-00497-1. **Historical tables, fiscal year [yr.].** $22. S/N 041-001-00498-0. **A citizen's guide to the federal budget, fiscal year [yr.].** $2.50. S/N 041-001-00499-8. **The budget system and concepts, fiscal year [yr.].** $2.25. S/N 041-001-00500-5. **Budget information for states, fiscal year [yr.].** Price n/a. S/N n/a. PrEx2.8:yr.
■ micro cd
353.007 HJ2051.A59

The *Budget of the United States government, fiscal year [yr.]* contains the president's budget message and budget proposals. The *Appendix* contains more detailed information than any of the other documents. It includes for each agency proposed text of appropriations, budget schedules for each account, new legislative proposals, and explanations of the work to be performed and the funds needed. *Analytical perspectives* contains economic and accounting analyses that are designed to highlight specific program areas as well as information on federal receipts, collections, borrowing, and debt. *Historical tables* provides data on budget receipts, outlays, surpluses, deficits, debt, and federal employment for an extended time period—in many cases beginning in fiscal year 1940. *Budget information for states* provides data for the major federal formula grant programs (e.g., national school lunch program) to state and local governments. Tables are included for individual programs and also for each state. The *Citizen's guide* is a publication that contains a brief summary of the budget for the general public. The *Budget system and concepts* is a new publication describing the process by which the president's budget proposal is formed.

607 **Code of federal regulations.** Office of the Federal Register, National Archives and Records Administration. Govt. Print. Off. Annual. Paper $951. S/N 869-034-00000-2; microfiche $247. S/N 869-035-00000-9. SuDoc AE2.106/3.
■ micro cd tape
353.007 KF70.A3

Codification of the general and permanent rules published in the *Federal register* (Office of the Federal Register, National Archives and Records Administration. Govt. Print. Off. Daily. [1998 subscription $607.] S/N 769-004-00000-9. SuDoc AE2.106) by executive departments and agencies of the federal government. The fifty titles of the *Code* contain legally binding rules and regulations of importance to businesses, local governments, and a wide variety of social service agencies.

608 Historic documents of [yr.]. Congressional Quarterly, 1972– . Annual. $112. ISSN 0892-080X.
917.3 E839.5

Provides the text of important documents in the area of public affairs issued during the previous year. Introduction precedes each document. Volumes include detailed table of contents and cumulative five-year indexes.

609 The major international treaties, 1914–1945: a history and guide with texts. J. A. S. Grenville. 268p. Routledge, 1987. op.

The major international treaties since 1945: a history and guide with texts. J. A. S. Grenville and Bernard Wasserstein. 528p. Routledge, 1987. $85. ISBN 0-416-38080-8.
341.026 JX171.G7

This two-volume set, a major revision and updating of Grenville's 1974 *The major international treaties, 1914–1973,* provides the texts of selected treaties together with brief historical background and analysis of the diplomatic situation. Some treaty texts are reproduced in full. Longer documents have been edited to omit the more technical and purely formal portions. An important source for academic and larger public library collections. Smaller collections may be satisfied by *Treaties and alliances of the world.* Detailed index.

610 Public papers of the presidents of the United States. 1958– . U.S. Off. of the Federal Register. Govt. Print. Off., 1958– . Annual. Price varies. S/N 022-003- . SuDoc GS4.113:yr. ISSN 0079-7626.
■ micro
353.03 J80.A283

The public messages, speeches, and statements of the presidents from Truman (1945) on. Kept current by *Weekly compilation of presidential documents,* v.1- . Aug. 2, 1965- . Govt. Print. Off., 1965- . S/N 769-007-00000-8. SuDoc AE2.109:date. ISSN 0511-4187.

611 Treaties and alliances of the world. 5th ed. N. J. Renegger, comp. 579p. Gale, 1991. $120. ISBN 0-8103-9914-8.
341.026 JX4005.T72

Summarizes the main provisions of principal international treaties and agreements and provides excerpts from many. Includes early international agreements, such as the Geneva Conventions, as well as new treaties and agreements concluded up to September 1986 and descriptions of organizations involved in international cooperation. Summaries are grouped by subject within eighteen topical and geographic chapters. Subject and treaty-name index. Librarians with access to *The major international treaties . . .* volumes will find *Treaties and alliances of the world* useful for its coverage of pre-1914 agreements and because new editions have been produced more frequently than the Grenville work.

612 Treaties in force: a list of treaties and other international agreements of the United States in force on January 1 [yr.]. U.S. Dept. of State. Govt. Print. Off., 1929– . Annual. $41. S/N 044-000-02488-8. SuDoc S9.14:yr.
■ micro
341.273 JX231.U54

Lists bilateral and multilateral agreements to which the United States is a party in effect as of January 1 of each year. Issued annually.

613 United States Code, containing the general and permanent laws of the United States in force on January 4, 1995. 1994 ed. The Office of the Law Revision Counsel of the House of Representatives. 35v. Govt. Print. Off., 1994. Prices vary by volume. S/N 052-001- . SuDoc Y1.2/5:yr/v.
■ cd
345.2 KF62

Although the medium-sized library cannot satisfy all the needs of the legal specialist, it is important to supply the codified laws of the United States in addition to the appropriate state code. Updated by supplements. See *GPO sales publications reference file* for current availability, price, and order information.

Elections and Campaigns

614 America at the polls, 1920–1956: Harding to Eisenhower—a handbook of presidential election statistics; America at the polls, 1960–1996: Kennedy to Clinton—a handbook of presidential statistics. Alice V.

McGillvray and Richard M. Scammon, eds. 2v. Congressional Quarterly, 1998. $335/set. ISBN 1-56802-376-6.
■ disk
324.973 JK524.A73

America votes. Congressional Quarterly, 1956– . Biennial. 1998, $147. ISSN 0065-678X.
324.973 JK1967.A8

America at the polls is the most convenient source for state and, most significantly, county presidential returns from all elections since 1920. Volume 1 covers 1920 to 1956, and volume 2 contains election results from 1960 to 1996. *America votes* provides county-level data only for the most recent presidential election but adds congressional and gubernatorial returns by state, county, and, for the largest cities, by ward. County-level returns for president are also available in W. Dean Burnham's *Presidential ballots, 1836–1892* (956p. Johns Hopkins Univ. Pr., 1955. Reprint: Ayer Co., 1976. $78.95. ISBN 0-405-07678-9) and Edgar Eugene Robinson's *The presidential vote, 1896–1932* (Stanford Univ. Pr., 1934, op). More complete data in greater detail is available in machine-readable form from the Inter-university Consortium for Political and Social Research, University of Michigan.

615 Congressional Quarterly's guide to U.S. elections. 3d ed. 1543p. Congressional Quarterly, 1994. $275. ISBN 0-87187-996-4.
324.973 JK1967.C662

This first purchase for election statistics contains state-level data on elections for president, governor, senator, and representative through 1992. Valuable overviews of political parties, political conventions, and southern primaries as well as of presidential, gubernatorial, Senate, and House elections supplement the most complete one-stop source of U.S. election data available in print. Useful appendixes in addition to candidate and general indexes. Popular vote returns for president at the county level since 1836 can be found in *America at the polls* and *America votes* and other sources. County-level returns for senatorial candidates can be found in *America votes.*

616 Encyclopedia of the Republican Party, v. 1 and 2; Encyclopedia of the Democratic Party, v. 3 and 4. George Kurian and Jeffrey D. Schultz, eds. 4v. Sharpe Reference, 1997. $399. ISBN 1-56324-729-1.
324.2734 JK2352

Two volumes are devoted to each political party. The first volume presents a narrative history of some sixty-five pages; this is followed by a series of about fifty signed essays addressing various topics under the rubric of issues and ideology (e.g., abortion, affirmative action, gun control, term limits). Then follow biographies of varying lengths of presidents, vice presidents, unsuccessful presidential candidates, speakers, other notables, members of Congress, and governors. The second volume presents detailed information on party conventions, platforms, and elections. There are numerous appendixes and four indexes: general, biographical, geographical, and minorities and women.

617 National party platforms. 6th rev. ed. Donald B. Johnson, comp. 2v. Univ. of Illinois Pr., 1978. $64.95/set. ISBN 0-252-00692-5.

National party platforms of 1980. Donald B. Johnson, comp. 233p. Univ. of Illinois Pr., 1982. Paper $19.95. ISBN 0-252-00923-1.
324.2 JK2255.S64

Texts of the platforms of major and minor parties from 1840 through the campaign of 1980. Texts of subsequent Republican and Democratic Party platforms can be found in the *Congressional Quarterly almanac* and *CQ weekly report.*

618 Political parties and elections in the United States: an encyclopedia. L. Sandy Maisel, ed. 2v. 1345p. Garland, 1991. $150. ISBN 0-8240-7975-2.
324.273 JK2261.P633

A good starting point for research on political parties and elections. Alphabetically arranged entries cover political players, both major and minor; important events and elections; and broad concepts of modern politics. Most entries include cross-references to related articles, and all include biographic reference for further research. Among the eighteen appendixes are lists of female, Hispanic, and African American members of Congress; election commissioners; and chairs of national political committees.

Federal Executive Branch Sources

619 Biographical directory of the United States executive branch, 1774–1989. 3d ed. Robert Sobel, ed. 567p. Greenwood, 1990. $95.

ISBN 0-313-26593-3.
353.04 E176.B578

Gives biographical sketches of U.S. presidents, vice presidents, cabinet members, and presidents of the Continental Congress. Brief bibliographies. Appendixes list the presidents, vice presidents, and cabinet members; the cabinet members by presidential administration; and biographees by state of birth, military service, and marital status.

620 The complete book of U.S. presidents. 4th ed. William A. DeGregorio. 740p. Barricade Books, 1993. $30. ISBN 0-942637-37-2; paper $21. ISBN 0-942637-92-5.
E176.1 973.009

Similar in coverage to Kane's *Facts about the presidents,* with a chapter devoted to the biography of each U.S. president, from Washington through Clinton. DeGregorio provides more detailed information on the president and individuals in his life. Kane offers more data on the surrounding political environment. For libraries making a choice, DeGregorio's work will prove more useful.

621 Congressional Quarterly's guide to the presidency. 2d ed. Michael Nelson, ed. 2v. Congressional Quarterly, 1996. $299. ISBN 1-56802-018-X.
353.03 JK516.C57

In the authoritative and easily understood style of CQ publications, thirty-seven chapters grouped into seven parts examine the origin and development of the presidency, its powers, and its relationship to the branches of government and to the American people. Includes brief biographies of presidents and vice presidents through the Clinton administration. Cross-references within chapters relate discussions. Bibliographies at the end of each chapter suggest sources for further research. A valuable appendix includes documents and texts, votes of the Electoral College, summaries of the popular votes for president, a listing of cabinet members for each administration, and Gallup Poll ratings for presidents Truman through Reagan. Detailed subject index. Small collections may substitute *The presidency a to z: a ready reference encyclopedia* (574p. Congressional Quarterly, 1994. $145. ISBN 1-56802-056-2; paper $89.95. ISBN 1-56802-006-6).

622 Encyclopedia of the American presidency. Leonard Levy and Louis Fisher, eds. 4v. 1827p. Simon & Schuster, 1994. $355/set. ISBN 0-13-275983-7.
353.03 JK511.E53

A readable, interdisciplinary presentation of all aspects of the government's executive branch. Entries cover the "origin, evolution, and constant unfolding of the American presidency" from 1787 to 1992. Included in the more than 1,000 signed articles are biographies, definitions of terms, analysis of historical events, and discussion of the role of the presidency. Includes an extensive index and bibliographical references. More scholarly and in-depth than *Congressional Quarterly's guide to the presidency,* this is the single best source on the American executive branch.

623 Facts about the presidents. 6th ed. Joseph Nathan Kane. 493p. Wilson, 1993. $55. ISBN 0-8242-0844-5.
973.0992 E176.1

In part 1, individual chapters on each president from Washington through Clinton present data on the presidents' family history, elections, congressional sessions, cabinet and Supreme Court appointments, vice presidents, and highlights of the presidents' lives and administrations. Each chapter concludes with a brief bibliography for further reading. Part 2 presents comparative data on the president as an individual and on the office. Portraits, facsimile autographs, and index.

624 Presidential also-rans and running mates, 1788–1980. Leslie H. Southwick, comp. 722p. McFarland, 1984. $62.50. ISBN 0-89950-109-5.
324.973 E176.1

For each presidential election from 1788–89 through 1980, this unique source provides a one-page description showing nominees and election results followed by biographical sketches of each losing candidate for president and vice president. Southwick analyzes the qualifications of each losing candidate and provides a bibliography for further research. Useful, unique, and just plain interesting.

Federal Judicial Branch Sources

625 Congressional Quarterly's guide to the U.S. Supreme Court. 3d ed. Elder Witt. 2v. 1172p. Congressional Quarterly, 1997. $299. ISBN 1-56802-130-5.
347.73 KF8742.W567

Carefully researched, comprehensive, and completely updated source on the Court's organization and development from 1790 to 1996, its impact on the federal system of government, the effect of the Court's rulings on the individual, pressures on the Court, the characteristics (including brief biographical information) of the 104 justices, and summaries of the Court's major decisions. Appendixes include documents and texts related to the Court's history, a nominations chart, glossary, and a list of acts of Congress the Court has found unconstitutional. Footnotes conclude many articles, and extensive bibliographies accompany five of the seven major parts. Subject and case index. Indispensable for most collections. Although not as detailed, smaller libraries may want to substitute *The Supreme Court a to z: a ready reference encyclopedia* (528p. Congressional Quarterly, 1994. $129. ISBN 1-56802-053-8; paper $69.95. ISBN 1-56802-007-4).

626 Historic U.S. court cases, 1690–1990: an encyclopedia. John W. Johnson. 754p. (Garland reference library of the social sciences; 497. American law and society; 2.) $125. ISBN 0-8240-4430-4.
349.73 KF385.A4

Summarizes 171 of the most important U.S. court cases, from the Salem witchcraft trials to the notorious 1990 flag-burning case. The book is arranged in subject chapters, such as "Race and Gender in American Law" and "Freedom of Speech." Essays are several pages in length and avoid legal jargon. Each essay contains the legal citation for the case and a short bibliography of additional sources. A must for high school, public, and undergraduate collections.

627 The justices of the United States Supreme Court, 1789–1995: their lives and major opinions. Leon Friedman and Fred L. Israel, eds. 5v. Chelsea House, 1995. $450/set. ISBN 0-7910-1377-4.
347.73 KF8744.F75

The most extensive treatment of the lives, work, and influence of the justices of the United States Supreme Court. This source contains substantial biographical essays, selected bibliographies, and critical evaluations of the legal contributions of the justices, preceded by an introductory essay on the history and development of the Court. Smaller libraries may choose *The Supreme Court justices: a biographical dictionary* (Melvin I. Urofsky, ed. Garland, 1995. $75. ISBN 0-8153-1176-1) for its discussion of justices' legal opinions or *Supreme Court justices: illustrated biographies, 1789–1995* (Clare Cushman, ed. Congressional Quarterly, 1995. $46.95. ISBN 1-56802-127-5; paper $33.95. ISBN 1-56802-126-7) for its concentration on the lives and characters of the justices.

628 Leading constitutional decisions. 18th ed. Robert F. Cushman with Susan P. Koniak. 432p. Prentice-Hall, 1992. Paper $52. ISBN 0-13-529439-8.
342.73 KF4549.C83

A collection of the most important Supreme Court decisions on constitutional questions of lasting significance. For the use of students of American government and history.

629 Oxford companion to the Supreme Court of the United States. Kermit L. Hall, ed. 1032p. Oxford Univ. Pr., 1992. $49.95. ISBN 0-19-505835-6.
347.73 KF872.A35

A comprehensive guide to the work of the Court and its influence on American life. Biographical entries cover justices and nominees and famous lawyers who argued before the Court. About 400 entries discuss specific cases and include a *United States reports* citation as well as discussion of the case's legal impact. Other entries cover legal concepts and explain the Court's political, economic, and cultural history. Numerous appendixes include a useful case index. An essential purchase.

630 United States Supreme Court decisions: an index to excerpts, reprints, and discussions. 2d ed. Nancy Anderman Guenther. 856p. Scarecrow, 1983. $65. ISBN 0-8108-1578-8.
348.73 KF101.6

Essential for libraries dealing with Supreme Court cases. Entries for each decision of the Court are arranged chronologically and provide the name of the case, date of the decision, and a citation of the text of the decision. This is followed by references to pages within books where users can locate excerpts or reprints as well as discussions of the cases. A separate listing of periodical articles about each decision is new to this edition. Case name and invaluable subject index.

Federal Legislative Branch Sources

631 Biographical directory of the United States Congress, 1774–1989. U.S. Congress. 2104p. Govt. Print. Off.,

1989. $82. S/N 052-071-00699-1. SuDoc Y1.1/3:100-34.

Biographical directory of the American Congress, 1774–1996: the Continental Congress, September 5, 1774, to October 21, 1788, and the Congress of the United States from the First through the 104th Congress, March 4, 1789, to January 3, 1997. Joel D. Treese, ed. 2108p. Congressional Quarterly, 1997. $295. ISBN 0-87289-124-0.
973.3 JK1010.A5

The *Biographical directory of the United States Congress, 1774–1989,* provides brief biographies of members of Congress from the Continental Congress and from the first through the 100th Congress of the United States. Lists executive officers by administration and senators and representatives by Congress. Updated by the *Official congressional directory.* The *Biographical directory* is now being cumulated by Congressional Quarterly.

632 **Congressional district atlas.** 86th Congress. Bureau of the Census. Govt. Print. Off., 1960– . (1964, 1966, 1968, 1970, 1973, 1975, 1977, 1983, 1985, 1987). (103rd Congress. 1993, 2v. $42. S/N 003-024-08683-2. SuDoc C3.62/5:993.)
912 G1201.F7

The historical atlas of United States congressional districts, 1789–1983. Kenneth C. Martis. 302p. Macmillan, 1982. $195. ISBN 0-02-920150-0.
912.13 G1201.F

The *Congressional district atlas* provides maps showing the boundaries of congressional districts in more useful detail than those found in the *Almanac of American politics.* For each state, alphabetical listings place municipalities, county subdivisions, and counties in the appropriate district(s). *The historical atlas of United States congressional districts* provides maps showing all congressional districts for each Congress through the ninety-seventh (1981–82), along with alphabetical lists of members (state and district numbers appended), legal descriptions of every congressional district, and an introduction. Each volume includes an extensive bibliography and indexes.

633 **Congressional districts in the 1990s.** 1016p. Congressional Quarterly, 1993. $194. ISBN 0-87187-722-8.
328.73 JK1341.C64

Descriptive and statistical profiles of the 435 congressional districts based on the 1990 census and the subsequent congressional reapportionment. An easy-to-use source for maps of each state's congressional districts and tables of statewide demographic data in addition to district data including recent election returns, population, race, colleges and universities, newspapers, and industries.

634 **Congressional Quarterly almanac.** Congressional Quarterly, 1945– . Annual. $370. ISSN 0095-6007.
■ online
328.73 JK1.C66

CQ weekly report, 1945– . Congressional Quarterly, 1945– . ISSN 0010-5910. Contact publisher for price.
■ online
328.73 JK1.C15

Published after each annual session of Congress, the *Almanac* reorganizes into chapters (e.g., "Foreign Policy/National Security"; "Transportation/ Commerce") and indexes material in the *CQ weekly report.* Includes summaries of legislation, roll-call votes, texts of presidential messages, and a list of lobby registrations. The *CQ weekly report* is a succinct reporting source on the week in Congress: new bills, progress on pending bills, summaries of legislation of the year and session to date, and voting charts. Also provides information on executive branch activities. The most rapid and complete source for election results, the texts of presidential news conferences, and important Supreme Court decisions. Even though the *Almanac* reorganizes much of the information presented in the issues of the *CQ weekly report,* libraries should retain back issues of the weekly because they often provide more detail than is found in the *Almanac* in addition to significant articles indexed in *Public affairs information service bulletin.* Libraries unable to afford the *Almanac* may find useful the overview inexpensively provided by *Congressional yearbook* (Congressional Quarterly, 1993– . 1998, $23.95. ISSN 1079-8129).

635 **Congressional Quarterly's guide to Congress.** 4th ed. 1185p. Congressional Quarterly, 1991. $239. ISBN 0-87187-584-5.
328.73 JK1021.C565

A complete guide to the study of the origins, history, and procedures of Congress. Special features include, among many others, glossaries of terms, bibliographies, a biographical index of Congress, standing rules of the House and Senate, and texts of basic documents. Subject index. Smaller libraries may choose *Congress a to z: a ready reference encyclopedia* (2d ed. 560p. Congressional Quarterly, 1993. $129. ISBN 0-87187-826-7; paper $69.95. ISBN 0-87187-988-3). *Congress a to z* provides briefer, more simply stated descriptions of the legislative process and definitions of terms, committee profiles, and biographical sketches of selected members. Its information serves as an excellent supplement but cannot replace the depth of *Congressional Quarterly's guide to Congress.*

636 **The encyclopedia of the United States Congress.** Donald C. Bacon et al. 4v. 2360p. Simon & Schuster, 1995. $355. ISBN 0-13-276361-3.
328.73 JK1067.E63

The most comprehensive work and a grand overview of the history, development, and processes of Congress. Alphabetically arranged entries cover all aspects of this American institution: biographies of members, the buildings of Congress, its agencies and committees, and significant legislation and court cases, to name a few. Most of the contributors are scholars, and all articles are signed. Entries range from a few paragraphs to essays of several pages, but all contain brief citations to additional sources. Even libraries that own a one-volume congressional guide such as the fine *Congressional Quarterly's guide to Congress* will want to acquire this set for the scope and depth of its coverage.

637 **Historical atlas of political parties in the United States Congress, 1789–1988.** Kenneth C. Martis. 518p. Free Pr., 1999. $200. ISBN 0-02-920170-5.
912.13 G1201.F9

Produced by the United States Congress Bicentennial Atlas Project. Presents easy-to-read color maps depicting the political party of members of Congress for all districts and each Congress, accompanying membership lists for each Congress, political affiliation identification tables (1789–1837), political party identification tables (1789–1988), and extensive textual discussion of the history of political parties in the U.S. Congress.

638 **Official congressional directory.** U.S. Congress. Govt. Print. Off., 1809– . Biennial, 1977/78– . Formerly annual. $43. S/N 052-070-07112-5; paper $30. S/N 052-070-07111-7. SuDoc Y4.P93/1/cong/date.
328.73 JK1011.A1

Complete description of the organization of Congress and listing of current members with biographical sketches and committee assignments. Lists key congressional staff and principal personnel for executive departments and independent agencies. Provides information on the federal judiciary, diplomats and consular service, and press and other galleries and small maps of congressional districts. The *Official congressional directory* is a first purchase for all collections. Those able to invest additional dollars in congressional directory information will benefit from the *Congressional staff directory* (Staff Directories, 1959– . Annual. Paper $89. ISSN 0589-3178), which offers more extensive listings of staffers, more convenient organization, and more current information supplemented by 3,200 staff biographies.

639 **Open secrets: the encyclopedia of congressional money and politics.** 4th ed. Larry Makinson and Joshua F. Goldstein for the Center for Responsive Politics. 1348p. Congressional Quarterly, 1996. $200. ISBN 1-56802-229-8.
324.7 JK1991.063

A strikingly useful tool for penetrating the often murky world of congressional campaign finance and the burgeoning role of political action committees (PACs). The work is divided into sections that examine the overall patterns of PAC giving to congressional candidates, the role of key industry and interest groupings, and PAC giving to the membership of all thirty-seven House and Senate standing committees. The fourth edition also includes detailed analysis of contributions to both the winners and losers in the 1996 congressional and presidential elections, and previous editions should be retained for their analysis of the 1988, 1990, and 1992 elections. Extensive use of clear tables, pie charts, and graphs. Published biennially.

640 **Vital statistics on Congress, 1980– .** Norman J. Ornstein et al. Congressional Quarterly, 1987/88– . Biennial. $50.95. Paper $36.95. ISSN 0896-9469. (previously published by the American Enterprise Institute for Public Policy.)
328.73 JK1041.V58

A unique compilation of time-series data on congressional membership, elections, campaign finance, committees, congressional staff and operating expenses, workload, budgeting, and voting alignments. Most tables and charts describe Congress in the aggregate. The *Almanac of American politics* remains the choice for data on individual members of Congress.

9

Education

DEBORAH L. THOMAS

Education is a large and competitive industry as well as a field for study and research, and the reference literature that accompanies education has a pragmatic, businesslike quality. The reference sources in education tend to be practical, relatively inexpensive, and primarily serial in nature. For the most part, they have been developed to provide up-to-date information about educational institutions, research and statistical trends, educators, educational materials, and the education industry itself. Although there are extraordinary changes afoot in the field of education—distance learning, new nontraditional student populations, transformational learning, asynchronous learning, and interactive learning, to mention but a few—these trends find their proper forum in the journal and monographic literature and very little reflection in the traditional reference collection.

Bibliographies and Guides

General

641 Core list of books and journals in education. Nancy Patricia O'Brien and Emily Fabiano. 125p. Oryx, 1991. $39.95. ISBN 0-89774-559-0.
016.37 LB14.6

A recommended core collection, primarily useful to academic libraries, of 987 reference works, monographs, and journal titles relevant to education. Organized into eighteen subject chapters. Entries for books contain short annotations. Subject, author, and title indexes.

642 Education: a guide to reference and information sources. Lois J. Buttlar. 258p. Libraries Unlimited, 1989. $35. ISBN 0-87287-619-5.
011.02 LB15

Describes reference sources, online databases, major research centers and organizations, and selected periodical titles in education and related fields. Almost all selections are in English and published after 1980. The 676 entries are divided into twenty chapters devoted to broad disciplines, specific areas of education (e.g., special education, higher education, women's studies and feminist education), research centers and organizations, or periodicals, and then organized by type of source. Each entry includes a full bibliographic citation, price, LC number, ISSN or ISBN, and an extensive, informative annotation. Author, title, and subject index.

Media and Curriculum Materials

643 **Audiocassette and compact disc finder: a subject guide to educational and literary materials on audiocassettes and compact discs.** 3d ed. National Information Center for Educational Media (NICEM). 1419p. Plexus, 1993. $125. ISBN 0-937548-22-7.

Film and video finder. 5th ed. National Information Center for Educational Media (NICEM). 3v. Plexus, 1997. $295/set. ISBN 0-937548-29-4.
■ cd online
371.33 LB1044.4

Comprehensive and regularly updated bibliographical sources for nonprint media. The National Information Center for Educational Media (NICEM) was established in 1964 "to develop an automated storage and retrieval system containing bibliographic information on non-print educational media." The printed indexes and their database equivalent (*A-V online*) provide bibliographic information, brief annotations, producer, and distributor, although some entries do not give prices. *A-V online,* available through Dialog and on compact disc, has information on programs in the following formats: videotapes, slide sets, filmstrips, 16mm motion pictures, audiocassettes, slide and tape, overhead transparencies, 8mm film cartridges, phonographic records, interactive video, multimedia, and computer-based training.

644 **Educational media and technology yearbook.** v.1– . Libraries Unlimited (in cooperation with the Assn. for Educational Communications and Technology), 1973– . Annual. $65. ISSN 8755-2094. (*formerly* **Educational media yearbook.**)
371.3 LB10283

Articles by specialists provide state-of-the-art reviews of recent developments and trends, technology updates, and leadership profiles. Somewhat more than half are devoted to directories of media organizations and associations, graduate programs, funding sources, and producers, distributors, and publishers.

645 **Educators guide to free teaching aids.** 1st ed.– . Educators Progress Service, 1955– . Annual. Loose-leaf $45.95. ISSN 0070-9387.
016.3713 AG600

Educators guide to free films, filmstrips and slides. 1st ed.– . Educators Progress Service, 1941– . Annual. Paper $36.95. ISSN 0070-9395.
371.3352 LB1044

Educators guide to free guidance materials. 1st ed.– . Educators Progress Service, 1962– . Annual. Paper $28.95. ISSN 0070-9417.
016.37142 HF5381

Educators guide to free health, physical education, and recreation materials. 1st ed.– . Educators Progress Service, 1968– . Annual. Paper $27.95. ISSN 0424-6241.
371.335 Z6121

Educators guide to free home economics and consumer education materials. 1st ed.– . Educators Progress Service, 1984– . Annual. Paper $25.95. ISSN 0883-2811.
016.64 TX1

Educators guide to free science materials. 1st ed.– . Educators Progress Service, 1960– . Annual. Paper $27.95. ISSN 0070-9425.
507 Q181

Educators guide to free social studies materials. 1st ed.– . Educators Progress Service, 1961– . Annual. Paper $29.95. ISSN 0070-9433.
307 AG600

Educators index of free materials. 1st ed.– . Educators Progress Service, 1937– . Annual. Ring bindg. $49.95. ISBN 0-87708- .
011.03 AG600

Elementary teachers guide to free curriculum materials. 1st ed.– . Educators Progress Service, 1944– .

Annual. Paper $26.95. ISSN 0070-9980.
016.372 Z5817.2

Guide to free computer materials. 1st ed.– . Educators Progress Service, 1983– . Annual. Paper $39.95. ISSN 0748-6235.
001.64 QA76.16

These annotated lists give source, availability, and so forth; some arranged by form, with subject, title, and source and availability indexes; others by subject, subdivided by form, with the same indexes. Much of the material is from U.S. government agencies.

646 **T.E.S.S.: the educational software selector.** 1984– . EPIE Institute and Teachers College Pr., 1984– . $125. ISSN 8755-5107.
■ cd
371.3 LB1028.5

An extraordinarily useful CD-ROM guide to the educational software market. Describes some 17,000 programs from more than 960 suppliers. Entries provide name, type of program, grade-level range, uses, scope, grouping (i.e., how many can participate), description, configuration and price, distribution medium and price, components, availability, and, for some programs, rated reviews. Coverage includes more than 100 subjects and administrative computing for all of the microcomputers commonly found in schools. Directory of software suppliers. Subject and product name indexes.

Indexes and Abstracts

647 **Current index to journals in education.** v.1– . Oryx, 1969– . Monthly. $245. Semiannual cumulation. $245. ISSN 0011-3565.

Thesaurus of ERIC descriptors. 13th ed. 640p. Oryx, 1995. $69.50. ISBN 0-89774-788-7.
■ cd online
025.4 L11

Indexes to more than 750 education and education-related periodicals. *Current index to journals in education (CIJE)* and *Resources in education (RIE)* together comprise the Educational Resources Information Center (ERIC) system, which offers broad-based coverage of current education literature. Essential for education collections. The thesaurus is an indispensable key for fully utilizing *RIE* and *CIJE*. Contains the index terms (descriptors) used by the ERIC system.

648 **Education index.** v.1– . Wilson, 1929– . Monthly with quarterly and annual cumulations. Service basis. ISSN 0013-1385.
■ cd online
016.3705 L11

Indexes approximately 350 English-language serial publications, periodicals, yearbooks, and papers in all areas of education, as well as publications of the U.S. Department of Education. For many years, the only index in the field, and despite the merits of the other indexes now available, a necessary choice.

649 **Resources in education.** v.1– . Educational Resources Information Center (dist. by Govt. Print. Off.), 1966– . Monthly. $155. S/N 765-003-00000-8. SuDoc ED1.310:yr. Annual cumulations (4-volume set) available from Oryx. $415. ISSN 0197-9973. (*formerly* **Research in education**, 1966–75.)
■ cd online
370.5 L11

These indexes contain abstracts of educational research reports, conference papers, curriculum materials, and other unpublished documents of interest to educators. Cited documents, except where noted, are available from the ERIC Document Reproduction Service in both microfiche and paper copy. For subject index terms, consult *Thesaurus of ERIC descriptors.*

Dictionaries and Encyclopedias

650 **American educators' encyclopedia.** Rev. ed. David E. Kapel et al. 634p. Greenwood, 1991. $105. ISBN 0-313-25269-6.
370.3 LB15.O37

Convenient and reliable source of information on the names, terms, and topics most frequently used in elementary, secondary, and higher education. More than 1,900 alphabetically arranged entries cover all aspects of education. Bibliographical references are included for most entries. Extensive cross-references and index. More than 200 topics were added to the revised edition, while one-third of the original entries were deleted or updated.

651 Encyclopedia of American education. Harlow G. Unger. 3v. 1611p. Facts on File, 1996. $175. ISBN 0-8160-2994-6.

Covers the entire span of American education, from the colonial period to the present day. Includes some 2,500 alphabetical entries, each of which includes a bibliography of additional sources. An award-winning work; probably the best general encyclopedia available.

652 Encyclopedia of educational research. 6th ed. Marvin C. Alkin, ed. 4v. Free Pr., 1992. $400/set. ISBN 0-02-900431-4.
370.3 LB15

Sponsored by the American Educational Research Association, this standard source presents a critical synthesis and interpretation of reported research in about 250 articles contributed primarily by U.S. scholars. Article topics are broad, for example, "attitude measurement" and "motivation." Extensive bibliographies complete each article. Well indexed and illustrated.

653 Encyclopedia of special education: a reference for the education of the handicapped and other exceptional children and adults. Cecil R. Reynolds and Lester Mann, eds. 3v. Wiley, 1987. $425/set. ISBN 0-471-82858-0.
371.9 LC4007

Some 380 specialists contributed the more than 2,000 succinct, signed, alphabetically arranged entries on leaders in the field of special education, educational and psychological tests, techniques of intervention, handicapping conditions, major court cases and laws, and the services needed to support special education. Brief bibliographies accompany each entry. Extensive cross-referencing in addition to cumulative name and subject indexes. Smaller libraries may choose the *Concise encyclopedia of special education* (Wiley, 1990. $89.95. ISBN 0-471-51527-2).

654 The Facts on File dictionary of education. Jay M. Shafritz et al. 503p. Facts on File, 1988. $40. ISBN 0-8160-1636-4.
370.321 LB15.543

Brief, alphabetically arranged entries identify theories, practices, concepts, laws, court cases, organizations, periodicals, people, and the most commonly used, commercially available tests for preschool to high school. Many entries conclude with references to seminal literature or further reading. Extensive cross-references.

655 The international encyclopedia of education: research and studies. 2d ed. Torsten Husen and T. Neville Postlethwaite, eds. 12v. Pergamon, 1994. $3795/set. ISBN 0-08-041046-4.
370.3 LB15

This is a completely revised and expanded edition of this new standard reference. Well-documented overview of all aspects of education. Organized into twenty-two broad categories, the thorough, informative, signed, and jargon-free essays range in length from 2,000 to 5,000 words and include generous bibliographies. Most of volume 12 is an author and detailed subject index. Expensive, but the most comprehensive source in the field of education.

Directories

656 Athletic scholarships. 3d ed. Andy Clark and Amy Clark. 336p. Facts on File, 1993. $24.95. ISBN 0-8160-2892-3; paper $14.95. ISBN 0-8160-2893-1.
796.079 GV583

This invaluable resource for athletes seeking financial aid for college alphabetically lists four-year and two-year colleges in the United States by the name of the school. Entries include address, telephone numbers for both men's and women's athletic departments, amount of aid and number of grants available, school's affiliation, names of sports information and athletic directors, and a list of men's and women's sports programs with an indication of whether scholarships are offered. Introductory essays discuss recruiting rules and how to get a scholarship.

657 AV market place. Bowker, 1969– . Annual. $165. ISSN 1044-0445.
371.33 LB1043

Directory listings for about 7,500 companies offering audiovisual products and services. Entries include basic information such as address, telephone number, and catalog availability. Other sections include lists of associations, awards, and festivals; a calendar of meetings and conventions; and industry yellow pages.

658 The directory for exceptional children: a listing of educational and training facilities. v.1– . Porter Sargent, 1954– . Biennial. $60. ISSN 0070-5012.
371.92 LC4007

Contains questionnaire data on more than 2,600 public and private facilities and organizations. Fifteen lengthy sections, arranged by state, list resources for learning-disabled, emotionally disturbed, autistic, neurologically impaired, mentally retarded, blind, deaf, hard of hearing, and speech-handicapped persons. Entries include a brief, nonevaluative descriptive paragraph. Includes listings of associations, societies, foundations, and state agencies. Facility-organization index.

659 Directory of financial aids for minorities, 1984/85– . Gail Ann Schlachter. Reference Services Pr., 1984– . Biennial. $47.50. ISSN 0738-4122.

Directory of financial aids for women, 1978– . Gail Ann Schlachter. Reference Services Pr., 1978– . Biennial. $45. ISSN 0732-5215.

Financial aid for the disabled and their families, 1988/89– . Gail Ann Schlachter and R. David Weber. Reference Services Pr., 1988– . Biennial. $39.50. ISSN 0898-9222.
378.3 LB2337.2

Describe scholarships, fellowships, loans, grants, awards, and internships designed primarily or exclusively for minorities, women, and the disabled, respectively. Each directory lists state sources of educational benefits and offers an annotated bibliography of directories that list general financial aid programs. Program title, sponsoring organization, geographic, subject, and filing date indexes.

660 The equipment directory of video, computer, and audio-visual products. v.1– . International Communications Industries Assn., 1953– . Annual. Paper $95. ISSN 0884-2124. (*formerly* **Audio-visual equipment directory.** ISSN 0571-8759.)
778.55 TS2301

Directory of AV equipment designed to help buyers make purchase decisions. Comprehensive source of information for currently available products listed in equipment categories. Photos, specifications, and prices accompany the descriptions.

661 Financial aids for higher education. 16th ed. Judy Kesslar Santamaria, ed. 638p. Brown and Benchmark, 1995. Paper $28.95. ISBN 0-697-22262-4.
■ cd
378.3 LB2338

Alphabetically arranged guide to more than 3,000 financial assistance programs for undergraduates. Entries list sponsor, description, restrictions, value, eligibility, basis of award, application procedures and deadlines, and source of further information. Introductory essays offer advice on securing financial aid and descriptions of national qualifying exams. A unique program finder leads students to appropriate programs. Additional program name–subject index. New editions biennially.

662 The independent study catalog: NUCEA's guide to independent study through correspondence instruction. 7th ed. Peterson's Guides, 1977– . Biennial. Paper $21.95. ISSN 0733-6020. (*formerly* **Guide to independent study through correspondence instruction.**)
374.8 LC5951

Lists more than 10,000 high school, college, graduate, and noncredit correspondence courses offered by more than seventy members of the National University Continuing Education Association. Entries for each institution include contact person, address, telephone number, and information about the program, in addition to course names, sponsoring departments, credit values, levels, and special features. There is an index to subject matter areas and additional information on costs, financial aid, accreditation, applications, and so forth.

663 The Macmillan guide to correspondence study. Macmillan, 1983– . Irreg. (6th ed., 1996, $160.) ISSN 1068-2481.
374.473 L901.M26

An excellent comprehensive guide to correspondence study at all levels. Arranged in three sections: college and universities; proprietary schools; and private, nonprofit, and governmental institutions. Entries include contact information, admission requirements, costs, credit and grading information, and accreditations. Following is a list of course offerings, including brief course descriptions. Especially useful for its list of elementary and secondary school offerings.

664 The national faculty directory, 1970– . Gale, 1970– . Annual. $730. ISSN 0077-4472. Supplement, 1984– . Annual. $290. ISSN 0077-4472.
378.1 L901

Alphabetically arranged listing of some 597,000 members of teaching faculties at junior colleges, colleges, and universities in the United States and at selected Canadian institutions. Entries include name, department, institution, and mailing address. The interedition *Supplement* contains entries for new faculty and new addresses or other changes for those previously listed. Although expensive, it is typically in high demand on most campuses.

665 Peterson's internships. Peterson's Guides, 1981– . Annual. $29.95. ISSN 1082-2577.
331.25 L901

A comprehensive current guide to internship opportunities across the United States. Arranged by subject, each entry provides general contact information, number and duration of internships, basic job descriptions, salaries, benefits, and specific candidate requirements. Indexed by field of interest, geographic area, and employer.

666 Peterson's study abroad. Peterson's Guides, 1994– . Annual. $26.95. ISSN 1069-6504.
370.19 LB2376

Information on 1,300 international study programs offered by 350 colleges and universities in eighty countries. Many of these programs are offered by U.S. schools but taught at the campus of the foreign "host" university. Arranged by country, program descriptions include costs, admission requirements, fields of study, living arrangements, and other basic information. Not comprehensive, but accurate and up-to-date.

667 Scholarships, fellowships and loans. Gale, 1998. $161. ISBN 0-78761-675-3.
378.3 LB2338

Recently acquired by Gale, this familiar resource provides detailed information about financial aid for formal and informal degree and nondegree programs at all levels beyond secondary school. Includes information about awards, grants, loans, and contests sponsored by corporations, foundations, religious groups, professional associations, and a few government sources. The index directs students to sources identified by vocational goals, level of study, residence requirements, and sponsoring organizations.

668 World of learning. 48th ed. 2v. Europa (dist. by Gale), 1947– . Annual. $495/set. ISSN 0084-2117.
060.25 AS2.W6

The standard international directory for the nations of the world, covering learned societies, research institutes, libraries, museums and art galleries, and universities and colleges. Includes for each institution address, officers, purpose, foundation date, publications, and so forth. Index.

School and College Directories

Many adequate and similar directories are available. The list below is quite selective, and new titles appear frequently.

669 Accredited institutions of postsecondary education, programs, candidates. 1976/77– . American Council on Education, 1976– . Annual. Paper $54.95. ISSN 0270-1715.
378.73 L901

Provides name, address, phone number, and enrollment for accredited and candidate postsecondary institutions. Most useful for listing the accreditation for the institution as a whole and professional accreditation by subject field. Use with caution because some disciplines have no recognized specialized accreditation, especially for undergraduate programs, and such programs will not be listed here. This directory does not list all curricula offered by an institution. Appendixes list recognized accrediting bodies and discuss the accreditation process. Institutional index.

670 American universities and colleges. 15th ed. American Council on Education. 2200p. De Gruyter, 1997. $199.95. ISBN 3-11-014689-4.
378.73 L901

A directory of institutions organized by state forms the bulk of this compendium. Entries present characteristics, accreditation, structure, history, degree requirements, and additional information in somewhat greater detail than most directories. Particularly valuable for providing descriptions of individual colleges and schools within some institutions. Appendixes contain information on academic dress, a directory of ROTC units, and summary data for institutions. A separate section describes the accreditation activities in each professional field represented by an agency recognized by the Council on Postsecondary Education and lists the institutions offering accredited degrees. Index.

671 Barron's profiles of American colleges. 21st ed. 1636p. Barron, 1996. Paper $23.95. ISBN 0-8120-1752-8.
■ cd
378.73 L901

Descriptions of some 1,650 accredited four-year colleges in the United States. Profiles include data on admission requirements, application deadlines, housing, campus environment, financial aid, extracurricular activities, and other essential information. Features an "at-a-glance" chart with information on enrollments, costs, and standardized test scores for each college and a comprehensive index of college majors. Some editions include a supplementary disk that gives snapshot profiles of colleges and provides help with the application process.

672 Bear's guide to earning college degrees nontraditionally. 12th ed. John Bear. 336p. C & B, 1995. Paper $27.95. ISBN 0-89815-699-8.
378.73 L901

This popular guide to alternative education lists both accredited and nonaccredited schools offering bachelor's, master's, and doctoral degrees. The 1,600 school descriptions include information on cost, degree offerings, and residency requirements. Useful introductory sections discuss how to evaluate a nontraditional school, the meaning of accreditation, and alternative ways to earn college credit.

673 Black American colleges and universities: profiles of two year, four year, and professional schools. Levirn Hill, ed. 796p. Gale, 1994. $60. ISBN 0-8103-9166-X.
378.73 LC2781

A guide to 118 historically and predominantly Black colleges and universities. Entries include contact information, enrollment, admission requirements, accreditation, degrees offered, selectivity, brief history, and descriptions of campus life and activities. Some entries contain photographs and list notable alumni.

674 The Black student's guide to colleges. 5th ed. Barry Beckham, ed. 216p. Madison Books, 1999. $19.95. ISBN 1-56833-116-9.
378.15 L901

A selective guide to 158 institutions, some predominantly Black. Entries enumerate total enrollment, Black undergraduates, Black athletes, total students graduating, Blacks graduating, total faculty, and Black faculty. Also provides data for tuition, total expenses, percentage of Blacks receiving aid, percentage of total aid awarded to Black students, and average award. Narratives discuss each institution from the Black student's perspective.

675 College blue book. 26th ed. 5v. Macmillan, 1998. $245/set. ISBN 0-02-864758-0; v.1, Narrative descriptions. $48. ISBN 0-02-695961-5; v.2, Tabular data. $48. ISBN 0-02-695962-3; v.3, Degrees offered by college and subject. $48. ISBN 0-02-695963-1; v.4, Occupational education. $48. ISBN 0-02-695964-X; v.5, Scholarships, fellowships, grants, and loans. $48. ISBN 0-02-695976-3.
■ cd
378.73 L901

This perennial standard offers narrative descriptions of nearly 3,000 U.S. and Canadian colleges, easy-to-use tabular data, and a listing of degrees offered by subject and institution. The supplementary volume *Occupational education* provides the most complete available listing (just under 9,000 schools) for programs leading to technical and semiprofessional jobs in the service sector, health-related work, public service, fire and police protection, retailing, and secretarial and other business-related work.

676 College catalog collection on microfiche. v.1– . Career Guidance Foundation, 1977– . Annual, with semiannual updates. $698. ISSN 0733-1355.
■ micro cd online
378.C697 L900

National edition of more than 3,400 college catalogs from 3,000 American schools. Four regional editions: Eastern, Western, Southern, and North Central (1996, $298/ea.). International edition (1996, $266). Major four-year undergraduate collection (1996, $258). Financial aid collection (1996, $299). State education directories (1996, $89). Lower standing-order prices for all editions.

677 College handbook. 1st ed.– . College Entrance Examination Board, 1941– . Annual. Paper $20. ISSN 0069-5653.
371.214 LB2351

Index of majors and graduate degrees. 2d ed.– . College Entrance Examination Board, 1979/80– . Annual. Paper $17.95. ISSN 0192-3242.
378.1 L901

Official publication of the prestigious College Board. Describes more than 3,200 accredited institutions arranged by state, then alphabetically. Entries follow a common outline and include full name, address, percent of applicants admitted, percentages completing freshman year and those entering graduate study, type of school, degrees offered, enrollment, number of faculty, location, calendar, computing facilities, size of library, degrees awarded, majors, academic programs and requirements, admissions requirements, student life, athletics, expenses, financial aid, and name, address, and phone number of the director of admissions. The companion *Index of majors* lists institutions by degree program and indicates the level of degrees offered at each. Current, authoritative, and affordable.

678 Comparative guide to American colleges: for students, parents, and counselors. 16th ed. James Cass and Max Birnbaum. 800p. HarperCollins, 1994. Paper $19. ISBN 0-06-273295-1.
378.73 L901

Provides analytical and comparative data on individual colleges, with an emphasis on the scholastic achievements of the student body, academic opportunities offered, and the quality of faculty. State, selectivity, and religious indexes. Comparative listing of majors. *See The insider's guide to the colleges* for more subjective comments.

679 The electronic university: a guide to distance learning programs. 2d ed. 504p. Peterson's Guides, 1995. Paper $24.95. ISBN 1-56079-664-2.
378.1 L901

Profiles U.S. and Canadian institutions of higher education that offer at least one degree or certificate program using primarily electronic means for course delivery and class interaction. Entries for each degree or certificate program include information on admission requirements, program availability, residency requirements, media used to interact with professors and classmates, and accreditation. For those interested in continuing education without a degree in mind, specific courses offered at a distance are listed separately. Subject and geographic indexes.

680 Fiske guide to colleges. v.1– . Edward B. Fiske et al. Times Books, 1988– . Annual. Paper $20. ISSN 1042-7368.
378.73 L901.N48

This popular source features entertaining and informative 1,000–2,500 word essays on 317 of the "best and most interesting institutions in the nation." Many of the colleges included were chosen for high academic quality, but the guide includes a good mix of schools from all parts of the country. Information was provided primarily by the schools' administrators and students and gives prospective students a good feel for campus life.

681 Guide to summer camps and summer schools. 1st ed.– . Porter Sargent, 1936– . Biennial. $35; paper $25. ISSN 0072-8705.
796.54 GV193.G8

Listing of summer camping, travel, pioneering, recreational, and educational programs in the United States and abroad. Entries provide name, location, winter address, age and sex of participants, fees, length of camping period, and a description of important features. Programs are listed by special feature (e.g., mountain climbing, emphasis on science, etc.). Index.

682 The insider's guide to the colleges, 1996. 22d ed. Yale Daily News staff, eds. 760p. St. Martin's, 1995. Paper $14.95. ISBN 0-312-13522-X.
378.73 L901

No collection of college information should be without this subjective, sometimes irreverent guide to more than 300 U.S. and Canadian colleges. Each two- to three-page sketch was compiled from descriptions provided by students actually attending the schools. A useful contribution to the college search. *See Comparative guide to American colleges* for more traditional comparisons.

683 Lovejoy's college guide. 25th ed. ARCO, 1995. $50. ISBN 0-02-862489-0; paper $29.95. ISBN 0-02-862488-2.
■ cd
378.73 L901.S83

Guide to general enrollment, cost, and academic data on some 2,500 U.S. colleges and universities. Each entry provides a comprehensive profile, including helpful information on academic character and student life, except that only addresses are given for community colleges that do not offer dormitory facilities. Tabular information on institutions offering intercollegiate sports and a listing of institutions by career curricula and special programs. Indexed by intercollegiate sports and special activities.

684 Medical school admission requirements, United States and Canada. 1st ed.– . Assn. of American Medical Colleges, 1951– . Annual. Paper $20. ISSN 0066-9423.
610.7 R745

Provides address, telephone number, description of the curriculum, entrance requirements, selection factors, financial aid, brief information for minorities, application and acceptance policies for the current first-year class, expenses, and percentages of successful applicants. Introductory chapters discuss a variety of subjects of significance to those considering medical education. Essential for all academic and most public libraries.

685 Official GRE/CGS directory of graduate programs. Graduate Record Examinations Board. 4v. Educational Testing Service, 1973– . Biennial. Paper $80/set. ISSN 0743-0566; v.A, Natural sciences. Paper $20. ISBN 0-446-39591-9; v.B, Engineering, business. Paper $20. ISBN 0-446-39593-5; v.C, Social science, education. Paper $20. ISBN 0-446-39595-1; v.D, Arts, humanities and other fields. Paper $20. ISBN 0-446-39597-8.
378.1 L901

Comprehensive guide to graduate programs at accredited institutions in the United States. Each volume includes narrative descriptions of institutions arranged by state and provides brief coverage of application dates, degree requirements, accreditation, library holdings, research and computer facilities, housing options, financial aid, and student services. Tables arranged by program and institution provide a wealth of comparative data, including highest degree, enrollment by degree, number of faculty and students, department prerequisites, financial aid positions available, foreign-language requirement, degrees awarded, graduate tuition and fees, and application fee. Provides separate addresses for general information, applications, assistantships, fellowships, loans, and housing for each institution. Essential for all academic libraries.

686 The official guide to U.S. law schools. 1st ed.– . Law School Admission Council/Law School Admission Services in cooperation with the American Bar Assn. and the American Assn. of Law Schools, 1972– . Annual. Paper $20. ISSN 0886-3342. (*formerly* **Prelaw handbook.**)
340.07 KF273

Most complete information available about the application process at all ABA-approved law schools. A two-page description of each school covers library and physical facilities, program of study and degree requirements, special programs, activities, admissions process and dates, expenses and financial aid, housing, placement, and address and phone number. Data on applicant groups provided for many programs. Introductory essays discuss the legal profession, becoming a lawyer, applying to law schools, and other topics of interest to aspiring attorneys.

687 Patterson's American education. v.1– . Educational Directories, 1904– . Annual. $85. ISSN 0079-0230.
370.2 L901

Patterson's elementary education. v.1– . Educational Directories, 1989– . Annual. $85. ISSN 1044-1417.
372 L901

American education provides extremely basic directory information for more than 34,000 public, private, and church-affiliated secondary schools; 11,400 school districts; and some 6,000 colleges, universities, junior colleges, and vocational, technical, and trade schools. *Elementary education* does the same for 13,000 public school districts, 59,000 public elementary schools, and 10,000 private and church-affiliated elementary schools. Organized by state, both volumes list addresses and officials of statewide education agencies followed by community listings, which include a code for population, district name, a code for total system enrollment, superintendent's name and address, and a listing of schools, their addresses, and principals appropriate to each volume. Part 2 of *American education* classifies postsecondary institutions.

688 Peterson's annual guides to graduate study. v.1– . Peterson's Guides, 1966– . Annual.
■ cd online
378.1 L901.P46

Book 1. Peterson's guide to graduate and professional programs, an overview. Paper $27.95. ISSN 0894-9344.

Book 2. Peterson's guide to graduate programs in the humanities and social sciences. Paper $37.95. ISSN 0894-9352.

Book 3. Peterson's guide to graduate programs in the biological, agricultural and health sciences. Paper $44.95. ISSN 0894-9360.

Book 4. Peterson's guide to graduate programs in the physical sciences and mathematics. Paper $37.95. ISSN 0894-9379.

Book 5. Peterson's guide to graduate programs in engineering and applied sciences. Paper $37.95. ISSN 0894-9387.

Book 6. Peterson's guide to graduate programs in business, education,

health, and law. Paper $27.95. ISSN 0894-9352.

Book 1 provides general essays on graduate education, listings of programs by field, listings of institutions and offerings, and profiles of schools offering graduate and professional programs. Books 2–6 offer more detailed information on specific programs, including degrees, accreditation, expenses, language and thesis requirements, and contacts. Some descriptions are as long as two pages and include faculty and their areas of research. This is a popular and useful series, but users should be aware that the amount of information provided varies with the amount of payment from institutions.

689 **Peterson's colleges with programs for students with learning disabilities.** 5th ed. Charles T. Mangrum and Stephen S. Strichart, eds. 688p. Peterson's Guides, 1997. Paper $32.50. ISBN 1-56079-853-X. ■ disk
378.73 L901

A state-by-state listing of 800 two- and four-year colleges that offer special programs for students with learning disabilities. Includes brief profiles of the schools and special programs. Geographic index.

690 **Peterson's guide to four-year colleges.** Peterson's Guides, 1976– . Annual. Paper $24.95. ISSN 0894-9336.
378.73 L901

Peterson's guide to two-year colleges. Peterson's Guides, 1978– . Annual. Paper $21.95. ISSN 0894-9328.
378.73 L901.P448

Profiles more than 1,900 accredited four-year colleges in the United States and Canada and more than 1,400 accredited two-year colleges in the United States. Both volumes provide geographic and majors directories. The *Guide to four-year colleges* also offers entrance difficulty and cost-ranges directories as well as listings of Army and Air Force ROTC programs. The four-year *Guide* also includes information on campus computing requirements and facilities. Both volumes include longer, two-page descriptions of institutions paying for the service.

691 **Peterson's guide to private secondary schools.** 1st ed.– . Peterson's Guides, 1980– . Annual. Paper $29.95. ISSN 0894-9409.
373.2 L900.P48

Descriptive information on some 1,400 independent U.S. and Canadian secondary schools and similar foreign schools. A geographically arranged table presents basic data such as categories of students accepted, grades taught, enrollment, and course offerings, while the following section, arranged alphabetically by school name, offers detailed narrative profiles. As with other Peterson's guides, more detailed, two-page descriptions are provided for inclusion by some schools. Twenty-eight directories group schools by characteristics such as boy's day, girl's day, coeducational, and barrier-free campuses. School name index.

692 **Peterson's register of higher education, 1990– .** Peterson's Guides, 1989– . Annual. Paper $49.95. ISSN 1046-2406. (*formerly* **Peterson's higher education directory.**)
378.73 L901

A unique and especially useful directory to the more than 3,500 U.S. colleges and universities accredited to grant postsecondary degrees and to the administrators who run them. Rather than the state-by-state arrangement of most college directories, profiles are arranged alphabetically by name of the institution. Each includes the full name, address, telephone number, FICE code, entity number, degrees, calendar, type and number of enrollment, tuition, accreditation, and information on research facilities and affiliations. But most valuably, each entry also lists key administrative personnel classed according to sixty-three categories, from chief executive to administrator of vocational/technical education, giving name, title, and individual telephone number. Appendixes list U.S. Department of Education offices, state higher-education agencies, accrediting bodies, consortia, and membership lists of selected higher-education associations. Name, accreditation, and geographic indexes. Essential for academic collections.

693 **Peterson's vocational and technical schools and programs.** 2v. Peterson's Guides, 1996. Paper $34.95/v. ISBN 1-56079-484-4 (East); 1-56079-485-2 (West).
374.013 L903

A comprehensive guide to 7,500 public and private institutions that grant certificates, diplomas, or other credentials for less than two years of study. Volume 1 covers schools east of the Mississippi River, and volume 2 profiles schools west of the Mississippi. Schools must be accredited or state licensed and meet U.S. Department of Education qualifications to be included. Brief entries include address information, enrollment, cost, and programs offered. Each volume is indexed by field of study and institution name.

Handbooks, Yearbooks, and Almanacs

694 **American college regalia: a handbook.** Linda Sparks and Bruce Emerton, comps. 308p. Greenwood, 1988. $49.50. ISBN 0-313-26266-7.
378.73 LB3630

Organized by state, then alphabetically by college name, entries provide school nickname, colors, mascot, name of newspaper, yearbook, and the title and text of the alma mater for 469 schools with enrollments of 2,500 or more. Indexed by school name, school colors, and mascot. A must for academic collections.

695 **Baird's manual of American college fraternities.** 20th ed. Jack L. Anson and Robert F. Marchesani, eds. Various pagings. Baird's Manual Foundation, 1991. $59.95. (ISBN not available.)
378.73 LJ31

Comprehensive source of information about American college fraternities, sororities, professional fraternities, honor societies, recognition societies, and their campus homes. Includes descriptions of fraternities that "are no more."

696 **The college costs and financial aid handbook, 1994– .** College Entrance Examination Board, 1980– . Annual. Paper $16.95. ISSN 1073-1075.
378.3 LB2342

Practical information on financing a college education, including what college costs, how much a family will be expected to pay, tips for obtaining financial aid, sample cases and worksheets, and a glossary of terms. Part 2 provides a detailed listing of expenses and financial aid information for more than 3,100 colleges, universities, and proprietary schools. Includes financial aid deadlines.

697 **Private colleges and universities.** John F. Ohles and Shirley M. Ohles. (Greenwood encyclopedia of American institutions; 6.) 2v. Greenwood, 1982. $125/set. ISBN 0-313-21416-6.

Public colleges and universities. John F. Ohles and Shirley M. Ohles. (Greenwood encyclopedia of American institutions; 9.) 1014p. Greenwood, 1986. $95. ISBN 0-313-23257-1.
378.73 L901.033

Together, these volumes provide unique historical overviews of 1,291 private institutions, 547 public colleges and universities, and 31 state systems of higher education. Though more current information can be found readily in a variety of less expensive sources, these alphabetically arranged sketches will remain useful for the conveniently arranged histories and lists of references following each entry. Indexes and useful appendixes.

698 **Public schools USA: a comparative guide to school districts.** Charles Hampton Harrison. 483p. Peterson's Guides, 1991. $44.95. ISBN 0-56079-081-4.
371.01 LA217.2

A treasure for families considering relocation or anyone concerned with a community's education system. Presents comparative data and evaluative comments for school districts that are organized from kindergarten through twelfth grade, have an enrollment of at least 2,500, and are located within approximately twenty-five miles of fifty-two major metropolitan areas (e.g., Atlanta, Detroit, San Diego, Kansas City). Clearly formatted tables—organized by metropolitan area, then district—include name of district, address of central office, a composite indicator called Effective Schools Index, a statistical profile, and an appraisal of the quality of school leadership, instruction, and school environment.

699 **Requirements for certification of teachers, counselors, librarians, administrators for elementary schools, and secondary schools.** v.1– . Univ. of Chicago Pr., 1935– . Annual. $39. ISSN 1047-7071.
371.15 LB1771

The most current and thorough source for initial certification requirements in the public education field. Arranged by state, then by category. Appendix provides addresses of state offices of certification.

Statistical Sources

700 **Condition of education.** U.S. Dept. of Education. Govt. Print. Off., 1975– . Annual. $25. S/N 065-000-01196-4. SuDoc ED1.109:yr.
■ cd
375.37 L112

Annual data on sixty key education indicators that shed light on the condition of education in the United States. Data include student performance, resources in the schools, student characteristics, special education, and racial and ethnic composition of schools. Introductory text summarizes positive developments and discusses areas of concern. Essential for public and academic collections.

701 Digest of education statistics. v.1– . U.S. Dept. of Education. Govt. Print. Off., 1962– . Annual. $44. S/N 065-000-01174-3. SuDoc ED1.310/2:yr.
370.973 L111

Valuable abstract of statistical information covering the broad field of American education from prekindergarten through graduate school. Gives statistics on number of schools and colleges, enrollments, teachers, graduates, educational attainment, finances, federal funds for education, libraries, international education, research and development trends, women in education, and data on noncollegiate institutions.

Biographical Sources

702 Biographical dictionary of American educators. John F. Ohles, ed. 3v. Greenwood, 1978. $195/set. ISBN 0-8371-9893-3.
370.973 LA2311

Articles about 1,665 American teachers, reformers, theorists, and administrators, from colonial times to 1976, including many state and regional educators, women, and minorities. Many entries include bibliographical references. Individuals included must have reached the age of sixty, retired, or died by January 1, 1975.

703 Directory of American scholars. 9th ed. 5v. Gale, 1999. $495/set. ISBN 0-7876-3164-7.
923.733 LA2311.D598

This is a welcome new edition of the standard directory of U.S. and Canadian scholars active in teaching, research, and publishing—the first update since 1982. It has been completely revised and includes some 35,000 entries, more than 20,000 of which are new. The entries are arranged by academic discipline: (1) history; (2) English, speech, drama; (3) foreign languages, linguistics, philology; (4) philosophy, religion, law; and (5) geographic and institution indexes. Each entry provides name of scholar, primary discipline, vital statistics, education, honorary degrees and awards, past and present professional experience, concurrent positions, memberships, publications, and mailing address.

704 Who's who in American education, 1988–1989– . Publishers vary, 1988– . Annual. $159.95. ISSN 1046-7203.
370.92 LA2311

Contains alphabetically arranged sketches describing prominent contemporary Americans from adult, elementary, secondary, and teacher education. Each entry contains full name, basic biographical information, education, nature of work, areas of practice, professional positions, memberships, awards, publications, research, and home or office address. An appendix lists biographees by specialization (e.g., administration, elementary, gifted/talented) subdivided by state.

10

Words and Language

SCOTT E. KENNEDY

Encyclopedic reference sources focusing on the study of words and language have been relatively scarce until recently. However, style books, desk dictionaries, thesauri, and other practical writer's aids have been and continue to be in great demand: the supply has been robust and the products continually updated and augmented. Principal or unabridged dictionaries, the result of painstaking and time-consuming scholarship, are few and far between in any language; English is fortunate to have several excellent sources to turn to. Though revised on a less frequent basis than their thematic relatives, they are the sources from which the other products draw their data, and new editions are looked upon as great and significant events. Bilingual foreign language dictionaries are in a middle ground. The most studied languages—those listed in this chapter—provide the largest market and see the largest number of commercial players. When seeking a small- to middle-sized English-based bilingual dictionary for the more popular languages, a visit to the publications lists of Oxford University Press, Random House, HarperCollins, Macmillan, or Larousse generally reveals several viable options.

General

Bibliographies and Guides

705 Linguistics: a guide to the reference literature. Anna L. DeMiller. 256p. Libraries Unlimited, 1991. $45. ISBN 0-87287-692-6.
410 P121.D45

An annotated guide to more than 700 reference sources published prior to 1990. There are three principal divisions: general sources, including encyclopedias, biographies, periodical indexes and abstracts, and atlases; interdisciplinary and discipline-specific sources such as anthropological linguistics and sociolinguistics; and sources on individual languages or language groups. Author, title, and subject indexes.

Encyclopedias, Companions, and Atlases

706 Atlas of languages: the origin and development of languages throughout the world. Bill Louw. 244p. Facts on File, 1996. $35. ISBN 0-8160-3388-9.
409 P106.L67

Presents a popular yet authoritative account of language families throughout the world. More than thirty full-color maps provide graphical presentation of the contemporary and historical distribution of languages. Describes the evolution of languages, why they spread, and why they become extinct. Includes separate chapters on writing systems, including sign languages, as well as pidgin and creole linguistic forms. Includes 170 full-color illustrations. Index.

707 Blackwell encyclopedia of writing systems. Florian Coulmas. 603p. Blackwell, 1996. $83.95. ISBN 0-631-19446-0.
411 P211.C68

A masterful one-volume work providing clear and concise information on the writing systems, scripts, and orthographies of the world's major languages. Entries are in an *A* to *Z* format and vary in length from short explanations of terms and concepts to lengthy accounts of individual writing systems and theoretically important issues. Extensive bibliographies. Includes many figures and tables.

708 Cambridge encyclopedia of language. 2d ed. David Crystal. 496p. Cambridge Univ. Pr., 1997. Paper $29.95. ISBN 0-521-55967-7.
403 P29.C64

Divided into eleven thematic sections, this work covers the many aspects of human language. The attractive layout and generous use of illustrative materials, including photographs, maps, graphs, and diagrams, enhance its readability and appeal for the generalist as well as for students who are beginning their study of languages and linguistics and wish a general overview of the primary discoveries and issues. Appendixes include a glossary of terms, a table of the world's languages, and bibliographic notes. Indexes for languages, authors, and topics. Appropriate for both reference and circulating collections.

709 Encyclopedia of language and linguistics. R. E. Asher and J. M. Y. Simpson, eds. 10v. 5644p. Pergamon, 1994. $2400. ISBN 0-08-035943-4.
403 P29.C64

The most authoritative and comprehensive reference work in the field of language and linguistics, with contributions by more than 1,000 specialists from more than seventy-five countries. More than 2,000 articles, well indexed and referenced. Includes many diagrams and an extensive glossary. Combines both impeccable scholarship with readability and ease of use.

710 International encyclopedia of linguistics. William Bright, ed. 4v. 1664p. Oxford Univ. Pr., 1992. $475. ISBN 0-19-505196-3.
410.3 P29.I58

A major work in the field of linguistics. For those libraries unable to afford the ten-volume *Encyclopedia of language and linguistics,* this is an essential purchase. An alphabetical arrangement of entries addressing all aspects of the field, authoritative, up-to-date, and well illustrated.

711 The world's major languages. Bernard Comrie, ed. 1025p. Oxford Univ. Pr., 1987. Paper $29.95. ISBN 0-19-520521-9.
409 P371.W6

Presents the history, structure, and sociological context for fifty major languages and language groups. Describes phonology, morphology, and other linguistic features. Offers extensive bibliographic notes and references. A scholarly work accessible to the general reader.

English Language

Bibliographies and Guides

712 Kister's best dictionaries for adults and young people: a comparative guide. Kenneth F. Kister. 464p. Oryx, 1992. $46.75. ISBN 0-89774-191-9.
423 PE1611.K57

Reviews 300 English-language dictionaries, 132 for adults and 168 for children. Provides citation, purpose, scope, authority, and more for each source reviewed. Evaluates merit of work and often quotes from relevant reviewer's commentary. Author-title-subject index.

Encyclopedias and Companions

713 Cambridge encyclopedia of the English language. David Crystal. 489p. Cambridge Univ. Pr., 1995. $54.95. ISBN 0-521-40179-8; paper $27.95. ISBN 0-521-59655-6.
420 PE1072.C68

Organized thematically to describe the history of the language, the nature of its vocabulary, the grammar, its spoken and written variations, and how it is studied and learned. Frequent quotes from poems, ads, cartoons, and newspaper articles support or illustrate the text. Includes glossary, references for further reading, and index.

714 Oxford companion to the English language. Tom McArthur, ed. 1184p. Oxford Univ. Pr., 1992. $45. ISBN 0-19-214183-X.
420 PE31.O94

Part dictionary, part usage guide, part style manual, part grammar, this delightful companion serves as an authoritative, comprehensive, and highly readable sourcebook that illustrates—by means of more than 5,000 alphabetical entries prepared by some 100 scholars—the current state of the English language today. Highly recommended.

Dictionaries

PRINCIPAL ENGLISH-LANGUAGE DICTIONARIES

715 Oxford English dictionary. 2d ed. J. A. Simpson and E. S. C. Weiner. 20v. Oxford Univ. Pr., 1989. $3000. ISBN 0-19-861186-2.

Oxford English dictionary additions series. John Simpson and Edmund Weiner, eds. Oxford Univ. Pr., 1993– . v.1, 352p. 1993. $45. ISBN 0-19-861292-3; v.2, 384p. 1993. $45. ISBN 0-19-861299-0; v.3, 400p. 1997. $45. ISBN 0-19-860027-5.
■ cd
423 PE1625.O87

A complete revision of the monumental dictionary first published in 1933, this new edition integrates the text of the first edition published in twelve volumes, the four-volume supplement (1972–86), and approximately 5,000 new words or new senses of existing words. This edition contains general revisions and presents an alphabetical list of words in the English vocabulary from the time of Chaucer to the present day, with all the relevant facts concerning their form, history, pronunciation, and etymology. Also valuable for the 2,400,000 quotations that explain the definitions. Spellings are British, with American spellings listed as variants. The volumes in the *Additions series* offer definitions of approximately 3,000 new words each, incorporating illustrative quotations from around the world.

716 The Random House unabridged dictionary. 2d ed. 2478p. Random House, 1993. $100. ISBN 0-679-42917-4.
■ cd
423 PE1625.R3

Though the smallest of the unabridged dictionaries, *Random House,* originally published in 1966 and revised in 1987, is the most up-to-date. The second edition contains 50,000 new entries and 75,000 new definitions. Adhering to a descriptive approach, *Random House* emphasizes words in current use, including new scientific and technical terms, idiomatic phrases, slang and colloquialisms, and proper names. Stylistic labels employ such restrictive tags as "slang," "offensive," "vulgar," and "informal," and the most frequently used meaning is given first. Many entries also note the date of a word's first appearance in the language. Extensive encyclopedic features include biographical and geographical names and also works of art, music, and literature in the main body of the work, with appendixes providing bilingual dictionaries in French, Spanish, Italian, and German; a basic style manual; an atlas of the world; and other useful features. Not as comprehensive as *Webster's third* but an easy-to-use and authoritative unabridged dictionary.

717 Webster's third new international dictionary of the English language. Philip Babcock Gove, ed. 2662p. Merriam-Webster, 1993. $119. ISBN 0-87779-201-1.
423 PE1625.W36

The largest and most prestigious dictionary published in the United States, *Webster's third* was first published in 1961, covering English language in use since 1755. An addendum of new words is added to each subsequent printing (i.e., eight pages of new words appeared in the 1966 printing, sixteen pages in 1971, thirty-eight in 1976, forty-eight in 1981, fifty-six in 1988, and so on). *Webster's third* excludes biographical and geographical names and is much less prescriptive regarding usage than *Webster's second.* Clear, accurate definitions are given in historical order. Outstanding for its numerous illustrative quotations, impeccable authority, and etymologies, *Webster's third* is regarded as the most reliable, comprehensive general unabridged dictionary. Libraries owning *Webster's second* will want to retain it for its prescriptive usage labels and biographical and geographical names.

DESK DICTIONARIES

718 **The American Heritage dictionary of the English Language.** 3d ed. 2184p. Houghton, 1992. $45. ISBN 0-395-44895-6.
■ cd
423 PE1628.A623

The most practical and comprehensive of the desk dictionaries, the *American Heritage* contains more than 200,000 entries; bright, clear, easy-to-read definitions; numerous illustrations along the sidebars; and extensive illustrative quotations make this one of the most pragmatic tools in the collection. An excellent selection for the home or the ready reference collection.

719 **Merriam-Webster's collegiate dictionary.** 10th ed. 1600p. Merriam-Webster, 1996. $24.95. ISBN 0-87779-709-9.
423 PE1628.M36

The standard one-volume collegiate or office dictionary for many years. Reliable and up-to-date, it is the best of the no-frills dictionaries. Offers 160,000 entries, including 6,500 biographical names and 11,000 geographical names.

720 **New shorter Oxford English dictionary.** Leslie Brown, ed. 2v. 3828p. Oxford Univ. Pr., 1993. Thumb-indexed $135. ISBN 0-19-861271-0.
■ cd
423 PE1625.N39

Part abridgement of the *OED* and part entirely new work, this two-volume dictionary *(A-M, N-Z)* brings the scholarship and authority of the *OED* to the general reader and smaller library. Some 300,000 words are described, defined, and explicated. Prefers British pronunciation and usage, but remains international in scope. Traces every word back to the first documented use and makes extensive use of quotation to illustrate meaning. The most literate and scholarly of the desk dictionaries.

721 **Random House Webster's college dictionary.** Random House, 1996. 1568p. $23.95. ISBN 0-679-43886-6.
423 PE1628.R28

Based on the *Random House dictionary of the English language,* and following a similar format, this fine desk dictionary defines nearly 200,000 words, provides synonyms and etymologies, and includes more than 4,000 biographical and geographical entries within the main alphabet. Appendixes offer college directory information, definitions of English given names, and a concise manual of style.

ABBREVIATIONS AND ACRONYMS

722 **Abbreviations dictionary.** 9th ed. Ralph De Sola, Dean Stahl, and Karen Kerchelich. 1240p. CRC Pr., 1995. $94.95. ISBN 0-8493-8944-5.
423.1 PE1693.D4

This new edition of a standard reference work includes abbreviations, acronyms, geographical equivalents, nicknames, and lists of specialized terms. Although there is some overlap with *Acronyms, initialisms, and abbreviations dictionary,* reference collections will generally need both.

723 **Acronyms, initialisms, and abbreviations dictionary: a guide to acronyms, initialisms, abbreviations, contractions, alphabetic symbols, and similar condensed appellations.** 24th ed. 3v. 3166p. Gale, 1998. $610. ISBN 0-7876-2423-3.

Reverse acronyms, initialisms, and abbreviations dictionary. 3123p. in 3 pts. Gale, 1998. $375. ISBN 0-7876-2455-1.
423.1 P365.A28

More than 500,000 entries—acronyms, initialisms, abbreviations, and similar contractions—are expanded to their full context. Approximately 15,000 new terms have been added to the twenty-fourth edition. *Reverse acronyms, initialisms, and abbreviations dictionary* arranges terms alphabetically by meaning of the abbreviation.

724 **Barnhart abbreviations dictionary.** Robert K. Barnhart, ed. 434p. Wiley, 1995. $34.95. ISBN 0-471-57146-6.
423.1 PE1693.B3

Provides in one volume both an abbreviations dictionary and a reverse abbreviations and initialisms dictionary. Contains about 60,000 entries chosen for their currency and use. An excellent single-volume source.

725 **International acronyms, initialisms, and abbreviations dictionary.**

4th ed. 1374p. Gale, 1997. $225.
ISBN 0-8103-7437-4.
423.1 P365.I57

"Deciphers more than 150,000 English and non-English acronyms used internationally and in specific countries." This edition adds more than 40,000 new terms.

726 **World guide to abbreviations of organizations.** 11th ed. 1149p. Blackie Academic & Professional (dist. by Gale), 1997. $180. ISBN 0-7514-0261-3.
060 AS8.588

Expands abbreviations of more than 68,000 international, national, governmental, and individual organizations. This edition features 8,500 new entries, including many entries from newly independent countries of Eastern Europe.

CROSSWORD PUZZLE DICTIONARIES

727 **Crossword puzzle dictionary.** 6th ed. Andrew Swanfeldt. 858p. HarperCollins, 1994. $23. ISBN 0-06-270090-1; paper $15. ISBN 0-06-272053-8.
793.73 GV1507.C7

One of the oldest of such works currently available, Swanfeldt's dictionary continues to be a popular resource for crossword puzzle enthusiasts. Synonyms for words are grouped according to the number of letters they contain. Features 330,000 answer words, including expanded geographical and cultural entries, including continents, countries, U.S. states, actors, sports figures, and politicians.

728 **The New York Times crossword puzzle dictionary.** 3d ed. Thomas Pulliam and Clare Grundman. 618p. Times Books, 1995. $27.50. ISBN 0-8129-2606-4.
793.73 GV1507.C7

A popular crossword puzzle dictionary and one of the largest on the market, with some 50,000 main entries providing more than 500,000 answer words. Essentially a dictionary of undiscriminated synonyms, it is one of the more useful works of its kind.

729 **The Random House crossword puzzle dictionary.** 2d ed. Tony Geiss. 1093p. Random House, 1994. $23. ISBN 0-679-43376-7; paper $5.99. ISBN 0-804-11349-1.
797.73 GV1507.C7

Based on Random House dictionary files, this work provides an alphabetical list of terms, with synonyms, arranged according to the number of letters each term contains. Contains 700,000 clue and answer words, more than any other dictionary currently available. A useful and entertaining companion for both crossword puzzle and trivia buffs.

ETYMOLOGY AND WORD AND PHRASE ORIGINS

730 **The Barnhart dictionary of etymology.** Robert K. Barnhart, ed. 1284p. Wilson, 1988. $64. ISBN 0-8242-0745-9.
422 PE1580.B35

This is the most recent addition to the scholarly etymological dictionaries. It focuses on words used in contemporary American English and words of American origin and incorporates current American scholarship. Entries give spelling variations, pronunciation for difficult words, part of speech, definition, and information on word origins. Written for a wide audience, this is a very attractive, readable work suited for most library users.

731 **A comprehensive etymological dictionary of the English language: dealing with the origin of words and their sense development thus illustrating the history of civilization and culture.** Ernest Klein. 844p. Elsevier, 1971. $194. ISBN 0-444-40930-0.
422 PE1850.K47

A one-volume reprint of the original two-volume work published in 1966–67, this etymological dictionary covers more than 44,000 terms drawn from science, literature, the arts, technology, mythology, and history. It also includes the etymologies of numerous proper names. Although superseded in part by more recent works, Klein's dictionary remains a basic source of information on the origin of words.

732 **The Facts on File encyclopedia of word and phrase origins.** Rev. ed. Robert Hendrickson. 800p. Facts on File, 1997. $65. ISBN 0-8160-3226-1.
422 PE1689.H47

A popular comprehensive etymological dictionary covering some 9,000 words and phrases. Written in a nonacademic style, this work will appeal to the general reader curious about the origins of words or expressions used in everyday speech.

733 **Morris dictionary of word and phrase origins.** 2d ed. William Morris and Mary Morris. 669p. HarperCollins, 1988.

$37.50. ISBN 0-06-015862-X.
422.03 PE1580.M6

This edition traces the origins of several thousand words and phrases commonly used in the English language, including slang terms and clichés not usually found in more formal works. Entries are listed alphabetically by the first word in the phrase, with an index at the end.

734 Oxford dictionary of English etymology. C. T. Onions et al., eds. 1024p. Oxford Univ. Pr., 1992, c1966. $65. ISBN 0-19-861112-9.
422 PE1580.O5

Authoritative work tracing the history of common English words back to their Indo-European roots. The most complete and reliable etymological dictionary ever published, it serves as a complement to the *OED*. Also available in an abridged edition, *The concise Oxford dictionary of English etymology* (T. F. Hoad, ed. 522p. Oxford Univ. Pr., 1986. $24.95. ISBN 0-19-861182-X).

FOREIGN WORDS AND PHRASES USED IN THE ENGLISH LANGUAGE

735 Dictionary of foreign phrases and abbreviations. 3d ed. Kevin Guinagh, trans. and comp. 261p. Wilson, 1983. $44. ISBN 0-8242-0675-4.
422.4 PE1670.G8

Completely revised and updated, the third edition of this standard work contains more than 5,000 foreign phrases, proverbs, and abbreviations frequently used in written and spoken English. Provides translations and pronunciations, and for some entries brief explanatory notes; includes a list of phrases by languages.

736 The Harper dictionary of foreign terms: based on the original edition by C. O. Sylvester Mawson. 3d ed. Eugene Ehrlich, ed. 423p. HarperCollins, 1987. $20. ISBN 0-06-181576-4; paper $10.95. ISBN 0-06-091686-9.
422.4 PE1670.M3

A second revision of C. O. Sylvester Mawson's *Dictionary of foreign terms*, first published in 1934. Covers some 15,000 foreign words, phrases, and quotations from more than fifty languages, including Swahili, American Indian, ancient Greek, and modern Russian. Entries include foreign terms, plural and feminine forms as needed, and definitions. Authoritative, up-to-date, broad coverage.

737 Oxford dictionary of foreign words and phrases. Jennifer Speake. 512p. Oxford Univ. Pr., 1997. $30. ISBN 0-19-863159-6.
422.4 PE1582.A3

Covers more than 8,000 foreign words and phrases used in English today.

IDIOMS AND USAGE DICTIONARIES

738 American Heritage dictionary of idioms. Christine Ammer. 736p. Houghton, 1997. $30. ISBN 0-395-72774-X.
423.1 PE2839.A47

Includes nearly 10,000 figures of speech, phrases, clichés, and colloquialisms; for each entry there is a clear definition, an example of use, and an indication of historical origin. The most comprehensive and authoritative work currently available.

739 Columbia guide to standard American English. Kenneth G. Wilson. 482p. Columbia Univ. Pr., 1993. $31.50. ISBN 0-231-06988-X; paper $16.95. ISBN 0-231-06989-8.
428.0097 PE2835.W55

A superb addition to our English-language usage tools by one who, without being overly prescriptive, still advocates linguistic good manners. Wilson presents 6,500 entries, primarily American expressions, explaining appropriate uses, pointing out some of the finer nuances between words (e.g., *naked* and *nude*), clearly differentiating troublesome pairs (such as *disinterested* and *uninterested*), and generally setting the record straight in a delightful, easy, and familiar style. Essential for all.

740 A dictionary of American idioms. 3d ed. Rev. by Adam Makkai. 355p. Barron, 1995. Paper $12.95. ISBN 0-8120-1248-8.
423.1 PE2839.M34

This new edition, based on the 1975 publication edited by M. T. Boatner et al., lists more than 5,000 idioms used in contemporary American speech. Gives definitions, an illustrative sentence, and, in some cases, usage notes and etymology. Of particular interest to ESL students.

741 Dictionary of bias-free usage: a guide to nondiscriminatory language. Rosalie Maggio. 293p. Oryx, 1991. $25. ISBN 0-89774-653-8.
428 PE1460.M26

A practical guide for avoiding discriminatory words and word constructions in both speech and writing. Some 5,000 sex- and gender-specific words and phrases are considered, and effective, literate alternatives are clearly presented. Both a useful book and a consciousness raiser.

742 New Fowler's modern English usage. 3d ed. R. W. Burchfield, ed. 864p. Clarendon Pr., 1996. $25. ISBN 0-19-869126-2.
428.2 PE1628.F65

A modern version of a classic first published in 1926. Fowler's original work, revised by Gowers in 1965, has again been revised for a new generation of English speakers. Burchfield, a distinguished lexicographer, has in fact produced a totally new work, adding numerous entries that discuss recent foibles and perversities of usage. Provides comprehensive and clear advice on the correct use of the complex communication tool we call the English language. Libraries owning the earlier editions will want to obtain this one as well.

PRONUNCIATION DICTIONARIES

743 NBC handbook of pronunciation. 4th ed. Rev. and updated by Eugene Ehrlich and Raymond Hand Jr. 539p. HarperCollins, 1991. $15.95. ISBN 0-06-273056-8; paper $10.95. ISBN 0-06-096574-6.
423 PE1137.E52

A standard pronunciation reference tool originally compiled by James F. Bender. Listings for each of the 21,000 entries provide spelling and a simplified phonetic respelling to indicate proper pronunciation. Covers words frequently mispronounced or difficult to pronounce, plus numerous geographical and personal names.

744 Pronouncing dictionary of proper names. 2d ed. John K. Bollard, ed. 1097p. Omnigraphics, 1998. $80. ISBN 0-7808-0098-2.
423 PE1137.P82

Presents the proper pronunciation for more than 23,000 proper names. Each entry includes an identification or definition of the proper name entry and two representations of its pronunciation: the first is based on a simplified respelling and the second on the symbols and conventions of the International Phonetic Alphabet. This is the most comprehensive pronunciation dictionary currently available.

RHYMING DICTIONARIES

745 The complete rhyming dictionary and poet's craft book. Clement Wood. Rev. by Ronald Bogus. 627p. Doubleday, 1991. $25. ISBN 0-385-41350-5.
808.1 PE1519.W6

An expanded and updated edition of the classic 1936 rhyming dictionary. Authoritative and comprehensive, with more than 60,000 entries, including one-, two-, and three-syllable rhymes.

746 New comprehensive American rhyming dictionary. Sue Young. 622p. Avon, 1991. Paper $24.95. ISBN 0-688-10360-X.
423.1 PE1519.Y68

Compiled by a linguistics expert, this rhyming dictionary is arranged by word sound rather than by alphabetical order. Includes phrases and slang words. Contains 65,000 entries.

747 Words to rhyme with: for poets and song writers. Willard R. Espy. 656p. Facts on File, 1986. $55. ISBN 0-8160-1237-7.
423.1 PE1519.E87

"Including a primer of prosody; a list of more than 80,000 words that rhyme; a glossary defining 9,000 of the more eccentric rhyming words; and a variety of exemplary verses, one of which does not rhyme at all." The most comprehensive of the rhyming dictionaries.

SIGN LANGUAGE DICTIONARIES

748 American sign language: a comprehensive dictionary. Martin L. A. Sternberg. 1132p. HarperCollins, 1981. $49.50. ISBN 0-06-014097-6.
419.03 HB2475.S77

An excellent guide to American sign language; contains some 5,000 alphabetically arranged entries, each providing a pronunciation guide, grammatical notes, and a description and illustration of the appropriate sign and its formation. Extensive bibliography with a subject index, and indexes for translating seven foreign languages into sign.

749 American sign language dictionary. Martin L. A. Sternberg and Herbert Rogoff. 640p. HarperPerennial, 1995. Paper $19. ISBN 0-06-273275-7.
■ cd
419 HV2475.S78

A revised and abridged version of the Sternberg classic. Together with the accompanying CD-ROM, this dictionary provides a history of each sign and clearly indicates what each sign is intended to depict and, hence, to mean.

750 Random House American sign language dictionary. Elaine Costello and Lois Lenderman. 1067p. Random House, 1994. $55. ISBN 0-394-58580-1.
419.03 HV2475.C66

A compendium of more than 5,600 words and signs, prepared by the director and editor in chief of Gallaudet University Press. Used as the primary communication vehicle by some 500,000 Americans, the American Sign Language is our fourth most commonly used language. This dictionary includes a detailed introduction to the language, which clearly explains its origins, its use, and its structure.

SIMILES, METAPHORS, AND CLICHÉS

751 Have a nice day—no problem! a dictionary of clichés. Christine Ammer. 454p. Dutton, 1992. $25. ISBN 0-525-93394-8.
423.1 PE1689.A48

This phrase dictionary traces the origins, explains the meanings, and illustrates the use of some 3,000 clichés commonly found in American English. A delightful and engaging work, not as scholarly, perhaps, as Eric Partridge's *Dictionary of clichés* (Routledge, 1978) but a good deal more detailed and more fun.

752 Metaphors dictionary. Elyse Sommer and Dorrie Weiss, eds. 833p. Gale, 1995. $65. ISBN 0-8103-9149-X.
081 PE1689.M47

A dictionary collection of some 6,500 metaphoric comparisons from ancient times to the present organized in 500 alphabetically arranged thematic sequences. Includes author and subject indexes and a bibliography of sources.

753 Similes dictionary. Elyse Sommer and Mike Sommer, eds. 950p. Gale, 1988. $75. ISBN 0-8103-4361-4.
808.8 PN6084.S5

More than 16,000 similes are arranged alphabetically under some 500 thematic categories. Authors of similes are given, but not sources. Covers a wide range of materials from classical literature to contemporary film and television. Author index.

SLANG AND EUPHEMISMS

754 Dictionary of American slang. Robert L. Chapman, ed. 624p. HarperCollins, 1998. $23.95. ISBN 0-06-270107-X.
427 PE2846.C46

A revised edition of a standard work, *Dictionary of American slang* (2d supplemented ed. Harold Wentworth and Stuart Berg Flexner, comps. and eds. 766p. Crowell, 1975). This new version includes many older slang expressions from the original work along with hundreds of new words from the last twenty years. Notations include pronunciations, appropriate classification and dating labels, illustrative phrases, and numerous cross-references.

755 Dictionary of euphemisms. R. W. Holder. 496p. Oxford Univ. Pr., 1996. $35. ISBN 0-19-869275-7; paper $13.95. ISBN 0-19-280051-5.
428.1 PE1449.H548

A straightforward *A-Z* listing and translation of common euphemisms. Entries are accurate and succinct. A separate thematic index directs the user to appropriate euphemisms for several of the most commonly avoided spades, such as death, obesity, and urination.

756 A dictionary of slang and unconventional English: colloquialisms and catch-phrases, solecisms and catachreses, nicknames, and vulgarisms. 8th ed. Eric Partridge. Paul Beale, ed. 1400p. Macmillan, 1984. $85. ISBN 0-02-594980-2.
427.09 PE3721.P3

The standard work on the subject, updated and enlarged, Partridge's is the most scholarly work on English slang but has relatively little American slang. Available in an abridged edition, *A concise dictionary of slang and unconventional English* (Paul Beale, ed. 534p. Macmillan, 1990. Paper $35. ISBN 0-02-605350-0).

757 Random House historical dictionary of American slang. 3v. Random House, 1994– . v.1, A-G. 1994. $55. ISBN 0-394-54427-7; v.2, H-O. 1997. $65. ISBN 0-679-43464-X; v.3, S-Z forthcoming.
427.973 PE2846.H57

A monumental work, scrupulously researched, this is the first historical dictionary to be devoted exclusively to American slang. Each entry is followed by a succinct definition and illustrative quotations that give life and form to the words. The quotations are drawn from both oral and written tradition and range in time from the seventeenth century to the present day. A complete list of the 8,000 sources cited in the dictionary will appear in volume 3 (still forthcoming as of this writing). This is a work of such substance that, given the price, it deserves to find a home in every major library in the nation.

758 Rawson's dictionary of euphemisms and other doubletalk: being a compilation of linguistic fig leaves and verbal flourishes for artful users of the English language. Hugh Rawson and Brand Aymar, eds. Rev. ed. 463p. Crown, 1995. $25. ISBN 0-517-70201-0.
428.1 PE1449.R34

Offers erudite definitions and usage histories of hundreds of common euphemisms, from *abattoir* to *zounds*. This is a true study of euphemism, providing significant quotations from literary works, political statements, and social commentary. The discursive entries are captivating, witty, and thought-provoking.

759 Slang and euphemism: a dictionary of oaths, curses, insults, sexual slang and metaphor, racial slurs, drug talk, homosexual lingo, and related matters. Richard A. Spears. 448p. Jonathan David, 1981. $24.95. ISBN 0-8246-0259-5; paper $12.95. ISBN 0-8246-0273-0.
427 PE3721.S67

Covering 17,500 terms and including 40,000 definitions, this work provides a record of usage of prohibited words and subjects among speakers of English since the beginnings of the language.

760 The thesaurus of slang: 150,000 uncensored contemporary slang terms, common idioms, and colloquialisms arranged for quick and easy reference. Rev. ed. Ester Lewin and Albert E. Lewin, eds. 464p. Facts on File, 1994. $50. ISBN 0-8160-2898-2.
427.09 PE3721.L45

This thesaurus works as a reverse dictionary for identifying contemporary slang terminology: that is, it translates the standard English into slang. Slang equivalents and colloquialisms are listed for some 12,500 "standard words." Find 200 slang terms for automobile or 62 expressions for coffee. For those who want to find a more colorful means of expression, or who merely "delight in the vigor of the vernacular," this is a splendid resource.

THESAURI: SYNONYMS, ANTONYMS, AND HOMONYMS

761 Homophones and homographs: an American dictionary. 2d ed. James B. Hobbs, comp. 302p. McFarland, 1993. $29.95. ISBN 0-89950-776-X.
423.1 PE2833.H63

An extensive list of 7,000 homophones and 1,500 homographs drawn primarily from *Webster's third*. Homophones are arranged in alphabetical sequence, followed by homographs. The most comprehensive work of its kind.

762 Merriam-Webster's collegiate thesaurus. 894p. Merriam-Webster, 1996. $17.95. ISBN 0-97779-169-4.
423.1 PE1591.W38

Webster's includes more than 130,000 synonyms, related words, idioms, contrasted words, and antonyms among its 25,000 main entries. Alphabetically arranged, entries provide a brief definition, a list of synonyms, a list of related terms, and a list of contrasted terms and antonyms. An illustrative sentence is provided if further explanation is deemed necessary. Authoritative, current, and easy to use.

763 Merriam-Webster's dictionary of synonyms. 944p. Merriam-Webster, 1996. $21.95. ISBN 0-87779-341-7.
423.1 PE1591.M478

A model of a good synonym dictionary, *Webster's* carefully discriminates groups of similar words and provides more than 17,000 illustrative quotes from Merriam-Webster's large citation file. Antonyms and contrasted words are also listed. Alphabetically arranged with numerous cross-references.

764 Oxford thesaurus: American edition. Laurence Urdang. 1024p. Oxford Univ. Pr., 1992. $19.95. ISBN 0-19-507354-1.
423.1 PE2832.U7

The *Oxford thesaurus* is a remarkable achievement by one of America's premier lexicographers. It incorporates both the *A-Z* dictionary approach of modern thesauri with the comprehensive index of the traditional *Roget's*. The *Oxford* includes more than 275,000 synonyms, offering example sentences and other aids that guide the user to precise synonym choice.

765 The Random House college thesaurus. Jesse Stein and Stuart Berg Flexner, eds. Rev. by Fraser Sutherland. 792p. Random House, 1997. Thumb-indexed $14.95. ISBN 0-679-45280-X.
423.1 PE1591.R314

Based on the *Reader's Digest family word finder* (Random House, 1975), this thesaurus consists of 11,000 main entries. Synonymic words are discriminated with sample sentences when necessary to clarify shades of meaning. Includes helpful usage notes and for many entries a list of antonyms. The alphabetical arrangement of words makes this a quick and easy-to-use resource.

766 Random House word menu. Rev. ed. Stephen Glazier. 767p. Random House, 1997. $22. ISBN 0-679-44963-9.
423.1 PE1680.G58

Classifies some 65,000 words into relevant categories and subcategories. Though unclassifiable itself, the *Word menu* can be used by anyone seeking to find related terms, equivalent terms, or just interesting words that are common to certain fields of endeavor. Anyone who crafts with words or who loves words will find this work a longtime companion.

767 Roget's international thesaurus. 5th ed. Rev. by Robert L. Chapman. 1141p. HarperCollins, 1992. $18.95 ISBN 006-270014-6.
423.1 PE1591.R73

Thoroughly revised and updated, the fifth edition reflects contemporary vocabulary, including slang, technical terms, and idiomatic expressions. A true thesaurus based on the principles of Peter Mark Roget, it is arranged topically with an alphabetical index to the 300,000 entries. Within each section, words are grouped by part of speech in the following order: nouns, verb, adjectives, adverbs, prepositions, conjunctions, and interjections. Most important or commonly used terms are indicated by boldface type.

768 Roget's II: the new thesaurus. 3d ed. Peter Strupp, ed. 1280p. Houghton, 1995. $20. ISBN 0-395-68722-5.
423.1 PE1591.R715

The new, accessible format of *Roget's II* makes it an attractive addition for ready reference collections. Main entries with synonym lists are arranged alphabetically and are followed by indented subentries of related words. Variations in meaning are differentiated, with appropriate synonyms designated for each meaning. Cross-references and various guide labels are provided as needed.

Style Manuals

769 American Medical Association manual of style: a guide for authors and editors. 9th ed. Cheryl Iverson, ed. 660p. Williams & Wilkins, 1998. $35.95. ISBN 0-683-40206-4.
808 R119.A533

To promote "clarity, organization, and style," the principal AMA publications editors have prepared these guidelines for authors and editors engaged in writing and preparing articles for publication in the medical field. From style, usage, and nomenclature to advice on grammar and nonsexist language, the manual is vigilant in promoting clear, readable, reliable, and authoritative writing.

770 Associated Press stylebook and libel manual: including guidelines on photo captions, filing the wire, proofreaders' marks, copyright. Fully rev. and updated ed. Norm Goldstein, ed. Addison-Wesley, 1998. $15. ISBN 0-201-33985-4.
808.02 PN4783

Called the "journalist's bible," the *AP stylebook* is a dictionary, handbook, and style guide, all in one. The 5,000 alphabetically arranged entries lay out the AP rules on grammar, spelling, punctuation, and usage. This edition includes practical advice on libel and copyright.

771 The bluebook: a uniform system of citation. Harvard Law Review. Irreg. (16th ed. 1996, $9.) ISSN 1062-9971.
348.73 KF245

Bieber's dictionary of legal citations: reference guide for attorneys, legal secretaries, paralegals, and law students. 5th ed. Mary Miles Prince. 368p. W. S. Hein & Co., 1997. $39.50. ISBN 1-57588-285-X.
340.01 KF246

The bluebook is compiled by the editors of the *Harvard law review* in conjunction with the editors of the *Columbia law review*, the *University of Pennsylvania law review*, and the *Yale law review* and serves as the standard source for style formats in U.S. law journals. *Bieber's dictionary* is a companion to *The bluebook* and is meant to serve as a helpful interpretive tool when using that source. In this edition, for the first time, an exact reproduction of *The bluebook* is appended.

772 The Chicago manual of style. 14th ed. 921p. Univ. of Chicago Pr., 1993. $28. ISBN 0-226-10389-7.
808 Z253.U69

The fourteenth edition of this standard style manual reflects the latest technological developments, discusses the new copyright laws, and provides more sample citations of footnotes and bibliographic entries and more guidance on the basics of style, including proper pronunciation, quotation, and abbreviation. A basic "how-to" for authors and editors. Glossary of technical terms, bibliography, index.

773 Columbia guide to online style. Janice Walker and Todd Tyler. 256p. Columbia Univ. Pr., 1998. $35. ISBN 0-231-10788-9; paper $17.50. ISBN 0-231-10789-7.
808 PN171.F56

Provides rules for electronic citation, guidelines for formatting documents for online publication, and tips on preparing texts electronically for print publication.

774 Electronic styles: a handbook for citing electronic information. 2d ed. Xia Li and Nancy B. Crane. 213p. Information Today, 1996. Paper $19.99. ISBN 1-57387-027-7.
808 PN171.F56L5

This is a revised edition of the well-received *Electronic style,* which appeared in 1993, a lone voice seeking to guide us through the wilderness of the uncharted virtual landscape. Taking on the brave new world of electronic communication, the authors have helped to bring order out of chaos and to promote rational, pragmatic, and reliable citation models. Taking into account both APA and MLA style formats, the authors propose how to cite full-text information files, bibliographic databases, e-journals, discussion lists, e-mail, online documents, and web sites.

775 A manual for writers of term papers, theses, and dissertations. 6th ed. Kate L. Turabian. Rev. and expanded by John Grossman and Alice Bennet. 308p. Univ. of Chicago Pr., 1996. $27.50. ISBN 0-226-81626-5; paper $12.95. ISBN 0-226-81627-3.
808.02 LB2369.T8

The standard guide for students preparing formal papers, including term papers, theses, and dissertations, in both scientific and nonscientific fields. This edition reflects a trend toward simplification of documentation.

776 MLA handbook for writers of research papers. 4th ed. Joseph Gibaldi. 293p. Modern Language Assn., 1995. Paper $9.95. ISBN 0-87352-565-5.
808.02 LB2369.G53

Based on the 1951 *MLA style sheet* as revised in 1970, 1977, and 1988, this handbook contains style rules covering such matters as abbreviations, footnotes, and bibliographies. In addition it discusses such issues as how to choose a term paper topic, how to make effective use of the library, and articulates a process for composing the research paper. A new edition is scheduled for May 1999.

777 New York Public Library writer's guide to style and usage. 838p. HarperCollins, 1994. $35. ISBN 0-06-270064-2.
808 PE1421.N46

The most recent addition to the style and usage guide collection, this work is the first comprehensive guide to fully incorporate the world of electronic publishing. Within this context, it offers advice on everything from current usage, grammar, and style to manuscript construction and preparation. In contrast to the *Chicago manual,* which seeks to set the professional and academic standard, this volume addresses a general audience of everyday writers seeking reliable advice and practical guidelines.

778 Publication manual of the American Psychological Association. 4th ed. 368p. American Psychological Assn., 1994. $31.95. ISBN 1-55798-243-0; paper $21.95. ISBN 1-55798-241-4.
808 BF76.7

The standard style manual used in the social and behavioral sciences, this edition refines and reorganizes parts of the third edition (1983) and presents new material. Includes more examples as well as a more detailed index.

779 Scientific style and format: the CBE manual for authors, editors, and publishers. 6th ed. Style manual committee, Council of Biology Editors. 825p. Cambridge Univ. Pr., 1994. $39.95. ISBN 0-521-47154-0.
808 T11.S386

General guidance on writing and publishing scientific articles, with detailed sections on style in special fields.

Foreign-Language Dictionaries

Bibliographies and Guides

780 A guide to foreign language courses and dictionaries. 3d ed., rev. and enl. A. J. Walford and J. E. O. Screen, eds. 343p. Greenwood, 1977. $29.95. ISBN 0-313-20100-5.
418 P207.W3

Currently in need of revision, but still in print, this practical guide covers most of the major European languages, plus Arabic, Chinese, and Japanese. Intended for teachers, students, graduates taking up a language for the first time, scientists needing to acquire a reading knowledge of a language, tourists, businesspeople, and librarians. The book is arranged into sections by type and level of user, with the most strongly recommended item listed first in each section.

781 Guide to world language dictionaries. Arnold Dalby, ed. 500p. Fitzroy Dearborn, 1998. $95. ISBN 1-57958-069-6.
413.03 P361

This new work appraises the main general dictionaries of the world's 275 written languages. Organized in alphabetical order by language, it also includes a history of dictionaries and an explanation of the International Phonetic Alphabet.

Chinese

782 A new English-Chinese dictionary. Rev. ed. The Editing Group of A new English-Chinese dictionary. 1769p. Univ. of Washington Pr., 1988. $19.95. ISBN 0-295-96609-2.
495.1 PL1455.N49

A comprehensive dictionary compiled by a group of seventy Chinese scholars. Defines more than 80,000 words, including basic vocabulary, general terms, scientific and technical terms, abbreviations and contractions, foreign words, and geographic names. Contains a supplement of 4,000 new or revised words, plus nine appendixes.

783 A new English-Chinese dictionary. 2d rev. ed. Zheng Yi Li et al., eds. 1613p. Wiley, 1984. $125. ISBN 0-471-80896-2; paper $42.50. ISBN 0-471-80897-0.
495.1 PL1455.N4

An authoritative dictionary with more than 120,000 entries, this is the largest English language dictionary ever to be produced in the People's Republic of China. It is intended for Chinese readers or Chinese students learning English. Recommended for communities serving Chinese speakers or advanced ESL students.

784 The pinyin Chinese-English dictionary. Beijing Foreign Languages Institute. Wu Jingrong, ed. 976p. Wiley, 1982. $99.95. ISBN 0-471-27557-3; paper $59.95. ISBN 0-471-86796-9.
495.1 PL1455.H338

An outstanding desk dictionary compiled by a staff of more than fifty Chinese and English linguistic specialists. More than 125,000 entries divided into single and compound character entries. Reflects the more straightforward presentation of Chinese characters adopted by the pinyin system of English transliteration.

French

785 Cassell's French dictionary: French-English; English-French. Denis Girard et al., eds. 1440p. Macmillan, 1977. $21.95. ISBN 0-02-522610-X; thumb-indexed $24.95. ISBN 0-02-522620-7.
443 PC2640

Popular, reliable, and inexpensive, this work includes French-Canadianisms, phonetic pronunciation, and handy appendixes. Thoroughly revised.

786 Collins-Robert French-English, English-French dictionary. 3d ed. Beryl T. Atkins et al. 1848p. Collins, 1993. $50. ISBN 0-7859-7396-6.
443 PC2640.C688

Collaborative effort of the Collins staff with Paul Robert and the Société Nouveau Littré. Designed to meet the needs of students, teachers, businesspeople, and the general reader. Includes about 280,000 headwords and compounds, and approximately the same number of phrases and idioms in current usage, providing 490,000 translations in all.

787 Grand dictionnaire francais-anglais, anglais-francais/Larousse French-English, English-French dictionary. Faye Carney and Claude Nimmo, eds. 2064p. Larousse, 1993. $45.

ISBN 2-03-420100-0.
443 PC2640.L3

An excellent standard dictionary with more than 300,000 references and 500,000 translations. Definitions are detailed and usage examples are provided for key entries. Includes maps and geographical information.

788 Harrap's new standard French and English dictionary. J. E. Mansion, ed. Rev. and ed. by R. P. L. Ledésert and Margaret Ledésert. 4v. Harrap, 1972–80. $250/set. ISBN 0-317-62983-2.
443 PC2640.H317

A monumental work, exceptionally thorough, reliable, and accurate, indispensable to student and specialist alike. Uses International Phonetic Alphabet. Also available in a condensed one-volume edition, *Harrap's shorter French and English dictionary* (798p. Harrap, 1982. $64.75. ISBN 0-245-53926-3).

789 Oxford-Hachette French dictionary. 2d ed. Marie-Helene Correard and Valerie Grundy, eds. 1943p. Oxford Univ. Pr., 1994. $45. ISBN 0-19-864519-8.
■ cd
443 PC2640.O83

With more than 350,000 entries and 530,000 translations, this is a superb one-volume dictionary. Usage examples are drawn from the everyday world of newspapers and advertising. Includes an encyclopedic supplement with information on French history and culture.

German

790 Cassell's German-English, English-German dictionary. New rev. ed. Harold T. Betteridge, comp. 1580p. Macmillan, 1978. $21.95. ISBN 0-02-522920-6; thumb-indexed $23.95. ISBN 0-02-522930-3.
443 PF3640.B45

Consistent with quality of other Cassell dictionaries. Adequate reference for most public libraries. Enlarged typography and additional current terms in this edition.

791 Collins German-English, English-German dictionary. 3d ed. Peter Terrell, ed. 1728p. HarperCollins, 1997. $55. ISBN 0-06-270199-1.
433 PF3640.C68

An excellent one-volume contemporary German-English bilingual dictionary. More than 280,000 headwords.

792 Langenscheidt's new college German dictionary: German-English, English-German. Sonia Brough and Heinz Messinger, eds. 1515p. Langenscheidt, 1995. $29.95. ISBN 0-88729-028-3; thumb-indexed $34.95. ISBN 0-88729-019-1.
433.2 PF3640.L25

A collegiate bilingual dictionary aimed at the American market.

793 Langenscheidt's new Muret-Sanders encyclopedic dictionary of the English and German languages: based on the original work by E. Muret and D. Sanders. Otto Springer, ed. 2 pts. in 4v. Langenscheidt, 1962–75. $110/v. ISBN 3-468-01120-2.
433.2 PF3640.L257

The largest completed German and English dictionary. The German-English section of some 200,000 headwords is particularly valuable. Treats contemporary vocabulary and has useful appendixes, including abbreviations, biographies, gazetteer, and table of mathematical equivalents. More encyclopedic than *Oxford-Harrap* and better for specialized vocabulary. Also available in a one-volume condensation as *Langenscheidt's condensed Muret-Sanders German dictionary: German-English* (Heinz Messinger and the Langenscheidt editorial staff. 1296p. Langenscheidt, 1982. $74.95. ISBN 3-468-02125-9).

794 Oxford-Duden German dictionary: German-English, English-German. W. Scholze-Stubenrecht and J. B. Sykes, eds. 1696p. Oxford Univ. Pr., 1990. Thumb-indexed $45. ISBN 0-19-864171-0.
■ cd
433.2 PF3640.O94

A collaborative effort between two of the foremost dictionary publishers. More than 260,000 words and phrases and more than 450,000 translations.

795 The Oxford-Harrap standard German-English dictionary. Trevor Jones, ed. v.1– . Oxford Univ. Pr., 1977– . Part 1: German-English. v.1, A-E. $84. ISBN 0-19-864129-X; v.2, F-K. $84. ISBN 0-19-864130-3; v.3, L-R. $84. ISBN 0-19-864131-1; v.4, in progress.
433.2 PF3640.H3

Published in 1963 under the title *Harrap's standard German and English dictionary.* At present, covers German-English, *A* to *R*, in three volumes. Includes both general and specialized terms, many idioms, proverbs, and colloquialisms, including Swiss and Austrian forms. Outstanding for clear typography and fullness of context quotations. English-German volumes also planned. An important larger work.

Greek

796 Greek-English lexicon. 9th ed. Henry G. Liddell and Robert Scott, eds. 2111p. Oxford Univ. Pr., 1940. $89. ISBN 0-19-864214-8.

Greek-English lexicon: a supplement. Rev. ed. P. G.W. Glare, ed. 320p. Oxford Univ. Pr., 1996. $49.95. ISBN 0-19-864223-7.

Greek-English lexicon. 9th ed. with rev. supplement. Henry G. Liddell et al. 2446p. Oxford Univ. Pr., 1996. $125. ISBN 0-19-864226-1.
483 PA445.E5L6

Frequently reprinted (a 1996 printing is now available with the 1996 revised supplement bound in), this is the standard Greek and English lexicon, covering the language to about A.D. 600, omitting Patristic and Byzantine Greek.

797 Oxford dictionary of modern Greek: Greek-English, English-Greek. J. T. Pring, ed. 370p. Oxford Univ. Pr., 1986. Paper $13.95. ISBN 0-19-864148-6.
489.3 PA1139.E5

Concise, accurate, inexpensive dictionary. Includes about 20,000 words, emphasizing modern conversational and written Greek.

Hebrew

798 Webster's new world Hebrew dictionary. Hayim Baltsan, ed. 827p. Macmillan, 1994. $35. ISBN 0-13-944547-1; paper $18. ISBN 0-671-88991-5.
492.4 PJ4833.B26

A bilingual dictionary that presents transliterated Hebrew words in Latin alphabetical order. Entries include definition, usage, and proper Hebrew spelling.

Italian

799 Cambridge Italian dictionary. Barbara Reynolds, ed. 2v. Cambridge Univ. Pr., 1962–81. $180/set. ISBN 0-521-06059-1.
453 PC1640.R4

Provides word equivalents rather than definitions, emphasizing usage and idiom. Gives proper names, Tuscan words, technical terms, colloquialisms, contemporary and obsolete words, with a good representation of specialties such as economics, sociology, and philosophy. Also available in a one-volume condensation, *The concise Cambridge Italian dictionary* (1975. $44.50. ISBN 0-521-07273-5), with the same compiler and publisher.

800 Collins English-Italian, Italian-English dictionary. Vladmiro Macchi, ed. 2277p. HarperCollins, 1998. $29.95. ISBN 0-06-017803-5.
453.21 PC1640.I5

More than 240,000 entries and 500,000 translations. Clear and easy to use. Helpful appendixes. An excellent purchase.

Japanese

801 Kenkyusha's new Japanese-English dictionary. 4th ed. Koh Masuda, ed. 2110p. Kenkyusha, 1974. $195. ISBN 0-317-59317-X.
495.6 PL697.K4

Kenkyusha's new English-Japanese dictionary. 5th ed. Yoshio Koine, ed. 2477p. Kenkyusha, 1980. $250. ISBN 0-8288-1013-3.
495.6 PL679.K39

The fullest Japanese-English and English-Japanese dictionaries; romanized Japanese entries are alphabetized in transliterated form, followed by Japanese characters and their English equivalents.

802 Kodansha's romanized Japanese-English dictionary. Masatoshi Yoshida. 640p. Kodansha America, 1993. Paper $28. ISBN 4-7700-1603-4.
495.6 PL679.V36

More than 16,000 entries, followed by actual examples using both romanized and Japanese scripts, and then their English translations. Useful appendixes aid in understanding Japanese grammar, numbers, and numerals.

803 The modern reader's Japanese-English character dictionary. 2d rev. ed. Andrew N. Nelson. 1109p. C. E. Tuttle, 1966. $47.50. ISBN 0-8048-0408-7.
495.6 PL679.N4

Indispensable for English-speaking students of Japanese until they are able to use Japanese words. Based on the Radical Priority System; presents 4,775 characters and 671 variants for a total of 5,446 numbered entries plus cross-references. Covers current and common usage as well as older words still encountered in modern literature.

Latin

804 Cassell's Latin dictionary: Latin-English, English-Latin. D. P. Simpson, ed. 883p. Macmillan, 1977. Thumb-indexed $24.95. ISBN 0-02-522580-4.
473 PA2365.E5

An authoritative and durable favorite, first published in 1854. Frequently revised. First part is designed to assist the reader, second part the writer of Latin.

805 Oxford Latin dictionary. P. G.W. Glare, ed. 2126p. Oxford Univ. Pr., 1982. $195. ISBN 0-19-864224-5.
473.21 PA2365.E5O9

Originally published in eight fascicles between 1968 and 1982; available for the first time as a single bound volume in 1983. Based on fifty years of scholarship and an entirely fresh reading of original Latin sources, this comprehensive and authoritative dictionary follows the principles of the *OED*. Covers classical Latin from the earliest recorded words to the end of the second century A.D. with entries for approximately 40,000 words based on a collection of more than one million quotations. Includes proper names and major Latin suffixes. Definitions provided in modern English. Quotes appear chronologically within each entry, showing whenever possible the earliest known instance of a particular usage. The standard work.

Russian

806 English-Russian, Russian-English dictionary. Kenneth Katzner. 904p. Wiley, 1984. $86.95. ISBN 0-471-86763-2; paper $27.95. ISBN 0-471-84442-X.
491.73 PG2640.K34

A one-volume bilingual dictionary compiled and published in the United States for English speakers. Gives parts of speech, grammar, usage, synonyms, colloquial and idiomatic expressions, and a glossary of geographical and personal names.

807 Oxford Russian dictionary. Rev. ed. Russian-English: Marcus Wheeler and Boris Unbegaun, eds; English-Russian: Paula Falla and Colin Howlett, eds. Oxford Univ. Pr., 1997. $55. ISBN 0-19-860153-0.
491.73 PG2640.W5

An excellent, up-to-date, comprehensive, one-volume bilingual dictionary compiled and published in the United Kingdom for English speakers.

Spanish

808 The American Heritage Larousse Spanish dictionary: Spanish/English, English/Spanish. 1152p. Houghton, 1986. $21.95. ISBN 0-395-32429-7.
463.21 PC4640.A54

This bilingual dictionary, based on *The American Heritage dictionary* and the *Pequeño Larousse ilustrado,* covers Latin American usage as well as Iberian Spanish. Useful features include grammar and usage notes, irregular verbs, abbreviations, pronunciation guides, and synonyms to distinguish meanings.

809 Collins Spanish-English, English-Spanish dictionary. Colin Smith et al., eds. 1684p. HarperCollins, 1993. $50. ISBN 0-06-275510-2.
463.21 PC4640.S595

A current and reliable bilingual dictionary. Presents more than 230,000 entries and 440,000 translations. Includes regional and slang usage. Differentiates between European and American Spanish pronunciation.

810 Larousse Spanish-English, English-Spanish dictionary. Ramon Garcia-Pelayo y Gross, ed. 804p. Larousse, 1993. $40. ISBN 2-03-420200-7.
463.21 PC4640.G73

More than 220,000 entries and 400,000 translations. Covers grammar extensively, and includes color atlases with both Spanish and English names. Up-to-date literary, political, and technical terms are included.

811 The new world Spanish/English, English/Spanish dictionary. 2d ed. Salvatore Ramondino, ed. 1296p. Penguin, 1997. Paper $24.95. ISBN 0-670-86962-7.
■ cd
463.21 PC4640.N4

This dictionary focuses upon usage in the Western Hemisphere, for both the English and the Spanish lexicography. The aim is to concentrate the word selection on the most important words currently in use and to prepare definitions based upon descriptive, as opposed to prescriptive, principles. An up-to-date and practical bilingual dictionary.

812 Oxford Spanish dictionary: Spanish-English, English-Spanish. Beatriz Jarman and Roy Russell, eds. 1920p. Oxford Univ. Pr., 1994. Thumb-indexed $45. ISBN 0-19-864503-1.
463.21 PC4640.O94

A standard, comprehensive single-volume bilingual dictionary. More than 275,000 words and phrases; more than 450,000 translations.

813 The University of Chicago Spanish dictionary. 4th ed. Carlos Castillo et al. Rev. and enl. by D. Lincoln Canfield. 476p. Univ. of Chicago Pr., 1987. $19.95. ISBN 0-226-10400-1; paper $6.95. ISBN 0-226-10402-8.
463.21 PC4640.U5

"A concise Spanish-English and English-Spanish dictionary of words and phrases basic to the written and spoken languages of today, plus a list of 500 Spanish idioms and sayings, with variants and English equivalents." Compiled for the American learner of Spanish and the Spanish American learner of English. Emphasizes usage found in the United States and Spanish America and includes some 15,000 entries in each part, plus pronunciation, parts of speech, grammar guide, and a list of idioms and proverbs.

11

Science and Technology

JACK O'GORMAN

There are many exciting new titles in science and technology, particularly in the areas of environmental awareness, global weather patterns, emerging technologies, and the Internet. Included here are key reference works in astronomy, chemistry, computer science, engineering, environment, life sciences, manufacturing, mathematics, physics, and weapons that were specifically chosen as suitable for the budgets of small and medium-sized public and academic libraries.

General

Bibliographies and Guides

814 Information sources in science and technology. 2d ed. C. D. Hurt. 450p. Libraries Unlimited, 1997. $55. ISBN 1-56308-528-3.
■ disk
016.5 Q158.5

This bibliography covers information sources in eighteen major scientific disciplines, providing generally short and primarily descriptive annotations along with recommendations as to audience. The second edition is reorganized by broad subject areas; computer science now is included as a separate discipline. Internet resources have been included, but it is difficult to keep up with this rapidly changing area. Author, title, and subject indexes.

815 Journal literature of the physical sciences: a manual. Alice Lefler Primack. 209p. Scarecrow, 1992. $29.50. ISBN 0-8108-2592-9.
500.2 Q158.5

The physical scientist is the audience for this guide to the literature. It describes the processes involved with the scientific journal, from indexes and databases to writing, refereeing, and copyright. Included is a list of core journals in physics, astronomy, chemistry, and earth sciences. The chapters on how to get the articles and how to publish a paper will be useful to scientists new to a field.

816 Reference sources in science, engineering, medicine, and agriculture. H. Robert Malinowsky, ed. 368p. Oryx, 1994. $49.95.

ISBN 0-89774-742-9; paper $47.25.
ISBN 0-89774-745-3.
026.6 Q158.5

Malinowsky is a well-known author in science and technology literature. This latest work is a bibliographic guide to 2,400 titles in science, engineering, medicine, and agriculture. Part 1 contains three short chapters on issues facing sci/tech librarians; part 2 is a selective bibliography in each discipline. This book will be useful for librarians doing collection development, library science students, and researchers looking for information in one of these fields.

Indexes and Abstracts

817 Applied science and technology index. Wilson, 1958– . Monthly except July. Quarterly cumulations; permanent bound annual cumulations. Volumes from 1980, service basis.
ISSN 0003-6986.
■ cd online tape
620.5 Z7913

A cumulative subject index to English-language periodicals in the fields of aeronautics and space science, computer technology and applications, chemistry, construction industry, energy resources and engineering, and so forth. Cumulative index with subject entries to periodical articles arranged in one alphabet with a separate listing of citations to book reviews.

818 General science index. Wilson, 1978– . Monthly except June and Dec. Quarterly cumulations and permanent bound annual cumulations. Service basis.
ISSN 0162-1963.
■ cd online tape
650 Q1.G4

Cumulative subject index to English-language science journals covering 150 essential periodicals. Its accessible subject headings, extremely broad coverage, and identification of articles on current topics in widely owned periodicals are helpful for high school and college students and public library patrons alike.

Dictionaries and Encyclopedias

819 Academic Press dictionary of science and technology. Christopher Morris, ed. 2432p. Academic Pr., 1992. $115.
ISBN 0-12-200400-0.
503 Q123

This title is the largest scientific dictionary in the English language, and English is the language of worldwide scientific discourse. With 133,007 entries contained in 2,432 pages, it defines most of the scientific terms a reader is likely to encounter. The 124 scientific fields included range from acoustical engineering to zoology. The entries include field of science, definition, cross-references, and occasional illustrations and color panels. This title is a comprehensive scientific dictionary.

820 Concise science dictionary. 3d ed. 800p. Oxford Univ. Pr., 1991. Paper $12.95. ISBN 0-19-280033-7.
503 Q123

The broad coverage of the chosen scientific disciplines makes this dictionary useful to public libraries and for undergraduates in college and university libraries. It contains about 7,000 definitions from the fields of physics, chemistry, biology, biochemistry, paleontology, and earth sciences. Also covered are common terms from astronomy, mathematics, computer technology, environmental science, and genetics. The entries are jargon free and contain cross-references.

821 The dictionary of science. Peter Lafferty and Julian Rowe, eds. 678p. Simon & Schuster, 1994. $45.
ISBN 0-13-304718-0.
503 Q123

The facts and figures of modern science for students and general readers alike. Along with 5,000 alphabetically arranged entries, it includes more than twenty chronologies and 400 diagrams. Should be in the collections of both large and small libraries.

822 A dictionary of scientific units: including dimensionless numbers and scales. 6th ed. H. G. Jerrard and D. B. McNeill. 255p. Chapman & Hall, 1992. $29.95. ISBN 0-412-46720-8.
530.8 QC82

Units form the backbone of scientific investigation. This dictionary defines temperature, time, mass, length, and electromagnetic forces and the units used to measure them. It includes metric or SI units, American (Imperial) units, and some unusual units, such as how many pennyweights in a Troy pound. The sixth edition includes more units, along with more precise definitions, and the most recently accepted values of physical constants.

823 Illustrated dictionary of science. Rev. ed. Michael Allaby, ed. 256p. Facts on File, 1995. $29.95. ISBN 0-8160-3253-X.
503 Q123

The language of science permeates our daily lives. To make sense of our world, we must come to grips with the terminology of matter, energy, substances, living things, medicine, the earth, and the stars. This dictionary can help the reader comprehend scientific terms in everyday use, from aa (lava) to zymase (enzyme found in yeast). Useful in public, school, and college libraries.

824 McGraw-Hill dictionary of scientific and technical terms. 5th ed. Sybil P. Parker, ed. in chief. McGraw-Hill, 1993. $110.50. ISBN 0-07-042333-4.
503.21 Q123

The fifth edition of this source is an outstanding dictionary in all areas of science. As in previous editions, each of the 122,000 entries identifies the field of science of the item and provides a nontechnical definition. This title provides authoritative and broad-ranging scientific information to students and the general public alike.

825 McGraw-Hill encyclopedia of science and technology: an international reference work in twenty volumes including index. 8th ed. McGraw-Hill, 1997. $1900. ISBN 0-07-911504-7.
■ cd
503 Q121

This encyclopedia is indispensable in answering scientific reference questions. In either print or multimedia format, it provides authoritative, clear information without being too technical. McGraw-Hill has produced other titles based upon this title in chemistry, astronomy, engineering, environmental science, and physics. Belongs in the reference collection of all libraries.

826 The new book of popular science. 6v. Grolier, 1996. $249. ISBN 0-7172-1219-X.
500 Q162

The wonder of the natural world is the subject of this six-volume set. It provides a logical, step-by-step presentation of astronomy, mathematics, earth sciences, energy, environmental and physical sciences, biology, plant life, animal life, mammals, humans, and technology. Essay-length articles with sidebars, a subject index, and plentiful photos and illustrations make this set visually attractive and easy to use. Suitable for school and public libraries.

827 The Raintree Steck-Vaughn illustrated science encyclopedia. 18v. Raintree Steck-Vaughn, 1996. $470. ISBN 0-8172-3800-X.
503 Q121

This encyclopedia can serve as an introduction to science for the young reader. Alphabetically arranged entries, subject index and cross-references, illustrations and photos, and a large-font text all create a very readable work. Some articles refer to projects that the young reader can do with minimal adult assistance. A useful addition to juvenile collections.

828 Van Nostrand's scientific encyclopedia. 8th ed. Douglas M. Considine and Glenn D. Considine, eds. 2v. 3632p. Van Nostrand Reinhold, 1995. $249.95. ISBN 0-442-01864-9.
■ cd
503 Q121

This eighth edition continues a long tradition as a comprehensive source of scientific and technical information. The editors have endeavored to keep pace with the rapidly expanding basis of scientific knowledge. Entries are arranged alphabetically by subject and cover earth sciences, life sciences, energy and the environment, materials science, physics, chemistry, and mathematics. Valuable for libraries of all sizes.

829 When technology fails: significant technological disasters, accidents, and failures of the twentieth century. Neil Schlager, ed. 659p. Gale, 1994. $59.95. ISBN 0-8103-8908-8.
363.1 TA169.5

A technological failure is often abrupt and deadly. This title chronicles the failures of aircraft, bridges, buildings, dams, spacecraft, and chemicals and nuclear disasters in the twentieth century. Each entry includes photographs or illustrations and a detailed explanation of how the disaster happened and its impact. A bibliography at the end of each entry guides the reader to more information about the calamity. Useful for college and public libraries.

830 World of invention. Bridget Travers and Jeffrey Muhr, eds. 770p. Gale, 1994. $75. ISBN 0-8103-8375-6.
608.7 T15

The number of inventions and their impact on modern life is staggering. This title includes 785 inventions entries and 361 biographical entries. The intended audience is the high school student and the general public. Although it covers ancient inventions, such as the wheel and axle, its focus is on inventions from the industrial revolution to the present. The entries are concise and informative but in a nontechnical style. The arrangement, extensive cross-references, and indexing make this title easy to use.

Handbooks, Yearbooks, and Almanacs

831 General information concerning patents: a brief introduction to patent matters. U.S. Department of the Interior, U.S. Patent and Trademark Office. Govt. Print. Off., 1922– . Annual. $4.95. S/N 003-004-00661-7. SuDoc C21.26/2.
608.7 T223

Contains a vast amount of general information on the application for and granting of patents expressed in nontechnical language for the layperson. Expressly intended for inventors, prospective applicants for patents, and students, this attempts to answer the most commonly asked questions about patents and the operation of the Patent and Trademark Office. Contains blank copies of patent application forms. A similar work, *General information concerning trademarks,* presents essentially the same material for trademarks. For all libraries.

832 Science and technology desk reference: 1,700 answers to frequently-asked or difficult-to-answer questions. 2d ed. The Carnegie Library of Pittsburgh Science and Technology Department staff. Gale, 1996. $45. ISBN 0-8103-8884-7.
500 Q173

Compiled from other reference sources, this title provides brief entries with some illustrations. It originated in the quick-reference file of the Science and Technology Department in the Carnegie Library in Pittsburgh. A one-volume sci/tech ready reference tool, useful for smaller libraries without extensive science collections.

Biographical Sources

833 American men and women of science: a biographical directory of today's leaders in physical, biological and related sciences. 20th ed. 8v. Bowker, 1906– . $900. ISSN 0000-1287.
■ cd online
509.2 Q141

Brief biographical sketches of about 124,000 scientists and engineers active in the United States and Canada. Arranged alphabetically, with discipline index using headings from the National Science Foundation's Standard Taxonomy of Degree and Employment Specialties. Useful in all libraries for biographical information of scientists.

834 American women in science: a biographical dictionary. Martha J. Bailey. 463p. ABC-Clio, 1994. $60. ISBN 0-87436-740-9.
509.2 Q141

The lives of 400 women scientists who began their careers before 1950 and made significant contributions to their fields are chronicled here. Each biography includes education, employment, bibliography, and a discussion of the scientist's life and contributions to science. This source can help locate information on people whose contributions have too often been overlooked.

835 The biographical dictionary of scientists. 2d ed. Roy Porter, ed. 960p. Oxford Univ. Pr., 1994. $85. ISBN 0-19-521083-2.
509.2 Q141

Presents the biographies of prominent historical and modern scientists alphabetically. The 1,200 biographies chronicle the scientific contributions and personal lives of these experimental and theoretical pioneers. A glossary of terms, a subject index, and appendixes of Nobel Prize winners round out this useful source.

836 Biographical encyclopedia of scientists. 2d ed. John Daintith et al., eds. 2v. 1100p. Institute of Physics, 1994. $190. ISBN 0-7503-0287-9.
509.2 Q141

Our accumulated scientific and technical knowledge is the result of contributions by scientists varying as widely as ancient Greeks, medieval Arabs, and modern astrophysicists and medical technologists. This encyclopedia contains 2,000 biographies of these contributors. Useful to students, scientists, and historians who need factual information on the lives and ideas of influential scientists.

837 Biographical index to American science: the seventeenth century to 1920. Clark A. Elliott, comp. 344p. Greenwood, 1990. $75. ISBN 0-313-26566-6.
509.2 Q141

This index, designed as a retrospective companion to *American men and women of science,* includes major entries for nearly 600 scientists not included in *AMWS* and minor entries for about 300 others who were included but reached prominence in their careers before 1900. A useful complement to the *Dictionary of scientific biography.*

838 Collins biographical dictionary of scientists. 4th ed. Trevor Williams, ed. 576p. HarperCollins, 1995. $40. ISBN 0-00-470109-7.
509.22 Q141

Details of more than 1,000 scientists from ancient Greece to the modern day. This edition adds 250 entries, including many living scientists, such as Stephen Hawking and Francis Crick. Subject index, timetable, and list of Nobel laureates.

839 Larousse dictionary of scientists. Hazel Muir, ed. 608p. Larousse, 1996. Paper $16.95. ISBN 0-7523-0036-9.
509 Q141

Details on the diverse backgrounds of scientists from the ancient world to the present day. The 2,200 entries cover physicists, biologists, astronomers, geologists, mathematicians, and many others, as well as all Nobel Prize winners. Arranged alphabetically by name. Concept index.

840 Who's who in technology. 7th ed. Amy Unterberger, ed. 1701p. Gale, 1995. $195. ISBN 0-8103-7467-6.
■ online
609.2 TA139

Biographies of about 40,000 men and women in technological and scientific fields in North America. Researchers are selected by their contributions to their fields, as evidenced by technical publications, patents awards, and positions of responsibility in businesses, universities, and research and development firms. Geographic index, employer index, technical discipline index, and expertise index help the reader locate the alphabetically arranged biographees.

841 Women in science: antiquity through the nineteenth century: a biographical dictionary with annotated bibliography. Marilyn Bailey Ogilvie. 254p. MIT Pr., 1986. Paper $14.95. ISBN 0-262-65038-X.
509.22 Q141

This work is primarily a biographical dictionary although it contains a lengthy introductory historical essay and a classified annotated bibliography. Alphabetically arranged sketches summarize the lives and contributions of 186 female scientists, many of whom are not covered in any other biographical dictionaries. An appendix covers twenty-six nineteenth-century women for whom only partial information was available; personal name index.

History of Science

842 Ancient inventions. Peter James and Nick Thorpe. 672p. Ballantine, 1994. $29.95. ISBN 0-345-36476-7.
609 T16

The ingenuity of the ancient world is chronicled in this source. Articles about clever machines, labor-saving devices, and feats of technology are organized thematically in medicine, communication, high-tech, city life, military, sports, transportation, and human sexuality sections. Written by a historian and an archaeologist, it focuses upon inventions up to 1492. This lively reference shows the antiquity of everyday objects and technologies.

843 Breakthroughs: a chronology of great achievements in science and mathematics, 1200–1930. Claire L. Parkinson. 576p. Hall, 1985. $40. ISBN 0-8161-8706-1.
509 Q125

Meant more for students and general readers than scholars, this chronological listing presents concise statements about events, accomplishments, discoveries, and achievements in the development of Western science. The name and subject indexes and the extensive cross-references allow easy tracking of trends in the development of specific subjects.

844 Dictionary of the history of science. William F. Bynum et al., eds. 528p. Princeton Univ. Pr., 1981. $75. ISBN 0-691-08287-1; paper $24.95. ISBN 0-691-02384-0.
509 Q125

Alphabetically arranged, more than 700 entries cover the origins, meaning, and significance of the chief theories and concepts in the development of science. Subjects of these entries include histories of medicine, mathematics, and the sciences. It has an emphasis on Western science over the last 500 years. Includes extensive cross-references, bibliographic references, and biographical index. Useful for undergraduate and public libraries.

845 Historical first patents: the first United States patent for many everyday things. Travis Brown. 224p. Scarecrow, 1994. $39.50. ISBN 0-8108-2898-7.
608.773 T223

This title presents the author's opinion of first U.S. patents for everyday technologies. Eighty-four entries cover such important inventions as the AC induction motor, FM radio, and frozen food. The impact of the technology, the patent process, the life of the inventor, and many illustrations from patent applications are included. Subject index and bibliography.

846 Instruments of science: an historical encyclopedia. Robert Bud and Deborah Jean Warner, eds. 709p. Garland, 1998. $150. ISBN 0-8253-1561-9.
502.8 Q184.5

A fascinating scholarly history of scientific instruments from the beginnings of science to the present day, with 327 entries, from "Abacus" to "X-ray Machine." Wonderfully illustrated. Signed articles, each with a bibliography for further study.

847 Milestones in science and technology: the ready reference guide to discoveries, inventions, and facts. 2d ed. Ellis Mount and Barbara A. List. 206p. Oryx, 1994. $34.50. ISBN 0-89774-671-6.
500 Q199

With significant updating and additions from the first edition, this title chronicles 1,250 important events in science and technology. The short entries provide summaries of the events and a recommended source for further reading. Frequent *see* and *see also* references, as well as extensive indexing, help guide the reader to the desired information.

848 Mothers of invention: from the bra to the bomb: forgotten women and their unforgettable ideas. Ethlie Ann Vare and Greg Ptacek. Quill, 1989. Paper $8.95. ISBN 0-688-08907-0.
609.2 T36

The subtitle of this source says it all. Sometimes the contributions of women inventors are not recognized. Includes short biographies and a discussion of the contribution women have made in DNA studies, stage lighting, and nuclear fission, to name a few examples. Subject index.

849 Oxford illustrated encyclopedia of invention and technology. Sir Monty Finniston, ed. 391p. Oxford Univ. Pr., 1992. $49.95. ISBN 0-19-869138-6.
603 T9

As part of the nine-volume set *Oxford illustrated encyclopedia,* this volume presents a broad conspectus of technology, with an international outlook. Alphabetically arranged entries range from 50 to 1,000 words focusing on technology and eminent technologists. Cross-references, color photos, and illustrations.

850 The timetables of technology: a chronology of the most important people and events in the history of technology. Bryan Bunch and Alexander Hellemans. 512p. Simon & Schuster, 1993. $35. ISBN 0-671-76918-9.
609 T15

A chronological time line of significant events in the history of technology, plus profiles of important figures and essays on key subjects and trends. With more than 5,000 entries on such subjects as architecture, communication, energy, agriculture, and medical technology, access is provided to key events by year. Cross-references and indexes make this title easy to use. For students of the history of technology.

851 World of scientific discovery. Bridget Travers and Jeffrey Muhr, eds. 776p. Gale, 1994. $75. ISBN 0-8103-8492-2.
500 Q126

Written from a nontechnical point of view, this source contains subject and biographical entries focusing on the process of scientific discovery. Its 1,083 entries cover history's best-known milestones and the people responsible for them, mostly from the start of the scientific revolution to the present day. Useful for libraries of all sizes.

AGRICULTURE

852 Agricultural statistics. U.S. Department of Agriculture. Govt. Print. Off., 1936– . Annual. $25. S/N 001-000-04563-6. SuDoc A1.47:yr.
■ cd
630 HD1751

"Intended as a reference book on agricultural production, supplies, consumption, facilities, costs, and returns." Tables on national and state data arranged by topic usually contain annual statistics for three to ten years, and occasionally give foreign data for comparison. Prior to 1936, data were issued as part of the *United States Department of Agriculture yearbook.*

853 **Black's agricultural dictionary.** 2d ed. D. B. Dalal-Clayton. 432p. Barnes & Noble, 1985. $54. ISBN 0-389-20556-7.
630.2 S411

This dictionary is recommended for libraries whose patrons are interested in agriculture. There is a British slant, although references are made to American usage. Agronomy, agricultural engineering, veterinary medicine, and botanical and horticultural terms are among the topics included. Definitions vary in length; cross-references are extensive; many graphics are included. Acronyms and abbreviations are listed separately.

854 **Encyclopedia of agricultural science.** Charles J. Arntzen and Ellen M. Ritter, eds. 4v. 2744p. Academic Pr., 1994. $595/set. ISBN 0-12-226670-6.
630 S411

An extensive compendium of current agricultural knowledge, covering such topics as plant science, animal science, forestry, soil science, entomology, horticulture, natural resources, agricultural engineering, and agricultural economics. Peer-reviewed extended articles (average length, ten pages). Glossary, illustration, charts, and photos included. A subject index and up-to-date bibliography round out this authoritative source. Students and agricultural professionals alike will find this encyclopedia very useful.

855 **Farm chemicals handbook.** Meister, 1908– . Annual. $96. ISSN 0430-0750.
668.6 S633

This annual publication is of great value to workers with agricultural chemicals. It includes a pesticide dictionary, a fertilizer dictionary, and a buyer's guide. The pesticide dictionary gives chemical names, synonyms, application, toxicity, and protective clothing recommendations. The text of the detailed fertilizer dictionary is accompanied by charts, graphs, and drawings. The indexed buyer's guide includes names and addresses of farm chemical manufacturers and suppliers. Useful for libraries serving agricultural clientele.

856 **The insecticide, herbicide, fungicide quick guide.** 1971– . Thomson, 1971– . Annually updated. $17.50.
632.95 SB951

Especially good for the library in an agrarian community, this inexpensive guide, updated annually since 1971, will provide assistance for the person recommending or searching for an appropriate insecticide, herbicide, or fungicide. Divided into three main sections by type of agent; within each section, specific crops are listed alphabetically along with the effective products for that crop. Information is taken from the manufacturer's label and the USDA and EPA pesticide summaries. Includes appendixes and manufacturers' addresses.

857 **The pesticide manual: incorporating the agrochemicals handbook.** 10th ed. Clive Tomlin, ed. 1341p. Crop Protection, 1994. $175. ISBN 0-948404-79-5.
632.9 SB951

The British Crop Protection Council has compiled a listing of chemical compounds used as pesticides. Entries include nomenclature, development, properties, formulation, uses, toxicology, and a structure diagram. Compounds in use or being developed are indexed by CAS Registry Number, molecular formula, common and chemical names, and code number. Superseded compounds are also listed separately.

Gardening

858 **American Horticulture Society: A-Z encyclopedia of garden plants.** Christopher Brickell and Judith D. Zuk, eds. 1092p. Dorling Kindersley, 1997. $79.95. ISBN 0-7894-1943-2.
635.9 SB403.2

A comprehensive dictionary describing more than 15,000 ornamental plants, with nearly 6,000 full-color illustrations, prepared by a team of 100 horticultural experts. Alphabetically arranged by botanical name, each description includes information on garden use, cultivation, propagation, pests, and diseases. The most authoritative single-volume reference source available.

859 **The American Horticultural Society encyclopedia of gardening.** 1st American ed. Christopher Brickell et al., eds. 648p. Dorling Kindersley, 1993. $59.95. ISBN 1-56458-291-4.
635 SB450.95

An illustrated guide to gardening techniques for the horticulturalist and weekend gardener alike. A clear presentation of information that a gardener needs to know about designing gardens, cultivation, maintenance, and propagation of plants of all types. Color photographs and illustrations and an extensive index add to its usefulness.

860 Encyclopedia of perennials: a gardener's guide. Christopher Woods. 350p. Facts on File, 1992. $50. ISBN 0-8160-2092-2.
635.9 SB434

Perennials, or nonwoody plants that take more than one year to complete their life cycle, are the most popular garden plants in North America and Europe. This encyclopedia is an illustrated guide to the many species of perennials. Entries include color photographs of the plants, common name and family name, physical characteristics, landscaping, and propagation. Arranged alphabetically by genera. Includes bibliography, appendixes, and subject index.

861 Exotica series 4 international: a treasury of indoor ornamentals for home, the office, or greenhouse—in warm climates the patio and the garden outdoors. 12th ed. Alfred Byrd Graf. 2v. 2576p. Roehrs, 1985. $187. ISBN 0-911266-20-8.
635.9 SB407

Intended as a pictorial record of ornamental exotic plants to be grown indoors, or outdoors in temperate climates, this groups more than 12,000 photographs by family to cover more than 8,500 species. Describes each plant, emphasizing growth and observable characteristics; gives origins when known, synonyms, and cross-references. Includes key to care, bibliography, and indexes. A standard authoritative work useful to horticulturalists, hobbyists, botany students, and others.

862 Garden literature: an index to periodical articles and book reviews. v.1– . Garden Literature Pr., 1992– . Quarterly. $98. ISSN 1061-3722.
016.635 Z5996

Covers 100 journals including gardening newsletters and newspapers of interest to gardeners, designers, growers, and garden retailers. Smaller libraries may want to consider *Garden literature sprout,* published annually, which indexes a baker's dozen of the leading garden magazines beginning in 1994. Either index will be useful to libraries serving gardening enthusiasts.

863 Gardening by mail: a source book: everything for the garden and gardener. 5th ed. Barbara J. Barton. Various pagings. Houghton, 1997. $24. ISBN 0-395-87770-9.
635 SB450.943

The full subtitle explains most of the contents of this tool aimed at both professional and recreational gardeners: "a directory of mail-order resources for gardeners in the United States and Canada, including seed companies, nurseries, suppliers of all garden necessaries and ornaments, horticultural and plant societies, magazines, libraries, and a list of useful books on plants and gardening." Five different indexes give access to more than 2,000 entries in seven major sections by plant, geography, products, society interests, and magazine title.

864 Hortus third: a concise dictionary of plants cultivated in the United States and Canada. Liberty Hyde Bailey Hortorium staff. 1290p. Macmillan, 1976. $150. ISBN 0-02-505470-8.
635.93 SB450

The goal of this "Bible of nurserymen" is to provide an inventory of accurately described and named plants of ornamental and economic importance in continental America north of Mexico, including Puerto Rico and Hawaii. Brief directions for use, propagation, and culture of more than 20,000 species are included. Index lists over 10,000 common plant names.

865 The National Arboretum book of outstanding garden plants: the authoritative guide to selecting and growing the most beautiful, durable, and care-free garden plants in North America. Jacqueline Heriteau. 292p. Simon & Schuster, 1990. $39.95. ISBN 0-671-66957-5.
635.9 SB407

A directory of more than 1,700 flowers, herbs, trees, and other proven plants selected by the Arboretum as the most beautiful, durable, and carefree plants of their kind to grow in North America. Entries include plant description, growing information, gardening tips, and many color photographs. Gardeners will enjoy this title.

866 The New Royal Horticultural Society dictionary of gardening. A. Huxley et al. Stockton Pr., 1992. $795. ISBN 1-56159-001-0.
635 SB450.95

Horticulture and gardening have advanced significantly since the *Dictionary of gardening* was published in 1951. This edition reflects these changes by bringing together international horticultural and botanical experts to write about gardens. The entries are in alphabetical order by genus, interfiled with entries on plant families, plant science, garden history, and biographies of prominent botanists and gardeners. Appendixes include botanical terms, pests and diseases, list of authors cited, bibliography, and index of popular names. This marvelous reference will be useful for many years.

867 10,000 garden questions answered by twenty experts. 4th ed. Marjorie J. Dietz, ed. 1057p. Random House Value, 1995. $19.99. ISBN 0-517-12226-X.
635 SB453

A well-known garden guide, with botanical names revised in the fourth edition to conform to *Hortus third.* Each chapter begins with introductory material, in which questions with answers by specialists are grouped by subject (e.g., soils and fertilizers, perennials, houseplants). A good all-purpose garden book, particularly appropriate for public library collections. Indexed.

ASTRONOMY

868 The amateur astronomer's handbook. 3d ed. James Muirden. 472p. HarperCollins, 1983. $10.95. ISBN 0-06-091426-2.
522 QB64

An excellent guide "intended to be a survey of the technique of amateur astronomy, from the selection of an instrument to the conduct of actual observation." Geared to Northern Hemisphere readers, this work assumes some basic astronomical knowledge. Bonuses include a section on astronomical photography, a glossary, reading lists, tables of recurring astronomical phenomena, and illustrations. Indexed.

869 The astronomical almanac for the year [yr.]: data for astronomy, space sciences, geodesy, surveying, navigation and other applications. Govt. Print. Off., 1981– . Annual. $38. S/N 008-054-00140-8. SuDoc D213.8:yr.
■ disk
528.1 QB8

Beginning in 1981, this joint production of Her Majesty's Nautical Almanac Office, Royal Greenwich Observatory, and the Nautical Almanac Office, U.S. Naval Observatory, replaced both *The American ephemeris and nautical almanac* and *The nautical almanac and astronomical ephemeris*. With basic information contributed by the ephemeris offices of a number of countries, this collection of tables is the authoritative source for annual astronomical data from the movement of heavenly bodies to the calculation of calendars. *Astronomical phenomena for the year [yr.]* (1950– . Annual. $17. S/N 008-054-00128-9. SuDoc D213.8/3:yr.), a booklet published two years in advance, is a useful digest of *Astronomical almanac* information.

870 The Cambridge atlas of astronomy. 3d ed. Jean Audouze and Guy Israel, eds. 470p. Cambridge Univ. Pr., 1994. $95. ISBN 0-521-43438-6.
520 QB65

This edition of the *Cambridge atlas of astronomy* continues the tradition of excellence established by the previous editions. Beginning with the sun and proceeding through the solar system, the stars of our galaxy, and on to the extragalactic domain, the cosmos is systematically presented. The *Atlas* contains exceptional photographs, illustrations, and charts, along with informative text. The new edition includes revision of planetary information on Venus, Neptune, Pluto, and solar system debris, with new photographs from the Hubble space telescope. Forty pages of text and a twenty-four-page glossary were added to this edition. *Search* magazine says, "If you wish to have just one book on astronomy, this is the one to get."

871 The Cambridge photographic atlas of the planets. Geoffrey Briggs and Fredric Taylor. 256p. Cambridge Univ. Pr., 1986. $47.50. ISBN 0-521-23976-1.
523.49 QB605

Intended as an atlas for the general reader, this work provides official maps and more than 200 of the best NASA photographs of planets from Mercury to Uranus and their satellites. Captions and clear text summarize information through 1986 about the planets from both international space exploration and Earth-based observation: surface features, chemical composition, atmosphere, and so forth. Its unique approach makes this an excellent addition to any reference collection.

872 Encyclopedia of astronomy and astrophysics. Robert A. Meyers, ed. 807p. Academic Pr., 1989. $95. ISBN 0-12-226690-0.
520.3 QB14

An in-depth treatment of developments in astronomy and astrophysics, including instrumentation and observations of the solar system. Intended for the undergraduate, graduate, or practicing professional. Access includes subject index and major subject entries. Offers 300 glossary entries, 300 longer entries, and numerous illustrations and tables.

873 Encyclopedia of the solar system. Paul Weissman, Lucy-Ann McFadden, and Torrence Johnson, eds. 794p. Academic Pr., 1998. $99.95. ISBN 0-12-226805-9.
523.2 QB501

The encyclopedia offers forty thematically organized chapters, further subdivided into authoritative articles written by more than fifty scientists. The work incorporates information gathered through the planetary explorations of *Voyagers I* and *II, Magellan, Galileo, Pathfinder,* and the Hubble orbiting telescope. Includes references to related studies, a glossary, and clear contents tables for each chapter. Well illustrated with magnificent color images, figures, and tables.

874 Facts on File dictionary of astronomy. 3d ed. Valerie Illingworth, ed. 528p. Facts on File, 1994. $29.95. ISBN 0-8160-3229-7.
520.3 QB14

Clear and concise definitions make this work an excellent choice as a good basic dictionary of astronomy. Numerous cross-references, line drawings, and tables enhance its reference value.

875 The friendly guide to the universe. Nancy Hathaway. 480p. Viking, 1994. Paper $13.95. ISBN 0-14-015381-0.
520 QB43.2

This easy-to-read almanac covers astronomical topics from a chronology of the universe to celestial art. It includes illustrations and sidebars and has a glossary and bibliography.

876 The new atlas of the universe. 2d ed. Patrick Moore. 271p. Random House Value, 1998. $29.99. ISBN 0-517-55500-X.
523 QB44.2

For school and public libraries seeking a less demanding text than *The Cambridge atlas of astronomy.*

877 Norton's 2000.0: star atlas and reference handbook (epoch 2000.0). 18th ed. Ian Ridpath, ed. Wiley, 1989. $44.95. ISBN 0-582-03163-X.
523 QB65

This standard reference work for amateur and professional astronomers is considered "indispensable" by the editor of a major astronomy magazine. It includes computer-generated star charts and practical information on astronomy. The article on comets, for example, is clear and informative. The unusual title reflects a problem faced by celestial cartographers: the coordinates of stars gradually change, so the eighteenth edition chose the reference date 2000. This practical reference book will not quickly go out-of-date.

878 Patrick Moore's A-Z of astronomy. Patrick Moore. 240p. Norton, 1987. $13.50. ISBN 0-393-30505-8.
520.3 QB14

A completely revised version of *The A-Z of astronomy* (1977), itself a revision of *The amateur astronomer's glossary* (1966), this concise, nontechnical work is a good introductory dictionary for the nonspecialist in the field. The more than 400 entries include terms from basic astronomy and astronomers, observatories, and events. Simple but clear definitions, numerous cross-references, an index, and helpful illustrations make it especially valuable for smaller collections.

CHEMISTRY

Bibliographies and Guides

879 Chemical information management. Wendy Warr and Claus Suhr. 261p. Wiley, 1992. $90. ISBN 3-527-28366-8.
540 QD8.5

Chemical information is very document intensive. This title is a survey of the techniques of managing chemical information from both scientific literature and patent literature. Methods of monitoring, indexing, storing, and retrieving information are explained, with emphasis placed on electronic formats and online searching. Useful to libraries with chemistry collections.

Dictionaries and Encyclopedias

880 Concise chemical and technical dictionary. 4th ed. H. Bennett, ed. 1271p. Chemical, 1986. $160. ISBN 0-8206-0310-4.
540 QD5

About 100,000 entries covering trademark products, chemicals, drugs, and terms mark this comprehensive guide to the vocabulary of chemistry and related trades. Prefatory material touches on nomenclature and formulas of organic chemicals and on pronunciation of chemical words; entries are brief, often less than a full line, and rely on abbreviations to convey critical information. Many useful appendixes plus the volume's extensive coverage make it valuable to every library requiring basic technical data.

881 The encyclopedia of chemistry. 4th ed. Douglas M. Considine and Glenn D. Considine, eds. 1082p. Van Nostrand Reinhold, 1984. $149.95. ISBN 0-442-22572-5.
540 QD5

A unique one-volume encyclopedia covering 1,300 topics in the field of chemical knowledge with surprising depth. This edition contains more than 85 percent new text to reflect the growing interdisciplinary character of chemistry. Topics emphasized include advanced processes, energy sources, wastes, new materials, plant chemistry, molecular biology, and use of food chemicals. Includes bibliographic references and an alphabetical index.

882 Exploring chemical elements and their compounds. David L. Heiserman. 376p. TAB Books, 1992. $29.95. ISBN 0-8306-3018-X; paper $18.95. ISBN 0-8306-3015-5.
546 QD466

Designed to be usable by high school and college chemistry students. Entries are arranged by atomic number of each element. The book progresses up the periodic table. Each entry includes a summary of basic physical properties, history of the element, chemical properties, a summary of important compounds, a list of known isotopes, and a diagram of the most common crystalline structure of the element.

883 Facts on File dictionary of chemistry. Rev. ed. John Daintith, ed. 256p. Facts on File, 1988. $24.95. ISBN 0-8160-1866-9; paper $12.95. ISBN 0-8160-2367-0.
540 QD5

Written with the student in mind, this dictionary defines about 2,500 chemical terms clearly and concisely. The revised edition incorporates new materials, techniques, applications, and topics affecting the environment. This is a reasonably priced chemistry dictionary.

884 Hawley's condensed chemical dictionary. 13th ed. Richard J. Lewis Sr. 1275p. Van Nostrand Reinhold, 1997. $99.95. ISBN 0-442-02324-3.
540 QD5

More a compendium of descriptive information and technical data than a dictionary in the strictest sense, the *CCD* has been a standard source almost since its introduction in 1919. The main body covers many thousands of chemicals and raw materials, processes and equipment, chemical phenomena and terminology, and trademarked chemical products; and appendixes list accepted chemical abbreviations, short biographies of important chemists, and descriptions of the nature and location of American technical societies and trade associations. This edition also incorporates Chemical Abstract Service's Registry Numbers. A Spanish-language edition is published by Ediciones Omega of Barcelona, Spain.

885 Macmillan encyclopedia of chemistry. Joseph J. Lagowski, ed. 4v. Macmillan, 1997. $400. ISBN 0-02-897225-2.
540.3 QD4.M33

Comprehensive, up-to-date encyclopedia. Longer essays provide overviews of key concepts and chemical processes. Element definitions and biographical entries are included.

Handbooks, Yearbooks, and Almanacs

886 Chemical exposure and human health: a reference to 314 chemicals with a guide to symptoms and a directory of organizations. Cynthia Wilson. 339p. McFarland, 1993. $55. ISBN 0-89950-810-3.
615.9 RB152

Many medical doctors are not trained to recognize the adverse effects of chemicals on the human body. This source is a guide intended to assist doctors and patients in identifying possible problems. It has sections on chemicals, symptoms, target organs, sources of chemical exposure, and organizations that provide information about chemical hazards. More than 300 chemicals are included.

887 CRC handbook of chemistry and physics: a ready-reference book of chemical and physical data. David R. Lide, ed. CRC Pr., 1913– . (78th ed. 1997, $110. ISBN 0-8493-0478-4.)

ISSN 0147-6262.
541.9 QD65

A compilation of essential tables of physical and chemical data and some frequently used mathematical tables, this is a standard source for all but the smallest of libraries. For those, a wise investment is the *CRC handbook of chemistry and physics, student ed.* (1st student ed. Robert C. Weast, ed. 1261p. CRC Pr., 1988. Paper $32.95. ISBN 0-8493-0740-6), which "provides certain core data and information that are constant or which change only slightly over an extended period of time."

888 Hazardous chemicals desk reference. 4th ed. Richard J. Lewis Sr. 1742p. Van Nostrand Reinhold, 1997. $125.95. ISBN 0-471-28779-2.
604.7 T55.3

This title contains introductory chapters on aspects of safety and a body of entries on more than 5,500 materials chosen for their importance in industry, for their toxicity, for their fire and explosion hazard, or for their having generated widespread interest. Cross-references by synonym and Chemical Abstract Service's Registry Number.

889 Hazardous substances resource guide. 2d ed. Richard P. Pohanish and Stanley A. Greene, eds. 800p. Gale, 1996. $198. ISBN 0-8103-9062-0.
604.7 T55.3

Citizens concerned with hazardous substances encountered in the home, community, and workplace can turn to this source to help identify toxic chemicals and to locate organizations providing further information about these chemicals. Lists 1,047 hazardous substances along with Chemical Abstract Service's Registry Numbers, synonyms, uses, appearance, effects of exposure, danger profile, and a first-aid guide, where available. It also includes information on more than 1,500 organizations, agencies, and publications, including hot lines and poison control centers.

890 The Merck index: an encyclopedia of chemicals, drugs, and biologicals. 12th ed. Susan Budavari et al., eds. Merck, 1996. $45. ISBN 0-911910-12-3.
■ online
615 QV772

A source of basic information on chemical substances. Entries give physical properties, chemical structure, and synonyms. To reflect the growing interdependence of chemistry, biology, and medicine, the work incorporates information on biochemistry, pharmacology, toxicology, and agriculture and the environment. The publisher expects future print editions to remain at 10,000 substances, although the online file will continue to grow. A standard reference source.

891 NIOSH pocket guide to chemical hazards. 251p. Govt. Print. Off., 1994. Paper $14. ISBN 0-16-045338-0. S/N 017-033-00473-1. SuDoc HE20.7108:C42/994.
363 T55.3

This guide to the 400 most-common workplace chemical hazards belongs in the glove compartment of every construction and transportation vehicle, fire truck, and every library, depository or not, in the country. This GPO best-seller includes a wealth of chemical information including chemical structures, formulas, legal exposure limits, reactions, measurement methods, personal protective equipment, symptoms of exposure, and first-aid recommendations.

Biographical Sources

892 Nobel laureates in chemistry, 1901–1992. Laylin K. James, ed. 798p. American Chemical, 1993. $69.95. ISBN 0-841-22459-5; paper $34.95. ISBN 0-841-22690-3.
540 QD21

Nobel Prizes symbolize superlative achievement in science. This book, part of the History of modern chemistry series, presents biographies and scientific achievements of individuals who received the Nobel Prize in chemistry from 1901 through 1992, except for the years when no prize was awarded. Arranged by year of award, the signed biographies give information about these famous chemists, along with a bibliography for each laureate.

893 Women in chemistry and physics: a biobibliographic sourcebook. Louise S. Grinstein et al., eds. 721p. Greenwood, 1993. $115. ISBN 0-313-27382-0.
540 QD21

Obtaining information about women is not always easy. This source presents biographies of prominent women in chemistry and physics whose intelligence and strength of will allowed them to contribute in largely male fields. Entries include a discussion of their lives, their work, and bibliography by and about the scientist. Useful for public and college libraries.

Computer Science

Indexes and Abstracts

894 ACM guide to computing literature. Assn. for Computing Machinery, 1977– . Annual. $210. ISSN 0149-1199.
■ online
016 QA75.5

Bibliographic listing. Indexes by author, key word, category, proper noun subject, reviewer, and source. The 1994 edition contains more than 24,000 entries and listing for more than 34,000 authors. Comprehensive index to the literature of computer science.

895 Literature analysis of microcomputer publications: LAMP. v.1– . Mort Wasserman, ed. Soft Images (200 Route 17, Mahway, NJ 07430), 1983– . Bimonthly. $89.95; microfiche $69.95. ISSN 0735-9721.
■ micro
016.00164 QA76.5

Directed toward computer users, with an index of articles on computer programs, technical topics, and reviews from international periodicals. Index to articles in more than 130 American and international periodicals. It covers all technical articles, computer programs, features, monthly columns, and reviews. The author index lists names as they appear in the articles. The subject index is typical, with *see* and *see also* references. Part 3, the review index, is divided into five sections: books and periodicals, educational courseware and films, hardware, software, and video and computer games. Some items are rated by the reviewer with a number of stars ranging from one to five, poor to excellent. The first index to cover information on computers effectively.

Dictionaries and Encyclopedias

896 The computer glossary: the complete illustrated dictionary. 7th ed. Alan Freedman. 465p. AMACOM, 1995. Paper $39.95. ISBN 0-8144-0127-9.
■ disk
004 QA76.15

This important computer glossary provides plain definitions for complex terms. Now in its seventh edition, it continues to improve and keep up with rapid technical and terminology changes, without losing its historical perspective. The 6,000 terms and 200 illustrations and photographs define hardware, software, PCs, mainframes, and networking terms. This dictionary will be useful to everyone from computer neophyte to computer guru and should be in every library, large or small.

897 Encyclopedia of computer science. 4th ed. Anthony Ralston et al., eds. 1558p. Van Nostrand Reinhold, 1997. $160.99. ISBN 1-85032-814-5.
004 QA76.15

The new edition of this standard in the field is a welcome addition to any computer science collection. This massive work is still an excellent starting place in almost any library for background information on practical and theoretical aspects of computer science. Hardware, software, languages, applications, and people are some of the topics covered in the 550 signed articles presented in alphabetical order, most with bibliographies and illustrations. Extensive cross-references, detailed index, and useful appendixes, including a multilingual glossary. A basic source for almost every library.

898 IBM dictionary of computing. 10th ed. G. McDaniel, comp. 758p. McGraw-Hill, 1994. Paper $24.95. ISBN 0-07-031489-6.
004 QA76.15

Originated as a dictionary for IBM technical writers, this dictionary contains terms from "the full range of IBM's hardware and software products." Included are terms from American National Standards Institute and International Standards Organization computer standard dictionaries. The total number of entries (22,000) makes this dictionary exhaustive. If the reader remembers that the dictionary has an IBM "accent," he or she will find it very useful.

899 Macmillan encyclopedia of computers. Gary G. Bitter, ed. 2v. 1120p. Macmillan, 1992. $200. ISBN 0-02-897045-4.
004 QA76.15

Contains 200 articles on the impact of computers on our daily lives. Technical information, design considerations, and historical and biographical information is also included. Many diagrams and bibliographies.

900 McGraw-Hill encyclopedia of personal computing. Stan Gibilisco, ed. 1216p. McGraw-Hill, 1995. $89.95. ISBN 0-07-023718-2.
004.16 QA76.15

Intended for personal computer users: high school students, electronic hobbyists, or businesspeople. Entries are arranged alphabetically, with most acronyms listed under the full term. Entries are straightforward and not too technical. Includes illustrations and frequent cross-references. Suitable for academic and public libraries.

901 Microsoft Press computer dictionary: the comprehensive standard for business, school, library, and home. 3d ed. Microsoft Pr., 1997. $29.95. ISBN 1-57231-446-X.
004 QA76.15

As the subtitle suggests, this dictionary is intended for business, school, library, and home use. Its 5,000 definitions include illustrations, pronunciation guide, and cross-references where applicable. It uses letter-by-letter alphabetization with numbers and symbols at the beginning of the book in ascending ASCII order. It does not include company makes and models but does include computer jargon and some slang. For libraries of all types.

902 Webster's new world dictionary of computer terms. 5th ed. Donald D. Spencer. 624p. Macmillan, 1994. Paper $9.95. ISBN 0-671-89993-7.
004 QA76.15

Including more than 4,500 terms, this up-to-date, straightforward dictionary aimed at novice and experienced computer users covers the basics of computer science, acronyms, languages, organizations, popular hardware brands, and selected best-selling programs. Little jargon, no biographies; cross-references. Especially useful for libraries with smaller collections.

Directories

903 Data sources: the comprehensive guide to the information processing industry: equipment, software, services, companies, and people. Ziff-Davis, 1981– . Quarterly or semiannual (subtitle varies). $595 for annual subs. (issued 2 times per year). $365 for single set. ISSN 0744-1673.
001.64 HD9696

A comprehensive guide to the data-processing industry: hardware, data communications products, software, company profiles. Lists more than 43,000 hardware, software, and data communications products and profiles 10,000 companies. Very useful to libraries of all sizes.

904 Datapro directory of microcomputer software. Datapro, 1981– . Monthly updates. $877 to new subs. ISSN 0730-8795.
338 QA76.6

One of several publications from McGraw-Hill/Datapro that provides computer information in three-ring binders. Other titles include *Datapro directory of small computers, Datapro reports on microcomputers,* and *Datapro management small computer systems.* Pages are updated depending on changes in the computer industry. Entries include name of software, vendor address and phone number, function of software, hardware, source language, price, and a one-paragraph description of the software. For example, the entries on operating systems (DOS, Windows, OS/2 Warp, etc.) provide up-to-date, evaluative information.

905 Gale directory of databases. 1998 ed. Kathleen Nolan, ed. 2v. Gale, 1998. $370/set. ISBN 0-8103-4931-0.
■ disk cd online tape
025 QA76.9

A standard reference source on machine-readable databases. Its scope has grown, as indicated by its statement of purpose: "covers all publicly available electronic databases, including online and transactional, CD-ROM, bulletin boards, offline files available for batch processing, and databases on magnetic tape and diskette." Volume 1 is devoted to online databases; volume 2, to CD-ROMs. Thoroughly profiles close to 13,000 databases, nearly 3,900 database producers, and more than 2,400 online and CD-ROM services and vendors. Subject and master name indexes.

906 Microcomputer index. Learned Information, 1980– . Quarterly. $140. ISSN 8756-7040.
■ online tape
016 QA75.5

Contains abstracts of literature on the use of microcomputers in business, education, and the home. New products announcements and software and hardware reviews are included. Provides citations and abstracts of some 2,000 articles from more than seventy-five English-language microcomputer journals. Deals with all aspects of microcomputer systems and industry and microcomputer use in business, education (all levels), libraries, and the home. Includes buyer and vendor guides, program listings, and other features from such popular titles as *Byte* and *PC World* and applications-oriented titles such as *Classroom computer learning and small computers in libraries*. Four different indexes in each issue; subscription includes annual cumulative index.

907 The software encyclopedia [yr.]: a comprehensive guide to software packages for business, professional or personal use. Bowker, 1985– . $290.50. ISSN 0000-006X.
■ online tape
005.3 QA76.753

Annotated listings for microcomputer software, plus contact information. Indexed by title, compatible systems, and applications. Directory of more than 20,000 available microcomputer software packages from more than 4,000 publishers, giving for each complete bibliographic and ordering information, hardware and other requirements, and so forth, along with a brief descriptive annotation. Access is through five indexes: title, publisher, guide to systems, guide to applications, and system compatibility and applications. With the 1989 edition, excludes software aimed specifically at the scholastic market (which appears in the companion edition *Software for schools* [1987–88, $49.95. ISBN 0-8352-2369-8]). This guide has improved with age and is a good buy for most academic and public libraries.

908 Software reviews on file. v.1– . Looseleaf. Facts on File, 1985–1995. Monthly. $239. ISSN 8755-7169.
531.2 QA76.75

Software and CD-ROM reviews on file. v.12– . Loose-leaf. Facts on File, 1996– . $259. ISSN 1087-6367.
530.29 QA76.75

Excerpts of several thousand reviews a year, from more than 300 computer publications, of more than 600 new programs for microcomputers are arranged by topic, giving author of the program, contents, brand name, copyright date, system requirements, and price. An attempt to fill the insatiable need for software reviews in libraries that have not been able to keep up with the proliferation of microcomputing magazines. The arrangement is by broadly defined classifications (e.g., business, programming languages). Access to reviews is through cumulative indexes by software and computer brand names, program name, software producers, and general subject categories. Since 1996, includes CD-ROM reviews.

Internet

909 Gale guide to Internet databases. 4th ed. Joanna Zakalik and Sara Burak, eds. 1100p. Gale, 1998. $104. ISBN 0-7876-1632-X.
004.67 TK5105.875

With the phenomenal growth of the Internet, its decentralization, and its lack of standardization, it has become unwieldy for users. This guide describes 2,000 domestic and international databases providing authoritative information and offering unrestricted access. Includes specialized home pages section, glossary of Internet terms, and subject index. Useful for all libraries.

910 Harley Hahn's Internet and web yellow pages. 5th ed. Harley Hahn. 914p. Osborne McGraw-Hill, 1998. Paper $34.99. ISBN 0-07-882387-0.
■ cd
384.3025 TK5105.875

Using the Internet without a guide is something like using a library without an organizational scheme or a catalog. *Harley Hahn's Internet and web yellow pages* provides subject arrangement and description of Internet addresses for more than 5,000 Internet information sources. Easy-to-read text and a stylish layout make this source fun to use. For libraries of all sizes providing Internet information.

911 The whole Internet user's guide and catalog. 2d ed. Ed Krol. 574p. O'Reilly & Associates, 1994. Paper $9.95. ISBN 1-56592-063-5.
004.6 TK5105.875

No area of science and technology has received so much attention as the Internet. Professional publications, newspapers, TV ads, and even highway billboards tout World Wide Web addresses. But where can patrons, and librarians, find information on how to use the Internet, and where to go once they know how to use it? This is an indispensable guide to the Internet. Chapters in the second edition include e-mail, ftp, telnet, and the World Wide Web. The "Resources on the Internet" section provides subject arrangement of selected Internet sites and their addresses. Useful in all libraries.

Earth Sciences

912 The concise Oxford dictionary of earth sciences. Ailsa Allaby and Michael Allaby, eds. 432p. Oxford Univ. Pr., 1991. Paper

$12.95. ISBN 0-19-286125-5.
550 QE5

The term *earth science* covers a lot of ground. Climatology, meteorology, geography, geology, geochemistry, geomorphology, geophysics, oceanography, and petrology are among the topics covered by this dictionary. More for the undergraduate, graduate, or professional, this title defines its terms in alphabetical order with frequent cross-references. Useful for academic and larger public libraries.

913 Earth sciences reference. Mary McNeil. 709p. Flamingo Pr., 1991. $55. ISBN 0-938905-00-7; paper $49. ISBN 0-938905-01-5.
550 QE5

A dictionary of geology, ecology, energy, oceanography, meteorology, and related subjects. Suitable for high school and undergraduate students, it may also appeal to general adult readers. Its alphabetical arrangement, formatting, detailed subject index, geographic index, and bibliography make this book easy to use.

914 Encyclopedia of earth sciences. E. Julius Dasch, ed. 2v. 1273p. Macmillan, 1996. $200. ISBN 0-02-883000-8.
550 QE5

This encyclopedia covers issues and principal facts from the fields of geology, oceanography, and meteorology. In addition, it seeks to relate Earth to the other astronomical bodies and phenomena in the solar system, galaxy, and universe. An excellent source for any medium-sized library.

915 Encyclopedia of the solid earth sciences. Philip Keareyed. 736p. Blackwell Scientific, 1994. $69.95. ISBN 0-632-03699-0.
550.3 QE5

The goal of earth sciences is to understand the earth both from a practical and theoretical viewpoint. This encyclopedia furthers that goal. The 2,700 entries contain illustrations, bibliographies of principles, and many cross-references. The extensive indexing makes information easy to locate. A useful purchase for geology collections.

Geology

916 The Audubon Society field guide to North American rocks and minerals. Charles W. Chesterman. 850p. Knopf, 1978. $19. ISBN 0-394-50269-8.
552.097 QE443

Although "older," this title has retained its usefulness and remained in print. It is designed to be used in three ways: "as a tool for identifying minerals, as a guide to identifying rocks, and as a convenient reference source for mineral collecting in the field." The small format, designed to be carried into the field, contains full-color plates identifying rocks and minerals and text describing color, hardness, occurrence, and other information. Indexes are by name and location.

917 Challinor's dictionary of geology. 6th ed. John Challinor and Antony Wyatt, eds. Oxford Univ. Pr., 1986. $35. ISBN 0-19-520506-5; paper $9.95. ISBN 0-19-520505-7.
550 QE5

A standard work "examining the meaning and usage of names and terms that stand for the more significant things, facts, and concepts of the science." Most definitions are technical, although some of the 3,000 terms are identified only by selected quotes. Many are accompanied by first usage or an example of usage. Although there is a slight British slant, the work is scholarly and accurate. Includes classified index and some cross-references.

918 Color encyclopedia of gemstones. 2d ed. Joel E. Arem. Chapman & Hall, 1987. $76.95. ISBN 0-412-98911-5.
553.8 QE392

Tabulates all known gemstone species and varieties, including synthetics. Includes 300 full-color photographs and details about gems such as color crystallography, occurrence, density, and sizes. Useful for anyone working with gems or interested in learning more about them.

Meteorology

919 Dictionary of global climate change. 2d ed. W. John Maunder, comp. Chapman & Hall, 1995. Paper $24.95. ISBN 0-412-99581-6.
551.603 QC981.8

Students, scientists, journalists, and an informed public can use this dictionary to make sense out of the rapidly evolving field of global climate change. The first edition grew out of a lexicon presented at the Second World Climate Conference in 1991. This edition added more than 250 entries. Written with the nonspecialist in mind, it presents clear definitions of technical terms and includes sources of information and an acronym list. For libraries with meteorological collections.

920 Encyclopedia of climate and weather. Stephen H. Schneider. 2v. 929p. Oxford Univ. Pr., 1996. $195. ISBN 0-19-509485-9.
551.503 QC854

Presents a remarkably thorough picture of the global environment, past and present. The author bases his findings not only upon traditional meteorology, but also upon social and economic factors that have become increasingly influential on the environment in general. Draws significant conclusions about the future of our weather systems.

921 The Times Books world weather guide. Rev. ed. E. A. Pearce and C. G. Smith. Random House, 1990. $17.95. ISBN 0-8129-1881-9.
551.6 QC982

This guide provides weather data not usually given in travel brochures and covers seasonal conditions for nearly 500 cities. Arranged roughly by continent and then alphabetically by country or major climatic region. Preliminary surveys of the climate are followed by charts for one or more representative cities, showing month-by-month extremes, average daily highs and lows, and other climate data.

922 The weather almanac: a reference guide to weather and climate of the United States and its key cities. 8th ed. Frank Bair, ed. Gale, 1998. $130. ISBN 0-8103-5522-1.
551.69 QC983

Provides information on the weather in the United States, including tabular data for 108 selected cities. Topics such as air pollution, earthquakes, and jet lag are also included.

923 Weather America: the latest detailed climatological data for over 4,000 places with rankings. Alfred N. Garwood, ed. 1412p. Toucan Valley, 1996. $99.95. ISBN 1-884925-60-X.
551.6973 QC983

Organized by state, *Weather America* provides summaries of climatological conditions; includes maps showing the location of the state's weather stations. Provides principal weather data items from a selection of stations for each month plus yearly average. National rankings are an interesting feature.

924 Weather of U.S. cities. 5th ed. Frank E. Bair, ed. Gale, 1996. $210. ISBN 0-8103-5525-6.
551.6973 QC983

Arranged by state and city, this work provides both narrative information and statistical tables based upon local climatological data from 268 cities and weather observation stations throughout the United States. Thirty-year annual summaries provide comparative data on rainfall, temperature, snowfall, and so forth.

Oceanography

925 The Facts on File dictionary of marine science. Barbara Charton, ed. 336p. Facts on File, 1988. $25.95. ISBN 0-8160-1031-5; paper $15.95. ISBN 0-8160-2369-7.
551.46 GC9

This dictionary fills a gap in most collections by providing a nontechnical introductory lexicon on marine sciences for general readers and students. The entries vary in length from a sentence to a couple of columns, covering not only the expected oceanographic terms and locations, but also navigators and explorers, ships in general, marine plants and animals, and terms from related sciences. Cross-references and appendixes.

926 The Times atlas and encyclopedia of the sea. 2d ed. Alastair Couper, ed. 272p. Harper, 1989. $65. ISBN 0-06-016287-2.
551.46 G2800

In a magnificent compilation of maps and photos accompanied by lucid text, this unique and comprehensive resource offers something for all readers, from students and sports persons to naval strategists, businesspeople, and marine specialists. The scope of the work is massive, containing seventeen thematic chapters, eleven appendixes, glossary, bibliography, and index. Libraries owning the original edition can probably get by without the second edition.

ENERGY

927 Chambers nuclear energy and radiation dictionary. P. M. B. Walker, ed. 260p. Chambers, 1992. $40. ISBN 0-550-13246-5; paper $20. ISBN 0-550-13247-3.
621.48 TK9009

This dictionary could function as an introductory text on nuclear energy and as a dictionary of nuclear- and radiation-related terms. The eleven chapters preceeding the dictionary proper present nuclear concepts in simple language with frequent illustrations. Dictionary entries can be used as an index to refer readers to the introductory chapters.

928 Energy and American society: a reference handbook. E. Willard Miller and Ruby M. Miller. 418p. ABC-Clio, 1993. $39.50. ISBN 0-87436-689-5.
333.79 TJ163.235

This volume begins with chapters on petroleum, coal, nuclear power, and renewable energy. It proceeds by presenting an energy chronology, statistics, and energy-related laws and regulations. It contains an organizational directory and an annotated bibliography and subject index.

929 Energy supply A-Z. Arthur Godman. 144p. Enslow, 1991. $18.95. ISBN 0-89490-262-8.
333.79 TJ163.16

Defines terms used in the field of energy, including applicable laws and agencies. It also provides references to energy-related organizations and associations. Useful in high school, public, and college libraries.

930 Nuclear power plants worldwide. Peter Dresser. 500p. Gale, 1993. $129. ISBN 0-8103-8880-4.
621.483 TK9202

"Profiles of 741 commercial nuclear power units explain, in nontechnical language, the operations, performance, output, ownership, current status, newsworthy events, and other key facts for sites around the world." Thirty-nine countries involved in the nuclear industry are included, along with an explanation of how nuclear power plants work and definitions of nuclear power terms. Alphabetical index lists plant names, company names, and other details.

ENGINEERING

931 Index and directory of industry standards. 12th ed. Global Engineering Documents, 1995. $435/set. U.S. standards only, $230. International and non-U.S. national standards, $315. ISBN 1-57053-020-3/set.
602.18 T59.2

With the wide variety of professional-standards-producing agencies, the challenge for smaller or medium-sized libraries is not so much having the industry standards available, but identifying them. This index provides subject and numeric access to U.S. and international standards agencies. Industry standards, such as IEEE, ASTM, or ANSI, are indexed. Includes 11,000 new standards and 23,000 updated standards in the 1995 edition. U.S. and international standards volumes can be purchased separately.

932 International directory of engineering societies and related organizations. 15th ed. 370p. American Assn. of Engineering Societies, 1996. $185. ISSN 1067-9014.
620 TA1

The American Association of Engineering Societies has compiled this international directory of 950 organizations in 70 countries. Entries from Eastern Europe, Asia, and Africa mean it is a global listing of engineering organizations. Each entry includes name, acronym, address, telephone, and fax. Also included are elected and executive officers, a detailed description of the society, publications, conventions, and mailing list availability. This directory will be useful for all libraries with an engineering collection.

Aerospace and Aeronautics

933 ACAD: airman's civil aviation dictionary: "V" speeds, abbreviations, drawn illustrations, quick easy reference, easy to understand definitions. Frank "Beau" Artuso. 234p. ACAD, 1992. Paper $13.95. ISBN 0-9634854-4-X.
■ disk
629.13 TL509

ACAD is a civil aviation dictionary designed for pilots and student pilots studying for their checkride. Its large print, simple-language definitions, and clear drawings make aviation terms easy to understand. Also available as flash cards and on diskette.

934 Air and space history: an annotated bibliography. Dominick A. Pisano and Cathleen S. Lewis, eds. 571p. Garland, 1988. $93. ISBN 0-8240-8543-4.
016.6291 TL515

Compiled by the curatorial staff of the Smithsonian Institution's National Air and Space Museum, this authoritative and scholarly annotated bibliography of some 1,800 items will be the cornerstone upon which researchers in the years to come will build, and to which space and flight buffs will turn.

935 The aviation/space dictionary. 7th ed. Larry Reithmaier. 461p. Aero, 1990. $32.95. ISBN 0-8306-8092-6.
629.13 TL509

An unusual dictionary in that it covers both aviation and space fields, this title has been available since 1939. Hard-to-find terms, acronyms, and industry jargon are included among the 6,000 entries. Diagrams, photographs, and sixteen appendixes complete the aeronautical.

936 Cambridge air and space dictionary. P. M. B. Walker et al., eds. 3366p. Cambridge Univ. Pr., 1990. Paper $14.95. ISBN 0-521-39763-4.
629.13 TL509

The sciences and technologies of everything about the surface of the earth is the scope of this dictionary, which contains 6,000 definitions in aeronautics, astronomy, meteorology, and radar, along with acoustics, physics, telecommunications, and engineering. Entries are derived from the *Cambridge dictionary of science and technology.* Entries are arranged alphabetically with occasional longer, boxed articles. Cross-references and appendixes are included.

937 Flight and flying: a chronology. David Baker. 559p. Facts on File, 1993. $65. ISBN 0-8160-1854-5.
629.13 TL515

A chronicle of the history of aviation, from earliest attempts through Kitty Hawk to the end of 1991. It covers significant events from the lives of individual flyers and inventors, commercial airlines, and military air forces. It is arranged in chronological order, with a subject index, glossary, and abbreviations list. A comprehensive record for historians and aviation enthusiasts alike.

938 The illustrated encyclopedia of general aviation. 2d ed. Paul Garrison. 462p. TAB Books, 1990. $24.95. ISBN 0-8306-8316-X.
629.13 TL509

Defines terms and phrases and identifies acronyms and abbreviations used in aviation. Also includes directory information and 400 charts, tables, and photographs. More for the layperson than the worker in the aviation field.

939 The illustrated encyclopedia of space technology: a comprehensive history of space exploration. 2d ed. Kenneth Gatland et al. 306p. Crown, 1989. $29.95. ISBN 0-517-57427-6.
629.4 TL788

An authoritative yet popular treatment of space pioneers, communications satellites, meteorological observation, lunar exploration, manned flight, the space shuttle, and so forth. This source provides a comprehensive look at space exploration and space sciences throughout the eighties. Numerous color illustrations, a chronology of space exploration, glossary, and index. For both reference and circulating collections.

940 Jane's space directory, [yr.]. 13th ed. 550p. Jane's Information Group, 1997–1998. Annual. $320. ISSN 1352-0660.
629.4 TL787

This annual is devoted primarily to space programs listed by nation. Separate sections cover international projects, military space, the solar system, world space centers, space contractors, and satellite launch tables. Profusely illustrated, indexed. Smaller libraries can consider purchasing it at intervals.

941 Who's who in space: the international space station edition. 3d ed. Michael Cassutt. 496p. Macmillan, 1998. $110. ISBN 0-02-864965-6.
629.45 TL788.5

A comprehensive biographical dictionary depicting the men and women who have participated in space exploration. Biographies are arranged within the context of nationality and space program. Each section includes an account of the technical and historic developments that have occurred within the space program. Color illustrations throughout.

Electronics and Electrical Engineering

942 The ARRL handbook for the radio amateur. American Radio Relay League, 1991– . Annual. $30. ISSN 0890-3565.
621.3841 TK6550

The bible for hams, this handbook contains a wealth of information on equipment, operations, and regulations. It also explains concepts from basic theories and principles and provides instructions for advanced projects. It is also valuable for the amateur who wishes to obtain a license.

943 Communications standard dictionary. 2d ed. Martin H. Weik. 1168p. Van Nostrand Reinhold, 1989. $54.95. ISBN 0-442-20556-2.
001.5 TK5102

"A comprehensive compilation of terms and definitions used in communications and related fields." Sixty-four fields and hundreds of subtopics in all areas of communication systems and their applications are addressed. Includes terms from the technical literature and with definitions consistent with national, international, federal, military, industrial, educational, and scientific usage. Provides synonyms, some examples, illustrations, and extensive cross-references. For all academic and most public libraries.

944 The electronics dictionary for technicians. Tom Adamson. 395p. Macmillan, 1992. Paper $16.60. ISBN 0-023-00820-2.
621.381 TK7804

Electronics terms are defined for a student majoring in electronics technology or for a technician on the job. The focus is on current terms for technology, not historical usage of older electronic terms. For community college libraries with electronics technology programs.

945 Encyclopedia of electronics. 2d ed. Stan Gibilisco and Neil Sclater, eds. 960p. McGraw-Hill, 1990. $69.50. ISBN 0-8306-3389-8.
621.381 TK7804

Understandable for students and dabblers, yet not too general for professionals, this useful source covers all aspects of electricity, electronics, and communications technology. The more than 3,000 articles are in alphabetical order, although each is also listed one or more times in the classified index to seventeen general fields. A detailed index provides further access to articles, illustrations, and tables. Includes schematic symbols.

946 Handbook of electronic formulas, symbols, and definitions. 2d ed. John R. Brand. 403p. Van Nostrand Reinhold, 1992. $39.95. ISBN 0-442-00302-1.
621.38 TK7825

This handbook is divided into five sections: passive circuits English letters, passive circuits Greek letters, transistors, operational amplifiers, and appendixes. In each section formulas are arranged alphabetically by symbol. If the symbol for an electronic term is unknown to the reader, appendix C acts as a guide. This is a technical source useful to advanced electrical and electronics students and practicing engineers.

947 The illustrated dictionary of electronics. 7th ed. Stan Gibilisco. McGraw-Hill, 1994. $28.95. ISBN 0-07-024186-4.
621.381 TK7804

Provides short, clear definitions of electrical and electronics terms. Cross-references and line drawings help the reader find and understand the terminology in a jargon-free way. Comprehensive coverage.

948 Master handbook of electronic tables and formulas. 5th ed. Martin Clifford. 576p. McGraw-Hill, 1992. $22.95. ISBN 0-8306-2129-X.
621.381 TK7825

Designed for engineers, technicians, students, experimenters, and hobbyists. Covers electronics formulas and laws, constants and standards, conversion factors, symbols and codes, series and installation data, design data, and mathematical tables and formulas. This edition also emphasizes calculations and conversions using computers.

949 McGraw-Hill electronics dictionary. 5th ed. John Markus and Neil Sclater. 596p. McGraw-Hill, 1994. $49.50. ISBN 0-07-040434-8.
621.38 TK7804

With 14,000 easy-to-understand definitions, this dictionary is a single-volume reference for electronics and computer science. Many new terms and acronyms are included in the fifth edition. The expected audience consists of undergraduates, graduate students, and professionals working with electronics.

950 National electrical code: 1996. 1069p. National Fire Protection Assn., 1995. $39.50. ISBN 0-87765-402-6.
621.319 KF5704

The National Fire Protection Association (NFPA) began publishing this well-known title in 1911. The 1995 edition has been approved as a national standard by the American National Standards Association (ANSI) and supersedes all previous editions. Changes from the 1993 edition are noted by vertical lines in the margin. The purpose of the *Code* is the practical safeguarding of persons and property from hazards arising from the use of electricity. Coverage includes electrical equipment in homes, businesses, public buildings, and other structures such as mobile homes, recreational vehicles, and industrial substations. Recommended for all libraries.

951 National electrical safety code handbook: a discussion of the grounding rules, general rules, and parts 1, 2, 3, and 4 of the 3rd (1920) through 1993 editions of the National electrical safety code, American national standard C2. 4th ed. Allen L. Clapp, ed. 456p. IEEE Standards Pr., 1997. Paper $89. ISBN 1-55937-724-0.
621.319 TK152

The Institute of Electrical and Electronics Engineers (IEEE) wrote this title, and the American National Standards Institute (ANSI) approved it as a national standard. It covers basic provision for safeguarding of persons from hazards arising from the installation, operation, or maintenance of (1) conductors and equipment in electric supply stations and (2) overhead and underground electric supply and communications lines. It also includes work rules for the construction, maintenance, and operation of electric supply and communication lines and equipment.

952 The new IEEE standard dictionary of electrical and electronics terms (including abstracts of all current IEEE standards). 5th ed. Gediminas P. Kurpis and Christopher J. Booth, eds. 1619p. Institute of Electrical and Electronics Engineers, 1993. ISBN 1-55937-240-0.
621.3 TK9

IEEE is a world leader in the development and publication of industry standards involving today's leading-edge electronics technologies. This dictionary defines more than 30,000 terms from electronics and electrical and computer engineering. It also includes abstracts of IEEE standards. Definitions are arranged alphabetically and include variations in meanings, cross-references, the field of application, and the source of the definition. Useful for electrical engineers, computer scientists, and students in these fields.

Mechanical and Civil Engineering

953 Construction glossary: an encyclopedic reference and manual. 2d ed. J. Stewart Stein. 1137p. Wiley, 1993. $115. ISBN 0-471-56933-X.
690 TH9

Every specialized area has its own jargon, but construction jargon has different interpretations at different times and in different areas of the country. The book is divided into sections, such as finishes, wood and plastics, and professional services. Each section has an alphabetical arrangement of words related to that application. The subject index is also arranged by section; the reader may have to look in several places to find a particular term.

954 Dictionary of ceramic science and engineering. 2d ed. Ian J. McColm. Plenum, 1994. $75. ISBN 0-306-44542-5.
666 TP788

This dictionary reflects the fact that *ceramics* is more than sinks and bathtubs. Ceramics, or "nonmetallic inorganic products heated to temperatures over 540 degrees," are used in electronics, materials science, manufacturing, testing, and even high-temperature superconductors. Entries present definitions of terms and acronyms used in ceramic science. Pronunciations and derivations are not included. SI units are used throughout. Appendixes and bibliography are included. Useful for students and scientists working with ceramic materials.

955 The VNR dictionary of civil engineering. 4th ed. John S. Scott. 533p. Van Nostrand Reinhold, 1993. $19.95. ISBN 0-442-01414-7.
624 TA9

Civil engineering is a broad field covering airfields, bridges, docks, foundations, railways, roads, sewage treatment, structural design, traffic engineering, and other disciplines. A field with such a wide impact needs a dictionary to define its terms authoritatively. British spellings are used. American, British, and metric (SI) units are included. Alphabetical arrangement, cross-references, line drawings, and appendixes of dates and great engineers make this dictionary useful to all libraries with engineering collections.

ENVIRONMENT

956 Access EPA. Office of Information Resources Management, U.S. Environmental Protection Agency. Govt. Print. Off., 1991– . Annual. $19.95. S/N 055-000-00509-5. SuDoc EP1.8/13:995-96.
■ online
027.6 TD171

Access EPA is a directory of the U.S. Environmental Protection Agency (EPA) and other public sector environmental information resources. Citizens, scientists, and federal, state, and local government workers can all use this title as a pathfinder to major environmental resources. Clearinghouses, hot lines, and sources of information can be located through the indexes and color-coded sections. Useful for all libraries.

957 Atlas of the environment. 3d ed. Geoffrey Lean and Don Hinrichsen. 192p. ABC-Clio, 1994. $39.50. ISBN 0-87436-768-9.
363.7 G1046

With more than 200 color maps and charts, this title gives a graphic representation of today's environmental concerns to students and researchers. Each of the forty-two chapters provides an overview of a problem, such as acid rain or biodiversity, and discusses the likelihood that the problem will be resolved in the near future. Access is through table of contents only.

958 Choose to reuse: an encyclopedia of services, businesses, tools, and charitable programs that facilitate reuse. Nikki Goldbeck and David Goldbeck. 450p. Ceres Pr., 1995. Paper $15.95. ISBN 0-9606138-6-2.
363.72 TD794.5

Reuse is one of the three Rs of the environmental movement—reduce, reuse, recycle. It reduces waste, conserves energy, and can save money. This title makes suggestions on how to reuse at home, at work, and for charity. It includes entries for items from air filters to zippers and information on the used marketplace and "reuse for free." For libraries of all sizes.

959 The concise Oxford dictionary of ecology. Michael Allaby, ed. 424p. Oxford Univ. Pr., 1994. Paper $12.95. ISBN 0-19-286160-3.
574.5 QH540.4

Ecology, or the relationship between organisms and their environment, is a rapidly developing science. This dictionary defines 5,000 terms in sufficient detail to explain the concepts to undergraduates, graduate students, and professionals. Its companion volumes are *The concise Oxford dictionary of earth sciences, The concise Oxford dictionary of zoology,* and *The concise Oxford dictionary of botany.*

960 The consumer's good chemical guide: a jargon-free guide to the chemicals of everyday life. John Emsley. 347p. Freeman, 1994. $22.95. ISBN 0-7167-4505-4.
615.9 RA1213

The news is full of alarming stories with vague statistics about health risks encountered in daily life. Where can an individual turn to find accurate information? This guide deals with perfumes, sweeteners, alcohols, cholesterol, pain killers, PVC, dioxins, nitrates, and carbon dioxide. Each chapter discusses in a nontechnical way how these substances both positively and negatively impact the consumer's health. If readers want more-detailed chemical information, a glossary of chemicals mentioned in the text is included. For both public and academic libraries.

961 Deserts: the encroaching wilderness; a world conservation atlas. Tony Allan and Andrew Warren, eds. Oxford Univ. Pr., 1993. $39.95. ISBN 0-19-520941-9.
508.315 GB611

After the ocean, deserts make up the largest part of Earth. This title chronicles the ecological and social impact of the world's deserts. With striking color photographs and maps, it discusses the arid landscape, life in the desert, and peoples of the arid world and presents an atlas of the deserts. *Deserts* will be a welcome addition to public and university libraries.

962 The dictionary of ecology and environmental science. Henry W. Art et al., eds. 640p. Henry Holt, 1995. Paper $19.95. ISBN 0-8050-3848-5.
363.7 GE10

Eight thousand terms of all aspects of environmental science are included in this dictionary. Ecology, biodiversity, genetic resources, toxicology, air and water pollution, climatology, and the greenhouse effect are all included. Alphabetically arranged entries are clearly written and include cross-references. Useful for high school and college students, as well as the general public.

963 Encyclopedia of environmental information services: a subject guide to about 34,000 print and other sources of information on all aspects of the environment. Sarojini Balachandran, ed. 1813p. Gale, 1993. $130. ISBN 0-8103-8568-6.
016.3637 TD170

Information about the environment can be difficult to locate in a single place. This guide is an annotated bibliography of environmental issues. It contains more than 34,000 citations for 1,100 topics. Entries are arranged by subject and include cross-references. A sources-cited listing helps readers to locate information on a particular source or organization. Useful in all libraries.

964 Environmental encyclopedia. William P. Cunningham et al., eds. 1100p. Gale, 1993. $200. ISBN 0-8103-4986-8.
363.7 GE10

This one-volume encyclopedia of the environment will find plenty of use on the reference shelves of academic and public libraries. The alphabetically arranged and extensively cross-referenced and indexed articles will appeal to students and the general public. Organizations profiled include contact points. Two appendixes provide readers with an environmental chronology and a summary of environmental legislation. This title is part of the Gale Environmental Library.

965 The environmentalists: a biographical dictionary from the seventeenth century to the present. Alan Axelrod and Charles Phillips. 277p. Facts on File, 1993. $45. ISBN 0-8160-2715-3.
363.7 S926

A guide to individuals and organizations that have influenced the environmental movement in the United States and the world. Included are addresses for organizations. The guide contains about 600 profiles of the most significant individuals in the development of ecology from the seventeenth century to the present.

966 The environmentalist's bookshelf: a guide to the best books. Robert Merideth. 272p. Hall, 1993. $45. ISBN 0-8161-7359-1.
016.3637 GF41

The best books on nature and the environment were determined by a questionnaire survey sent to environmental leaders and experts around the world. The guide contains an annotated bibliography of the 500 most recommended environmental books. It is divided into four parts: core books, strongly recommended books, other recommended books, and respondents to the questionnaire.

967 The Facts on File dictionary of environmental science. L. Harold Stevenson and Bruce Wyman. 304p. Facts on File, 1991. $24.95. ISBN 0-8160-2317-4; paper $12.95. ISBN 0-8160-3066-9.
628 TD9

Concern for the environment has increased over the last few years. A basic dictionary can help high school and college students and the general public to a better understanding of environmental topics. Some of the subject areas covered by this title include control, remediation, prevention of harm, chemical contamination to the air and water, species preservation, environmental impact on human health, and ionizing radiation. This dictionary will be useful in almost all libraries.

968 The [yr.] information please environmental almanac. World Resources Institute, comp. Houghton, 1991– . Annual. $11.95. ISSN 1057-8293.
363.7 TD176.4

An almanac of the environment will fill a need in almost all reference collections. Environmental justice, home toxins, world population, saving energy, and biodiversity are some of the many topics covered by this source. The subject index leads the reader to entries with text, tables, and charts of environmental facts and figures.

969 The McGraw-Hill recycling handbook. Herbert F. Lund, ed. McGraw-Hill, 1992. $87.50. ISBN 0-07-039096-7.
363.72 TD794.5

It can be daunting for businesses, local governments, and consumers to try to keep up with the changes in recycling. This title is designed to be one place to look that covers every aspect of recycling procedures and technologies. Sections include an overview of recycling, including federal, state, and local laws; specific recyclable materials; and facilities, design, and recycling equipment. Includes case histories, appendixes, and a glossary.

970 Toxics A to Z: a guide to everyday pollution hazards. J. Harte. 576p. Univ. of California Pr., 1991. $75. ISBN 0-520-07223-5; paper $22.50. ISBN 0-520-07224-3.
615.9 RA1213

More than 100 commonly encountered toxins are described in this guide. It includes what they are, how they are measured, where they are found, and what the risks are. Cross-references help readers to identify toxic chemicals in major groups. Glossary, abbreviation guide, and introductory chapters about pollution hazards round out this source.

971 World resources 1996–97: a report. World Resources Institute staff. 400p. Oxford Univ. Pr., 1996. $24.95.

ISBN 0-19-521161-8. ISSN 0887-0403.
333.705 HC10

The World resources series is published to meet the need for accessible, accurate information on environment and development. This exhaustive report is prepared jointly by the World Resources Institute, the United Nations Environmental Programme (UNEP), and the United Nations Development Programme (UNDP). It is published in three parts in English and six other world languages. Part 1 features people and the environment. Part 2 focuses on the natural resources issues facing India and China, the world's two most populous countries. Part 3 reports on environmental conditions and efforts to resolve problems posed by these conditions. Subject index.

LIFE SCIENCES

Biology

972 Biological and agricultural index.
Wilson, 1964– . Monthly except Aug. Quarterly cumulations and permanent bound annual cumulations. Service basis. ISSN 0006-3177. 1964–89, $250. ISBN 0-685-22239-X; 1989–94, ISBN 0-315-56450-5.
■ cd online tape
016.63 S1

A detailed alphabetical subject index to more than 200 English-language periodicals. Useful for periodical articles in the fields of agriculture, biology, microbiology, ecology, veterinary medicine, and related fields.

973 Biology digest. v.1– . Plexus, 1974– . Monthly (Sept.–May). $22.50.
ISSN 0095-2958.
574 QH301

This index scans some 200 foreign and domestic periodicals for information relevant to all aspects of biology. About 400 abstracts are included in each issue, presenting enough information to enable readers who may not have access to the original documents to understand the work described. Each issue is organized by broad chapters and has one feature review article. Keyword and author indexes.

974 Chambers dictionary of biology. Peter M. B. Walker, ed. 324p. Cambridge Univ. Pr., 1989. $17.50. ISBN 1-85296-152-X; paper $8.95. ISBN 1-85296-153-8.
574 QH302.5

Some 10,000 biological terms are defined, including 3,000 in zoology, 2,500 in botany, and 1,200 in biochemistry, molecular biology, and genetics. Meanings and derivations of the many biological prefixes and suffixes are included. Some entries include illustrations and longer "special articles." Alphabetical arrangement, with Greek letters found in their nearest anglicized form. For chemical formulas, numbers are ignored. Useful for college, university, and larger public libraries.

975 Concise encyclopedia biochemistry.
2d ed. Thomas Scott and Mary Eagleson, eds. 649p. De Gruyter, 1988. $99.95.
ISBN 3-11-011625-1.
574.19 QD415

Approximately 4,500 entries range from two or three sentences to a couple of columns and cover all areas of biochemistry and biotechnology. Much of the emphasis in the second edition is on genetic engineering, cloning of DNA, and metabolic biochemistry. There is also attention given to animal, medical, microbial, and plant biochemistry. Graphics, cross-references, and references to the literature add to the value of this technical tool for researchers, teachers, and students. Belongs in most academic libraries.

976 Dictionary of biology. 3d ed.
Elizabeth Martin, Michael Ruse, and Elaine Holmes, eds. 553p. Oxford Univ. Pr., 1996. Paper $13.95.
ISBN 0-19-280032-9.
570.3 QH302.5

Designed for the high school biology student, this dictionary contains 5,000 biological terms. Alphabetical arrangement, pronunciation guide, page layout, and clearly written definitions all contribute to the readability of this dictionary. Useful for public libraries and undergraduate college libraries.

977 Encyclopedia of microbiology. Joshua Lederberg, ed. 4v. 2650p. Academic Pr., c1992. $734/set. ISBN 0-12-226890-3.
576 QR9

This encyclopedia surveys the field of microbiology, including viruses, bacteria, and other unicellular organisms. Articles are arranged by subject. The set includes a glossary, illustrations and tables, and a bibliography. The subject indexing will guide advanced undergraduates, graduate students, and professionals to in-depth articles in microbiology, including biotechnology, biochemistry, and genetics. A second edition of this authoritative reference work is planned for 1999.

978 The Facts on File dictionary of biology. Rev. ed. Elizabeth Tootill, ed. 326p. Facts on File, 1988. $24.95. ISBN 0-8160-1865-0; paper $12.95. ISBN 0-8160-2368-9.
574 QH13

Defines more than 3,000 terms used in the life sciences, from the elementary to the theoretical. Much of the material in this edition comes from the ever-changing fields of genetics, immunology, and molecular biology. Includes illustrations of life cycles, organ structures, and so forth. For libraries serving high school and college students in the life sciences.

979 The Facts on File dictionary of biotechnology and genetic engineering. Mark L. Steinberg and Sharon Cosley, eds. 224p. Facts on File, 1994. $27.95. ISBN 0-8160-1250-4.
660 TP248.16

Application of new technology is rapidly expanding, from university laboratories to biotech businesses. This dictionary presents the basic vocabulary of biotechnology and genetic engineering. Basic and technical terms have been included, with more specific terms referring back to basic concepts. The intended audience includes students, lawyers, physicians, scientists, teachers, and librarians. Useful for all libraries.

980 Five kingdoms: an illustrated guide to the phyla of life on earth. 3d ed. Alexander Margulis and Karlene V. Schwartz. 376p. Freeman, 1997. $39.95. ISBN 0-7167-3026-X; paper $29.95. ISBN 0-7167-3027-8.
■ disk
574 QH83

This description of the world's biodiversity covers about 100 phyla belonging to the five biological kingdoms. Readable chapters meant to be understood at the high school level discuss each division and provide representative drawings and photographs along with bibliographies for further reading. An appendix classifies about 1,000 genera to phylum level and includes many common names. Glossary and subject index.

981 The HarperCollins dictionary of biology. W. A. Hale and J. P. Margham. 569p. HarperPerennial, 1991. $14. ISBN 0-06-461015-2.
574 QH302.5

This title is intended for undergraduate and high school students as well as the general reader wishing to know more about biology. It includes 5,600 entries with about 300 illustrations. Cross-references are capitalized.

982 Index to illustrations of animals and plants. Beth Clewis. 217p. Neal-Schuman, 1991. $49.95. ISBN 0-55570-072-1.
574 QH46.5

Indexes by common name pictures of animals and plants from all over the world found in books published in the 1980s.

983 The official World Wildlife Fund guide to endangered species of North America. David W. Lowe et al., eds. 4v. 2319p. Beacham, 1990–94. v.1&2, 1258p. $195. ISBN 0-933833-17-2; v.3, 546p. $85. ISBN 0-933833-29-6; v.4, 690p. $85. ISBN 0-933833-33-1.
574.5 QL84.2

The study and conservation of endangered species is an important task if we are to preserve our habitat and biodiversity. This four-volume set consolidates information on native North American plants and animals that have been placed on the list of threatened and endangered species. Two-page entries give full information on threatened species, including description, habitat, food, and bibliography. Indexes are by state, family, common, and scientific name. Glossary, bibliography, and photographs are included. Helpful to planners, scientists, and educators.

Botany

984 The concise Oxford dictionary of botany. Michael Allaby, ed. 448p. Oxford Univ. Pr., 1992. Paper $13.95. ISBN 0-19-286094-1.
581 QK9

Amateur botanists, students, and professionals can use this dictionary to find terms in areas such as biogeology, ecology, genetics, plant physiology, biochemistry, and cytology. One-third of the 5,000 entries are devoted to taxonomy. Brief biographical sketches of important botanists are included.

Paleontology—Dinosaurs

985 The complete dinosaur. James O'Farlow and M. K. Brett-Surman,

eds. 752p. Indiana Univ. Pr., 1997. $59.95. ISBN 0-253-33349-0.
567.9 QE862.D5

This scholarly yet eminently readable work is divided into six parts: "The Discovery of Dinosaurs," "The Study of Dinosaurs," "The Groups of Dinosaurs," "The Biology of Dinosaurs," "Dinosaur Evolution," and "Dinosaurs and the Media." An appendix provides a useful chronological history of dinosaur paleontology. Numerous illustrations throughout.

986 **The Dinosaur Society's dinosaur encyclopedia.** Don Lessem et al., eds. 533p. Random House, 1993. $25. ISBN 0-679-41770-2.
567.9 QE862

The Dinosaur Society has compiled a compendium of most of the species that have been formally named, including some of doubtful validity. Each entry includes species name, pronunciation, what is known about the dinosaur, and an illustration of its skeleton or drawing of what it may have looked like. Dinosaurs are arranged alphabetically by genus (e.g., *Tyrannosaurus rex* is listed under *Tyrannosaurus*). Period index and geographic indexes are included. There is also a listing of extinct animals that are not considered dinosaurs and, thus, are not included in the main text.

987 **Dinosaurs: the encyclopedia.** Donald F. Glut. 1088p. McFarland, 1997. $145. ISBN 0-89950-917-7.
567.9 QE862.D5

Presents the most current information available on dinosaurs and their world. Appeals to both the scholar and the educated lay reader. Describes the origins of dinosaurs and current theories on their extinction; provides thorough systematics, listing all known species as well as doubtful and no longer substantiated genera. Includes more than 1,400 illustrations. Exhaustive index and massive bibliography.

988 **Encyclopedia of dinosaurs.** Phillip J. Currie and Kevin Padlan, eds. 870p. Academic Pr., 1997. $99.95. ISBN 0-12-226810-5.
567.91 QE862

An award-winning work with alphabetically arranged, signed entries and detailed bibliographies. Added features include a classified list of dinosaur genera, a list of further readings, a glossary, and a chronology of events related to the study of prehistoric life.

Zoology

989 **The concise Oxford dictionary of zoology.** Michael Allaby, ed. 512p. Oxford Univ. Pr., 1992. Paper $13.95. ISBN 0-19-286093-3.
591 QL9

The recent interest in conservation and ecology demonstrates the need for more readily available zoological information. This dictionary, with its concise definitions of zoological terms and organisms, can fulfill this need. Entries are based on *The Oxford dictionary of natural history*. Many new terms are included. Alphabetical arrangement with frequent cross-references.

990 **Encyclopedia of endangered species.** 2d ed. Mary Emanoil, ed. 1230p. Gale, 1998. $75. ISBN 0-8103-8857-X.
574.529 QH75

About 700 animals and plants have been included from lists of the U.S. Fish and Wildlife Service, the convention of International Trade in Endangered Species, and the World Conservation Union. Entries for plants and animals include status of the animal, taxonomic classification, and geographic range. Includes popular and scientific name indexes and color and black-and-white photographs. Recommended for public and high school libraries.

991 **The encyclopedia of snakes.** Chris Mattison. Facts on File, 1995. $35. ISBN 0-8160-3072-3.
597.96 QL666

This informative and comprehensive book includes details on snake classification, evolution, diversity, size, shape, and coloration. Also included are articles on physiology, ecology, feeding, breeding, and human superstitions about snakes. Extensive color photographs. For the herpetologist as well as interested students. Recommended for large and small libraries.

992 **Endangered wildlife of the world.** 11v. 1600p. Marshall Cavendish, 1993. $399.95. ISBN 1-85435-489-2.
591.52 QL83

Covers animals listed on the U.S. Fish and Wildlife Endangered Species List or on the "Red List" of the International Union for the Conservation of Nature. Arranged alphabetically by common name, entries include scientific name, status in the wild, taxonomic classification, and a description of the animal. The last volume contains charts, indexes, appendixes, and a bibliography.

993 **The great book of the sea: a complete guide to marine life.** Francesco Guerrini. 277p. Courage Books, 1993. $19.98. ISBN 1-56138-270-1.
591.92 QL121

Originally published in Italy in 1988, this source is a valuable reference on life in or near the sea. It includes sections on birds, fish, reptiles, mammals, and marine invertebrates. Includes 1,000 full-color illustrations, species distribution maps, and subject index.

994 **Grzimek's encyclopedia of mammals.** 2d ed. 5v. McGraw-Hill, 1989. $525. ISBN 0-07-909508-9.
599 QL701

An outstanding feature of this beautiful set is the 3,500 color photographs. Entries are arranged by order and suborder but not by evolutionary complexity. There is no overall index to the set; users must depend on the indexes at the end of each volume.

995 **The Merck veterinary manual.** v.1– . Merck, 1955– . Irreg. (8th ed. 1998, $32. ISBN 0-911910-29-8.) ISSN 0076-6542.
636.0896 SF748

Technical manual for use by veterinarians in the diagnosis and treatment of animal diseases. Authoritative, up-to-date information presented in a brief, convenient format; includes recommended prescriptions. Thumb-indexed. Instructions for use of the manual are included.

996 **Venomous reptiles of North America.** Carl H. Ernst. 248p. Smithsonian, 1992. $35. ISBN 1-56098-114-8.
597.96 QL666.O6

Presents the natural history of twenty-two venomous species native to the United States and Canada. Arranged by family and species, each entry includes a range map, recognition guide, and habitat, behavior, and reproductive information. Color plates of all species are included. By extensively reviewing the literature, the author has created a valuable herpetological reference.

997 **Whales, dolphins, and porpoises.** Mark Carwardine. 256p. Dorling Kindersley, 1995. $29.95. ISBN 1-56458-621-9; paper $18.95. ISBN 1-56458-620-0.
599.5 QL737

This handbook is more than just "a visual guide to all the world's cetaceans"; it is also a true field guide, based upon direct marine observation, providing clear and distinct identification information on all seventy-nine species known to the author. Includes information on diet, habitat, anatomy, and behavior. Beautifully illustrated.

MANUFACTURING

998 **Dictionary of manufacturing terms: compiled from Tool and manufacturing engineers handbook, 4th edition.** Raymond F. Veilleux, ed. 121p. Society of Manufacturing Engineers, 1987. $21. ISBN 0-87263-279-2.
670.42 TS9

As manufacturing technology develops in a global market, there is a need for a clear reference for manufacturing terminology. This title will be useful in the office, on the shop floor, and in libraries serving manufacturers. Examples of manufacturing processes included are turning, drilling, reaming, milling, grinding, threading, forging, and casting.

999 **Dictionary of materials and manufacturing.** Vernon John, ed. 400p. Nichols, 1990. $59.95. ISBN 0-89397-371-8.
620.1 TA402

This dictionary contains an extensive discussion of materials and processes used in manufacturing and civil engineering construction: metals, ceramics, polymers, and composite materials. Entries for manufacturing cover machine processes and manufacturing systems. The intended audience is engineers, scientists, and students. Recommended for libraries with engineering collections.

1000 **Encyclopedia of textiles.** Judith Jerde. 260p. Facts on File, 1992. $45. ISBN 0-8160-2105-8.
677 TS1309

Textiles are all around us. This title presents the history and manufacturing of plant, animal, and synthetic fibers. Articles cover fabric types, production, technical terms, and key figures in textile history. With 200 photos, some of which are full page, this encyclopedia will appeal to everyone with an interest in fabrics and textiles.

MATHEMATICS

1001 A concise Oxford dictionary of mathematics. 2d ed. Christopher Clapham. 320p. Oxford Univ. Pr., 1996. $11.95. ISBN 0-19-290041-8.
510 QA5

Pure mathematics is the focus of this dictionary. It defines terms that high school and undergraduate mathematics students are likely to encounter in their studies. Alphabetical arrangement, boldface cross-references, formulas and graphs, and seven appendixes.

1002 CRC standard mathematical tables and formulae. 30th ed. Daniel Willinger, ed. 832p. CRC Pr., 1996. $44.95. ISBN 0-614-29956-X.
510 QA47

A standard reference source for students, mathematicians, and scientists. Mathematical tables are taken from the *CRC handbook of chemistry and physics*. Belongs in the reference collection of larger and smaller libraries.

1003 Encyclopedic dictionary of mathematics. 2d ed. Mathematical Society of Japan staff and Kiyosi Ito, eds. 2v. MIT Pr., 1993. Paper $75. ISBN 0-262-59020-4.
510 QA5

Under the auspices of the Mathematical Society of Japan, with assistance from the American Mathematical Society, MIT Press has published the most important mathematical encyclopedia in English—a concise, up-to-date collection of significant results in pure and applied mathematics. It has boldface cross-references and a lengthy subject index. Specialized libraries may also want to consider *Encyclopedia of mathematics,* a 1988 translation of a Soviet mathematical encyclopedia. The publication of a paperback edition in 1993 should make the *Encyclopedic dictionary of mathematics* more affordable to libraries.

1004 The Facts on File dictionary of mathematics. Rev. ed. Carol Gibson, ed. 240p. Facts on File, 1988. $24.95. ISBN 0-8160-1867-7.
510 QA5

The breadth of subject coverage and extensive cross-references make this book ideal for the general public. More than sixty-five line drawings complement the 1,200 entries in mathematics, computer science, artificial intelligence, robotics, banking, physics, cartography, and electronics. Among the tables are those presenting major mathematical symbols, powers and roots, and important constants. A solid dictionary for the nonmathematician.

1005 Handbook of mathematical, scientific, and engineering formulas, tables, functions, graphs, transforms. Research and Education Association staff; M. Fogiel, director. 1030p. Research and Education Assn., 1994. $34.95. ISBN 0-8789-1521-4.
502 QA40

Solving problems in mathematics and science requires application of appropriate formulas, functions, and transforms. Designed for professional scientists and engineers, this handbook will guide users to the correct formula. Mathematical chapters cover algebra, geometry, trigonometry, derivatives, integrals, probability, and other advanced mathematical topics. Scientific and engineering formulas include physical constants, thermodynamics, optics, mechanics, structural design, and electrical, chemical, and biomedical technologies. Useful for libraries with scientific collections.

1006 The Macmillan dictionary of measurement. Mike Darton and John Clark. 512p. Macmillan, 1994. $27.50. ISBN 0-02-525750-1.
389.1 QC82

This handy compilation brings together terms of measurement from thirty-five different categories, such as mathematics, engineering, sports, and coins. Entries are arranged alphabetically with cross-references. The British focus does not detract from the utility of this volume.

1007 Mathematics dictionary. 5th ed. Robert C. James et al., eds. 600p. Chapman & Hall, 1992. $42.95. ISBN 0-442-00741-8; paper $29.95. ISBN 0-442-01241-1.
510 QA5

Over the last fifty years this dictionary has defined mathematical terms for undergraduates, graduates, scientists, and mathematicians. The fifth edition includes terms and concepts that have gained in importance over the last few years, such as *chaos, catastrophe theory,* and *nonstandard numbers.* Includes tables of French, German, Russian, and Spanish mathematical terms and their English equivalents.

1008 Mathematics illustrated dictionary: facts, figures, and people. Rev. ed. Jeanne Bendick. 247p. Watts, 1989. $15.82. ISBN 0-531-10664-0.
510 QA5

Written with mathematics students in mind, the 2,000 entries in this title define terms and identify persons in geometry, algebra, statistics, trigonometry, and business math. Formulas are given for standard calculations (e.g., the quadratic formula). Line drawings selectively illustrate the text. Large font, clear entries, and a how-to-use introduction help even young students to consult this tool unassisted.

1009 The words of mathematics: an etymological dictionary of mathematical terms used in English. Steven Schwartzman. 262p. Mathematical Assn. of America, 1994. Paper $34. ISBN 0-88385-511-9.
510 QA5

This title is an etymological guide to 1,500 common mathematical terms, defined not in a technical sense, but rather by their origins and literal meanings. As mathematics developed, words were borrowed and minted from Greek, Latin, Arabic, and English. Entries are arranged alphabetically, some with line drawings, and include forms and origins of terms with their modern meaning. Useful for students and teachers of mathematics.

Physics

1010 A concise dictionary of physics. New ed. 308p. Oxford Univ. Pr., 1990. Paper $10.95. ISBN 0-19-286111-5.
530 QC5

Derived from the *Concise science dictionary,* this title defines about 2,700 terms in physics, astronomy, and physical chemistry, as well as mathematics, metal science, and quantum mechanics. SI (metric) units are used throughout. Line drawings are used to clarify entries. Useful for both undergraduate and graduate physics students.

1011 Encyclopedia of modern physics. Robert A. Meyers, ed.; Steven N. Shore, scientific consultant. 773p. Academic Pr., 1989. $116. ISBN 0-12-226692-7.
530 QC5

This encyclopedia is devoted to topics on the cutting edge of physics, along with related long-standing areas of research. New discoveries and technologies are emphasized. Articles are on such topics as chaos, plasma science, quasi crystals, and superconductivity. Valuable for scientists, students, and professionals wishing to find information on the more contemporary questions in physics.

1012 Encyclopedia of physics. 2d ed. Rita G. Lerner and George L. Trigg, eds. 1408p. Wiley, 1990. $125. ISBN 0-471-18719-4.
530.03 QC5

Perhaps more than for other sciences, physics publications are anchored in the time they are printed. Advances in knowledge can change the approach to phenomena by physicists. This encyclopedia shows these changes with updated articles in topics such as superconductivity, fractals, and supersymmetry. Signed entries are alphabetically arranged and include cross-references and bibliographies at the end of the entry. Reading level of items in the bibliography (elementary, intermediate, advanced) is included. Useful for college and larger public libraries.

1013 The Facts on File dictionary of physics. Rev. ed. John Daintith et al., eds. 240p. Facts on File, 1988. $24.95. ISBN 0-8160-1868-5; paper $12.95. ISBN 0-8160-2366-2.
530 QC5

In a field as expansive as physics, a good dictionary is a necessity. The 3,000 definitions presented here cover advances in solid-state and quantum physics. More than fifty line drawings help define the more complex concepts. A short appendix includes conversion factors and physical quantity symbols. The clear text has imbedded cross-references. Can be used by students and by technical professionals.

1014 Macmillan encyclopedia of physics. 4v. Macmillan, 1996. $400. ISBN 0-02-897359-3.
530.03 QC5

These 900 articles, arranged alphabetically, offer clear explanations of the concepts, laws, and phenomena of physics as they relate to topics ranging from rainbows to earthquakes. Accessible and yet still profound, these essays do much to open the world and work of physics to the general reader. Includes numerous biographical entries, tables, and an index.

Transportation

1015 AAMA motor vehicle facts and figures. American Automobile Manufacturers Assn., 1976– . Annual. $20. ISSN 0272-3395.
338.4 HD9710

From an overview of the past year's events in the automobile industry, this primary statistical compilation looks at production, sales, and registrations; at ownership and usage; and at economic and social impact of passenger cars, motor trucks, and motor buses. Most data are reported for multiple years, allowing easy comparison. The work is indexed. Larger libraries may also want to invest in the heftier *World motor vehicle data* (ISSN 0085-8307).

1016 Automotive dictionary: a complete glossary of terms for automotive enthusiasts, racers, and engineers. John Edwards and Michael Lufty, eds. 208p. HP Books, 1993. Paper $16.95. ISBN 1-55788-056-5.
629.2 TL9

Engineering terms, automotive components, racing jargon, and hot-rodding slang have all been assembled into this attractive dictionary. Many black-and-white photographs and line drawings help the text bring automotive terms into alignment. This dictionary will be popular in both public and university libraries.

1017 NADA official used car guide. National Automobile Dealers Used Car Guide Co., 1992– . Quarterly. $9.95. ISSN 1061-9054.
629 HD9710

One of several NADA value guides, this is the ubiquitous "blue book" prized by car dealers, shoppers, and traders, not to mention consumers with insurance problems. The latest edition lists seven years of used-car values. Should be in every library serving patrons old enough to drive.

Vehicular Maintenance and Repair

1018 Chilton's auto repair manual. Kerry A. Freeman et al., eds. Chilton Book Co., 1968– . Annual. (1995–99 ed. $59.95. ISBN 0-8019-7922-6.) ISSN 0069-3634.
629.28 TL152

Chilton is the most familiar name in automobile repair manuals. This title covers mass-produced American-made autos. It breaks the car down into engineering, brakes, drivetrain, suspension, and other components. For the do-it-yourself auto mechanic. The backlist of titles covers auto repair manuals for U.S. autos to 1940. Manuals in Spanish for domestic and import cars are available for autos made from 1976 to 1991.

1019 Chilton's easy car care. 3d ed. Kerry A. Freeman, ed. Chilton Book Co., 1990. $17.95. ISBN 0-8019-8619-2.
629.28 TL152

This title should find a place in every reference collection, as it provides easy, basic instructions on maintenance and repair that assume no prior knowledge or experience with automobiles. Thirty-five chapters cover the fundamentals, from tools and supplies to buying and owning a car; the car components, from the electrical system to wheels and tires; and cosmetics, from interior care to body care and repair. Tune-up specifications, glossary, and index are included.

1020 Chilton's import car repair manual. Chilton Book Co., 1986– . Annual. $28.95. (1993–97 [1996]: ISBN 0-8019-7920-X.) ISSN 1044-2456.
629.28 TL152

This is the companion volume to *Chilton's auto repair*, with recent editions including the last five model years for automobiles imported into the United States and Canada. The arrangement is similar to that of the domestic volume. Earlier editions provide repair instructions back to 1964.

1021 Chilton's motorcycle and ATV repair manual. Chilton Book Co., 1985– . Irreg. $34.95. ISSN 1050-0251.
629.28 TL444

In addition to vehicular specifications given in the standard Chilton arrangement of manufacturer, then model, the copious illustrations, and the usual notes and warnings, there is also a general information section and glossary for novices. The scope here is popular street, off-road, and all-terrain vehicles (ATVs). Historical volume available for model years 1945–85.

1022 Chilton's truck and van repair manual, 1993–97. Chilton staff. Freeman, 1996. $28.95. ISBN 0-8019-7918-8.
629.28 TL230.2

This biennial volume is the equivalent for trucks and vans of *Chilton's auto repair manual* and *Chilton's import car repair manual*. It covers the last five model years for gasoline- and diesel-powered domestic and imported pickup trucks, vans, RVs, four-wheel drives, and utility vehicles. It is similar in arrangement to the volume on autos. Earlier editions should be kept to provide coverage back to 1961.

1023 Motor auto repair manual, [yr.]. 2v. Motor, 1937– . Annual. v.1, General Motors Corp.; v.2, Chrysler Corp., Ford Motor Co. (59th ed. 1995, $192/set. v.1, ISBN 0-87851-860-6; v.2, ISBN 0-87851-861-4.) ISSN 0098-1745.
629.28 TL152

Written for the mechanic with some experience, this title presents mechanical repair procedures as well as tune-up and performance specifications for American-made automobiles. A general section on procedures is followed by specific instructions, arranged by make of car. Each annual volume covers models for the current year plus at least five previous years and includes a detailed table of contents.

1024 Motor light truck and van repair manual. Professional service trade ed. Motor, 1984– . Annual. $104. ISSN 0077-1724.
629.28 TL230.2

This volume, popular with the mechanically experienced, includes some 3,000 models of American manufacturers' pickups, four-wheel drives, vans, RVs, campers, motor homes, and delivery trucks from the latest several years. Mechanical specifications, arranged by make, and service procedures, arranged by system, are accompanied by tables, charts, illustrations, troubleshooting diagrams, and step-by-step instructions.

Weapons and Warfare

1025 Dictionary of military terms. 3d rev. ed. U.S. Department of Defense, comp. 512p. Stackpole Books, 1995. $44.95. ISBN 1-85367-217-3.
■ cd
355 U24

Terms included in this dictionary are words of general military significance not usually found in standard dictionaries. Technical terms are included if they can be easily understood. This dictionary was created to cover the standard military terminology used in joint military operations of multinational forces such as NATO and the UN.

1026 Directory of U.S. military bases worldwide. 3d ed. William Evinger. 456p. Oryx, 1998. $125. ISBN 1-57356-049-9.
355.7 UA26

With stories about bases closing and American military personnel around the globe appearing daily in newspapers, interest in U.S. bases is high. This directory lists all U.S. military bases, alphabetically by state for bases in the United States and alphabetically by country for overseas bases. Each entry includes name, address, phone number, major commands, history of the base, visitor attractions, names and numbers of key contacts, and a summary of housing, medical, and other on-base facilities.

1027 International military and defense encyclopedia. Trevor N. Dupuy et al., eds. 6v. 3132p. Brassey's, 1993. $1300. ISBN 0-02-881011-2.
355 U24

This title is the first comprehensive English-language encyclopedia of international defense information. The six-volume set has 768 entries on military topics from the ancient world to the conflicts in the Persian Gulf and Bosnia. Students of political and military history will enjoy this tremendous compilation. It contains well-written entries, authoritative bibliographies, and a subject index. Its international, panhistorical coverage adds to its usefulness.

1028 Weapons: an international encyclopedia from 5000 B.C. to 2000 A.D. Updated ed. 336p. St. Martin's, 1990. $29.95. ISBN 0-312-03951-4; paper $19.95. ISBN 0-312-03950-6.
623.4 U800

People have been arming themselves for a very long time. This title brings together in one volume all of the different armaments used throughout history. Similar weapons are grouped together. Entries include a discussion of the history and use of individual weapons along with illustrations of the weapon and its use. Appendixes include regional and historical indexes, famous names glossary, bibliography, and subject index.

12

Health and Medicine

BARBARA M. BIBEL

Because health science information changes rapidly, it is important to maintain a current collection. Works listed here were the latest available editions at the time, but many are updated regularly. When ordering, always request the latest edition.

General

Bibliographies and Guides

1029 Consumer health information source book. 5th ed. Alan M. Rees. 232p. Oryx, 1997. $59.50. ISBN 0-57356-047-2.
016.613 RA776

Designed to help consumers make informed choices, this is also a useful source for collection development. It includes health information, information access, materials on specific health issues and conditions, and a core list of recommended consumer health publications. Electronic publications and databases are listed in this edition. There are author, title, and subject indexes and a directory of publishers' addresses.

1030 Consumer health USA: essential information from the federal health network. Alan M. Rees, ed. 543p. Oryx, 1995. $55. ISBN 0-89774-889-1.
616 RC81

Information reproduced from federal publications on various diseases and conditions, including a referral list of hot lines and state agencies. It is very useful for lay readers making health care decisions; it will be most appropriate for libraries without federal depository collections.

1031 Encyclopedia of health information sources: a bibliographic guide to over 13,000 citations for publications, organizations, and databases on health-related subjects. 2d ed. Alan M. Rees, ed. 521p. Gale, 1993. $175. ISBN 0-8103-6909-5.
016.61 R118

More than 13,000 citations from 6,715 sources covering the medical specialties, allied health professions, alternative health disciplines, health care administration, and education. The text is arranged alphabetically by subject and within subject by type of publication. There is no index, but a detailed table of contents and ample cross-references facilitate access.

Indexes and Abstracts

1032 Index medicus. National Library of Medicine, 1960– . Monthly with annual cumulations. $260/yr.; $55/yr. abridged. Depository item. ISSN 0019-3879.
■ cd online tape
016.61 R5

The principal index for the field of medicine. Provides access to thousands of academic and professional biomedical journals. It is arranged by subject, using the standard Medical Subject Headings (MESH) developed by the National Library of Medicine. All articles have English-language abstracts. Both professionals and lay readers will find this an extremely useful tool for locating the latest medical information.

Dictionaries and Encyclopedias

1033 The American Heritage Stedman's medical dictionary. 923p. Houghton, 1995. $24.95. ISBN 0-395-69955-X.
610.3 R121

A desk dictionary for lay readers that contains 45,000 entries, including biographical information about important scientists and physicians. There are charts and tables of anatomy, weights and measures, and recommended daily allowances of nutrients. Illustrated with line drawings.

1034 Black's medical dictionary. 38th ed. 656p. Barnes & Noble Imports, 1996. $130.75. ISBN 0-389-20145-5.
610.3 R121

This dictionary, illustrated with line drawings and graphs, has longer entries than most. Many are several paragraphs long, with extensive information on diseases and parts of the body. The language is accessible to educated lay readers.

1035 Cecil textbook of medicine. 20th ed. James Wyngarden, ed. 2380p. Saunders, 1996. $105. ISBN 0-7216-3573-3; 2v. ed. $130. ISBN 0-7216-3561-X.
■ cd

Harrison's principles of internal medicine. 14th ed. Anthony S. Fauci et al. 2569p. McGraw-Hill, 1998. 2v. ed. $135. ISBN 0-97-912913-X; 1v. ed. $105. ISBN 0-07-020291-5.
616.22 RC46

These standard medical textbooks offer detailed information about the diagnosis and treatment of diseases affecting all the systems of the human body. Although they are technical, lay readers use them, often with a medical dictionary, to learn more about various conditions and illnesses. Libraries should consider purchasing one of these.

1036 The dictionary of modern medicine. J. C. Segen, comp. and ed. 900p. Parthenon, 1992. $75. ISBN 1-85070-321-3.
610.3 R121

A sourcebook of currently used medical expressions, jargon, and technical terms. There are many words here that are not included in more traditional medical dictionaries. Some abbreviations are defined.

1037 Dorland's illustrated medical dictionary. 28th ed. 1940p. Saunders, 1994. $45.95. ISBN 0-7126-2859-1.

Dorland's pocket medical dictionary. 25th ed. Saunders, 1995. Paper $22.95. ISBN 0-7126-5738-9.
610.3 R121

The new edition of *Dorland's illustrated* for professional and educated lay users contains 115,000 entries, and 7,500 are new. Improvements include two-color anatomy plates, a better typeface, and seven appendixes with medical abbreviations; weight, measure, dosage, and temperature conversion; and reference laboratory values. This is the standard professional source and the authority for the Medical Subject Headings (MESH). The pocket dictionary has about 50,000 entries.

1038 Encyclopedia of medical devices and instrumentation. John J. Webster, ed. in chief. 4v. Wiley, 1988. $625. ISBN 0-471-82936-6.
610.28 R856

A unique encyclopedia that explains the structure and function of medical instruments and devices. It contains articles on everything from dialysis machines to CAT and MRI scanners. The language is somewhat technical but accessible to most readers.

1039 Gale encyclopedia of medicine. 5v. Gale, 1999. $499. ISBN 0-7876-1868-3.
610.3 RC81

Compiled by experienced medical writers, this new addition to the medical reference area seeks to describe some 1,500 of the most common medical disorders, conditions, tests, and treatments with both authority and thoroughness. The text and its language are aimed at the general reader, and the editors have provided definitions and illustrations to enhance comprehension. Reference librarians have long sought a medical encyclopedia appropriate for the lay reader, and Gale's encyclopedia is the first to address this need.

1040 International dictionary of medicine and biology. Sidney I. Landau, ed. 3v. 3200p. Churchill Livingstone, 1987. $495. ISBN 0-471-01849-X.
610.3 R121

An unabridged dictionary of the biomedical sciences. It is written for professionals, but informed lay readers will be able to use it.

1041 The inverted medical dictionary. 2d ed. Mary J. Stanaszek et al., eds. 322p. Technomic, 1991. $59.95. ISBN 0-87762-825-4.
610.3 R121

This dictionary allows users to find medical terms for something described in lay language. The brief entries include drug and prescription terms; most medical, chemical, and pharmacological abbreviations; and weights and measures.

1042 Macmillan encyclopedia of health. 8v. Macmillan, 1993. $375. ISBN 0-02-897439-5.

Marshall Cavendish encyclopedia of family health. 12v. Marshall Cavendish, 1991. $459.95. ISBN 1-85435-420-5.
610.3 RA776

These profusely illustrated encyclopedias provide brief articles on a broad range of medical and health topics. They are written in lay language and are very useful for students doing reports. *Marshall Cavendish* is a British publication, using British spelling and style, but this is not a problem for most readers.

1043 Melloni's illustrated medical dictionary. 3d ed. B. John Melloni et al., eds. 550p. Williams & Wilkins, 1993. $28.95. ISBN 1-85070-479-1.
610.3 R121

The outstanding feature of this dictionary is the use of illustration as an integral part of the definitions. There are more than 2,500 high-quality line drawings sharing equal space with the text of the 26,000 entries. The definitions are written for lay readers.

1044 Mosby's medical, nursing, and allied health dictionary. 5th ed. Mosby staff. 1968p. Mosby, 1997. $31.95. ISBN 0-8151-4800-3.
610.3 R121

This dictionary for paraprofessional and lay readers has been updated with the addition of 6,000 new entries, 2,000 full-color illustrations, and many tables. The appendixes contain diagnostic and procedural information, abbreviations, and anatomical classifications. An excellent general medical dictionary.

1045 The Oxford companion to medicine. John Walton et al., eds. 1038p. Oxford Univ. Pr., 1995. $50. ISBN 0-19-262355-9.
610.3 RC41

The new edition of this classic reference has been reduced to one volume and written for anyone with an interest in medicine. It is a cross between a dictionary and a one-volume encyclopedia with articles on medical fields and broad topics such as "Art and medicine." Libraries owning the old two-volume edition will want to retain it because it contains useful material not found in the new version. The new edition also has material not in the old one.

1046 The Oxford dictionary of sports science and medicine. Michael Kent, ed. 512p. Oxford Univ. Pr., 1994. $21.95. ISBN 0-19-262263-3.
617.1 RC1206

Growing interest in sports and fitness makes this dictionary timely as well as useful. It contains 7,500 entries with brief definitions of terms used in sports science and medicine.

1047 Stedman's abbreviations, acronyms, and symbols. 674p. Williams & Wilkins, 1991. $24. ISBN 0-683-07926-3.
610.14 R123

Definitions of more than 20,000 terms and symbols. There is an alphabetical section for letter abbreviations and a separate visual section for symbols organized by type: arrow, statistical symbols, genetic symbols, Greek alphabet, and so forth.

1048 Stedman's medical dictionary. 26th ed. various pagings. Williams & Wilkins, 1995. $55. ISBN 0-683-07922-0.
610.3 R121

A standard dictionary for health professionals. The definitions are brief, but they include pronunciation. Line drawings supplement the text.

1049 The wellness encyclopedia. Editors of the Univ. of California Wellness Letter. 624p. Houghton, 1995. Paper $25. ISBN 0-395-73345-6.
613 RA776

The title is self-explanatory. This is a manual of health maintenance with detailed information about diet, exercise, stress reduction, and disease prevention.

Directories

1050 American dental directory. American Dental Assn. Annual. $187.50. ISSN 0065-8073.
617.6 RK37

Lists dentists in the United States who are members of the American Dental Association and gives information about their training and specialties. Organized alphabetically by state and city.

1051 American Hospital Association guide to the health-care field. American Hospital Assn., 1945– . Annual. $280. ISSN 0094-8969.
362.1 RA977.A1

Geographical listing of accredited hospitals, long-term care facilities, and American military hospitals. Codes designate available services and facilities. A companion volume, *Hospital statistics* (Annual. $139. ISSN 0090-6662), supplies data on utilization, expenses, revenues, and personnel.

1052 The best hospitals in America. 2d ed. John W. Wright and Linda Sunshine. 630p. Gale, 1995. $39.95. ISBN 0-8130-9874-5; paper $18.95. ISBN 0-614-21991-4.

America's best hospitals. 560p. Wiley, 1996. $19.95. ISBN 0-471-12614-4.
362.1 RA981

Lists of the major medical centers in the United States and Canada. Information about distinguished physicians who are on their staffs and their specialties. These books also offer advice on choosing health care facilities. *America's best hospitals* gives detailed rankings by specialty for every state.

1053 Directory of nursing homes. Health Care Investment Analysts, 1993– . Annual. $225. ISSN 0888-7624.
362.16 RA997

Licensed long-term care facilities in the United States listed by state and city. Provides information about available services, admission requirements, facilities, Medicare and Medicaid certification, and number of beds.

1054 Directory of physicians in the United States. 35th ed. 4v. American Medical Assn., 1995. $495. ISBN 0-89970-389-5.
■ cd
610.2 R712

Licensed physicians and Doctors of Osteopathy who are members of the American Medical Association. There are alphabetical and geographic indexes. Numerical codes indicate medical schools attended, residencies, and type of practice for each physician.

1055 HMO/PPO directory from Medical Device Register. Heidi Stegenthaler Garret, ed. Various pagings. Medical Economics, 1993– . Annual. $199. ISSN 0887-4484.
362.04 RA13.5

Organized geographically by state, this directory provides detailed information about managed health care organizations in the United States. Listings for key decision makers are included.

1056 Medical and health information directory. 9th ed. Karen Backus, ed. 3v. Gale, 1998. $569/set. ISBN 0-7876-1556-0; v.1, $235. ISBN 0-7876-1557-9; v.2, $235. ISBN 0-7876-1558-7; v.3, $235. ISBN 0-7876-1559-5.
610 R712

Provides access to a wide range of health-related information. Volume 1 covers agencies and institutions, including associations, government agencies, HMOs, insurance companies, drug companies, and schools. Volume 2 lists publishers, libraries, and other information services. Volume 3 lists health services, such as home health care, substance abuse treatment, organ transplant services, and special clinics. The volumes are available separately.

1057 National directory of chiropractic. One Directory of Chiropractic, 1990– . Annual. $26.
615.5 RZ233

Lists chiropractors, colleges of chiropractic, suppliers of equipment and services, state associations, and state licensing boards and information for the United States. Access is alphabetical and geographic.

1058 The official ABMS directory of board certified medical specialists. 28th ed. 4v. Marquis Who's Who, 1996. $439.95. ISBN 0-8379-0539-7.
■ cd
610 R712

Information about board-certified medical specialists is organized by specialty and geographically within each specialty. There are instructions for use and a list of abbreviations in each volume. Lists of state medical boards, certifying boards, tables of numbers of specialists, and a master name index are included.

Handbooks, Statistics, and Diagnosis

1059 Accident facts. Statistics Department, National Safety Council staff, comp. National Safety Council, 1921– . Annual. $37.95. ISSN 0148-6039.
614.8 HA217

An annual compendium providing a wealth of statistical information on different types of accidents in the United States. The majority are transportation related, but occupational and home accidents are also included. A bargain that belongs in all collections.

1060 The American Medical Association family medical guide. 3d ed. Charles B. Clayman, ed. Random House, 1994. $37.50. ISBN 0-679-41290-5.
■ cd
616 RC81

This illustrated lay medical guide offers current basic medical information. It is well illustrated and uses flowcharts to guide users through self-diagnosis and treatment decisions. A first-aid guide, glossary, and index complete the work. A good source for unsophisticated readers.

1061 The Columbia University College of Physicians and Surgeons complete home medical guide. 3d ed. Donald Tapley et al., eds. 976p. Crown, 1995. $50. ISBN 0-517-59610-5.
613 RC81

This outstanding source has been completely revised and updated. New features include a table of commonly prescribed drugs, sidebars with information on alternative therapies, sections on different treatments for men and women, and many new illustrations, charts, and graphs. There are also directories of resources and poison control centers and information on using the health care system effectively.

1062 Conn's current therapy. Robert J. Rakel, ed. 1204p. Saunders, 1982– . Annual. $59.95. ISSN 8755-0070.
616 RM101

Each year this book provides an overview of the latest developments in treating diseases and chronic conditions. It is written for physicians, but lay readers will also find it useful.

1063 Current medical diagnosis and treatment. 1490p. Appleton & Lange, 1961– . Annual. (37th ed. 1998, $45. ISBN 0-8385-1542-X.) ISSN 0092-8682.
616.075 RC46

Current obstetric and gynecological diagnosis and treatment. 9th ed. 1230p. Appleton & Lange, 1997. $41.95. ISBN 0-8395-1401-4.
618 RG526

Current pediatric diagnosis and treatment. 13th ed. Appleton & Lange, 1996. $45. ISBN 0-8385-1400-6. ISSN 0093-8556.
618.92 RJ50

Current surgical diagnosis and treatment. 11th ed. 1426p. Prentice-Hall, 1997. Paper $45. ISBN 0-8385-1456-1.
618 RG526

The Current diagnosis and treatment series keeps medical practitioners informed about the latest developments in their fields. Librarians and their patrons use them as ready reference sources for current medical information. The medical volume is annual. The others are revised on an irregular schedule.

1064 **Everyone's guide to outpatient surgery.** James Macho and Greg Cable. 178p. Andrews & McMeel, 1994. $24.95. ISBN 0-8362-2422-1; paper $14.95. ISBN 0-8362-2421-3.
617.02 RD110

The surgery book: an illustrated guide to seventy-three of the most common operations. 448p. St. Martin's, 1993. $27.95. ISBN 0-312-09398-5.
617 RD31.3

These books explain preparation for surgery, operating room procedures, the specifics of common operations, and the advantages and disadvantages of outpatient and inpatient treatment. They also offer advice about choosing practitioners and facilities. *The surgery book* has line drawings showing surgical procedures.

1065 **Everything you need to know about diseases.** Matthew Cahill, ed. 928p. Springhouse, 1996. $24.95. ISBN 0-87434-822-6.
616 RC81

Everything you need to know about medical tests. SPC staff. 691p. Springhouse, 1997. $24.95. ISBN 0-97434-933-8.
616.07 RC81

Everything you need to know about medical treatment. Matthew Cahill, ed. 628p. Springhouse, 1996. $26.95. ISBN 0-87434-821-8.
616 RC81

These three books provide information about 500 diseases, 400 tests, and 300 treatments in lay language, including symptoms, diagnosis, normal and abnormal results, self-help information, advice for caregivers, and traveler's advisory.

1066 **The home health guide to poisons and antidotes.** Carol Turkington. 384p. Facts on File, 1994. $27.95. ISBN 0-8160-2825-7; paper $12.95. ISBN 0-8160-3316-1.
615.9 RA1216

Covers poisonous snakes, spiders, plants, chemicals, drugs, and agricultural chemicals. It also deals with food poisoning. Symptoms, treatments, and descriptions are given for each of the substances. There are directories of poison control centers, hot lines, organizations, and sources of educational materials. Indexes of toxicity ratings and poisons by symptoms complete the book.

1067 **Johns Hopkins symptoms and remedies: the complete home medical reference.** Simeon Margolis, ed. 830p. Rebus, 1995. $39.95. ISBN 0-929661-19-2.
612.02 RC81

Symptoms and early warning signs: a comprehensive guide to more than 600 medical symptoms and what they mean. Michael Apple et al. 496p. Dutton, 1994. $24.95. ISBN 0-525937-32-3; paper (1995) $15.95. ISBN 0-452-27113-4.
616.047 RC69

These two books explain symptoms and their possible causes. *Johns Hopkins* has two sections. The first is in chart format showing symptoms with diagnostic possibilities. The second is a list of diseases with symptoms, diagnosis, treatment, prevention, and when to call a physician. *Symptoms* is arranged by body system and uses a narrative format.

1068 **Mayo Clinic family health book.** 2d ed. David E. Larson, ed. in chief. 1500p. Morrow, 1996. $42.50. ISBN 0-688-14478-0.
■ cd
613 RC81

An excellent general overview of human anatomy and physiology, diseases, symptoms, and treatments. A second edition has been released on CD-ROM.

1069 **Medical tests and diagnostic procedures: a patient's guide to just what the doctor ordered.** Philip Shtasel. 316p. HarperCollins, 1991. Paper $10.95. ISBN 0-06-272001-5.
616.075 RC82

This book explains medical tests and their risks and benefits. A unique feature is a rating system using plus signs (+) to denote the level of discomfort to the patient.

1070 **The Merck manual of diagnosis and therapy.** Robert Berkow, ed. Merck, 1950– . (17th ed. 1999, $35. ISBN 0-911910-10-7.) ISSN 0076-6526.
615.5 RC55

A ready reference source for health care professionals providing the latest information on the diagnosis and treatment of diseases and chronic conditions. Educated lay readers will be able to use it. Spanish-language edition available.

1071 The Mount Sinai Medical Center family health guide to dental health. Jack Klatell et al. 304p. Macmillan, 1991. $29.95. ISBN 0-025-63675-8.
617.6 RK61

This guide explains oral anatomy, basic dental health, and dental treatments, including orthodontia and implants, in lay language. It is the only current source on this subject.

1072 People's Medical Society health desk reference: information your doctor can't or won't tell you; everything you need to know for the best in health care. Charles B. Inlander and the People's Medical Society staff. 672p. Hyperion (dist. by Little, Brown), 1996. Paper $19.95. ISBN 0-7868-8167-4. (*formerly* **The consumer's medical desk reference.**)
362.1 RC81

This book focuses on helping the public to make informed decisions and take control of medical treatment. It provides a great deal of information on the types of practitioners, facilities, and insurance coverage available; lists of professional and government organizations for referral; information on risks involved in treatments, tests, and drugs; travel information; and a glossary. Much of this information is not found in more traditional medical guides. A reasonably priced, useful source.

1073 Physician's guide to rare diseases. 2d ed. Jess G. Thoene, ed. 1200p. Dowden, 1995. $129.99. ISBN 0-9628716-1-3.
616.07 RC69

This book contains information about exotic and less-common diseases not found in most medical guides (e.g, rare genetic syndromes, tropical diseases). It fills a genuine need in medical collections.

1074 Professional guide to diseases. 6th ed. 1330p. Springhouse, 1998. $39.95. ISBN 0-87434-926-5.
616 RT65

An illustrated text written for nurses but also useful to lay readers. It is divided into broad chapters (e.g., genetic disorders, neoplasms) with a general introduction and sections on specific diseases.

1075 Statistical record of health and medicine. 2d ed. Charity Anne Dorgan, ed. 1200p. Gale, 1998. $115. ISBN 0-7876-1608-X. ISSN 1078-6961.
613 RA407

Health United States. U.S. Department of Health and Human Resources. National Center for Health Statistics, 1975– . Annual. $19. ISSN 0361-4468. SuDoc HE320.7042/6:yr.
362 RA407

Information about the general health of Americans. The Gale source contains statistics from both government and private sources, including international comparisons. *Health United States* covers trends in disease prevalence and health determinants with racial and ethnic detail, utilization of health resources, and expenditures. Every third year a prevention profile is included.

1076 Toxics A to Z. John Harte. 479p. Univ. of California Pr., 1991. $75. ISBN 0-520-07223-5; paper $22.50. ISBN 0-520-07224-3.
615.9 RA1213

This book provides an overview of toxic substances and pollution at home and in the workplace, the environmental implications of their use, methods of exposure, management, and regulation. There is an alphabetical listing of common toxics with their characteristics and how to prevent exposure and protect oneself and a bibliography.

1077 The Yale University School of Medicine patient's guide to medical tests. Barry L. Zaret, ed. Houghton, 1997. $40. ISBN 0-395-76536-6.
616.07 RC71

Describes in detail the most common diagnostic procedures currently in use. A welcome addition to the health collection of any public library.

AIDS

1078 AIDS information sourcebook. 3d ed. H. Robert Malinowsky and Gerald J. Perry. 224p. Oryx, 1991. Paper $39.95. ISBN 0-89774-598-1.
616.9792 RC607

This directory and bibliography lists more than 700 government and private agencies, hospitals, programs, and groups that provide education and support to AIDS patients and their families. It also contains a bibliography of books, journals, articles, and films and a chronology of the AIDS epidemic.

1079 **The AIDS knowledge base: a textbook on HIV disease from the University of California, San Francisco, and the San Francisco General Hospital.** 2d ed. P. T. Cohen and Paul A. Volberding. Various pagings. Lippincott-Raven, 1994. $125. ISBN 0-316-77067-1.
616.9792 RC607

A comprehensive source of the latest clinical, legal, ethical, and psychosocial information on the care of HIV/AIDS patients. Although written for health professionals, educated lay readers will appreciate it.

1080 **AIDS sourcebook.** 2d ed. Karen Bellenir, ed. Omnigraphics, 1998. $78. ISBN 0-7808-0225-X.
362.1 RC607

Provides for the lay reader clear and direct information about AIDS and HIV infection; includes historical and statistical data, current research, prevention measures, and special topics of interest for persons living with AIDS. Sources for further assistance are listed for each topic.

ALTERNATIVE HEALTH CARE

1081 **The alternative health and medicine encyclopedia.** 2d ed. James Marti. 400p. Gale, 1998. $45. ISBN 0-7876-0073-3.
616.53 R733

Alternative medicine: the definitive guide. Burton Goldberg Group staff. 1068p. Future Medicine, 1995. $59.95. ISBN 0-9636334-3-0.
615.5 R733

These two sources provide an overview of alternative health care. The Gale source is less detailed, but it contains an interesting essay on the future of health care. *Alternative medicine: the definitive guide* contains in-depth articles on alternative therapies by acknowledged experts in the field.

1082 **Alternative medicine yellow pages: the comprehensive guide to the new world of health.** Melinda Bonk, ed. 225p. Future Medicine, 1994. Paper $12.95. ISBN 0-9636334-2-2.
615.5 R733

Alternative practitioners are listed by therapy and, within each section, geographically. Despite its title, it is not a complete listing of alternative therapists.

1083 **The doctor's book of home remedies: thousands of tips and techniques anyone can use to heal everyday health problems.** Debora Tkac. 676p. Rodale, 1990. $27.95. ISBN 0-87857-873-0.

The doctor's book of home remedies II: over 1,000 new doctor-tested tips anyone can use to heal hundreds of everyday health problems. Sid Kricheimer. 613p. Rodale, 1993. $27.95. ISBN 0-87596-158-4.
610 RC81

Two books full of simple things that can make you feel better: using heat, cold, exercise, herbs, and even chicken soup. The authors are careful to indicate when medical care is needed. Both are available in Spanish.

1084 **Encyclopedia of natural medicine.** Michael Murray and Joseph Pizzorno. 640p. Prima, 1991. Paper $19.95. ISBN 1-55958-091-7.
615.5 RZ433

Written by two naturopaths, this encyclopedia provides detailed information about alternative therapy for common illnesses and chronic conditions. The authors are careful to indicate when the services of a traditional physician are needed (appendicitis, fractures, etc.).

1085 **The healing herbs: the ultimate guide to the curative power of nature's medicines.** Michael Castleman. 448p. Rodale, 1991. $27.95. ISBN 0-87857-934-6.
615.321 RM66

An herbal written by a respected alternative health educator, this book contains color illustrations of healing plants and clear explanations of how and when to use them. There is a Spanish-language edition.

1086 **New choices in natural healing: over 1,000 of the best self-help remedies from the world of alternative medicine.** Bill Gottlieb et al., eds. 687p. Rodale, 1995. $27.95. ISBN 0-87596-257-2.
615.5 RA776.95

This book offers information about twenty different natural therapies and treatments for 163 common health problems. The author always advises when to consult a physician.

Anatomy and Physiology

1087 **Atlas of human anatomy.** 2d ed. Frank Henry Netter and Arthur F. Dalley, eds. 525p. Novartis, 1997. $84.95. ISBN 0-914168-80-0.

Grant's atlas of anatomy. 9th ed. J. C. Boileau Grant and James Edward Anderson. Various pagings. Williams & Wilkins, 1991. $50. ISBN 0-683-03702-3.

The human body on file. Diagram Group staff. Loose-leaf. 300p. Facts on File, 1983. $155. ISBN 0-87196-706-5.
611 QM25

Basic anatomy atlases are heavily used in both public and academic libraries. The Netter and Grant atlases provide very detailed coverage of the whole body by organ system and in layers, starting from the outside and working inward. But because these books are bound and in color, their illustrations are not easy to reproduce. *The human body on file* offers clear black-and-white line drawings in a loose-leaf format, which makes photocopying easy.

1088 **Gray's anatomy.** 38th ed. Peter L. Williams et al., eds. 2092p. Churchill Livingstone, 1995. $175. ISBN 0-443-04560-7. Luxury ed. $435. ISBN 0-443-05327-8.
611 QM23.2

The classic text and standard reference tool for human anatomy. It contains more than 1,000 illustrations—approximately half are in color—and a very detailed index. It is frequently revised.

1089 **The human body: an illustrated guide to its structure, function, and disorders.** Charles Clayman, ed. in chief. 240p. Dorling Kindersley, 1995. $29.95. ISBN 1-56458-992-7.
612 QP38

A basic introduction, written in lay language and profusely illustrated with drawings, photographs, X rays, and scans. It is organized by organ system and includes a section on the human life cycle and genetics. A glossary and index complete the book.

1090 **The human body explained: a guide to understanding the incredible living machine.** Philip Whitefield, ed. 192p. Henry Holt, 1995. $40. ISBN 0-8050-3752-7.
612 QP38

This book explains basic human physiology in lay language. Chapters are color coded with many sidebars and cross-references. Color illustrations are abundant.

1091 **Textbook of medical physiology.** 9th ed. Arthur C. Guyton and John E. Hall. 1072p. Saunders, 1995. $57.95. ISBN 0-7216-5944-6.
616.07 QP34.5

A classic textbook and standard reference source. It is written in technical language, but educated lay readers will be able to understand it. Functions of all human organs and systems are explained in great detail.

Cancer

1092 **American Cancer Society's complete book of cancer.** Arthur I. Holleb, ed. 650p. Doubleday, 1986. op.
616.99 RC263

A good overview of cancer: biology, diagnosis, treatment, rehabilitation, and prevention. It includes lists of agencies, organizations, and regional cancer centers for referral.

1093 **Cancer sourcebook: basic information on cancer types, symptoms, diagnostic methods, and treatments, including statistics on cancer occurrences worldwide and the risks associated with known carcinogens and activities.** Frank E. Bair, ed. Omnigraphics, 1995. $80. ISBN 0-7808-0041-9.
616.994 RC263

The latest information on cancer incidence worldwide as well as on diagnosis, treatment, and risk factors. Statistics are taken from government publications. The international comparisons are an interesting feature useful for research.

1094 **Cancer: what cutting-edge science can tell you and your doctor about the causes of cancer and the impact on diagnosis and treatment.** Robert M. McAllister et al. 329p. Basic Books/

HarperCollins, 1993. $22.
ISBN 0-465-00845-3; paper $13.
ISBN 0-465-00846-1.
616.99 RC261

An excellent overview of the latest developments in cancer research and treatment. Written in lay language, it is a useful source for cancer patients and their families who need to make decisions about treatment.

1095 Everyone's guide to cancer therapy. 2d ed. Malin Dollinger et al. 848p. Andrews & McMeel, 1998. $29.95. ISBN 0-8362-3617-3; paper $19.95. ISBN 0-8362-3709-9.
616.994 RC263

This book explains various cancer treatments in common use, how they work, and their side effects, risks, and benefits. It is a useful, reassuring source accessible to all users.

Children's Health

1096 Columbia University College of Physicians and Surgeons complete guide to early child care. 514p. Crown, 1990. $32.50. ISBN 0-517-57217-6.
618.92 RJ16

An excellent overview of child development, childhood illness, and basic parenting skills. It includes information about disabilities affecting children, child abuse, and divorce.

1097 The doctor's book of home remedies for children: from allergies and animal bites to toothaches and TV addiction: hundreds of doctor-proven techniques and tips to care for your kid. Prevention Magazine editors. 450p. Rodale, 1993. $27.95. ISBN 0-87596-183-5.
618.92 RJ61

Like *The doctor's* two volumes on home remedies for adults, this offers many simple techniques for treating common childhood ailments at home as well as clear advice on when medical attention is needed. A Spanish-language edition is available.

1098 Smart medicine for a healthier child: a practical A-to-Z reference to natural and conventional treatments for infants and children. Janet Zand et al. 464p. Avery, 1994. Paper $19.95. ISBN 0-89529-545-8.
618.92 RJ61

A unique text on children's health written by a physician, a registered nurse, and a naturopath, this book assumes that conventional medicine and alternative treatments can complement each other. The book has three sections: an explanation of the various therapies, an alphabetical listing of diseases and conditions with suggested treatments, and illustrated instructions for applying the treatments. A glossary, bibliography, referral list of hot lines and organizations, and list of suppliers of alternative health products complete the book.

Drugs

1099 The complete drug reference. U.S. Pharmacopeia. 1760p. Consumer Reports Books, 1980– . Annual. $39.95. ISBN 0-89043-850-1.
615.58 RS55

Objective information about prescription and nonprescription drugs. It includes detailed instructions about the proper way to take medication and a color drug-identification guide. It is written in lay language and is easy to use.

1100 Encyclopedia of drugs and alcohol. Jerome H. Jaffe, ed. 4v. Macmillan, 1995. $350. ISBN 0-02-897185-X.
362.29 HV5804

This set offers detailed coverage of all types of drugs, their use, and their abuse. The signed articles by experts in their fields include chemical, medical, and social aspects of drug use. Articles are on specific drugs, drug use in geographic areas, treatment techniques, and sociological and criminological subjects.

1101 The essential guide to psychiatric drugs. 3d ed. Jack M. Gorman. St. Martin's, 1997. Paper $15.95. ISBN 0-312-16824-1.
615.788 RM15

This book provides the latest information on psychiatric drugs in current use, such as the new antidepressants Prozac and Zoloft. It explains their action, proper use, side effects, and signs of overdose.

1102 The handbook of over-the-counter drugs and pharmacy products. Max Leber et al. 464p. Celestial Arts, 1994.

Paper $14.95. ISBN 0-89087-734-3.
615.1 RM671

A useful source containing basic information about nonprescription drugs and their effectiveness as well as about cosmetics, shampoos, bottled water, and other pharmacy products not included in most drug books. It even has information about pet-care products.

1103 **Herbal drugs and phytopharmaceuticals: a handbook for practice on a scientific basis.** Trans. and ed. Norman Granger Bisset from the German edition by Max Wichtl, ed. 568p. CRC Pr., 1994. $189. ISBN 0-8493-7192-9.
615.32 RM666

For the serious herbalist. Describes 181 herbal drugs arranged by Latin names with synonyms, origin, composition, illustrations, indications, side effects, proper use, and how to test for purity. There is a bibliography.

1104 **People's guide to deadly drug interactions.** Joe Graedon and Teresa Graedon. 432p. St. Martin's, 1995. $25.95. ISBN 0-312-13243-3.
615.7 RM302

This guide fills a genuine need in medical collections. It explains potentially fatal interactions that can occur when patients use several drugs at the same time or combine certain drugs with certain foods. Written in lay language with color-coded charts, it is easy to understand and use.

1105 **Physician's desk reference.** Medical Economics, 1947– . Annual. $74.95. ISSN 0093-4461.
■ cd online
615.1 QV772

Physician's desk reference for nonprescription drugs. Medical Economics, 1980– . Annual. $74.95. ISSN 1044-1305.
■ cd online
615.1 RM671

PDR generics. Medical Economics, 1995– . Annual. $79.95. ISSN 1084-4325.
615.1 RS655

Physician's GenRx. Mosby, 1993– . Annual. $69.95. ISSN 1064-7783.
■ disk cd
615.1 RS55

All of these sources provide detailed drug information. The *PDR* contains package insert data from pharmaceutical companies. The *PDR generics* and *Physician's GenRx* contain information from the FDA on both generic and brand-name medications. The *Physician's GenRx* also includes company profiles.

1106 **Psychedelics encyclopedia.** 3d ed. Peter Stafford. 420p. Ronin, 1992. Paper $24.95. ISBN 0-914171-51-8.
362.293 HV5822

Detailed information about mind-altering substances from all over the world. It is written in lay language—a useful source for student reports.

1107 **Zimmerman's complete guide to nonprescription drugs.** 2d ed. David R. Zimmerman. 1128p. Visible Ink/Gale, 1992. $45. ISBN 0-8103-8874-X; paper $19.95. ISBN 0-8103-9421-9.
615.7 RM671

Organized by type of drug with a narrative introduction explaining different medications and charts to compare their safety and effectiveness.

Nutrition and Diet

1108 **Bowe's and Church's food values of portions commonly used.** 17th ed. Anna De Planter Bowes; rev. by Helen Nichols Church. 481p. Lippincott, 1998. Paper $29.95. ISBN 0-397-55435-4. (*formerly* **Food values of portions commonly used.**)
641.1 TX551

Lists of food values compiled from databases, tables in journal articles and textbooks, and from the food industry are presented in tabular form. The tables are organized by food categories (e.g., cereals, beverages, fast food). Brand names are provided to help identify foods. Items listed include calories, fats, carbohydrates, fiber, vitamins, minerals, and amino acids in an average portion. More than 3,500 foods are listed.

1109 **The concise encyclopedia of foods and nutrition.** Audrey H. Ensmonger et al. 1184p. CRC Pr., 1995. $132.95. ISBN 0-8493-4455-7.
613.2 TX349

Comprehensive coverage of nutrition, foods and their composition, vitamins, additives, and metabolic and nutritional diseases. It contains many charts and graphs.

1110 The Mount Sinai School of Medicine complete book of nutrition. Victor Herbert et al. 796p. St. Martin's, 1990. $35. ISBN 0-312-05129-8.
613.2 RM217.2

All aspects of human nutrition for various age groups, diseases, and special situations (weight loss, eating disorders) are discussed in this book. It also offers practical advice on shopping, restaurant dining, food storage, and reading labels.

1111 The wellness encyclopedia of food and nutrition: how to buy, store, and prepare every variety of fresh food. Sheldon Margen. 512p. Rebus, 1992. $29.95. ISBN 0-929661-03-6.
613.2 TX353

This is a fine guide to maintaining health by eating properly. The author, a professor of nutrition at the University of California, Berkeley, takes readers from the market to the kitchen, and, finally, to the table, showing them how to select, store, and prepare fresh foods in a healthy, appetizing manner.

Physical Impairments

1112 Accent on living buyer's guide: your number one source of information on products for the disabled. Betty Garee, ed. 132p. Cheever, 1989– . Annual. Paper $15. ISSN 0272-2461.
681.761 HQ1064

Resources for people with disabilities: a national directory. Elizabeth H. Oakes and John Bradford, eds. 2v. Ferguson, 1998. $89.95. ISBN 0-89434-242-8.
■ cd
362.4 HV1553

Accent on living is a directory of products for the disabled. Organized by specific problems area (e.g., sports, dressing, drinking), it lists both manufacturers and retail outlets with their addresses. There are also advertisements for products and an index by product name. *Resources for people* is a directory of organizations, corporations, and associations serving people with disabilities. Provides more than 8,000 entries arranged under 26 categories giving name, address, telephone, fax, and information on disability served. Indexes by type of disability, state, city, and organization name. Large-print format.

1113 The encyclopedia of blindness and vision impairment. Jill Sardegna and T. Otis Paul. 340p. Facts on File, 1990. $45. ISBN 0-8160-2153-8.
362.4103 RE91

This book provides an overview of vision impairment. Entries cover medical, historical, and psychosocial subjects. There is a bibliography as well as a list of agencies for referral.

1114 The encyclopedia of deafness and hearing disorders. Carol Turkington and Allen E. Sussman. 288p. Facts on File, 1992. $45. ISBN 0-8160-2267-4.
617.8 RF290

An overview of hearing impairment. Medical, historical, and psychosocial subjects are covered. There is a bibliography and a list of agencies for referral.

1115 Gallaudet encyclopedia of deaf people and deafness. John V. Van Cleve, ed. 3v. McGraw-Hill, 1987. $355. ISBN 0-07-079229-1.
362.4 HV2368

This encyclopedia provides in-depth coverage of the deaf community. Signed articles include information on sign languages, life and culture of deaf people, acoustics, and sociolinguistics. All articles have references.

1116 Making life more liveable: a practical guide to over 1,000 products and resources for living well in the mature years. Ellen Lederman. 384p. Fireside/Simon & Schuster, 1994. Paper $14. ISBN 0-671-87531-0. Large-type ed.: Irving R. Dickman. 96p. American Foundation for the Blind, 1983. Paper $19.95. ISBN 0-89128-115-0.
646.7 HQ1064

This book contains information on products for low-vision and hearing- and mobility-impaired people. It also contains listings of books, pamphlets, and organizations that help people live with these problems. It has a very good index.

Women's Health

1117 Conception, pregnancy, and birth. Miriam Stoppard. 352p. Dorling Kindersley, 1993. $29.95. ISBN 1-56458-182-9.

Mayo Clinic book of pregnancy and baby's first year. 750p. Morrow, 1994. $30. ISBN 0-688-11761-9.
618.2 RG525

Two excellent, illustrated sources in lay language explaining conception, fetal development, labor, childbirth, and care of the newborn. The Mayo Clinic book offers more depth and coverage of the first year of life along with parenting information, advice on returning to work after giving birth, and grandparenting.

1118 Contraceptive technology. 16th rev. ed. Robert A. Hatcher et al. 730p. Irvington, 1994. $39.30. ISBN 0-8290-3173-1; paper $22.95. ISBN 0-8290-3171-5.
613.9 RG136

This book offers the latest information on contraception, sexuality, sexually transmitted diseases, and family planning. It is frequently revised.

1119 Harvard guide to women's health. Karen J. Carlson et al. 718p. Harvard Univ. Pr., 1996. $39.95. ISBN 0-674-36768-5.
616 RA778

A comprehensive, thoughtful, clearly written encyclopedia covering more than 300 topics of special concern to women, from coffee and cancer to cosmetics and mental health. Well-depicted illustrations enhance the text. Suggestions for further information include Internet sites, videos, and organizations. Highly recommended.

1120 Menopause and midlife health. Morris Notelovitz and Diana Tonnesson. 480p. St. Martin's, 1993. $24.95. ISBN 0-312-09337-3; paper $15.95. ISBN 0-312-11314-5.
618.1 RG186

An encyclopedia of midlife health for women written by a physician doing research in this field. It emphasizes health maintenance and clearly explains hormonal changes that occur as women age. It offers objective information about hormone replacement therapy and sound advice about diet, exercise, and osteoporosis prevention.

1121 The new A to Z of women's health. 3d ed. Christine Ammer. 576p. Facts on File, 1995. $40. ISBN 0-8160-3121-5.
613 RA778

A concise encyclopedia of women's health arranged alphabetically. It includes both traditional and alternative treatment information. There are line drawings to illustrate anatomy and charts to summarize some information. There is no bibliography, but there is a list of resource organizations.

1122 Our bodies, ourselves for the new century: a book by and for women. Rev. ed. Boston Women's Health Collective. 780p. Simon & Schuster, 1998. $24. ISBN 0-684-84231-9.

Woman's body: a manual for life. Miriam Stoppard, ed. 224p. Dorling Kindersley, 1994. $29.95. ISBN 1-56458-617-0.

The women's complete healthbook. Roselyn P. Epps and Susan C. Stewart, eds. 720p. Delacorte, 1995. $39.95. ISBN 0-385-31382-9.
613.04 RA778

Three fine sources on women's health. The new *Our bodies, ourselves* offers the most depth, addressing political and psychosocial issues as well as medical problems. It is also the only one with bibliographies. *Woman's body* has beautiful color illustrations and interesting historical notes. *The women's complete healthbook* has an outstanding article on gender differences in drug treatment.

1123 A woman's guide to coping with disability. 2d ed. 224p. Resources for Rehabilitation, 1997. Paper $42.95. ISBN 0-929718-19-4.
362.4 RA778

Written especially for women, this book covers federal laws, housing, coping with daily activities at home and in the workplace, and the most common conditions that disable women. Each chapter covers a specific disorder and includes a bibliography, referral list of organizations, and a resource list of books, audio- and videotapes, and vendors of assistive devices.

13

Household

CAROLE DYAL

Many of the works in this chapter are appropriate not only for the reference collection, but also for the circulating collection and for the home library.

Beverages, Cooking, and Foods

Beverages

1124 The complete beverage dictionary. 2d ed. Robert A. Lipinski and Katheleen A. Lipinski. 416p. Wiley, 1997. $39.95. ISBN 0-471-28746-6.
663 TP503

Defines 6,100 specialized terms relating to the beverage industry, identifying the qualities of a beverage, production techniques, the natural materials from which beverages are derived, regions where the materials are produced, implements used for serving, laws regulating production and consumption, business practices of the industry, and more. Covering both alcoholic and nonalcoholic beverages and international in scope, this volume is an excellent addition to any comprehensive reference collection.

1125 Complete world bartender guide: the standard reference to 2,000 drinks. Rev. ed. Bob Sennett, ed. 544p. Bantam, 1993. Paper $6.99. ISBN 0-553-29900-X.

Mr. Boston: official bartender's and party guide. 64th ed. Renee Cooper and Charles Morris. 288p. Warner, 1994. $9.99. ISBN 0-446-67042-1.
641.8 TX951

In addition to the mixed-drink recipes arranged from *A* to *Z* for low-calorie and nonalcoholic as well as alcoholic drinks, the *Complete world bartender guide* includes pictures and names of bar glasses, hints on stocking a bar, a minidictionary, and guidelines for responsible drinking. The drink recipes are indexed by main ingredient and type of drink. *Mr. Boston* serves as an excellent alternative, providing more than 1,000 recipes, the stories behind the concoctions, food and drink combinations, and party suggestions.

1126 Encyclopedia of beer. Christine P. Rhodes, ed. 502p. Henry Holt, 1997. Paper $18.95. ISBN 0-8050-5554-1.
641 TP568

More than 900 entries in an *A* to *Z* format, with hundreds of illustrations and helpful cross-references. Includes brewers and their products, beer styles (stout, scotch ale), brewing terminology and equipment, ingredients and flavorings, festivals and traditions, and the history of beer. Appendixes list relevant organizations, collectors clubs, educational institutions, mail-order beer clubs, importers, and associated magazines, newsletters, and journals.

1127 Guide to the best wineries of North America. Andre Guyot. Gault Millau, 1993. Paper $18. ISBN 1-881066-02-9.
641.2 TP557

Sponsored by the American Automobile Association, this guide provides a geographic overview to some 1,700 wineries in Canada, the United States, and Mexico; introductory histories of the wine regions; a glossary of terms, including grape varieties; a section on how wine is made; and food and wine pairing suggestions, from appetizers through desserts.

1128 Larousse encyclopedia of wine. Christopher Foulkes, ed. 608p. Larousse, 1994. $40. ISBN 2-03-507022-8.
641.2 TP548

The *Larousse encyclopedia* incorporates the contributions of more than 100 experts from around the world and discusses everything from the history and chemistry of wines to choosing and tasting wines and how to read labels. Although focusing on the wines of France, the work includes prominent wines of North America (primarily California), Australia, South America, and Africa. Well illustrated. Good glossary and index.

1129 New Sotheby's wine encyclopedia. Tom Stevenson. 600p. Dorling Kindersley, 1997. $50. ISBN 0-7894-2079-1.
641.22 TP548

This work serves both as a comprehensive reference guide to the wines of the world and an illustrated introduction to the wine-making regions of the world. Introductory material describes tasting and assessing wines, factors affecting taste and quality, vine cultivation, grape varieties, and wine-processing methods. The main body of the text includes information on some 2,000 wine producers from all the major wine-producing regions of the globe. Wonderfully and lavishly illustrated. Includes a glossary and an extensive index.

1130 The Oxford companion to wine. Jancis Robinson, ed. 1040p. Oxford Univ. Pr., 1994. $60. ISBN 0-19-866159-2.
820.9 PR8706

Generally hailed as the single most essential reference source on wines, this *A* to *Z* companion contains more than 3,000 entries covering everything from the chemistry of wine making to the role of wine in lyric poetry. Prepared by an international team of experts, this work is at once scholarly and eminently readable. Though offering fewer illustrations than the *Larousse encyclopedia, The Oxford companion* provides considerably more detail and depth on the history, culture, industry, and science of the grape.

Cooking

1131 American Heart Association cookbook. 6th ed. Random House, 1998. Large-type ed. $29.95. ISBN 0-679-42920-4. Paper $16. ISBN 0-8129-2954-3.
641.5631 RC684.D5

Prepared under the guidance of heart specialists, this cookbook provides, aside from 600 healthy recipes, important information on the proper selecting, cooking, and storing of foods. There is a good introduction to low-fat and low-cholesterol cooking and extensive information on the physical effects that various foods have on the body and the heart in particular. Includes advice on changing to a more healthy diet, substituting ingredients, dining out, and analyzing nutrients. It is an established classic.

1132 The complete book of herbs, spices, and condiments: from garden to kitchen to medicine chest. Carol Ann Rinzler. 199p. Facts on File, 1990. $19.95. ISBN 0-8160-2008-6.
641.3 TX406

Provides fascinating information about nutritional plants, herbs, and food flavorings. Includes nutritional profiles and dietary cautions. Describes how herbs affect the body as well as how to use them in cookery. Warns of hazardous herbs. This is not a cookbook but an alphabetical sourcebook. Includes a bibliography of relevant books and magazine articles. Indexed by adverse effects, alternate uses, chemical reactions, chemicals in products, drugs, and medical test effects.

1133 The encyclopedia of herbs, spices, and flavorings. Elizabeth Lambert

Ortiz. 288p. Dorling Kindersley, 1992. $34.95. ISBN 1-56458-065-2.
641.3 TX406

Splendidly illustrated (with more than 750 full-color photographs), this encyclopedia of more than 200 herbs, spices, essences, edible flowers and leaves, aromatics, vinegars, oils, teas, and coffees is a pure delight. Each entry contains instructions on the growth and storage of the substance, its use as an ingredient, its affinity with other foods, special preparation techniques, and decorative applications.

1134 Fannie Farmer cookbook. 13th rev. ed. Marion Cunningham. 874p. Knopf, 1996. $30. ISBN 0-679-45081-5.

Joy of cooking. Rev. ed. Irma S. Rombauer. 1136p. Simon & Schuster, 1997. $29.50. ISBN 0-684-81870-1.
641.5 TX715

The above are time-tested basic cookbooks that provide methods of preparation and describe ingredients for most common American dishes. Arranged in categories of foods; detailed indexes. Indispensable.

1135 The food professional's guide: the James Beard Foundation directory of people, products, and services. Irene Chalmers. Wiley, 1990. $35. ISBN 0-471-52460-3.
641.025 TX650

Lists specialty food wholesalers alphabetically by product, provides biographical sketches of chefs and restaurant owners, provides directory information on food and product promoters, discusses cooking schools, and describes government resources and consumer resources.

1136 The Garland recipe index. Kathryn W. Torgeson and Sylvia Weinstein. (Garland reference library of the humanities; 414.) 314p. Garland, 1984. $39. ISBN 0-8240-9124-8.
016.6415 Z5776

The international cookery index. Rhonda H. Kleiman and Allan M. Kleiman. 230p. Neal-Schuman, 1987. $65. ISBN 0-918212-87-1.
641.5 TX651

The American regional cookery index. Rhonda H. Kleiman. (Neal-Schuman cookery index series.) 221p. Neal-Schuman, 1989. $59.95. ISBN 0-55570-029-2.
641.5 TX751.5

The contents of forty-eight popular cookbooks are indexed by ingredient, recipe name, and cooking style in *The Garland recipe index.* Vegetarian, regional, and ethnic cookbooks are analyzed, as well as standard works by James Beard, Craig Claiborne, and Julia Child. To expand on and complement the coverage in *The Garland,* libraries should consider the Cookery index series. Of the fifty-two cookbooks covered in *The international cookery index,* only twelve are also covered in *The Garland.* Access points include names of well-known dishes, type of dishes (e.g., soups), major ingredients, preparation (e.g., pickled), and nationality. As well as indexing the selected cookbooks, *The international cookery index* suggests other titles of interest and so can serve as a selection tool. The second book in the series concentrates on American regional cooking.

1137 Guide to cooking schools: cooking schools, vacations, apprenticeships, and wine instruction courses throughout the world. 360p. Shaw Guides, 1989– . Annual. $22.95. ISBN 0-945834-25-X. ISSN 1040-2626.
641.50705 TX667

A comprehensive directory and guide to more than 1,000 international culinary schools. The *Guide* is divided between career and professional programs and recreational cooking schools. Listings include vocational schools, apprenticeships, cooking vacations, wine courses, food and wine organizations, and publications worldwide. Provides rankings by tuition costs and size of student body.

1138 The kitchenware book. 2d ed. Steve Ettlinger. 466p. Macmillan, 1995. Paper $14.95. ISBN 0-02-860424-5.

The well-tooled kitchen. Fred Bridge and Jean Tibbets. Morrow, 1992. $10. ISBN 0-688-12064-4.
683 TX656

The kitchenware book describes the universe of cooking utensils, organized by four general categories: preparation, cooking, beverage, and serving. Provides buying tips and suggested uses. Very clear illustrations (line drawings). *The well-tooled kitchen* describes more than 500 gadgets and utensils, noting the purpose and important features of each; provides black-and-white photographs to depict items. Recipes are scattered throughout. Good guide for selecting tools and utensils by use. Includes bibliography and index by name of utensil.

1139 Recipex: every cook's master index. Annie Gilbar. 671p. Simon & Schuster, 1990. $15.95. ISBN 0-671-66827-7.
016.6415 Z5776.G2

Provides, in a single source, access to 35,000 recipes contained in fifty-two classic cookbooks, coded by title, degree of difficulty, and number of servings. The thorough presentation, easy use, and good indexing make this a truly excellent source for libraries that have regular cookery questions.

1140 The Vegetarian Times complete cookbook. Editors of *Vegetarian Times* and Lucy Moll. 506p. Macmillan, 1995. Paper $29.95. ISBN 0-02-621745-7.

The American vegetarian cookbook from the Fit for Life kitchen. Marilyn Diamond. 422p. Warner, 1990. $26.95. ISBN 0-446-51561-2.

The new Laurel's kitchen: a handbook for vegetarian cookery and nutrition. 2d ed. Laurel Robertson, Carol Finders, and Brian Ruppenthal. 512p. Ten Speed Pr., 1986. $27.95. ISBN 0-89815-167-8; paper $19.95. ISBN 0-89815-166-X.
641.5 TX837

The Vegetarian Times *complete cookbook* provides insightful discussions of basic issues, including what is a vegetarian diet, why be a vegetarian, and types of vegetarianism. Discusses menu planning, the basic pantry, ready-made menus, and kitchen techniques. Recipes include nutritional information per serving. Indexed by ingredients and categories of foods. *The American vegetarian cookbook from the Fit for Life kitchen* describes the serious effects of diet on health. It provides vegetarian alternatives to traditional nonvegetarian recipes. It describes how to outfit a vegetarian kitchen and how to shop for appropriate foods. Appendixes include tables for nutritional information, general lists of protein sources, substitution charts, and recommended periodicals. Good bibliography and index. *The new Laurel's kitchen* is an updated edition of a classic vegetarian cookbook focusing on nutrition. (Nutrition tables in back are keyed to recipes.) It is thoroughly indexed by both ingredient and recipe name. For those not familiar with vegetarianism, this an excellent beginning reference source.

Foods

1141 The book of food: a cook's guide to over 1,000 exotic and everyday ingredients. Frances Bissell. 276p. Henry Holt, 1994. $40. ISBN 0-8050-3006-9.
641.3 TX353

Describes foodstuffs and where they come from; illustrates how to choose, store, and prepare ingredients. Color photographs, short glossary, and index. Does not include recipes, but does illustrate general techniques of food preparation.

1142 The dictionary of American food and drink. Rev. ed. John F. Mariani. DIANE, 1997. Paper $15. ISBN 0-788-15073-1.
641.5 TX349

Describes more than 2,000 terms, and provides insight—often amusing insight—into the origins and meaning of our ever-expanding and delightful vocabulary of food. Includes some interesting recipes along the way.

1143 Larousse gastronomique: the new American edition of the world's greatest culinary encyclopedia. Prosper Montague. Jenifer Harvey Lang, ed. 1193p. Crown, 1988. $50. ISBN 0-517-57032-7.
641.03 TX349

This is a completely updated edition, adapted to the American kitchen, of the standard reference source for chefs and homemakers of all nations. Alphabetically arranged, with many cross-references, this culinary bible includes more than 8,500 recipes and information on cooking terms, foods, wines, preservation, serving, organizing, and anything else related to the kitchen. Recipe index and more than 1,000 illustrations, most in full color.

Calendars, Festivals, and Holidays

Calendars

1144 Chase's calendar of events. Contemporary Books, 1958– . Annual. Paper $47.95. ISSN 1083-0588. (*formerly* **Chase's annual events.**)
■ cd
523.9 GT4803

This yearly almanac and survey of dates chronicles more than 10,000 American and international holidays, festivals, celebrity birthdays, anniversaries, astronomical phenomena, and other traditional observances. Provides name, purpose, inclusive dates, sponsor's name and address, and contact person or organization for each event.

1145 Holidays and anniversaries of the world: a comprehensive catalogue containing detailed information on every month and day of the year. 3d ed. Beth A. Baker, ed. 1080p. Gale, 1999. $105. ISBN 0-8103-5477-2.
394.2 CE76

The book is organized by month; each month begins with a description of the special "weeks" (e.g., National Library Week is noted for April) and movable religious holidays. The remainder of the entry for each month is a chronological listing of saints' days, dates of major historical events, famous births, and every religious and civil observance celebrated in modern times. Not as much explanation about each holiday as in Hatch's *American book of days*, but a user will not find a more comprehensive listing of observances in any other source. The latest edition lists more than 23,000 regional, national, and international holidays and anniversaries; includes a perpetual calendar and projection dates for major movable religious holidays. Extensive index provides additional access.

Festivals and Holidays

1146 Folklore of American holidays: a compilation of more than 600 beliefs, legends, superstitions, proverbs, riddles, poems, songs, dances, games. 3d ed. Hennig Cohen and Tristram Potter Coffin, eds. 500p. Gale, 1998. $105. ISBN 0-8103-8864-2.
394.2 GT4803

Provides, in calendar order, historical background and general characteristics (customs, rituals, stories, beliefs) associated with some 125 American holidays. Includes source and bibliographic information.

1147 The folklore of world holidays. 2d ed. Robert Griffin and Ann H. Shurgin, eds. 750p. Gale, 1999. $105. ISBN 0-8103-8901-0.
394.2 GT3930

Identifies and describes legends and folklore relating to 340 holidays and festivals observed in more than 150 nations. Excludes political holidays. Entries are in Gregorian calendar order, but there is reference to Jewish, Hindu, Chinese, Buddhist, Islamic, and lunar calendar traditions. Each entry is keyed to an extensive list of sources for additional reading. Combined ethnic, subject, and geographic index concludes the work.

1148 Holidays and festivals index. Helene Henderson and Barry Puckett, eds. 1100p. Omnigraphics, 1995. $65. ISBN 0-7808-0012-5.
394.2 GT3925

A comprehensive index to more than 3,000 commemorative events from 150 countries, keyed to twenty-seven basic reference tools published between 1962 and 1994. Provides ethnic, geographical, name, religion, and chronological access. Exhaustive in coverage.

1149 Holidays, festivals, and celebrations of the world dictionary. Sue E. Thompson and Barbara W. Carlson, eds. 536p. Omnigraphics, 1994. Lib. bindg. $58. ISBN 1-55888-768-7.
394.2 GT3925

Describes more than 1,400 holidays, festivals, celebrations, holy days, feasts and fasts, and other observances around the world. Introductory material includes descriptions of non-Gregorian calendar systems and lists of legal holidays by state and country. Entries are arranged alphabetically by key word, followed by the date of the event, and range from one paragraph to half a page. Indexed by subject, key word, fixed and movable holiday, and religious observance. An excellent choice for the general reference collection.

Consumer Affairs

1150 Buy wholesale by mail. Print Project and the Enlightened Shopper. HarperPerennial, 1997– . $19. ISSN 1049-0116.
381.142 HF5465.5

How consumers can save 30 to 90 percent off list prices. This directory provides brief listings by type of product or service including address, phone number, descriptions of products, comparative data, and tips on particularly good buys. There are also valuable sections on buying by mail, warranties, and returning merchandise.

1151 The catalog of catalogs V: the complete mail-order directory. Edward L. Palder. 513p. Woodbine House, 1997. Paper $24.95. ISBN 0-933149-88-3.
381 HF5466

Lists 12,500 catalogs of interest to consumers, arranged in 650 broad categories. Provides basic ordering information: company name, address, products, availability of catalog (free or fee), and phone number. Updated every two years, this source remains current and inexpensive and remarkably handy.

1152 Consumer Reports buying guide issue. (Dec. issue of *Consumer reports.*) *Consumer reports* editors. Consumers Union, 1937– . Annual. Paper $8.99. ISSN 0010-7174.
339.4 TX335.41

The *Buying guide* contains summary information on consumer goods and services arranged by areas such as recreation, gardening, automobiles, household appliances, personal care, food, and general consumer information. Includes ratings of products and prices, with citations to original report.

1153 Consumer sourcebook. A. H. Brennan. 1700p. Gale, 1974– . Irreg. (11th ed. 1998, $255. ISBN 0-7876-2087-4.) ISSN 0738-0518.
339.4 HC110

This directory describes more than 15,000 programs and services available to the American consumer at little or no cost. Lists federal, state, county, and local governmental agencies, nongovernmental consumer organizations and associations, and consumer affairs and customer services departments of corporations. Describes consumer publications and multimedia products and provides consumer tips and recommendations. Includes a master index providing name- and subject-term access.

1154 Consumers' guide to product grades and terms. Susan B. Gall and Timothy L. Gall, eds. 603p. Gale, 1993. $75. ISBN 0-8103-8898-7.
381.3 TX335

Explains terms and grades (such as PG-13) used to class and describe more than 8,000 consumer products. Chapter 1: describes advertising standards and sources of standards and defines how terms are meant to be used. Chapter 2: environmental section, defines very clearly what can and cannot be included in a product description. Chapters 3 through 21: specific subject areas such as apparel, housewares, and dairy products. Definitions are extensive and sources clearly identified. The book is intelligently presented with a thorough table of contents, a detailed index, and an appendix listing 200 standard setting organizations.

1155 The smart consumer's directory, 1994. Nelson, 1993. $9.99. ISBN 0-8407-6321-2.
381.33 HC110

Provides detailed strategies for wise buying as well as helpful instructions for filing unhappy complaints. Packed with information aimed to assist consumers who wish to better survive and even to thrive in our complex material world. Provides purchasing tips, suggestions for finding assistance, travel information, and advice on personal finance.

Etiquette

1156 The Amy Vanderbilt complete book of etiquette. Nancy Tuckerman and Nancy Dunnan. 786p. Doubleday, 1995. $32. ISBN 0-385-41342-4.
395 BJ1853

A contemporary guide to family relationships, teenagers, drugs, alcohol and tobacco, adopted children, the single life, ceremonies (graduation, engagement, weddings, etc.), entertaining, business letters, forms of address, dress, gift giving, and travel. Updated to include tips on accepted "modern" phenomena such as cellular phones, cohabitation, and women engaging in business travel.

1157 Emily Post's etiquette. 16th ed. Elizabeth L. Post. 800p. HarperCollins, 1997. $35. ISBN 0-06-270078-2.
395 BJ1853

A complete, up-to-date, well-indexed guide to correct behavior in a wide variety of situations. Reflects today's relaxed, informal approach to matters that formerly required a strict code. Includes a new section on teaching manners to children.

1158 Letitia Baldridge's new complete guide to executive manners. Rev. ed. Letitia Baldridge. 590p. Scribner, 1993. $35. ISBN 0-89256-362-1.
395 HF5389

How to perform in business-related situations. Personal qualities for effectiveness. Communications, including letter writing, phone protocols. Dressing. International business. Manners, including how to handle gifts. Business protocol while entertaining. Retirements. Notes on the changing business world. Thorough index.

1159 Miss Manners rescues civilization: from sexual harassment, frivolous lawsuits, dissing and other lapses in civility. Judith Martin. 497p. Crown, 1996. $30. ISBN 0-517-70164-2.

Miss Manners' guide for the turn of the millennium. Judith Martin. 742p. Fireside, 1990. $17. ISBN 0-671-72228-X.

Miss Manners' guide to excruciatingly correct behavior. Judith Martin. 768p. Warner, 1988. Paper $16.99. ISBN 0-446-38632-4.
395 BJ1853

Miss Manners, our wittiest and most erudite commentator on social behavior, leads even the most intractable of us to see the world through the eyes of an informed, understanding, stalwart, and yet gracious mind. One of the true proponents of a civilized life.

1160 Protocol: the complete handbook of diplomatic, official, and social usage. 4th rev. ed. 414p. Devon, 1997. Paper $20. ISBN 0-941402-04-5.
399 BJ1853

Twelve chapters elucidate the nuances of public protocol by describing order of precedence, table seating, forms of address, the etiquette of calling cards, flag displays, proper formal attire, and so on. Both government and commercial publications appear in the bibliography. Well indexed.

Home Maintenance

Construction

1161 Building a multi-use barn: for garage, animals, workshop, studio. John Wagner. 192p. Williamson, 1994. Paper $19.95. ISBN 0-912589-76-4.
690 TH4930

Anatomy of a building from start to finish. Design, purpose, site considerations. Foundation, framing, roofing, siding. Wiring, plumbing, heating. Good close-up detail. Illustrations. Answers frequently asked questions. Lists sources and associations for advice. Good index.

1162 The home design handbook: the essential planning guide for building, buying, or remodeling a home. June C. Myrvang and Steve Myrvang. 256p. Henry Holt, 1992. Paper $14.95. ISBN 0-0850-1833-6.
728 NA7115

Designed to aid novices in planning their home design. Provides advice by asking a series of questions intended to get one thinking about all the many details involved in making a comfortable, practical, and inviting home. Provides useful checklists to consider when working on both the exterior and interior of the structure.

1163 Homeowners' complete outdoor building book: wood and masonry construction. 3d ed. John Burton Brimer. Popular Science Books, 1985. $29.95. ISBN 0-943-82247-5.
690 TH4961

Provides much useful information including several small, basic projects for the novice. More complex projects for experienced workers. Simple, straightforward text. Many photographs and illustrations.

1164 Means illustrated construction dictionary. R. S. Means. 691p. R. S. Means, 1991. $99.95. ISBN 0-87629-218-X; paper $54.95. ISBN 0-87629-219-8.
624 TH9

Workers, hobbyists, and home builders will discover more than 13,000 brief, nontechnical definitions in this valuable new guide to the specialized and changing vocabulary of the construction industry. Black-and-white sketches, abbreviations at the beginning of each letter section, and the inclusion of some slang and regionalisms add to an already useful package. Includes practical tables of weights, measures, conversions, size determinations, and symbols, as well as a list of professional associations concerned with the construction industry. A must for libraries serving either professionals or just weekend putterers.

1165 Ortho's basic home building: an illustrated guide. Jill Fox and Ron Hildebrand. 325p. Meredith Books, 1992. $29.95. ISBN 0-89721-235-5.
690.837 TH4815

All steps of housebuilding: planning, foundations, roofs, utilities, exterior finish, heating, cooling, steps, stairs, interior finish, preparation for occupancy. Good line drawings, explicit narrative. Tools and permits needed. Thorough glossary of building terms. Good index.

Home Improvement

1166 Adding on: how to design and build a beautiful addition to your home. Roger Yepsen, ed. 373p. Rodale, 1996. $17.95. ISBN 0-87596-769-8.
690.837 TH4816.2

Guides you, step-by-step, through a major building project, from the design phase to a very detailed how-to. Discusses what to look for in contracts and how to draw them up. Excellent illustrations, glossary, and index.

1167 The complete home renovation manual. 224p. Smithmark, 1993. $19.95. ISBN 0-831-71588-X.
643.7 TH4816

Provides an overview of home structure, covering both inside and outside construction: roofing, replacing windows, installing lighting, reconstructing attics and bathrooms, insulating, and adding carports and decks. Provides useful checklists and discussion options. Many illustrations. Good index; good descriptions.

1168 Home improvement cost guide. 2d ed. Consumer Union editors. 257p. R. S. Means, 1989. $24.95. ISBN 0-87629-173-6.
643 TH4816

The Means name is well known to professional builders; this guide brings the company's expertise to the consumer wanting to embark on home improvement projects. Although the information about the costs of materials may vary, this guide offers much of value beyond dollar figures: the installation time estimates, the material quantity estimates, and the pointers and precautions for each of the seventy-four projects detailed here will provide practical and difficult-to-find information for the do-it-yourselfer.

1169 Ortho's home improvement encyclopedia. Rev. ed. Ortho Books staff; Alan Ahlstrand, ed. 511p. Ortho Books, 1994. $24.95. ISBN 0-89721-270-3.
643.7 TH4816

Alphabetical arrangement of home improvement projects with useful cross-references to other sections. Clear drawings and illustrations. The narrative instructions are very easy to follow. Good index.

1170 Renovation: a complete guide. 2d ed. Michael W. Litchfield. 592p. Sterling, 1997. $24.95. ISBN 0-8069-9775-3.
643.7 TH4816

Arranges projects in sequential order: first things first. Provides very specific details (e.g., what blade to use, how to space nails). Possible problems discussed and resolved. Very good annotated bibliography.

1171 Year-round house care: a seasonal checklist for basic home maintenance. Graham Blackburn. 176p. Consumer Reports Books, 1991. $24.95. ISBN 0-89043-448-4; paper $14.95. ISBN 0-89043-352-6.
643 TH4817

This book alerts the vigilant homeowner to the signs of deterioration, both interior and exterior, and suggests corrective steps.

Housekeeping

1172 The Good Housekeeping household encyclopedia. Good Housekeeping magazine editors. Hearst Books, 1993. $25. ISBN 0-688-12036-9.
640 TX158

This handbook will help you take excellent care of your home—covering everything from household budgeting to maintaining your computer. Discusses how to clean, maintain, organize, decorate, and repair virtually everything. Approximately one-third is devoted to cleaning. Includes safety and health tips, home financing, first aid. Provides an extensive index and sources for more information.

1173 How to clean practically anything. 4th ed. Consumer Reports Books editors. 256p. Consumer Reports Books, 1996. Paper $11.95. ISBN 0-89043-843-9.
648 TX158

A practical resource for the clean at heart. Details what kind of detergents and cleaners to use and their effectiveness in attacking ovens, appliances, floors, and fabrics. Discusses cleaning strategies. Includes an extensive stain-removal chart. Provides in-depth product analysis. The table of contents takes you to the right section; the index takes you to the right page.

1174 Mary Ellen's clean house! The all-in-one-place encyclopedia of contemporary housekeeping. Mary Ellen Pinkham. 358p. Crown, 1994. Paper $12. ISBN 0-517-88185-3.
640 TX158

Everything you should know about general housekeeping and maintenance: laundering, stain removal, pest control, furnishing the home, protecting the home when you leave, learning to do minor repairs. Easy to use, though not a lot of illustrations.

Interior Decoration

1175 Complete home decorating book. Nicholas Barnard. 288p. Dorling Kindersley, 1994. $29.95. ISBN 1-56458-667-7.
747 TT387

Divided in two sections. Section 1: soft furnishings: basic sewing (e.g., curtains, shades, bed furnishings, cushions, simple upholstery). Photographs lead one step-by-step through each process. Section 2: decorating (e.g., painting; wallpapering; tiling; treatment of hard floors, carpets, and rugs; shelving; lighting; and houseplants). Begins with photographs of basic household tool kit, exclusive of carpenters' tools. Equipment and "how-to" for each section. Thorough index.

Maintenance and Repair

1176 Basic home repairs. 2d ed. Sunset Books staff. 96p. Sunset, 1995. $9.99. ISBN 0-376-01581-0.
643 TH4817.3

A step-by-step guide to both indoor and outdoor repairs. Discusses tools and their uses. Describes what to do in emergencies. Provides a short glossary and index.

1177 Basic plumbing. 4th ed. Sunset Books staff. 96p. Sunset, 1995. $12.95. ISBN 0-376-01583-7.
696 TH6124

Begins with a description of plumbing systems; explains basics such as how to read the water meter; provides photographs of standard plumbing tools. Discusses how to work with tubing and other materials. More illustration than narrative. Plumbing glossary and basic index.

1178 Basic plumbing with illustrations. Rev. ed. Howard C. Massey. 381p. Craftsman Book Co., 1994. $33. ISBN 0-934041-99-7.
696 TH6122

High-level narration. Instructions for installing code-approved plumbing in residential and light commercial buildings. Definitions of terms, elucidation of fitting symbols, very extensive index.

1179 Basic wiring. 3d ed. Sunset Books staff. 96p. Sunset, 1995. $12.95. ISBN 0-376-01584-5
621.319 TX3271

Illuminates the world of wiring. Lists tools, types of cables and wires, testing devices. Extremely clear illustrations for each household project. Glossary and index.

1180 Better Homes and Gardens do-it-yourself home repairs. Better Homes and Gardens editors. 320p. Meredith Books, 1985. Paper $16.95. ISBN 0-696-01520-X.
643 TH4817.3

Home improvements manual. Rev. ed. Reader's Digest editors. 384p. Reader's Digest, 1992. $30. ISBN 0-89577-410-0.
643.7 TH4816

Both excellent sources for learning the basics of carpentry, general maintenance, appliance repair, painting, plumbing, and electrical work.

1181 The carpenter's manifesto. Rev. ed. Jefferey Ehrlich and Marc Mannheimer. 320p. Henry Holt, 1990. Paper $19.95. ISBN 0-8050-1299-0.
694 TH5606

Presents basic techniques of carpentry, providing clear conceptualizations of structural design and construction principles. Describes the form and use of tools, types of materials used in carpentry, and joining methods for every type of carpentry, from cabinets and shelves to doors and windows. Glossary, bibliography, and handy tables.

1182 The family handyman easy repair: over 100 simple solutions to the most common household problems. Reader's Digest editors. 192p. Reader's Digest, 1994. $19.95.

ISBN 0-89577-624-3.
643 TH4817.3

Designed to help the most inexperienced handyman succeed in basic repair: replacing broken glass, fixing faucets, mending gutters, restoring furniture. The work is profusely illustrated so that anyone can understand the 100 or so tasks detailed. This is for repairing, not remodeling, the home.

1183 Fix it fast, fix it right: hundreds of quick and easy home improvement projects. Gene Hamilton and Katie Hamilton. 320p. Rodale, 1991. $24.95. ISBN 0-87857-859-5; paper $14.95. ISBN 0-87857-860-9.
643.7 TH4816

Describes the most common home repair projects (painting, wallpapering, lighting). Useful charts for calculating what is needed for projects. Good illustrations (line drawings) and clear comprehensible narrative. Step-by-step instruction. Includes consolation notes on why, even with the best planning, things can go wrong.

1184 Fix it yourself for less: one hundred fifty money-saving repairs for appliances and household equipment. Consumer Reports editors and Mort Schultz. 224p. Consumer Reports Books, 1992. Paper $16.95. ISBN 0-89043-482-4.
643 TX298

Each chapter begins with a list of repairs, tools, and materials needed. Appendixes include descriptions of troubleshooting instruments and how they work, a list of dealers for old and new appliance parts, and a brand-name directory. Black-and-white photographs. Detailed index.

1185 Home Magazine's how your house works. Don Vandervoort. 222p. Ballantine, 1997. Paper $14. ISBN 0-614-27595-4.
643.7 TH4817

Blueprints of structural systems. Diagrams of house systems from plumbing through phone lines; shows systems from beginning to end. Clearly illustrated with good diagrams. Useful for developing an understanding of processes from start to finish. Good index.

1186 The home repair emergency handbook. Gene Schnaser. 174p. Taylor, 1992. $14.95. ISBN 0-87833-797-0.
643 TH4817

Covers 118 home emergencies: electrical wiring; plumbing, heating, and cooling systems; appliances. Simple line drawings. Useful, nontechnical narrative. Helpful hints with each section, including preventive measures and making do until the professional arrives.

1187 How things work in your home (and what to do when they don't). Time-Life Books editors. 368p. Henry Holt, 1987. $19.95. ISBN 0-0850-0126-3.
643 TH4817.3

Describes how home appliances and systems work and what to do when things do not. Colorful and easy-to-follow steps. Covers everything from heating systems to electric toothbrushes.

1188 Major appliances: operation, maintenance, troubleshooting, and repair. Billy C. Langley. Prentice-Hall, 1993. $49. ISBN 0-13-544834-4.
683 TK7018

Washing machines, refrigerators, dishwashers, ovens, and so on. Describes real installations in textbook fashion. Very detailed instructions, including electrical schematics. Arranged by type of appliance. Coverage very thorough. Short index.

Tools

1189 Bob Vila's toolbox: the ultimate illustrated guide to portable hand and power tools. Bob Vila. 235p. Morrow, 1993. $25. ISBN 0-688-11735-X.
621.9 TJ1195

Describes and lists all types of tools in a basic tool kit. Illustrates and explains use of each. Arranged by function of tool: measuring, cutting, drilling, and so forth. Section on specialty tools. Gives tips for using tools and construction tips. Very detailed glossary. Index.

1190 The complete illustrated guide to everything sold in hardware stores. Steve R. Ettlinger. 432p. Simon & Schuster, 1993. $15. ISBN 0-02-043005-1.
683 T5405

Correctly identifies and describes tools and hardware. Organized like a hardware store: plumbing supplies, paints, electrical products, and so on. Each entry includes a line drawing, a brief description, alternative names, and instructions for use.

1191 How to sharpen every blade in your woodshop. Don Geary. 144p. Betterway Books, 1994. $17.99. ISBN 1-55870-342-X.
684 TT186

How to care for and sharpen all of your blades, routers, bits, chisels, and other woodworking tools. Thorough and authoritative.

1192 The illustrated hardware book. Consumer Reports editors and Tom Philbin. 224p. Consumer Reports Books, 1992. $16.95. ISBN 0-89043-417-4.
683 TS400

Categorizes and describes hundreds of common hardware items. Entries include name, description, purpose, and tips. Well illustrated. Good index.

1193 Reader's Digest book of skills and tools. Reader's Digest editors. 360p. Reader's Digest, 1993. $29. ISBN 0-89577-469-0.
643.7 TT155

Tools described are grouped by function, starting with basic tools and hardware, then woodworking, masonry, ceramics, painting, and flooring. Includes description of how tools are used in very specific step-by-step projects. Includes buyer's guide and directory of manufacturing companies. General index.

Parenting

1194 The childwise catalog: a consumer guide to buying the safest and best products for your children: newborns through age five. 3d ed. Jack Gillis and Mary Fise. 448p. HarperCollins, 1993. Paper $14. ISBN 0-06-273182-3.
649 RJ61

Prepared under the auspices of the Consumer Federation of America. Specific advice and suggestions on choosing toys, equipment, and child-care facilities; foods and diet; traveling with children; safety (e.g., Halloween, the laundry room); and protecting the child in today's technologically hazardous society. Where applicable, problems associated with particular brand names are enumerated. Ends with resource guide including organizations dealing with children, catalog sources, and government agencies. Index.

1195 Parent's choice: a sourcebook of the very best products to educate, inform, and entertain children of all ages. Diane H. Green. 208p. Andrews & McMeel, 1993. Paper $35. ISBN 0-8362-8036-9.
790.1 GV1218.5

By the editors of *Parent's Choice* and Parent's Choice Awards. Information to familiarize parents with education and learning. Discusses toys, books, videos, audios, computer programs, and magazines. Good bibliography, company addresses. Indexes by ages, categories.

1196 Parents' resource almanac. Beth DeFrancis. 779p. B. Adams, 1994. Paper $15. ISBN 1-55850-394-3.
649 HQ755.8

Designed to guide parents through the labyrinth of resources and information available on children and child rearing. Opposing points of view of child care presented. Provides descriptions of free and inexpensive materials. Entries are in alphabetical order by type of resource within each chapter. Chapters range from child development to grandparents to grooming, nutrition, education, computers, travel, and television. Includes chapters on the best books, magazines, and products for children. Useful appendixes on museums, aquariums, zoos, national parks, national forests, and more. Index.

1197 Sourcebook on parenting and child care. Kathryn H. Carpenter. 272p. Oryx, 1994. Paper $35. ISBN 0-89774-780-1.
016.649 HQ755.8

A bibliography of the 900 most practical books, journals, and audiovisuals on parenting—most from 1990 to 1994. Entries include summary of contents, intended audience, and special features. Provides directory information on professional and parenting organizations and useful statistics.

1198 Who to call: the parent's source book. Dan Starer. 654p. Morrow, 1992. $30. ISBN 0-688-10044-9.
649 HQ769

Telephone access, including toll-free numbers and hot lines, for thousands of organizations providing information on children and adolescents. Describes how to get results and answers through the phone. Arranged by general category (education, recreation, medical and psychological needs), then explicit subject breakdown. A thirty-page index helps one find anything by name or by subject.

Pets

1199 Complete book of pet care. Peter Roach. 272p. Howell Books, 1995. Paper $17.95. ISBN 0-87605-484-X.
636.0887 SF413

Covers birds, cats, dogs, fish, guinea pigs, hamsters, horses, mice, rabbits, reptiles, and amphibians. Arranged alphabetically. Selecting, housing, breeding, general care of sick pets (common ailments), when to consult a veterinarian. Color photographs, drawings. Straightforward narrative, no jargon; comprehensible, but not overly simple. Detailed index.

Birds

1200 The complete bird owner's handbook. 2d rev. ed. Gary Gallerstein. 352p. Howell Books, 1994. $27.50. ISBN 0-87605-903-5.
636.6 SF461

The standard source for bird owners. Everything from purchasing at the shop to caring for wild orphaned birds. Emphasizes the creation of healthy avian environments; provides tips on nutrition and grooming. Describes common diseases and what to do in emergencies. Provides a species guide, information on breeding, and a directory of relevant organizations.

Cats

1201 ASPCA complete cat care manual. Andrew Edney. 192p. Dorling Kindersley, 1992. $24.95. ISBN 1-56458-064-4.
636.8 SF447

A standard care manual for cats; everything from daily essentials to crisis management. Well illustrated, easy to follow.

1202 Cats. David Alderton. 256p. Dorling Kindersley, 1993. $29.95. ISBN 1-56458-073-3; paper $17.95. ISBN 1-56458-070-9.
636.8 SF442

Describes more than 250 types of cats, with more than 700 color photographs. Traces the evolution of the domestic cat. Provides systematic classification and historical discussion including country of origin and ancestry of various cat breeds. Section 1, longhaired; section 2, shorthaired. Each entry provides a general description of body shape and face, fur, and temperament. Offers hints on how to select a cat, sexing kittens, grooming, handling, and showing.

1203 The complete cat book. Richard Gebhardt. 224p. Howell Books, 1991. $19.95. ISBN 0-87605-841-1; paper $14.95. ISBN 0-87605-919-1.
636.8 SF442

A reference to principal breeds as recognized by the Cat Fancier's Association and other recognized registries. Discusses care, breeding, showing, history, and anatomy of cats.

1204 Cornell book of cats: a comprehensive medical reference for every cat and kitten. 2d ed. Siegal Mordecai, ed. 508p. Villard, 1997. $35. ISBN 0-679-44953-1.
636.8 SF985

The well cat book: the classic comprehensive handbook of cat care. 2d ed. Terri McGinnis. 292p. Random House, 1996. $15.95. ISBN 0-679-77000-3.
636.8 SF427

Both books discuss cat care, cat development, and feline medical reference information, including symptoms and signs of illness and medical treatments. The *Cornell book of cats* provides the more comprehensive and authoritative entries.

1205 Encyclopedia of the cat. Bruce Fogle. 250p. Dorling Kindersley, 1997. $34.95. ISBN 0-7894-1970-X.
636.8 SF442.2

A sourcebook that describes the cat family and its evolution, cats in human culture and religion, cats in folklore and literature, cat anatomy and behavior, cat breeds, and cat care. Well illustrated and well organized.

1206 The Reader's Digest illustrated book of cats. Reader's Digest editors. 256p. Reader's Digest, 1993. $25. ISBN 0-88850-198-6.
636.8 SF442

Divided into six sections that describe the history, anatomy, physiology, behavior, breeds, and care of cats. Describes forty-four breeds as recognized by the International Cat Association (TICA). Lists countries where the breed is registered or recognized. Provides much information on the cat world, including cat shows and cat associations. Comprehensive.

Dogs

1207 ASPCA complete dog care manual. Bruce Fogle. 192p. Dorling Kindersley, 1993. $24.95. ISBN 1-56458-168-3.
636.7 SF427

A complete sourcebook for dog owners, from dog equipment to diet and obedience. Dogs, start to finish. Well illustrated.

1208 Atlas of dog breeds of the world. 5th ed. Bonnie Wilcox and Chris Walkowicz. 912p. T.F.H., 1995. $89.95. ISBN 0-79381-284-4.
636.71 SF422

The mini-atlas of dog breeds. Andrew de Prisco. 573p. T.F.H., 1990. $39.95. ISBN 0-86622-091-7.
636.7 SF427

The *Atlas of dog breeds of the world* is the most comprehensive breed book available, covering more than 400 breeds with color photographs or portraits accompanying each informative entry. *The mini-atlas* provides a less expensive and nearly as thorough alternative.

1209 The complete dog book: the photograph, history and official standard of every breed admitted to AKC registration. 18th ed. AKC staff. 832p. Howell Books, 1992. $27.50. ISBN 0-87605-464-5.
636.7 SF427

The American Kennel Club (AKC) maintains the registry of pedigree dogs in North America, and its publication offers the official standard for each recognized breed, a photograph, the history of the breed, and organizations of breeders. In the "Healthy Dog" section, the book covers the general topics of nutrition, illness, training, and first aid. No further reading is suggested, but the text is indexed. A basic guide needed in every public library.

1210 Dog owner's home veterinary handbook. 2d rev. ed. Delbert G. Carlson and James M. Giffin. 423p. Howell Books, 1992. $25. ISBN 0-87605-537-4.
636.7 SF991

Easy-to-use, quick reference. Provides index of symptoms and signs of problems and includes description and treatment of common maladies. General index.

1211 Dogs. David Alderton. 320p. Dorling Kindersley, 1993. $29.95. ISBN 1-65458-179-9; paper $17.95. ISBN 1-56458-176-4.
636.7 SF426

More than 300 entries from a half page to two pages in length describing all breeds of dog. Photographs show mature dog; graphics indicate size in relation to humans; swatches show typical hairs; includes historical narrative, country of origin, and traditional employment of breed. Additional features include a glossary, directory of organizations, and an index.

Fish

1212 Dr. Axelrod's atlas of freshwater aquarium fishes. 9th ed. Herbert R. Axelrod. 1152p. T.F.H., 1997. $99.95. ISBN 0-79380-033-1.
639.34 SF457

More than 7,000 photographs with captions provide basic information such as scientific name, feeding habits, reproduction, temperament, swimming habits, size, recommended pH, and so on. Uses an arrangement by geographical region. Lacks narrative and references for further reading.

1213 Dr. Axelrod's mini-atlas of freshwater aquarium fishes. Herbert R. Axelrod et al. 992p. T.F.H., 1995. $29.95. ISBN 0-86622-385-1.
639.34 SF457

Intended as a resource for the identification and maintenance of the different varieties of freshwater and marine fishes collected by hobbyists. Provides information on aquarium setup, species compatibility, feeding, breeding, and care. Indexed both by popular and scientific name.

1214 Dr. Burgess's atlas of marine aquarium fishes. Warren Burgess et al. 768p. T.F.H., 1990. $69.95. ISBN 0-86622-896-9.
639.342 SF457.1

Hundreds of full-color photographs. Captions identify fish, their families, range, feeding habits, temperament, swimming habits, optimum aquarium lighting, and aquarium decor. Symbols used in captions make finding information easy. The scientific name and family are indicated. Divided into common fish and unusual fish.

1215 Dr. Burgess's mini-atlas of marine aquarium fishes. Warren Burgess and Herbert R. Axelrod. 1023p. T.F.H., 1991. $29.95. ISBN 0-86622-404-1.
639.3 SF457.1

More than 1,800 full-color photographs. Captions identify feeding habits, reproduction, aquarium lighting, temperament, aquarium setup (including decoration), swimming habits, and water needs. A third of the book is dedicated to setting up aquariums and caring for fish, health of fish, and plants for aquariums. Indexes for setup and maintenance of aquariums; for common names of fish; and for scientific names of fish.

1216 Illustrated encyclopedia of aquarium fish. Gina Sandford. 256p. Howell Books, 1995. $29.95. ISBN 0-87605-947-7.
639.3 SF456.5

Includes a long and useful introduction on how to choose a tank; describes decorating and filling the tank, food preferences (e.g., omnivores, herbivores, insectivores, carnivores), and breeding. Includes both freshwater fish and marine fish. Color photographs accompany narrative entries. Indexed by scientific name and common name.

1217 The Macmillan book of the marine aquarium. Nick Dakin. 400p. Macmillan, 1993. $75. ISBN 0-02-897108-6.
639.3 SF457.1

A guide for the beginner, lavishly illustrated, on how to set up and maintain a marine aquarium. Includes information on the natural marine environment, the aquarium replica, marine fish, and their care. Includes compatibility chart, glossary, and indexes.

Horses

1218 The encyclopedia of the horse. Elwyn H. Edwards and Bob Langris. 400p. Dorling Kindersley, 1994. $39.95. ISBN 1-56458-614-6.
636.1 SF285

One of the best reference books on horses. Provides a chronicle of the role of the horse throughout history. Offers narrative entries on more than 150 breeds, including sporting horses. More than 1,000 full-color illustrations. Glossary, index.

1219 Horse industry directory. 186p. American Horse Council, 1972– . Annual. $20. ISSN 0890-233X.
636.1 SF277

An annual publication covering breeding associations, businesses, riding and show associations, libraries and museums, and so forth. Includes state veterinarians, race tracks, steeplechase meets, health requirements, and federal sources. Extremely useful information.

1220 Horses. Elwyn H. Edwards. 320p. Dorling Kindersley, 1993. $29.95. ISBN 1-56458-180-2; paper $17.95. ISBN 1-56458-177-2.
636.1 SF285

A compact guide. Easy to use, well illustrated. Tells how to identify more than 100 breeds; provides an identification key by geographic origin. Indexed.

Reptiles and Amphibians

1221 The completely illustrated atlas of reptiles and amphibians for the terrarium. Fritz Jurgen Obst. 832p. T.F.H., 1988. $129.95. ISBN 0-86622-958-2.
639.3 QL640.7

Describes, depicts, and provides instruction for the care of reptiles and amphibians that can be kept in captivity. For both hobbyists and students alike.

1222 The proper care of reptiles. John Coborn. 256p. T.F.H., 1993. $16.95. ISBN 0-86622-345-2.
639.3 SF459.R4

Section 1 deals with care of reptiles: general facts, housing, management, health and hygiene, captive breeding, foods, and feeding. Section 2 discusses selection of species likely to be kept at home, including tortoises, turtles, snakes, and lizards. Index includes names as well as topics.

Unusual Pets

1223 Exotic pets. Arthur Rosenfeld. 288p. S & S Trade, 1987. $21.45. ISBN 0-671-63690-1; paper ISBN 0-671-47654-8. op.
636.08 SF413

Manual of exotic pets. New ed. Peter H. Benyon and John E. Cooper, eds. 312p. Univ. of Iowa Pr., 1994. Paper $69.95. ISBN 0-8138-2294-7.
636.089 SF981

The Rosenfeld book provides good general overviews for those starting out with snakes, lizards, turtles, parrots, amphibians, and fishes. It discusses housing, handling, and general care and includes prices. The *Manual*, copublished with the British Small Animal Veterinary Association, provides a wealth of information about exotic pets and their management, husbandry, physiology, and diseases—all in a very readable form. Individual chapters deal with chinchillas, chipmunks, gerbils, hamsters, hedgehogs, rabbits, rats and mice, ferrets, primates, wild mammals, cage and aviary birds, pigeons, wild birds, birds of prey, reptiles, chelonians, lizards and snakes, and amphibians. Indexed.

1224 Exotic pets: a veterinary guide for owners. Shawn Messonnier. 144p. Seaside, 1994. Paper $8.95. ISBN 1-55622-381-1.
636 SF413

A reference manual describing the most common facts and problems encountered. Deals with a variety of species including bull python, box turtle, iguana, ferret, birds, and small rodents. For each includes general information, special anatomical features, selecting your pet, first veterinary visit, housing, diet, and common diseases.

1225 Keeping unusual animals as pets. Jef Hewitt. 120p. Sterling, 1990. $15.95. ISBN 0-8069-7278-5.
636.088 SF459

Provides basic descriptions of and proper care for creatures such as tomato frogs and scorpions. Discusses the ethics of keeping unusual animals as pets. This is a general guide that ideally would need to be supplemented by specific handbooks for specific types of pets.

1226 Practical guide to exotic pets. Chris Mattison. 128p. Courage Books, 1994. $15.98. ISBN 1-56138-370-8.
636.088 SF413

Deals with three categories of exotic pets: invertebrates, amphibians, and reptiles. More than fifty of the most common exotic pets are discussed. A general overview is followed by entries on specific pets and on handling, housing, and feeding exotic animals. Includes numerous photographs. Step-by-step directions. Indexed by species.

1227 Practical guide to impractical pets. Barbara Burn. 352p. Macmillan, 1997. $27.95. ISBN 0-87605-724-5.
636.088 SF413

Focuses on eighty-four exotic pets and describes how one might live with them. Divides pets into three categories: easy, difficult, and impossible. Photos, index, charts.

14

Visual Arts

DONALD W. MAXWELL

Visual arts are nonverbal in nature. They communicate through symbol: on two-dimensional surfaces, by three-dimensional objects, through architecture, or with useful, everyday objects like clothing and furniture.

Bibliographies and Guides

1228 Art information: research methods and resources. 3d ed. Lois Swan Jones. 373p. Kendall/Hunt, 1990. $35.95. ISBN 0-8403-5713-3. (*formerly* **Art research methods and resources.**)
707 N85

More than 19,000 sources are cited in this guide to the methodology of art research and bibliography of research tools. Includes a list of art research centers in the United States, Canada, and Europe and several helpful appendixes.

1229 Arts in America: a bibliography. Bernard Karpel, ed. 4v. Smithsonian, 1980. op.
016.7 Z5961.U5

This set is a standard reference source for locating information about the arts in America. The first three volumes are divided into twenty-one sections providing more than 24,000 annotated entries on such subjects as Native American art, architecture, decorative arts, nineteenth-century painting, twentieth-century graphic art, photography, film, theater, dance, and music and separate sections on serials and periodicals, dissertations and theses, and visual resources. Materials cited include monographs, reference works, catalogs, discographies, and many rare items; good coverage is provided up to 1975. The fourth volume is a complete and detailed index that facilitates an interdisciplinary study of the arts in America.

1230 Guide to the literature of art history. Etta Arntzen and Robert Rainwater. 616p. American Library Assn., 1981. $20. ISBN 0-8389-0263-4.
016.709 N380

With more than 4,100 annotations, this work is the most complete of bibliographies on the study of art. A wide variety of sources comprises general reference works, directories, sales records, visual sources, dictionaries and encyclopedias, iconographies, historical materials, books on specific art media, and serials. Annotations cover both the content of sources and an evaluative comment; many nonart resources are also treated. A new edition, *Guide to the literature of art history 2*, is being edited by Max Marmor and Alex Ross, art library directors of Yale University and Stanford University, and is expected from ALA in the near future.

1231 Visual arts research: a handbook. Elizabeth B. Pollard. 165p. Greenwood, 1986. $49.95. ISBN 0-313-24186-4.
707.2 N85

A dated but useful guide to research in visual art. Bibliographic essays cite more than 400 books and databases and 100 periodicals. Suggests sources for locating information about artists, periods, media, works, materials, techniques, and art education.

Indexes and Abstracts

1232 Art index. Wilson, Jan. 1929/Sept. 1932– . Quarterly with annual cumulations. Service basis. ISSN 0004-3222.
■ cd online
016.7 Z5937

Author-subject index to the contents of approximately 270 domestic and foreign periodicals, yearbooks, and museum bulletins, including those recommended for indexing by subscribers. Archaeology, architecture, art history, crafts, graphic arts, industrial design, landscape architecture, museology, photography and films, and related subjects are indexed. Book reviews are indexed in a separate section.

Indexes to Reproductions and Illustrations

1233 Catalogue of reproductions of paintings prior to 1860 with fifteen projects for exhibitions. 10th ed. 346p. UNESCO, 1979. op.

Catalogue of reproductions of paintings 1860 to 1979 with seventeen projects for exhibitions. 11th rev. ed. 275p. UNESCO, 1981. Paper $16. ISBN 92-3-001924-0.
769.9 ND189

Good-quality reproductions of more than 3,000 paintings, with details about the original work, the artist's dates and nationality, and information about the reproductions, including availability. There is also a section on organizing exhibits. The text is in English, French, and Spanish.

1234 Contemporary art and artists: an index to reproductions. Pamela Jeffcott Parry, comp. 327p. Greenwood, 1978. $59.95. ISBN 0-313-20544-2.
709 N6490

Includes works in all media, except architecture, and most crafts for the period 1940 to the mid-1970s. Some of the sixty books indexed are also found in other indexes, but many are found only here. Most entries include artist's name, nationality, and dates; title and date of the work; and a location symbol. Artists who died before 1950 are generally excluded. There is a good subject index.

1235 Dictionary of American portraits: 4045 pictures of important Americans from earliest times to the beginning of the twentieth century. Hayward Cirker and Blanche Cirker. 756p. Dover, 1967. $80. ISBN 0-486-21823-6.
704.9 N7593

Illustrations of portraits of important American citizens and others who have made a significant contribution to American national life. Presidents and four other categories of prominent public persons have been continued beyond 1900. The portraits selected represent their subjects in characteristic poses. Includes a bibliography and an occupation index.

1236 Illustration index. 2d ed. Lucile E. Vance and Esther M. Tracey. 527p. Scarecrow, 1966. op; 3d ed. Roger C. Greer. 164p. Scarecrow, 1973. op; 4th ed. Marsha C. Appel. 458p. Scarecrow, 1980. $34. ISBN 0-8108-1273-8.

Illustration index V, 1977–1981. Marsha C. Appel. 411p. Scarecrow, 1984. $34. ISBN 0-8108-1656-3.

Illustration index VI, 1982–1986. Marsha C. Appel. 531p. Scarecrow, 1988. $42.50. ISBN 0-8108-2146-X.

Illustration index VII, 1987–1991. Marsha C. Appel. 492p. Scarecrow, 1993. $59.50. ISBN 0-8108-2659-3.

Illustration index VIII, 1992–1996. Marsha C. Appel. 480p. Scarecrow, 1998. $65. ISBN 0-8108-3484-7.
011 N7525

Comprehensive guide to more than 100,000 photographs, paintings, drawings, and diagrams appearing in popular periodicals, chosen for richness of illustration and availability of back issues in libraries. The second edition covers the period 1950 to June 1963 and completely replaces the first edition (1957) and its supplement (1961). Coverage of the third edition is from July 1963 to December 1971. The fourth edition covers 1972–76. Later titles indicate the years covered. Arrangement is by subject.

1237 **Index to illustrations.** Jessie Croft Ellis. 682p. Faxon, 1966, c1967. $13. ISBN 0-87305-095-9.
741.6 NC996

An index to illustrations in widely owned books and periodicals such as *Current biography* and *National geographic*. Arranged by subject.

1238 **Index to reproductions of American paintings: a guide to pictures occurring in more than eight hundred books.** Isabel Stevenson Monro and Kate M. Monro. 731p. Wilson, 1948. op.

Index to reproductions of American paintings, first supplement: a guide to pictures occurring in more than four hundred works. Isabel Stevenson Monro and Kate M. Monro. 480p. Wilson, 1964. op.
759.13 ND205

An index to reproductions in more than 1,200 books and exhibition catalogs, providing the name of the artist, title of painting, and subject. Location of the original paintings is noted when known.

1239 **Index to reproductions of European paintings: a guide to pictures in more than three hundred books.** Isabel Stevenson Monro and Kate M. Monro. 668p. Wilson, 1956. op.
016.759 ND45

A guide to pictures by European artists that are reproduced in 328 books. Paintings are entered under the name of the artist, title of painting, and, in many cases, subject. Location of original painting is noted when known.

1240 **Slide buyers' guide: an international directory of slide sources for art and architecture.** 6th ed. Norine D. Cashman, ed. 190p. Libraries Unlimited, 1990. $35. ISBN 0-87287-797-3.
026 N4040.V57

The most complete publication on this subject available, it lists and evaluates slide vendors and classifies them by country. The detailed subject index is divided according to historical periods, art forms, and geographical areas.

1241 **World painting index.** Patricia Pate Havlice. 2v. Scarecrow, 1977. $125. ISBN 0-8108-1016-6.

World painting index. First supplement, 1973–1980. Patricia Pate Havlice. 2v. Scarecrow, 1982. $95. ISBN 0-8108-1531-1.

World painting index. Second supplement, 1980–1989. Patricia Pate Havlice. 2v. Scarecrow, 1995. $149.50. ISBN 0-8108-3020-5.
750 ND45

The original volume and its supplements index 2,475 books and catalogs published between 1940 and 1989. They provide a means for locating paintings from all over the world, with emphasis on those in the Western tradition. The first volume of each set contains a numbered bibliography, an alphabetical listing by artist of paintings, and a list of works whose creators are not known. The second volumes are alphabetical listings of paintings by title.

Dictionaries and Encyclopedias

1242 **Art: a history of painting, sculpture, architecture.** 4th ed. Frederick Hartt. 1127p. Abrams, 1993. $60. ISBN 0-8109-1921-4; paper 2v. $43.95/v. Prentice-Hall/Abrams, 1993. v.1, ISBN 0-13-052416-6; v.2, ISBN 0-13-052424-7.
709 N5300

Chronologically arranged encyclopedia covers prehistoric times through the early 1990s. Authoritative and attractive, with descriptions and facts synthesized with historical, social, and critical commentary. Emphasis is placed on women artists in the revised edition. Color and black-and-white reproductions are integrated with the text. Includes a glossary, bibliography, and thorough index.

1243 **Dictionary of art.** Jane Turner, ed. 34v. Grove's Dictionaries, 1996. $8000/set.

ISBN 1-884446-00-0.
■ online
703.20 N31.D5

With more than 41,000 entries, 15,000 illustrations, 300,000 bibliographic citations, 6,700 contributors from 120 countries, and a 670,000 entry index, this encyclopedic work is the single most comprehensive art reference source to date. The price will seem prohibitive for many budgets, but this award-winning set is all that one would expect from Grove's and more. The Friends of your library will surely want to help you acquire this magnificent work of scholarship.

1244 Dictionary of ornament.
Phillippa Lewis and Gillian Darley. 319p. Pantheon, 1986. $29.95. ISBN 0-394-50931-5.
745.4 NK1165

An alphabetical survey of ornament, pattern, and motif in the applied arts and architecture. It is thoroughly cross-referenced, with 1,020 entries illustrated by 1,150 small photographs. The descriptions are somewhat fuller than Maureen Stafford and Dora Ware's out-of-print *An illustrated dictionary of ornament.* The coverage is mainly of European and North American objects from the Renaissance to the present day.

1245 Encyclopedia of aesthetics. Michael Kelly. 4v. Oxford Univ. Pr., 1998. $495. ISBN 0-19-511307-1.
111 BH56

Featuring more than 600 articles, each with extensive bibliographies, this magnificent encyclopedia provides detailed information on the critical issues and figures in the history of art, culture, and society.

1246 The encyclopedia of American comics: from 1897 to the present.
Ron Goulart, ed. 408p. Facts on File, 1990. op.
741.5 PN6725

Signed entries about American comic strips, their artists, writers, creators, and others. Many black-and-white illustrations and several color plates. Includes cross-references and an index. An older comprehensive encyclopedia on world comics is *The world encyclopedia of comics.*

1247 The encyclopedia of visual art.
Lawrence Gowing, ed. 10v. Grolier, 1983. Reprint: 2v. Prentice-Hall, 1985, c1983. Reprint: 10v. Encyclopaedia Britannica Educational Corp., 1989. $279/set. ISBN 0-85229-187-6. Reprint (rev. ed.): **A biographical dictionary of artists.** Lawrence Gowing, ed. 784p. Facts on File, 1995, c1983. $50. ISBN 0-8160-3252-1.
709 N25

The first five volumes of this well-illustrated set are arranged chronologically with articles describing important developments and genres, as well as information about individual objects of art. The next four volumes provide biographies of both classical and contemporary artists and a glossary of art terms. The final volume contains three sets of illustrated studies, a directory of galleries and museums, and an index. The Prentice-Hall reprint combined the chronology into one volume, the biographies into a second, each with separate indexes, and omitted the studies and directory. The revised edition contains only the biographies and glossary.

1248 Encyclopedia of world art. 15v. McGraw-Hill, 1959–87. $1495/set. ISBN 0-07-019467-X. v.16, Supplement. World art in our time. 1983. $99.50. ISBN 0-318-00457-7. v.17, Supplement II. New discoveries and perspectives in the world of art. 681p. J. Heraty & Associates, 1987. $99.50. ISBN 0-910081-01-8.
703 N31

Survey containing signed articles with extensive bibliographies. Based on the Italian *Enciclopedia universale dell' arte,* this definitive English-language encyclopedia embraces architecture, sculpture, painting, and the minor arts. There are numerous cross-references and many illustrations. Volume 15 of the set is a detailed index to volumes 1 to 14. Volumes 16 and 17 update the original set.

1249 Graphic arts encyclopedia.
3d ed. George A. Stevenson. Rev. by William A. Pakan. 582p. McGraw-Hill, 1990. $57.95. ISBN 0-07-048113-X. Reprint: Design Pr., 1992. $57.95. ISBN 0-8306-2530-5.
686.2 TR665

A useful source of information on terms, processes, equipment, products, and techniques used in the reproduction of words and pictures, updated to include desktop publishing information. Photographs and drawings assist in the identification of objects. Supplemented by a bibliography, tables, and charts.

1250 The HarperCollins dictionary of art terms and techniques. 2d ed. Ralph Mayer. Steven Sheehan, rev. and ed. 474p. HarperPerennial, 1991. Paper $16. ISBN 0-06-461012-8.
703 N33

Definitions of more than 3,200 terms from the study and practice of visual art, including materials and methodology of painting, drawing, sculpture, graphic arts, ceramics, computer-generated art, and photography. Includes many line drawings and a select bibliography. Mayer also was the author of *The artist's handbook of materials and techniques.*

1251 History of art. H. W. Janson. 5th ed. rev. and ex. by Anthony F. Janson. 960p. Abrams, 1995. $60. ISBN 0-8109-3421-3.
709 N5300

The fifth edition of this classic on Western art has more changes than the previous editions combined, particularly for after 1520. It extends the discussion of twentieth-century art, particularly of architecture and sculpture, and increases the discussion of women and African American artists. It is arranged chronologically and has maps, time lines, more than 1,250 black-and-white and color illustrations, 119 reproduced excerpts from primary sources, an extensive bibliography, glossary, and index. Its intention is to provide "the framework for how to look at and respond to art in museums and galleries."

1252 Museum of American Folk Art encyclopedia of twentieth-century folk art and artists. Chuck Rosenak and Jan Rosenak. 416p. Abbeville, 1990. $49.98. ISBN 1-55859-041-2.
709 NK808

American folk art of this century is described through the paintings, drawings, sculptures, pottery, and other works of 257 artists, four essays, and numerous color plates. Lists of public folk art collections, footnotes, a bibliography, and an index round out this authoritative work.

1253 New dictionary of modern sculpture. Robert Maillard, ed. Bettina Wadia, trans. 328p. Tudor, 1971. op.
730 NB50

A sympathetic survey of twentieth-century sculpture that includes signed articles with brief biographies. There is also some technical information and criticism. The arrangement is alphabetical by sculptor. Based on the French *Nouveau dictionnaire de la sculpture moderne* (1970).

1254 The Oxford companion to art. Harold Osborne, ed. 1277p. Clarendon Pr., 1970. $49.95. ISBN 0-19-866107-X.
703 N33

More than 3,000 articles of varying lengths on the visual arts and artists, designed for the nonspecialist. Handicrafts and the practical arts are not included. Most articles have a coded reference to the 3,000-item bibliography. Numerous cross-references.

1255 The Oxford companion to twentieth-century art. Harold Osborne, ed. 656p. Oxford Univ. Pr., 1988. Paper $22.50. ISBN 0-19-282076-1.
709 N6490

Provides sketches of hundreds of artists who have done their most significant work between 1900 and 1975. International in scope, it covers artists in more depth than other volumes in the Oxford series. Illustrations and bibliographies add to the value of the book, which is designed primarily for ready reference. Information on movements, trends, and the state of art during the twentieth century is included.

1256 The Oxford dictionary of art. Rev. ed. Ian Chilvers and Harold Osborne, eds. 672p. Oxford Univ. Pr., 1997. $49.95. ISBN 0-19-860084-4.
703 N33

This newly updated dictionary offers a comprehensive, if succinct, guide to all aspects of Western art, excluding architecture. There are more than 3,000 entries of one to three paragraphs in length covering individual artists, important institutions, art historians, movements, art terms, and so on. The dictionary does not include bibliography or provide illustrations, but there is a useful chronology at the end and a brief directory of the very largest museums and galleries worldwide.

1257 Twentieth century American folk, self-taught, and outsider art. Betty-Carol Sellen with Cynthia J. Johanson. 462p. Neal-Schuman, 1993. $90. ISBN 1-55570-142-6.
745 NK805

This source lists places where American folk art can be viewed and learned, organizations and publications devoted to the genre, and a bibliography of print and audiovisual sources on folk art. Includes profiles of contemporary folk artists and several black-and-white and color illustrations.

1258 **World encyclopedia of comics.** 2d ed. Maurice Horn, ed. 7v. Chelsea House, 1997. $245/set. ISBN 0-7910-4854-3. Also available in a one-volume edition (1061p. $59.95. ISBN 0-7910-4856-X).
741.5 NC1325

More than 1,300 entries, with half on American subjects, covering biographical data on noted cartoonists and bibliographic information on their works. Includes histories of political humor, animation, strips, and individual characters. Indexes to proper names, illustrations, subjects, and geography.

Directories

1259 **American art directory.** Bowker, 1898– . Biennial. $262.50. ISSN 0065-6968.
705.8 N50

More than 6,000 entries on U.S. and Canadian art museums, libraries, associations, schools, and corporations with art holdings, arranged alphabetically by state or province, then city. Museum listings include addresses, phone numbers, names of key personnel, hours of operation, income, and description of exhibitions, activities, and publications. School listings include names of administrator and faculty, registration information, majors, degrees granted, and courses. Other sections list art publications, state art councils, scholarships, exhibition booking agencies, and other information. Indexes to subjects, personnel, and organizations.

1260 **Art in America. Annual guide to galleries, museums, artists.** Aug. issue of Art in America. Brant (575 Broadway, New York, NY 10012), 1913– . $39.95. ISSN 0004-3214.
708 N510

Directory information on all aspects of art activity in the United States, including more than 3,700 galleries, museums, "alternative spaces," dealers, and consultants, including names, addresses, contact persons, hours, telephone numbers, descriptions, and lists of artists exhibited. There is a review of the highlights of the previous museum season with a record of major events and exhibitions and an advertising directory of auction houses, art services, and schools.

1261 **Artist's and graphic designer's market: where and how to sell your illustration, fine art, graphic design and cartoons.** F & W Pub. for Writer's Digest, 1994– . Annual. $24.99. ISSN 1075-0894.
706 N8600

This merger of *Artist's market* and *Guide to literary agents and art/photo reps* lists places where art can be marketed in the United States and Canada, including studios, galleries, publishers of art prints, books, and magazines, as well as businesses like public relations firms and greeting-card and record companies. Articles cover topics in the business of art and insider information from art directors and artists. The 1998 edition contained 2,500 listings of names, addresses, phone numbers, submission details, and pay rates.

1262 **Museums of the world.** 6th ed. 750p. K. G. Saur, 1997. $425. ISBN 3-598-20605-4.
069 AM1

Arranged alphabetically by country, and then by city within the country, 24,624 museums in 191 countries are listed by name (in original language and translated into English), with address, phone, fax, and telex numbers; e-mail address; type of museum; founding date; director; and description of collections and facilities. Includes indexes to names of institutions (in original language and English), persons with works featured in a museum, and subjects.

1263 **The official museum directory.** American Assn. of Museums/ Bowker, 1971– . Annual. 2v. $229/set. ISSN 0090-6700.
069 AM10.A2

This comprehensive directory of more than 7,300 U.S. museums is arranged by state and then by city and includes such information as address, key personnel, hours, major holdings, activities, and publications. Includes nearly 2,000 listings of products and services suppliers as well as indexes to names, subjects, collection emphases, and personnel.

1264 **The world's master paintings: from the early Renaissance to the present day.** Christopher Wright, comp. 2v. Routledge, 1992. $399. ISBN 0-415-02240-1.
750 ND40

This source lists publicly accessible works (i.e., not in private collections) by 1,300 Western painters and their locations throughout the world as of May 1991. The first main section of this source arranges paintings first by century; then by school; then alphabetically by painter (accompanied by a biographical sketch, citations for catalogues raisonné[s] or other major book[s], and the location of other major collections); then by city in which works can be found; then alphabetically by title of painting. The second section contains the same information as the first, but arranged now by location (i.e., city or town in which the collection can be found); then by institution, with a description of holdings, including a select bibliography (especially catalogs); then by nationality; and finally by painter.

Handbooks

1265 **The artist's handbook of materials and techniques.** Ralph Mayer. 5th ed., rev. and updated by Steven Sheehan. 761p. Viking, 1991. $40. ISBN 0-670-83701-6.
751 ND1500

This excellent guide for the amateur and professional encompasses all aspects of the materials and techniques employed by contemporary artists, as well as traditional methods of the past. Mayer was also the author of *The HarperCollins dictionary of art terms and techniques.*

Biographical Sources

1266 **Contemporary artists.** 4th ed. Joann Cerrito, ed. 1340p. St. James, 1996. $149. ISBN 1-55862-183-0.
709 N6490

Some 850 painters, sculptors, and graphic and performance artists of international renown are included, with some deceased artists (who died since 1960) whose work is still influential on the current art scene. Each entry consists of a biography, complete list of individual shows, selected list of group exhibitions and collections, bibliography, signed critical essay, and, in many cases, comments by the artists on their own works.

1267 **Dictionary of contemporary American artists.** 6th ed. Paul Cummings. 786p. St. Martin's, 1994. $85. ISBN 0-312-08440-4.
709 N6512

Information on more than 900 artists: birth and death dates and places, where they studied art and with whom, teaching positions, memberships, commissions, awards and scholarships won, dealers, exhibitions and collections of work, addresses, and extensive bibliographical information. Supplemented with cross-references to artists who appeared in the previous five editions, black-and-white illustrations, a pronunciation guide to names, and a general bibliography.

1268 **Mantle Fielding's dictionary of American painters, sculptors and engravers.** 2d ed. Glenn B. Opitz, ed. 1081p. Apollo Books, 1986. $95. ISBN 0-938290-04-5.
709 N6536

More than 12,000 biographies arranged alphabetically, covering artists from colonial times to the mid-1980s. Entries include birth and death dates, education, exhibitions, collections, awards, and last known address. A useful source for information on minor artists that may be difficult to find elsewhere. This 1986 imprint is a revision of the 1983 second edition.

1269 **Who's who in American art.** 1521p. Bowker, 1936–37– . Biennial. $210. ISSN 0000-0191.
■ online tape
709 N6536

The twenty-second edition contains listings of more than 11,900 living visual artists and other contributors to art of the United States, Canada, and Mexico, including administrators, educators, historians, librarians, critics, curators, collectors, and dealers. Listings include vital statistics, education and training, media of work, positions held, memberships, honors, commissions, major works in public collections, exhibitions, and publications. Indexes locate entries by geographical designation and professional classification. A necrology is cumulative from 1953. Available online as a part of *Bowker biographical directory online.*

Architecture

1270 **American shelter: an illustrated encyclopedia of the American home.** Lester Walker. 320p. Overlook Pr.,

1981. $40. ISBN 0-87951-131-1.
728.3 NA7205

In his chronologically arranged encyclopedia of American houses, A.D. 300 through 1980, Walker has illustrated ninety-nine different structures, using floor plans and isometric drawings. Explanatory notes accompany each drawing. Small drawings in the table of contents can lead to the correct structure if users do not know the name of the style. Includes a glossary, select bibliography, and an index to architects. Complemented by *The visual dictionary of American domestic architecture.*

1271 Contemporary architects. 3d ed. Muriel Emanuel, ed. 1125p. St. James, 1994. $149. ISBN 1-55862-182-2.
720 NA680

Includes entries on 585 of the world's greatest living architects, landscape architects, and architectural engineers and theorists, as well as early-twentieth-century architects who died after 1960 and whose work continues to influence modern architecture. Entries include biographical details, awards and other honors received, a chronological list of works and projects, major exhibitions, publications by and about the architect, the biographee's comments about his or her own work, an evaluative essay written by an architectural critic or historian, and a photograph or drawing of a representative work. Includes a geographical index to 1,000 major works by the biographees.

1272 Dictionary of architecture and construction: over 2,000 illustrations. 2d ed. Cyril M. Harris, ed. 924p. McGraw-Hill, 1993. $59.50. ISBN 0-07-026888-6.
720 NA31

Approximately 22,500 terms from the working language of architecture and construction. Particular emphasis placed on changes in the industry in the previous two decades in architectural styles, building trades and materials, urban planning, landscape architecture, and the conservation, preservation, and restoration activities of historic architecture. Line drawings throughout the work.

1273 Encyclopedia of American architecture. 2d ed. Robert T. Packard and Balthazar Korab. 724p. McGraw-Hill, 1995. $89.50. ISBN 0-07-048010-9.
720 NA705

This revised edition of William Dudley Hunt Jr.'s 1980 work is a nontechnical, selective view with 232 articles about architects, firms, building types, systems, materials and structures, periods and movements, the building industry, and architectural practice. Includes numerous cross-references, line drawings and color photographs, suggestions for further reading and information, and a good index.

1274 Encyclopedia of architecture: design, engineering and construction. Joseph A. Wilkes, ed. 4v. Wiley, 1988–90. $950/set. ISBN 0-471-63351-8.
720 NA31

Covering both construction and design, this work will be worthwhile for both technology and art collections. Broad coverage and illustrations, plans, bibliographies, and signed articles, together with an index in the final volume, make this a title highly recommended for those who need such a tool. A supplement in the last volume brings the material up-to-date.

1275 A history of architecture. 19th ed. Banister F. Fletcher. John Musgrove, ed. 1621p. Butterworths, 1987. $110. ISBN 0-408-01587-X.
720 NA200

This complete revision of a standard work describes, through artifacts, the principal patterns of architectural development and then places them in their proper historical and cultural setting. Material has been expanded to include Africa, the Americas, Asia, the Far East, and Australia. Seven chapters on twentieth-century architecture have been added. Colored maps, photographs, glossary, and extensive index.

1276 International dictionary of architects and architecture. Randall J. Van Vynckt, ed. 2v. St. James, 1993. $260/set. ISBN 1-55862-089-3.
720 NA40

Volume 1 covers 523 architects, and volume 2 covers 467 buildings and sites that are prominent in Western architectural history. Entries for architects list biographical information, a chronology of major built works, a bibliography of books and articles by and about the architect, and an original, signed, scholarly essay. Entries for architecture note dates of construction, the architect(s) (if known), notable alterations, a bibliography, and an essay. Includes 964 photographs and 169 floor plans and indexes to geography, building, and architect.

1277 Macmillan encyclopedia of architects. Adolf K. Placzek, ed. 4v. Free Pr., 1982. $425/set.

ISBN 0-02-925000-5.
720 NA40

Signed articles profile the lives of 2,400 architects from ancient times through the early 1980s with birth dates prior to 1931. Entries include a brief biographical sketch, a list of architectural works, and a bibliography of printed works by and about the architect. Supplemented by a chronological table of contents, a glossary of 600 terms, 1,400 illustrations, a 15,000-entry index of personal names, and a 30,000-entry index of names of architectural works.

1278 The visual dictionary of American domestic architecture. Rachel Carley. 272p. Henry Holt, 1994. $40. ISBN 0-8050-2646-0; paper $19.95. ISBN 0-8050-4563-5.
728 NA7205

More than 600 line drawings and floor plans of interiors, exteriors, and structures of homes make up this field guide. Brief narrative about the development of housing styles helps explain not only what structures looked like, but why they looked the way they did. Arranged chronologically from "Native American Dwellings" and "Continental Influences" to "Contemporary Trends." Indexed. Complements Lester Walker's *American shelter.*

1279 A visual dictionary of architecture. Francis D. K. Ching. 319p. Van Nostrand Reinhold, 1995. $42.95. ISBN 0-442-00904-6.
720 NA31

More than 1,000 line drawings are arranged into sixty-nine broad aspects of architecture (e.g., history, hardware, wall, stair, geometry, light) and surrounded by captions with words and their definitions. Access to specific words can be gained through the index, which contains more than 6,000 entries.

Ceramics

1280 Encyclopedia of pottery and porcelain, 1800–1960. Elisabeth Cameron. 366p. Facts on File, 1986. op.
666 NK3920

International in scope, this reference covers techniques, styles, movements, marks, artists, and manufacturers. There are 2,500 concise entries, 500 black-and-white photographs and drawings, and a separate section of color illustrations. This encyclopedia is arranged alphabetically and concludes with a list of references.

1281 An illustrated dictionary of ceramics: defining 3,054 terms relating to wares, materials, processes, styles, patterns, and shapes from antiquity to the present day. George Savage and Harold Newman. 319p. Thames & Hudson, 1985. Paper $24.95. ISBN 0-500-27380-4.
738 NK3770

Precise definitions of more than 3,000 terms relating to the physical aspects of ceramics: material, pattern, decoration, type, and glaze. All periods are covered, with emphasis on Europe, the Middle and Far East, and some American ceramics.

Costume

Material found under Sewing, in chapter 17, Crafts and Hobbies, may be helpful here also.

1282 The book of costume. Millia Davenport. 976p. Crown, 1964. $39.95. ISBN 0-517-03716-5.
391.09 GT513

A one-volume edition, formerly in two volumes, this work covers up to 1867. Costumes of the Orient, Europe, and America are included as well as ecclesiastical vestments and habits of monastic orders. Arranged chronologically. There are many illustrations, with the location of the original listed for most. Detailed index.

1283 Contemporary fashion. Richard Martin, ed. 575p. St. James, 1995. $135. ISBN 1-55862-173-3.
746.9 TT505.A1

Nearly 400 entries with information and assessment of fashion designers, design houses (e.g., Hermes), and clothing corporations (e.g., L. L. Bean) active from 1945 to the present. Entries contain personal and professional biography, bibliographical citations to works by as well as about the designer, a critical essay by an authority on fashion, and, sometimes, a personal statement from the designer. Includes several full-page black-and-white photographs of designs and indexes to names and nationalities.

1284 The dictionary of costume. R. Turner Wilcox. 406p. Scribner, 1969. $60. ISBN 0-684-15150-2.
391 GT507

This fully illustrated dictionary of historic costume covers all facets on a worldwide basis. The entries are primarily succinct descriptions of items of clothing. Bibliography.

1285 Encyclopedia of world costume. Doreen Yarwood. 471p. Scribner, 1978. op. Reprint: Bonanza, 1986. Paper $16.99. ISBN 0-517-61943-1.
391 GT507

With more than 2,000 drawings and eight pages of color illustrations, this is a comprehensive guide to costume from ancient times to the present day. There are 650 articles on such topics as hairstyles, fabrics, baby clothes, eyeglasses, cosmetics, political influences, and costumes of various countries. A bibliography and list of sources for further information add to the value of the work.

1286 Five centuries of American costume. R. Turner Wilcox. 207p. Scribner, 1963. $40. ISBN 0-684-15161-8.
391.0973 GT605

Arranged chronologically; emphasis is on the dress of American men, women, and children from the Vikings, Eskimos, and early settlers to 1960. Clear line drawings illustrate the text. Bibliography, but no index.

1287 The history of costume: from ancient Mesopotamia through the twentieth century. 2d ed. Blanche Payne et al. 659p. HarperCollins, 1992. $68.50. ISBN 0-06-047141-7. Reprint: Watson-Guptill, 1994. $65. ISBN 0-8230-4958-2. (*formerly* **History of costume: from the ancient Egyptians to the twentieth century.**)
391.009 GT510

Fully illustrated with photographs of paintings, statuary, and actual costumes, as well as line drawings. Information on accessories and fifty pages of draft patterns are helpful. Bibliography and detailed index.

Decorative Arts and Design

Price and hobby guides to antiques and collectibles may be found in chapter 17, Crafts and Hobbies.

1288 American furniture: 1620 to the present. Jonathan L. Fairbanks and Elizabeth Bidwell Bates. 561p. R. Marek, 1981. op.
749.213 NK2405

Separate chapters treat the development of stylistic changes up to 1835, with an introductory essay that emphasizes the changing technology of furniture construction and production. Individual examples of the furniture follow, with representation from private and public collections. There is also extensive coverage of frontier and vernacular furniture up to contemporary times. A lengthy bibliography. The illustrations are especially useful.

1289 Book of old silver, English, American, foreign: with all available hallmarks. Seymour B. Wyler. 447p. Crown, 1937. $26. ISBN 0-517-00089-X.
739 NK7230

A comprehensive indexed table of hallmarks facilitates the identification of silver. Contains chapters on various types of silver articles (e.g., tea and condiment sets, flat- and tableware, boxes, etc.).

1290 The Bullfinch illustrated encyclopedia of antiques. Paul Atterbury and Lois Tharp, eds. 332p. Little, Brown, 1994. $50. ISBN 0-8212-2077-2.
745.1 NK30

Covers six major areas—pottery and porcelain, glass, silver, furniture, clocks and watches, and oriental wares—that were a part of the development of decorative design of Western Europe and North America through the early twentieth century. Includes more than 1,000 quality illustrations of items from the photographic libraries of Sotheby's and Christie's auction houses accompanied by descriptive text and explanations of their significance. Supplemented with time lines, tables of marks, descriptions of how items work or were made, a glossary, and an index.

1291 Complete guide to furniture styles. Enl. ed. Louise Ade Boger. 500p. Scribner, 1969. op. Reprint: Macmillan,

1982. Paper $31. ISBN 0-684-17641-6.
749.2 NK2270

A chronological arrangement that concentrates on the European and American traditions. Many illustrations and a bibliography are included. Index of artists and craftspeople.

1292 Contemporary designers. 3d ed. Sara Pendergast, ed. 981p. St. James, 1997. $189. ISBN 1-55862-184-9.
745.2 NK1390

Biographical directory of 690 designers from around the world who were active in 1990 or, if they had died since 1970, are still considered highly influential. Covers primarily architectural, fashion, graphic, industrial, interior, product, and stage designers. Entries contain personal and professional biographies, a list of their important works, a bibliography of print material by or about the designers, and, in some cases, an autobiographical statement or evaluative essay by a critic or historian. Includes numerous black-and-white illustrations, a Nationality Index, and a Design Field Index.

1293 Dictionary of antiques. 2d ed. George Savage. 534p. Barrie and Jenkins, 1978. op.
745.1 NK30

Designed for collectors and dealers who need to date or attribute antiques of all kinds, including plate, glassware, furniture, embroidery, and so forth. The 1,500 entries have numerous illustrations and cross-references. It contains an appendix of marks and a bibliography.

1294 Dictionary of twentieth-century design. John Pile. 312p. Facts on File, 1990. $35. ISBN 0-8160-1811-1. Reprint: Da Capo Pr., 1994. $18.95. ISBN 0-306-80569-3.
745.4 NK1390

For both public and academic libraries, this tool covers "product, industrial, graphic, interior, exhibition, typographic, and advertising design." As defined by the author, design is making decisions to determine a form (shape, texture, color, size, and pattern) of an object that is functional. His definition relates to many fields (e.g., fine arts, architecture, inventions, crafts, etc.). More than 1,000 entries, varying from sixty words to two pages, extend to styles, periods, movements, designers, manufacturers, firms, and techniques. Includes photographs, a bibliography, and a detailed index.

1295 Field guide to American antique furniture. Joseph T. Butler. 399p. Facts on File, 1985. op. Reprint: Henry Holt, 1986. Paper $19.95. ISBN 0-8050-0124-7.
749.213 NK2405

This impressive visual guide begins with a section on the anatomy of furniture featuring fourteen easy-to-read diagrams. The main body is a history from the seventeenth to the early twentieth century arranged by type of furniture, chronologically, and by geographic region. More than 1,700 detailed line drawings identify the furniture and its characteristics. A list of major collections of American antique furniture, a lengthy glossary, selected bibliography, and an excellent index.

1296 A handbook of ornament. 4th ed. Franz S. Meyer. 548p. Duckworth, 1974. Paper $8.95. ISBN 0-486-20302-6.
745.4 NK1510

This work is a grammar of art, industrial, and architectural design in all its branches for both practical and theoretical use. Based on the German *Handbuch der ornamentic,* it was originally published in 1892 and is still a standard. Well illustrated with 300 plates containing 3,000 illustrations. Indexed.

1297 An illustrated dictionary of jewelry: 2,530 entries, including definitions of jewels, gemstones, materials, processes, and styles, and entries on principal designers and makers from antiquity to the present day. Harold Newman. 334p. Thames & Hudson, 1987. Paper $24.95. ISBN 0-500-27452-5.
739.27 NK7304

Considers jewelry as personal ornament throughout history and the world. Entries include definitions of terms and processes, styles, designers, famous stones and gems, and biographies of jewelers past and present. Bibliographical notes are included.

1298 The Oxford companion to the decorative arts. Harold Osborne, ed. 865p. Clarendon Pr., 1975. op. Reprint: Oxford Univ. Pr., 1985. Paper. op.
745 NK30

Similar in format to other Oxford companions, this work has articles of varying lengths on specific crafts, periods, cultures, techniques, materials, schools, styles, and well-known craftspersons. There is an extensive bibliography. The 1985 paper edition corrects errors made in the original 1975 edition.

1299 The Penguin dictionary of decorative arts. New ed. John Fleming and Hugh Honour. 935p. Viking, 1989. $65. ISBN 0-670-82047-4.
745 NK30

Entries on furniture and furnishings in the Western tradition. Definitions of terms, some biographies of well-known craftspeople and designers, articles on materials and processes, and short histories of factories are included, with 1,000 black-and-white illustrations.

Photography

1300 Contemporary photographers. 3d ed. Martin Marix Evans, ed. 1234p. St. James, 1995. $155. ISBN 1-55862-183-0.
770 TR139

Detailed information on more than 600 photographers with an international reputation is given, with coverage of all aspects of the field: studio art, commercial portraiture, journalism, and advertising. Entries consist of biographical information, a photograph from the person's work, a list of shows and exhibitions, a bibliography, critical information, and, in many cases, a statement by the photographer about his or her work.

1301 Dictionary of contemporary photography. Leslie Stroebel and Hollis N. Todd. 217p. Morgan & Morgan, 1974. $15. ISBN 0-87100-065-2.
770 TR9

Definitions for about 4,500 terms.

1302 Encyclopedia of practical photography. 14v. Amphoto, c1977–79. op.
770 TR9

Eastman Kodak and Amphoto collaborated on this work, which covers virtually every aspect of photography: motion pictures, exposure processing, history, legal and scientific aspects, and so forth. Some entries are new and some have been taken from other Kodak publications. A system of symbols is used to classify the material into categories: biography, exposure, optics, theory of photography, storage and care, and so forth. For the amateur, hobbyist, professional, teacher, and student. Index, many cross-references, and many color and black-and-white illustrations.

1303 The Focal encyclopedia of photography. 3d ed. Leslie Stroebel and Richard Zakia, eds. 914p. Focal Pr., 1993. $125. ISBN 0-240-80059-1.
770 TR9

Considers photography as both art and science and as it relates to other fields such as business, chemistry, communications, computer science, education, history, and physics. Entries range from short definitions to longer surveys, with 75 percent new material since the second edition of 1969. Cross-references.

1304 The International Center of Photography encyclopedia of photography. William L. Broecker, ed. International Center of Photography. 607p. Crown, 1984. op.
770 TR9

This one-volume reference work provides the general reader with a comprehensive view of the field. The editor conducted a worldwide search for significant photographs, and the resulting collection of black-and-white and color plates is outstanding. More than 1,300 alphabetized entries cover types of photography, equipment, methods, and aesthetic matters from earliest times to the present. Biographical sketches include nineteenth- and twentieth-century photographers (born before 1940) plus individuals involved in developing new photographic products or techniques. There are two appendixes: a biographical supplement of more than 2,000 photographers and an alphabetical list of photographic societies and associations. This tome brings together a wealth of current information not found in previously published single-volume encyclopedias.

1305 Photographer's market. Writer's Digest, 1978– . Annual. $23.99. ISSN 0147-247X.
381 TR12

Lists of potential markets for photography: books and periodicals, card and calendar companies, record companies, and more. Listings include names, addresses, and terms and conditions. Other information includes agencies, contests, workshops, schools, organizations, and feature articles of interest to photographers. Includes bibliography, glossary, and general and subject indexes.

1306 Photography books index: a subject guide to photo anthologies. Martha Moss. 286p. Scarecrow, 1980. $25. ISBN 0-8108-1283-5.

Photography books index II: a subject guide to photo anthologies. Martha Moss. 261p. Scarecrow, 1985. $23.50. ISBN 0-8108-1773-X.
779 TR199

Photography books index covers twenty-two sources (ten of which are also in *Photography index*). However, the strength of this work is the subject approach. Headings are based on the eleventh edition of *List of subject headings* (Minnie Earl Sears. Barbara M. Westby, ed. Wilson, 1977). The works indexed are of a general and popular nature, expected to be found in the smaller library. Each subject index entry provides photograph title, date, photographer, and source. Volume 2 continues the same format but adds twenty-eight new sources.

1307 Photography index: a guide to reproductions. Pamela Jeffcott Parry, comp. 372p. Greenwood, 1979. $42.95. ISBN 0-313-20700-3.
779 TR199

This is a guide to photographic reproductions in more than eighty heavily illustrated books and exhibition catalogs. Both artistic and documentary photographs are covered. Citations appear in two sections: a chronological listing of anonymous photographs and an alphabetical listing by photographer or firm. More than 1,700 individuals or firms are listed, with nationalities and dates in most cases. Access to these two sections is provided by a detailed title and subject index.

15

Performing Arts

DONALD W. MAXWELL

Performing arts require public performance to be appreciated, unlike visual arts, which only need to be seen. The performing arts included here are dance; film and video; television, radio, and telecommunications; and theater. Music is treated separately in the next chapter because of the large number of reference books in that field.

General Sources

Bibliographies and Guides

1308 The performing arts: a guide to the reference literature. Linda Keir Simons. 244p. Libraries Unlimited, 1994. $42. ISBN 0-87287-982-8.
016.791 PN1584

An annotated bibliography of 757 reference sources, primarily in English and published since the mid-1960s, on theater, dance, and musicals, but not film or television. Lists bibliographies, indexes, encyclopedias, and so forth, as well as electronic discussion groups, core periodicals, libraries and archives, and professional organizations and societies. Indexes to author and title and to subject.

Indexes and Abstracts

1309 A guide to critical reviews. James M. Salem. Scarecrow. Part 1: American drama, 1909–1982. 3d ed. 657p. 1984. $49.50. ISBN 0-8108-1690-3; Part 2: The musical, 1909–1989. 3d ed. 820p. 1991. $72.50. ISBN 0-8108-2387-X; Part 3: Foreign drama, 1909–1977. 2d ed. 420p. 1979. $37.50. ISBN 0-8108-1226-6; Part 4: The screenplay, from The jazz singer to Dr. Strangelove. 2v. 1971. $72.50/set. ISBN 0-8108-0367-4; Part 4, Supplement 1: The screenplay, 1963–1980. 708p. 1982. $55. ISBN 0-8108-1553-2.
016.8092 PN2266

These volumes provide citations to reviews in general periodicals and the *New York Times*, with some coverage of regional and specialty periodicals. These are reviews to particular productions, rather than general literary criticism. Each volume has a variety of special lists on awards, long runs, and so forth and several indexes.

Directories

1310 Musical America. International directory of the performing arts. K-III Directory Corp., 1974– . Annual. $90. ISSN 0735-7788.
780.25 ML12

Available separately from the monthly magazine, this issue, which appears each December, is an international directory of the performing arts. Included are highlights of the year in the areas of music, dance, opera, and concerts. There are listings for orchestras, dance and opera companies, music publishers, periodicals and newspapers, booking organizations, and more. There is also a listing by city of the performing arts activities in each U.S. city that has significant activity. The international listings cover the major cities, orchestras, festivals, and activities around the world.

1311 Stern's performing arts directory. DM, 1988– . Annual. $65. ISSN 0070-2684. (*formerly* **Dance Magazine annual, Performing arts directory.**)
791 GV1580

Contains listings for U.S., Canadian, and international dance companies, theaters, schools, individual artists, and support professions (e.g., choreographers, accompanists, etc.), as well as opera companies, symphony orchestras, composers, stage directors, and theater companies and productions. A second section lists performing arts resources: services (e.g., ad agencies, financial services, etc.), service organizations, merchandise, government agencies, sponsors, and periodicals. Index to advertisers.

Biographical Sources

1312 Contemporary theatre, film, and television. Gale, 1984– . v.1, 1984. $128. ISBN 0-8103-2064-9; v.2, 1985. $128. ISBN 0-8103-0241-1; v.3, 1986. $128. ISBN 0-8103-2066-5; v.4, 1987. $128. ISBN 0-8103-2067-3; v.5, 1988. $128. ISBN 0-8103-2068-1; v.6, 1989. $128. ISBN 0-8103-2069-X; v.7, 1989. $128. ISBN 0-8103-2070-3; v.8, 1990. $128. ISBN 0-8103-2071-1; v.9, 1992. $128. ISBN 0-8103-2072-X; v.10, 1993. $128. ISBN 0-8103-2073-8; v.11, 1994. $128. ISBN 0-8103-2074-6; v.12, 1994. $128. ISBN 0-8103-6902-8; v.13, 1995. $128. ISBN 0-8103-5729-1; v.14, 1996. $146. ISBN 0-8103-9374-3; v.15, 1996. $146. ISBN 0-8103-9958-X; v.16, 1997. $146. ISBN 0-7876-1065-8; v.17, 1997. $146. ISBN 0-7876-1153-0; v.18, 1998. $146. ISBN 0-7876-2056-4. ISSN 0749-064X.
■ online
791 PN2285

Comprehensive biographical guide succeeds and expands on the seventeen editions of *Who's who in the theatre* (1912–81) by including not only theater, film, and television performers, but also choreographers, composers, critics, dancers, designers, executives, producers, and technicians from the United States and Great Britain. Biographies are provided for approximately 6,600 people. Entries are modeled after those in *Contemporary authors*. Beginning with volume 3, there are cumulative indexes in each volume that also index *Who's who in the theatre* and *Who was who in the theatre* (Gale, 1978).

Awards

1313 Entertainment awards: a music, cinema, theatre and broadcasting reference, 1928 through 1993. Don Franks. 536p. McFarland, 1995. $75. ISBN 0-7864-0031-5.
792 PN2270.A93

List of the more than 10,000 winners of major performance awards through 1993: Golden Globes, Grammys, Country Music Association Awards, Oscars, New York Film Critics, Pulitzer Prizes for theater, Tonys, Obies, New York Drama Critics' Circle, Emmys, and Peabodys. Indexed.

1314 Variety's directory of major U.S. show business awards. Mike Kaplan, ed. 750p. Bowker, 1989. $59.95. ISBN 0-8352-2666-2.
791 PN2270.A93

Lists each nomination and award for performance as well as technical Oscars, Emmys, Tonys, Grammys, and Pulitzers. The comprehensive index lists writers, titles, artists, producers, and other personnel. Don Franks's *Entertainment awards* lists more recent winners of these and several other awards.

Dance

1315 **Biographical dictionary of dance.** Barbara Naomi Cohen-Stratyner. 970p. Schirmer Books, 1982. $75. ISBN 0-02-870260-3.
793.3 GV1785.A1

A basic biographical source on dance that covers four centuries of European and American dance (including ballet, Broadway, burlesque, and television) through sketches of approximately 3,000 notable figures, including major dancers, choreographers, composers, designers, and impresarios. Entries are frequently supplemented by bibliographies and lists of major works or roles. Macmillan has announced a new edition to appear in 1999 entitled *The Schirmer biographical dictionary of dance* ($95. ISBN 0-02-862677-0).

1316 **The concise Oxford dictionary of ballet.** Updated 2d ed. Horst Koegler. 458p. Oxford Univ. Pr., 1987. op.
792.803 GV1585

Short entries on all aspects of ballet, including people, companies, technical terms, places, events, and so forth, as well as some consideration of modern, ethnic, and ballroom dance. Originally translated and adapted from *Friedrichs ballett lexicon von A-Z* (1972), this is an update of the second edition, originally published in 1982.

1317 **Dance classics: a viewer's guide to the best-loved ballets and modern dances.** Nancy Reynolds and Susan Reimer-Torn. 297p. a capella books, 1991. Paper $14.95. ISBN 1-55652-106-5.
792.8 GV1790.A1

Originally published in 1980 as *In harmony*, this guide describes the choreography, sets, and costumes of forty-four traditional and modern ballets and nine contemporary dances. The described pieces are arranged chronologically and represent 150 years of Western dance—its major historical phases, choreographers, styles, and innovations. Short essays, a glossary of dance terms, and an index complete the work.

1318 **Dance film and video guide.** Deirdre Towers, comp. 233p. Dance Films Assn., Dance Horizons/Princeton Book Co., 1991. Paper $24.95. ISBN 0-87127-171-0.
792.8 GV1595

A film- and videography of more than 2,000 commercially available works on all styles of dance (e.g., ballet, ballroom, folk, ethnic). Includes a directory of distributors and indexes to subjects, choreographers, composers, companies, dancers, and directors.

1319 **The dance handbook.** Allen Robertson and Donald Hutera. 278p. Hall, 1990. $25. ISBN 0-8161-9095-X; paper $16.95. ISBN 0-8161-1829-9.
792.8 GV1601

This handbook contains entries for 200 major dancers, dance companies, choreographers, and dances. Describes how dance moved from the romantic era in ballet to present avant-garde experiments. Sections deal with significant characteristics of each era. Critical commentary is interspersed with factual information. The work is supplemented by a brief glossary of terms; a bibliography; a directory of magazines, companies, and festivals; photographs; and an extensive index.

1320 **International dictionary of ballet.** Martha Bremser, ed. 2v. St. James, 1993. $230/set. ISBN 1-55862-084-2.
792.8 GV1585

Contains 750 entries on artists (dancers, choreographers, designers, teachers, et al.), ballet companies, and ballets, all accompanied by a list of related publications and a signed, critical essay. Black-and-white photographs and other illustrations. Indexes to nationalities and to professions and institutions.

1321 **International encyclopedia of dance.** 6v. Oxford Univ. Pr., 1998. $1250. ISBN 0-19-509462-X.
792.6 GV1585

Fifteen years in the making, this long-awaited encyclopedia includes more than 2,000 articles representing the work of some 600 scholars from around the globe. The six-volume set incorporates detailed entries on virtually every kind of dance, dance production, and dance company from every country, culture, and period of world history. With more than 2,100 illustrations, many of them quite stunning, the encyclopedia serves to bring the art and the story of dance to mind and to life. A seminal work.

1322 **One hundred one stories of the great ballets.** George Balanchine and Francis Mason. 541p. Dolphin Books, 1975. op. Reprint: Anchor Books Doubleday, 1989. Paper $12.95. ISBN 0-385-03398-2.
792.8 MT95

This includes old favorites and some of the newer ballets up to 1975. Production information contains orchestration, choreographer, music, principal dancers, designers, and date and place of premiere. Detailed, concise stories sometimes with critical notes. Based on *Balanchine's complete stories of the great ballets* (rev. ed. George Balanchine and Francis Mason. 838p. Doubleday, 1977. op), which describes 404 ballets and is perhaps the better source, but it is out-of-print.

Film and Video

Sources listed in chapter 16, Music, may be useful for information related to musical films and film soundtracks.

Indexes

1323 Film review index. Patricia King Hanson and Stephen L. Hanson. 2v. Oryx, 1986–87. $139.50/set. ISBN 0-317-49429-6; v.1, 1882–1949. 1986. ISBN 0-89774-153-6; v.2, 1950–85. 1987. ISBN 0-89774-331-8.
016.79143 PN1995

Arranged alphabetically by film title, this index covers about 8,000 U.S. and foreign feature films. Each entry includes title, alternate titles, year produced, director, country of origin, and an average of ten citations to reviews. A bibliography and indexes by director, year, and country of production are appended. For films after 1986, consult *Media review digest* or *Readers' guide to periodical literature*.

Dictionaries and Encyclopedias

1324 The American film industry: a historical dictionary. Anthony Slide. 431p. Greenwood, 1986. $65. ISBN 0-313-24693-9. Reprint: Limelight Editions, 1990. $19.95. ISBN 0-87910-139-3.
384 PN1993.5.U6

Diverse topics and terms are defined. Film techniques are described. Through a network of extensive cross-references, the user can follow the development of significant American film events, companies, organizations, and genres. Good for beginning research and company addresses, yet scholars will find the list of locations of archival materials particularly worthwhile.

1325 The complete film dictionary. Ira Konigsberg. 420p. New American Lib., 1987. op. Reprint: Meridian, 1989. Paper $15.95. ISBN 0-452-00980-4.
791.43 PN1993.45

Intended for filmmakers, film students, and film buffs. More than 3,500 entries cover film as art, technology, and industry. More than 200 line drawings and black-and-white photographs supplement the text.

1326 Encyclopaedia of the musical film. Stanley Green. 344p. Oxford Univ. Pr., 1988. Paper $15.95. ISBN 0-19-505421-0.
791.43 PN1995.9.M86

A selective arrangement of the most important and well-known aspects of the musical film. Articles on American and British musical films, individual songs and performers, composers, lyricists, film directors, and other major figures. A bibliography and a discography conclude the work.

1327 The film encyclopedia. 2d ed. Ephraim Katz, ed. 1496p. HarperCollins, 1994. Paper $25. ISBN 0-06-273089-4.
791.43 PN1993.45

More than 7,000 entries provide information about stars, directors, producers, screenwriters, cinematographers, studios, styles, genres, and schools of filmmaking; give short histories of national cinemas, organizations and events; and define jargon and technical terms.

1328 Halliwell's filmgoer's companion. Leslie Halliwell. John Walker, ed. 514p. HarperPerennial, 1997– . Biennial. $25. ISSN 1066-2912.
791 PN1993.45

This standard source provides brief entries in dictionary format on American, British, and European actors, directors, producers, writers, and other film personnel, as well as cinematic themes and fictional characters. Entries include quotations and filmographies. Supplementary material includes lists of award winners and other top films, a bibliography, and a time line. Compare with *Halliwell's film and video guide*.

1329 The Hollywood musical. 2d ed. Clive Hirschhorn. 456p. Crown, 1991. op. Reprint: Random House, 1991. $29.99. ISBN 0-517-06035-3.
791.4375 PN1995.9.M86

Heavily illustrated, chronological descriptions of 1,344 films from 1927 to 1980. For each film, there is a critical synopsis, photograph, and listing of the songs and musical numbers; some credits are given but not full production information. A variety of helpful indexes encompass film titles, songs, performers, composers, and other personnel.

1330 International dictionary of films and filmmakers. 3d ed. 4v. St. James, 1996. $500/set. ISBN 1-55862-199-7. v.1, Films. $140. ISBN 1-55862-300-0; v.2, Directors. $140. ISBN 1-55862-301-9; v.3, Actors and actresses. $140. ISBN 1-55862-302-7; v.4, Writers and production artists. $140. ISBN 1-55862-303-5.
791.43 PN1997.8

This set provides detailed and authoritative information on films and their personnel that "represent the current concerns of North American, British, and West European film scholarship and criticism." Volume 1, *Films*, comprises 680 entries, 130 of which are entirely new to this edition. Volume 2, *Directors*, comprises more than 500 entries on directors, 65 of which are entirely new to this edition. Volume 3, *Actors and actresses*, contains 652 entries, of which 86 are new to this edition. Volume 4, *Writers and production artists*, contains 520 entries, 45 of which are new. Entries are substantial, clearly organized, and well illustrated. Each entry in volume 1, for example, contains "production information, lists of cast and crew, a selected bibliography of works about the film, and an essay by a specialist in the field." New to this edition is a geographic index for identifying films by their country of origin.

1331 Magill's survey of cinema—English language films, first series. Frank N. Magill, ed. 4v. Salem, 1980. op.
■ cd online
791.43 PN1993.45

Magill's survey of cinema—English language films, second series. Frank N. Magill, ed. 6v. Salem, 1981. op.
■ cd online
791.43 PN1993.45

Magill's survey of cinema—foreign language films. Frank N. Magill, ed. 8v. Salem, 1985. $350/set. ISBN 0-89356-243-2.
■ cd online
791.43 PN1995.9

Magill's survey of cinema—silent films. Frank N. Magill, ed. 3v. Salem, 1982. op.
■ cd online
791.43 PN1995.75

Magill's cinema annual. Salem, 1982–94. Gale, 1995– . Annual. $39.95. ISSN 0739-2141.
■ cd online
791.43 PN1993.3

Provides coverage for silent films from 1902 to 1936 and for English-language sound films from 1927 to 1980. *English language films* and *Silent films* provide a total of more than 1,500 essay-reviews on individual films, analyzing production background, story line, direction, performances, technical merits, critical response, popular reception, and awards. Data are given for cast, credits, running time, and release date. Indexes cover titles, directors, screenwriters, cinematographers, film editors, performers, and chronologies. *Foreign language films* covers 700 films in languages other than English. *Magill's cinema annual* makes available the same depth of information on about 100 contemporary English- and foreign-language films released in the United States during the year and provides brief synopses and personnel for about 100 other films. Since 1995, it includes a comprehensive index to all titles in this series. *Magill's American film guide* covered 1,000 films from the original set (5v. Magill, 1983. op). The entire combined set is available on CD-ROM as *Magill's survey of cinema.*

1332 The motion picture guide, 1927–1984. Jay Robert Nash and Stanley Ralph Ross. 12v. Cinebooks, 1985–87. $600/set. ISBN 0-933997-00-0.
■ cd
791.43 PN1993

The motion picture guide annual. Edmond Grant and Ken Fox, eds. Cinebooks, 1985– . Annual. $180. ISBN 0-933997-39-6.
■ cd
011 PN1993

The motion picture guide is a major source for all film questions, for casual to serious research. The first nine volumes cover every movie made in English, along with notable foreign films. Volume 10 covers silent films. Volumes 11 and 12 cover major film awards, title changes, and film series and have proper name indexes. Information for each of the 35,000 titles includes detailed production credits, casts and roles, a synopsis, other factual material, and critical commentary. *The motion picture guide annual* keeps *The motion picture guide* up-to-date and contains indexes to awards, names, and country of film origin.

1333 The New York Times film reviews. 1913–68. 6v. Times Books, 1971. Biennial. 1969–1970– . Garland, 1998. $165. ISBN 0-8153-3052-9. ISSN 0362-3688. Reprint: Garland, 1970. $3200/original 6v. plus first 11 biennial v. ISBN 0-8153-0350-5.
791.43 PN1995

Reviews of films evaluated by critics of the *New York Times,* arranged by their date of publication in the newspaper. The original 1913–68 volume contained 18,000 reviews. Biennial volumes, beginning in 1969, contain approximately 700 reviews each. Each volume reproduces the original newspaper photographs and contains title and personal and corporate indexes. The reviews are also indexed in *The New York Times index.*

Directories

1334 An actor guide to the talkies: a comprehensive listing of 8,000 feature-length films from January, 1949, until December, 1964. Richard B. Dimmitt. 2v. Scarecrow, 1967. op.

An actor guide to the talkies, 1965 through 1974. Andrew A. Aros. 771p. Scarecrow, 1977. $52.50. ISBN 0-8108-1052-2.

A title guide to the talkies: a comprehensive listing of 16,000 feature-length films from October, 1927, until December, 1963. Richard B. Dimmitt. 2v. Scarecrow, 1965. op.

A title guide to the talkies, 1964 through 1974. Andrew A. Aros. 336p. Scarecrow, 1977. $35. ISBN 0-8108-0976-1.

A title guide to the talkies, 1975 through 1984. Andrew A. Aros. 347p. Scarecrow, 1986. $35. ISBN 0-8108-1868-X.
016.79143 PN1998

The volumes on actors and actresses list films, arranged by title, with the name of the producer and studio, year of release, and complete cast listing. Both U.S. and foreign films are covered. Another set of listings is by actor or actress with a reference to the films in which he or she appeared. The volumes on titles serve as a source for finding the novel, play, or nonfiction work that served as the basis of the film, with information about the film and the original source material.

1335 Bowker's complete video directory. 3v. Bowker, 1990– . Annual. $229.95. ISSN 1051-290X.
■ cd
016.29143 PN1992.95

Volume 1 lists more than 41,000 entertainment videos; volumes 2 and 3 list more than 65,000 educational and special-interest videos. Ten indexes enable users to search by genre, cast, director, and so forth. Includes a directory of services and suppliers. Also available as a part of the CD-ROM *Variety's video directory plus.*

1336 Halliwell's film and video guide [yr.]. HarperPerennial, 1997– . Annual. $22.50. ISSN 1098-206X.
■ cd
791 PN1993.45

Descriptions of around 20,000 films. Arranged alphabetically by film title, entries include a critical rating of one to four stars; country of origin; year of release; running time; color or black and white; special film techniques (e.g., Technicolor, Todd-AO); availability of videotape, laser disc, and soundtrack on CD; producer and distributor; alternative titles; synopsis of plot; short critical assessment; writing, directing, photography, music, and other credits; principal actors; comments from professional critics; and Academy Award nominations and wins. Cross-references to alternative titles and English-language titles of foreign film. Compare with *Halliwell's filmgoer's companion.*

1337 Leonard Maltin's movie and video guide. Leonard Maltin, ed. Plume, 1993– . Annual. Paper $19.95. ISSN 1082-9466. (*formerly* **Leonard Maltin's TV movies and video guide.**)
■ disk
791.43 PN1992.8.F5

Roger Ebert's video companion. Roger Ebert. Andrews & McMeel, 1994– . Annual. $17.95. ISSN 1072-561X. (*formerly* **Roger Ebert's movie home companion.**)
791.43 PN1995

Video movie guide. Mick Martin and Marsha Porter. Ballantine, 1985– . Annual. $16; paper $7.99. ISSN 1095-6190.
■ cd
791.43 PN1992.93

VideoHound's golden movie retriever. Visible Ink Pr., 1991– . Annual. Paper $21.95. ISSN 1095-371X.
■ cd
791.43 PN1992.95

These inexpensive paperback video guides are indispensable for information about theatrical films on video. All have standard directory information (title, year, length in minutes, director, cast members, critical ratings, plot descriptions, and MPAA ratings). Television film critic Maltin's *Guide* contains 19,000 entries arranged into a single alphabet, indicates laser disc availability, and has indexes to stars (but not entire casts) and directors. Television and newspaper film critic Ebert's *Companion* contains longer essays on fewer films, supplemented with essays and actor profiles, lists of top films, and indexes to reviews appearing in previous editions and to persons and films. Newspaper and radio film critic Martin and writer Porter's *Guide* contains 13,000 entries, is arranged alphabetically within broad genres, and includes indexes to casts, directors, award winners, highly rated films, and titles. *VideoHound* contains 22,000 reviews arranged by title. Its entries contain descriptions and reviews, lists of songs (if any), alternate titles, country of origin, writers, lyricists, composers, awards, tape and disc formats, price, and distributor. There are several unique indexes among its thirteen: honors from twelve national and international awards bodies, series, song titles, and music videos. It is available in abridged form as *VideoHound's pocket movie guide* and as a part of the *VideoHound multimedia* CD-ROM.

1338 **Video source book.** Gale, 1979– . Annual. $315/2v. set. ISSN 0748-0881.
■ disk online tape
011 PN1992.95

Directory of more than 160,000 videos. Entries include standard video directory information plus suggested audience and purpose; availability for broadcast, home, and classroom use; and availability in other languages, broad subject category, major awards won, and how and from where to purchase. Includes indexes to alternate titles, subject, director/cast, and special formats (e.g., closed-captioned, laser disc, etc.) as well as a directory of distributors. Also distilled into the 22,000-entry *VideoHound's golden movie retriever.* Compare with *Bowker's complete video directory.*

1339 **VideoHound's family video retriever.** 563p. Visible Ink Pr., 1995. Paper $11.95. ISBN 0-8103-7866-3.
791.43 PN1992.945

Reviews 4,000 films and made-for-kids videos appropriate for viewing by children and families. Entries are arranged in alphabetical order and list critical and MPAA ratings, year and country of release, descriptions and reviews, suggested viewing age range, cast, composers, writers, directors, titles of songs in musical films, running time, awards and nominations, available tape and disc formats, price, distributor, and an advisory if the film contains profane language references or illustrates alcohol, drugs, sex, nudity, or violence. Contains black-and-white illustrations and indexes to MPAA ratings, cast and director, 300 category classifications, and a distributor guide. Based on *VideoHound's golden movie retriever.*

Handbooks

1340 **International motion picture almanac.** Quigley, 1956– . Annual. $110. ISSN 0074-7084.
791.43 PN1993.3

Includes biographical sketches of movie personalities, lists of services, distributors, film corporations, companies, theaters, suppliers, organizations, markets, and government agencies, primarily in the United States. Lists of films of the previous decade and a review of the previous year in film: awards, polls, and festivals.

1341 **Screen world.** John Willis. Crown, 1949–91. Applause, 1993– . Annual. $49.95; paper $27.95. ISSN 0080-8288. (*formerly* **John Willis' screen world.**)
■ cd
791.43 PN1993.3

Each volume provides release date, running time, rating, full cast and partial production credits, brief plot capsules, and black-and-white photographic stills from major domestic and foreign films released in the United States in the previous year. Supplemented by lists of the past year's Academy Award nominations and past years' winners, box office statistics, brief biographical data on more than 2,000 actors and actresses, a necrology, and several color photos.

Biographical Sources

1342 A biographical dictionary of film. 3d ed. David Thomson. 834p. Random House, 1994. $40. ISBN 0-394-58165-2. Reprint: Knopf, 1994. Paper $25. ISBN 0-679-75564-0.
791.43 PN1998.2

More than 900 entries describe the lives and careers of actors and actresses, directors, writers, and producers important in the history of cinema.

1343 Who was who on screen. Abridged ed. Evelyn Mack Truitt. 438p. Bowker, 1984. Paper $29.95. ISBN 0-8352-1867-8.
791.43 PN1998.A2

An authoritative and comprehensive alphabetically arranged biographical directory of 13,000 screen personalities who died between 1905 and 1981. Each entry gives name and variant names; birth and death dates and places; cause of death; well-known parents, children, or marriages; positions held within the movie industry; awards; and a year-by-year list of all screen credits. Included are lesser-known actors, directors, screenwriters, producers, extras, vaudeville stars, burlesque actors, radio performers, child actors, animal actors, and so forth. Illustrated. Condensed from *Who was who on screen* (3d ed. Evelyn Mack Truitt. 788p. Bowker, 1983. op).

Television, Radio, and Telecommunications

Dictionaries and Encyclopedias

1344 The broadcast communications dictionary. 3d ed. Lincoln Diamant, ed. 255p. Greenwood, 1989. $49.95. ISBN 0-313-26502-X. Reprint: **Dictionary of broadcast communications.** NTC Business Books, 1991. Paper $27.95. ISBN 0-8442-3325-0.
384.54 PN1990.4

A dictionary of 6,000 common, technical, and slang terms from radio and television programming and production, local station and network operations, cable TV, audio and videotape production, broadcast engineering and equipment, media usage, advertising, performing talent, satellite communications technology, communications research, and defense, government, and trade groups. Cross-references and a select bibliography.

1345 Children's television, 1947–1990: over 200 series, game and variety shows, cartoons, educational programs and specials. Jeffrey Davis. 285p. McFarland, 1995. $42.50. ISBN 0-89950-911-8.
791.45 PN1992.8.C46

A select encyclopedia of children-oriented programming, beginning with 1947's "Small Fry Club" to 1990. Entries are arranged in alphabetical order within broad categories such as "Cartoon Shows," "Kindly Hosts and Hostesses," "Puppets, Marionettes, and Dummies," and more. Appendixes list awards, a chronology, and children's shows in prime time or originating in radio or movies. Black-and-white illustrations. Index.

1346 The complete directory to prime time network and cable TV shows, 1946–present. 6th ed. Tim Brooks and Earle Marsh. 1385p. Ballantine, 1995. Paper $23. ISBN 0-345-39736-3.
791.45 PN1992.18

Provides coverage of more than 5,000 nighttime series on commercial networks, with information on the type of show, broadcast history, cast, spin-offs, and plot or format. Index to actors and actresses. Appendixes list each season's prime time schedules, Emmy award winners, long-running and highly rated programs, and spin-offs. Coverage of original cable series began with the sixth edition.

1347 Encyclopedia of television. Horace Necomb, ed. 3v. Fitzroy Dearborn, 1997. $300. ISBN 1-884964-26-5.
791.45 PN1992.18

Commissioned by the Museum of Broadcast Communications, in Chicago, and drawing heavily upon its archives, this 1,948-page encyclopedia provides an excellent starting point for any topic related to television or the television industry. Extensive essays in alphabetical arrangement; includes many biographical entries, with large, crisp portraits. Suggestions for further reading follow each entry.

1348 Encyclopedia of television: series, pilots, and specials. Vincent Terrace. 3v. New York Zoetrope, 1985–86. v.1, 1937–1973. 480p. op; v.2, 1974–1984. Rev. ed. 500p. op; v.3, The index: who's who in television 1937–1984. op.
791.45 PN1992.9

A detailed alphabetical listing of 7,000 televised series, pilots, specials, and experimental programs broadcast from 1937 through 1984. Each listing includes credit and cast information, a story line, number of episodes, running times, networks, syndication, and cable information. Volume 3, which serves as the index, contains 18,000 performers, 5,000 producers, 5,000 writers, and 3,500 directors, each with a list of lifetime credits.

1349 The Facts on File dictionary of television, cable, and video. Robert M. Reed and Maxine K. Reed. 226p. Facts on File, 1994. $24.95. ISBN 0-8160-2947-4.
384.55 PN1992.18

More than 1,600 words and terms from three electronic media that share communication as their main objective as well as the same production techniques and engineering equipment. Many cross-references.

1350 Les Brown's encyclopedia of television. 3d ed. Les Brown. 723p. Gale, 1992. $55. ISBN 0-8103-8871-5. Reprint: Visible Ink Pr., 1992. Paper $22.95. ISBN 0-8103-9420-0.
791.45 PN1992.18

Almost 3,000 brief, informative articles on people, programs, companies, technology, legal cases, and the television industry throughout the world, with emphasis on U.S. television. Includes a bibliography of books and journals, tabular data, black-and-white illustrations, and an index.

1351 NTC's mass media dictionary. R. Terry Ellmore. 668p. National Textbook Co., 1991. $39.95. ISBN 0-8442-3185-1; paper $24.95. ISBN 0-8442-3186-X.
302.23 P87.5

Definitions of more than 20,000 words from mass media: radio, television, cable, film, newspapers, magazines, direct mail, and advertising.

1352 Same time . . . same station: an A-Z guide to radio from Jack Benny to Howard Stern. Ron Lackmann. 370p. Facts on File, 1996. $45. ISBN 0-8160-2862-1.
791.44 PN1991.3.U6

The more than 1,000 entries include biographies (performers, writers, directors, and technicians), profiles of programs (synopses, air dates, times, networks, cast lists, sponsors, and theme songs), and profiles of major U.S. and Canadian networks, spanning from the 1920s to the present. Includes black-and-white photographs, cross-references, select bibliography, index, and appendixes with chronologies, sponsors, and other information.

1353 Television cartoon shows: an illustrated encyclopedia, 1949 through 1993. Hal Erickson. 659p. McFarland, 1995. $75. ISBN 0-7864-0029-3.
791.45 PN1992.8.A59

More than 500 entries list show titles, network, studio, production information, including voice credits, and a critical essay with plot description, critical commentary, and other information. These entries are sandwiched between essays on the history of television cartoon shows and cartoon voices. A select bibliography and thorough index conclude the work.

1354 Webster's new world dictionary of media and communications. 2d ed. Richard Weiner. 678p. Macmillan, 1996. $39.95. ISBN 0-02-861474-7.
302.23 P87.5

More than 35,000 technical terms, abbreviations, and slang words from advertising, broadcasting, computers, direct marketing, exhibitions, film, graphic arts, journalism, library science, mail, marketing, newspapers, photography, printing, public relations, publishing, radio, recording, telecommunications, telephone, television, theater, and other fields. Includes cross-references and some pronunciations.

Directories

1355 Broadcasting and cable yearbook. 2v. Bowker, 1993– . Annual. Paper $199.95. ISSN 0000-1511. (*formerly* **Broadcasting-cable yearbook; Broadcasting-cablecasting yearbook; Broadcasting yearbook; Broadcasting and cable market place.**)
384.54 HE8689

The most comprehensive directory to the Fifth Estate, covering the history and continuing growth of every field in the industry. There are nine major sections: "The Fifth Estate," "Radio," "Television," "Cable," "Satellites," "Programming," "Advertising and Marketing," "Technology," and "Professional Services." Includes extensive equipment listings and a buyer's guide. The standard directory of AM and FM radio stations in the United States, Canada, Mexico, and the Caribbean and of U.S. and Canadian television stations.

1356 Television and cable factbook: the authoritative reference for the television, cable and electronics industries. 3v. Warren, 1983– . Annual. $510/set. ISSN 0732-8648. (*formerly* **Television factbook.**)
384.55 TK6540

Three separate volumes for stations, cable, and TV and cable services. The stations volume includes directory information on 1,500 U.S. television stations, arranged by state, including maps of broadcast areas. The cable volume provides brief information on 11,200 cable systems. The services volume contains statistical and directory information on organizations, agencies, associations, equipment, revenues, expenses and earnings, advertising, TV households, cable systems, and so forth. Also includes public and international TV directories.

Handbooks

1357 International television and video almanac. Quigley, 1987– . Annual. $110. ISSN 0539-0761. (*formerly* **International television almanac.**)
384.55 HE8700

Lists TV and cable industry personalities, services, government agencies, services, organizations, and a review of the previous year in the industry: news, statistics, awards, and festivals. For television also lists statistics, history, producers, distributors, programs, shows, series, movies, stations, ad agencies, and press contacts. Also lists companies, retailers, equipment manufacturers, and publications for the home video industry.

1358 World radio TV handbook. Billboard, 1961– . Annual. $24.95. ISSN 0144-7750.
621.3811 TK6540

Listings of long-, medium-, and shortwave television and radio broadcast frequencies, operating times, and addresses for every country in the world. Lists English-language and world satellite broadcasts. Maps of principal transmitter sites.

THEATER

Sources listed in chapter 16, Music, may be useful for information related to musical theater and cast recordings.

Bibliographies and Guides

1359 Basic catalogue of plays and musicals. Samuel French (25 W. 45th St., New York, NY 10010), 1994– . Annual supplements. $5. ISSN 0361-6495.
016.80882 Z5785

Complete catalogue of plays. Biennial with annual supplement. Dramatists Play Service (440 Park Ave. S., New York, NY 10016), 1957– . Free. ISSN 0419-7178.
792 PN6110.7.A5

These catalogs are published by the major American publishers of plays, which are also the major rights organizations for copyright and royalties. Several thousand plays are described with entries that include plot, setting, number of characters, and so forth. Access is also available by the number of characters in a cast, topical lists, and general indexes to titles and authors. Some bibliographical information is omitted; these are often the only readily available sources to identify titles and other information about plays.

Indexes

1360 Index to children's plays in collections. 2d ed. Barbara Kreider. 227p. Scarecrow, 1977. op.

Index to children's plays in collections, 1975–1984. 3d ed. Beverly Robin Trefny and Eileen C. Palmer. 108p. Scarecrow, 1986. $20. ISBN 0-8108-1893-0.
016.80882 PN1627

About 950 plays from sixty-two collections have been added to the first edition (1972). Several collections published from 1965 to 1969 but not covered in the first edition are indexed. The 1986 edition extends access by indexing 540 plays from forty-eight collections published between 1975 and 1984, to bring the series total to 1,990 plays. Combined author, title, and subject listing, arranged alphabetically. Number of characters is noted in the author entry. An added feature is an analysis of casts by number of characters, gender of characters, and so forth. A bibliography of collections is in the appendix.

1361 An index to one-act plays for stage, radio and television. Hannah Logasa and Winifred Ver Nooy, comps. 327p.

Faxon, 1924. op; Supplement, 1924–1931. 1932. op; Second supplement, 1932–1940. 1941. op; Third supplement, 1941–1948. 1950. op; Fourth supplement, 1948–1957. 1958. $12. ISBN 0-87305-087-8; Fifth supplement, 1956–1964. 1966. $11. ISBN 0-87305-094-0.
016.8082 Z5781

Title, author, and subject indexes to one-act plays in collections and editions published separately. With the third supplement, radio plays begin to be indexed, and with the fourth supplement, television plays start to appear.

1362 **Index to plays, 1800–1926.** Ina Ten Eyck Firkins, comp. 307p. Wilson, 1927. Reprint: AMS Pr., 1971. $24.50. ISBN 0-404-02386-X; Supplement, 1927–34. Ina Ten Eyck Firkins, comp. 140p. Wilson, 1935. op.
■ micro
016.80882 Z5781

A comprehensive index of 7,872 plays by 2,203 authors, and in the supplement, of 3,284 plays by 1,335 authors, indicating where the text of play can be found in anthologies or other sources. Full bibliographic information is provided with a brief characterization such as comedy, tragedy, domestic, and so forth. A title and subject index. This predecessor to *Play index* is useful for older plays.

1363 **Index to plays in periodicals.** Rev. and exp. ed. Dean H. Keller. 824p. Scarecrow, 1979. $60. ISBN 0-8108-1208-8.

Index to plays in periodicals, 1977–1987. Dean H. Keller. 391p. Scarecrow, 1990. $42.50. ISBN 0-8108-2288-1.
016.80882 PN1721

The 1979 volume contains references to more than 9,500 entries found in 267 periodicals through 1976. The 1990 volume has 4,605 plays from 104 periodicals. Both volumes are arranged by author and contain citations to plays, an indication to the number of acts, and language if not English. Both contain title indexes.

1364 **Ottemiller's index to plays in collections: an author and title index to plays appearing in collections published between 1900 and 1985.** 7th ed. Billie M. Connor and Helene G. Machedlover. 564p. Scarecrow, 1988. $42.50. ISBN 0-8108-2081-1.
016.80882 PN1655

This standard work for locating plays in collections provides locations of more than 10,000 copies of more than 4,000 different plays by 2,000 different authors as found in about 2,000 anthologies. Coverage is of full-length plays from all periods and literatures and one-acts; radio and television dramas are included when found in the anthologies of full-length plays. Access is by author, collection, and title.

1365 **Play index.** Wilson. 1949–52 v. Dorothy Herbert West and Dorothy Margaret Peake, comps. 239p. 1953. $20. ISBN 0-686-66657-7; 1953–60 v. Estelle A. Fidell and Dorothy Margaret Peake, eds. 404p. 1963. $25. ISBN 0-686-66658-5; 1961–67 v. Estelle A. Fidell, ed. 464p. 1968. $28. ISBN 0-686-66659-3; 1968–72 v. Estelle A. Fidell, ed. 403p. 1973. $33. ISBN 0-686-66660-7; 1973–77 v. Estelle A. Fidell, ed. 457p. 1978. $41. ISBN 0-686-66661-5; 1978–82 v. Juliette Yaakov, ed. 459p. 1983. $48. ISBN 0-317-01196-0; 1983–87 v. Juliette Yaakov and John Greenfieldt, eds. 522p. 1988. $58. ISBN 0-685-45835-0; 1988–92 v. Juliette Yaakov and John Greenfieldt, eds. 542p. 1993. $80. ISBN 0-685-70308-8. ISSN 0554-3037.
016.80882 Z5781

Index of full-length, one-act, radio, television, and Broadway plays; plays for amateurs, children, young adults, and adults. Arrangement is by author, title, and subject in one index, with such information as number of acts and scenes, size of cast, number of sets, bibliographic information, and a brief synopsis. Includes a list of plays by type of cast and number of players, a list of collections indexed, and a directory of publishers and distributors. Combined, the eight volumes index more than 31,500 plays.

1366 **Plays for children and young adults: an evaluative index and guide.** Rashelle S. Karp and June H. Schlessinger. 580p. Garland, 1991. $78. ISBN 0-8240-6112-8.

Plays for children and young adults: an evaluative index and guide. Supplement 1, 1989–1994. Rashelle

S. Karp, June H. Schlessinger, and Bernard S. Schlessinger. Garland, 1996. $83. ISBN 0-8153-1493-0.
016.812 PN1627

Alphabetically arranged entries for 3,560 plays published between 1975 and 1989 indicate bibliographic citation, audience grade level, cast number and gender required for production, number of acts, production time, setting, plot summary, royalty, and source. Includes indexes to author, title, casts, grade level, subject, and playing time. The supplement describes and evaluates some 2,000 additional plays published between 1989 and 1994 that are appropriate for young people to produce.

Dictionaries and Encyclopedias

1367 **American musical theatre: a chronicle.** 2d ed. Gerald Bordman. 821p. Oxford Univ. Pr., 1992. $60. ISBN 0-19-507242-1.
782.1 ML1711

A comprehensive history covering influences on American musical theater prior to its birth in 1866 through the 1989–90 Broadway season. The book moves year by year to describe every musical, citing opening date, theater, plot synopsis, and notable performers, directors, producers, and musicians. Three indexes cover shows and sources, songs, and people.

1368 **Book of the musical theatre.** Kurt Ganzl and Andrew Lamb. 1353p. Schirmer Books, 1989. $90. ISBN 0-02-871941-7.
782.81 MT95

Detailed plot synopses follow features of first productions and a list of characters. Entries are arranged by country and then chronologically. An essay on the history of musical theater in each geographic area opens every section. The time period spans 1728 to 1987. Criteria used: is likely to be produced, is of historical significance, or is a favorite of the authors. A selective discography and indexes of titles, authors, composers, lyricists, and song titles increase its reference value.

1369 **Cambridge guide to American theatre.** Don B. Wilmeth and Tice L. Miller, eds. 547p. Cambridge Univ. Pr., 1993. $49.95. ISBN 0-521-40134-8.
792 PN2220

The U.S.-related entries from *The Cambridge guide to world theatre* were revised and updated for this source, which includes 2,300 signed entries on people, shows, and theaters, as well as topics such as vaudeville, burlesque, circus, and off-off Broadway; African American, Asian American, and Hispanic theater; frontier theater; and theater of various U.S. cities. Includes a twenty-page introductory survey to American theater, a select bibliography, a biographical index, and more than 150 black-and-white illustrations.

1370 **The Cambridge guide to theatre.** Martin Banham, ed. 1233p. Cambridge Univ. Pr., 1995. $49.95. ISBN 0-521-43437-8.
792 PN2035

This is a comprehensive revision of *The Cambridge guide to world theatre* (1988) and its slightly revised paperback edition (1992). It includes 200 new entries as well as many revised old ones. Covers the history and current practice of theater throughout the world, both in those areas with long traditions (Germany, Japan, Britain, United States) and those that are lesser known or have shorter histories (e.g., Finland, Malawi). A broad interpretation of theater allows this work, directed toward theatergoers and theater students, to include other popular staged entertainment such as puppetry and the circus. Articles are signed, alphabetically arranged, and contain cross-references. Includes about 100 black-and-white illustrations. Broader in scope than *The Oxford companion to the theatre.*

1371 **The encyclopedia of the musical theatre.** Kurt Ganzl. 2v. Schirmer Books, 1994. $175. ISBN 0-02-871445-8.
782.1 ML102.M88

Nearly 3,000 articles about popular and internationally renowned plays from the Western musical theater tradition. Entries cover shows and people who wrote, performed, produced, and lent other artists' skills to them. Supplemented with lists of recordings and works written, a select bibliography, and black-and-white illustrations.

1372 **The New York Times theater reviews.** 1870–1919. 6v. Times Books, 1975. 1920–70. 10v. Times Books, 1971. Garland, 1971–72– . Biennial. $165. ISSN 0160-0583. Reprint: Garland, 1992. $3555/original 16v. plus first

10 biennial v. ISBN 0-8153-0351-3.
792 PN1581

Reprints of all the theater reviews that have appeared in the *New York Times* in the order in which they appeared in the newspaper. Includes title, production-company, and personal-name indexing. Gives a complete citation for all reviews and biographical information about the critics who wrote the reviews. The reviews are also indexed in the *New York Times index*.

1373 The Oxford companion to American theatre. 2d ed. Gerald Bordman. 735p. Oxford Univ. Pr., 1992. $49.95. ISBN 0-19-507246-4.
792 PN2220

An *A* to *Z* listing of American plays of major importance or commercial success, foreign plays with long runs or significant influence, major actors, authors, producers, and other theatrical notables. The more than 3,000 entries include theater groups, genres, issues, and a few other uniquely American forms of entertainment: vaudeville, Wild West shows. Many cross-references.

1374 The Oxford companion to the theatre. 4th ed. Phyllis Hartnoll, ed. 934p. Oxford Univ. Pr., 1983. $55. ISBN 0-19-211546-4.

The concise Oxford companion to the theatre. 2d ed. Phyllis Hartnoll and Peter Found, eds. 568p. Oxford Univ. Pr., 1992. Paper $40. ISBN 0-19-866136-3.
792 PN2035

A pair of alphabetically arranged, heavily cross-referenced one-volume encyclopedias covering all aspects of the theater worldwide: theaters, persons, genres, companies. The more concise 1992 companion has 2,500 entries, is more up-to-date, and contains a select bibliography, but it confines itself to mostly mainstream U.S. and British theater. The 1983 volume has 3,500 entries, more international scope, and several plates of black-and-white illustrations, but it is more dated.

1375 Stage it with music: an encyclopedic guide to the American musical theatre. Thomas S. Hischak. 341p. Greenwood, 1993. $45. ISBN 0-313-28708-2.
792.6 ML102.M88

This comprehensive one-volume work presents factual information and subjective commentary in nearly 900 entries covering 1866 to 1992. These include 335 on individual shows; 500 on actors, directors, producers, composers, choreographers, and other personnel; and more than 30 on musical series, genres, and subjects. Includes a chronology, select bibliography, and an index to subjects, names, shows, and song titles.

1376 Two hundred years of the American circus: from Aba-Daba to the Zoppe-Zavatta troupe. Tom Ogden. 402p. Facts on File, 1993. $50. ISBN 0-8160-2611-4.
791.3 GV1815

Entries cover performers, types of acts, animals, circus jargon, history, and related subjects. Cross-references, black-and-white illustrations, bibliography, and an index to names, places, and subjects.

Handbooks

1377 The best plays of . . . [yr.]. Limelight Editions, 1993– . Annual. $47. ISSN 1071-6971.
792 PN6112

This important set offers summaries of the theater season for Broadway, off Broadway, off-off Broadway, national touring companies, and theater in cities around the United States. "Ten Best Plays" includes a synopsis of the story and actual dialogue of principal scenes. Complete credits for each play produced in New York each year; statistics of runs, awards, and prizes; a necrology; and a list of best plays from 1894 to the current year. The index is substantial. This source has existed with various names and publishers since 1899 and has been an annual since 1920.

1378 Theatre world. Crown, 1945–91. Applause, 1992– . Annual. (v.50. 1994–95. Applause, 1997. $49.95. ISBN 1-55783-250-1; paper $25.95. ISBN 1-55783-251-X.) ISSN 0082-3856. (*formerly* **John Willis' theatre world.**)
792 PN2277.N5

Long-standing publication edited by John Willis that provides a record of performances, casts, and other production information for New York theater and regional theater around the country. There are many photographs and a listing of actors and actresses with brief biographical information.

16

Music

DONALD W. MAXWELL

Music is a performing art with a great amount of reference literature. Here, general sources on music are followed by sources on classical music and then on nonclassical. Effort has been made here to provide a greater number of sources on nonclassical genres of music.

General Sources

Bibliographies and Discographies

1379 **A basic music library: essential scores and sound recordings.** 3d ed. Elizabeth Davis, ed. 665p. American Library Assn., 1997. $85. ISBN 0-8389-3461-7.
016.78 ML113

This collection-building guide has been compiled by a team of experts under the auspices of the Music Library Association. Its listing of basic music books, scores, and recordings serves as an excellent tool for both developing and evaluating music collections of all sizes. New to this edition is a section describing some 7,000 sound recordings, including 2,500 classical compositions; 1,000 non-Western pieces; and 4,500 recordings of "vernacular music" (e.g., blues, jazz, rock, and country and western). More than 3,000 printed scores for all types of performance (e.g., single instrument, ensemble, voice, and vocal group) are also listed. Entries are ranked as recommended for small, medium-sized, or large libraries and provide information on uniform title, composer, publisher, and price. A distributor directory is included for user convenience.

1380 **The literature of American music in books and folk music collections: a fully annotated bibliography.** David Horn. 556p. Scarecrow, 1977. $45. ISBN 0-8109-0996-6. **The literature of American music in books and folk music collections: supplement 1.** David Horn with Richard Jackson. 570p. Scarecrow, 1988. $55. ISBN 0-8108-1997-X.

Literature of American music in books and folk music collections, 1983–1993. Guy A. Marco. 472p. Scarecrow, 1996. $69.50.

ISBN 0-8108-3132-5.
016.7817 ML120.U5

With the appearance of the third volume, this essential series now provides an extensive bibliography of books on American music (composers, performers, styles) from the colonial era up through 1993. Entries are critically annotated and provide all essential bibliographic information. Author, title, and subject indexing.

1381 **Music reference and research materials: an annotated bibliography.** 5th ed. Vincent H. Duckles and Ida Reed, eds. 812p. Schirmer Books, 1997. $45. ISBN 0-02-870821-0.
016.78 ML113

Comprehensive 3,500-entry bibliography, including 1,500 new to this edition, divided into sections covering dictionaries and encyclopedias, histories and chronologies, bibliographies of music and music literature, discographies, yearbooks, and directories, among others. Three separate indexes for authors, editors, and reviewers; subjects; and titles. This standard guide to source literature in music has only gotten better over the years. An essential purchase.

1382 **Schwann opus.** Stereophile, 1992– . Quarterly. $12.95. $39.95/yr. ISSN 1066-2138. (*formerly* **inMusic, Opus.**)
016.7816 ML156.2

Schwann spectrum. Stereophile, 1993– . Quarterly. $9.95. $24.95/yr. ISSN 1066-9161. (*formerly* **inMusic, Spectrum.**)
016.78026 ML156.2

These list recordings currently in print. Both titles include lists of new releases, feature articles and columns, book and record reviews, formats (e.g., compact disc, cassette, record) in which recordings are available, label and catalog number, date of release or recording, and whether digital or analog, stereo or monaural. *Schwann opus* lists classical recordings arranged by composer name. Entries include piece title, opus or catalog number, composition date, recording title and date, performer(s), and conductors. A collection section is arranged by subject and lists recordings by one or more artists of multiple composers' works. No prices are given. *Schwann spectrum* lists nonclassical recordings in several sections: popular (rock, rhythm and blues, country, blues, rap, folk, reggae) and jazz; musicals, movies, and TV shows; gospel and religious; new age; spoken and miscellaneous; children's; international; Christmas; laser discs; and CD-ROMs. Arrangement is primarily by performer name or collection title. Retail prices are given for most recordings.

Indexes

1383 **Music index: the key to current music periodical literature.** Harmonie Park, 1949– . Monthly with annual cumulation and subject heading list. $1375/yr. ISSN 0027-4348.
■ micro cd
016.78 ML118

Indexes approximately 350 current periodicals by author and subject, including geographic places, performers, performing groups, book, music, performance, and recording reviews; discographies; and festivals.

Dictionaries and Encyclopedias

1384 **The book of world-famous music: classical, popular, and folk.** 4th ed. James J. Fuld. 718p. Dover, 1995. Paper $19.95. ISBN 0-486-28445-X.
016.78 ML113

Approximately 6,000 songs, tunes, and melodies are arranged alphabetically by name. Words, where applicable, are printed along with a brief musical excerpt. The history of the melody is traced to its original printed source and documented through extensive footnotes. There is also brief biographical information on composers and lyricists, who are indexed along with original, alternative, and translated titles.

1385 **Garland encyclopedia of world music.** Bruno Nettl and Ruth Stone, eds. 10v. Garland, 1998–2000. $1650/set. ISBN 0-8153-1865-0. $165/v.
780.9 ML100

This is a major new encyclopedia dedicated to exploring the social and cultural context of music around the world. Individual volumes are devoted to specific regions of the world (e.g., *Africa,* volume 1; *South Asia: the Indian subcontinent,* volume 5; and *Australia and the Pacific Islands,* volume 9), and each has an accompanying audio compact disc of representative examples keyed to the text. Articles are authoritative, well illustrated, and provide cultural and historical perspectives on the musical styles, genres, and performances of each of the nine regions covered (volume 10 will be devoted to *The world's music: general perspectives and reference tools*).

1386 Music: an illustrated encyclopedia. Neil Ardley. 192p. Facts on File, 1986. $18.95. ISBN 0-8160-1543-0.
780 ML3928

Discusses the technical, historical, geographical, and biographical aspects of music. Inserts list composers, famous musicians, and first performances. Detailed drawings of instruments, diagrams of sound systems, and black-and-white and color photographs.

1387 Music since 1900. 5th ed. Nicolas Slonimsky. 1260p. Schirmer Books, 1994. $125. ISBN 0-02-872418-6.
780 ML197

This work contains a descriptive chronology, brief biographies, a glossary of musical terms, and selected documents from the history of twentieth-century music through 1991.

1388 Musical instruments of the world: an illustrated encyclopedia. Diagram Group. 320p. Sterling, 1997. Paper $19.95. ISBN 0-8069-9847-4.
781.9 ML102.I5

This reissue of a popular Facts on File publication of 1978 is an illustrated encyclopedia of musical instruments from all periods and places. With more than 4,000 drawings and diagrams, this work provides historical information and details on the origins, construction, and operation of instruments. Also contains brief information about ensembles (e.g., bands, orchestras) and biographies of persons instrumental in this field. Indexed. Anthony Baines's *The Oxford companion to musical instruments* (404p. Oxford Univ. Pr., 1992. $45. ISBN 0-19-311334-1) is a more scholarly work, based almost entirely on articles on instruments from *The new Oxford companion to music*. Some entries have been revised and longer entries broken into shorter ones.

1389 National anthems of the world. 9th ed. W. L. Reed and M. J. Bristow, eds. 608p. Cassell, 1997. $95. ISBN 0-304-43925-9.
784.7 ML1627

This edition includes 182 anthems listed alphabetically by country and reflects new anthems, new words to old music, and anthems of former Soviet republics that have gained or regained independence, the divisions of Yugoslavia and Czechoslovakia, and unifications of Yemen and Germany. Each anthem is arranged for voice and piano and includes composer's name, date of composition and adoption, lyricist, arranger, name of anthem if it has one, and words to all verses in their original language and a literal translation of them into English. Occasional footnotes. Appendix lists national days by country.

1390 The new Grove dictionary of American music. H. Wiley Hitchcock and Stanley Sadie, eds. 4v. Grove's Dictionaries of Music, 1986. $725. ISBN 0-943818-36-2.
781.773 ML101.U6

A major source of information on American music. Extensive coverage of musical genres from every historical period, with more than 1,000 articles on classical and avant-garde composers and more than 1,500 entries on composers and performers in jazz, rock, country, and blues. Accounts of the history, musical life, and traditions of various American cities and instruments, dance, and publishers. This revision, by 900 American contributors, updates 70 percent of the material of an earlier edition. Includes bibliographic essays and many illustrations and music examples.

1391 The new Grove dictionary of music and musicians. Stanley Sadie, ed. 20v. Grove's Dictionaries of Music, 1980. $2300/set. ISBN 0-333-23111-2; paper $500/set. 1995. ISBN 1-56159-174-2.
780 ML100

This monumental work is the sixth edition of *Grove's dictionary of music and musicians*. It is both a dictionary and encyclopedia for all types of music and performers. There are 22,500 articles, 7,500 cross-references, and 3,000 illustrations, including tables, technical diagrams, family trees, maps, instruments, places, musical autographs, and portraits. There are 2,500 musical examples and 16,500 biographies of composers, writers, instrument makers, and so forth, from all historical periods up to the present. There are extensive bibliographies and complete lists of works for many figures. This work is essential for any academic institution that offers a music curriculum and is desirable for any library that wants to provide an in-depth and comprehensive reference source on music.

1392 The new Grove dictionary of musical instruments. Stanley Sadie, ed. 3v.

Grove's Dictionaries of Music, 1984. $550/set. ISBN 0-943818-05-2.
781.91 ML102.I5

This set supersedes all other reference books on this subject. More than just a dictionary, it includes the history of the field, profiles of more than 1,000 instrument makers and inventors, bibliographies, and comprehensive coverage of ancient and modern, Western and non-Western musical instruments. Although derived in part from *The new Grove dictionary of music and musicians,* this is a new work that updates, revises, and expands, particularly in the area of non-Western instruments. More than 1,600 black-and-white photographs and drawings enhance the articles.

1393 **The new Harvard dictionary of music.** Don Michael Randel, ed. 942p. Belknap, 1986. $39.95. ISBN 0-674-61525-5.

Harvard concise dictionary of music. Don Michael Randel, comp. 577p. Belknap, 1978. $22.50. ISBN 0-674-37471-1; paper $14. ISBN 0-674-37470-3.
780 ML100

An authoritative and concise work for laypeople, students, performers, composers, scholars, and teachers that carries on the tradition of its earlier incarnation, the two editions of Willi Apel's *Harvard dictionary of music,* with a greatly expanded scope that includes broader coverage of recent music. The 6,000 newly written entries feature all things musical: jazz, rock, world music, genre, form, and definitions, with 222 instrument drawings and 250 musical examples. The concise version is based on the second edition (1969) of Apel's *Harvard dictionary of music.* The bibliographies from the former work have been omitted, but 2,000 biographical entries on composers and musicians are included.

1394 **The new Oxford companion to music.** Denis Arnold, ed. 2v. Oxford Univ. Pr., 1983. $135. ISBN 0-19-311316-3.
780 ML100

Written for the general reader, this standard dictionary covers all areas of musical interest. Articles of varying lengths about composers and music, covering forms, terms, instruments, acoustical principles, and notation. Numerous cross-references and illustrations. Based on Percy A. Scholes's *The Oxford companion to music* (10th ed. Oxford Univ. Pr., 1970. $49.95. ISBN 0-19-311306-6).

Directories

1395 **Billboard's international buyer's guide.** Billboard, 1971– . Annual. $129. ISSN 0067-8600. (*formerly* **International buyer's guide; Billboard international music-record-tape buyer's guide; Billboard international music-record directory.**)
338.4 ML18

This guide is the basic source for directory information in the music industry. Music and video companies, retail suppliers, industry services, manufacturing plants, services and equipment, materials and supplies, and international listings are all covered. The entries include company name, address, phone, names of principal executives, trade and brand names, and list of products and services.

1396 **Songwriter's market.** Writer's Digest, 1979– . Annual. $22.99. ISSN 0161-5971.
338.4 MT67

Listings of song buyers, publishers, and others who offer opportunities and services to songwriters. Included are such firms as advertising agencies, audiovisual producers, music publishers, play producers and publishers, and record companies and producers. Each listing has information such as name and address, contact person, how to contact, how to submit music, kinds of music wanted, and names of artists and companies under contract. There are brief articles giving an overview of the field and a guide to awards and grants, managers and agents, festivals, book publishers and publications, and workshops.

Handbooks

1397 **This business of music.** 7th ed. M. William Krasilovsky and Sidney Shemel. 698p. Watson-Guptill, 1995. $29.95. ISBN 0-8230-7755-1.
338.4 ML3790

A handbook to the music industry, covering general aspects of copyrights, trademarks, contracts, and taxation and matters specific to recording artists and companies and music writers and publishers. Includes several appendixes and sample legal forms. Indexed.

Biographical Sources

1398 **Baker's biographical dictionary of musicians.** 8th ed. Nicolas Slonimsky. 2115p. Schirmer Books, 1992. $125. ISBN 0-02-872415-1.
780 ML105

Brief articles about composers, performers, critics, conductors, and teachers arranged alphabetically under surname with pronunciation, list of musical works, and a bibliography of print sources. Includes classical, jazz, rock, country, blues, and other popular musicians. The eighth edition is the first substantial rewrite since the fifth (1971): 1,300 entries were revised and 1,100 were added, with emphasis on female, Asian, and multimedia composers, ethnomusicologists, and performance artists. Two abridgements are available: *The portable Baker's biographical dictionary of musicians* (Nicolas Slonimsky. Richard Kostelanetz, ed. 291p. Schirmer Books, 1995. $20. ISBN 0-02-871225-0) and *The concise edition of Baker's biographical dictionary of musicians* (8th ed. Nicolas Slonimsky. 1155p. Schirmer Books, 1994. $50. ISBN 0-02-872416-X).

1399 **Biographical dictionary of Afro-American and African musicians.** Eileen Southern. 478p. Greenwood, 1982. $85. ISBN 0-313-21339-9.
780 ML105

Biographical information on more than 1,500 people active in the musical world: composers, performers, educators, and so forth. Each entry has a bibliography, and many have discographies. Besides a general name index, appendixes list persons by date of birth and musical occupation. Covers people born from 1640 to 1945 and includes all types of musical activity—popular, classical, folk, and so forth.

1400 **Composers since 1900: a biographical and critical guide.** David Ewen, ed. 639p. Wilson, 1969. $69. ISBN 0-8242-0400-X. First supplement. David Ewan, comp. and ed. 328p. Wilson, 1981. $49. ISBN 0-8242-0664-9.
780 ML390

The two volumes cover 219 international composers, both living and deceased, who have written music since the beginning of the twentieth century and who are notable because of significant, oft-performed, or honored work. Biographical sketch, list of musical compositions, bibliography of books and articles by and about the composer, some black-and-white photos.

1401 **Great composers, 1300–1900: a biographical and critical guide.** David Ewen. 429p. Wilson, 1966. $62. ISBN 0-8242-0018-7.
780.922 ML105

Lists of principal works by and works about each composer accompany the biographies. Portraits and appendixes containing chronological and geographical lists add to the value of the work.

Classical Music

Discographies

1402 **The Penguin guide to compact discs and cassettes.** Rev. ed. Ivan March, ed. 1580p. Penguin, 1996. $23.95. ISBN 0-14-051367-1.
780.26 ML156.9

The object of this book is "to give the serious collector a comprehensive survey of the finest recordings for permanent music on CD." Arranged alphabetically by composer (and sometimes subdivided by genre), this guide provides an evaluation of one to three stars and notes superlative recordings; an indication of digital and bargain-priced recordings; record label and catalog number; names of the individual artists, performing groups, and conductors; and brief critical narrative. Also lists selective recordings of multiple composers by individual performers and performing groups: orchestral and concertante concerts and instrumental and vocal recitals. No index. Updated by *The Penguin guide to compact discs yearbook* (Penguin, 1991– . Annual. $19.95. ISBN 0-14-051381-7).

Indexes

1403 **Cross index title guide to classical music.** Steven G. Pallay, comp. 206p. Greenwood, 1987. $59.95. ISBN 0-313-25531-8.
016.78 ML113

Cross index title guide to opera and operetta. Steven G. Pallay, comp. 214p. Greenwood, 1989. $49.95. ISBN 0-313-25622-5.
016.7821 ML128.O4

The classical music volume refers users from popular names and nicknames of pieces to the "true" name of the work. It includes more than 6,000 entries by 220 composers. A select bibliography includes composer catalogs and other sources used to compile the work. The opera volume indexes more than 5,500 vocal and instrumental excerpts with popular or distinct titles from more than 1,400 works by 535 composers. It includes an index to composers and their works and a select bibliography.

Dictionaries and Encyclopedias

1404 Heritage of music. Michael Raeburn and Alan Kendall, eds. 4v. Oxford Univ. Pr., 1989. $225/set. ISBN 0-19-520493-X. v.1, Classical music and its origins. $60. ISBN 0-19-505370-2; v.2, The romantic era. $60. ISBN 0-19-505371-0; v.3, The nineteenth-century legacy. $60. ISBN 0-19-505372-9; v.4, Music in the twentieth century. $60. ISBN 0-19-505373-7.
780 ML160

Arranged chronologically from the Middle Ages to the present day, these volumes each contain about two dozen chapters with signed articles of about twenty pages each. Principal composers for each period are treated, as are pertinent subjects pertaining to the time period and place. Biographies of additional composers complete the final chapter in each volume. A detailed index in each volume, even to illustrations; a cumulative index in volume 4.

1405 The new Grove dictionary of opera. Stanley Sadie, ed. 4v. Grove's Dictionaries of Music, 1992. $850/set. ISBN 0-935859-92-6.
782.1 ML102.O6

This comprehensive encyclopedia was developed from *The new Grove dictionary of music and musicians,* but more than 80 percent of the material is new. The signed entries describe composers, their operas, singers, conductors, librettists and other writers, producers, directors, designers, and other personnel; cities with opera houses; countries with operatic traditions; terminology; history; and the practice of opera (e.g., casting, costumes, seating, etc.). Entries are supplemented with black-and-white illustrations, bibliographies (including scores and libretti), musical examples, and tables. Entries for individual operatic works include a list of roles and their ranges, a description by plot, and music by act or by scene. Many cross-references. Appendixes include a list of role names and arias and ensembles and the opera in which they appear. The *International dictionary of opera* (C. Steven Larue, ed. 2v. St. James, 1993. $250/set. ISBN 1-55862-081-8) is a smaller, less expensive, but still thorough and authoritative alternative.

1406 The Oxford dictionary of opera. John Warrack and Ewan West. 782p. Oxford Univ. Pr., 1992. $45. ISBN 0-19-869164-5.
782.1 ML102.O6

Encyclopedic treatment of opera with entries on operas, composers, librettists, producers, performers and other persons, places, characters, songs, and terminology. Some entries have select bibliographies or lists of works or both. Select bibliography and some cross-references.

1407 The Viking opera guide. Amanda Holden et al., eds. 1305p. Viking, 1993. $69.95. ISBN 0-670-81292-7.
■ cd
782.1 ML102.O6

More than 800 articles on opera composers, arranged alphabetically by composer name, with a biographical sketch and bibliography and a list of complete operatic works. Major operas have detailed entries: title (and translation into English); subgenre (e.g., tragedy, comedy, etc.); duration; librettist; source of libretto; world, U.S., and U.K. premiere dates; synopsis of the opera and musical commentary; cast list and orchestration; and available sound and video recordings and scores. The volume is supplemented with a glossary of technical terms, black-and-white photographs, and an index to librettists and titles. The CD-ROM version (*The Viking opera guide on CD-ROM.* Amanda Holden, ed. Viking, 1993. $99.95 with print version. ISBN 0-14-088319-3) includes three hours of musical excerpts and color pictures. An alternative is *The definitive Kobbe's opera book* (The Earl of Harewood, ed. 1404p. Putnam, 1987. $40. ISBN 0-399-13180-9).

Handbooks

1408 Evenings with the orchestra: a Norton companion for concertgoers. D. Kern Holoman. 734p. Norton, 1992. $29.95. ISBN 0-393-02936-0.
784.2 MT125

Not-too-technical descriptions of what to listen for in 275 musical works most likely to be heard at the symphony. Entries include brief information about the composers, original and translated titles, instrumentation, when composed and first performed, publisher of full and inexpensive editions of the score, and duration of the piece. Also provides guidance for neophyte concertgoers: what (not) to wear, when (not) to clap, when (not) to arrive and leave, descriptions of orchestral instruments and their players, and basics of musical theory and history. Includes a glossary and a good index.

Biographical Sources

1409 **Contemporary composers.** 2d ed. Brian Morton, ed. 1200p. St. James, 1998. $170. ISBN 1-55862-238-1.
780 ML105

Entries on 600 living or recently deceased composers of "serious" music, including biographical information, list of works, an assessment of their role in contemporary music, selective bibliographies and discographies, and, in some cases, personal statements by the composers.

1410 **Musicians since 1900: performers in concert and opera.** David Ewen, comp. and ed. 974p. Wilson, 1978. $82. ISBN 0-8242-0565-0.
780 ML105

Biographical essays are included on 432 performers, both living and dead, who have been important in the musical life of the twentieth century. Includes family background, education, professional training, early appearances, important engagements, major roles, and critical reception. A brief bibliography and usually a photograph accompany each entry.

1411 **The Norton/Grove dictionary of women composers.** Julie Anne Sadie and Rhian Samuel, eds. 548p. Norton, 1994. $45. ISBN 0-393-03487-9.
780.92 ML105

This source aims "to repair a deficiency in existing reference materials on the subject" and in doing so, uses the methodology of *The new Grove dictionary of music and musicians*. The 900 signed entries cover composers of achievement in Western classical and popular music born before 1959. Each includes a biographical sketch, usually followed by a list of works and a bibliography. Includes a chronology, black-and-white illustrations, cross-references, and index.

1412 **The Penguin dictionary of musical performers: a biographical guide to significant interpreters of classical music, singers, solo instrumentalists, conductors, orchestras, and string quartets ranging from the seventeenth century to the present day.** Arthur Jacobs. 250p. Penguin, 1991. $9.95. ISBN 0-14-051160-1.
780 ML105

Identifies more than 2,500 famous performers of classical music from the sixteenth century to the present. Index.

1413 **Who's who in American music: classical.** 2d ed. 2v. Bowker, 1985. $124.95. ISBN 0-8352-2074-5.
780 ML106.U3

Provides biographical information on 9,308 professional musicians active in "the creation, performance, preservation, or promotion of serious music in America" in 1985. It identifies each person's specialty (e.g., conductor, writer, director, composer, librarian, educator, critic) and lists, as appropriate, the person's birthdate, place of birth, education, debut performances, works, recorded performances, professional and teaching experience, honors, major publications, address, and other pertinent information. Geographic and professional classifications indexes.

Nonclassical Music

Bibliographies and Discographies

1414 **All music guide to rock: the experts' guide to the best recordings in rock, pop, soul, r&b, and rap.** 2d ed. Michael Erlewine, ed. 1232p. Miller Freeman, 1997. $26.95. ISBN 0-87930-494-4.
■ disk cd online
016.78164 ML156.9

Reviews of 15,000 recordings by 2,500 performers. Each artist's entry provides biographical information, a description of his or her music, signed capsule reviews, and a rating of one to five stars. Suggests essential, first-purchase, and landmark recordings. Supplemented with surveys of pop music styles that are illustrated with lineage charts. Concludes with a select bibliography and an index to artists. For jazz recordings, see *All music guide to jazz: the best CDs, albums, and tapes. All music guide: the experts' guide to the best recordings from thousands of artists in all types of music,* 3d ed. (Michael Erlewine, ed. 1400p. Miller Freeman, 1997. Paper $27.95. ISBN 0-87930-423-5) covers all types of music.

1415 The Billboard book of top forty hits. 6th ed. Joel Whitburn. 674p. Billboard, 1996. $21.95. ISBN 0-8230-7632-6.
016.78164 ML156.4.P6

Listing of the more than 80,000 singles (45 rpm records through the late 1980s, cassettes from then on) that have made their way onto the Billboard top-forty list of best-selling records of the rock era between January 1, 1955, and July 27, 1995. Arranged alphabetically by artists' names, with their top-forty songs listed chronologically with record label and number, each song's highest position and number of weeks on the chart, and whether the song achieved gold or platinum status. Index to song titles. Lists of top artists and record achievements.

1416 The Rolling Stone album guide: completely new reviews: every essential album, every essential artist. 3d ed. Anthony DeCurtis et al., eds. 838p. Random House, 1992. Paper $20. ISBN 0-679-73729-4. (*formerly* **The new Rolling Stone record guide; The Rolling Stone record guide.**)
781.66 ML156.4.P6

This work has been completely rewritten by a quartet of music critics since its second edition of 1983 and is based on albums that were in print as of 1992. Rock, pop, soul, rap, blues, jazz, gospel, and country are covered, with emphasis on rock. Entries are arranged by artist and include a discography (one-half- to five-star rating, album title, label, catalog number, and year of release) and an essay with critical evaluation that puts artists and recordings in historical context. Sections on anthologies and soundtracks lurk at the back of the volume.

Dictionaries and Encyclopedias

1417 The encyclopedia of popular music. 3d ed. Colin Larkin, ed. 8v. Grove's Dictionaries, 1998. $750. ISBN 1-56159-237-4.
781.64 ML102.P66

Comprehensive work on all forms of twentieth-century nonclassical music, including pop, rock, metal, country, rhythm and blues, rap, reggae, jazz, ragtime, big band, Latin, folk, and gospel. The more than 18,500 entries, ranging from 150 to 3,000 words, cover performers, songwriters and other personnel, genres, organizations, record companies, and so forth. Includes select discographies and extensive cross-references, bibliography, and a 50,000-name index. New to this edition are a five-star album rating and a complete song-title index.

1418 The Oxford companion to popular music. Peter Gammond. 739p. Oxford Univ. Pr., 1991. $45. ISBN 0-19-311323-6.
781.64 ML102.P66

Covers Anglo-American and European popular music since 1850, including jazz, blues, ragtime, country and western, operetta, musicals, rhythm and blues, military, rock, pop, folk, and film music. Numerous biographical entries and extensive cross-references. Some entries include filmographies and bibliographies. Indexes to people and groups, shows and films, and songs and albums.

1419 The Penguin encyclopedia of popular music. Donald Clarke, ed. 1378p. Penguin, 1990. Paper $20. ISBN 0-14-051147-4.
781.64 ML102.P66

A one-volume encyclopedia with nearly 3,000 entries, mostly on performers of all genres of nonclassical music: rock, country, jazz, gospel, metal, reggae, rap, ragtime, new age, folk, zydeco, blues, and so forth, as well as songwriters, producers, record labels, and histories of genres themselves. Entries note album titles, chart places, compare artists, and make many cross-references. Thoroughly indexed.

Biographical Sources

1420 American songwriters: an H. W. Wilson biographical dictionary. David Ewen. 489p. Wilson, 1987. $60. ISBN 0-8242-0744-0.
784.5 ML390

The 146 biographies include lyricists and composers and the performance history of individual songs and major stage musicals. An index lists the 5,600 song titles found in the text.

Songs

1421 American popular songs from the Revolutionary War to the present. David Ewen, ed. 507p. Random House, 1966. $19.95. ISBN 0-394-41705-4.
016.784 ML128.N3

Approximately 3,600 songs are listed, with such information as date of composition, composer, lyricist, and films or Broadway musicals in which they have been featured.

1422 The children's song index, 1978–1993. Kay Laughlin et al., comps. 153p. Libraries Unlimited, 1996. $37.50. ISBN 1-56308-332-9.
016.78242 ML128.S3

This index, listing 2,654 children's songs found in seventy-seven books published between 1977 and 1994, is intended for use by teachers and librarians. It is divided into indexes by song title, first line, and subject. The subject index has a helpful thesaurus. Updates *Index to children's songs* (1979).

1423 Find that tune: an index to rock, folk-rock, disco, and soul in collections. Vol. 1. William Gargan and Sue Sharma, eds. 340p. Neal-Schuman, 1984. $55. ISBN 0-918212-70-7.

Find that tune: an index to rock, folk-rock, disco, and soul in collections. Vol. 2. Sue Sharma and William Gargan, eds. 387p. Neal-Schuman, 1989. $55. ISBN 1-55570-019-5.

Find that tune: an index to rock, folk-rock, disco, and soul in collections. Vol. 3. William Gargan and Sue Sharma, eds. 390p. Neal-Schuman, 1998. $59.95. ISBN 1-55570-196-5. Available as a set. $149.95/3v. set. ISBN 1-55570-199-X.
784.5 ML128.R6

Volumes 1 and 2 each index some 4,000 songs in more than 200 collections of sheet music, covering music published from 1950 to 1985. Volume 3 concentrates on music published since that time, including new categories of rap, rockabilly, and blues. Volumes provide collection, title, first-line, composer-lyricist, and performer indexes.

1424 Folk song index: a comprehensive guide to the Florence E. Brunnings collection. Florence E. Brunnings. 357p. Garland, 1981. op.
784.4 ML128.F75

More than 50,000 song titles are indexed from a variety of collections, some of which are relatively obscure and not widely available. Subtitles, nicknames, and first lines are also included and coverage extends to some popular and classical songs.

1425 The great song thesaurus. 2d ed. Roger Lax and Frederick Smith. 774p. Oxford Univ. Pr., 1989. $85. ISBN 0-19-505408-3.
784.5 ML128.S3

This source is unique in that it provides information not only about songs, but about history and culture as well. It lists more than 11,000 of the most popular and significant songs from English-speaking countries from the sixteenth century through 1986. The main section lists song titles chronologically, then alphabetically by title, lyricist and composer, and key lyric lines. A thesaurus lists songs by subject, key word, and category. Other sections list award winners; theme, trademark, and signature songs; plagiarized songs; songs from theater, film, radio, and television; and other hard-to-find categories.

1426 Index to children's songs: a title, first line, and subject index. Carolyn Sue Peterson and Ann D. Fenton, comps. 318p. Wilson, 1979. $38. ISBN 0-8242-0638-X.
016.7846 ML128.S3

A numbered, indexed list of 298 children's songbooks published between 1909 and 1977, identifying more than 5,000 songs (both American and foreign) and variations, arranged alphabetically by author. There are also a title and first-line index and a subject index using more than 1,000 subject headings. The titles are likely to be held in schools and public libraries. Updated by *The children's song index, 1978–1993.*

1427 Popular music 1920–1979: a revised cumulation. Nat Shapiro and Bruce Pollock, eds. 3v. 2839p. Gale, 1985. $270/set. ISBN 0-8103-0847-9.

Popular music 1980–1989: an annotated guide to American popular songs. 911p. Gale, 1995. $132. ISBN 0-7876-0205-1.

Popular music: an annotated guide to American popular songs. Gale, 1974– . Annual. 1985– . $75. ISBN 0-7876-1178-6. ISSN 0886-442X.
784.5 ML120.U5

This title has been an annual since 1985 but is periodically cumulated. The two cumulative volumes list more than 20,000 song titles in a single alphabet and add indexes for important performances and awards. Typical entries include title and alternate title(s), country of origin for non-U.S. songs, author(s) and composer(s), current publisher, copyright date, and notes about each song's origin and performance history. Subsequent volumes are arranged alphabetically by title as in the 1920–79 cumulation, with the same categories of information included for each song. Indexes to lyricists and composers, important performances, chronology, and awards; and list of publishers. The annual update volumes are arranged and indexed in the same way.

1428 Popular song index. Patricia Pate Havlice. 933p. Scarecrow, 1975. $59.50. ISBN 0-8108-0820-X. First supplement. 386p. 1978. $42.50. ISBN 0-8108-1099-9. Second supplement. 530p. 1984. $37.50. ISBN 0-8108-1642-3. Third supplement. 875p. 1989. $59.50. ISBN 0-8108-2202-4.
016.784 ML128.S3

The original volume indexes 301 song collections published between 1940 and 1972. The supplements add 253 collections, mainly from the 1970–87 period but with some published earlier. "Popular" includes folk songs, hymns, children's songs, and more. The index is by title, first line of verse, and first line of chorus, all coded to the song collections.

1429 Song finder: a title index to 32,000 popular songs in collections, 1854–1992. Gary L. Ferguson, ed. 368p. Greenwood, 1995. $79.50. ISBN 0-313-29470-4.
782.42 ML128

An indispensable title-only index to more than 32,000 popular songs appearing in 621 books published between 1854 and 1992. Some 75 percent of these books have never been indexed before. The work is divided into two parts: a list of books indexed and an alphabetical listing of songs by title. Identifying features, such as composer name, are provided for each entry.

1430 Song index: an index to more than 12,000 songs in 177 song collections comprising 262 volumes. Minnie Earl Sears, ed. 650p. Wilson, 1926. op.

Song index supplement: an index to more than 7,000 songs in 104 song collections comprising 124 volumes. Minnie Earl Sears, ed. 366p. Wilson, 1934. op. Reprint of both volumes: **Song index.** Reprint Services, 1990. $109. ISBN 0-7812-9019-8.
■ micro
016.784 ML128.S3

This early Wilson work lists titles, first lines, and names of authors and composers in a single alphabet, with fullest information under title entry. This source can be used to find words and music of a song, lists of songs by an author or composer, and poems that have been set to music.

1431 The song list: a guide to contemporary music from classical sources. James L. Limbacher, ed. 229p. Pierian, 1973. $16.50. ISBN 0-87650-041-6.
016.784 ML113

The first section provides the adapter or lyricist of a classical composition; the second section gives composers' works known by more than one title or by a "popular" title. A useful ready reference source.

1432 Songs in collections: an index. Desiree de Charms and Paul F. Breed. 588p. Harmonie Park, 1966. $38. ISBN 0-911772-53-7.
783.6016 ML128.S3

Analyzes 411 collections for more than 9,000 songs, including folk songs, carols, and sea chanties. Serves as a supplement to Sears's *Song index*.

1433 Songs of the theater. Richard Lewine and Alfred Simon. 897p. Wilson, 1984. $82. ISBN 0-8242-0706-8.
016.78281 ML128.S3

More than 12,000 songs from musical stage productions, with selected titles from film and television productions. For stage productions, coverage is complete for the years 1925 to 1971 and selective for 1900 to 1924. For each song, the composer, lyricist, show title, and year are listed. A second section lists productions with cast and credits and information on vocal scores and cast albums. Chronological list of productions and index to composers and lyricists.

Blues

1434 The big book of blues: a biographical encyclopedia. Robert Santelli. 419p. Penguin, 1993. $16.95. ISBN 0-14-015939-8.
781.643 ML102.B6

More than 600 entries including biographical sketches noting contributions to the genre and lists of currently available albums for "essential listening" with label and stock number. Information was drawn from existing sources and interviews conducted by the author. Includes cross-references, bibliography, and index.

1435 Encyclopedia of the blues. Gerard Herzhaft. Brigitte DeBord, trans. 513p. Univ. of Arkansas Pr., 1992. Paper $18.95. ISBN 1-55728-253-6.
781.643 ML102.B6

Entries cover musicians, producers, trends, movements, major regions, and instruments important and influential in the genre. Includes profiles of approximately 350 artists, select bibliographies, discographies, a list of 200 important blues records available on CD in 1992, and an appendix that traces 300 standard blues songs back to their probable origins. Indexes to blues instruments and the artists who play(ed) them and to groups and individual performers.

Country and Folk

1436 The Blackwell guide to recorded country music. Bob Allen, ed. 411p. Blackwell, 1994. $24.95. ISBN 0-631-19106-2.
016.781642 ML156.4.C7

A select discography of 405 good, representative, and definitive recordings divided into ten broad subgenres. Includes essays on the subgenres, discographical details of the recordings, a list of recommended readings, a glossary, and an index to artists and song and album titles.

1437 The comprehensive country music encyclopedia. Editors of Country Music magazine. 449p. Times Books, 1994. $25. ISBN 0-8129-2247-6.
781.642 ML102.C7

Contains 680 entries on individuals and groups, genres, events, places, and other things that have helped to shape country music. Includes photographs.

1438 Definitive country: the ultimate encyclopedia of country music and its performers. Barry McCloud. 1132p. Perigee, 1995. $40. ISBN 0-399-51890-8; paper $20. ISBN 0-399-52144-5.
781.642 ML102.C7

More than 1,200 biographical entries cover all styles and trends in country music from the 1920s to the present. Includes lists of recommended recordings for each artist, award winners, hall of fame inductees, and gold and platinum singles and albums. Directory information includes fan clubs, fairs, agents, radio stations, and other industry contacts. Several hundred black-and-white photos, filmography, and select discography.

1439 Encyclopedia of folk, country, and western music. 2d ed. Irwin Stambler and Grelun Landon. 902p. St. Martin's, 1983. $17.95. ISBN 0-312-24819-9.
781.773 ML102.F66

Provides detailed information on individual artists and groups, major variety shows, definitions of terms, instruments, and other areas. Information on awards, a selective discography, and a bibliography are included.

1440 The folk music sourcebook. Updated ed. Larry Sandberg and Dick Weissman. 272p. Da Capo Pr., 1989. Paper $18.95. ISBN 0-306-80360-7.
016.78162 ML12

Definitive guide to folk music, both popular and scholarly, this traces the origins, instruments, artists, recordings, books, periodicals, organizations, retail outlets, film archives, and terms in the field.

Jazz

1441 All music guide to jazz: the best CDs, albums, and tapes. Ron Wynn, ed. 3d ed. 1378p. Miller Freeman, 1998. $29.95. ISBN 0-87930-530-4.
781.65 ML156.4.J3

A comprehensive guide to more than 18,000 recordings of some 1,700 jazz artists. Introductory glossaries describe various subgenres (e.g., bebop, world fusion, Harlem stride, etc.) and musical terms. Artists are listed alphbetically, with a brief biographical sketch, then a list of their albums. Album entries include recording dates; record label and numbers; a signed, authoritative review; and a symbol indicating whether it is a landmark recording, essential for a good collection, or a first purchase. Appendixes list record labels, producers, venues, magazines, and mail-order sources. A select bibliography and a thorough index conclude the work.

1442 The Harmony illustrated encyclopedia of jazz. 3d ed. Brian Case and Stan Britt. Rev. by Chrissie Murray. 208p. Harmony, 1987. Paper

$13.95. ISBN 0-517-56443-2.
785.42 ML102.J3

More than 500 entries on individual and group performers in this genre. Profusely illustrated with black-and-white and color photographs. Entries include discographies. Indexed. Old, classic reference sources in this genre are Leonard Feather's *Encyclopedia of jazz* (527p. Horizon, 1960. Reprint: Da Capo Pr., 1984. Paper $19.95. ISBN 0-306-80214-7), *Encyclopedia of jazz in the sixties* (312p. Horizon, 1967. Reprint: Da Capo Pr., 1986. Paper $14.95. ISBN 0-306-80263-5), and *Encyclopedia of jazz in the seventies* (Leonard Feather and Ira Gitler. 393p. Horizon, 1976. Reprint: Da Capo Pr., 1984. Paper $16.95. ISBN 0-306-80290-2).

1443 The new Grove dictionary of jazz. Barry Kernfeld, ed. 2v. Grove's Dictionaries of Music, 1988. op. Reprint: St. Martin's, 1994. $50. ISBN 0-312-11357-9.
785.42 ML102.J3

Not just a spin-off of *The new Grove dictionary of music and musicians;* 90 percent of the material in this work is new. Entries treat musicians, composers, record producers, musical terms and instruments, recording studios, and other topics. Bibliographies and discographies are appended to most entries.

Rock

1444 The Harmony illustrated encyclopedia of rock. Mike Clifford, ed. 7th ed. 208p. Harmony, 1992. Paper $19. ISBN 0-517-59078-6.
781.66 ML102.R6

A heavily illustrated source of information on all aspects of the rock music world. Entries concentrate on personalities and groups, giving biographical, historical, and career information and including discographies. A helpful index and cross-references assist in tracing the work of an individual or group throughout rock history.

1445 The new Rolling Stone encyclopedia of rock and roll. Patricia Romanowski and Holly George-Warren, eds. 1120p. Fireside, 1995. Paper $25. ISBN 0-684-81044-1.
781.66 ML102.R6

This is a revised edition of *The Rolling Stone encyclopedia of rock and roll* (1983). It contains 1,800 entries, some describing styles and trends but most biographical, arranged alphabetically by individual or group name. Essays describe lives and careers and place work in critical and historical perspective. Includes lists of Grammy Award winners and Rock and Roll Hall of Fame inductees, black-and-white photographs, and cross-references.

1446 Rock stars/pop stars: a comprehensive bibliography, 1955–1994. Brady J. Leyser, comp. 302p. Greenwood, 1994. $59.95. ISBN 0-313-29422-4.
016.78166 ML128.R6

Lists 3,600 books published in the United States, Canada, and Britain, including biographies, bibliographies, discographies, even fiction, about individuals and groups associated with rock and pop music, including performers, record company executives, producers, managers, and deejays. Arranged by name. Subject, author, and title index.

17

Crafts and Hobbies

CAROLE DYAL

Many of the works in this chapter are appropriate not only for the reference collection, but also for the circulating collection and for the home library.

INDEXES

1447 **Index to handicraft books, 1974–1984.** Carnegie Library of Pittsburgh Science and Technology staff. 424p. Univ. of Pittsburgh Pr., 1986. $49.95. ISBN 0-8229-3532-5. 016.7455 Z6151

Index to handicrafts, modelmaking, and workshop projects. Eleanor C. Lovell and Ruth M. Hall. 698p. Faxon, 1936. Lib. bindg. $14. ISBN 0-87305-057-6. (Supplements 1, 2, 4, and 5 also in print, 1943–75). 016.7455 Z7911

Make it: an index to projects and materials. Joyce F. Shields. 485p. Scarecrow, 1975. $39.50. ISBN 0-8108-0772-6. 016.7455 Z7911

Make it II: an index to projects and materials, 1974–1987. Mary E. Heim. 552p. Scarecrow, 1989. $49.50. ISBN 0-8108-2125-7. 016.7455 Z7911

These titles index thousands of handicraft materials and handicraft projects appearing in hundreds of books and periodicals. The alphabetically arranged entries include such activities as needlework, electronics, woodworking, toy making, and fence building. Useful for the hobbyist, for schools that offer craft classes, or for anyone desiring to come up with creative or practical answers to questions about virtually any craft or hobby.

1448 **Index to how to do it information: a periodical index, 1963–1989.** 2v. Norman M. Lathrop, comp. Lathrop, 1993. Paper $100. ISBN 0-910868-57-3. 1994 Supplement. $35. ISBN 0-910868-90-5. 1995 Supplement. $35. ISBN 0-910868-94-8. 1997 Supplement. $35. ISBN 0-910868-95-6. 016.7455 Z7913

Indexes sixty-three magazines that regularly feature "how-to" articles.

Handbooks

1449 The artist's complete health and safety guide. 2d ed. Monona Rossel. 344p. Allworth Pr., 1994. Paper $19.95. ISBN 1-880559-18-9.
700 RC963

Supplies commonly used by artists and crafters are often highly toxic. This guide describes the relationship of such toxic materials to specific diseases and gives the threshold limit values for many common chemicals used in art and hobby materials, including raw materials, pigments and dyes, solvents, and plastics. Safe substitutes for toxic materials are listed. Precautions are clearly articulated. Organizations and published works of relevance are described.

1450 Craft supply sourcebook: a comprehensive shop-by-mail guide for thousands of craft materials. 4th ed. Margaret Ann Boyd. Betterway Books, 1996. Paper $18.99. ISBN 1-55870-441-8.
680 TT12

Provides addresses and other directory information on more than 3,000 companies selling craft supplies.

1451 Favorite hobbies and pastimes: a sourcebook of leisure pursuits. Robert S. Munson. 366p. American Library Assn., 1994. Paper $55. ISBN 0-8389-0638-9.
790.1 GV1201.5

A book of information sources for eighty-four hobbies and pastimes from skiing to stamp collecting. Offers three- to six-page entries, alphabetically arranged by subject, that describe the specifics of the hobby or pastime, followed by a bibliography of books and periodicals and a directory of associations affiliated with the topic. Subject index.

1452 Hobbyist's sourcebook. 2d ed. Gale, 1995. $55. ISBN 0-8103-7614-8.
790.1 GV120.5

Covers forty-three hobbies, alphabetically arranged, from caving to wine making. Provides a basic overview, describing costs and equipment, statistics, and participating community. Identifies key resources, including books, periodicals, catalogs, and videos.

Crafts

Beading

1453 The bead directory: the most comprehensive collection of bead sources available. 4th ed. Milton Firestone and Alice Scherer. Linda Benmour, ed. 308p. Artstone Pr., 1996. Paper $22.95. ISBN 1-883153-20-4.
745.58 TT860

A guide to bead shops and mail-order suppliers in the United States, Canada, and Britain. Stores are listed by state. Entries include name of store, description, address, phone and fax, contact persons, hours, type of payment accepted, and so on. Appendixes list associations, organizations, museums, classes, conferences, and periodicals devoted to beadwork.

Embroidery

1454 The complete encyclopedia of needlework. 3d ed. Thérèse de Dillmont. 704p. Running Pr., 1996. $24.40. ISBN 1-56138-702-9; paper $14.98. Courage Books, 1998. ISBN 0-7624-0388-8.
746.4 TT760

Originally published in France in the nineteenth century, this work offers a very traditional approach to stitchery, describing needlework ranging from linen and silk embroidery to tapestry. Provides directions for both simple and advanced techniques of every kind of needlework, including sewing and knitting.

1455 Complete encyclopedia of stitchery. Mildred Graves Ryan. 685p. Adams, 1995. $15.95. ISBN 1-55850-474-5.
746.4 TT760

Includes sections on crocheting, embroidering, knitting, rug making, sewing, and tatting. Entries are arranged alphabetically by stitch. Provides black-and-white block illustrations and step-by-step instructions that are clear and easy to follow.

1456 Complete stitch encyclopedia. Jan Eaton. 173p. Barron, 1986. $24.95. ISBN 0-81209-257-0.
746.4 TT760

More than 400 stitches are clearly presented, most showing the position of the needle as the stitch is made. Stitches are arranged in groups and graded as easy, medium, or difficult to perform. Includes stitch reference number, written description, recommended fabrics and threads, historical information, and variant names. Well indexed.

1457 **Reader's Digest complete book of cross stitch and counted thread techniques.** Eleanor Van Zandt. 160p. Reader's Digest, 1995. $25. ISBN 0-89577-621-9.
746.44 TT778.C76

Provides clear directions for basic cross-stitching as well as more advanced stitching techniques. Presents pages of traditional motifs, borders, numerals, flowers, and so forth. Includes pattern darning, black work, pulled work, Hardanger, and other drawn thread work. Describes several challenging projects. Useful descriptions of materials and equipment required. Well illustrated.

1458 **Reader's Digest complete book of embroidery.** Melinda Cross. 192p. Reader's Digest, 1996. $25. ISBN 0-89577-874-2.
746.44 TT770

Describes more than 100 embroidery stitches and shows how to incorporate them into practical projects. Features seventy-five traceable motifs. Well illustrated.

Knitting

1459 **Reader's Digest knitter's handbook: a comprehensive guide to the principles and techniques of handknitting.** Montse Stanley. 318p. Reader's Digest, 1993. $28. ISBN 0-89577-467-4.
746.43 TT820

A truly comprehensive compendium of knitting techniques. At once clearly written and remarkably detailed, this work will appeal to both beginners and advanced students. Includes gauge charts and pattern instructions. All techniques discussed are well illustrated.

1460 **A treasury of knitting patterns.** Reprint ed. Barbara G. Walker. 320p. Simon & Schuster, 1981. Paper $20. ISBN 0-684-17314-X.
746.4 TT820

A second treasury of knitting patterns. Barbara G. Walker. 433p. Simon & Schuster, 1981. Paper $26. ISBN 0-684-16938-X.
746.4 TT820

Charted knitting designs: a third treasury of knitting patterns. Barbara G. Walker. 304p. Scribner, 1986. $21. ISBN 0-684-12566-8; paper $14.95. ISBN 0-684-17462-6.
746.432 TT820

These are classic knitting stitch pattern compendia illustrated with close-up photographs of stitches along with explicit directions on how to knit more than 500 patterns. Includes simple knit-purl combinations, ribbings, color-change patterns, slip-stitch patterns, twist-stitch patterns, fancy texture patterns, patterns made with yarn-over stitches, eyelet patterns, lace, cables, and cable-stitch patterns. Includes information on the origin and use of patterns. Indexed.

1461 **Vogue knitting: the ultimate knitting book.** 288p. Pantheon, 1989. $35. ISBN 0-394-57186-X.
746.9 TT820

A basic encyclopedia of knitting that is clearly written and easy to comprehend. Includes a history of knitting and a stitch dictionary that illustrates more than 120 popular stitches. Describes knitting supplies and basic techniques, including how to design garments. Includes 1,600 full-color illustrations.

Quilts

1462 **The complete quilting course.** Gail Lawther. 176p. Chilton Book Co., 1992. $27.95. ISBN 0-8019-8358-4.

The quilter's companion: everything you need to know to make beautiful quilts. Mimi Dietrich et al. 314p. That Patchwork Place, 1994. $29.95. ISBN 1-56477-040-0.

Quilter's complete guide. Marianne Fons and Liz Porter. 255p. Oxmoor House, 1993. $29.99. ISBN 0-8487-1099-1; paper $19.95. ISBN 0-8487-1152-1.
746.9 TT835

All the above are excellent comprehensive guides to quilting, describing requisite equipment and supplies and introducing quilting skills in an accessible how-to approach. In each case, instruction by means of practical projects reinforces skills learned.

1463 Encyclopedia of pieced quilt patterns. Barbara Brackman, comp. 551p. American Quilter's Society, 1993. $34.95. ISBN 0-89145-815-8.
746.46 TT835

Spanning the years 1830–1980, this encyclopedia presents the most complete index to published American quilt designs in existence. A simple graphic illustration is provided for each pattern indexed. Designs are presented in twenty-five clearly differentiated categories (one patch, strip, four patch, wheels, fans, and so on), each with several subdivisions. Provides source of reference for each pattern. Both a practical tool and a historical catalog. A masterpiece. Extensive bibliography.

1464 Quilt groups today: who they are, where they meet, what they do, and how to contact them. American Quilter's Society staff. 336p. Collector Books, 1992. Paper $14.95. ISBN 0-89145-999-5.
746.46 TT835

This directory was compiled under the auspices of the American Quilter's Society from survey forms completed by individual quilt groups around the world. Entries are arranged by state or country (for those outside the United States) and include address, area served, group size and expertise, and meeting location and frequency. A survey form is included for those who would like to be included in the next edition.

1465 The quilt I.D. book: 4,000 illustrated and indexed patterns. Judy Rehmel. 368p. Prentice-Hall, 1986. op.
746.9 TT835

Identifies more than 4,000 patterns in fifteen basic categories. "Unknown" patterns included. Black-and-white drawings. Indexed by name.

Sewing

1466 Claire Shaeffer's fabric sewing guide. Updated ed. Claire B. Shaeffer. 531p. Chilton Book Co., 1994. Paper $24.95. ISBN 0-8019-7802-5.
646.2 TT713

This is the most comprehensive guide to the selection, wear, care, and sewing of all fabrics. Part 1 describes fiber content, including natural fibers, man-made fibers, leathers, synthetic suedes, vinyls, furs, and feathers. Part 2 discusses fabric structure: woven fabrics, knits, and stretch-woven fabrics. Part 3 discusses all manner of fabric surface characteristics, including special-occasion fabrics such as satin and taffeta, sequined and beaded fabrics, lace and net; napped and pile fabrics; felt and felted fabrics; reversible fabrics; quilted fabrics; and fabrics with designs, such as plaids, stripes, and prints. Part 4 discusses linings and interfacings. Part 5 describes sewing techniques, such as seams, hems, edge finishes, closures, and hand stitches. Part 6 is a fabric and fiber dictionary. There are several useful appendixes, a glossary, a bibliography, and an index.

1467 Complete book of sewing: a practical step-by-step guide to sewing techniques. 320p. Dorling Kindersley, 1996. $39.95. ISBN 0-7894-0419-2.

Complete guide to sewing: step-by-step techniques for making clothes. Rev. ed. 432p. Reader's Digest, 1995. $30. ISBN 0-88850-247-8.
646.4 TT705

These two basic sewing guides complement one another well. The Dorling Kindersley volume illustrates steps and techniques primarily through numerous color photographs; the Reader's Digest volume provides more extensive commentary and includes a section on tailoring for men, lacking in the former.

1468 The complete step-by-step guide to home sewing. Jeanne Argent. 240p. Chilton Book Co., 1990. Paper $32.95. ISBN 0-8019-8080-1.
646.2 TT713

An overall guide to home sewing projects by the former crafts editor of *Family Circle*. Step-by-step directions for curtains, blinds, cushions, bed linens, kitchen- and tableware, lampshades, upholstery, loose covers, garden ideas, and more.

1469 Fairchild's dictionary of fashion. 2d rev. ed. Charlotte Mankey Calasibetta, ed. 685p. Fairchild, 1998. $42. ISBN 1-56367-169-7.
391.03 TT503

This work provides 15,000 definitions along with about 500 well-executed line drawings and 500 biographical sketches of designers.

1470 Fairchild's dictionary of textiles. 7th ed. Phyllis G. Tortora and Robert S.

Merkel, eds. 662p. Fairchild, 1996. $72. ISBN 1-87005-707-3.
677 TS1309

Includes more than 14,000 definitions relating to textiles. A primary reference source for those working with textiles or those interested in the words or the history of words relating to textiles, fibers, fabrics, and dyes.

1471 The Vogue/Butterick step-by-step guide to sewing techniques. Vogue Patterns editors. 3d ed. 415p. Simon & Schuster, 1998. Paper $20. ISBN 1-57389-004-9.
646.2 TT705

Demonstrates more than 500 of the 2,000 dressmaking procedures regularly used in Vogue and Butterick patterns. Alphabetical organization. Very well illustrated. Easy reference, good index. Vocabulary list linked to page numbers. The forty-seven sections focus on specific garment pieces or specific techniques (e.g., appliqués, basting, buttonholes, collars, linings, marking, ruffles).

Woodworking

1472 Creating your own woodshop. Charles Self. 128p. Betterway Books, 1994. Paper $18.99. ISBN 1-55870-326-8.
684 TT185

Shows how to design, arrange, and fill work space. How to choose a space and equip it with tools. How to arrange space to accommodate the most important work flows. How to select proper tools. How to build freestanding workshops.

1473 Encyclopedia of wood joints. Wolfram Graubner. 160p. Taunton, 1992. Paper $24.95. ISBN 1-56158-004-X.
684 TT185

The most comprehensive source on wood joining, detailing more than 600 joints. Arranged according to four major processes: splicing joints, oblique joints, corner and cross joints, and end joints. Provides an understanding of the craft of joining and a rationale for choosing one technique over another.

1474 The encyclopedia of woodworking techniques. Jeremy Broun. 176p. Running Pr., 1993. $24.95. ISBN 1-56138-209-4.
684 TT185

Arranges thirty-two woodworking procedures (clamping, gluing, measuring, etc.) in alphabetical order and describes each one in detail, commenting on the tools required and the skill.

1475 Hand tools: their ways and workings. Aldren A. Watson. 424p. Lyons & Burford, 1993. Paper $21.95. ISBN 1-55821-224-8.
684 TJ1195

How to identify and use hand tools. Very clear drawings. Includes workbench plans and hand-tool shop inventory. Indexed by name of tool. Clear text and good working hints (e.g., practice clamping with dry wood). Step-by-step instructions.

1476 How to carve wood: a book of projects and techniques. Richard Butz. 224p. $25.75. Peter Smith, 1991. ISBN 0-8446-6439-1.
731.4 TT199.7

Begins with tool selection and design of work space. Recommends and illustrates tools for different kinds of carving. Section on sharpening tools. Common woods and finishes: name, hardness, texture, description. Carving designs. Bibliography for more specifics.

1477 Working with wood: the basics of craftsmanship. Peter Korn. 208p. Taunton, 1993. Paper $24.95. ISBN 1-56158-041-4.
784 TT180

Describes the physical properties of wood and how these affect joining. Describes the processes of joining and the tools used in joining. Black-and-white photographs, good line drawings. Clear instructions, safety tips. Projects build on one another. Recommends sources of supply. Simple, straightforward index.

Hobbies

Antiques and Collectibles

1478 Kovels' antiques and collectibles price list. 29th ed. Ralph M. Kovel, Ralph Kovel, and Terry H. Kovel. 800p. Crown, 1996. $14.95. ISBN 0-517-88777-0.
745.1 NK805

The area of prices in the antiques and collectibles market is extremely volatile, but this standard work is helpful in that it states what costs what and when. Encompasses more than 50,000 appraiser-approved prices for furniture, ceramics, toys, glassware, and other collectibles as well as helpful tips on identification.

1479 The official price guide to antiques and collectibles. 15th ed. 704p. House of Collectibles, 1997. $15. ISBN 0-876-37960-9.
745.1 NK805

Covers a wide variety of collectibles from furniture and china to Barbie and G.I. Joe. More than 60,000 items: chalkware, combs, nautical gear, nursery collectibles, weather vanes, American eagles, and more—all are represented with updated prices and market information. Includes a full-color section on record-setting auction items for the year.

1480 Warman's antiques and collectibles price guide: the essential field guide to the antiques and collectibles marketplace. Ellen T. Schroy, ed. 640p. Warman, 1976– . Annual. $16.95. ISSN 0196-2272.
745.1 NK1133

Lists antique objects alphabetically by category, providing a capsule history of the object, bibliographic references, periodicals, clubs, museums, photographs, and marks. Within each category, objects that are actively being sold in the antiques market are listed with descriptions and prices. Index.

Coins and Paper Money

1481 The coin atlas: the world of coinage from its origins to the present day. Joe Cribb et al. 336p. Facts on File, 1990. $40. ISBN 0-8160-2097-3.
737.494 CJ59

A historical atlas of coinage. Provides a political history of each country's coinage through text and photographs; maps indicate location of mints and general circulation of coins. Includes glossary; selective bibliography; and an index of persons, places, events, metals, and minting processes.

1482 Coin world almanac: a handbook for coin collectors. 6th ed. Beth Deisher, ed. 752p. Pharos Books, 1990. $29.95. ISBN 0-88687-462-9; paper $15.95. ISBN 0-88687-460-2.
737.4 CJ1

This work contains "the essential facts which form the permanent record of numismatics." Twenty-two chapters record this information through essays, tables, statistics, and directories. Topics covered include coin collecting, investing, paper money, counterfeits, rarities, and coin design. Lists museums, societies, and organizations of interest to collectors.

1483 Collecting coins for pleasure and profit: a comprehensive guide and handbook for collectors and investors. Barry Krause. 224p. Betterway Books, 1991. Paper $18.95. ISBN 1-55870-207-5.
737.4 CJ1751

Collecting paper money for pleasure and profit: a comprehensive guide and handbook for collectors and investors. Barry Krause. 240p. Betterway Books, 1992. Paper $18.95. ISBN 1-55870-256-3.
769.5 HG353

Excellent guides on the art of collecting; they include interesting chapters on currency gradation, errors, and forgeries.

1484 The comprehensive catalog of U.S. paper money: all U.S. paper federal currency since 1812. 6th ed. Gene Hessler. 520p. BNR Pr., 1997. Paper $29.95. ISBN 0-931960-50-9.
769.5 HG591

The official 1998 blackbook price guide of U.S. paper money. 30th ed. Marc Hudgeons. 272p. House of Collectibles, 1997. Paper $6. ISBN 0-67660-970-0.
769.55 HG591

Standard catalog of U.S. paper money. 16th ed. Chester Krause et al., eds. 248p. Krause, 1997. $24.95. ISBN 0-87341-536-1.
769.5 HG591

Standard catalog of world paper money: volume 1: specialized issues. 8th ed. Albert Pick, ed. 1184p. Krause, 1998. $60. ISBN 0-87341-648-1.
769.55 HG591

Standard catalog of world paper money: volume II: general issues. 8th ed. Albert Pick. 1232p. Krause, 1997. $55. ISBN 0-87341-469-1.
769.55 HG591

Standard catalog of world paper money: volume III: modern issues. 4th ed. Colin Bruce, ed. 768p. Krause, 1998. $60. ISBN 0-87341-592-2.
769.55 HG591

These catalogs describe paper money, the use of which dates as far back as the eighteenth century. They provide listings of prices for paper money in various conditions. There is also a variety of supplementary data in each book, depending on the particular specialty that is being covered. Length of treatment and depth of coverage are fairly consistent with the length and price of the book.

1485 The official blackbook price guide to U.S. coins. 33d ed. Marc Hudgeons. 320p. Ballantine, 1994. Paper $6. ISBN 0-87637-936-6.
737.4 CJ1735

Standard catalog of world coins. 25th ed. Chester L. Krause and Clifford Mishler. Colin R. Bruce, ed. 1712p. Krause, 1997. Paper $47.95. ISBN 0-87341-497-7.
737.4 CJ1755

Standard catalog of world coins: seventeenth century, 1601–1700. Chester L. Krause, Clifford Mishler, and Colin R. Bruce, eds. Krause, 1996. Paper $65. ISBN 0-87341-271-0.
737.4 CJ1755

Standard catalog of world coins: eighteenth century, 1701–1800. 2d ed. Chester L. Krause and Clifford Mishler. 1304p. Krause, 1997. $145. ISBN 0-87341-260-5; paper $65. ISBN 0-87341-526-4.
737.4 CJ1751

Standard directory of world coins: nineteenth century, 1801–1900. 2d ed. Clifford Mishler, Colin Bruce, and Chester L. Krause. 1032p. Krause, 1998. $45. ISBN 0-87341-652-X.
737.4 CJ1751

The purpose of these catalogs is to help collectors identify coins and to list the market prices for coins in various conditions. They generally provide a history of each coin, date of minting, size, and identification marks. There is also a variety of supplementary data in each book, depending on the particular specialty that is being covered.

1486 Walter Breen's complete encyclopedia of U.S. and colonial coins. Walter Breen. 754p. Doubleday, 1988. Paper $100. ISBN 0-385-14207-2.
737.4 CJ1830

A comprehensive history describing the more than 8,000 coins that have been used in the United States. An essential purchase.

Stamps

1487 Linn's world stamp almanac: a handbook for stamp collectors. 5th ed. Linn's Stamp News staff, eds. 756p. Amos Pr., 1989. $19.95. ISSN 0146-6887.
769.56 HE6194

Essential facts on philately intended to aid both research and hobby activities. Historical and directory information, biographical and bibliographical material, stamp production, law, and postal administration are some of the features of this useful tool.

1488 The Micarelli identification guide to U.S. stamps: regular issues, 1847–1934. Charles Micarelli. 156p. Scott, 1991. $34.95. ISBN 0-89487-177-3.
769.56973 HE6185.U6

A manual and identification guide to regular issues from 1847 to 1934. Clear illustrations and well-designed tables.

1489 The official 1998 blackbook price guide of U.S. postage stamps. 20th ed. Marc Hudgeons. 220p. House of Collectibles, 1997. Paper $7.99. ISBN 0-67660-064-6.
383 HE6185

Easy-to-use basic guidebook with valuations of more than 20,000 stamps. How to buy, sell, and care for stamps. Many color photographs.

1490 Scott's specialized catalogue of United States stamps. Scott, 1867– . Annual. $35. ISSN 0161-5084.

Scott's standard postage stamp catalogue. 6v. Scott, 1923– .

Annual. $35/v.
769.56 HE6226

Scott provides the most comprehensive catalog of stamps printed in the United States. Gives minute details, such as date of issue, design, denomination, color, perforation, and watermark on all stamps issued. Most of the stamps are given a valuation. Volume 1 covers United States and affiliated territories, United Nations, Canada, and British America; volumes 2 through 6 cover the rest of the world. Illustrated.

1491 Stamp collecting: an illustrated guide and handbook for adult collectors. Barry Krause. 152p. Betterway Books, 1989. $9.95. ISBN 1-55870-127-3.
769.56 HE6215

Begins with basics: starting a collection; storing, handling, and preserving; buying and selling collectibles; and popular collecting areas. Lists relevant books, periodicals, societies, museums, and libraries.

1492 U.S. first day cover catalogue and checklist. Michael A. Mellone. 300p. Scott, 1984– . Annual. $7.95. ISSN 0747-5381.
769.565 HE6184

First day covers are "commemorative covers with stamps, cancellations, and cachets from the first day that a stamp is issued." Explains the process of producing and the reasons for collecting first day covers. Includes prices. The authoritative guide.

18

Games and Sports

CAROLE DYAL

As our leisure time increases, we frequently turn to games and sports for recreation and entertainment. The world of reference publishing provides many excellent sources that aid our analytical study of these areas and add to our personal enrichment.

Guides

1493 Can you name that team: a guide to professional baseball, football, soccer, hockey, and basketball teams and leagues. David B. Biesel. 240p. Scarecrow, 1991. $37.50. ISBN 0-8108-2458-2.
796 GV583

An essential work for those interested in tracking the ups and downs, the transitions and metamorphoses, and the multiple peregrinations of professional sports teams and their names. In all, more than 950 teams playing in thirty-eight professional leagues are followed. Section 1 lists teams by geographical affiliation (city, state, or region) and presents a brief history of how each team received its name. Section 2 provides a fascinating genealogy for each team, indicating where each team name came from and what it subsequently became; for example, the Brooklyn Dodgers were originally the Brooklyn Bridegrooms (1890–98), then the Brooklyn Superbas (1899–1910), the Brooklyn Infants (1911–13), the Brooklyn Robins (1914–31), the Brooklyn Dodgers (1932–57), and became the Los Angeles Dodgers in 1958. Section 3 serves as a master index to the other two sections.

Indexes

1494 Index to The Sporting News, 1975–1990. Ned Kehde, ed. 448p. J. G. Burke, 1992. $40. ISBN 0-934272-28-2; paper $24.95. ISBN 0-934272-18-X. Serial: ISSN 1041-2859.
796 GV583

Indexes feature stories and obituaries that have appeared in the premier sporting news source from 1975 through 1990.

Encyclopedias

History

1495 The encyclopedia of North American sports history. Ralph Hickok. 528p. Facts on File, 1992. $55. ISBN 0-8160-2096-5.
796 GV1202

Fast, easy access to a wide variety of information about the history of North American sports. Outlines the general history of sports, focusing on the evolution of sports and sports government. Entries: (1) Sports—modern organized competitive sport; summary of the history of sports before they began in North America. (2) General history of broad subjects relating to sports (e.g., "Drugs in Sports," "Player Drafts"). (3) Biography of sports figures of genuine historic importance. (4) Sporting events, with emphasis on their history. (5) Major awards. (6) Cities—lists each North American city that has ever had a sports team. (7) Stadiums, fields, and arenas. (8) Sports organizations.

1496 Encyclopedia of world sport: from ancient times to the present. David Levinson and Karen Christenson, eds. 3v. ABC-Clio, 1996. $225. ISBN 0-87436-819-7.
796 GV567

A comprehensive encyclopedia, with more than 250 alphabetical entries ranging from 500 to 8,000 words. Everything from bobsledding and boomerang throwing to Tai Chi and tug-of-war. Citations for further reading at the end of each entry. Large print, clear layout, useful graphics, and extensive bibliography. Includes relevant passages from literary works, which give life to the sport being discussed.

1497 Professional sports team histories. Michael L. LaBlanc, ed. 4v. Gale, 1994. $149. v.1, NBA, $49. ISBN 0-8103-8859-X; v.2, Major league baseball, $49. ISBN 0-8103-8860-X; v.3, NFL, $49. ISBN 0-8103-8861-8; v.4, NHL, $49. ISBN 0-8103-8862-6.
796.09 GV861

Each volume presents a brief history of the professional sport dealt with, followed by individual team histories arranged alphabetically within leagues and divisions. Highlights notable persons, events, and seasons.

1498 Women's sports encyclopedia. Robert Markel, Susan Waggonere, and Marcella Smith, eds. 340p. Henry Holt, 1997. $30. ISBN 0-8050-4494-9.
796 GV709

A sourcebook outlining women's participation in sports, from traditional team events such as basketball and soccer to swimming, golf, billiards, yachting, combat sports, luge, sled-dog racing, and many more. Provides biographies, records, and sports histories.

Rules

1499 Rules of the game: the complete illustrated encyclopedia of all the major sports of the world. Diagram Group. 320p. St. Martin's, 1995. Paper $15.95. ISBN 0-312-11940-2.
796 GV861

Written in clear, concise language, enhanced by some 2,000 pictorial displays. More than 150 sports are covered. Includes rules and laws published by governing sports bodies for each sport, brief history, description of the playing area and equipment, and a synopsis of players and officials for each sport. Includes section on misconduct and the consequences of misconduct. Index by sport and general index.

1500 Sports rules encyclopedia. 2d ed. Jess R. White, ed. 732p. Leisure Pr., 1990. $42. ISBN 0-88011-363-4.
796 GV731

A general reference to the rules of fifty-one sports. Arranged alphabetically by sport. Includes rules for the sport, description of the governing body of each sport, and names and addresses of selected magazines that cover the sport. The articles vary in length and complexity depending on how rules are published by each organization. Appendix A covers organizations concerned with sports for the handicapped; appendix B is arranged alphabetically by sport. Includes additional rules and sources (organizations or sports not in the main encyclopedia).

Sports Science

1501 Encyclopedia of sports science. John Zumerchick, ed. 2v. Macmillan, 1997. $220. ISBN 0-02-897506-5.
613.7 GV558

Part 1 describes the physics and mechanics of more than thirty different sports in terms all can understand. Entries are arranged in alphabetical order by sport, focusing on the unique elements of each (e.g., bow dynamics and arrow dynamics for archery; hull design and air forces for sailing; buoyancy and flotation and propulsion in water for swimming). Part 2 is devoted entirely to the human body and how it performs, reacts, and gets conditioned, injured, and healed. Entries are arranged alphabetically under seventeen broad headings and describe everything from the effects of aging on performance to the physiology of vision. This is an excellent addition to the sports reference collection.

Directories

1502 **Sports fan's connection: an all-sports-in-one directory.** 584p. Gale, 1992. $62. ISBN 0-8103-7954-6.
796 GV583

Directory to more than 4,000 informational sources for professional, collegiate, and Olympic sports. Entries on specific teams, college and university programs, U.S. and international organizations, associations, fan clubs, and halls of fame. Also includes radio and TV stations, sports videos, books, magazines, newsletters, and so forth. Covers about fifty sports. Entries are listed alphabetically by sport and include master name and keyword indexes.

1503 **Sports Halls of Fame: a directory of over 100 sports museums in the United States.** Doug Gelbert. 176p. McFarland, 1992. $38.50. ISBN 0-89950-660-7.
796 GV583

A very useful directory organized in three sections: national sports museums, museums of individual sports and sports heroes, and regional (local attraction) sports museums. Each entry provides a history of the sport in question, a description of the museum, location, telephone number, hours of operation, admission charges, and major highlights. Includes black-and-white photographs and indexing by name, city, and subject.

Handbooks and Almanacs

1504 **The [yr.] ESPN Information Please sports almanac.** John Hassan. 832p. Warner, 1998– . Annual. Paper $11.95. ISSN 1046-4980.
796 GV741

Sports Illustrated 1998 sports almanac. Sports Illustrated editors. 848p. Little, Brown, 1992– . Annual. Paper $13.95. ISSN 1056-7887.
796.05 GV741

Good general references for all sports, year-by-year. Sport-by-sport key statistics, top stories and anecdotes, final standings, and awards. Some historical treatment, but mostly current information.

1505 **The Guinness book of sports records, 1997–98.** Mark Young, ed. 960p. Guinness Media, 1997. $24.95. ISBN 0-9652383-2-6.
796 GV741

Comprehensive ready reference source, useful in all libraries that serve sports enthusiasts. Based on information gathered from associations, leagues, sports editors, and experts in specific sports, it provides a balanced coverage of male and female athletics. Photographs, illustrations, and statistics are featured for individual sports and games as well as for Olympic, world, national, and collegiate championships and tournaments.

1506 **Professional sports statistics: a North American team-by-team and major nonteam events, year-by-year reference, 1896 through 1996.** K. Michael Caschnitz. 1338p. McFarland, 1997. $85. ISBN 0-7864-0299-7.
796.04 GV581

Many reference sources offer statistics based upon individual achievement; here is a compendium of statistics devoted primarily to team performance. The work is divided into two sections: (1) a chronological arrangement describing highlights of major team sports, with some attention devoted to significant nonteam sports (e.g., golf, boxing, and horse racing); and (2) a listing of individual team statistics arranged alphabetically by team. A welcome addition to the collection.

1507 **Sports and recreation for the disabled: a resource handbook.** 2d ed. Jeffrey Jones. 550p. Cooper, 1994. Paper $30. ISBN 1-884125-04-2.
796 GV709.3

More than fifty major sports are covered, from all-terrain vehicles to wilderness experiences. Entries give rule modifications, organizations sponsoring competitive events, rationale for disabled competition, adaptive equipment, supplies, references, and bibliography. Appendixes provide additional general information on events and suppliers.

Atlases

1508 **Atlas of American sport.** Robert Singer et al., eds. 984p. Macmillan, 1992. $75. ISBN 0-02-897195-7.
796 G1201

Displays the phenomena of sport in cartographic images. Divided into five sections containing 251 color maps. Shows the location of teams, degree of participation, championship success, and other graphical data for the most common American sports.

1509 **USA Today sports atlas: where to find every sport in America.** Will Balliett, ed. 224p. H. M. Gousha, 1993. Paper $12.95. ISBN 0-13-948258-X.
796 G1201

Pinpoints venues for professional and collegiate sports on city and state road maps.

Biographical Sources

1510 **Biographical dictionary of American sports: baseball.** David L. Porter, ed. 730p. Greenwood, 1987. $75. ISBN 0-313-23771-9.
796.356 GV865

Biographical dictionary of American sports: basketball and other indoor sports. David L. Porter, ed. 826p. Greeenwood, 1989. $75. ISBN 0-313-26261-6.
796.0973 GV697

Biographical dictionary of American sports: football. David L. Porter, ed. 783p. Greenwood, 1987. $75. ISBN 0-313-25771-X.
796.332 GV939

Biographical dictionary of American sports: outdoor sports. David L. Porter, ed. 748p. Greenwood, 1988. $75. ISBN 0-313-26260-8.
796.092 GV697.A1

Biographical dictionary of American sports: 1989–1992 supplement for baseball, football, basketball, and other sports. David L. Porter, ed. 784p. Greenwood, 1992. $79.95. ISBN 0-313-26706-5.
796.092 GV697

Biographical dictionary of American sports: 1992–1994 supplement for baseball, football, basketball, and other sports. David L. Porter, ed. 784p. Greenwood, 1995. $89.50. ISBN 0-313-28431-8.
796.092 GV697

A cumulative index to The biographical dictionary of American sports. David L. Porter, ed. 352p. Greenwood, 1993. $47.95. ISBN 0-313-28435-0.
796.092 GV697.A1

Sports fans, librarians, educators, sports historians, and writers will welcome these biographical dictionaries covering America's most popular team sports. One- and two-page alphabetically arranged biographies not only illustrate the subjects' important athletic and professional achievements, but also discuss aspects of their personal lives. Primary focus is on individuals who are retired or deceased, with approximately 5 percent of the entries dedicated to active sports figures. Features notable professional and college athletes, coaches, executives, managers, umpires, writers, sports announcers, and promoters. All entries include concise bibliographies for additional sources of information. Several appendixes and indexes in each volume. A useful acquisition for scholars and browsers.

1511 **Sports stars, series 1.** Michael A. Pare. 622p. 2v. Gale, 1994. $49.95/set. ISBN 0-8103-9859-1.

Sports stars, series 2. Michael A. Pare. 574p. 2v. Gale, 1996. $49.95/set. ISBN 0-7876-0867-X.

Sports stars, series 3. Michael A. Pare. 342p. Gale, 1997. $39. ISBN 0-7876-1749-0.

Sports stars, series 4. Michael A. Pare. 350p. Gale, 1998. $39.

ISBN 0-7876-2784-4.
796.092 GV697.A1

The lives and careers of contemporary sports stars. Includes information on the early life of each athlete and his or her ambitions, training, setbacks, success, and future outlook. Highlights major accomplishments. Provides an address at which the athlete may be contacted and a brief bibliography.

1512 A who's who of sports champions: their stories and records. Ralph Hickok. 928p. Houghton, 1995. $29.95. ISBN 0-395-68195-2; paper $19.95. ISBN 0-395-73312-X.
796.092 GV697.A1

Provides biographical information on 2,200 influential American and Canadian athletes engaged in fifty different sports. A superb one-volume source.

Video Guides

1513 Sport on film and video: the North American Society for Sport History guide. Daryl Alder, ed. 204p. Scarecrow, 1993. $32.50. ISBN 0-8108-2739-5.
796.029 GV576

Describes more than 1,800 productions dealing with sport history, chronology, biography, psychology, and sociology. Entries are arranged alphabetically and indicate subject matter, audience level, release date, length, format, color or black and white, distributor, and historical period. Omits feature films. Well indexed.

1514 The sports video resource guide. Bob Carroll. 245p. Simon & Schuster, 1992. $12. ISBN 0-671-73446-6.
384.55 GV742.34

A comprehensive guide to popular sports videos. Includes list price and distributor.

Backpacking

1515 Backpacker's handbook. Hugh McManners. 160p. Macmillan, 1995. $19.95. ISBN 1-56458-852-1.
796.5 GV199.6

A comprehensive how-to for backpackers addressing the hundreds of questions about wilderness living. Step-by-step color illustrations throughout. Divided into five sections: getting started, equipment and techniques, moving on the trail, camping in the wild, and dealing with emergencies. A beautiful book.

Baseball

1516 The ballplayers: baseball's ultimate biographical reference. Mike Shatzkin, ed. 1230p. Arbor House/Morrow, 1990. $39.95. ISBN 0-87795-984-6.
796.357 GV865.A1

Biographical sketches and career information on more than 5,000 major-league players and managers from the beginning of baseball through the 1980s. Entries include player position, career stats, awards, nicknames, and anecdotes. Additional entries on umpires, sports writers, fans, scouts, ballparks, broadcasters, and others associated with the sport.

1517 Baseball: a comprehensive bibliography. Myron J. Smith, comp. 934p. McFarland, 1986. $110. ISBN 0-89550-222-9.

Baseball: a comprehensive bibliography. Supplement 1 (1985–May 1992). Myron J. Smith. 437p. McFarland, 1993. $68.50. ISBN 0-89950-799-9.
016.796357 Z7514.B3

Scholarly bibliographies, comprehensive and authoritative. Broad in scope, including baseball history, baseball in art and literature, equipment, rules, and commerce. Biographical entries predominate.

1518 The [yr.] baseball almanac. 672p. Publications International, 1992– . Annual. Paper $6.99.
796.357 GV865.A1

Alphabetic listing and profiles of current players. Rookie prospects. Team overviews by league. Hall of Fame members. All-time awards and highlights. Team and individual stats and annual awards.

1519 Baseball America's [yr.] directory. Baseball America staff. 256p. Baseball America, 1990– . Annual. $12.95.
796.357 GV865

Major- and minor-league names, addresses, schedules, ticket information, and phone and fax numbers. Includes independent leagues, foreign leagues (e.g., Mexico, Japan), winter baseball, college baseball, and amateur leagues (including high school and youth leagues).

1520 The baseball encyclopedia: the complete and definitive record of major league baseball. 10th ed. 2857p. Macmillan, 1996. $59.95. ISBN 0-02-860815-1.
■ cd
795.357 GV877

A complete statistical record, from 1876. Players, pitchers, managers, lifetime team rosters, all-star games, play-offs, World Series, special records and awards, trades, history (including the Negro leagues), rules, and sources of information are covered. Exhaustive in detail, with good cross-references.

1521 Baseball guide [yr.]: the almanac of the [yr.] season. Sporting News staff. 535p. Sporting News, 1940– . Annual. Paper $15.95. ISSN 0078-3838.
796.357 GV877

Standard annual that reviews the previous "baseball year": pitching and batting statistics; individual team statistics; league championships, World Series, and all-star game; major- and minor-league transactions and draft; and a necrology. There is a schedule for the current year and a useful index.

1522 The biographical encyclopedia of the Negro baseball leagues. James Riley. 1280p. Carroll & Graf, 1994. $39.50. ISBN 0-7876-0065-3.
796.357 GV865.A1

Biographical and statistical information on the careers of more than 4,000 Negro baseball league players compiled by a recognized authority. Alphabetical arrangement. Entries vary from one line to several pages. Includes team histories and a massive bibliography.

1523 Cultural encyclopedia of baseball. Jonathan Fraser Light. 896p. McFarland, 1997. $75. ISBN 0-7864-0311-X.
796.357 GV862.3

Focuses on the cultural, as opposed to the statistical, aspects of baseball. More than seven years in the making. Includes entries on a broad range of topics from advertising, superstitions, and tripleheaders to broadcasters, commissioners, and owners. At once anecdotal and informative. Well illustrated; complements nicely the more traditional baseball reference sources.

1524 Encyclopedia of major league baseball team histories: American League. Peter C. Bjarkman, ed. 624p. Meckler, 1991. $65. ISBN 0-88736-373-3.

Encyclopedia of major league baseball team histories: National League. Peter C. Bjarkman, ed. 600p. Meckler, 1990. $65. ISBN 0-88736-374-1.
796.357 GV875

Team histories from their founding through 1985. Includes annotated bibliography for each team, year-by-year standings, and season summaries. All-time career and single-season records for each team. Alphabetized by city, then team.

1525 Encyclopedia of major league baseball teams. Donald Dewey and Nicholas Acocello. 640p. HarperCollins, 1993. $35. ISBN 0-06-270049-9.
796.357 GV875.A1

Provides histories of the 121 major-league baseball teams. Entries are arranged alphabetically by city and vary from a single page in length to more than twenty-five pages. Includes interesting anecdotes as well as straight narrative and stats. Provides a listing of the team's standing each year, its win-lose record, and manager.

1526 The Negro leagues book. Dick Clark. 382p. Society for American Baseball Research, 1994. $49.95. ISBN 0-910137-59-5; paper $24.95. ISBN 0-910137-55-2.
796.357 GV863.A1

Photos, histories, rosters, player records. Lists teams and their cities, and includes biographies of the great ones. Comprehensive bibliography.

1527 Official baseball register [yr.]: baseball bios from A to Z. Sporting News staff. 600p. Sporting News, 1940– . Annual. Paper $14.95. ISSN 0162-542X.
796.357 GV877

Baseball biographies, including pronunciations of names. Year-by-year team and individual statistics, starting with professional records. Major-league players with at least one major-league game. Listing of signed players.

1528 Official rules of major league baseball [yr.]. Major League Baseball staff. 201p. Triumph Books, 1995. Annual. Paper $8.95. ISBN 1-57243-220-9.
796.357 GV877

Playing rules and interpretations by the Official Playing Rules Committee. Provides insight into the committee's intent when drafting rules. Gives specific penalties and approved rulings for umpires for specific game situations. Now, you make the call.

1529 The rules of baseball. David Nemic. 272p. Lyons & Burford, 1994. $24.95. ISBN 1-55821-279-5; paper $16.95. ISBN 1-55821-280-9.
796.357 GV877

An annotated version of the official rules by a respected baseball historian. Puts the rules into plain English and provides clear examples and rationale. Extremely helpful.

1530 Total baseball: the official encyclopedia of major league baseball. 4th ed. John Thorn and Pete Palmer, eds. 2650p. Viking Penguin, 1995. $59.95. ISBN 0-670-86099-9.
796.357 GV863.A1

Individual player and team statistics. History of the game, team histories, diagrams of ballparks. Year-by-year registers of players, pitches, situations. All-time leaders, managers, coaches. Negro baseball rosters. Rules and rule changes over the years. Game scores, from 1982 to 1994, day by day. Baseball lore. Packed with information. Even explains how to calculate averages. Glossary.

Basketball

1531 Basketball almanac, 1997–98. Consumer Guide editors. 608p. NAL-Dutton, 1997. Paper $6.99. ISBN 0-451-19245-1.
796.323 GV885.1

Arranged alphabetically by NBA team. Includes veterans, the year's draft, rookies (listed alphabetically), team overviews, awards, year-by-year results, Hall of Famers, top college stars (alphabetical listing), top college teams, and college review.

1532 Basketball biographies: 434 U.S. players, coaches, and contributors to the game, 1891–1990. Martin Taragno. 336p. McFarland, 1991. Lib. bindg. $49.95. ISBN 0-89950-625-9.
796.323 GV884.A1

Brief biographies in a straightforward alphabetical listing. Includes statistics and statements on the player's contribution to the sport.

1533 Basketball resource guide. 2d ed. Jerry V. Krause and Stephen J. Brennan. 248p. Human Kinetics, 1990. Paper $25. ISBN 0-88011-369-3.
016.796323 Z7514.B34

Lists books, periodicals, theses, dissertations, visuals, and pamphlets concerned with the sport of basketball. Index.

1534 Encyclopedia of college basketball. Michael Douchant. 615p. Gale, 1994. $42.95. ISBN 0-8103-9640-8.
796.323 GV885.7

Early years and history of college basketball, beginnings of NCAA tournament. Year-by-year tournament statistics (through 1995), including coaches, women's games, and NIT. New rules listed for each season. Best players register, best coach directory (both acting and former). Conference directory, school directory (nicknames, addresses, colors, and basketball history). NCAA records, odd and interesting statistics. Thirty-three-page index.

1535 The encyclopedia of pro basketball team histories. Peter C. Bjarkman. 420p. Carroll & Graf, 1994. $24. ISBN 0-7867-0126-9.
796.323 GV885.515.N37

Presents team histories in a lively and rich narrative. Includes bibliography for each team, retired numbers, and year-by-year summary of performance, as well as individual career, season, and game records.

1536 The official NBA basketball encyclopedia. 2d ed. Alex Sachane, ed. 842p. Random House, 1994. $39.95. ISBN 0-679-43293-0.
796.323 GV885.7

Early history of basketball; time line 1891–1994. Tree of teams, 1946–94. History of the NBA and of the ABA (1967–76). Season-by-season statistics, many black-and-white photographs. Olympic competitions. NBA all-star games, year-by-year, player-by-player. Lists coaches and referees, official rules, Hall of Famers, NBA draft and lottery (by year, by team), all-time records. Statistics of players arranged alphabetically comprise more than half of the book.

1537 Official NBA rules: 1998–99 edition. Craig Carter, ed. 60p. Sporting News, 1998. $6.95. ISBN 0-89204-602-3.
796.323 GV855.55

The official rule book used by NBA referees. Includes a detailed index and diagrams of referee signals.

1538 Official rules of basketball (NCAA). NCAA staff. 184p. Triumph Books, 1997. Paper $9.95. ISBN 1-57243-222-5.
796.323 GV885.A1

Official rules, including interpretations, referee's official signals, and detailed court diagrams. New rules for the year are highlighted. Both men's and women's rules. Index by key word.

1539 The Sporting News official NBA guide, 1997–98: the NBA from 1946 to today. 648p. Sporting News, 1997. Paper $15.95. ISBN 0-89204-585-X.
796.32 GV885

Player and team statistics and schedules. Year-by-year review of the past and view of current activities. Includes rules. Indexed.

1540 The Sporting News official NBA register, 1997–98: the book used by the men in stripes. 400p. Sporting News, 1997. Paper $15.95. ISBN 0-89204-587-6.
796.32 GV885

Alphabetical listing of all players on team rosters for the designated year, listing their total career statistics, including college records. Reports points, shooting percentages, rebounding, blocks, steals, assists, and turnovers. Sections on rookies and coaches.

Bicycling

1541 Bicycling Magazine's complete guide to bicycle maintenance and repair. Rev. ed. Bicycling Magazine editors and Mountain Bike editors. 352p. Rodale, 1994. $24.95. ISBN 0-87596-218-1; paper $16.95. ISBN 0-87596-207-6.
629.28 TL430

Includes information on road bikes and mountain bikes. Recommended maintenance. Step-by-step repair, illustrated with black-and-white drawings. Lists tools needed. Extensive glossary. Good index (glossary helps).

1542 Richards' ultimate bicycle repair manual. Richard Ballantine and Richard Grant. Dorling Kindersley, 1994. Paper $8.95. ISBN 1-56458-484-4.
629.28 TL430

Includes illustrations of tools and step-by-step photographs. Not as thorough as *Bicycling Magazine's complete guide,* but the superior illustrations clarify steps better for the more visual minded. Service charts, emergency repairs, and troubleshooting chart. Brief glossary; adequate index.

Billiards and Pool

1543 Byrne's new standard book of pool and billiards. New ed. Robert Byrne. 416p. Harcourt Brace, 1998. $35. ISBN 0-15-100325-4; paper $20. ISBN 0-15-600554-9.
794.7 GV891

From basic to advanced play. Includes pool, pocket billiards, and billiards. Sections on technique, such as how to play overhead shots. Close-up photographs of all shots. Many line drawings. Selected master shots illustrated. Thorough table of contents (in lieu of index). Appendix 1: where to go for more information about pool. Appendix 2: where to go for more information about billiards.

1544 The illustrated encyclopedia of billiards. Michael L. Shamos. 320p. Lyons, 1993. $35. ISBN 1-55821-219-1.
794.7 GV891

Alphabetically arranged entries from a single line to several pages. This encyclopedia of billiards, pool, and snooker is written by a well-known devotee for those afficionados who truly love the game. Covers 2,500 terms, abbreviations, and organizations. More than 200 illustrations.

1545 Pocket billiard guidebook for pool players, tournament directors, and spectators. James R. Lawson, ed. 192p. Lawco, 1994. Paper $39.95. ISBN 0-945071-55-8.
794.7 GV891

A guidebook providing information on everything from etiquette to hustling: rules; game variants; equipment; cues; associations; books, videos, and magazines; forms of tournament play; glossary; and index.

Card Games

1546 Ainslie's complete Hoyle. Tom Ainslie. 544p. Simon & Schuster, 1979. Paper $15. ISBN 0-671-24779-4.
795 GV1243

Includes all indoor games played today, with suggestions for good play, illustrative hands, and all official laws to date, revised and enlarged with complete laws of contract bridge and canasta.

Divided into four sections: card games, board and table games, gambling casino games, and "Games for club car and tavern."

1547 A dictionary of card games. David Parlatt. 400p. Oxford Univ. Pr., 1992. Paper $13.95. ISBN 0-19-869173-4.
795.4 GV1243

A treasury of Western card games arranged in alphabetical order. Includes an appendix of terms and a bibliography.

1548 Goren's new bridge complete. Charles H. Goren. 720p. Doubleday, 1985. $29.95. ISBN 0-385-23324-8.
795.41 GV1282.3

Describes innovations, changes, and modern developments in clear and simple language for the neophyte or the advanced player. Appended: laws of contract bridge, brief refresher on how bridge is played, glossary, and index.

1549 New complete Hoyle: the authoritative guide to the official rules of all popular games of skill. Rev. Alfred H. Morehead. 720p. Doubleday, 1991. $25.95. ISBN 0-385-24962-4.
794 GV1243

In addition to rules, includes the brief history and origin of each game. Includes historical or obsolete games mentioned in literature. Extensive glossary.

Chess

1550 Chess: an annotated bibliography of works published in the English language, 1850–1968. Douglas A. Betts. 659p. Hall, 1974. $35. ISBN 0-8161-1094-8.

Chess: an annotated bibliography, 1969–1988. A. S. Lusis. 350p. Cassell, 1991. $100. ISBN 0-7201-2079-9.
016.7941 Z5541

Together these works describe the bibliographic world (in English) of chess more completely than any other source. Entries include title, author, imprint, physical description, and annotation. Indexes by name, title, subject, and series.

1551 The Oxford companion to chess. 2d ed. David Hooper and Kenneth Whyld. 480p. Oxford Univ. Pr., 1992. $45. ISBN 0-19-866164-9; paper $22.50. ISBN 0-19-280049-3.
794.1 GV1445

Alphabetical arrangement includes terminology, biographies, openings, games, and compositions. Embraces all branches of chess and includes historical, sociological, and technical information. Recommends books for further reading; includes an appendix illustrating 650 opening chess moves (discussed in the text) and a glossary of terms in six foreign languages. Exceptionally thorough coverage for both the beginner and the serious player.

Exercise

1552 The Weight Watchers complete exercise book. Judith Zimmer. 144p. Macmillan, 1995. Paper $14. ISBN 0-02-860081-9.
613.7 RA781.6

Designed to help individuals create their own lifetime fitness programs. Offers five complete home workouts that focus on calorie burning, toning, promoting flexibility, reducing stress, aerobic fitness, and overall fitness. Information on walking, swimming, cycling, and other forms of popular exercise. More than 150 illustrations. Spiral-bound.

Fishing

1553 The Dorling Kindersley encyclopedia of fishing. 288p. Dorling Kindersley, 1994. $39.95. ISBN 1-56458-492-5.
799.1 SH411

The six chapters cover all the basics: tackle, bait, flies, fish species, techniques, and fishing venues. There are lengthy descriptions of everything from appropriate clothing to endangered species. A beautifully illustrated volume, almost a work of art. Describes essential items of tackle, basics of fly tying with illustrations, techniques and bait to catch each type of fish. Pictures of 250 species of fish, both fresh and saltwater, illustrated in full color with details of distribution, habitat, food size. Glossary and index.

1554 The illustrated encyclopedia of fly-fishing: a complete A-Z of terminology, tackle, and techniques. Silvio Calabi. 336p. Henry Holt, 1995. Paper $19.95. ISBN 0-8050-3809-4.
799.12 SH456

More than 500 entries describing all things connected with fly-fishing, including history, equipment, species, techniques, terminology, biographies, and associations. Entries may cover several pages; most are about 300 words. Environmental concerns presented.

Football

1555 The college football bibliography. Myron J. Smith Jr., comp. 968p. Greenwood, 1993. $125. ISBN 0-313-29026-1.
016.796332 GV950

Describes reference works, general works, works about conferences, individual teams, rivalries and bowl games, and biographies. A listing of more than 12,000 books, annuals, yearbooks, collections, and periodical articles covering 300 college teams from 1869 to the 1990s. Author and subject indexes.

1556 Football encyclopedia: the complete history of professional football from 1892 to the present. 2d ed. David S. Neft et al. 1088p. St. Martin's, 1994. $49.95. ISBN 0-312-11435-4.
796.332 GV954

Provides both a narrative history and statistical tables.

1557 NCAA football: the official [yr.] college football records book. NCAA staff. National Collegiate Athletic Association, 1994– . Annual. Paper $16.95. ISSN 0735-5475.
796.33 GN955

The official account from the National Collegiate Athletic Association.

1558 Official [yr.] National Football League record and fact book. NFL staff, comp. 392p. Workman, 1984– . Annual. Paper $15.95. ISSN 0883-4199.
796.332 GV955

Digest of rules and official signals. Includes team-by-team records, team statistics, and a schedule and calendar. Statistical leaders. Individual statistics by position category. Draft choices. Super Bowl records.

1559 Official rules of the NFL. NFL staff. Triumph Books, 1996. Paper $8.95. ISBN 1-57243-142-3.
796.332 GV955

The complete National Football League rules of play, from markings on the field to number of captains allowed for each squad. Index.

1560 Professional football: the official pro football Hall of Fame bibliography. Myron J. Smith Jr. 432p. Greenwood, 1993. $85. ISBN 0-313-28928-X.
796.332 Z7514.F7

A comprehensive bibliography of professional football writing. Contains more than 15,000 entries covering books, documents, dissertations and theses, yearbooks, and periodical articles arranged in four broad categories: reference works, general works, professional leagues, and biography. Author and subject indexing.

1561 Sports encyclopedia: pro football: the modern era, 1973–1997. 16th ed. David S. Neft, Richard M. Cohen, and Robert Korch. 628p. St. Martin's, 1998. $19.99. ISBN 0-312-18761-0.
796.332 GV955

Contains complete rosters and statistics for every player and every year, including the January 1998 Super Bowl.

Gambling

1562 Scarne's new complete guide to gambling. Rev. ed. John Scarne. 871p. Simon & Schuster, 1986. Paper $18. ISBN 0-671-63063-6.
795 GV1301

Expert advice on betting, state lotteries, contract bridge, backgammon, roulette, dice games, gin rummy, carnival games, sweepstakes, raffles, and much more.

Golf

1563 The American golfer's guide: over 500 of the best American golf courses open to the public. Hubert Padroli and Mary Tiegreen, eds. 304p. Turner, 1996. Paper $21.95. ISBN 1-57036-301-3.
796.352 GV981

Describes more than 500 public access courses in the United States, Bermuda, and the Caribbean. Includes practical information such as fees, phone numbers, accommodations, reservation policies, course style, yardage, and par. Provides details of course architecture, often with illustrations. A source for both the traveler and the dreamer.

1564 **Encyclopedia of golf techniques: the complete step-by-step guide to mastering the game of golf.** Paul Foston, ed. 431p. Courage Books, 1994. $29.95. ISBN 1-56138-445-3. 796.352 GV965

A real encyclopedia of technique. Color photographs from all angles. Step-by-step directions. Includes advice and tips for all surfaces and conditions. Specific examples from famous courses.

1565 **The Golf Digest almanac.** 512p. Random House, 1984– . Annual. $6.95. ISSN 0742-4485. 796.352 GV981

No index, but a detailed table of contents leads the user to tournament schedules; college, junior, and international golf; list of winners; men, women, and senior amateurs and professionals; and state and club champions. Short biographies of professionals; some information on selected courses and equipment is given. Complete rules conclude the book.

1566 **Golf Digest's best places to play.** 3d ed. Fodor's Travel, 1997. $19.50. ISBN 0-679-03025-5. 796.352 GV981

Listed alphabetically by state, then by name of course. Star rating includes comments by some of 10,000 subscribers. Courses judged by the quality of the experience and the relation of the course to others in the area. Geographical directory by town or city. Best seventy-five courses listed. Index, alphabetic by course.

1567 **Golf Magazine's encyclopedia of golf: the complete reference.** 2d ed. Golf Magazine editors. 517p. HarperCollins, 1993. $40. ISBN 0-06-270019-7. 796.352 GV965

History, rules, equipment, fundamentals, championship courses, worldwide tournaments, and personalities are described. Statistics, records, facts, and fancies are included. Photographs and drawings illustrate the text. Information is easily accessible from either the detailed table of contents or the index. Glossary.

1568 **Official rules of golf.** Rev. ed. USGA staff and Royal and Ancient Golf Club of St. Andrews. 208p. Triumph Books, 1996. Paper $8.95. ISBN 1-57243-140-7. 796.353 GV971

Two ruling bodies of golf, the U.S. Golf Association and the Royal and Ancient Golf Club of St. Andrews, jointly write the rules. Changes since the last edition are listed. Also listed are golf etiquette, definitions, and rules of play. The index points to where a rule will be found. Appendixes cover local rules, design of clubs, the ball, and rules for amateur status.

1569 **The PGA manual of golf: the professional way to play better golf.** PGA staff and Gary Wiren. 480p. Macmillan, 1997. Paper $19.95. ISBN 0-02-861682-0. 796.352 GV965

The most popular instruction book. Endorsed by the PGA. Well illustrated.

Hiking

1570 **A hiker's companion: 12,000 miles of trail-tested wisdom.** Cindy Ross and Todd Gladfetter. 224p. Mountaineers, 1993. Paper $12.95. ISBN 0-89886-353-8. 796.5 GV199.4

Excellent tips and practical information on backpacks, sleeping bags, tents, appropriate dress, cooking, itinerary planning, sanitation, first aid, and much more.

Hockey

1571 **The complete encyclopedia of hockey.** 4th ed. Zander Hollander, ed. 604p. Visible Ink Pr., 1992. Paper $22.95. ISBN 0-8103-8869-3. 796.962 GV847.8

Covers the World Hockey Association, collegiate, and Olympic hockey as well as the National Hockey League. Chronological presentation of players, Stanley Cup, officials, Hall of Fame, records, coaches. Historical information about the National Hockey League and team records. Career statistics, including play-off statistics, are given for 4,200 players. Glossary, official signals, rules. Thorough index.

1572 **The National Hockey League official guide and record book, 1997–98.** NHL staff. 448p. Triumph Books,

1984– . Annual. Paper $18.95. ISBN 1-57243-226-8.
796.96 GV847.8

An annual publication. Provides information on clubs, statistics, individual and team records, the Stanley Cup, and team rosters.

1573 Official rules of the National Hockey League. Rev. ed. NHL staff, ed. 160p. Triumph Books, 1996. Paper $8.95. ISBN 1-57243-141-5.
796.962 GV847.5

Regularly updated, the official rules are essential for those who wish to understand and interpret the game.

1574 Twentieth century hockey chronicle. David Barrett et al. 576p. Publications International, 1994. ISBN 0-7853-0176-3.
796.96 GV963

Presents the essence of every season in the twentieth century from 1900 to 1994. Photographs progress from black and white to high-resolution color. Covers early clubs from 1900, National Hockey League from 1917, and World Hockey Association, NCAA, and Olympic Games.

Martial Arts

1575 The original martial arts encyclopedia: tradition, history, pioneers. Rev. ed. John Corcoran and Emil Farkas. Stuart Sobel, ed. 450p. Pro Action, 1993. $29.95. ISBN 0-9615126-3-6.
796.962 GV847.5

The best single source on martial arts. Presents detailed descriptions of thirty-three major martial arts, and briefly describes others. Explains equipment, training, and weaponry. Includes biographies of principal figures, and provides a list of organizations and associations.

Olympics

1576 The complete book of Winter Olympics. 1998 ed. David Wallechinsky. 248p. Overlook Pr., 1998. $27.95. ISBN 0-87951-849-9; paper $14.95. ISBN 0-87951-818-9.

Sports Illustrated presents the complete book of the Summer Olympics. Rev. ed. David Wallechinsky. 205p. Little, Brown, 1997. $29.95. ISBN 0-316-92093-2; paper $15.95. ISBN 0-316-92094-0.
796.98 GV841.5

These books cover, respectively, the winter games through 1994 (including a preview of the 1998 Tokyo games) and the summer games through 1996. Each presents a short summary of the basic rules, an introduction to most of the events, and a brief history of the modern games. Includes summaries of significant and unusual events, complete records of all medalists, and numerous black-and-white photographs. The information is extensive and current; the anecdotes and trivia make them delightful for browsing. Though the books' titles may continue to vary, these publications are likely to become the definitive serial treatments of the games. Look for updates every two years.

Recreational Games

1577 Best games: 188 active and quiet, simple, and sophisticated games for preschoolers through adults. Linda Jennings et al. 141p. McFarland, 1985. Paper $24.95. ISBN 0-89950-159-1.
794 GV1201

Basic guide for all kinds of games—for living rooms, spacious backyards, and for large and small groups, both active and sedentary. A master index includes activity level (much, little, or moderate), age level, number of players, and indoor or outdoor play. The games are listed alphabetically, each with a short paragraph of instruction.

1578 Family fun and games. Diagram Group staff. 800p. Sterling, 1994. Paper $19.95. ISBN 0-8069-8777-4.
795.4 GV1234

The first half of this wonderful encyclopedia of games provides instructions for general amusements, including fifty board games, thirty-four dice games, twenty versions of dominoes, thirty versions of marbles and jacks, educational games, and party games of all sorts. The second half is devoted to card games, listing them alphabetically by primary name (e.g., *gin rummy* appears under *rummy*). Good cross-references; the twenty-two-page main index includes alternative names. Additional indexes sort games by number of players.

1579 New rules for classic games. R. Wayne Schmittberger. 256p. Wiley, 1992. Paper

$9.95. ISBN 0-471-53621-0.
793 GV1201.42

Offers hundreds of variant ways of playing traditional games such as Scrabble, chess, and checkers, as well as many dice, card, and word games. Some of the modifications make the games more challenging; some, more interesting; some, just more fun.

1580 Pick-up games: the rules, the players, the equipment. Deborah Crisfield. 208p. Facts on File, 1992. $27.95. ISBN 0-8160-2700-5.
790.1 GV1201.42

A *pickup game* is "an offshoot of an established sport" with flexible rules and a relatively informal flavor. Here one finds Frisbee golf, flag football, freeze tag, and kick the can—more than 250 games in all. Arranged in fifteen chapters—fourteen established sports (badminton, basketball, and so on, in alphabetical order) and one miscellaneous chapter for those without any obvious parent. Presents a history of the parent game, rules, and diagram of the playing field and then concise descriptions of all the variants.

Rock Climbing and Mountaineering

1581 Climbing: the complete reference. Greg Child, comp. 264p. Facts on File, 1995. $39.95. ISBN 0-8160-2692-0.
796.522 GV200

More than 1,000 substantial entries, alphabetically arranged. Describes important climbing areas and famous routes; relates climbing history; portrays geographic regions and mountain groups; presents biographies of notable climbers; details equipment and techniques. A solid, comprehensive single-volume source.

1582 Handbook of climbing. Allen Fyffe and Ian Peter. Viking, 1997. $34.95. ISBN 0-7207-2054-0.
797.522 GV200

Technical handbook. Describes equipment, techniques, and safety precautions. Lots of clear photographs. Extensive glossary and index.

1583 Mountaineering, the freedom of the hills. 6th ed. Don Graydon and Mountaineers Books staff, eds. 528p. Mountaineers, 1997. Paper $12.95. ISBN 0-89886-427-5.
796.5 GV200

The bible of the mountain-climbing world and the standard text for climbing courses. Completely updated and revised. Presents safety principles and accepted techniques of mountaineering. Covers rock, snow, and ice climbing. Describes requisite equipment, foot gear, knots, and first aid. A classic.

1584 Rock climbing basics. Turlough Johnson. Stackpole Books, 1995. $16.95. ISBN 0-8117-2420-4.
796.5 GV200.2

Straightforward basic climbing for beginners. Color photographs portray the most basic and important skills. Safety, safety, safety. Explains equipment and knots and emphasizes training regimen.

1585 Rock 'n road: rock climbing areas of North America. Tim Toula. 420p. Chockstone Pr., 1995. Paper $30. ISBN 0-934641-35-8.
796.5223 GV199.44

A guide to all the climbing areas of North America, including gym walls, fabricated cliffs, boulders, and cliff faces. Lists more than 2,000 locations, indicating climbability, rock type, and height.

Running

1586 The essential runner: a concise guide to the basics for all runners. John Hanc. 160p. Lyons & Burford, 1994. Paper $12.95. ISBN 1-55821-289-2.
796.42 GV1061

Outlines fundamentals: training schedules, injury prevention, and nutrition. Describes equipment and accessories. Includes sample running programs.

1587 New York Road Runners Club complete book of running and fitness. 3d ed. New York Road Runner's Club staff. Random House, 1997. Paper $18. ISBN 0-679-78010-6.
796.426 GV1061

Advice on sports nutrition, medical treatments, prevention of injuries, exercise, health, and equipment from the world's largest running club. Includes training models for runners of all levels, from beginners to advanced. Lists races for children, women-only races, and great road races by month. Extensive resource list including books, organizations, and running camps.

1588 Running injury-free: how to prevent, treat, and recover from dozens of painful problems. Joe Ellis and Joe Henderson. 288p. Rodale, 1994. Paper $14.95. ISBN 0-87596-221-1.
617.1 RC1220.R8

Written by a podiatrist and an editor of *Runner's world.* Describes symptoms; explains first aid. Aims to describe what pain means and how to avoid it. Presents relevant exercises, stretching, and warm-ups. Includes basics, such as how to lace shoes. Emphasizes home remedies. Good index.

Sailing

1589 Sailing for beginners: the classic manual of small-boat sailing, revised and updated. Moulton M. Farnham. 256p. Macmillan, 1986. Paper $18. ISBN 0-02-079870-9.
797.1 GV811

Still the classic manual. Step-by-step coverage.

Soccer

1590 Official rules of soccer. Federation Internationale de Football Association staff, ed. 190p. Triumph Books, 1997. Paper $9.95. ISBN 1-572431-84-0.
796.334 GV943

All the rules. Also signals made by referees and linesmen (photographs, not line drawings). Appendixes include diagrams illustrating offside points and instructions on taking kicks from the penalty mark. Amendments to laws and decisions since the last edition are indicated by double underline.

1591 The simplest game: intelligent fan's guide to the world of soccer. 3d ed. Paul Gardner. 384p. Macmillan, 1996. Paper $14.95. ISBN 0-02-860401-6.
796.334 GV943

Provides historical background on the origins of soccer. Chronicles World Cup activities to date. Details evolution of the game, including defensive and offensive strategies. Includes international rules and glossary.

1592 Soccer handbook for players, coaches, and parents. Albert M. Luongo. McFarland, 1996. $22.50. ISBN 0-7864-0159-1.
796.334 GV943

A complete handbook to the world's most popular sport. Aimed at those who serve the youth of today. Rules, basic and advanced skills, sportsmanship, fairness, and team play.

1593 World encyclopedia of soccer. 2d ed. Michael L. LaBlanc and Richard Henshaw. 430p. Gale, 1993. $42. ISBN 0-8103-8995-9.
796.334 GV943

History of the game, complete rules, overview of strategies and tactics, biographies of great players, worldwide team profiles, U.S. and international soccer associations, and Olympic competitions. Includes charts, statistics, drawings, diagrams. Appendix A: basic chronology from 2500 B.C. to 1994. Appendix B: glossary of terms and concepts (thirty-nine pages). Appendix C: early rules. Appendix D: cup competition, listed alphabetically by city, followed by a chronological listing. Appendix E: stadiums and their capacities. Appendix F: witchcraft's role in soccer, as in some East African nations. Appendix G: pre-Columbian games. The book is easy to read and has a good index.

Swimming

1594 Swimming for total fitness: a progressive aerobic program. Rev. ed. Jane Katz and Nancy P. Bruning. 384p. Doubleday, 1993. $17.50. ISBN 0-385-46821-0.
797.21 GV837

A step-by-step program for learning swimming. (1) Fundamentals—includes both narrative and illustrations. (2) Techniques—more illustrations. (3) Starts, dives, and turns. (4) Progressive workout programs—beginners to advanced—including warm-up, main set, and cool down. Offers four levels of workout, progressing to super workouts. (5) Equipment; includes lists of suppliers. (6) Questions and answers: Why chlorine? Aches and pains. Sickness. Appendixes with various exercises and workout logs.

Tennis

1595 Bud Collins' modern encyclopedia of tennis. 2d ed. Bud Collins and Zander Hollander, eds. 666p. Gale, 1994. $39.95. ISBN 0-8103-8988-6.

Visible Ink Pr., 1994. Paper $14.95. ISBN 0-8103-9443-X.
796.342 GV992

Offers a year-by-year history, including tournament records from 1874, profiles of more than 250 players, a guide to equipment, and a glossary of terms. Presents international and U.S. official rules. Appendix containing statistics, dates, and names.

1596 Tennis sourcebook. Dennis J. Phillips. 584p. Scarecrow, 1995. $80. ISBN 0-8108-3001-9.
016.796 GV995

A compilation of important information sources intended to cover all aspects of the sport. First section: general works arranged by format, then by author. Second section: topical bibliographies. Third section: biographies, with more than 100 entries. Fourth section: videos—all produced since 1980, including videos depicting tennis history, rules, instructions, and biographies of popular players. Fifth section: associations—United States, international, world—listed alphabetically. A comprehensive sourcebook.

Wilderness Training

1597 The complete wilderness training book. Hugh McManners. 192p. Dorling Kindersley, 1994. $29.95. ISBN 1-56458-488-7.
613.9 GF86

Teaches basic skills of survival: mental conditioning, proper equipment, basics of camp living (e.g., lighting fires), traveling in the wild. Describes edible plants; distinguishes edible fish and dangerous fish. Describes how to preserve food and how to ensure potability of water. Navigating by stars. Crossing deserts: proper clothing, carrying water. Crossing water: building rafts. Basic survival kit checklist; signaling techniques; first aid. Describes how to build shelters, from bamboo tents to igloos. Step-by-step color photographs.

19

Literature

SCOTT E. KENNEDY

New, updated, or revised reference sources in the area of literature seem to appear almost daily. In order to feature significant new works and still maintain a broad representation of time-tested standards, three well-known multititled critical series listed in the previous edition of this work have been omitted here. These are the Chelsea House Library of literary criticism, the Ungar Library of literary criticism, and the Magill Critical survey series. Those interested in building the literary criticism areas of their collection are encouraged to request these publishers' catalogs.

General Works

Bibliographies and Guides

1598 The Cambridge guide to literature in English. Ian Ousby, ed. 1061p. Cambridge Univ. Pr., 1993. $49.95. ISBN 0-521-44086-6.
820.9 PR85.C29

This scholarly one-volume reference guide to literature in English contains alphabetical entries for authors, titles, characters, literary terms, genres, movements, and critical concepts. Covers the literature of Great Britain and the United States, as well as the English-language literature of Canada, Africa, Australia, New Zealand, Ireland, India, and the Caribbean. This work appears to be a revision of *The Cambridge guide to English literature* (Cambridge Univ. Pr., 1983). Each work provides some entries not found in the other edition.

1599 Literary research guide: a guide to reference sources for the study of literatures in English and related topics. 2d ed. James L. Harner. 776p. Modern Language Assn., 1993. $45. ISBN 0-87352-558-2; paper $19.50. ISBN 0-87352-559-0.
820.9 PR83.H34

The successor to Margaret Patterson's *Literary research guide* (2d ed. Modern Language Assn., 1983), this is an excellent annotated guide to information on English and American literature. The book is in two main sections: types of reference works (databases, biographical sources, etc.) and works relating to particular national literatures (English, Irish, etc.). Beginning students may want to use Nancy L. Baker's *Research guide for undergraduate students: English and American literature* (4th ed. Modern Language Assn., 1995. $10.50. ISBN 0-87352-566-3), which has a much narrower scope and takes a how-to approach.

1600 Reference guide for English studies. Michael J. Marcuse. 790p. Univ. of California Pr., 1990. Paper $45. ISBN 0-520-05161-0.
820.9 PR56.M37

A guide to English and American literatures for the advanced researcher. The guide is divided into twenty-four sections that cover all aspects of literary research, from very general and very specific reference sources to descriptions of specific libraries, union catalogs, retrospective and current national biography, and manuscript archives. Provides very detailed descriptions of each reference work discussed, giving publication history and often listing contents. Recommends key works for each major topic.

1601 Reference works in British and American literature. 2d ed. James K. Bracken. 2v. Libraries Unlimited, 1998. $90. ISBN 1-5630-8518-6.
820.9 PR83.B74

Volume 1 presents an annotated guide to the most important and useful general reference works in British and American literature, aimed at the novice scholar as well as the more sophisticated literary researcher. Entries cover a wide variety of reference sources as well as core journals and research centers and associations. Volume 2 provides critical annotations on reference works devoted to individual authors. Author-title and subject indexes.

Indexes and Abstracts

1602 MLA international bibliography of books and articles on modern language and literature. Harrison T. Meserole, comp. Modern Language Assn., 1921– . Annual. $850. ISSN 0024-8215.
■ cd online
405 PB1.M29

A major bibliography covering scholarship for modern languages and literatures. Since 1981, this work has appeared in two volumes. The first is a bibliography of books and journal articles relevant to the study of language and literature. The second volume consists of a subject index and an index to authors. Essential for all libraries that support original research or an undergraduate collegiate curriculum. Volumes from 1970 to the present are available online.

Encyclopedias

1603 Benét's reader's encyclopedia. 4th ed. Bruce Murphy, ed. 1144p. HarperCollins, 1996. $36. ISBN 0-06-181088-6.
803 PN41.B4

A completely revised edition of a basic reference book, *The reader's encyclopedia,* this is a useful companion to world literature. Entries cover authors, titles, plots, characters, allusions, literary movements and terms, historical events, and other relevant topics.

1604 Encyclopedia of literary epics. Guida M. Jackson. 660p. ABC-Clio, 1996. $65. ISBN 0-87436-773-5.
809.1 PN56.E65

A comprehensive reference work devoted to the world's literary epics (e.g., *Paradise Lost, The Divine Comedy,* Pope's *Dunciad*). Main entries present the epic story, its characters, and themes, as well as the relevant social, political, and historical context. Other entries are devoted to authors, themes, epic characters, and mythological types. Each entry contains bibliographic references for further study. Subject index.

1605 Encyclopedia of traditional epics. Guida M. Jackson-Laufer. 732p. ABC-Clio, 1994. $65. ISBN 0-87436-724-7.
398.22 PN56.E65

This award-winning work covers epics of all nations and all time periods, presenting the social, political, and historical context as well as the literary and thematic material. Epics here are those originating in the oral, as opposed to the literary, tradition and include such works as the *Chanson de Roland, Beowulf,* and the Norse *Sagas.*

1606 Encyclopedia of utopian literature. Mary Ellen Snodgrass. 644p. ABC-Clio, 1995. $65. ISBN 0-87436-757-3.
809 PN56.U8

Covers utopian and anti-utopian writing from ancient mythology to contemporary science fiction. Alphabetical in arrangement, some 300 articles cover authors, specific works, themes, and styles. Entries include "Black Muslims," *Camelot, A child's garden of verses, Don Quixote, 1984,* "Timaeus," *Walden,* and the *Wonderful world of Oz.*

1607 **Encyclopedia of world literature in the twentieth century.** Rev. ed. Leonard S. Klein, ed. 5v. Ungar, 1981–93. $470/set. v.1, ISBN 0-8044-3135-3; v.2, ISBN 0-8044-3136-1; v.3, ISBN 0-8044-3137-X; v.4, ISBN 0-8044-3131-8; v.5, ISBN 0-8044-3131-0.
803 PN771.E5

A major revision of the 1967 edition edited by Wolfgang Bernard Fleischmann, this multivolume encyclopedia provides extensive coverage on international developments in twentieth-century literature. Although emphasis is given to writers of Europe and North America, this work also represents one of the most valuable sources of information on national literatures, including Third World countries. Volume 5 is a detailed index to names and subjects.

Handbooks

1608 **Brewer's dictionary of phrase and fable.** 15th ed. Adrian Room, ed. 1182p. HarperCollins, 1995. $45. ISBN 0-06-270133-9.
803 PN43.B65

A revised and expanded edition of Ebenezer Cobham Brewer's classic dictionary, first published in 1870, this work contains terms and phrases for linguistic, literary, historical, and biographical subjects. The present edition has added more than 300 new entries, some on current usage. Because of the numerous revisions that this work has undergone, earlier editions may prove useful as unique sources for some items.

1609 **A glossary of literary terms.** 6th ed. M. H. Abrams. 301p. Henry Holt, 1993. $12.95. ISBN 0-03-054982-5.
803 PN41.A184

An excellent guide to literary terms used with American, British, foreign, and comparative literature. Terms are discussed in essay-type entries. Index covers all terms included.

1610 **A handbook to literature.** 6th ed. C. Hugh Holman and William Harmon. 615p. Macmillan, 1992. $30. ISBN 0-02-553440-8.
803 PN41.H6

Based on the original edition by William Flint Thrall and Addison Hibbard, this useful manual gives an alphabetical listing of 1,800 words and phrases peculiar to the study of English and American literature, with explanations, definitions, and illustrations. Includes an outline of English and American literary history and a listing of Nobel Prizes for literature and Pulitzer Prizes for fiction, poetry, and drama. Index of proper names.

1611 **Johns Hopkins guide to literary theory and criticism.** Michael Groden and Martin Kreiswirth, eds. 775p. Johns Hopkins Univ. Pr., 1994. $65. ISBN 0-8018-4560-2.
■ online
809 PN81.J64

A comprehensive survey of ideas and persons (from Aristotle to Chomsky) that have made their mark in the world of literary theory. Substantive entries on literary critics, theorists, schools, and movements. The 226 entries are arranged alphabetically; each entry is signed, and most include a bibliography of both primary and secondary sources.

Digests

1612 **Magill's literary annual.** Frank N. Magill, ed. Salem, 1977– . Annual. $70. ISSN 0163-3058.
803 PN44.M32

Essay reviews of 200 fiction and nonfiction books of the previous year, published in two volumes. Articles, arranged alphabetically by title, are from three to five pages long and include bibliographic information, a plot summary, some criticism, and sources of further information. Annual volumes now contain a list of titles by category, a cumulative author index, and a list of biographical works by subject. Provides an update to Magill's *Masterplots*.

1613 **Masterplots.** Rev. 2d ed. Frank N. Magill, ed. 12v. Salem, 1996. $600. ISBN 0-89356-084-7.
■ cd
808.8 PN44.M3

A complete revision of earlier *Masterplots* (1976). Many titles of "less critical significance" have been dropped and 425 new titles added. The current work contains 1,801 plot synopses of world literature, followed by critical evaluations. Plot digests are preceded by ready reference data on author, type of work, setting, and principal characters. A chronology and author, title, and geographic indexes are located at the end of volume 12. Updated by *Magill's literary annual* and the various *Masterplots II* series. A standard and extremely popular work.

Literary Characters

1614 Cyclopedia of literary characters. Rev. ed. Frank N. Magill and A. J. Sobczak, eds. 5v. Salem, 1998. $350/set. ISBN 0-89356-438-9.
809 PN44.M3

This work identifies and describes more than 29,000 characters drawn from more than 1,400 novels, dramas, and epics of world literature. Arrangement is alphabetical by title of the literary work in which characters appear. The title index, author index, character index, and pronunciation guide facilitate ready reference use.

1615 Cyclopedia of literary characters II. Frank N. Magill, ed. 4v. Salem, 1990. $300/set. ISBN 0-89356-517-2.
809 PN44.M3

Following the pattern of the original *Cyclopedia of literary characters,* published in 1963, this four-volume set covers approximately 5,000 characters cited in the *Masterplots II* series—*American fiction, British and Commonwealth fiction, World fiction, Drama*—and selected works from the *Short story series.* Main entries are arranged alphabetically by title of the work, with characters listed in order of importance. Character descriptions vary in length from a few words to 100 to 150 words. Includes author, title, and character indexes, all with cross-references.

1616 Dictionary of fictional characters. William Freeman. Rev. by Martin Seymour-Smith. 598p. The Writer, 1991. Paper $18.95. ISBN 0-87116-166-4.
820.3 PN56.4S49

This dictionary identifies 50,000 characters taken from more than 3,000 works created by some 800 authors. It spans six centuries of British, Commonwealth, and American literature, covering novels, short stories, plays, and poems.

Literary Prizes

1617 Literary and library prizes. 10th ed. Olga S. Weber and Stephen J. Calvert, eds. 651p. Bowker, 1980. $26.95. ISBN 0-8352-1249-1.
807.9 PN171.P75

Lists 454 awards, including 97 new to the tenth edition. Divided into four sections: international, American, British, and Canadian. Subdivided by genre, such as poetry, drama, library, and so forth. Lists past winners and discontinued awards.

Quotations

1618 Columbia Granger's world of quotations on CD-ROM. Robert Andrews, Mary Biggs, and Michael Seider, eds. Columbia Univ. Pr., 1996. $350. ISBN 0-231-10518-5.
808.88 PN6081.C65

More than 65,000 quotations (five million words); features notable lines from some 5,000 authors—writers, poets, scholars, statesmen, journalists, and wits—including lines from official documents, press releases, movies, television, literature, and memorable speeches. Searching is by subject, author, key word, author's birthdate, nationality, occupation, and gender. Authoritative and user-friendly.

1619 Familiar quotations: a collection of passages, phrases, and proverbs traced to their sources in ancient and modern literature. 16th ed. Justin Kaplan, ed. 1405p. Little, Brown, 1992. $40. ISBN 0-316-08277-5.
808.88 PN6081.B27

A standard collection with quotations arranged chronologically and then by author. Focuses almost exclusively on literary sources. One of the most popular and best-researched quotation books. Excellent index.

1620 The home book of quotations, classical and modern. 10th ed. Burton Stevenson. 2816p. Dodd, 1967. op.
808.88 PN6081.S73

One of the most comprehensive and useful of the many books of quotations. Arrangement is by subject, with a very detailed index. More than 50,000 quotations.

1621 Magill's quotations in context. Frank N. Magill and Tench Francis Tilghman, eds. 2v. Salem, 1965. $75/set. ISBN 0-89356-132-0.

Magill's quotations in context, second series. Frank N. Magill and Tench Francis Tilghman, eds. 2v. Salem, 1969. $75/set. ISBN 0-89356-136-3.
808.8 PN6081.M29

The original work contains 2,020 entries; the *Second series,* 1,500 additional quotations. Entries give source of quote, author, date of publication, type of work, brief explication of source of quote, and quote in context. Keyword and author indexes.

1622 The new quotable woman: the definitive treasury of notable words by women from Eve to the present. Elaine Partnow, ed. 714p. Meridian, 1993. Paper $15. ISBN 0-452-01099-3.
808.8 PN6081.5.N49

Originally published by Facts on File in 1989, and based on two earlier collections, this revised edition contains more than 20,000 quotations from more than 2,500 women. Entries are arranged chronologically by sources' birth dates and are indexed by subject, nationality and ethnicity, occupation, and name.

1623 Oxford dictionary of modern quotations. Tony Augarde, ed. 384p. Oxford Univ. Pr., 1991. $45. ISBN 0-19-866141-X.
808.8 PN6080.O98

In an alphabetical arrangement by author, this dictionary provides more than 6,000 popular quotations from twentieth-century novels, speeches, plays, poems, films, radio, and television.

1624 The Oxford dictionary of quotations. 4th ed. rev. Angela Partington, ed. Oxford Univ. Pr., 1996. $39.95. ISBN 0-19-860058-5.
808.8 PN6080.O95

Recently updated, containing more than 17,000 quotations from more than 2,500 individuals. Alphabetical arrangement by author. Includes classical writers and quotations from the Bible, film, song, and non-English-speaking authors, for whom quotations are given both in the original and in translation. Includes appendixes covering sayings of the nineties, advertising slogans, and mottoes.

1625 Quotations in black. Anita King, ed. and comp. 344p. Greenwood, 1981. $45. ISBN 0-313-22128-6.
808.8 PN6081.3Q67

Arranged chronologically by the birth date of the speaker, *Quotations in black* provides an international selection of more than 1,100 quotations from more than 200 individuals, plus a brief biographical sketch of each. An additional section includes proverbs. Access to all quotations is provided by both author and subject-keyword indexes. A unique work, which should stand beside standard collections of quotations.

Proverbs

1626 Dictionary of American proverbs. Wolfgang Mieder, ed. 719p. Oxford Univ. Pr., 1992. $49.95. ISBN 0-19-505399-0.
398.9 PN6426.D53

This dictionary, the result of many years of scholarship, includes 15,000 proverbs currently in use in the United States and Canada. Arranged alphabetically by key word. Includes variants.

1627 The Macmillan book of proverbs, maxims, and famous phrases. Burton Stevenson. 2957p. Macmillan, 1987, c1948. $75. ISBN 0-02-614500-6.
808.8 PN6405.H66

Formerly entitled *The home book of proverbs, maxims, and familiar phrases,* this work follows the pattern of the author's *Home book of quotations.* Subject arrangement and detailed index. Covers more than 73,000 expressions. Includes foreign quotations with English translations.

1628 Modern proverbs and proverbial sayings. Bartlett Jere Whiting, comp. 709p. Harvard Univ. Pr., 1989. $39.95. ISBN 0-674-58053-2.
398.9 PN6403.W49

Presents more than 5,500 proverbs, arranged by key word, collected from writings published between 1930 and 1985. Includes citations for each entry.

1629 Multicultural dictionary of proverbs: over 20,000 adages from more than 120 languages, nationalities, and ethnic groups. Harold V. Cordy. 416p. McFarland, 1997. $47.50. ISBN 0-7864-0251-2.
398.9 PN6405.C67

More than 20,000 proverbs from more than 120 languages, nationalities, and ethnic groups. Includes keyword, subject, and name indexes and bibliography.

1630 The Oxford dictionary of English proverbs. 3d ed. F. P. Wilson, ed. 950p. Oxford Univ. Pr., 1970. $55. ISBN 0-19-869118-1.
808.88 PN6421.O9

A scholarly work, detailing date and source of earliest recorded use, with examples of usage from literature. Proverbs are arranged by the most significant word, with many cross-references to other words of significance.

Multivolume Criticism

1631 Contemporary literary criticism. v.1– . Gale, 1973– . $140/v. ISSN 0091-3421.
■ online
809.04 PN771.C59

This multivolume, ongoing series offers significant passages from contemporary criticism on authors who are now living or who have died since December 31, 1959. More than 100 volumes are now available. Brief author sketches are followed by critical excerpts, presented in chronological order. The number of authors covered in each volume has varied over the years, but recent volumes provide criticism on some eight to twelve literary figures, including novelists, playwrights, short-story writers, scriptwriters, and other creative writers. Nearly 5,000 authors have been included since the series began publication. *Contemporary literary criticism yearbook* first appeared in 1984 as part of this series. This annual publication seeks to give an overview of current literary activities and trends through critical excerpts and lengthy essays by prominent literary figures, who survey the year's literary production in their respective fields. Cumulative indexes to authors, nationalities, and titles facilitate use of this well-organized, award-winning work.

1632 Literature criticism from 1400 to 1800. v.1– . Gale, 1984– . $140/v. ISSN 0740-2880.
809.03 PN86.L53

Each volume provides critical excerpts on some ten to twenty literary figures from the period 1400 to 1800. Thirty-nine volumes are now available. Entries are arranged alphabetically by author and include a biographical and critical essay followed by a chronological list of the author's main works and excerpts from English-language criticism. A cumulative author index provides references to previous volumes in this and other Gale series.

1633 Nineteenth-century literature criticism. v.1– . Gale, 1981– . $140/v. ISSN 0732-1864.
809.034 PN761.N56

Excerpts from nineteenth- and twentieth-century criticism in English on writers of all nationalities and genres who died between 1800 and 1900. More than sixty-four volumes are now available. Gives pseudonyms, birth and death dates, biography, list of principal works, annotated bibliography of criticism, and a portrait of each subject. Each volume covers approximately twenty to thirty authors; every fourth volume covers topics, as opposed to specific authors or works, such as Catholicism or Irish famine. This work is similar in both scope and format to Gale's *Contemporary literary criticism.* Cumulative indexes to authors, nationalities, and critics.

1634 Twentieth-century literary criticism. v.1– . Gale, 1978– . $140/v. ISSN 0276-8178.
809.04 PN771.G27

A companion series to Gale's *Contemporary literary criticism,* these studies contain excerpts of criticism on notable authors who died between 1900 and 1960. More than seventy-three volumes have been published. Recent volumes cover some eight to twelve authors and include for each writer an opening paragraph and list of principal works, followed by a chronological listing of criticism. Every fourth volume covers topics such as movements or trends of significance. Cumulative indexes for authors, nationalities, and critics in each volume, with cross-references to entries in other Gale series.

Biography

1635 Contemporary authors: a bio-bibliographical guide to current writers in fiction, general nonfiction, poetry, journalism, drama, motion pictures, television, and other fields. v.1– . Gale, 1962– . $140/v. ISSN 0010-7468.
■ online
810.9 PN451.C59

Brief, factual articles record biobibliographical information for a large number of creative writers in a variety of fields, including literature, journalism, television, and film, in more than 130 volumes. Only two volumes of a *CA permanent series* were issued. Its purpose was to remove deceased or retired authors from the regular volumes. The *First revision series,* begun in 1967 and continued through volumes 41–44 (1979), was both an updating and a cumulation of volumes in the original set. *CA new revision series* (v.1– . Gale, 1981– . $140/v. ISSN 0275-7176) updates information on authors listed in earlier volumes of *Contemporary authors* but does not replace individual volumes. A cumulative author index, with references to *CA* and to other Gale series, appears in alternate new volumes of *CA* through volume 126. Gale now issues a separately published cumulative index to citations in *CA* and in other Gale publications. One hundred sixty volumes now in print.

1636 Contemporary authors autobiography series. v.1– . Gale, 1984– . $140/v. ISSN 0748-0636.
809 PN453.C63

Autobiographical essays by contemporary writers provide unique insights into the life, works, and thought of each author. Each volume covers some twenty to thirty writers. A chronological bibliography of the author's works accompanies each essay. Cumulative index to essayists, personal and geographical names, titles, and subjects. The twenty-eight volumes now in print provide autobiographical essays by more than 450 contemporary writers.

1637 Contemporary foreign language writers. James Vinson and Daniel Kirkpatrick, eds. 439p. St. Martin's, 1984. $39.95. ISBN 0-312-16663-X.
809 PN771.C585

Great foreign language writers. James Vinson and Daniel Kirkpatrick, eds. 714p. St. Martin's, 1984. $49.95. ISBN 0-312-34585-2.
809 PN524.G74

These companion volumes provide biographical and bibliographical information for nearly 400 major foreign-language poets, novelists, and dramatists. For each author there is a biographical sketch, a bibliography of primary works, a selected list of secondary sources, and a signed critical essay. Title index.

1638 Contemporary literary critics. 2d ed. Elmer Borklund. 600p. St. James, 1982. $75. ISBN 0-912289-33-3.
801 PN75.A1

Included for each of 124 modern American and British critics are biographical data, a bibliography of the author's criticism and other publications, a list of secondary sources, and an essay on the critic's theories and position.

1639 Contemporary popular writers. Dave Mote, ed. 528p. St. James, 1997. $130. ISBN 1-55862-216-0.
820.9 PR478.P66

Authoritative coverage of 300 of today's most popular and best-known novelists, playwrights, poets, short-story, and nonfiction writers (e.g., Michael Crichton, Agatha Christie, Stephen King, and Toni Morrison). Each entry provides detailed personal biographical information, a bibliography of works by the author, a list of key works about the author, and a critical essay. Author, nationality, genre, and title indexes.

1640 Cyclopedia of world authors. Rev. 3d ed. Frank N. Magill, ed. 5v. Salem, 1997. $350/set. ISBN 0-89356-434-6.
809 PN451.M36

Provides 200 1,000-word biographical sketches of 1,000 world authors. Entries are in alphabetical order and include a chronological list of principal works and biographical data. Index in volume 5.

1641 Dictionary of literary biography. Gale, 1978– . $146/v. ISSN 0731-7867.
■ online
810.9 PS21

An excellent multivolume series, currently in more than 195 volumes, covering the lives and works of those who have contributed to the greatness of literature in America, England, and elsewhere. Each volume examines a particular group of writers organized by topic, period, or genre. Major biographical and critical essays on the most important writers are accompanied by briefer entries on lesser figures in a single alphabetic sequence. In both cases information covered includes each subject's life, work, and critical reputation. *DLB* is updated by *Dictionary of literary biography yearbook* (Gale, 1981– . $146/v. ISSN 0730-3793), which includes both revised entries and new entries. *Dictionary of literary biography documentary series: an illustrated chronicle* (Gale, 1982– . $146/v.) provides reproductions of illustrative materials, including photographs, letters, manuscript facsimiles, and reprints of reviews, interviews, and obituaries. Cumulative indexes to all three sets are contained in each new volume. In 1987–89, in response to requests from smaller libraries, Gale issued the *Concise dictionary of American literary biography* (Gale, 1987–89. $380/set). This six-volume set covers major American authors from the seventeenth century to the present. In 1991–92, Gale issued the *Concise dictionary of British literary biography* (Gale, 1991–92. $500/set). This eight-volume work covers the major British literary figures of all eras. Articles selected from the parent set, *DLB*, are reprinted in full with some updating and revisions.

1642 European writers. William T. H. Jackson and George Stade, eds. 14v. Scribner, 1983–91. $1060/set. ISBN 0-684-19267-5.
809 PN501.E9

This fourteen-volume study on major European authors from medieval times to the present serves as a companion series to *Ancient writers: Greece and Rome* as well as to *American writers* and *British writers*. Scholarly essays of approximately 15,000 words provide both a biographical sketch and a critical review of individual writers, as well as an overview of a few broader literary topics. Articles conclude with a selected bibliography of major editions, translations, and secondary studies. The last volume is an index to the set. For smaller libraries, a three-volume selection of the sixty-eight most studied European writers is also available (*European writers: selected authors*. 3v. Scribner, 1993. $300. ISBN 0-684-19583-6).

1643 Research guide to biography and criticism. Walton Beacham, ed. 6v. Research Pub., 1985–91. $129/set. ISBN 0-933833-00-8.
820.9 PN466.R47

These annotated guides cite biographical and critical sources for 335 of the "most often studied" American, English, and Canadian poets and fiction writers and 146 world dramatists. The *Updates* (volumes 4 to 6) include additional citations to studies published since 1984 on English and American authors represented in the original volumes for literature and drama. Entries provide exact bibliographic information and a description of the contents of each book reviewed. Sources described are those readily available in U.S. libraries. A very useful resource for the beginning researcher and an important acquisition for libraries that do not subscribe to Gale's *Dictionary of literary biography*.

Special Interest

Black American Literature

1644 African American writers. Lea Baechler and A. Walton Litz, eds. 544p. Scribner, 1991. $75. ISBN 0-684-19058-3.
810.9 PS153.N5

Presents thirty-four scholarly essays on the lives and works of noted African American writers from James Baldwin to Richard Wright.

1645 Black authors: a selected annotated bibliography. James Edward Newby. 720p. Garland, 1991. $80. ISBN 0-8240-3329-9.
015.73 PS153

A comprehensive bibliography of the writings of Black American authors from 1773 to 1990, arranged by genre. Includes title and author indexes.

1646 Contemporary Black American playwrights and their plays: a biographical directory and dramatic index. Bernard L. Peterson Jr. 625p. Greenwood, 1988. $75. ISBN 0-313-25190-8.
812.54 PS153.N5

Provides information on more than 700 contemporary dramatists, screenwriters, and scriptwriters. Depending upon availability of data, entries include biographical and bibliographical information, together with annotations of dramatic works. Title index and a selective general index to names, organizations, and awards.

1647 Masterpieces of African-American literature. Frank N. Magill. 593p. HarperCollins, 1992. $45. ISBN 0-06-270066-9.
810.9 PS153.N5

Critical summaries of about 3,000 words of 149 literary works by ninety-six African American writers. Includes works of all genres from the eighteenth, nineteenth, and twentieth centuries. Includes author and title indexes.

1648 Oxford companion to African American literature. William L. Andrews, Francis Smith Foster, and Trudier Harris, eds. 896p. Oxford Univ. Pr., 1997. $55. ISBN 0-19-506510-7.
810.8 PS153.N5

Incorporating the contributions of more than 300 scholars, this comprehensive reference work provides entries on major works of literature, on literary characters, on character types, on literary genres, on icons of the African American world, and on virtually every aspect of the recorded African American experience.

1649 Schomburg Center guide to Black literature from the eighteenth

century to the present. Roger M. Valade, ed. Gale, 1996. $75. ISBN 0-7876-0289-2.
810.9 PN841.V36

Presents in a convenient *A* to *Z* format authoritative discussions of more than 500 Black authors and their works. Includes a chronology, a subject index, and a history of the Schomburg Center, the leading repository for Black studies in the United States.

Gay and Lesbian Literature

1650 Gay and lesbian literary heritage: a reader's companion to the writers and their works, from antiquity to the present. Claude J. Summers, ed. 704p. Henry Holt, 1995. $45. ISBN 0-8050-2716-5; paper $25. ISBN 0-8050-5009-4.
809 PN56.H57

Presents some 400 alphabetically arranged essays by 150 scholars; these include overviews within national or ethnic contexts, essays addressing specific issues or genres, and essays on individual authors from Plato to Fierstein. All entries conclude with bibliographic information.

1651 Gay and lesbian literature. Sharon Malinowski, ed. 2v. St. James, 1994. v.1, $99. ISBN 1-55862-174-1; v.2, $99. ISBN 1-55862-350-7.
809 PN56.E65

Each volume presents authoritative biographies, bibliographies, and criticism of more than 200 internationally renowned gay or lesbian authors. Entries include such notable writers as James Baldwin, C. P. Cavafy, Tennessee Williams, and Virginia Woolf.

Women's Literature

1652 American women writers: a critical reference guide from colonial times to the present. Lina Mainiero, ed. 5v. Ungar, 1979–82. $75/v. ISBN 0-8044-3150-7.
810.9 PS147.A4

Provides biobibliographical and critical information about American women, prominent and less well known, who, from colonial days to 1975, contributed to American writing in many subject areas, including literature, psychology, anthropology, politics, and children's literature. Written primarily by women from the academic community, and alphabetically arranged by the name of the subject, the articles vary in length from one to four pages. Each includes a selected bibliography of secondary sources. A supplement, identified as volume 5 and edited by Carol Hurd Green and Mary Grimley Mason, was published in 1994 (Continuum Pr., 1994. $75. ISBN 0-8264-0603-3).

1653 Bloomsbury guide to women's literature. Claire Buck, ed. 1184p. Macmillan, 1994. Paper $20. ISBN 0-13-089665-9.
809 PN471.B57

More than 5,000 *A* to *Z* entries; included are biographical notes on individual authors from the classical world to the present day, detailed descriptions of hundreds of literary works, and thematic entries on literary genres. Provides black-and-white illustrations, bibliographies, and a useful chronology.

1654 Dictionary of British and American women writers, 1660–1800. Janet Todd, ed. 344p. Rowman, 1985. $48.50. ISBN 0-8476-7125-9.
820.9 PR113.D5

Signed articles on some 500 women writers give a brief biographical sketch, a list of known works by the author, and a short critical evaluation.

1655 Encyclopedia of feminist literary theory. Elizabeth Kowaleski-Wallace. 472p. Garland, 1997. $95. ISBN 0-8153-0824-8.
801.95 PN98.W64

Provides definitions of critical terms, summaries of the work of feminist literary critics, and descriptions of the development of the feminist perspective over time. Entries emphasize American and British views since 1970.

1656 The feminist companion to literature in English: women writers from the Middle Ages to the present. Virginia Blain et al. 1231p. Yale Univ. Pr., 1990. $49.95. ISBN 0-300-04854-8.
820.9 PR111.B57

This biographical dictionary provides brief articles of 500 words or less for more than 2,700 women writing in English. Covers not only British and American authors but also those of Africa, Australia, Canada, the Caribbean, New Zealand, the South Pacific, and the British Isles. Children's literature, diaries, letters, and other popular forms are represented here, along with traditional genres (novels, plays, poetry, and short stories). Entries also discuss topics relevant to the development of women's writing. This source is particularly useful for identifying lesser-known figures. Indexed by topic and names (grouped chronologically).

1657 Feminist writers. Pamela Kester-Shelton. 641p. St. James, 1996. $130. ISBN 1-55862-217-9.
809 PN451.F46

Arranged alphabetically, entries provide biographical, biobibliographical, and critical information on more than 300 feminist writers. Includes author, title, nationality, genre, and subject indexes.

1658 Masterpieces of women's literature. Frank N. Magill. 594p. HarperCollins, 1996. $50. ISBN 0-06-270138-X.
809 PS147.M37

Provides summaries and evaluations of the principal works of women's literature from *Adam Bede* and *The bell jar* to *Sexual politics* and *The wide Sargasso Sea.* Each of the 175 entries is written by a recognized scholar and includes a section on the form and content of the work, critical analysis, the literary and social context, and sources for further study.

1659 Modern American women writers. Lea Baechler and A. Walton Litz. 583p. Scribner, 1991. $75. ISBN 0-684-19057-5.
810.9 PS151.M54

Signed essays on forty-one twentieth-century women writers from Maya Angelou to Edith Wharton. Includes a feminist chronology (1640–1990) and index.

Specific Genres

Children's Literature

1660 Children's books and their creators. Anita Silvy, ed. 800p. Houghton, 1995. $40. ISBN 0-395-65380-0.
028.1 PN1009.A1

The 800 entries discuss the most important authors, illustrators, genres, issues, and works of children's literature.

1661 Children's literature: a guide to information sources. Margaret W. Denman-West. 187p. Libraries Unlimited, 1998. $38.50. ISBN 1-56308-448-1.
808.8 PA1009.A1

Written for all who are interested in children's literature—researchers, librarians, teachers, parents, and young people themselves—this information guide covers reference materials published between 1985 and 1997. Chapters include "Guides to Award Winning Books," "Recommended Reading," "Multicultural Literature," "Subject Bibliographies," "Reference Books," "Biographies," "Core Periodicals," "Nonprint Media," "Special Collections," "Professional Associations," and "Information Superhighway."

1662 Children's literature: a guide to the criticism. Linnea Hendrickson. 696p. Macmillan, 1987. $38.50. ISBN 0-8161-8670-7.
011.62 Z2014.5

An annotated bibliography of criticism arranged in two parts: by authors, illustrators, and their works; and by subjects, themes, and genres. Works considered range from the picture book to the young adult novel. The major emphasis is on twentieth-century children's literature, although some earlier classics are included. An index of critics and an index of authors, titles, and subjects contribute to the ease of use.

1663 Children's literature review. Gerard J. Senick, ed. Gale, 1976– . $131/v. ISSN 0362-4145.
028.52 PN1009.A1

This continuing series presents excerpts from criticism on some 600 authors and illustrators of books for children and young adults. Coverage is international in scope and includes a variety of genres. Approximately fifteen authors are represented in each volume. Forty-eight volumes have been published to date. Entries consist of brief sketches of the authors, commentaries by the authors, and excerpts from reviews and criticism. Illustrations; author portraits; cumulative indexes to authors, nationalities, and titles.

1664 Dictionary of American children's fiction, 1859–1959: books of recognized merit. Alethea K. Helbig and Agnes Regan Perkins. 666p. Greenwood, 1985. $65. ISBN 0-313-22590-7.

Dictionary of American children's fiction, 1960–1984: recent books of recognized merit. Alethea K. Helbig and Agnes Regan Perkins. 914p.

Greenwood, 1986. $67.95.
ISBN 0-313-25233-5.

Dictionary of American children's fiction, 1985–1989: books of recognized merit. Alethea K. Helbig and Agnes Regan Perkins. 368p. Greenwood, 1993. $57.95.
ISBN 0-313-27719-2.

Dictionary of American children's fiction, 1990–1994: books of recognized merit. Alethea K. Helbig and Agnes Regan Perkins. 473p. Greenwood, 1996. $79.50.
ISBN 0-313-28763-5.
813.54 PR85.C29

These volumes give brief biographical and bibliographical information as well as plot summaries for American children's fiction written between 1859 and 1994. Entries are provided for titles, authors, characters, significant settings, and other unique elements. A detailed index provides access to all main entries, to major characters for whom there are no separate entries, and to settings, themes, topics, pseudonyms, illustrators, and genres.

1665 Index to fairy tales, myths and legends. 2d ed., rev. and enl. Mary Huse Eastman. (Useful reference series; 28.) 610p. Faxon, 1926. op.

Index to fairy tales, myths and legends: supplement. Mary Huse Eastman. (Useful reference series; 61.) 566p. Faxon, 1937. op.

Index to fairy tales, myths and legends: 2d supplement. Mary Huse Eastman. (Useful reference series; 82.) 370p. Faxon, 1952. op.

Index to fairy tales, 1949–1972: including folklore, legends and myths in collections. Norma Olin Ireland. 741p. Faxon, 1973. Reprint: Scarecrow, 1985. $45. ISBN 0-8108-2011-0.

Index to fairy tales, 1973–1977: including folklore, legends and myths in collections. Norma Olin Ireland, comp. 259p. Faxon, 1979. Reprint: Scarecrow, 1985. $29.50.
ISBN 0-8108-1855-8.

Index to fairy tales, 1978–1986: including folklore, legends and myths in collections. Norma Olin Ireland and Joseph W. Sprug, comps. 575p. Scarecrow, 1989. $49.50.
ISBN 0-8108-2194-X.

Index to fairy tales, 1987–1992: including 310 collections of fairy tales, folktales, myths, and legends: with significant pre-1987 titles not previously indexed. Joseph W. Sprug, comp. 587p. Scarecrow, 1994. $62.50.
ISBN 0-8108-2750-6.
398.2 GR550.S67

Although this is an essential reference book for the children's department, it is also a valuable source for the location of much folklore and fairytale material and should be available in adult book collections as well. Versions of material suitable for small children are indicated. Recent supplements include folklore, legends, and myths in collections; subject index to stories.

1666 The Oxford companion to children's literature. Humphrey Carpenter and Mari Prichard. 586p. Oxford Univ. Pr., 1984. $55. ISBN 0-19-211582-0.
809 PN1008.5.C37

This one-volume handbook to children's literature contains nearly 2,000 entries for authors, titles, characters, literary terms and genres, and a variety of personal and place-names associated with the study of children's literature. Emphasis is on British and American literature, with brief summaries of the state of children's literature in other countries. Numerous cross-references and illustrations.

1667 The Oxford dictionary of nursery rhymes. 2d ed. Iona Archibald Opie and Peter Opie, eds. 560p. Oxford Univ. Pr., 1998. $45. ISBN 0-19-860088-7.
398 PN6110.C4

A scholarly collection of nursery rhymes, songs, nonsense jingles, and lullabies with notes and explanations concerning history, literary associations, social uses, and possible portrayal of real people. Both standard and earliest recorded versions (where available) are included. Indexes for "notable figures" and first lines. Eighty-five illustrations.

1668 Something about the author: autobiography series. v.1– . Gale, 1986– . $100/v. ISSN 0885-6842.
028.5 PN497.S66

A companion series to *Something about the author: facts and pictures* this is a collection of autobiographical essays by prominent authors and illustrators of books for children and young adults. Each of the twenty essays per volume contains approximately 10,000 words, and each volume contains 300 pages. Personal photos have been included that show the author at various ages and special people and moments in the author's life. Each entry is followed by a bibliography of the author's book-length works. Cumulative index for subjects, personal names, geographical names, essayists' names, and titles of works. Twenty-six volumes currently in print.

1669 Something about the author: facts and pictures about contemporary authors and illustrators of books for young people. Anne Commire, ed. Gale, 1971– . $100/v. ISSN 0276-816X.
028.52 PN451.S6

All volumes of this continuing series of illustrated biographical and autobiographical sketches of authors and illustrators of children's books are identical in plan and format. Among data presented are personal information of home or office addresses or both, childhood reminiscences, hobbies, education, family, and so forth. Cumulative indexes to characters, illustrations, and authors. Ninety-eight volumes available.

1670 Twentieth-century children's writers. 4th ed. Laura Standley Berger, ed. 1272p. St. James, 1995. $140. ISBN 1-55862-177-6.
820.9 PN1009.A1

Information is provided for approximately 800 English-language authors of fiction, poetry, and drama for children and young people. The alphabetically arranged entries cover writers most of whose work was published after 1900. Each entry contains biographical information, a bibliography of publications, and a signed critical evaluation. The appendix includes representative writers of the nineteenth century and a section on foreign-language writers. A title index and a list of advisers and contributors conclude this valuable survey of contemporary writers for children.

1671 Writers for children: critical studies of major authors since the seventeenth century. Jane M. Bingham, ed. 661p. Scribner, 1987. $75. ISBN 0-684-18165-7.
809 PN1009.A1

This critical guide to selected children's classics contains eighty-four signed essays on important writers from the seventeenth century to the twentieth century. Essays range from 2,500 to 6,000 words and conclude with selected bibliographies of primary and secondary sources. Index to authors and titles.

PRIZES AND AWARDS

1672 Children's book prizes: an evaluation and history of major awards for children's books in the English-speaking world. Ruth Allen. Ashgate, 1998. $84.95. ISBN 1-859-28237-7.
820.9 PR990

An evaluation and history of children's book awards.

1673 Children's books: awards and prizes, includes prizes and awards for young adult books. Children's Book Council, 1996. $75. ISSN 0069-3472.
809 PN1009.A1

This is the most complete, cumulative listing of the winning titles of extant awards programs. The 125 awards are divided into five sections: U.S. awards selected by adults, U.S. awards selected by children, British Commonwealth awards, international and multinational awards, and awards classified. The main entries are arranged alphabetically by award and contain a brief description of the award and a chronological listing of the winners and, in some cases, honor books. Title and person indexes are appended.

1674 The Newbery and Caldecott awards: a guide to the medal and honor books. Assn. for Library Service to Children. American Library Assn., 1988– . Annual. Paper $16. ISSN 1070-4493.
011.62 PS374.C454

Lists, with brief descriptions, all award-winning titles from the inception of the awards. Indexed by author, illustrator, and title. Published annually.

1675 Newbery and Caldecott medal and honor books: an annotated bibliography. Linda Kauffman Peterson and Marilyn Leathers Solt. 427p. Hall, 1982. $50. ISBN 0-8161-8448-8.
011 PN1009.A1

The complete bibliographic information (including suggested grade level and category of literature) together with a brief summary and critical commentary. Chronicles all the Newbery and

Caldecott medal and honor books from 1922 through 1981. This indispensable record of distinguished contributions to American literature for children is arranged by year of award and has author, title, and illustrator indexes.

1676 Newbery and Caldecott medalists and honor book winners: bibliographies and resource material through 1991. 2d ed. Muriel Brown and Rita Schoch Foudray, comps. 511p. Neal-Schuman, 1992. $85. ISBN 1-55570-118-3.
011 Z1037.A2

Arranged by author or illustrator, this work provides background information on the 325 authors and illustrators who have received recognition as medalists and honor book winners. Indicates the work for which they were recognized, as well as relevant biographical and bibliographic information.

Drama

1677 Contemporary dramatists. 6th ed. K. A. Berney, ed. 850p. St. James, 1998. $140. ISBN 1-55862-371-X.
822.9 PN1625.V5

Biographical notes on some 300 living playwrights writing in English, with signed critical essays and bibliographies of each dramatist's published works. Supplemental sections cover screenwriters, radio writers, television writers, musical librettists, and theater groups. Comprehensive title index.

1678 Dramatic criticism index: a bibliography of commentaries on playwrights from Ibsen to the avant-garde. Paul F. Breed and Florence M. Sniderman, comps. and eds. 1022p. Gale, 1972. $66. ISBN 0-8103-1090-2.
808 PN2021.B8

This bibliography of twentieth-century criticism, selected from some 630 books and 200 periodicals, contains nearly 12,000 entries. The 300 American and foreign playwrights covered are primarily twentieth-century authors, although some nineteenth-century dramatists are also included. Authors of the commentaries cited here include scholars, critics, playwrights, directors, and journalists. Arrangement is alphabetical by author. Indexes for titles and critics.

1679 European drama criticism 1900–1975. 2d ed. Helen H. Palmer, comp. 653p. Shoe String Pr., 1977. $49.50. ISBN 0-208-01589-2.
809 PN1721.P2

This selective bibliography of critical writings on major European playwrights provides a listing of criticisms published in English and foreign languages from 1900 to 1975. Arranged alphabetically by author and then by title. Cross-references; lists of books and journals indexed; index of plays and authors.

1680 McGraw-Hill encyclopedia of world drama: an international reference work. 2d ed. Stanley Hochman, ed. 5v. McGraw-Hill, 1984. $380/set. ISBN 0-07-079169-4.
809.2 PN1625.M3

Outstanding multivolume encyclopedia of dramatic literature. More than 900 entries for authors both major and minor and 100 nonbiographical articles defining terms. Emphasis is on the Western European tradition, but it includes material of Asia, Africa, and Latin America. Features theater movements, genres, styles, and surveys of major national dramas. Glossary; illustrations; index.

Fiction

1681 Eighty years of best sellers, 1895–1975. Alice Payne Hackett and James Henry Burke. 265p. Bowker, 1977. $15. ISBN 0-8352-0908-3.
011 Z1033.B3

Annual lists of best-sellers published in the United States from 1895 through 1975, with brief, entertaining commentaries on each year. Arranged by number of copies sold, by subject, and by year. Title and author indexes.

1682 Fiction catalog. 13th ed. 973p. Wilson, 1996. $98. ISBN 0-8242-0894-3. (Price includes main volume plus four annual supplements.)
808.3 PN3451

A standard annotated bibliography of some 5,000 works of classical and popular fiction. Serves both as a selection aid and as a source for identifying outstanding works of fiction. Entries, arranged alphabetically by author, contain full bibliographic information and brief descriptive summaries, along with excerpts from critical reviews. Includes out-of-print titles and a special section for large-print books. Title and subject indexes. New editions are published every five years.

1683 Genreflecting: a guide to reading interests in genre fiction. 4th ed. Diana Tixier Herald, ed. 367p. Libraries Unlimited, 1995. $38. ISBN 1-56308-343-X.
813.09 PS374.P63

Annotated guide to genre fiction, including westerns, thrillers, romance, science fiction, fantasy, and horror. Written to familiarize librarians with popular-reading interests of the public as well as to aid libraries and bookstores in identifying and selecting genre fiction. Arranged by genre and then by themes and types. Indexes to genre authors and to secondary materials.

NOVEL

1684 The contemporary novel: a checklist of critical literature on the English language novel since 1945. 2d ed. Irving Adelman and Rita Dworkin. 666p. Scarecrow, 1996. $125. ISBN 0-8108-3103-1.
823 PS379

A selective bibliography of critical literature on the contemporary English-language novel. For the second edition the scope was enlarged to include English-language writers outside Britain and America, including, for example, writers from Ghana, Nigeria, the Caribbean, and India. Surveyed are novelists whose major work appeared after 1945 or who wrote earlier but gained full recognition after that date. All of the works of each qualified author are entered, followed by critical citations published through 1982, regardless of the publication date of the original works.

1685 Contemporary novelists. 6th ed. Susan Windisch Brown, ed. St. James, 1996. $160. ISBN 1-55862-189-X.
823 PR881.C69

Covers English-language contemporary novelists. Provides a biographical sketch, an address, a bibliography of works published, a signed scholarly essay on each of the writers covered, and, in many cases, a comment by the novelist.

1686 Sequels: an annotated guide to novels in series. 3d ed. Janet Husband and Jonathan F. Husband. 688p. American Library Assn., 1997. $79. ISBN 0-8389-0696-6.
808 PN3488.S47

A selective, annotated list of the best, most enduring, and most popular novels in series. Short stories and children's books are excluded; classics, mysteries, and science fiction are included. Each work is listed in the best current edition, in the preferred order for reading. Arranged by author, with a title and subject index.

MYSTERY

1687 A catalogue of crime. Rev. ed. Jacques Barzun and Wendell Hertig Taylor. 952p. HarperCollins, 1989. $50. ISBN 0-06-015796-8.
808 PN3448.D4

This revised, enlarged edition of Barzun's *Comprehensive bibliography of crime and detective fiction* provides bibliographic information and brief plot summaries for novels, short stories, criticism, and true crime. Arrangement is alphabetical by author and then by title, with indexes to authors, titles, and names.

1688 Crime fiction II: a comprehensive bibliography, 1749–1990. Allen J. Hubin. 2v. Garland, 1994. $250. ISBN 0-8240-6891-2.
823 PR830.D4

This is a revised and updated edition of Hubin's well-received 1984 bibliography and 1988 supplement dealing with mystery, detective, thriller, spy, suspense, and gothic fiction. Compiled to provide information concerning all English-language adult crime fiction published between 1749 and 1990, this comprehensive bibliography cites more than 81,000 novels (English-language as well as translations of non-English works), plays, and short stories in which crime or the threat of crime is a major plot element. Entries are arranged alphabetically by author, with access provided by title, settings, series, series character, author pseudonyms, and film adaption. This is the most reliable, useful, and authoritative bibliography on the genre to date.

1689 Mystery and suspense writers: the literature of crime, detection, and espionage. Robin W. Winks and Maureen Corrigan, eds. 2v. Scribner, 1998. $225. ISBN 0-684-80492-1.
823.08 PR830.D4

These two volumes offer in-depth narrative essays on sixty-nine of our most revered mystery and suspense writers, from Margery Allingham to Edgar Wallace. Essays are written by noted experts in the field and range in length from 5,000 to

12,000 words. There are also studies of themes and subgenres such as "The Female Detective" and "Religious Mysterie" and three appendixes ("Pseudonyms and Series Characters," "Some Mystery and Suspense Subgenres," and "Major Prizewinners"). Indexed.

1690 Twentieth-century crime and mystery writers. 3d ed. Lesley Henderson, ed. (Twentieth-century writers series.) 1100p. St. James, 1991. $115. ISBN 0-55862-031-1.
823 PR830.D4

A brief biography, an evaluative essay, and a bibliography of an author's crime publications and other works are included in each entry in this impressive work. The main part of the book covers English-language writers whose works appeared since the time of Sir Arthur Conan Doyle. The appendixes include selective representations of earlier mystery writers and foreign-language authors whose books are well known in English translation.

ROMANCE

1691 Twentieth-century romance and historical writers. 2d ed. Lesley Henderson, ed. 900p. St. James, 1990. $115. ISBN 0-912289-97-X.
823 PR888.L69

This bibliography of 530 twentieth-century writers of romance and historical fiction is similar in format and appearance to other works in the Twentieth-century writers series. Brief biographical information is followed by a bibliography covering the author's total work. The entry frequently includes a comment by the author and always concludes with a well-written, signed critical essay. Title index.

SCIENCE FICTION, FANTASY, AND THE GOTHIC

1692 Anatomy of wonder 4: a critical guide to science fiction. 4th ed. Neil Barron, ed. 912p. Bowker, 1995. $39. ISBN 0-8352-3288-3.
808.3 PN3433.8

A selective annotated bibliography of science fiction and research aids for science fiction. Gives concise summaries and evaluations of more than 2,000 adult and juvenile science fiction titles. Includes sections on English-language science fiction, foreign-language science fiction, and research aids, covering history and criticism, science fiction magazines, science fiction on film and television, and a core collection checklist.

1693 Encyclopedia of fantasy. John Clute and John Grant, eds. 1049p. St. Martin's, 1997. $75. ISBN 0-312-15897-1.
809.3 PN3435.E53

A comprehensive survey of fantasy in all its forms including texts, film, art, opera, myth, comic books, authors, characters, and places. Specific authors include E. T. A. Hoffmann, E. A. Poe, George MacDonald, William Morris, Lewis Carroll, J. R. R. Tolkien, C. S. Lewis, the Grimm brothers, Cervantes, Chaucer, and Dante. A thorough and authoritative treatment of the genre.

1694 Encyclopedia of science fiction. John Clute and Peter Nicholls. 1370p. St. Martin's, 1993. $75. ISBN 0-312-09618-6.
809.3 PN3433.E53

A companion to the *Encyclopedia of fantasy,* this monumental work includes, in a convenient alphabetical arrangement, more than 4,300 entries offering authoritative information on authors, themes, terminology, films, television, magazines, comics, illustrators, publishers, and awards and everything else having to do with the ever-fascinating world of science fiction.

1695 Reference guide to science fiction, fantasy, and horror. Michael Burgess. 403p. Libraries Unlimited, 1992. $45. ISBN 0-87287-611-X.
809.3 PN3433.5.B87

A standard work. Broadly divided into twenty-nine sections such as "encyclopedias and dictionaries," "award lists," "atlases and gazetteers," "character dictionaries," and "magazine and anthology indexes." Includes core collection recommendations. Indexed.

1696 St. James guide to horror, ghost, and gothic writers. David Pringle, ed. St. James, 1998. $140. ISBN 1-55862-206-3.
809 PN3448.S45

Covers more than 400 historic and contemporary horror, ghost, and gothic writers. Entries feature a biography, a complete list of the author's publications, selected critical and biographical studies, comments by the entrant, when available, and a critical essay by an expert in the field. Coverage includes Isak Dinesen, Nathaniel Hawthorne, Doris

Lessing, H. P. Lovecraft, Edgar Allen Poe, Anne Rice, Edith Wharton, and many others.

1697 Science fiction writers: critical studies of the major authors from the early nineteenth century to the present day. 2d ed. Richard Bleiler, ed. 816p. Scribner, 1999. $115. ISBN 0-684-80593-6.
823 PS373.S35

Ninety-six key authors of science fiction are treated in critical essays by science fiction authorities. Selected bibliographies have been prepared for each writer. Index of names and titles. This long-awaited second edition is a must for every science fiction collection.

1698 Supernatural fiction writers: fantasy and horror. E. F. Bleiler, ed. 2v. Scribner, 1985. $130/set. ISBN 0-684-17808-7.
809.3 PN3435.S96

Essays on writers of fantasy and horror from A.D. 125 to the present include an introduction and overview, a selected bibliography, and a list of critical studies. Commentaries, containing biographical and critical information, are generally five to ten pages in length. Emphasis is on English-language writers although some influential foreign-language authors are also covered. Index to names and titles.

1699 Twentieth-century science-fiction writers. 3d ed. Curtis C. Smith, ed. 1016p. St. James, 1991. $115. ISBN 1-55862-111-3.
823 PS374.S35

Covers primarily English-language writers of science fiction from H. G. Wells to the present. Author entries consist of biographical data, a bibliography of works (both science fiction and non–science fiction), and a signed critical essay. Appendixes include selective representations of authors in other languages whose works have been translated into English and major fantasy writers.

SHORT STORY

1700 Reference guide to short fiction. 2d ed. Thomas Riggs. 1197p. St. James, 1999. $140. ISBN 1-55862-222-5.
809.3 PN3373.R36

Provides detailed information on 375 writers and 400 works of short fiction published in the nineteenth and twentieth centuries. Entries are arranged alphabetically for both writers and works and average about 1,000 words in length. Entries provide authoritative information on critical dates in the author's life, degrees received, awards received, and bibliographic information about all the author's published works. The individual works discussed are all considered classics in the genre and include everything from "A Christmas Carol" to "The Marquise of O."

1701 Short story criticism: excerpts from criticism of the works of short fiction writers. Gale, 1988– . $104/v. ISSN 0895-9439.
809.3 PN3373.S386

This addition to the Gale literary criticism series presents significant critical excerpts on the most important short story writers of all eras and nationalities. Each entry gives a biographical and critical overview, a list of principal works, excerpts of criticism, and a selected bibliography. Beginning with volume 6, the series includes an appendix of general studies of short fiction and excerpted comments by authors, whenever available. A cumulative index lists all authors found in *SSC* or in any of Gale's other literary criticism or biographical series. Twenty-nine volumes currently in print.

1702 Short story index, 1900–1949. Dorothy Elizabeth Cook and Isabel S. Monro, comps. 1553p. Wilson, 1953. $45. ISBN 0-8242-0384-4. Annual short story index, 1974– . $85/yr. ISSN 0360-9774. Cumulative supplements issued approximately every five years. Variously priced. (Supplement 1984–88, $125.)
808.83 PN3373.C6

Short story index: collections indexed, 1900–1978. Juliette Yaakov, ed. 349p. Wilson, 1979. $40. ISBN 0-8242-0643-6.
808.83 PN3451

These indexes provide valuable access to short stories in collections published since 1900. The original volume indexes more than 60,000 stories published in 4,320 collections between 1900 and 1949. Indexing is by author, title, and subject of the short story. A list of collections indexed provides a useful buying guide for the library. Published annually since 1974, with five-year cumulations in print since 1955. *Short story index: collections indexed, 1900–1978* is an index to 8,355 collections containing more than 121,000 short stories. Access through author or editor and title. Numerous cross-references.

1703 Twentieth-century short story explication: an index to the third edition and its five supplements, 1961–1991. Warren S. Walker and Barbara K. Walker. 254p. Shoe String Pr., 1992. $47.50. ISBN 0-208-02320-8.

Twentieth-century short story explication: interpretations, 1900–1975, of short fiction since 1800. 3d ed. Warren S. Walker, comp. 880p. Shoe String Pr., 1977. $69.50. ISBN 0-208-01570-1. Supplement 1 to 3d ed. 257p. Shoe String Pr., 1980. $35. ISBN 0-208-01813-1; Supplement 2 to 3d ed. 348p. Shoe String Pr., 1984. $42.50. ISBN 0-208-02005-5; Supplement 3 to 3d ed. 486p. Shoe String Pr., 1987. $45. ISBN 0-208-02122-1. Supplement 4 to 3d ed. 342p. Shoe String Pr., 1989. $45. ISBN 0-208-02188-4. Supplement 5 to 3d ed. 408p. Shoe String Pr., 1991. $49.50. ISBN 0-208-02299-6.

Twentieth-century short story explication, new series. Shoe String Pr., 1993– . v.1, 1989–90. 336p. $49.50. ISBN 0-208-02340-2; v.2, 1991–93. 259p. $49.50. ISBN 0-208-02370-4; v.3, 1993–94. 347p. $49.50. ISBN 0-208-02419-0.
809.3 PN3373

More than 2,000 authors from around the world are represented in this index to critical analyses of short stories published in books and periodicals since 1900. Arranged by authors and then by stories. The five supplements cover new authors and extend coverage through the 1980s. The new series continues the coverage into the 1990s. Includes checklists of books and journals used and an index of short story writers.

Poetry

1704 The Columbia Granger's index to poetry in anthologies. 11th ed. Edith P. Hazen, ed. 2200p. Columbia Univ. Pr., 1998. $200. ISBN 0-231-11038-3.
808.8 PN1022.H39

The standard work for locating poems in anthologies. Ready access is provided by title, first line, last line, author, and subject to volumes of anthologized poetry. Formerly *Granger's index to poetry,* this edition indexes more than 80,000 poems, by 11,000 poets, from some 400 anthologies. Included in the 150 new anthologies are collections of poetry translated from other languages. Symbols for anthologies indexed are given in the titles and first-line index, with anthologies identified at the front of the volume. All previous editions should be retained.

1705 The Columbia Granger's index to poetry in collected and selected works. Nicholas Frankovich, ed. 2000p. Columbia Univ. Pr., 1996. $225. ISBN 0-231-10762-5.
808.8 PN1022

Indexes more than 50,000 poems by 262 leading poets that appear in selected and collected works—as opposed to anthologies. Indexing is by author, title, first line, last line, and subject. Serves as a complement to *The Columbia Granger's index to poetry in anthologies.*

1706 The Columbia Granger's world of poetry 1995 on CD-ROM. CD-ROM, release 2.1. Columbia Univ. Pr., 1995. $495. ISBN 0-231-10158-9.
808.8 PN1022.C65

Cites more than 135,000 poems by some 20,000 poets found in more than 700 anthologies and 72 volumes of collected and selected works. This CD-ROM product allows author, title, subject, keyword, first line, last line, and category searching and incorporates the full texts for 10,000 poems now in the public domain and 7,500 selected lines from poems still under copyright. The most commonly researched, recognized, and requested poems were chosen. User-friendly software.

1707 Contemporary poets. 6th ed. Thomas Riggs, ed. 1336p. St. James, 1996. $189. ISBN 1-55862-191-1.
821 PR603.C6

A biographical handbook of contemporary poets, arranged alphabetically. Entries consist of a short biography, full bibliography, comments by many of the poets, and a signed critical essay.

1708 Guide to American poetry explication. (A reference publication in literature.) 2v. Hall, 1989. v.1, Colonial and nineteenth century. James Ruppert. 252p. $40. ISBN 0-8161-8919-6; v.2, Modern and contemporary. John R. Leo. 546p. $50. ISBN 0-8161-8918-8.
811 PS221

A successor to the very popular Kuntz and Martinez *Poetry explication* (1980), this expanded and completely revised series provides a comprehensive index to American poetry explication published from 1925 through 1987, incorporating all appropriate entries from the three earlier editions of *Poetry explication*. Entries are arranged alphabetically by name of the poet, followed by an alphabetical list of titles, with citations to criticisms listed below each title.

1709 Guide to British poetry explication. 4v. Nancy Martinez and Joseph G. R. Martinez. Hall, 1991–95. v.1, Old-English, medieval. 310p. $65. ISBN 0-8161-8921-8; v.2, Renaissance. 540p. $65. ISBN 0-8161-8920-X; v.3, Restoration-romantic. 576p. $65. ISBN 0-8161-1997-X; v.4, Victorian-contemporary. 310p. $65. ISBN 0-8161-8988-9.
821 PR311.M37

A successor to the very popular Kuntz and Martinez *Poetry explication* (1980), this expanded and completely revised series indexes poetry explications found in books, journal articles, anthologies, and dissertations. Entries are arranged alphabetically by name of the poet, followed by an alphabetical list of titles, with citations to criticisms listed below each title.

1710 International index to recorded poetry. Herbert H. Hoffman and Rita Ludwig Hoffman, comps. 529p. Wilson, 1983. $75. ISBN 0-8242-0682-7.
011 PN1022.H63

This valuable index to the world's recorded poetry provides access by author, title, first line, and reader to some 1,700 recordings issued through 1980 in the United States and abroad. The work identifies approximately 15,000 poems by some 2,300 authors and represents more than twenty languages on phonodiscs, tapes, audiocassettes, filmstrips, and videocassettes. Includes a "List of Recordings Analyzed."

1711 Last lines: an index to last lines of poetry. Victoria Kline. 2v. Facts on File, 1991. $145/set. ISBN 0-8160-2765-2.
808.8 PN1022.K55

Covers more than 174,000 poems written in or translated into English. Indexes each poem by title, last line, author, and key word.

1712 New Princeton encyclopedia of poetry and poetics. 3d ed. 1383p. Princeton Univ. Pr., 1993. $125. ISBN 0-691-03271-8; paper $29.95. ISBN 0-691-02123-6.
808.1 PN1021.N39

The authoritative, scholarly encyclopedia of poetics and poetry. Provides surveys of the poetry of 106 nations, descriptions of poetic genres and forms, explanations of prosody and rhetoric, discussions of major schools and movements, and discussions on the use and place of poetry in the broader context of civilization.

1713 Poetry criticism. v.1– . Gale, 1991– . $98/v. ISSN 1052-4851.
809.1 PN1010.P499

Using the same successful format as the other titles in Gale's literary criticism series, this biannual publication reprints selected criticism on poets from many countries and all time periods (e.g., Pindar, John Milton, and Nikki Giovanni are featured in recent volumes). Twenty-one volumes currently in print.

1714 Poetry handbook: a dictionary of terms. 4th ed. Babette Deutsch. 203p. Barnes & Noble, 1981. $8.95. ISBN 0-06-463548-1.
808.1 PN44.5.D4

Definitions are clear and concise and cover not only terminology and poetic forms, but broader topics such as romanticism and nonsense verse. Entries are in alphabetical order and include many illustrative examples from literature. Cross-references. Also includes an index of poets cited in the body of the work.

Speech and Rhetoric

1715 Encyclopedia of rhetoric and composition: communication from ancient times to the information age. Theresa Enos. 832p. Garland, 1996. $100. ISBN 0-8240-7200-6.
808 PN172.E53

Provides an overview of rhetoric and its role in contemporary life. Discusses the application of rhetoric, and illustrates its practical benefits. Includes 467 signed entries, including entries on major rhetoricians from all time periods.

1716 Encyclopedia of the essay. Tracy Chevalier, ed. 1000p. Fitzroy Dearborn, 1997. $130. ISBN 1-884964-30-3.
808 PN6141.E53

The encyclopedia focuses on biographical entries for noted essayists such as Montaigne, Addison, Hazlitt, Woolf, E. B. White, Hannah Arendt, Edmund Wilson, and Susan Sontag. Also included are geographic and historical surveys in entries such as the "French Essay" and the "German Essay." Entries on literary figures include a signed scholarly evaluation, a chart of biographical facts, selected writings, and sources for further reading.

1717 Speech index: an index to 259 collections of world famous orations and speeches for various occasions. 4th ed., rev. and enl. Roberta Briggs Sutton. 947p. Scarecrow, 1966. $59.50. ISBN 0-8108-0138-8.

Speech index: an index to collections of world famous orations and speeches for various occasions. 4th ed. supplement, 1966–80. Charity Mitchell. 466p. Scarecrow, 1982. $45. ISBN 0-8108-1518-4.
808.8 AI3.S85

The fourth edition of *Speech index* incorporates all the materials in the three previous editions: 1935, 1935–55, and 1956–62, with additional titles in this field published from 1900 through 1965. The supplement cumulates the 1966–70 and 1971–75 supplements to the fourth edition and adds titles from 1976 to 1980. Speeches are indexed by orator, type of speech, and by subject, with a selected list of titles given in the appendix. Particularly useful for amateur speakers in locating examples to use in preparing a speech and models they can adapt to their needs.

National and Regional Literatures

American

1718 American drama criticism: interpretations, 1890–1977. 2d ed. Floyd Eugene Eddleman, comp. 488p. Shoe String Pr., 1979. $42.50. ISBN 0-208-01713-5.

American drama criticism: supplement I to the 2nd ed. Floyd Eugene Eddleman, comp. (Drama explication series.) 255p. Shoe String Pr., 1984. $34.50. ISBN 0-208-01978-2.

American drama criticism: supplement II to the 2nd ed. 240p. Shoe String Pr., 1989. $47.50. ISBN 0-208-02138-8.

American drama criticism: supplement III to the 2nd ed. 436p. Shoe String Pr., 1992. $55. ISBN 0-208-02270-8.

American drama criticism: supplement IV to the 2nd ed. 239p. Shoe String Pr., 1996. $45. ISBN 0-208-02393-3.
812 PS332.P3

This revised edition of the 1967 bibliography, together with its supplements, lists interpretations of American plays published primarily between 1890 and 1995. Entries are arranged by playwright and then by title. The work concludes with a "List of Books Indexed" and a "List of Journals Indexed," followed by indexes for critics, adapted authors and works, titles, and playwrights.

1719 American nature writers. John Elder, ed. 2v. Macmillan, 1996. $225. ISBN 0-684-19692-1.
810.9 PS163.A6

Seventy writers are featured in this biographical-critical set including Emerson, Thoreau, Muir, Leopold, Carsons, Matthiessen, and Lewis Thomas. Sixty-four scholars participated in this effort to describe the contributions of writer-naturalists who have contributed significantly to the way we interpret the world around us.

1720 American writers: a collection of literary biographies. Leonard Unger, ed. 4v. plus five supplements. Scribner, 1974– . $1000/set. ISBN 0-684-19594-1.
810.9 PS129

American writers presents lengthy authoritative essays on more than 200 major American authors (novelists, poets, short-story writers, playwrights, critics, and philosophers) in four base volumes (ninety-seven essays published in 1974) and a series of supplementary volumes (ongoing). Following each biocritical essay is a selected bibliography of the author's work, a list of studies for further reading, and, if applicable, a list of published interviews.

1721 American writers before 1800: a biographical and critical dictionary. James A. Levernier and Douglas R. Wilmes, eds. 3v. Greenwood, 1983.

$285/set. ISBN 0-313-22229-0.
810.9 PS185.A4

Signed articles for more than 786 early American writers provide valuable information on many lesser-known figures as well as major authors. Each entry contains a brief biographical sketch, a critical evaluation, a list of the author's major publications, and a selective bibliography of secondary sources. Entries are arranged under separate appendixes by date of birth, place of birth, and principal residence; a fourth appendix provides a chronology of the period. Detailed forty-page index to people and subjects.

1722 **Articles on American literature, 1900–1950.** Lewis Leary, comp. 437p. Duke Univ. Pr., 1954. $60. ISBN 0-8223-0241-1.

Articles on American literature, 1950–1967. Lewis Leary, comp., with Carolyn Bartholet and Catharine Roth. 751p. Duke Univ. Pr., 1970. $60. ISBN 0-8223-1239-X.

Articles on American literature, 1968–1975. Lewis Leary, comp., with John Auchard. 745p. Duke Univ. Pr., 1979. $60. ISBN 0-8223-0432-5.
813 PS88.L4

A bibliography of criticism in English that appeared in periodicals between 1900 and 1975. Arranged alphabetically by author, with a separate listing of articles by topic, such as literary trends, regionalism, and humor.

1723 **Benét's reader's encyclopedia of American literature.** George Perkins, Barbara Perkins, and Phillip Leininger. HarperCollins, 1991. $45. ISBN 0-06-270027-8.
810.9 PN41.B4

Some 6,500 authoritative entries on novelists, playwrights, poets, short-story writers, essayists, critics, places, events, characters, and other relevant subjects pertaining to American literature. Includes writers from Canada and Latin America as well as the United States dating from the era of European exploration to the 1990s.

1724 **Chicano literature: a reference guide.** Julio A. Martinez and Francisco A. Lomeli, eds. 492p. Greenwood, 1985. $55. ISBN 0-313-23691-7.
810.9 PS153.M4

Signed critical essays on the life and works of Chicano authors and on other topics relevant to the history and development of Chicano literature, including articles on the novel, poetry, theater, children's literature, and Chicano philosophy. Selected bibliographies; brief index.

1725 **Dickinson's American historical fiction.** 5th ed. Virginia Brokaw Gerhardstein. 352p. Scarecrow, 1986. $32.50. ISBN 0-8108-1867-1.
813 PS374.H5

First published in 1956, *Dickinson's American historical fiction* classifies, under chronological periods from colonial days to the 1970s, 3,048 historical novels published largely between 1917 and 1984. Selective classics of historical fiction published earlier are also included. Brief annotations place works in historical perspective. Author-title and subject indexes.

1726 **Fifty southern writers after 1900: a bio-bibliographical sourcebook.** Joseph M. Flora and Robert Bain, eds. 628p. Greenwood, 1987. $75. ISBN 0-313-24519-3.

Fifty southern writers before 1900: a bio-bibliographical sourcebook. Robert Bain and Joseph M. Flora, eds. 601p. Greenwood, 1987. $75. ISBN 0-313-24518-5.
810 PS261.F54

These two volumes offer bio-bibliographical essays by noted scholars on 100 southern writers. Each essay consists of a biographical sketch, a discussion of the author's major themes, an assessment of the scholarship, a chronological list of the author's works, and a bibliography of selected criticism. Alphabetically arranged; index for names and titles.

1727 **The Oxford companion to American literature.** 6th ed. James D. Hart and Phillip Leininger. 800p. Oxford Univ. Pr., 1995. $55. ISBN 0-19-506548-4.
810 PS21.H3

This handbook to American literature includes short biographies of American authors, brief bibliographies, plot summaries of novels and plays, entries on literary schools and movements, and brief entries for those social and economic movements that formed the background for much literary protest. Arranged by specific subject in dictionary format with numerous cross-references. Chronological index.

1728 Reference guide to American literature. 3d ed. Jim Kamp. 1202p. St. James, 1994. $145. ISBN 1-55862-310-8.
810.9 PS129.R44

Provides an authoritative bibliography and commentary for American literature. Presents writers and relevant topics alphabetically. Each personal entry lists biographical data, publications, and critical studies and presents a signed scholarly essay on the author's contributions to literature. Incorporates 131 essays on the best-known American works, including *Civil Disobedience, Lolita, Death of a Salesman,* and "The Waste Land." Includes an exhaustive chronology and title index.

1729 Twentieth-century western writers. 2d ed. James Vinson, ed. 1000p. St. James, 1991. $115. ISBN 0-912289-98-8.
810.9 PS271.T84

Entries for writers contain a biography, bibliography, and signed critical essay. Notations also provide information about available bibliographies, manuscript collections, and critical studies. Title index.

Arabic

1730 Encyclopedia of Arabic literature. Julie Scott Meisami and Paul Starkey, eds. 2v. 896p. Routledge, 1998. $290. ISBN 0-415-06808-8.
892 PJ7510

Edited by two Middle Eastern scholars, this encyclopedia will be of interest to all who wish to explore Arabic culture and civilization. The 1,300 signed entries are arranged alphabetically and aim to provide information on "the most important authors, works, genres, key terms, and issues in the Arabic literary tradition—classical, transitional, and modern." Sources for further reading are provided for most entries. A comprehensive index and a glossary are also included.

British

1731 British writers. Ian Scott-Kilvert, ed. 7v. plus four supplements. Scribner, 1979– . $1100/set. ISBN 0-684-80587-1.
820 PR85.B688

A companion to Scribner's *American writers,* this work presents articles by distinguished contributors on major British writers from the fourteenth century to the present. Published earlier as separate works, the twenty-one essays in volume 1 have been entirely revised. The biographical sketch that opens each entry is followed by a survey of the author's principal works, a critical evaluation, and an updated bibliography. Indexed.

1732 English novel explication: criticisms to 1972. Helen H. Palmer and Anne Jane Dyson, comps. 329p. Shoe String Pr., 1973. $24.50. ISBN 0-208-01322-9.

English novel explication: supplement I. Peter L. Abernethey et al., comps. 305p. Shoe String Pr., 1976. $32.50. ISBN 0-208-01464-0.

English novel explication: supplement II. Christian J. W. Kloesel and Jeffrey R. Smitten, comps. 326p. Shoe String Pr., 1981. $35. ISBN 0-208-01464-0.

English novel explication: supplement III. Christian J. W. Kloesel, comp. 533p. Shoe String Pr., 1986. $57.50. ISBN 0-208-02092-6.

English novel explication: supplement IV. Christian J. W. Kloesel, comp. 351p. Shoe String Pr., 1990. $55. ISBN 0-208-02231-7.

English novel explication: supplement V. Christian J. W. Kloesel, comp. 431p. Shoe String Pr., 1994. $59.50. ISBN 0-208-02308-9.

English novel explication: supplement VI. Christian J. W. Kloesel, comp. Shoe String Pr., 1998. $59.50. ISBN 0-208-02418-2.
823 PR821

Continuing the work begun by Bell and Baird, the present series provides a checklist of interpretive criticism on the English novel published from 1957. Includes an index of authors and titles and a list of books indexed.

1733 The English novel 1578–1956: a checklist of twentieth-century criticisms. Inglis F. Bell and Donald Baird. 168p. Swallow, 1958. Reprint: Shoe String Pr., 1974; Bingley, 1974. op.
823 PR821

Covers criticism published in books and periodicals from the beginning of the twentieth century through 1956. Arranged alphabetically by author, then by title, followed by a list of critical studies. Continued by *English novel explication*.

1734 **The Oxford companion to English literature.** Rev. 5th ed. Margaret Drabble, ed. 1184p. Oxford Univ. Pr., 1995. $55. ISBN 0-19-866221-1.
820.9 PR19.D73

A thorough revision of this standard handbook to English literature, first compiled by Sir Paul Harvey in 1932 and revised in 1967 by Dorothy Eagle (fourth edition). Contains brief articles on authors, titles, characters, literary allusions, and related literary topics.

SHAKESPEARE

1735 **The essential Shakespeare: an annotated bibliography of major modern studies.** 2d ed. Larry S. Champion. 568p. Hall, 1993. $70. ISBN 0-8161-7332-X.
822.3 PR2894.C53

A convenient annotated checklist of the most significant Shakespearean scholarship in English from 1900. Some 2,000 entries are arranged under general studies or under individual works. A very useful guide for students and nonspecialists interested in Shakespeare.

1736 **The Folger book of Shakespeare quotations.** Burton Stevenson. 776p. Folger Books, 1979. $75. ISBN 0-918016-00-2.
822.3 PR2892.S64

Originally published by Funk & Wagnalls in 1953 under the title *The standard book of Shakespeare quotations*, this work serves as a subject guide with exact citations to the 1911 Globe edition of *Shakespeare's plays and poems*. A concordance is also provided.

1737 **The Harvard concordance to Shakespeare.** Marvin Spevack. 1600p. Belknap/Harvard Univ. Pr., 1973. $75. ISBN 0-674-37475-4.
822.3 PR2892.S62

A computer-produced concordance based on volumes 4 through 6 of the author's *A complete and systematic concordance to Shakespeare* (Hildeshein, Georg Olms, 1968–70). A thorough piece of scholarship: 29,000 words, statistics on the number of occurrences of words in verse and prose passages, and their relative frequency.

1738 **The quotable Shakespeare: a topical dictionary.** Charles DeLoach, comp. 544p. McFarland, 1988. $39.95. ISBN 0-89950-303-9.
822.3 PR2892.D37

A compilation of 6,516 quotations arranged under some 1,000 topics; title, character, and topical indexes.

1739 **The reader's encyclopedia of Shakespeare.** Oscar James Campbell and Edward G. Quinn, eds. 1014p. Crowell, 1966. op.
822.3 PR2892.C3

Criticism and information on all aspects of Shakespeare's works. Sources are given at the end of many articles. Among the appendixes are a chronology of events related to the life and works of Shakespeare, transcripts of documents, genealogical table of the Houses of York and Lancaster, and a thirty-page selected bibliography.

1740 **Shakespeare A to Z: the essential reference to his plays, his poems, his life and times, and more.** Charles Boyce. 742p. Facts on File, 1990. $55. ISBN 0-8160-1805-7.
822.3 PR2892.B69

Presents a scene-by-scene synopsis of each play, a critical commentary, a discussion of the play's sources, a history of the text, and the play's theatrical history. Includes entries on all the major characters; Shakespeare's contemporaries; theatrical terms; Shakespearean actors, producers, and directors; and Shakespeare's nondramatic poetry.

1741 **A Shakespeare glossary.** C. T. Onions. Enl. and rev. by Robert D. Eagleson. 326p. Oxford Univ. Pr., 1986. $34. ISBN 0-19-811199-1; paper $10.95. ISBN 0-19-812521-6.
822.3 PR2892.O6

Gives definitions of words or senses of words now obsolete, as well as explanations for unfamiliar allusions and for proper names. Illustrative citations from Shakespeare are included for each definition.

1742 **Shakespeare on screen: an international filmography and videography.** Kenneth S. Rothwell and Annabelle Henkin Melzer. 404p. Neal-Schuman, 1990. $75. ISBN 1-55570-049-7.
822.3 PR3093.R68

The principal work on film adaptations of Shakespeare.

1743 Shakespearean criticism. v.1– . Gale, 1984– . $146/v. ISSN 0883-0123.
822.3 PR2965.S44

Intended as an introduction to Shakespearean criticism for students and nonspecialists, this Gale series presents significant passages from the most important critical commentaries on Shakespeare. Thirty-eight volumes are now in print. The first nine volumes each contain criticism on three to six plays. Each entry consists of an introduction, excerpts of criticism, and a selected bibliography. Later volumes are devoted to performance criticism and special topics, including the sonnets and other poetry, stage history of the plays, and other general subjects. Beginning with volume 13 (*Yearbook 1989*), *SC* published an annual volume containing approximately fifty essays representing the best scholarship published on Shakespeare during the previous year. Beginning with volume 27, the series focused on thematic specific criticism, such as kingship or gender roles, published since 1960. Cumulative indexes to topics and critics.

1744 William Shakespeare: his world, his work, his influence. John F. Andrews, ed. 3v. Scribner, 1985. $300/set. ISBN 0-684-17851-6.
822.3 PR2976.W5354

This three-volume study on the Elizabethan poet and dramatist constitutes a multifaceted view of Shakespeare and his world. Critical essays by British and American scholars examine Shakespeare's life and works, the historical and cultural aspects of the era in which he wrote, and his subsequent influence on literature, theater, and popular culture. Index to names and titles in volume 3.

Classical

1745 Ancient writers: Greece and Rome. T. James Luce, ed. 2v. Scribner, 1982. $200/set. ISBN 0-684-16595-3.
880 PA3002.A5

The forty-seven articles found in this important handbook of Greek and Roman literature were written by noted classicists and vary in length from ten to fifty pages. Arranged chronologically, they primarily treat individual authors, although some cover groups of authors. Each article consists of biographical information, a critical analysis of the author's works, and a selective bibliography of primary and secondary sources. An important resource for libraries supporting an interest in classical studies.

1746 Classical and medieval literature criticism: excerpts from criticism of the works of world authors, from classical antiquity through the fourteenth century, from the first appraisals to current evaluations. v.1– . Gale, 1988– . $140/v. ISSN 0896-0011.
809 PN681.5.C57

Following the pattern of other Gale series for literature criticism, this work provides an introduction to literary works from antiquity to the fourteenth century. Each entry contains a historical and critical introduction, a list of principal English translations, and excerpts from major critical writings. Cumulative index. Twenty-three volumes published so far.

1747 The classical epic: an annotated bibliography. Thomas J. Sienkewicz. 265p. Salem, 1991. $40. ISBN 0-89356-633-2.
883.01 PA3022.E6

A bibliography "directed toward the first time reader of Classical epics in English translation." This work aids the advanced high school student and general college student to find study materials on the *Iliad, Odyssey,* and *Aeneid.* Targeting easily accessible materials, the bibliography describes items that discuss social conditions, geographical conditions, composition techniques, translations, characters, and influence of the great classical epics.

1748 Classical Greek and Roman drama: an annotated bibliography. Robert J. Forman, ed. 239p. Salem, 1989. $40. ISBN 0-89356-659-4.
882.01 PA3024

An annotated bibliography of translations and commentaries and accessible English-language criticism of works by Aeschylus, Aristophanes, Ennius, Euripides, Menander, Plautus, Seneca, Sophocles, and Terence.

1749 Classical studies: a guide to the reference literature. Fred W. Jenkins. 263p. Libraries Unlimited, 1996. $43. ISBN 1-56308-110-5.
882 PA91

Part 1 describes bibliographical sources, research guides, indexes and abstracts, review journals, topical bibliographies, and individual bibliographies.

Part 2 describes other information resources such as dictionaries, handbooks, biographical sources, geographical sources, directories, and Internet resources. Part 3 describes relevant organizations to classical studies, providing an address and other directory information.

1750 Greek and Latin authors, 800 B.C.–A.D. 1000. Michael Grant. 490p. Wilson, 1980. $55. ISBN 0-8242-0640-1.
880 PA31.G7

This dictionary adds more than 370 important and representative authors from 1,800 years of classical literature to the Wilson authors series. An expert on the ancient world, Grant supplies in each entry the pronunciation of the author's name, biographical background, an overview of major works with critical commentary on the nature and quality of those works, and, where relevant, a brief discussion of the influence of the author's works on later literature. A bibliography of the most useful editions of the author's works, together with selective critical studies, completes each sketch.

1751 Greek and Roman authors: a checklist of criticism. 2d ed. Thomas Gwinup and Fidelia Dickinson. 280p. Scarecrow, 1982. $17.50. ISBN 0-8108-1528-1.
880 PA3001

A valuable compilation of English-language criticism on seventy authors of ancient Greece and Rome published in books and periodicals. Alphabetical by author, with citations to general criticism followed by critical studies of individual works. Not indexed.

1752 The Oxford classical dictionary. 3d ed. Simon Hornblower and Antony Spawforth, eds. 1640p. Oxford Univ. Pr., 1997. $99. ISBN 0-19-866172-X.
938 DE5.O9

Brief, succinct entries in dictionary format on all facets of classical studies, including biography, literature, geography, and historical events. Signed articles, many with useful bibliographies. Index of names that are not titles of entries.

1753 The Oxford companion to classical literature. 2d ed. M. C. Howatson, ed. 627p. Oxford Univ. Pr., 1989. $55. ISBN 0-19-866121-5.
880.9 PA31.H69

The first completely revised and enlarged edition of Sir Paul Harvey's standard handbook to classical antiquity, originally published in 1937. Although much of the original has been retained, revisions have been made to reflect new discoveries as well as recent advances in scholarship. This work continues to serve as a valuable resource for identifying geographical, historical, mythological, and political backgrounds relevant to the study and understanding of the literature of Greece and Rome. Appendixes include maps and a chronology.

Latin American

1754 Encyclopedia of Latin American literature. Verity Smith, ed. 926p. Fitzroy Dearborn, 1997. $125. ISBN 1-884964-18-4.
860.09 PQ7081.A1

A guide to authors, works, and literary issues relevant to the literary culture of Latin America presented in an alphabetical arrangement. Most of the 500 entries are about 1,500 words long, but survey articles on individual countries may be as long as 10,000 words.

1755 Handbook of Latin American literature. 2d ed. David William Foster, ed. 799p. Garland, 1992. $100. ISBN 0-8153-0343-2; paper $18.95. ISBN 0-8153-1143-5.
860.9 PQ7081.A1

Provides separate scholarly essays on all Latin American countries as well as Latino writing in the United States and includes a separate essay on literature and film. Discusses literary movements and issues, principal figures, and major works from the colonial period to the present. Each essay concludes with an annotated bibliography. Index.

1756 Latin American writers. Carlos A. Sole and Maria Isabel Abreu, eds. 3v. Scribner, 1989. $250/set. ISBN 0-684-18463-X.
860.9 PQ7081.A1

This award-winning set provides a scholarly overview of Latin American literature from the colonial period to the present. Entries are lengthy and cover 176 writers of Spanish America and Brazil and include a signed biographical and critical essay, followed by a selected bibliography of primary and secondary sources. Volume 3 contains a general index, lists of subjects arranged alphabetically and by country, and a list of contributors.

1757 Masterpieces of Latino literature. Frank N. Magill. 655p. HarperCollins,

1994. $45. ISBN 0-06-270106-1.
860.9 PQ7081.A1

Covers the works of 105 Latino authors from South, Central, and North America, who lived from the seventeenth century to the present. Entries are arranged alphabetically by title. Provides an overview of the plot of each work considered and a reliable critical commentary.

African

1758 African writers. C. Brian Cox. 2v. 936p. Scribner, 1997. $220. ISBN 0-684-19651-4.
896 PL8010.A453

Incorporating the work of an international team of scholars, the sixty-five writers featured in this two-volume set came from or spent critical periods of their lives on the African continent during the nineteenth or twentieth centuries. Works may have originally appeared in English, French, Portuguese, Arabic, or an indigenous language. Writers include Chinua Achebe, Albert Camus, Doris Lessing, Najib Mahfuz, Alan Paton, Wole Soyinka, and Laurens van der Post. The set provides a list of writers by country of residence and provides a historical chronology of the African continent from 1830 to 1996. Author entries average about fifteen pages and include substantial biographical information, a scholarly analysis of the author's works, and an extensive bibliography, incorporating interviews, critical studies, and translations.

Australian

1759 The Oxford companion to Australian literature. 2d ed. William H. Wilde et al. 833p. Oxford Univ. Pr., 1995. $85. ISBN 0-19-553381-X.
820.9 PR9600.2.W55

Provides a comprehensive account of Australian literature from 1788 to the present. Alphabetical entries provide information on authors, works, important literary characters, literary journals, awards, societies, movements, and historical events with relevance to the study of Australian literature.

Canadian

1760 The Oxford companion to Canadian literature. 2d ed. William Toye, ed. 1168p. Oxford Univ. Pr., 1998. $65. ISBN 0-19-541167-6.
809 PR9180.2.O94

A successor to the *Oxford companion to Canadian history and literature,* this comprehensive dictionary consists of some 800 entries on English-language and French-Canadian literature. Entries, contributed by some 200 scholars, cover ethnic and regional literatures as well as other topics and aspects of Canadian literary culture.

Chinese

1761 Indiana companion to traditional Chinese literature. William H. Nienhauser Jr., ed. 1056p. Indiana Univ. Pr., 1986. $95. ISBN 0-253-32983-3.

Indiana companion to traditional Chinese literature. Vol. 2. William H. Nienhauser Jr., ed. 576p. Indiana Univ. Pr., 1998. $59.95. ISBN 0-253-33456-X.
895.1 PL2264.I5

The original volume was compiled by more than 170 scholars of Chinese literature and covers Chinese literature through 1911. Consists of some 500 signed entries on authors, schools, movements, and genres. Includes, for each entry, a bibliography of editions, translations, and criticism. Lengthy essays on broad topics serve to establish a context for the work as a whole. Volume 2 supplements the entries found in the original volume. The first half of volume 2 presents 63 newly researched entries, many of which offer information on general topics such as the printing and circulation of texts, children's literature, and literary Chinese; the second half of volume 2 presents updated bibliographies for the entries found in the original volume. Both volumes provide name, title, and subject indexes.

French

1762 Guide to French literature. Anthony Levi. 2v. St. James, 1992. v.1, Beginnings to 1789. $140. ISBN 1-55862-159-8; v.2, 1789 to the present. $140. ISBN 1-55862-086-9.
840 PQ226.L48

An exhaustive and authoritative work. In an *A* to *Z* format, provides biographical, critical, and scholarly information on principal figures in French literature and discusses topics, issues, schools, and movements in lengthy essays. Includes a thorough bibliography for each author discussed.

1763 New Oxford companion to literature in French. Peter France, ed. 926p. Oxford Univ. Pr., 1995. $55. ISBN 0-19-866125-8.
840.9 PQ41.N49

An outstanding, award-winning companion to literature in the French language. Discusses cultural and literary movements and those who participated in them. Includes entries for authors, titles of works, literary terms, festivals, literary movements, and historical events with relevance to literature in French.

German

1764 The Oxford companion to German literature. 3d ed. Mary Garland and Henry Garland. 968p. Oxford Univ. Pr., 1997. $75. ISBN 0-19-815896-3.
830.3 PT41.G3

This new revision of the standard work presents entries of varying lengths pertinent to German culture and literature in a single alphabetical order. Includes entries for authors, titles of works, literary terms, festivals, literary movements, and historical events with relevance to German literature.

Irish

1765 Dictionary of Irish literature. Rev. ed. Robert Hogan, ed. 2v. Greenwood, 1996. $135. ISBN 0-313-29172-1.
820.9 PR8706.D5

Irish literature in English and in Gaelic is explored in two introductory essays, followed by more than 500 biocritical sketches about important Irish literary figures, with primary and secondary bibliographies, and articles on significant related subjects and institutions. In addition to a chronology that relates political and literary events from the years 432 to the present, an extensive bibliography cites general works on Irish literature, and an index provides access to names, titles, and subjects in the book.

1766 Modern Irish writers: a bio-critical sourcebook. Alexander G. Gonzalez, ed. Greenwood, 1997. $95. ISBN 0-313-29557-3.
820.9 PR8727.G66

Provides alphabetically arranged entries on more than seventy Irish writers from 1885 to the present, including Joyce, Yeats, Heaney, and Beckett. Entries include biographical information, a discussion of each writer's work, critical reception, and a bibliography of both primary and secondary sources.

1767 The Oxford companion to Irish literature. Robert Welch and Bruce Stewart. 648p. Oxford Univ. Pr., 1996. $55. ISBN 0-19-866158-4.
820.9 PR8706.O88

Covers sixteen centuries of literature from the emerald isle. Alphabetically arranged entries provide a comprehensive guide to the evolution and history of Irish literature, framed within the context of the unique culture that is Ireland.

Italian

1768 Dictionary of Italian literature. Rev. ed. Peter Bondanella and Julia Conaway Bondanella, eds. 716p. Greenwood, 1996. $99.50. ISBN 0-313-27745-1.
850.3 PQ4006.D45

Introduction to authors and genres of Italian literature from the twelfth century to the present and to literary periods, problems, schools, and movements. Entries are arranged alphabetically, with cross-references and full indexing. Bibliographies include English translations of primary texts as well as critical studies in various languages.

Japanese

1769 Princeton companion to classical Japanese literature. Earl Miner, Hiroko Odagiri, and Robert E. Morrell. 570p. Princeton Univ. Pr., 1985. $45. ISBN 0-691-06599-3; paper $24.95. ISBN 0-691-00825-6.
895.6 PL726.1.M495

Provides essential information on classical Japanese literature. An opening section provides a historical context for the text and is followed by, among other things, a chronology, a description of major authors and their works, and entries on literary terms, theaters, reference tools, literary symbols, relevant geographical information, and costume.

Russian

1770 Handbook of Russian literature. Victor Terras, ed. 558p. Yale Univ. Pr., 1985. $55. ISBN 0-300-03155-6; paper $24.95. ISBN 0-300-04868-8.
891.3 PG2940.H29

This well-researched companion to Russian literature covers authors, critics, genres, literary movements, journals, newspapers, institutions, and other topics of literary interest. Most of the nearly 1,000 articles include bibliographies of secondary studies; author entries also provide a list of major works and important translations. Indexed.

Spanish

1771 The Oxford companion to Spanish literature. Philip Ward, ed. 629p. Oxford Univ. Pr., 1978. $49.95. ISBN 0-19-866114-2.
860.3 PQ6006.O95

Readers of Spanish-language literature from the period of Roman Spain to 1977 will find in this comprehensive reference work a richness of information relating to authors from Spain and Spanish America (excluding Brazil), movements, themes, and a variety of other pertinent subjects. The majority of the articles present biographical and bibliographical information about authors, including writers of creative, historical, philosophical, and critical works.

20

History

BETSY HOAGG

The dynamic world changes since the end of the cold war have contributed to an increased interest in the history of other nations and peoples. The challenges for the small or medium-sized library are to find sources that suit the interests of its clientele and to try to keep abreast of increasing diversity. Among the traditional subjects, some multivolume encyclopedias continue to be the standard, although concise editions of many works are viable alternatives.

Included in this chapter are historical atlases. Other types of thematic atlases, as well as political atlases, are covered in chapter 21.

Bibliographies and Guides

1772 Guide to historical literature. 3d ed. Mary Beth Norton, ed. 2v. Oxford Univ. Pr., 1995. $150. ISBN 0-19-505727-9.
016.9 D20

This edition is an extensive revision of the 1961 version, with more space given to Asian, African, and American literature. Almost 27,000 entries are divided into forty-eight sections. The work is cross-referenced, annotated, with authority. Well indexed by author and subject, it contains citations chiefly to works published between 1961 and 1992.

1773 Guide to the study of the United States of America. U.S. Library of Congress. General Reference and Bibliography Div. 1193p. Govt. Print. Off., 1960. op. Supplement 1956–65. 526p. Govt. Print. Off., 1976. $12. S/N 030-010-00042-7.
917.3 E156

A valuable guide to every phase of American life. Annotated bibliography with excellent descriptive annotations that list representative books reflecting the development of American life and thought. Brief biographies of many of the authors included.

1774 Harvard guide to American history. Rev. ed. Frank Freidel and Richard K. Showman. 2v. in one. 1312p. Belknap,

1974. Paper $20. ISBN 0-674-37555-6.
016.9173 E178

Standard bibliographic guide to books and articles on American history. Current paper edition combines original two volumes: sections on research methods, histories of special subjects (demography, law, social manners, religion), biographies, and area histories comprised the first volume. The second volume contained a chronological listing. Personal name and subject indexes.

Indexes and Abstracts

1775 America: history and life.
ABC-Clio, 1964– . 5/yr. Price varies. Formerly published in four parts. ISSN 0002-7065.
■ cd online
973 E171

Historical abstracts. ABC-Clio, 1955– . Price varies. Part A: modern history abstracts, 1450–1914. 4/yr. ISSN 0363-2717. Part B: twentieth century abstracts, 1914 to the present. 4/yr., including index. ISSN 0363-2725. Annual index also available separately.
■ cd online
909 D299

These comprehensive standard indexes for American and world history cover the breadth of literature in many languages. *America: history and life* deals with history of the United States and Canada from prehistory to the present. *Historical abstracts* deals with world history outside North America in two chronological divisions. For libraries with a need for extensive scholarly literature. Most small and medium-sized libraries will be well served by Wilson's *Social sciences index*.

1776 Index to America: life and customs.
Norma O. Ireland. v.1, 17th century. 250p. Scarecrow, 1978. op. ISBN 0-8108-2013-7; v.2, 18th century. 187p. Scarecrow, 1976. op. ISBN 0-8108-2014-5; v.3, 19th century. 374p. Scarecrow, 1974. $35. ISBN 0-8108-1661-X; v.4, 20th century to 1986. 361p. Scarecrow, 1989. $37.50. ISBN 0-8108-2170-2.
016.973 [970.016] E178

This set indexes nearly 500 general books on American history and culture. Employing several thousand straightforward subject terms, the set is successful in providing access to materials for the junior and senior high school student that may have otherwise been overlooked. An excellent place to begin searching for difficult-to-find material on the history of American culture.

Chronologies

1777 American chronicle: seven decades in American life, 1920–1989. Lois Gordon and Alan Gordon. 709p. Simon & Schuster, 1987. $35. ISBN 0-689-11899-6.
973.9 E169.1

The American years: a chronology of United States history. Ernie Gross. 655p. Scribner, 1999. $95. ISBN 0-684-80590-1.
973.02 E174.5

The *American chronicle* is a wonderful resource. Packed into the nine pages allotted for each year are facts and figures, sample consumer-goods prices, major news headlines, quotations, and lists of popular radio shows, TV shows, and movies, as well as significant fashion trends and advertising themes. Highly useful for school assignments and fascinating to browse. *The American years* provides a year-by-year overview of American life from 1776 to 1997. Each year is divided into subject categories, under which key events are listed. Categories for each year are consistent (e.g., "Transportation," "Science/Medicine," "Education," "Religion," "Art," "Sports"), and there is a "Miscellaneous" section for special events. The detailed index helps make this a handy ready reference tool.

1778 Chronicle of the twentieth century.
Clifton Daniel et al., eds. 1438p. International, 1992. $69.95. ISBN 1-872031-02-1.
909.02 CB425

The editors have included in each annual entry monthly calendars with a brief event listed per day. There are summaries of major news stories complemented with extensive illustrations and maps.

1779 Day by day: the eighties. Ellen Meltzer and Marc Aronson. 2v. Facts on File, 1995. $195/set. ISBN 0-8160-1592-9.

Day by day: the seventies. Thomas M. Leonard et al. 2v. Facts on File, 1988. $195/set. ISBN 0-8160-1020-X.

Day by day: the sixties. Douglas Nelson and Thomas Parker. 2v. Facts on File, 1983. $195/set. ISBN 0-87196-648-4.

Day by day: the fifties. Jeffrey Merritt. 1036p. Facts on File, 1979. $145. ISBN 0-87196-383-3.

Day by day: the forties. Thomas M. Leonard. 1072p. Facts on File, 1977. $145. ISBN 0-87196-375-2.
909.82 D840

This set of chronologies is laid out in a two-page format, showing on a day-by-day basis events in ten broad categories. On the left page the focus is on international affairs, while the right page covers U.S. events in politics, foreign policy, military affairs, the economy, science, lifestyles, and culture. Based primarily on the Facts on File yearbooks. Two pages of illustrations begin each year.

1780 The people's chronology: year-by-year record of human events from prehistory to the present. Rev. and updated ed. James Trager, ed. 1237p. Henry Holt, 1992. $45. ISBN 0-8050-1786-0; paper $25. ISBN 0-8050-3134-0.
902 D11

Human-interest and trivia events as well as major political, military, economic, and social happenings are included in this massive chronology. Events from 1,000,000 B.C. until 1991 are listed, with a large majority of the entries from the nineteenth and twentieth centuries. Comprehensive index.

1781 Smithsonian timelines of the ancient world: a visual chronology from the origins of life to A.D. 1500. Chris Scarre. 256p. Dorling Kindersley (dist. by Houghton), 1993. $49.95. ISBN 1-56458-305-8.
930 D54.5

A colorful resource, this work encompasses a wide range of subjects in the ancient world. The threads of civilization in five major areas are charted.

1782 The timetables of history: a horizontal linkage of people and events. New 3d ed. Bernard Grun. 724p. Simon & Schuster, 1987. $17.95. ISBN 0-671-63435-6; paper $20. ISBN 0-671-74271-X.
902 D11

These clearly laid-out timetables relate significant events occurring in various fields of endeavor to their historical and political milieu. Daily life as well as science, literature, religion, the arts, and music are charted in a two-page format that facilitates an easy comparison. More recent times are covered in greater detail. Indexed.

Dictionaries and Encyclopedias

1783 The American Revolution, 1775–1783: an encyclopedia. Ed. Richard L. Blanco. 2v. Garland, 1993. $175. ISBN 0-8240-5623-X.
973.3 E208

The focus is on the military history of the subject, placing the event in a worldwide context, but much ancillary material is also covered. Maps of major battles; biographies of participants from many ethnic backgrounds. Bibliographies; glossary; index of major entries.

1784 Atlas of the North American Indian. Carl Waldman. 288p. Facts on File, 1985. $35. ISBN 0-87196-850-9; paper $18.95. ISBN 0-8160-2136-8.
970.004 E77

Although called an atlas, this volume more appropriately should be classed with encyclopedias. The text is clearly written and well supported with about 100 thematic maps covering historical, military, and cultural events. Appendixes contain a chronology, a listing of Indian tribes, and their contemporary locations. Also includes an extensive bibliography and index.

1785 Brassey's battles: 3500 years of conflict, campaigns, and wars from A to Z. John Laffin. 484p. Brassey's, 1995. $23.95. ISBN 1-85753-176-0.
904 D25

About 7,000 listings identifying campaigns. A few military actions are included for minor wars in which there were no single important battles. Describes some sea battles. Some excellent battle maps.

1786 Cambridge ancient history. 2d ed. 14v. Cambridge Univ. Pr., 1971– . Prices vary, $82.50–$150/v. Some volumes available in paper.
930 D57

Excellent reference history. Each chapter written by a specialist; full bibliographies at end of volume. Libraries owning the set will want to fill in gaps; smaller collections might want to consider less costly and voluminous alternatives.

1787 The Cambridge historical encyclopedia of Great Britain and Ireland. Christopher Haigh, ed. 392p. Cambridge Univ. Pr., 1985. op. ISBN 0-521-25559-7; paper $27.50. ISBN 0-521-39552-6.
941 DA34

Broad chronological overview of seven themes ranging from government to culture. The essays on topics such as government and politics, warfare, society, the economy, and international relations are supported by short identification paragraphs in the margins. The time period covered extends from 100 B.C. to 1975. There is a biographical section with about 800 entries. Includes a detailed index.

1788 The Cambridge history of Latin America. Leslie Bethell, ed. 10v.– . Cambridge Univ. Pr., 1985– . $79.95–$120/v.
980 F1410

Another in the respected multivolume history series from Cambridge. Long essays by recognized scholars cover political, economic, and social history. Women's studies, art, architecture, and music are also included. Good use of maps and charts to assist the reader in understanding the basic forces that led to today's Latin America. Long bibliographical essays for each chapter are gathered at the end of the volume.

1789 Cambridge medieval history. 9v. Cambridge Univ. Pr., 1911–36. Various pricing, availability. ISBN 0-318-51274-2.
940.1 D117

Survey of the period written by experts in each area. Readable, concise information for students and informed laypersons. Extensive bibliographies and index in each volume. Most volumes are op. The *New Cambridge medieval history* is projected for seven volumes, at an anticipated cost of $95 per volume. As of this date, volumes 2, 5, and 7 are complete.

1790 Civil War dictionary. Rev. ed. Mark Mayo Boatner III. 974p. Times Books, 1988. $30. ISBN 0-8129-1689-1; paper $19. ISBN 0-679-73392-2.
973.7 E468

More than 4,000 brief entries dealing with people, places, military engagements, and special subjects. Maps, diagrams, and an atlas of sectional maps covering the Civil War area are features.

1791 Civilizations of the ancient Near East. Jack M. Sasson, ed. 4v. Scribner, 1995. $449. ISBN 0-648-19279-9.
939 DS57

This set covers the cultures of the Near East from the Bronze Age to the time of Alexander the Great. Signed, scholarly essays are complemented by extensive bibliographies. The arrangement is topical, rather than by civilization. The detailed index is essential for locating specifics.

1792 Dictionary of American diplomatic history. 2d ed., rev. and exp. John E. Findling. 707p. Greenwood, 1989. $69.95. ISBN 0-313-26024-9.
327.73 E183.7

The people, places, terminology, and events that make up the history of American diplomacy from the Revolution to 1988 are identified and explained in this easy-to-use encyclopedic source. About half the entries are biographical. Five useful appendixes enhance the volume.

1793 Dictionary of American history. Rev. ed. Louise B. Ketz, ed. 8v. Scribner, 1976. $625/set. ISBN 0-684-13856-5. Supplement, 1996. 2v. $180/set. ISBN 0-684-19579-8.
973 E174

The set contains more than 6,200 readable articles that explain the concepts, events, and places of American history. It covers political, economic, social, industrial, and cultural history. It does not include biographical sketches. Articles are signed and include bibliographical citations. The two-volume *Supplement* brings the set up to 1975. The *Concise dictionary of American history* (1983. $100. ISBN 0-684-17321-2) is a single-volume abridgment.

1794 Dictionary of American immigration history. Francesco Cordasco, ed. 810p. Scarecrow, 1990. $97.50. ISBN 0-8108-2241-5.
325.73 JV6450

This unique dictionary contains 2,500 well-cross-referenced, signed entries, including major themes, movements, ethnic groups, associations, unions, legislation, and biographical sketches. It covers the period from the 1880s, when the U.S. Congress began to administer immigration policy actively, to 1986 and the passage of the Immigration and Control Act. Bibliographies.

1795 Dictionary of the American West. Winfred Blevins. Facts on File, 1993. $40. ISBN 0-8160-2031-0; paper $17.95. ISBN 0-8160-2858-3.
427 PE2970

More than 5,000 terms pertaining to the history and culture of the American West, including cowboys and ranching, Native American peoples, flora and fauna, and more.

1796 Dictionary of the Middle Ages. Joseph R. Strayer, ed. 13v. Scribner, 1982–89. $990/set. ISBN 0-684-19073-7.
909.07 D114

Covering the sixth through sixteenth centuries in thirteen volumes, this impressive work of scholarship contains more than 5,000 entries dealing with political, religious, and cultural history. The well-written articles run from a few lines to several pages; they are signed and include bibliographies.

1797 Encyclopedia of Africa south of the Sahara. John Middleton, ed. 4v. Scribner, 1997. $475. ISBN 0-684-80466-2.
967.003 DT351.E53

The best single reference work on Africa. An alphabetical arrangement of signed articles presenting the current state of knowledge of the culture and history of Africa. Includes bibliographies. Essential.

1798 Encyclopedia of African-American culture and history. 5v. 3203p. Macmillan, 1996. $495. ISBN 0-02-897345-3.
973.04 E185

An authoritative work covering the African American experience from 1619 to the present. More than 2,300 entries, enhanced by clear and accurate photographs, charts, and maps; includes numerous biographical entries as well as historical and thematic essays. An essential purchase.

1799 Encyclopedia of American economic history: studies of the principal movements and ideas. Glenn Porter, ed. 3v. Scribner, 1980. $295/set. ISBN 0-684-16271-7.
330.9 HC103

This encyclopedia includes seventy-one signed articles on topics in American economic history, articles covering chronological periods, economic topics (such as tariff), and the institutional and social framework. The articles include extensive bibliographical essays, and the seventy-five-page index provides good subject access.

1800 Encyclopedia of American history. 7th ed. Richard B. Morris and Jeffrey B. Morris, eds. 1285p. HarperCollins, 1996. $50. ISBN 0-06-270055-3.
973 E174.5

Now back in print, the one-volume work is a standard.

1801 Encyclopedia of Asian history. Ainslie Embree, ed. 4v. Scribner, 1988. $380/set. ISBN 0-684-18619-5.
950 DS31

Covers all aspects of Asian civilization from early history to the present, from Iran on the west to Indonesia on the east. More than 2,000 pages contain more than 3,000 articles. It is an excellent overview of the subject.

1802 An encyclopedia of battles: accounts of over 1560 battles from 1479 B.C. to the present. Rev. ed. David Eggenberger. 533p. Dover, 1985. Paper $14.95. ISBN 0-486-24913-1.
904 D25

This encyclopedia contains short, one- or two-paragraph entries that are clearly written and well illustrated. The author very effectively places the battle within a broader political or military context. This is a revision of *A dictionary of battles*. The new entries in this edition, covering 1976 to 1985, are placed in an appendix. A sound, affordable volume for smaller libraries.

1803 Encyclopedia of Jewish history: events and eras of the Jewish people. Joseph Alpher, ed. 288p. Facts on File, 1986. $40. ISBN 0-8160-1220-2.
909 DS118

Contains signed articles, glossary, and chronologies. Each two-page format focuses on a theme. The editors have managed to maintain a fair degree of continuity in spite of the fragmentation of the format and the heavy use of illustrations.

1804 Encyclopedia of Latin American history and culture. Barbara A. Tenenbaum. 5v. 3192p. Scribner, 1996. $525. ISBN 0-684-19253-5.
980.003 F1406

This monumental work, with contributions from more than 800 scholars, includes more than 5,300 essays on the places, peoples, events, history, art, language, economics, and culture of the Latin American region. Illustrations include photographs, maps, and charts. This encyclopedia provides a comprehensive study of Latin American culture and history. Accessible to all intelligent readers.

1805 Encyclopedia of the American West. Charles Phillips and Alan Axelrod, eds. 4v. Macmillan, 1996. $507.50. ISBN 0-02-897495-6.
978 F591

An authoritative work presenting more than 1,700 entries in alphabetical arrangement. The signed entries vary in length from a few paragraphs to as many as forty pages; most offer suggestions for further reading. Topics range from "Alamo" to "Architecture," "Bonanza Farming," "Chinatowns," "Log Cabins," "Mining," "Saloons," "Wolves," "Wounded Knee Massacre," and "Rufus Fairchild Zogbaum." The writing is both scholarly and enjoyable. At the end there is a comprehensive index and a list of biographical entries by profession.

1806 Encyclopedia of the Confederacy. 4v. Ed. Richard N. Current and Paul D. Escott. Simon & Schuster, 1994. $365. ISBN 0-13-275991-8.
973.7 E487

An ambitious work, with almost 1,500 articles covering biography, campaigns, politics, childhood, medicine, industry, music, and every other aspect of life in the Confederacy. Complemented by almost 600 illustrations, including sixty-seven maps, it is a comprehensive treatment. Well indexed; cross-references.

1807 Encyclopedia of the holocaust. Israel Gutman, ed. 4v. Macmillan, 1990. $360/set. ISBN 0-02-896090-4. Also available as a two-volume set; 1990. $175/set. ISBN 0-02-864527-8.
940.53 D804.3

This set provides a wealth of information about a major event in the history of Western civilization. More than 1,000 entries treat countries, people, reflections in the arts and theology, sites of camps and massacres, and contemporary documentation centers.

1808 Encyclopedia of the Middle Ages. Matthew Bunson. 512p. Facts on File, 1995. $50. ISBN 0-8160-2456-1.
940.1 D114

A dictionary format, brief entries, with cross-references. Includes glossary, bibliography, and chronology. A useful, if somewhat abbreviated, treatment, for libraries not requiring the *Dictionary of the Middle Ages* and not owning *The Middle Ages: a concise encyclopedia* (Lyons, op).

1809 Encyclopedia of the North American colonies. Jacob Ernest Cooke, ed. 3v. Scribner, 1993. $330/set. ISBN 0-684-19269-1.
940.03 E45

Exploring every aspect of colonial life, and considering not only British, but French, Dutch, Spanish, Russian, and Native American experiences, this award-winning set is well organized, authoritative, and accessible to senior high school students and beyond. Thematic articles with substantial bibliographies, cross-references, and a thorough index make this a valuable source.

1810 Encyclopedia of the Roman Empire. Matthew Bunson. Facts on File, 1994. $50. ISBN 0-8160-2135-X.
937 DG270

Covering more than 500 years of Roman history, this work delves into the art and architecture, religion, culture, science, and sociology of the empire. Includes glossary, bibliography, chronology, and stemmata of ruling families.

1811 Encyclopedia of the Third Reich. 2v. Christian Zentner and Friedemann Bedurftig, eds. Macmillan, 1991. $195. ISBN 0-02-897500-6.
943.086 DD256.5

Gathering a vast amount of information into one source, this work combines twenty-seven in-depth essays with more than 3,000 shorter entries to provide broad coverage of its subject. More than 1,000 illustrations complement the text. Extensive bibliography, organized by topic, cross-referenced. Deeply indexed.

1812 Encyclopedia of world history: ancient, medieval and modern, chronologically arranged. 5th ed. William Leonard Langer, ed. 1569p. Houghton, 1972. $45. ISBN 0-395-13592-3.
902 D21

Events of world history concisely presented in an arrangement that is first chronological, then geographical, and then chronological again. Devoted primarily to political, military, and diplomatic history. Includes maps and genealogical tables. Latest edition includes developments up to 1970.

1813 Handbook of American Indians north of Mexico. Frederick Webb Hodge. 2v.

(Reprint of Bureau of American Ethnology bulletin; 30.) Reprint Services, 1995. $250. ISBN 0-87471-004-9.
9970.1 E51

An encyclopedic survey providing specific subject access to all facets of American Indian cultures. Indexed. A classic.

1814 Handbook of North American Indians. Smithsonian (dist. by Govt. Print. Off.), 1978– . $25–$47/v. S/N 047-000– . SuDoc SI1.20/2:.
909 E77

This projected twenty-volume set (v.4, *History of Indians/White relations;* v.5, *Arctic;* v.6, *Subarctic;* v.7, *Northwest coast;* v.8, *California;* v.9 and 10, *Southwest;* v.11, *Great Basin;* and v.15, *Northeast,* now available) gives an encyclopedic summary of current historical-cultural knowledge of North American Indians. Extensively researched, readable essays are accompanied by illustrations, maps, and bibliographies. For a complete and comprehensive encyclopedia on Native American tribes, *see* the *Gale encyclopedia of Native American tribes,* described in chapter 6, entry 388.

1815 The Harper encyclopedia of military history from 3500 B.C. to the present. 4th ed. R. Ernest Dupuy and Trevor N. Dupuy. 1680p. HarperCollins, 1993. $65. ISBN 0-06-270056-1.
355 D25

Divided into twenty-two chronologically and geographically arranged chapters, this volume surveys the history of war from the dawn of conflict to the civil strife of the late 1980s into 1991. Bibliography at the end of the work; arranged by chapters. A general index, index of wars, and index of battles and sieges.

1816 Historical encyclopedia of world slavery. Junius P. Rodriguez, ed. 2v. ABC-Clio, 1997. $150. ISBN 0-87436-885-5.

Macmillan encyclopedia of world slavery. Paul Finkelman and Joseph C. Miller. 2v. Macmillan, 1998. $195. ISBN 0-02-864607-X.
306.3 HT861

The award-winning *Historical encyclopedia of world slavery* deserves to be on every public and academic library shelf. "Throughout time," the introduction tells us, "practically all of the world's civilizations and cultures have experienced some type of slavery, and peoples both ancient and modern in societies ranging from the simplest to the most complex have coped with the practice and with the many manifestations of its legacy." Within the two volumes, there are some 700 entries, most about a double-column page or two in length, covering all aspects of the subject from Asian/Buddhist monastic slavery, to Irish slaves in the Caribbean, to sexual enslavement by the Japanese military, to antebellum wage slavery in the United States. The work has clear, readable, and authoritative signed articles; an excellent bibliography; and a detailed master index. The *Macmillan encyclopedia of world slavery* contains more than 550 signed articles ranging from "Amistad" to "White Slavery." This *A* to *Z* encyclopedia covers all aspects of human slavery from antiquity to the present day, including entries from geographical, historical, legal, biographical, cultural, social, and religious perspectives. Well indexed and cross-referenced, with bibliographic references for further study.

1817 Japan: an illustrated encyclopedia. 2v. Kodansha (dist. by Macmillan), 1993. $250/set. ISBN 0-02-897203-1.
952 DS805

With more than 3,500 illustrations, most in color, this two-volume version of the definitive nine-volume work is a satisfying, dazzling source. More than 11,000 entries range from several paragraphs to many pages. Very readable. Extensive cross-references. Atlas and gazetteer, chronology, and lengthy bibliography. Essential.

1818 Louis L. Snyder's historical guide to World War II. Louis L. Snyder. 838p. Greenwood, 1982. $95. ISBN 0-313-23216-4.
940.53 D740

Snyder, a distinguished scholar of European history, has written a well-balanced guide to the war years, covering social, military, and political events. His articles provide the background of the events described and a paragraph explaining their significance.

1819 Native America in the twentieth century: an encyclopedia. Mary B. Davis, ed. 787p. Garland, 1994. $95. ISBN 0-8240-4846-6; paper $29.95. ISBN 0-8153-2583-5.
970.004 E76.2

Essays focus on present-day tribal groups, contemporary as well as historical issues. Topics include daily life, art, economic development, and government policy. Cross-referenced and extensively indexed.

1820 New Cambridge modern history. 14v. Cambridge Univ. Pr., 1957–79. $44.95–$89.95/v. ISBN 0-521-08787-0.
909 D208

An excellent reference history that ranges from the Renaissance (ca. 1493) through the close of World War II (1945). Chapters were written by scholars in the field. Each volume is indexed but lacks extensive bibliographies. Most volumes are out-of-print. A second edition is planned.

1821 New encyclopedia of the American West. Howard R. Lamar, ed. 1324p. Yale Univ. Pr., 1998. $60. ISBN 0-300-07088-8.
978 F591

This is the long-awaited revised edition of the *Reader's encyclopedia of the American West* (HarperCollins, 1987). Included in this book's conception of the West is any part of the continental United States in its formative period and all of the trans-Mississippi West from its first exploration to the present day. This edition discusses the territory, the people, the geography, the events, the organizations, the terms, and the history of the West in more than 2,400 authoritative and signed entries, many of which have bibliographic references. An excellent resource.

1822 Oxford companion to American history. Thomas Herbert Johnson, ed. 906p. Oxford Univ. Pr., 1966. $55. ISBN 0-19-500597-X.
973.03 E174

A biographical and historical guide to American civilization. Biographical entries for major figures whether living or dead. Entries for literary movements, social protests, associations, philanthropic institutions, and so forth. A good choice for ready reference.

1823 Vietnam War almanac. Harry G. Summers Jr. 416p. Facts on File, 1985. $27.95. ISBN 0-8160-1017-X.
959.704 DS557

Summers begins with two broad chapters establishing for the reader the physical and historical realities of Vietnam. He then provides 500 entries that identify people, events, equipment, and social aspects of the war. He focuses primarily on the American perspective. Most entries have suggestions for further reading. Summers is also the author of *Korean War almanac* (288p. Facts on File, 1990. $29.95. ISBN 0-8160-1737-9).

1824 World history: a dictionary of important people, places, and events from ancient times to the present. 1173p. Henry Holt, 1994. $60. ISBN 0-8050-2350-X.
903 D9

A comprehensive and timely revision of the *Concise dictionary of world history,* this work lists more than 10,000 alphabetical entries current through 1992. The 135 chronologies put events into historical context. An essential purchase.

Directories

1825 Directory of historical organizations in the United States and Canada. American Assn. for State and Local History, 1956– . Every four years. (1995, $79.95.) ISSN 0070-5659. (*formerly* **Directory of historical societies and agencies in the United States and Canada.**)
970 E172

Libraries should acquire the latest edition of this publication, which lists historical societies geographically, giving mailing address, number of members, museums, hours and size of library, publication program, and so forth. It is possible to locate societies devoted to a special phase of history through the index.

Handbooks, Yearbooks, and Almanacs

1826 The encyclopedia of American facts and dates. 9th ed. Gorton Carruth, ed. 1039p. HarperCollins, 1993. $45. ISBN 0-06-270045-6.
973.2 E174.5

Items are chronologically arranged, with parallel columns to show concurrent events in varied fields of endeavor.

1827 Handbook of American women's history. Angela Howard Zophy, ed. 763p. Garland, 1990. $95. ISBN 0-8240-8744-5.
305.4 HQ1410

Clearly written and concise entries make this a great starting point for beginning researchers. Many of the entries are biographical; others are about associations, laws and court cases, social movements, and many aspects of popular culture. Good cross-references and an extensive index.

1828 **Hispanic-American almanac.** 2d ed. Nicolas Kanellos, ed. 884p. Gale, 1996. $110. ISBN 0-8103-8595-3.
973.0468 E184

An overview of Hispanic American life and culture in twenty-five subject chapters. A multifaceted source, covering the history, culture, politics, and more. Topical essays by scholars; biography and chronology. More than 400 illustrations.

1829 **Historical statistics of the United States: colonial times to 1970.** Bureau of the Census. 2v. Govt. Print. Off., 1976. $56/set. S/N 003-024-00120-9. SuDoc C3.134/2:H62/970/pt.1-2.
■ cd
317.3 HA202

A valuable compilation of data from both governmental and nongovernmental sources. Range of data on many varied subjects. Sources are given; much is from the *Statistical abstract of the United States*. Now available on CD-ROM.

1830 **Historical tables: 58 B.C.–A.D. 1990.** 12th ed. John Paxton, ed. 352p. Garland, 1991. $80. ISBN 0-8153-0259-2.
902.02 D11

Tabular chronology of world history arranged in parallel columns by period. Concentrates on political history and has a European focus.

1831 **Japanese American history: an A-to-Z reference from 1868 to the present.** Brian Niiya, ed. 400p. Facts on File, 1993. $50. ISBN 0-8160-2680-7.
973 E184

Divided into three parts: an overview, chronology, and encyclopedia. Signed entries cover more than 400 significant individuals, events, organizations, and movements in Japanese American history. Chronology; pronunciation guide. Annotated bibliography of about 100 books and journal articles.

Primary Sources

1832 **Album of American history.** Rev. ed. James Truslow Adams, ed. 3v. Scribner, 1969. $295/set. ISBN 0-684-16848-0. Supplement 1. 267p. Scribner, 1985. $75. ISBN 0-684-17440-5.
973.92 E178.5

A pictorial history of the United States from the first colonial settlements through 1968 with the original set, up to 1983 with the *Supplement*. Well-selected photographs, drawings, prints, and pictorial reconstructions. Printed text consists of commentary on the illustrative matter and connecting narrative. Cumulative subject index; more than 20,000 cross-references.

1833 **Annals of America.** 24v. Encyclopaedia Britannica, 1987. $549/set. ISBN 0-87827-199-6.
973 E173

Volumes 1 through 21 comprise approximately 2,300 selections from speeches, diaries, journals, books, and articles illustrating and documenting the history of America from 1493 to 1986. Companion volumes include a name index and a conspectus.

1834 **Documents of American history.** 10th ed. Henry Steele Commager and Milton Cator, eds. 2v. Prentice-Hall, 1988. v.1, $66. ISBN 0-13-217274-7; v.2, $61. ISBN 0-13-217282-8.
973 E173

Includes significant documents arranged chronologically from 1492 to 1987. Index by topic and personal name. See *Historic documents* and the other legal and political documents listed in chapter 8, Political Science and Law, for contemporary primary source material.

1835 **Lend me your ears: great speeches in history.** Rev. and ex. ed. William Safire, ed. 1055p. Norton, 1997. $39.95. ISBN 0-393-04005-4.
808.85 PN6122

Presents 225 of history's most memorable speeches, from Demosthenes to Bill Gates, grouped in thematic categories. Introductions by Safire place the speech in its historical context and explain the reasons for its impact on events.

1836 **100 key documents in American democracy.** Peter B. Levy, ed. Greenwood, 1994. $59.95. ISBN 0-313-28424-5.
973 E173

This careful selection of documents is arranged chronologically, with commentary and context. Contributions come from labor leaders, songwriters, presidents, poets, and slaves. Indexed.

Historical Atlases

1837 Atlas of African history. Colin McEvedy. 148p. Facts on File, 1980. op; paper $10. Penguin, 1980. ISBN 0-14-051083-4.
911 G2446

Clearly explained series of fifty-nine maps in three colors that chart the historical events in the development of the African continent. Useful for students. An alternative to the *Historical atlas of Africa* (Ajayi and Crowder) now out-of-print.

1838 Atlas of American history. 2d rev. ed. Kenneth T. Jackson, ed. 306p. Scribner, 1984. $75. ISBN 0-684-18411-7.
911.73 E179

This is the standard atlas for American history. It is a revision of the James Truslow Adams 1953 edition, with added maps reflecting national monuments, missile sites, nuclear power plants, and water supplies. More than 5,000 cross-references and well indexed.

1839 Atlas of early American history: the revolutionary era, 1760–1790. Lester J. Cappon, ed. 157p. Princeton Univ. Pr., 1976. $275. ISBN 0-691-04634-4.
911.73 G1201

Maps show the development of political boundaries, economic activity, cultural activity, the rise of cities, and the locations of Native American settlements. Extensively indexed.

1840 Atlas of North American exploration: from the Norse voyagers to the race to the Pole. 224p. Prentice-Hall, 1992. $40. ISBN 0-13-297128-3.
911.7 G1106

A collection of both historical and current maps, showing routes of European exploration. Augmented by journals and letters. The intent is to show the "clash of culture" at points of contact. A similar treatment to that of *Atlas of the historical geography of the United States* (op).

1841 Atlas of the Civil War. James McPherson, ed. 224p. Macmillan, 1994. $40. ISBN 0-02-579050-1.
973.7 G1201

The text by McPherson, a Pulitzer Prize winner, accompanies colorful maps, time lines, photographs, and personal accounts.

1842 Atlas of the Islamic world since 1500. Francis Robinson. 238p. Facts on File, 1982. $40. ISBN 0-87196-629-8.
911 DS35.6

The history of Islam is treated in this atlas, which combines illustrations, text, and maps to portray Islamic civilization. Includes bibliography and index.

1843 Historical atlas of World War I. Anthony Livesey. 192p. Henry Holt, 1994. $45. ISBN 0-8050-2651-7.
940.4 G1037

The introduction to this volume discusses the events leading up to the war, followed by five chapters chronicling each year, and closing with an epilogue. A month-by-month time line in each chapter charts the progress of the war—or lack thereof. Detailed maps.

1844 Historical atlas of World War II. John Pimlott. 224p. Henry Holt, 1995. $45. ISBN 0-8050-3929-5.
940.5 G1038

Similar to the work above, with more than 100 maps, a chronology of important dates, and general and place-names indexes.

1845 Shepherd's historical atlas. 9th rev. ed. William Robert Shepherd. 353p. Barnes & Noble, 1980. $35.95. ISBN 0-389-20155-3.
911 G1030

Standard historical atlas. This edition contains all maps from previous editions and a special supplement of historical maps for the period 1929–80.

1846 The Times atlas of the Second World War. John Keegan, ed. 254p. HarperCollins, 1989. $50. ISBN 0-06-016178-7; paper $29.99. ISBN 0-517-12377-0.
911 G1038

This oversize atlas contains 450 maps, 150 photographs, a chronology, and a narrative that gives a good overview of the war. Stunning maps treat all parts of the world involved in this long and bloody conflict.

1847 The Times atlas of world history. 4th ed. Geoffrey Barraclough, ed. 360p. Hammond, 1993. $95. ISBN 0-8437-1146-9.
911 G1030

Outstanding historical atlas. Maps are striking and supplemented with informative text and occasional illustrations. Stresses economic and social as well as political history.

Biographical Sources

The titles listed below have a decidedly historical flavor. For general biography, *see* chapter 22, Biography, Genealogy, and Names.

1848 **Biographical dictionary of the Confederacy.** Jon L. Wakelyn. 601p. Greenwood, 1977. $57.50. ISBN 0-8371-6124-X.
973.7 E467

Provides biographical information on political, business, intellectual, and military leaders of rebel society. Appendixes classify figures by occupation, religious affiliation, education, party affiliation, and geographical mobility. Includes bibliographical references.

1849 **Encyclopedia of western gunfighters.** Bill O'Neal. 386p. Univ. of Oklahoma Pr., 1979. $37.95. ISBN 0-8061-1508-4; paper $19.95. ISBN 0-8061-2335-4.
364.1 F596

This encyclopedia contains brief biographies of 256 gunfighters and descriptions of 587 gunfights. Entries always include references to sources of further information. Includes an introduction that classifies the gunfighters by vital statistics and profession and gives gunfight statistics and chronology.

1850 **Explorers and discoverers of the world.** Daniel B. Baker. Gale, 1993. $59.95. ISBN 0-8103-5421-7.
910.92 G200

Brief biographies of 320 world explorers, with an effort to include women and non-Europeans. Includes bibliographies, maps, photos, and chronologies. Indexed. Also lists of explorers by place of birth and areas explored.

1851 **Pirates and privateers of the Americas.** David F. Marley. 458p. ABC-Clio, 1994. $60. ISBN 0-87436-751-4.
910 E18

An intriguing volume, this *A* to *Z* look at the life and times of its colorful subjects includes biography, battles, ships, and stories, covered in about 350 entries. The historical period is mid–seventeenth to early eighteenth century. Extensively cross-referenced. The bibliography of more than 130 items includes not only English-language, but also Spanish, Dutch, and French sources as well.

1852 **Who was who in world exploration.** Carl Waldman and Alan Wexler. 720p. Facts on File, 1992. $65. ISBN 0-8160-2172-4.
910.92 G200

More than 800 figures profiled. Brief entries, cross-referenced. Includes list of sponsors. Bibliography at end, organized by region of exploration.

1853 **World explorers and discoverers.** Ed. Richard Bohlander. 532p. Macmillan, 1992. $85. ISBN 0-02-897445-X.
910.2 G200

More than 300 persons, covering exploration from ancient times to the present. Entries lengthy, listing nationality, territory, short bibliography. Glossary, illustrated with more than fifty maps and 170 photographs.

21

Geography, Area Studies, and Travel

BETSY HOAGG

The impact of world events on these subjects has been astounding over the past ten years. Mapmakers, in particular, have been hard-pressed to keep up with political changes. Libraries will want to consider atlas purchases carefully and weed collections of outdated materials.

Dictionaries, Encyclopedias, and Gazetteers

1854 **American place names: a concise and selective dictionary for the continental United States of America.** George R. Stewart. 550p. Oxford Univ. Pr., 1970. $35. ISBN 0-19-500121-4.
917.3 E155

Gives brief derivations of about 12,000 American place-names. Names were chosen because they were either well known, commonly repeated, or unusual.

1855 **Cambridge encyclopedia of Africa.** Roland Oliver and Michael Crowder, eds. 492p. Cambridge Univ. Pr., 1981. $49.50. ISBN 0-521-23096-9.
960 DT3

Cambridge encyclopedia of Australia. Susan Bambric, ed. 400p. Cambridge Univ. Pr., 1994. $54.95. ISBN 0-521-36511-2.
994 DU90

Cambridge encyclopedia of China. 2d ed. Brian Hook, ed. 492p. Cambridge Univ. Pr., 1991. $49.50. ISBN 0-521-35594-X.
951 DS705

Cambridge encyclopedia of India, Pakistan, Bangladesh, Sri Lanka, Nepal, Bhutan, and the Maldives. Francis Robinson, ed. 520p. Cambridge Univ. Pr., 1989. $49.50. ISBN 0-521-33451-9.
954 DS334.9

Cambridge encyclopedia of Japan. 400p. Ed. Richard Bowring and Peter Kornicki. Cambridge Univ. Pr., 1993.

$49.95. ISBN 0-521-40352-9.
952 DS805

Cambridge encyclopedia of Latin America and the Caribbean. 2d ed. Simon Collier et al., eds. 479p. Cambridge Univ. Pr., 1992. $49.50. ISBN 0-521-41322-2.
980 F1406

Cambridge encyclopedia of the Middle East and North Africa. Trevor Mostyn and Albert Hourani, eds. 456p. Cambridge Univ. Pr., 1988. $49.50. ISBN 0-521-32190-5.
956 DS44

Cambridge encyclopedia of Russia and the former Soviet Union. 2d ed. Archie Brown et al., eds. 604p. Cambridge Univ. Pr., 1994. $49.50. ISBN 0-521-35593-1.
947 DK14

The volumes in the Cambridge regional encyclopedia series are excellent one-volume treatments. Signed articles, written by scholars, are arranged in narrative format and are well illustrated. Detailed tables of contents and extensive indexes provide access. Bibliographies at end of volumes.

1856 Cambridge gazetteer of the United States and Canada: a dictionary of places. Archie Hobson, ed. 743p. Cambridge Univ. Pr., 1995. $49.95. ISBN 0-521-41579-9.
917.3 E154

Includes all incorporated municipalities of more than 10,000 people (United States) or 8,000 (Canada); this work was, in the words of the preface, "written to be read." After locating each place, the entries give qualitative information that might be of interest. Extensive cross-referencing.

1857 The Canadian encyclopedia. 2d ed. James H. Marsh, ed. 4v. Hurtig, 1988. $175/set. ISBN 0-88830-326-2.
■ cd
971 F1006

This second edition contains more than 10,000 signed articles, covering all aspects of Canadian history and culture. Biographical coverage is extensive. Illustrations are attractively done. The indexing and cross-references are extensive.

1858 Columbia gazetteer of the world. Saul B. Cohen, ed. 3v. Columbia, 1998. $750. ISBN 0-231-11040-5.
910.3 G103.5

This new three-volume set replaces the classic *Columbia Lippincott gazetteer of the world* (1952), long a standard in many ready reference collections. Includes more than 160,000 entries, 30,000 of which are wholly new to this edition.

1859 The cowboy encyclopedia. Richard W. Slatta. 474p. ABC-Clio, 1994. $60. ISBN 0-87436-738-7.
978 E20

A well-rounded treatment of cowboy culture and lore, with such topics as dress, equipment, and recreation, as well as history and myth. Bibliography and index. A good balance to the *Encyclopedia of western gunfighters*.

1860 Dictionary of human geography. 3d ed. R. J. Johnston et al., eds. 724p. Blackwell, 1994. $89.95. ISBN 0-631-18141-5; paper $22.95. ISBN 0-631-18142-3.
304.2 GF4

This work contains more than 700 entries, 100 of them new to this edition, written by forty-five authors. An effort has been made to broaden perspective: although still predominantly British in flavor, sixteen of the authors are American or Canadian, and the editors "have paid particular attention to the importance of feminist perspectives." Articles are signed, with references and a brief list of further readings. Deeply indexed and cross-referenced, this volume is very usable, concise yet detailed.

1861 Encyclopedia of southern culture. Charles Reagan Wilson and William Ferris, eds. 1634p. Univ. of North Carolina Pr., 1989. $69.95. ISBN 0-8078-1823-2; paper, Anchor Books: v.1, $14.95. ISBN 0-385-41545-1; v.2, $14.95. ISBN 0-385-41546-X; v.3, $16. ISBN 0-385-41547-8; v.4, $16. ISBN 0-385-41548-6.
975 F209

This wide-ranging interdisciplinary study treats topics as narrow as fried chicken and as broad as the Civil War. All entries conclude with bibliographies, making the work useful for students and scholars, but this well-written work will also appeal to general readers with an interest in the South.

1862 Encyclopedia of the Third World. 4th ed. George Thomas Kurian. 3v. Facts on File, 1992. $225/set.

ISBN 0-8160-2261-5.
909.09 HC59.7

Basic facts, location, weather, population, ethnicity, and language are given for nations of the Third World. Political, economic, educational, military, legal, cultural, and social information is supplied. Each entry also incorporates an attractive basic-fact section, organizational chart, useful glossary, chronology of events starting in 1945 or at year of independence, and a short bibliography of titles since 1970. Comprehensive, well organized, and convenient, set in large type, with an introduction of relevant international organizations, several valuable appendixes, and a good index, this tool will meet the demands placed on libraries for current Third World data. A fifth edition is anticipated.

1863 Longman dictionary of geography: human and physical. Audrey N. Clark. 724p. Longman, 1985. $36.95. ISBN 0-582-35261-4; paper $25.60. ISBN 0-582-01779-3.
910.3 G63

Where previous works separated the fields of human and physical geography, Clark has done a fine job of combining the two related fields. The 10,000 entries can easily be understood by nonspecialists. The appendix includes Greek and Latin roots and conversion charts. Not illustrated. A good substitute for Monkhouse's *Dictionary of the natural environment* (op).

1864 Modern geography: an encyclopedic survey. Gary S. Dunbar. Garland, 1991. $45. ISBN 0-8240-5343-5.
910 G63

An overview of the developments in the field of geography, from 1890 to the present. Almost 100 contributors, with signed articles and brief bibliographies. Includes biographies, from several paragraphs to several pages. Index of personal names.

1865 Muslim peoples: a world ethnographic survey. 2d ed. Richard V. Weekes, ed. 2v. Greenwood, 1984. $150/set. ISBN 0-313-23392-6.
305.6 DS35

The Oxford encyclopedia of the modern Islamic world. John L. Esposito, ed. 4v. Oxford Univ. Pr., 1995. $465. ISBN 0-19-506613-8.
909.097 DS35.53

Muslim peoples contains essays covering the life and culture of all major ethnic groups having a Muslim population in excess of 100,000; they together comprise more than 92 percent of all Muslims. Extensive bibliographies accompany each readable essay, along with maps of the location of the group. *The Oxford encyclopedia of the modern Islamic world* is the first truly comprehensive encyclopedia on modern Islamic life and culture. It is worldwide in scope and focuses upon Islamic life as it has evolved over the past 200 years. There are some 750 entries ranging in length from 500 to 10,000 words, featuring articles on religion, technology, politics, science, philosophy, and law, as well as numerous biographical studies and lengthy pieces on recognized Islamic countries and larger regions (e.g., "Islam in Europe" and "Islam in America"). Entries are followed by scholarly bibliographies. The fourth volume contains a synoptic outline of contents as well as an extensive index.

1866 Nicknames and sobriquets of U.S. cities, states, and counties. 3d ed. Joseph Kane and Gerald L. Alexander. 429p. Scarecrow, 1979. $35. ISBN 0-8108-1255-X.
917.3 E155

Comprehensive listing of nicknames of cities, counties, and states. Indexed geographically by city and state and alphabetically by nickname.

1867 Reference handbook on the deserts of North America. Gordon L. Bender, ed. 594p. Greenwood, 1982. $135. ISBN 0-313-21307-0.
917.3 GB612

Covers the seven major desertic areas of North America as geographical, topographical, geological, and ecological entities through essays on animal and plant adaptations, desert riparian ecosystems, sand dunes, desert varnish, and research facilities. Detailed appendixes to chapters provide lists of flora and fauna, sources of information on wind and climate, and so forth. The best available treatment of North American arid lands. Similar works that treat various aspects of geomorphology and geography are no longer in print: *Rand McNally encyclopedia of world rivers* (1980), *Rolling rivers: an encyclopedia of America's rivers* (Bartlett, 1984), *Standard encyclopedia of the world's mountains* (Huxley, 1962), and *World atlas of geomorphic features* (Snead, 1980).

1868 Webster's new geographical dictionary. Rev. ed. 1376p. Merriam-Webster, 1988. $24.95. ISBN 0-87779-446-4.
910 G103.5

A high-quality, one-volume gazetteer, revised frequently. Gives pronunciation of place-names. A viable alternative to the *Columbia gazetteer of the world.*

1869 **World encyclopedia of cities: North America.** 2v. ABC-Clio, 1994. $75/v., $120/set. ISBN 0-87436-649-6. v.1, ISBN 0-87436-650-X; v.2, ISBN 0-87436-651-8.
917.3 HT108.5

These first two volumes of a projected six-volume set draw data primarily from government publications. For each state and province, one to five cities are profiled. A map, general demographics, and information on climate, crime, economy, education, health, housing, recreation, transportation, and so forth.

1870 **Worldmark encyclopedia of the nations.** 9th ed. 5v. Gale, 1998. $345/set. ISBN 0-7876-0074-1.
903 G63

Factual and statistical information on the countries of the world, exhibited in uniform format under such rubrics as topography, population, public finance, language, and ethnic composition. Country articles appear in volumes 2 through 5, arranged geographically by continent. Volume 1 is devoted to the United Nations and its affiliated agencies. Illustrations and maps. Brief index of countries and territories.

1871 **Worldmark encyclopedia of the states.** 4th ed. 956p. Gale, 1998. $150. ISBN 0-7876-0080-6.
973 E156

This convenient source for accurate and reliable information on each of the fifty U.S. states and on U.S. dependencies is similar in format to the *Worldmark encyclopedia of the nations.* Each state is presented with facts arranged under fifty uniform subheadings. The sections on state and local government, environmental protection, ethnic groups, and languages will be especially useful.

Handbooks, Yearbooks, and Almanacs

1872 **America suburbs rating guide and fact book.** Alan Willis and Bennett Jacobstein. 846p. Toucan Valley, 1993. Paper $74. ISBN 0-9634017-5-0.
307.74 HA214

Encompassing 1,770 suburban communities in fifty metropolitan areas, based on the 1990 census. Communities of 10,000 or more in population are listed. Rankings include median household income, home value, rents, population density, and crime statistics.

1873 **The American counties: origins of county names, dates of creation and organization, area, population including 1980 census figures, historical data, and published sources.** 4th ed. Joseph Nathan Kane. 546p. Scarecrow, 1983. $52.50. ISBN 0-8108-1558-3.
973 E180

Alphabetic listing of each county, state-by-state, giving statistical data and brief information on the person, tribe, or feature for which it is named. Following are tables of counties that include name changes, county seats, date created, and state act creating them. Also mentions county histories, if available.

1874 **Background notes.** Bureau of Public Affairs. U.S. Department of State. (Publication no. 7795.) Govt. Print. Off., 1980– . Irreg. $23/yr. S/N 844-002-00000-9. SuDoc: S1.123:– .
■ online
910 G59

These brief pamphlets on individual countries, issued periodically by the State Department, summarize statistical data on population, geography, government, the economy, and defense. Short narratives then tell about the people, culture, political conditions, and foreign relations. Travel information is also included. More than 170 countries and geographic entities are now covered. Index available. These are an inexpensive alternative to the Gale *Countries of the world* volumes.

1875 **Country study series.** Foreign Area Studies, American University. Govt. Print. Off. Dates and prices vary ($7.50–$39/v.). S/N 008-020– . SuDoc S18.2:– . (Individually classed.) (*formerly* **Area handbooks.**)

Extensive series of works on individual countries that provide basic facts about social, economic, political, and military conditions. They include extensive bibliographies and contain a wealth of information at a very affordable price.

1876 Europa world yearbook. 2v. Europa (dist. by Gale), 1959– . Annual. $705. ISSN 0956-2273. (*formerly* **Europa yearbook.**)
341.1 JN1

The best annual directory of the nations of the world. For each country it includes demographic and economic statistics and facts about constitution and government, political parties, press, trade and industry, publishers, and so forth. Also incorporates a substantive section with listings and information about international organizations. Europa also publishes six regional yearbooks: *Africa south of the Sahara* (1971– . Annual); *The Middle East and North Africa* (1948– . Annual); *The Far East and Australasia* (1969– . Annual); *Western Europe* (1989– . Annual); *South America, Central America, and the Caribbean* (1987– . Annual); and *Eastern Europe and the Commonwealth of Independent States* (1992– . Annual). Purchase these only as supplements in areas of strong interest.

1877 Places rated almanac. David Savageau and Geoffrey Loftus. 421p. Macmillan, 1997. $24.95. ISBN 0-028-61233-7.
307.7 HN60

Ranks 343 metropolitan areas as to factors that affect the quality of life: the arts, economics, education, crime, transportation, environment, housing, climate, and health care. Provides statistical information on American cities and towns. People planning to move will find it useful. Each chapter has an introduction, rates the cities on the factor under consideration, and sets up a profile of selected cities on that aspect of their urban environment. All the scores are totaled and the cities rated; the final list gives the best places to live in the United States. Not indexed.

1878 South American handbook. Trade and Travel, 1924– . Annual. Paper $39.95. ISSN 0081-2579.
918 F2211

A yearbook and guide to the countries and resources of South America, Central America, Mexico, the Caribbean, and the West Indies. Useful for general facts and statistics as well as travel information.

1879 Statesman's year-book: statistical and historical annual of the states of the world. St. Martin's, 1864– . Annual. $85. ISSN 0081-4601.
310 JA51

Excellent concise yearbook providing detailed information about constitution and government, finance, commerce, agriculture, religion, and more of the countries of the world. Bibliographies included for each country. Particularly good for Great Britain and members of the Commonwealth.

1880 World factbook. Central Intelligence Agency. Govt. Print. Off., 1982– . Annual. $59. S/N 041-015– . SuDoc PrEx3.15:– .
■ cd online
910 G122

Tailored primarily for government officials, this tool will nevertheless satisfy the needs of many others, because it treats the following topics for each country in the world: land, people, government, economy, communication, and defense forces, with many subdivisions under each topic. The small locational map of the country at the head of each article refers to the twelve large maps of various parts of the world at the end of the volume.

Atlases

Keeping abreast of changing political geography has been a challenge for mapmakers in recent years. The atlases included here are offered as a basic high-quality atlas collection, general enough to accommodate most needs. Special areas of interest should be added as budgets dictate. Historical atlases are found in chapter 20, History.

Bibliographies and Guides

1881 Kister's atlas buying guide: general English-language world atlases available in North America. Kenneth F. Kister. 236p. Oryx, 1984. $43. ISBN 0-912700-62-9.
912 Z6021

An essential purchase along with the other Kister reference-book-buying guides. Profiles 105 English-language atlases in depth. Includes listings of publishers, distributors, and dealers.

1882 The map catalog: every kind of map and chart on Earth and even some above it. 3d ed. Joel Makower, ed. 364p. Vintage, 1992. Paper $20. ISBN 0-679-74257-3.
912 GA105.3

Heavily illustrated, this volume is divided into topical sections: travel maps, boundary maps, scientific maps, maps of specific areas, and so forth. Cross-references and index. Appendixes include directories to state and federal map agencies, selected map stores, maps by mail, and selected map libraries. There are chapters on learning map skills and having maps made.

1883 Maps for America: cartographic products of the U.S. Geological Survey and others. 3d ed. Morris M. Thompson and U.S. Geological Survey. 279p. Govt. Print. Off., 1988. $25. S/N 024-001-03563-4. SuDoc I19.2:M32/12/987.
526 GA405

Excellent map reference work for most libraries. Contains a detailed breakdown of what is on U.S. Geological Survey maps and why it is there, a vast amount of background information, and information on what standards of accuracy are used. Also includes essays on various aspects of cartography, a glossary, and an index.

World

1884 Atlas of the world. 6th ed. 304p. Oxford Univ. Pr., 1998. $75. ISBN 0-1952-1464-1.
912 G1021

An excellent resource, this work features sections on the universe and solar system, climate, geology, landscape, environment, demography, agriculture, and manufacturing and trade. A selection of sixty-six city maps is also included.

1885 Book of the world. Kartographisches Institut Bertelsmann. 558p. Macmillan, 1996. $450. ISBN 0-02-860811-9.
912 G1021

A large, heavy, and utterly fascinating atlas that offers 264 pages of superb maps and 24 pages of stunning satellite pictures of natural landmarks such as the Grand Canyon and Mount Kilimanjaro. An object beautiful in itself. A 1999 edition is forthcoming.

1886 Macmillan centennial atlas of the world. 520p. Macmillan, 1996. $175. ISBN 0-02-861264-7.
■ cd
912 G1021

Offers 224 pages of detailed world maps, a 150,000 place-name index, up-to-date information, and a color-rich geographic display of the world's surface. Highlights points of interest and transportation routes and provides a uniform scale across continental displays.

1887 National Geographic atlas of the world. 6th ed. 2d rev. National Geographic Society. 269p. National Geographic Society, 1996. $100. ISBN 0-7922-3036-1.
912 G1021

Excellent general-purpose world atlas with focus on the United States. Maps are principally political but include much physical and cultural information as well. Most recent edition includes 200 metropolitan maps. Comprehensive index of 155,000 place-names.

1888 New international atlas. 25th anniversary. Rev. ed. 560p. Rand McNally, 1998. $99. ISBN 0-528-83808-3.
912 G1021

Up-to-date, excellent one-volume atlas. Well indexed.

1889 Rand McNally Goode's world atlas. 19th ed. Edward B. Espenshade, ed. 367p. Rand McNally, 1996. $34.95. ISBN 0-528-83130-5.
912 G1021

Updated and republished on a regular schedule, Goode's is an excellent small desk atlas at a reasonable price. Popular with students, it is frequently used to illustrate reports. It has fine thematic and regional maps. Indexed.

1890 Times atlas of the world. 10th ed. 392p. Random House, 1999. $175. ISBN 0-8129-2077-5.
912 G1021

The classic atlas. Very detailed with listings for most geographic and urban locations. Index gives longitude and latitude as well as map reference. Contains 123 plates and a 222-page index-gazetteer.

Regional

1891 Atlas of South America. Moshe Brawer. 144p. Simon & Schuster, 1991. $55. ISBN 0-685-39952-4.
912.68 G1700

The first part of this atlas is an overview of the continent, with chapters on the Andes, the Amazon, flora and fauna, mineral resources, and so forth. The second is a country-by-country treatment. Heavily illustrated; annotated bibliography. Index of place-names; brief index of personal names.

1892 **Atlas of the British empire.** C. A. Bayly. 256p. Facts on File, 1989. $40. ISBN 0-8160-1995-9.
909 DA16

Covering the period from 1500 to the Commonwealth, this work examines the changing meaning of *empire*. Essays on the various periods. Indexed.

1893 **Canada gazetteer atlas.** 174p. Univ. of Chicago Pr., 1980. $75. ISBN 0-226-09259-3.
912.71 G1115

Forty-eight maps and an index give the name, status, population, and position of the populated places recorded in the 1976 census of Canada. Comprehensive map and gazetteer information for all of Canada. Companion to the *National atlas of Canada*.

1894 **Cultural atlas of Africa.** Jocelyn Murray. 240p. Facts on File, 1981. $45. ISBN 0-87196-558-5.
960 DT14

Cultural atlas of China. Caroline Blunden and Mark Elvin. 237p. Facts on File, 1983. $45. ISBN 0-87196-132-6.
951 DS721

Cultural atlas of France. John Ardagh and Colin Jones. 240p. Facts on File, 1991. $45. ISBN 0-8160-2619-X.
912.44 G1844

Cultural atlas of Japan. Martin Collcutt et al. 240p. Facts on File, 1988. $45. ISBN 0-8160-1927-4.
952 DS821

Cultural atlas of Russia and the Soviet Union. Robin Milner-Gulland and Nikolai Dejevsky. 240p. Facts on File, 1989. $45. ISBN 0-8160-2207-0.
947 DK32

Cultural atlas of Spain and Portugal. Mary Vincent. 240p. Facts on File, 1995. $45. ISBN 0-8160-3014-6.
946 DP17

This attractive series offers a one-volume overview of each region or country, liberally illustrated with photographs, maps, and works of art. Included are a brief chronology, gazetteer, bibliography, and list of rulers. Indexed.

1895 **National atlas of Canada.** 5th ed. National Atlas Information Service, 1978– . $185/set; $9.75/ea.
912.71 G1115

The Canadian government produces this thematic atlas of the physical features and resources of Canada. It is now published in individual sheets rather than as a bound volume. Available as a boxed set of ninety-two maps. The project is moving into the digital environment and will be available in other formats in the future.

1896 **Rand McNally road atlas and city guide of Europe.** Rand McNally, 1984– . Annual. $19.95. ISBN 0-528-81188-6.
912.4 G1797.21

The atlas contains more than seventy large-scale road maps of Europe. In addition there are detailed street maps of almost 100 cities, an extensive index, a route planner, mileage charts, and a chart of international road signs.

United States

1897 **Atlas of the United States: a thematic and comparative approach.** Jilly Glassborow and Gillian Freeman, eds. 128p. Macmillan, 1986. $50. ISBN 0-02-922830-1.
912 G1201

This atlas contains seventy theme maps along with a page of explanatory text for each. Some of the subjects covered are geographical features, population data, sociological themes, economic data, and scientific information. There are also forty-nine pages of U.S. and worldwide data comparisons. A good source for middle school students trying to visualize their world.

1898 **National atlas of the United States.** U.S. Geological Survey. 417p. U.S. Geological Survey, 1970. op.
912.73 G1200.U57

The first national atlas of the United States. In addition to demographic, economic, and sociocultural maps that equal in cartographic skill those of any other atlas, it contains a unique section of "administrative" maps reflecting changing configurations of governmental districts, functions, and regions. Subject and place-name indexes. Though somewhat out-of-date, and difficult to obtain, it remains a landmark work.

1899 Rand McNally commercial atlas and marketing guide. Rand McNally, 1876– . Annual. $395. ISSN 0361-9723.
912 G1019

Primarily an atlas of the United States, with large, detailed, clear maps. Includes many statistical tables of population, business and manufacturers, agriculture, and other commercial features, such as indicators of market potential.

1900 Rand McNally road atlas. Rand McNally, 1924– . Annual. Paper $7.95. ISSN 0361-6509.
912.7 G1201

Road maps of each state in the United States, Canada, and Mexico. Distances shown on the maps. Index of place-names and mileage charts included.

1901 Rand McNally standard highway and mileage guide. 17th ed. 480p. Rand McNally, 1997. $135. ISBN 0-528-81603-9.
912.73 G1201

Essentially a series of charts used to calculate distances between reference points. Very popular with summer travelers. Computes the distance between 1471 "key point" cities.

Travel Guides

Libraries with an active traveling public will find that many travelers have their favorites and expect to find the guides on the circulating shelves. Reference departments may want to have some duplicates for the most popular destinations available for inhouse use. Local guides are always popular for day trips, and the growing bed-and-breakfast trend deserves some special consideration. Popular publishers and series such as Baedecker, Michelin, Let's Go, Birnbaum, the Phaidon cultural series, Robert Kane, Fielding, Fodor, the Blue Guides, Insight Guides, and the Rand McNally Guides all have their adherents. Libraries should consider the tastes of their own clientele in filling out collections.

For guidebook information about the United States, consider also the American guide series, a series of in-depth guides done by the Federal Writers Project in the 1930s and available in various reprint editions or from out-of-print sources.

1902 Access America: an atlas and guide to the national parks for visitors with disabilities. Peter Shea et al. 464p. Northern Cartographic, 1988. $89.95. ISBN 0-944187-00-5.
912 G1201

Those with disabilities face disappointments, frustrations, and sometimes barriers when attempting to enjoy parklands. Information concerning such issues as altitude, safety, weather, guide-dog regulations, transportation, sign language, TDD capabilities, and campgrounds is included for thirty-seven national parks. Basic facilities charts and highway and in-park maps conclude each chapter. Independent-living centers, dialysis programs, and hospitals are in the appendix.

1903 Historic landmarks of Black America. George Cantor, ed. 372p. Gale, 1991. $39.95. ISBN 0-8103-7809-4.
917.304 E185.53

Similar to *North American Indian landmarks* in organization, this is a listing of more than 300 sites chosen on the basis of their interest to travelers. Each entry gives the location, hours of operation, exhibits, fees, handicapped access, and telephone numbers. Contains photographs and maps. Indexed, with a bibliography of "further readings."

1904 Hotel and travel index: the world wide hotel directory. Murdoch, 1939– . Quarterly. $89. ISSN 0162-9972.
910.25 TX907

The index contains more than 1,000 pages of international hotel listings. It also has maps of international cities with hotel locator codes.

1905 Mobil travel guide: major cities. Fodor's Travel, 1991– . Annual. Paper $17.95. ISBN 0-679-03499-4. ISSN 0737-9153.
647.9473 E158

One of the Mobil Guides series, this follows the usual Mobil format. Rates lodging and restaurants for forty-six most-visited cities. Provides airport and neighborhood maps, local events, and attractions.

1906 **Mobil travel guides.** 7v. Fodor's Travel, 1960– . Annual. Paper $15.95/ea. (California and the West. ISSN 0076-9827; Great Lakes. ISSN 0076-9789; Mid-Atlantic. ISSN 1090-6975; Northeast. ISSN 1040-1075; Northwest and Great Plains. ISSN 0076-9819; Southeast. ISSN 1040-1067; Southwest and South Central. ISSN 0076-9843.)
917 F2.3

Seven regional guides to the United States that contain information about points of interest, annual or seasonal events, restaurant and lodging facilities (with ratings), and suggested auto tours. Organized by state and city. A good basic reference collection.

1907 **North American Indian landmarks: a traveler's guide.** George Cantor. 409p. Gale, 1993. $45. ISBN 0-8103-8916-9; paper $17.95. ISBN 0-8103-9132-5.
917.304 E77

Organized by region and then alphabetically by state, this work brings together information on 340 sites in forty-five states and six provinces. Each entry gives access routes, simple maps, hours of operation, cost, and special programs. Seventy black-and-white illustrations. Index and brief bibliography.

1908 **OAG business travel planner.** Official Airline Guides. North American edition. 1992– . Quarterly. $130. ISSN 1053-0002. European edition. 1992– . Quarterly. $130. ISSN 1075-1548. Pacific Asia edition. 1992– . $130. ISSN 1069-2150. (*formerly* **Official airline guide travel planner and hotel/motel redbook.**)
■ online
647 TX907

A gold mine of information for the traveler. Airport maps, travel document requirements, national holidays, embassies, consulates, toll-free numbers for travel businesses, city maps, listings of hotels with locations shown, time charts, and airport facilities are included. A mainstay for many years.

1909 **OAG desktop flight guide.** Official Airline Guides. North American edition. 1948– . Semimonthly. $380. ISSN 0191-1619. Worldwide edition. 1976– . Monthly. $250. ISSN 0364-3875. (*formerly* **Official airline guide.**)
387.742 HE9768

The guides include a compilation of current airline data that lists direct and connecting flights. Subscriptions are available in two editions: one with fares and a less expensive version without fares. The *North American edition* is also available in a monthly edition. *Pocket guides* also published.

1910 **Official railway guide: North American travel edition.** K-III Directory Corp., 1974– . 4/yr. $172. ISSN 0273-9658.
385 HE2727

Guide lists schedules and fares of passenger rail lines, including suburban services, connecting bus and ferry service, and rail tour operators. Also publishes a freight service edition.

1911 **Woodall's campground directory: North American edition.** Woodall, 1967– . Annual. $21.95. ISSN 0146-1362.
917.59 GV198.56

Comprehensive directory is divided geographically into eastern and western sections that include Canada and Mexico. Road maps of each state and province show location of each site listed. Brief descriptions are accompanied by evaluative ratings of facilities and recreation. Alphabetical index of sites. Also available in eastern, western, and other regional editions.

22

Biography, Genealogy, and Names

BETSY HOAGG

Biographical Sources

Biographical sources covering specific categories of subjects, such as authors, artists, or scientists, are included in the relevant subject chapters. The titles listed here are general or comprehensive indexes to biographical information, general collective biographies, and a few titles of narrower scope not covered in other subject chapters. Many multicultural titles are among the newer entries.

Indexes

1912 **Biography and genealogy master index.** 2d ed. Miranda C. Herbert and Barbara McNeil, eds. 8v. Gale, 1980. $975/set. ISBN 0-8103-1094-5. Supplement, 1981–85 cumulation. 5v. Gale, 1986. $925/set. ISBN 0-8103-1506-8. Supplement, 1986–90. Barbara McNeil, ed. 3v. Gale, 1990. $925/set. ISBN 0-8103-4803-9. Supplement, 1991–95. 3v. Gale, 1995. $925/set. ISBN 0-8103-8345-4. **Biography and genealogy master index [yr.].** Gale, 1999. Annual supplements. $348. ISBN 0-7876-1272-3. ISSN 0730-1316.
■ cd online
016.92 Z5305

Consolidated index to hundreds of current and retrospective biographical dictionaries containing more than 6,000,000 biographical sketches. Gale has published an abridged edition aimed at smaller libraries: *Abridged biography and genealogy master index* (2d ed. 3v. Gale, 1994. $432/set. ISBN 0-8103-6878-1). This edition covers about 260 more commonly held biographical sources, with citations to 2,150,000 entries. Gale also publishes eight subject spin-offs from the database.

1913 **Biography index: a cumulative index to biographical material in books and magazines.** v.1– . Wilson, 1946– . Quarterly. $125. ISSN 0006-3053. Forthcoming: **Biography index: 1946–1994.** Wilson, n.d. $190. ISBN 0-685-73471-4.
■ cd online
920.02 Z5301

Indexes biographical articles published in approximately 1,700 periodicals, current books of individual and collected biography, obituaries, letters, diaries, memoirs, and incidental biographical material in otherwise nonbiographical books. Includes an index by professions and occupations. Annual and three-year cumulations.

1914 The New York Times obituary index, 1858–1968. 1136p. UMI, 1970. $205. ISBN 0-667-00599-4.

The New York Times obituary index, 1969–1978. 131p. UMI, 1980. $205. ISBN 0-667-00598-6.
920.02 CT213

A cumulation in one alphabetical sequence of the names listed under "Deaths" in all issues of the *New York Times* from September 1858 through December 1978. Valuable for convenience.

Collective Biography

Here are listed general sources for world, regional, and national biography. Biographical sources that pertain to specific subject fields (e.g., Business, Music, or Literature) or to specific ethnic groups (e.g., African Americans, Asian Americans, or Native Peoples of North America) or to specific disciplines (e.g., Women's Studies) are listed within those sections of the book.

1915 An African biographical dictionary. Norbert C. Brockman. 440p. ABC-Clio, 1994. $60. ISBN 0-87436-748-4.
920.06 DT18

A welcome addition to biographical sources, this work contains entries on nearly 600 political, social, and cultural leaders of sub-Saharan Africa. Most are contemporaries. Brief bibliographies and index. Appendix of nations and leaders since their independence.

1916 Almanac of famous people. 6th ed. Susan L. Stetler, ed. 2v. Gale, 1998. $115/set. ISBN 0-7876-0044-X. (*formerly* **Biographical almanac.**)
■ online
920.02 CT103

Provides both quick identification and guidance to further information on more than 27,000 people in more than 300 widely held biographical dictionaries. Information provided for most subjects includes nationality, occupation, birth and death dates, and sources of other biographical information. Volume 1 contains the biographies; volume 2, indexes.

1917 American national biography. John A. Garraty and Mark C. Carnes. 24v. Oxford Univ. Pr., 1999. $2500. ISBN 0-19-520635-5.
920.73 CT213

More than 6,000 historians and scholars have contributed to this monumental work detailing the lives of more than 17,500 individuals who have shaped the life and pulse of our nation. A worthy successor to the *Dictionary of American biography*, and without equal anywhere.

1918 Current biography. v.1– . Wilson, 1940– . Monthly except Dec. $69. ISSN 0011-3344. Yearbook, 1940– . $69. ISSN 0084-9499. Cumulative index, 1940–85. 128p. 1986. $21. ISBN 0-8242-0722-X. Cumulated index, 1940–95. 133p. 1995. $27. ISBN 0-8242-0892-7.
920 CT100

Biographical articles, with portraits and bibliographies, of newsworthy individuals of various nationalities. Annual volumes cumulate all the articles in one alphabet and add new information when necessary. A necrology is included. Index by name and profession cumulates annually. Each volume cumulates the indexes until the tenth year, when a ten-year index is published.

1919 Dictionary of American biography. 20v. bound as 10v. Scribner, 1957–88. $1599/set. ISBN 0-684-19075-3.
■ cd
920.073 E176

Containing about 18,000 biographies, this remains the standard American biographical source. Supplements 9 and 10 extend the coverage to persons who died in 1980 or earlier. Each signed article is documented. The *Comprehensive index* lists people by occupation, birthplace, school, contributor, subject, and one integrated alphabetical sequence. Also available is the *Concise dictionary of American biography* (4th ed. 1990. $155. ISBN 0-684-19188-1), a one-volume condensation of the original. Libraries already owning the set will want to keep up with additional volumes as published. In early 1999, Oxford University Press will publish a new twenty-four-volume work entitled *American national biography*, produced under the auspices of the American Council of Learned Societies. This $2,500 set (ISBN 0-19-520635-5) is destined to supplement, if not supersede, the *Dictionary of American biography.*

1920 Dictionary of national biography. v.1– . Oxford Univ. Pr., 1882– . 22v. (incl. Supplement 1). $2350/set. ISBN 0-19-865101-5. Supplement 2 (1901–11). $165. ISBN 0-19-865201-1. Supplement 3 (1912–21). $145. ISBN 0-19-865202-X. Supplement 4 (1922–30). $145. ISBN 0-19-865203-8. Supplement 5 (1931–40). $145. ISBN 0-19-865204-6. Supplement 6 (1941–50). $150. ISBN 0-19-865205-4. Supplement 7 (1951–60). $89. ISBN 0-19-865206-2. Supplement 8 (1961–70). $89. ISBN 0-19-865207-0. Supplement 9 (1971–80). $89. ISBN 0-19-865208-9. Supplement 10 (1981–85). $89. ISBN 0-19-865210-0. **Dictionary of national biography: missing persons.** Oxford Univ. Pr., 1994. $120. ISBN 0-19-865211-9.
920.042 DA28

Concise dictionary of national biography from the beginnings to 1900. 1514p. Oxford Univ. Pr., 1953. $95. ISBN 0-19-865301-8.

Concise dictionary of national biography 1901–1970. 748p. Oxford Univ. Pr., 1982. $39.95. ISBN 0-19-865303-4.
920.72 DA28

Authoritative and comprehensive British biography. Well-documented and signed biographies of notable inhabitants of the British Isles and colonies. Each article includes a bibliography, and every supplement has a cumulative index to all entries beginning from 1901 in one alphabetical sequence. The *Concise DNB* offers condensed coverage of figures included in the *DNB.* It is both a self-contained ready reference tool and an access tool for the entire set.

1921 Encyclopedia of world biography. 2d ed. 17v. Gale, 1998. $975/set. ISBN 0-7876-2221-4. (*formerly* **McGraw-Hill encyclopedia of world biography.**)
920.02 CT103

Originally published by McGraw-Hill in 1973, this thoroughly revised and updated version features 7,000 signed articles about persons relevant to social and cultural history. Each article has a brief synopsis and includes portraits and illustrations. Text sections are headlined; brief bibliography follows each article. Volume 17 contains the index and study guides that place the individuals into historical and cultural perspective.

1922 International who's who. v.1– . Europa (dist. by International and also by Gale), 1935– . Annual. $310. ISSN 0074-9613.
920 CT120

Brief biographical information on 20,000 prominent persons from all countries. Includes tables of reigning royal families and obituary list of those deceased before publication.

1923 Merriam-Webster's biographical dictionary. 1170p. Merriam-Webster, 1995. $27.95. ISBN 0-87779-743-9.
920.02 CT103

Brief biographies of more than 30,000 figures from ancient times to the present. Pronunciation, dates, and chief contribution to civilization are given. Valuable for ready reference. An update of *Webster's new biographical dictionary.*

1924 Notable American women, 1607–1950: a biographical dictionary. 3v. Harvard Univ. Pr., 1971. op; paper $45. ISBN 0-674-62734-2.

Notable American women: the modern period. 795p. Harvard Univ. Pr., 1980. op; paper $32. ISBN 0-674-62733-4.
920.72 CT3260

Written with the same standards as the *Dictionary of American biography,* these volumes attempt to redress the gap left by the earlier work. Coverage in the original three-volume set is from 1607 to women who died no later than 1950. The volume on the modern period includes subjects who died between 1951 and 1975. Bibliographic essays follow each signed article. Classified lists of biographies.

1925 Notable Americans: what they did, from 1620 to the present. 4th ed. 733p. Gale, 1988. $155. ISBN 0-8103-2534-9.
920 E176

More than 50,000 individuals are arranged in nineteen broad subject areas covering politics, government, the military, education, business, religion, and cultural institutions. An organization and personal name index fills more than 160 pages.

1926 Who was who in America. 12v. Marquis Who's Who, 1942– . $75/v.; $767.50/set. ISBN 0-8379-0222-3.
■ cd online
920.073 E176

Now available through 1993, this set includes more than 122,000 listings for persons who were once included in *Who's who in America* (1928) but are no longer, because of death or other reasons.

1927 Who was who in the Greek world, 776 B.C.–30 B.C. Diana Bowder, ed. 227p. Cornell Univ. Pr., 1982. $42.50. ISBN 0-8014-1538-1.
920 DF208

Who was who in the Roman world. Diana Bowder, ed. 256p. Cornell Univ. Pr., 1980. op.
920 DG203

In these two similar volumes, Bowder has created "biographical reference works of scholarly accuracy and reliability that are easily accessible to the student and general reader." Each contains a chronology, bibliography, and an index for persons cited but without their own entries. Entries include citations and references to the other volume if an individual appears in both. Many entries are illustrated with portrait busts, coins, monuments, or maps.

1928 Who's who. v.1– . St. Martin's, 1849– . Annual. $210. ISSN 0083-937X.
920.03 DA28

Emphasis is on Britons, but notables of other countries are included. Small libraries may purchase at intervals of several years without losing major value.

1929 Who's who in America. v.1– . Marquis Who's Who, 1889– . Biennial. (1997–98, $509.95.) ISSN 0083-9396.
■ cd online
920.073 E176

The standard biographical source for currently prominent Americans. Marquis does accept information from the biographees, though the publisher may compile the facts independently. Besides the base volume, the company publishes several regional volumes (*Who's who in the East, Who's who in the Midwest, Who's who in the South and Southwest,* and *Who's who in the West*). Some of the subjects in the base volume also appear in the regional volumes. In addition, the company publishes several subject volumes in the areas of business, law, medicine, and entertainers. The CD-ROM version boasts a gathering of more than 490,000 entries from the various volumes.

1930 Who's who in the world. v.1– . Marquis Who's Who, 1970– . Annual. $369.95. ISSN 0083-9825.
■ cd online
920.02 CT120

Biographical information in the standard Marquis format. The latest edition contains more than 31,000 individuals worldwide. Although more expensive than St. Martin's *Who's who,* it does not have that work's strong British emphasis.

Genealogy

Genealogy is an area in which collection size could vary greatly depending on resources of the local community and patron interest. The titles included here give a general representation of the types of genealogical sources available; many other similar sources could be purchased to augment them. Libraries should acquire any existing tools of local scope for genealogical research.

Bibliographies and Guides

1931 A bibliography of American county histories. P. William Filby. 449p. Genealogical Pub., 1985. $24.95. ISBN 0-8063-1126-6.
016.973 E180

With the exception of Alaska, Hawaii, and Puerto Rico, Filby has collected 5,000 local histories, including many of those published since the Kaminkow set was published. In addition, Filby has identified county histories held by libraries other than the Library of Congress. Entries are by state and then chronological within the county. Important for libraries serving genealogists.

1932 Genealogical and local history books in print: family history volume. 5th ed. Marion Hoffman, ed. 449p. Genealogical Pub., 1996. Paper $25. ISBN 0-8063-1513-X.

Genealogical and local history books in print: general reference and world resources volume. 5th ed. Marion Hoffman, ed. 353p. Genealogical Pub., 1997. Paper $25. ISBN 0-8063-1538-5.

Genealogical and local history books in print: U.S. sources and resource volume—Alabama–New York. 5th ed. Marion Hoffman, ed. 539p. Genealogical Pub., 1997. Paper $25. ISBN 0-8063-1536-9.

Genealogical and local history books in print: U.S. sources and resource volume—North Carolina–Wyoming. 5th ed. Marion Hoffman, ed. 491p. Genealogical Pub., 1997. Paper $25. ISBN 0-8063-1537-7.
016.929 CS69

This seminal set is a fountain of information, listing general reference books, local histories (the bulk of the entries), and a well-indexed family genealogy list. Some of the titles are annotated. Publishers' names and addresses are included, and many of the publishers are societies, agencies, and so forth, which would otherwise be hard to track down.

1933 **Genealogical microfilm catalogs.** National Archives and Records Administration.
016.929 CS68

The National Archives has microfilmed more than 2,000 series of federal records that contain a wealth of valuable information for genealogists and other researchers. The genealogical microfilm catalog series include the *National Archives microfilm resources for research: a comprehensive catalog* (1996. $5. ISBN 0-911333-34-7), population census catalogs, and subject catalogs such as *Immigrant and passenger arrivals* (1991. $3.50. ISBN 0-911333-05-3), *Genealogical and biographical research* (1983. $3.50. ISBN 0-911333-06-1), *Black studies* (1984. $3.50. ISBN 0-911333-08-8), *American Indians* (1998. $3.50. ISBN 0-911333-09-6), and *Military service records* (1985. $3.50. ISBN 0-911333-07-X). Order from the National Archives Trust Fund Board, Washington, DC 20408, or visit the National Archives and Records Administration's Genealogical Web Site at http://www.nara.gov/publications/micfilm.html.

1934 **Genealogies in the Library of Congress: a bibliography.** Marion J. Kaminkow. 2v. Magna Carta, 1972. $175/set. ISBN 0-910946-15-9. Supplement, 1972–76. 1977. $25. ISBN 0-910946-19-1. Supplement, 1976–86. 1987. op.

A complement to Genealogies in the Library of Congress: a bibliography. Marion J. Kaminkow. 1118p. Magna Carta, 1981. $83.50. ISBN 0-910946-24-8.
016.929 CS69

A comprehensive listing of the holdings of the Library of Congress and, in the complement volume, of the holdings of twenty-four significant genealogical libraries across the nation. In areas with a strong interest in genealogy, libraries should also obtain the two volumes and supplement that list the holdings of the library of the National Society of the Daughters of the American Revolution (DAR). The DAR library contains printed genealogies not found elsewhere. Contact the DAR for ordering information.

1935 **Guide to genealogical research in the National Archives.** Rev. ed. 304p. National Archives Trust Fund Board, 1985. $35. ISBN 0-911333-00-2; paper $25. ISBN 0-911333-01-0.
016.929 CS68

Details the wide range of federal records important to genealogists and local historians. Records listed include census records, military service and pension files, ship passenger arrival lists, federal land records, and more.

1936 **In search of your European roots: a complete guide to tracing your ancestors in every country of Europe.** 2d ed. Angus Baxter. 292p. Genealogical Pub., 1994. Paper $16.95. ISBN 0-8063-1446-X.
929 CS403

Baxter begins with several chapters dealing with the broad scope of European history, the great treasure house of Mormon records, and European Jewish records. He then examines the records of each country, listing archival resources, military records, civil records, and church records. This revised edition includes new chapters on Germany and the countries of Eastern Europe.

1937 **Passenger and immigration lists bibliography, 1538–1900.** 2d ed. 324p. Gale, 1988. $115. ISBN 0-8103-2740-6.
016.929 CS47

Lists more than 1,300 published sources of names of persons arriving in the United States and Canada from 1538 to 1900. Includes all of the sources from which names were culled for *Passenger and immigration lists index* and hundreds of additional lists.

1938 Passenger and immigration lists index. P. William Filby, ed. 3v. Gale, 1981. $440/set. ISBN 0-8103-1099-6. Cumulative supplement, 1982–85. 1985. $530. ISBN 0-8103-1795-8. Cumulative supplement, 1986–90. 1990. $530. ISBN 0-8103-2579-9. Cumulative supplement, 1991–95. 1995. $530. ISBN 0-8103-8337-3.
929.3 CS68

A guide to the published arrival records of more than 1,400,000 passengers who came to the United States and Canada before 1900. The set and supplements index more than 1,000 books and articles containing passenger listings. Entries provide name, age, date, port of arrival, and a code indicating the source of the original record. Each annual supplement adds more than 100,000 new names.

1939 Project remember: a national index of gravesites of notable Americans. Arthur S. Koykka. 597p. Reference Pub., 1986. $59.95. ISBN 0-917256-22-0.
920 CT215

Among the 5,300 entries in this volume the reader will find artists, doctors, presidents, musicians, award winners, even prominent animals. Listings include birth and death information, the reason why the entry appears, and the site where the entrant is buried. Includes geographical index of grave sites.

1940 United States local histories in the Library of Congress. Marion J. Kaminkow, ed. 5v. Genealogical Pub., 1976. $300/set. ISBN 0-614-10566-8.
016.973 E180

An exhaustive bibliography of local histories, including regional, county, and town histories. The first four volumes, organized by geographic region, are all local histories received up to 1972; the fifth is a supplement listing U.S. local histories received between 1972 and 1976, with an index to all five volumes. Consult Filby's *Bibliography of American county histories* for more recent material. Also consider the recently published catalog of the National Society of the Daughters of the American Revolution (DAR). The DAR library has one of the best collections in the United States.

Indexes and Abstracts

1941 Genealogical periodical annual index. v.1– . Heritage, 1962– . Annual. $20. ISSN 0072-0593.
929.1 HC929

A subject, surname, and locality index to about 300 genealogical periodicals. Each year the editors try to include magazines that have newly appeared. A valuable and affordable finding aid for libraries with any genealogical demand. Some of the earlier volumes released by a different publisher are out-of-print. Libraries with strong interest in genealogy may wish to consider the *Periodical source index* (1995. $45. ISSN 1065-9056), published by the Allen County Library Foundation. *PERSI* indexes more than 3,200 genealogical and local history periodicals. The first twelve volumes cover materials published from 1847 to 1985. It has been published annually since 1986.

Directories

1942 County courthouse book. 2d ed. Elizabeth Bently. 400p. Genealogical Pub., 1992. $34.95. ISBN 0-8063-1485-0. (Temporarily op.)
347.73 KF8700

A compilation of information on 3,125 county jurisdictions and 1,577 New England towns and independent Virginia cities, this work lists contact persons, current addresses and telephone numbers, coverage, and the availability of key records, including probate, land, tax, and vital statistics.

1943 Genealogist's address book. 3d ed. Elizabeth Petty Bently. 650p. Genealogical Pub., 1995. $34.95. ISBN 0-8063-1292-0.
929 CS44

The third edition boasts changes to more than 80 percent of existing entries and is one-third larger than the previous publication. Arranged by subject, it is cross-referenced and provides addresses, names, telephone numbers, hours of operation, and other information on organizations, libraries, archives, historical societies, and other research centers of interest.

1944 Meyer's directory of genealogical societies in the USA and Canada. Libra, 1976– . Biennial. $28. ISSN 0732-3395.
929 CS44

A listing of genealogical societies, many of which are small and can be difficult to locate. For most of the societies Meyer has identified a contact person. A useful supplement to the *Directory of historical agencies in the United States and Canada.*

Handbooks, Yearbooks, and Almanacs

1945 **African American genealogical sourcebook.** Paula K. Byers, ed. 244p. Gale, 1995. $69. ISBN 0-8103-9226-7.
929.074 E185.96

Asian American genealogical sourcebook. Gale, 1995. $69. ISBN 0-8103-9228-3.
929.108 E184.06

Hispanic American genealogical sourcebook. Gale, 1995. $69. ISBN 0-8103-9227-5.
929.108 E184

Native American genealogical sourcebook. Gale, 1995. $69. ISBN 0-8103-9229-1.
929.1 E98

This new series focuses on each ethnic group, discusses the unique resources and problems, and provides basic methodology, methods of obtaining data, and interpretation. Directories of organizations and repositories are also provided. Also available as a four-volume set ($239. ISBN 0-8103-8541-4).

1946 **Ancestry's red book: American state, county, and town sources.** Rev. ed. Alice Eicholz, ed. 858p. Ancestry, 1992. $49.95. ISBN 0-916489-47-7.
929.1 CS49

Organized by state, this is a listing of locations for vital records, censuses, local history information, maps, land records, probate and tax files, and cemetery and church records. Includes periodical and newspaper listings. Directory of archives, libraries, and historical societies of note. Indexed.

1947 **The genealogist's handbook: modern methods for researching family history.** Raymond S. Wright III. 191p. American Library Assn., 1995. $48. ISBN 0-8389-0625-7.
929.1 CS9

This handbook aims to go beyond the search for mere pedigree in order to lead us to uncover the "story that details people's lives." Prepared by a historian, librarian, and genealogist, the work is clear, thorough, comprehensive, and courteous. It instructs as well as informs, and we are led to see our search for our ancestors as a search for our own vital history.

1948 **International vital records handbook.** 3d ed. Thomas Jay Kemp. 430p. Genealogical Pub., 1994. $29.95. ISBN 0-8063-1424-9.
929.1 CS42.7

Here is a collection of useful forms needed to obtain copies of vital records. The book is divided into sections covering the fifty states, U.S. territories, and the English-speaking Caribbean, the British Isles, and Europe. Forms may be photocopied for materials in the United States. Foreign document forms are supplied where available; where they are not, names and addresses of repositories are given, along with advice and lists of other organizations that might be of help.

1949 **Library of Congress: a guide to genealogical and historical research.** James Neagles. 382p. Ancestry, 1990. $35.95. ISBN 0-916489-48-5.
016.973 E180

A comprehensive guide to the resources of the Library of Congress, including the Local History and Genealogy Room and others. A good resource for libraries whose patrons travel to the nation's capital for their research needs.

1950 **Researcher's guide to American genealogy.** 2d ed., enl. and rev. Val D. Greenwood. 623p. Genealogical Pub., 1995 (reprint of 1990). $24.95. ISBN 0-8063-1267-X.
929 CS47

A complete reference work, this is a classic text.

1951 **Searching for your ancestors.** 6th ed. Gilbert H. Doane and James B. Bell. 334p. Univ. of Minnesota Pr., 1992. $17.95. ISBN 0-8166-1990-5.
929.1 CS16

Good introduction to the whys and how-tos of genealogical research.

1952 **Shaking your family tree.** Ralph Crandall. 256p. Yankee Books, 1988. Paper $10.95. ISBN 0-89909-148-2.
929 CS16

A popular beginner's guide. A companion workbook is available.

1953 The source: a guidebook of American genealogy. Arlene Eakle and Johni Cerny, eds. 786p. Ancestry, 1984. $49.95. ISBN 0-916489-00-0.
929 CS49

A range of genealogical material is gathered here under one cover. The authors provide chapters on major record types, major published sources, ethnic genealogy, and computers in genealogical research. An excellent basic volume.

Heraldry

The heraldry sources included are of general interest and basic.

1954 American badges and insignia. Evans E. Kerrigan. 286p. Viking, 1967. op; paper $14.95. Medallic, 1984. ISBN 0-9624663-2-8.
355.1 UC533

Explains all types of military insignia of the United States. Well illustrated, with diagrams. Includes bibliography and index.

1955 American war medals and decorations. Evans E. Kerrigan. 149p. Viking, 1971. op; paper $24.95. Medallic, 1990. ISBN 0-9624663-4-4.
355.1 CJ5805

Contains information about and colored illustrations of decorations of honor and service medals given to personnel of the U.S. armed services, as well as wartime awards given to civilians. Includes chronological table of awards, bibliography, and index.

1956 Basic heraldry. Stephen Friar and John Ferguson. 200p. Norton, 1993. $27.95. ISBN 0-393-03463-1.
929.6 CR151

A well-illustrated "basic" book on the subject. Bibliography and index. An alternative to Friar's *Dictionary of heraldry,* Neubecker's *Guide to heraldry,* and Puttock's *Dictionary of heraldry and related subjects,* all out-of-print. These should be added when they become available.

1957 Boutell's heraldry. Rev. ed. J. P. Brooke-Little, ed. 368p. Warne, 1983. op.
929.6 CR21

Since the first edition in 1863, this book has gone through many revisions. Now out-of-print, it is nevertheless regarded as the standard work of reference on heraldry, although the viewpoint is primarily British. Includes a glossary and many illustrations.

1958 Flags of the world. E. M. Barraclough, ed. 264p. Warne, 1981. op.
929.9 CR109

Standard source for the world's flags. Most recent edition has 370 colored pictures and 375 drawings. Includes regional and provincial flags as well as military flags. Libraries should watch for a new printing or edition.

1959 State names, seals, flags, and symbols: a historical guide. Benjamin F. Shearer and Barbara S. Shearer. 438p. Greenwood, 1994. $49.95. ISBN 0-313-28862-3.
929.9 E155

Arranged by subject and then by state, the volume provides information on names and nicknames, mottoes, seals, capitols, flowers, trees, birds, songs, and miscellaneous other state symbols. Includes a bibliography of state histories and color plates of seals, flags, birds, and flowers. New to this edition are Washington, D.C.; Puerto Rico; Virgin Islands; American Samoa; Guam; and the Northern Mariana Islands, as well as license plates, postage stamps, fairs, and festivals.

NAMES

Traditional sources for proper names continue to be the mainstay of collections, although some standards, such as the *New century cyclopedia of names,* are now out-of-print. Newer titles on the market have broadened their coverage to include more non-European and English-language entries.

1960 American given names: their origin and history in the context of the English language. George R. Stewart. 272p. Oxford Univ. Pr., 1986. $29.95. ISBN 0-19-502465-6; paper $8.95. ISBN 0-19-504040-6.
929.4 CS2375

Historical sketch of the frequency of given names followed by a dictionary arrangement of names that gives the sex, language derivation, meaning, and "a history of the name as it occurs in U.S. usage, popularity, etc."

1961 American nicknames: their origin and significance. 2d ed. George Earlie Shankle. 524p. Wilson, 1955. $44. ISBN 0-8242-0004-7.
929.4 E179

Includes the sobriquets and appellations of persons, places, objects, and events in American life, past and present. Numerous *see* references. Bibliographical footnotes are useful.

1962 Dictionary of eponyms. 2d ed. Cyril L. Beeching. 272p. Oxford Univ. Pr., 1988. Paper $9.95. ISBN 0-19-282156-3.
423 PE1596

Names of products, services, or concepts that are derived from proper names are defined with a brief history of the terms and their originators.

1963 A dictionary of first names. Patrick Hanks and Flavia Hodges. 320p. Oxford Univ. Pr., 1990. $39.95. ISBN 0-19-211651-7.
929.4 CS2367

This collection of 4,500 European and American first names also lists nicknames and variants in other languages. Appendixes list common Arabic names and names from the Indian subcontinent. Both male and female names are interfiled in one alphabet.

1964 A dictionary of surnames. Patrick Hanks and Flavia Hodges. 826p. Oxford Univ. Pr., 1989. $85. ISBN 0-19-211592-8.
929.4 CS2385

This book identifies and describes the origin and meaning of nearly 70,000 surnames of European derivation found in the English-speaking world. Names were selected based on the frequency of their appearance in telephone books in the United States, Canada, and Europe. The index lists all names in the text and is essential for locating variants.

1965 Eponyms dictionaries index: a reference guide to persons, both real and imaginary, and the terms derived from their names. 730p. Gale, 1977. $135. ISBN 0-8103-0688-3. Supplement, 1984. $94. ISBN 0-8103-0689-1.
423 PE1596

A listing of eponyms (such as Morse code, Hodgkin's disease) with references to the full names from which they were derived. For each person whose name is listed, brief biographical information and reference to sources of further information are given. Smaller libraries may well opt for the *Dictionary of eponyms.*

1966 The Facts on File dictionary of first names. Leslie Dunkling and William Gosling. 305p. Facts on File, 1984. $24.95. ISBN 0-87196-274-8.
929.4 CS2367

Contains more than 4,500 entries. Gives linguistic origin, history, and variants. The compilers also provide lists of the most popular names at various periods in history. Includes a lengthy bibliography.

1967 Handbook of pseudonyms and personal nicknames. Harold S. Sharp. 2v. Scarecrow, 1972. $59.50/set. ISBN 0-8108-0460-3. Supplement 1. 2v. Scarecrow, 1975. $82.50/set. ISBN 0-8108-0807-2. Supplement 2. 295p. Scarecrow, 1982. $35. ISBN 0-8108-1539-7.
929.4 Z1041

Standard ever-expanding source for identification of the real persons behind pen names, stage names, pseudonyms, aliases, sobriquets, and nicknames. Each real name entry contains dates, brief identification, a listing of all known pseudonyms, and so forth. Entries are listed by real name and by pseudonym.

1968 Pronouncing dictionary of proper names. 2d ed. John K. Bollard, ed. 1097p. Omnigraphics, 1998. $80. ISBN 0-7808-0098-2.
423 PE1137.P82

A comprehensive compilation of English-language names: countries, capitals, landmarks, given names, religions, languages, companies, products, and more. Designed to reflect the variations in American dialects and local pronunciations. Extensive cross-references for variant spellings.

1969 Pseudonyms and nicknames dictionary. 3d ed. Jennifer Mossman, ed. 2v. Gale, 1986. $235/set. ISBN 0-8103-0541-0.

New pseudonyms and nicknames. 306p. Gale, 1988. $110. op.
929.4 CT120

These sources attempt to include all countries and time periods, though Anglo-Americans predominate. Listings include brief biographical details and list references to further information. *Pseudonyms* gives wide-ranging coverage and includes about 135,000 entries. *New pseudonyms* adds another 9,000.

1970 Twentieth-century American nicknames. Laurence Urdang, ed. 398p. Wilson, 1979. $42.
ISBN 0-8242-0642-8.
929.4 CT108

Nicknames and the real names of persons, places, and so forth are listed in a single alphabet. Includes variant nicknames. The editor attempted to avoid duplication of nicknames appearing in Shankle's *American nicknames*.

INDEX

Compiled by Stuart Hoffman

Numbers refer to entries and not to pages, unless p. *appears before the number. An* n *after a number indicates that the work is mentioned in the annotation.*

1990 census of population and housing, Bureau of the Census, 407
1995 National directory of TTY numbers, 82
100 key documents in American democracy, P. B. Levy, ed., 1836
10,000 garden questions answered by twenty experts, M. J. Dietz, ed., 867
303 CD-ROMs to use in your library, P. R. Dewey, 21

AAMA motor vehicle facts and figures, 1015
Abbreviations dictionary, R. De Sola, D. Stahl, and K. Kerchelich, 722
ABI/INFORM Global, 448
Abingdon Bible handbook, E. P. Blair, 195
Abrams, M. H. Glossary of literary terms, 1609
Abridged biography and genealogy master index, 1912n
Abridged readers' guide to periodical literature, 126n
Aby, S. H. Sociology, 328
ACAD: airman's civil aviation dictionary, F. B. Artuso, 933
Academic American encyclopedia, L. T. Lorimer and K. A. Ranson, eds., p. 24, 148
Academic Press dictionary of science and technology, C. Morris, ed., 819
Accent on living buyer's guide, B. Garee, ed., 1112
Access America, P. Shea et al., 1902
Access EPA, Office of Information Resources Management, U.S. Environmental Protection Agency, 956
Accessing U.S. government information, J. Zwirn, comp., 132
Accident facts, Statistics Department, National Safety Council staff, comp., 1059
Accountants' handbook, D. R. Carmichael, S. B. Lilien, and M. Mellman, eds., 499
Accredited institutions of postsecondary education, programs, candidates, 669
Achtemeier, P., ed. HarperCollins Bible dictionary, 184n, 191
ACM guide to computing literature, 894
Acocello, N. *See* Dewey, D.
Acronyms, initialisms, and abbreviations dictionary, 723
Actor's guide to the talkies, 1949 through 1964, R. B. Dimmitt, 1334
Actor's guide to the talkies, 1965 through 1974, A. A. Aros, 1334
Adams, C. J., ed. Reader's guide to the great religions, 177
Adams, J. T., ed. Album of American history, 1832
Adamson, T. Electronics dictionary for technicians, 944
Adding on, R. Yepsen, ed., 1166
Adelman, I., and R. Dworkin. Contemporary novel, 1684
Adoption directory, E. Paul, ed., 343
Adventuring with books, W. Sutton, ed., 32
Advertising slogans of America, H. S. Sharp, comp., 456
African American genealogical sourcebook, P. K. Byers, ed., 1944

African American historic places, B. L. Savage, ed., 358
African American writers, L. Baechler and A. W. Litz, eds., 1644
African biographical dictionary, N. C. Brockman, 1915
African writers, C. B. Cox, 1758
African-American almanac, K. Estell, ed., 357
Afro-American reference, N. Davis, comp. and ed., 359
Agricultural statistics, U.S. Department of Agriculture, 852
Aharoni, Y., ed. Macmillan Bible atlas, 183
Ahlstrand, A., ed. Ortho's home improvement encyclopedia, 1169
AIDS information sourcebook, H. R. Malinowsky and G. J. Perry, 1078
AIDS knowledge base, P. T. Cohen and P. A. Volberding, 1079
AIDS sourcebook, K. Bellenir, ed., 1080
Ainslie, T. Ainslie's complete Hoyle, 1546
Ainslie's complete Hoyle, T. Ainslie, 1546
Air and space history, D. A. Pisano and C. S. Lewis, eds., 934
AKC staff. Complete dog book, 1209
Album of American history, J. T. Adams, ed., 1832
Alder, D., ed. Sport on film and video, 1513
Alderton, D. Cats, 1202; Dogs, 1211
Alexander, G. L. *See* Kane, J.
Alkin, M. C., ed. Encyclopedia of educational research, 652
All music guide, M. Erlewine, ed., 1414n
All music guide to jazz, R. Wynn, ed., 1414n, 1441
All music guide to rock, M. Erlewine, ed., 1414
All states tax handbook, 541
Allaby, A., and M. Allaby, eds. Concise Oxford dictionary of earth sciences, 912
Allaby, M., ed. Concise Oxford dictionary of botany, 984; Concise Oxford dictionary of ecology, 959; Concise Oxford dictionary of zoology, 989; Illustrated dictionary of science, 823; *see also* Allaby, A.
Allan, T., and A. Warren, eds. Deserts, 961
Allen, B., ed. Blackwell guide to recorded country music, 1436
Allen, J. P., and E. J. Turner. We the people, 356
Allen, R. Children's book prizes, 1672
Almanac of American politics, 579, 640n
Almanac of business and industrial financial ratios, L. Troy, ed., 484
Almanac of famous people, S. L. Stetler, ed., 1916
Almanac of state legislatures, W. Lilley III et al., 580
Alpher, J., ed. Encyclopedia of Jewish history, 1803
Alternative health and medicine encyclopedia, J. Marti, 1081
Alternative medicine, Burton Goldberg Group staff, 1081
Alternative medicine yellow pages, M. Bonk, ed., 1082
Alternative press index, 121
Alternative publications, C. S. Whitaker, ed., 46
Alternative realities, L. George, 308
Altman, E. I., ed. Handbook of corporate finance, 503; Handbook of financial markets and institutions, 503
AMA management handbook, J. J. Hampton, ed., 525
Amateur astronomer's glossary, 878n
Amateur astronomer's handbook, J. Muirden, 868
America at the polls, A. V. McGillvray and R. M. Scammon, eds., 614
America suburbs rating guide and fact book, A. Willis and B. Jacobstein, 1872
America votes, 614
America: history and life, 1775
American almanac of jobs and salaries, J. Wright, 550
American art directory, 1259
American badges and insignia, E. E. Kerrigan, 1954
American bench, J. J. Clapp and R. A. Kennedy, eds., 601
American book publishing record, 60
American book trade directory, Bowker staff, ed., 89
American Cancer Society's complete book of cancer, A. I. Holleb, ed., 1092
American chronicle, L. Gordon and A. Gordon, 1777
American college regalia, L. Sparks and B. Emerton, comps., 694
American Correctional Assn. Directory, 348
American counties, J. N. Kane, 1873
American dental directory, 1050
American drama criticism, F. E. Eddleman, comp., 1718
American educators' encyclopedia, D. E. Kapel et al., 650
American ephemeris and nautical almanac, 869n
American export register, 457
American film industry, A. Slide, 1324
American folklore, J. H. Brunvand, ed., 264
American furniture, J. L. Fairbanks and E. B. Bates, 1288
American given names, G. R. Stewart, 1960
American golfer's guide, H. Padroli and M. Tiegreen, eds., 1563
American Heart Association cookbook, 1131
American Heritage dictionary of idioms, C. Ammer, 738
American Heritage dictionary of the English Language, 718, 808n
American Heritage Larousse Spanish dictionary, 808
American Heritage Stedman's medical dictionary, 1033

American Horticulture Society: A-Z encyclopedia of garden plants, C. Brickell and J. D. Zuk, eds., 858
American Horticultural Society encyclopedia of gardening, C. Brickell et al., eds., 859
American Hospital Association guide to the health-care field, 1051
American immigrant cultures, D. Levinson and M. Ember, eds., 352
American Indian literatures, A. L. B. Ruoff, 387
American Indians, National Archives and Records Administration, 1933n
American Jewish yearbook, 229
American law yearbook, 578
American Library Association guide to information access, S. Whiteley, ed., 1
American library directory, 85
American Medical Association family medical guide, C. B. Clayman, ed., 1060
American Medical Association manual of style, C. Iverson, ed., 769
American men and women of science, 833, 837n
American musical theatre, G. Bordman, 1367
American Muslim, 249
American national biography, J. A. Garraty and M. C. Carnes, 1917, 1919n
American nature writers, J. Elder, ed., 1719
American nicknames, G. E. Shankle, 1961, 1970n
American place names, G. R. Stewart, 1854
American political dictionary, J. C. Plano and M. Greenberg, 560
American popular songs from the Revolutionary War to the present, D. Ewen, ed., 1421
American psychiatric glossary, 289
American Public Welfare Assn. Public welfare directory, 397
American Quilter's Society staff. Quilt groups today, 1464
American reference books annual, B. S. Wynar, ed., 2
American regional cookery index, R. H. Kleiman, 1136
American register of exporters and importers, 457
American Revolution, R. L. Blanco, ed., 1783
American shelter, L. Walker, 1270, 1278n
American sign language, M. L. A. Sternberg, 748
American sign language dictionary, M. L. A. Sternberg and H. Rogoff, 749
American social attitudes data sourcebook, P. E. Converse et al., 323
American songwriters, D. Ewen, 1420
American synagogue, K. M. Olitzky, 230
American universities and colleges, 670
American vegetarian cookbook from the Fit for Life kitchen, M. Diamond, 1140
American war medals and decorations, E. E. Kerrigan, 1955
American women in science, M. J. Bailey, 834
American women writers, L. Mainiero, ed., 1652
American writers, L. Unger, ed., 1720, 1731n
American writers before 1800, J. A. Levernier and D. R. Wilmes, eds., 1721
American years, E. Gross, 1777
America's ancient treasures, F. Folsom and M. E. Folsom, 439
America's best hospitals, 1052
Ammer, C. American Heritage dictionary of idioms, 738; Have a nice day—no problem, 751; New A to Z of women's health, 1121
Amy Vanderbilt complete book of etiquette, N. Tuckerman and N. Dunnan, 1156
Analytical perspectives, 606
Anatomy of wonder 4, N. Barron, ed., 1692
Ancestry's red book, A. Eicholz, ed., 1946
Anchor Bible dictionary, D. N. Freedman, 189
Ancient Golf Club of St. Andrews. *See* USGA staff
Ancient inventions, P. James and N. Thorpe, 842
Ancient writers, T. J. Luce, ed., 1745
Anderson, J. E. *See* Grant, J. C. B.
Andrews, R., M. Biggs, and M. Seider, eds. Columbia Granger's world of quotations on CD-ROM, 1618
Andrews, W. L., F. S. Foster, and T. Harris, eds. Oxford companion to African American literature, 1648
Annals of America, 1833
Anson, J. L., and R. F. Marchesani, eds. Baird's manual of American college fraternities, 695
Apel, W. Harvard dictionary of music, 1393n
Appel, M. C. Illustration index, 4th ed., 1236; Illustration index, V–VIII, 1236
Apple, M., et al. Symptoms and early warning signs, 1067
Applied science and technology, 450n
Applied science and technology index, 817
ARBA guide to subject encyclopedias and dictionaries, S. C. Awe, ed., 145
Ardagh, J., and C. Jones. Cultural atlas of France, 1894
Ardley, N. Music: an illustrated encyclopedia, 1386
Area handbooks, 1875
Arem, J. E. Color encyclopedia of gemstones, 918
Argent, J. Complete step-by-step guide to home sewing, 1468
Arkana dictionary of astrology, F. Gettings, 309
Arnold, A. L., and J. Kusnet. Arnold encyclopedia of real estate, 536
Arnold, D., ed. New Oxford companion to music, 1394

Arnold encyclopedia of real estate, A. L. Arnold and J. Kusnet, 536
Arnold encyclopedia of real estate yearbook, 536n
Arntzen, C. J., and E. M. Ritter, eds. Encyclopedia of agricultural science, 854
Arntzen, E., and R. Rainwater. Guide to the literature of art history, 1230
Aronson, M. *See* Meltzer, E.
Aros, A. A. Actor's guide to the talkies, 1965 through 1974, 1334; Title guide to the talkies, 1964 through 1974, 1334; Title guide to the talkies, 1975 through 1984, 1334
Arpan, J. S., and D. Ricks, eds. Directory of foreign manufacturers in the United States, 466
ARRL handbook for the radio amateur, 942
Art, F. Hartt, 1242
Art, H. W., et al., eds. Dictionary of ecology and environmental science, 962
Art in America, 1260
Art index, 1232
Art information, L. S. Jones, 1228
Articles on American literature, 1900–1950, L. Leary, comp., 1722
Articles on American literature, 1950–1967, L. Leary, C. Bartholet, and C. Roth, 1722
Articles on American literature, 1968–1975, L. Leary and J. Auchard, 1722
Artist's and graphic designer's market, 1261
Artist's complete health and safety guide, M. Rossel, 1449
Artist's handbook of materials and techniques, R. Mayer, 1250n, 1265
Artist's market, 1261n
Arts in America, B. Karpel, ed., 1229
Artuso, F. B. ACAD: airman's civil aviation dictionary, 933
Ash, L., and W. G. Miller, eds. Subject collections, 88
Asher, R. E., and J. M. Y. Simpson, eds. Encyclopedia of language and linguistics, 709
Asian American almanac, S. Gall and I. Natividad, eds., 374
Asian American encyclopedia, F. Ng, ed., 375
Asian American genealogical sourcebook, 1944
Asian Americans information directory, C. B. Montney, ed., 376
ASPCA complete cat care manual, A. Edney, 1201
ASPCA complete dog care manual, B. Fogle, 1207
Associated Press stylebook and libel manual, N. Goldstein, ed., 770
Astrology encyclopedia, J. R. Lewis, 310
Astronomical almanac for the year [yr.], 869
Astronomical phenomena for the year [yr.], 869n
Athletic scholarships, Andy Clark and Amy Clark, 656
Atkins, B. T., et al. Collins-Robert French-English, English-French dictionary, 786
Atlas of African history, C. McEvedy, 1837
Atlas of American history, K. T. Jackson, ed., 1838
Atlas of American sport, R. Singer et al., eds., 1508
Atlas of dog breeds of the world, B. Wilcox and C. Walkowicz, 1208
Atlas of early American history, L. J. Cappon, ed., 1839
Atlas of early man, J. Hawkes, 427
Atlas of human anatomy, F. H. Netter and A. F. Dalley, eds., 1087
Atlas of languages, B. Louw, 706
Atlas of North American exploration, 1840
Atlas of South America, M. Brawer, 1891
Atlas of the 1990 census, M. T. Mattson, 403
Atlas of the Bible, J. W. Rogerson, 181
Atlas of the British empire, C. A. Bayly, 1892
Atlas of the Christian church, H. Chadwick and G. R. Evans, eds., 212
Atlas of the Civil War, J. McPherson, ed., 1841
Atlas of the environment, G. Lean and D. Hinrichsen, 957
Atlas of the historical geography of the United States, 1840n
Atlas of the Islamic world since 1500, F. Robinson, 1842
Atlas of the North American Indian, C. Waldman, 1784
Atlas of the United States, J. Glassborow and G. Freeman, eds., 1897
Atlas of the world, 1884
Atlas of world cultures, G. P. Murdock, 428n
Atlas of world cultures: a geographical guide to ethnographic literature, D. H. Price, 428
Atterbury, P., and L. Tharp, eds. Bullfinch illustrated encyclopedia of antiques, 1290
Attwater, D. Penguin dictionary of saints, 226n; *see also* Butler, A.
Auchard, J. *See* Leary, L.
Audi, R., ed. Cambridge dictionary of philosophy, 160
Audiocassette and compact disc finder, National Information Center for Educational Media, 643
Audio-visual equipment directory, 660
Audiovisual market place, 90
Audouze, J., and G. Israel, eds. Cambridge atlas of astronomy, 870
Audubon Society field guide to North American rocks and minerals, C. W. Chesterman, 916
Augarde, T., ed. Oxford dictionary of modern quotations, 1623
Automotive dictionary, J. Edwards and M. Lufty, eds., 1016
AV market place, 90, 657
Aversa, E. *See* Blazek, R.
Aviation/space dictionary, L. Reithmaier, 935
Awards, honors, and prizes, 102

Awe, S. C., ed. ARBA guide to subject encyclopedias and dictionaries, 145
Axelrod, A., and C. Phillips. Environmentalists, 965
———. *See also* Phillips, C.
Axelrod, H. R. Dr. Axelrod's atlas of freshwater aquarium fishes, 1212; *see also* Burgess, W.
———, et al. Dr. Axelrod's mini-atlas of freshwater aquarium fishes, 1213
Aymar, B. *See* Rawson, H.
A-Z of astronomy, 878n

Background notes, Bureau of Public Affairs, U.S. Dept. of State, 1874
Backpacker's handbook, H. McManners, 1515
Backus, K., ed. Medical and health information directory, 1056
Bacon, D. C., et al. Encyclopedia of the United States Congress, 636
Baechler, L., and A. W. Litz. Modern American women writers, 1659
———, ———, eds. African American writers, 1644
Bahr, L. S., and B. Johnson, eds. Collier's encyclopedia, 151
Bailey, M. J. American women in science, 834
Bain, R., and J. M. Flora, eds. Fifty southern writers before 1900, 1726
———. *See also* Flora, J. M.
Baines, A. Oxford companion to musical instruments, 1388n
Bair, F. E., ed. Cancer sourcebook, 1093; Weather almanac, 922; Weather of U.S. cities, 924
Baird's manual of American college fraternities, J. L. Anson and R. F. Marchesani, eds., 695
Baker, B. A., ed. Holidays and anniversaries of the world, 1145
Baker, D. Flight and flying, 937
Baker, D. B. Explorers and discoverers of the world, 1850
Baker, N. L. Research guide for undergraduate students, 1599n
Baker's biographical dictionary of musicians, N. Slonimsky, 1398
Balachandran, S., ed. Encyclopedia of environmental information services, 963
Balanchine, G., and F. Mason. Balanchine's complete stories of the great ballets, 1322n; One hundred one stories of the great ballets, 1322
Balanchine's complete stories of the great ballets, G. Balanchine and F. Mason, 1322n
Balay, R., ed. Guide to reference books, 7
Baldridge, L. Letitia Baldridge's new complete guide to executive manners, 1158
Baldwin, J. M., ed. Dictionary of philosophy and psychology, 293
Ballantine, R., and R. Grant. Richards' ultimate bicycle repair manual, 1542
Balliett, W., ed. USA Today sports atlas, 1509
Ballplayers, M. Shatzkin, ed., 1516
Baltsan, H., ed. Webster's new world Hebrew dictionary, 798
Bamberger, B. J. *See* Plaut, W. G.
Bambric, S., ed. Cambridge encyclopedia of Australia, 1855
Banham, M., ed. Cambridge guide to theatre, 1370
Barabas, S. *See* Tenney, M. C.
Barker, R. L. Social work dictionary, 402
Barksdale, H. C., ed. Marketing information, 530
Barnard, N. Complete home decorating book, 1175
Barnhart abbreviations dictionary, R. K. Barnhart, ed., 724
Barnhart dictionary of etymology, R. K. Barnhart, ed., 730
Barnhart, R. K., ed. Barnhart abbreviations dictionary, 724; Barnhart dictionary of etymology, 730
Barraclough, E. M., ed. Flags of the world, 1958
Barraclough, G., ed. Times atlas of world history, 1847
Barrett, D., et al. Twentieth century hockey chronicle, 1574
Barron, N., ed. Anatomy of wonder 4, 1692
Barron's profiles of American colleges, 671
Bart, P., and L. Frankel. Student sociologist's handbook, 329
Bartholet, C. *See* Leary, L.
Barton, B. J. Gardening by mail, 863
Barzun, J., and W. H. Taylor. Catalogue of crime, 1687
Baseball almanac, 1518
Baseball America's [yr.] directory, 1519
Baseball encyclopedia, 1520
Baseball guide, Sporting News staff, 1521
Baseball, M. J. Smith, comp., 1517
Baseball: supplement 1, M. J. Smith, 1517
Basic catalogue of plays and musicals, S. French, 1359
Basic heraldry, S. Friar and J. Ferguson, 1956
Basic home repairs, Sunset Books editors, 1176
Basic music library, E. Davis, ed., 1379
Basic plumbing, Sunset Books staff, 1177
Basic plumbing with illustrations, H. C. Massey, 1178
Basic wiring, Sunset Books staff, 1179
Basketball almanac, Consumer Guide editors, 1531
Basketball biographies, M. Taragno, 1532
Basketball resource guide, J. V. Krause and S. J. Brennan, 1533
Bataille, G. M., ed. Native American women, 390
Bates, E. B. *See* Fairbanks, J. L.
Baxter, A. In search of your European roots, 1936
Baxter, P. M. Psychology, 287

Bayly, C. A. Atlas of the British empire, 1892
Beacham, W., ed. Research guide to biography and criticism, 1643
Bead directory, M. Firestone and A. Scherer, 1453
Bear, J. Bear's guide to earning college degrees nontraditionally, 672
Bear's guide to earning college degrees nontraditionally, J. Bear, 672
Bechert, H., and R. F. Gombrich. World of Buddhism, 263
Becker, L. C., ed. Encyclopedia of ethics, 284
Beckham, B., ed. Black student's guide to colleges, 674
Bedurftig, F. *See* Zentner, C.
Beeching, C. L. Dictionary of eponyms, 1962
Beit-Hallahmi, B. Illustrated encyclopedia of active new religions, sects, and cults, 255
Bell, J. B. *See* Doane, G. H.
Bell, R. E. Dictionary of classical mythology: symbols, attributes, and associations, 266
Bellenir, K., ed. AIDS sourcebook, 1080
Bender, G. L., ed. Reference handbook on the deserts of North America, 1867
Bendick, J. Mathematics illustrated dictionary, 1008
Benét's reader's encyclopedia, B. Murphy, ed., 1603
Benét's reader's encyclopedia of American literature, G. Perkins, B. Perkins, and P. Leininger, 1723
Bennet, A. *See* Turabian, K. L.
Bennett, H., ed. Concise chemical and technical dictionary, 880
Bentley, L. H., and J. J. Kiesl. Investment statistics locator, 517
Bently, E. County courthouse book, 1942
Bently, E. P. Genealogist's address book, 1943
Benyon, P. H., and J. E. Cooper, eds. Manual of exotic pets, 1223
Berger, L. S., ed. Twentieth-century children's writers, 1670
Berkow, R., ed. Merck manual of diagnosis and therapy, 1070
Berman, D. M. *See* Matthews, J. L.
Berney, K. A., ed. Contemporary dramatists, 1677
Bernhard, A. Value Line investment survey, 524
Best books for children, J. T. Gillespie and C. J. Naden, eds., 33
Best books for junior high readers, J. T. Gillespie, 34
Best books for senior high readers, J. T. Gillespie, 35
Best games, L. Jennings et al., 1577
Best hospitals in America, J. W. Wright and L. Sunshine, 1052
Best plays of . . . [yr.], 1377
Best reference books 1986–1990, B. S. Wynar, ed., 2
Best's Flitcraft compend, 508
Best's insurance reports, life-health . . , 509
Best's insurance reports, property-casualty, 509n
Best's key rating guide: property-casualty, 510
Best's review—life-health insurance edition, 509n
Best's review—property-casualty insurance edition, 509n
Bethell, L., ed. Cambridge history of Latin America, 1788
Better Homes and Gardens do-it-yourself home repairs, 1180
Betteridge, H. T., comp. Cassell's German-English, English-German dictionary, 790
Betts, D. A. Chess: an annotated bibliography of works published in the English language, 1850–1968, 1550
Bibliographic index, 113
Bibliography of American county histories, P. W. Filby, 1931, 1940n
Bibliography of bioethics, L. Walters, ed., 280
Bibliography of philosophy, psychology, and cognate subjects, B. Rand, 293n
Bicycling Magazine's complete guide to bicycle maintenance and repair, 1541
Bieber's dictionary of legal citations, M. M. Prince, 771
Biesel, D. B. Can you name that team, 1493
Big book of blues, R. Santelli, 1434
Biggs, M. *See* Andrews, R.
Billboard book of top forty hits, J. Whitburn, 1415
Billboard's international buyer's guide, 1395
Bingham, J. M., ed. Writers for children, 1671
Biographical dictionary of Afro-American and African musicians, E. Southern, 1399
Biographical dictionary of American cult and sect leaders, J. G. Melton, 210
Biographical dictionary of American educators, J. F. Ohles, ed., 702
Biographical dictionary of American labor, G. M. Fink et al., eds., 453n, 547
Biographical dictionary of American sports, D. L. Porter, ed., 1510
Biographical dictionary of artists, L. Gowing, ed., 1247
Biographical dictionary of dance, B. N. Cohen-Stratyner, 1315
Biographical dictionary of film, D. Thomson, 1342
Biographical dictionary of psychology, N. Sheehy, A. J. Chapman, and W. Conroy, eds., 290
Biographical dictionary of scientists, R. Porter, ed., 835
Biographical dictionary of the Confederacy, J. L. Wakelyn, 1848
Biographical dictionary of twentieth-century philosophers, S. Brown et al., eds., 168
Biographical directory of American colonial and revolutionary governors, 1607–1789, J. W. Raimo, 602n
Biographical directory of American territorial governors, T. A. McMullin and D. Walker, 602n

Biographical directory of the American Congress, J. D. Treese, ed., 631
Biographical directory of the governors of the United States, 1789–1978, R. Sobel and J. Raimo, eds., 602
Biographical directory of the governors of the United States, 1978–1983, J. W. Raimo, ed., 602
Biographical directory of the governors of the United States, 1983–1988, M. M. Mullaney, 602
Biographical directory of the governors of the United States, 1988–1994, M. M. Mullaney, 602
Biographical directory of the United States Congress, U.S. Congress, 631
Biographical directory of the United States executive branch, R. Sobel, ed., 619
Biographical encyclopedia of scientists, J. Daintith et al., eds., 836
Biographical encyclopedia of the Negro baseball leagues, J. Riley, 1522
Biographical index to American science, C. A. Elliott, comp., 837
Biography and genealogy master index, M. C. Herbert and B. McNeil, eds., 1912
Biography index, 1913
Biological and agricultural index, 972
Biology digest, 973
Birnbaum, M. *See* Cass, J.
Bishop, P. D., and M. Darnton, eds. Encyclopedia of world faiths, 174.
Bissell, F. Book of food, 1141
Bitter, M. G., ed. Macmillan encyclopedia of computers, 899
Bjarkman, P. C. ed. Encyclopedia of major league baseball team histories: American League, 1524
Bjarkman, P. C. ed. Encyclopedia of major league baseball team histories: National League, 1524
Bjarkman, P. C. Encyclopedia of pro basketball team histories, 1535
Black American colleges and universities, L. Hill, ed., 673
Black Americans information directory, W. S. Van de Sande, ed., 360
Black authors, J. E. Newby, 1645
Black firsts, J. C. Smith, 361
Black student's guide to colleges, B. Beckham, ed., 674
Black studies, National Archives and Records Administration, 1933n
Black women in America, D. C. Hine et al., eds., 362
Black's agricultural dictionary, D. B. Dalal-Clayton, 853
Black's law dictionary, J. R. Nolan and M. J. Connolly, 561
Black's medical dictionary, 1034
Blackburn, G. Year-round house care, 1171
Blackwell, B. Concise dictionary of classical mythology, 265
Blackwell encyclopedia of modern Christian thought, A. McGrath, ed., 213
Blackwell encyclopedia of writing systems, F. Coulmas, 707
Blackwell guide to recorded country music, B. Allen, ed., 1436
Blain, V., et al. Feminist companion to literature in English, 1656
Blair, E. P. Abingdon Bible handbook, 195
Blanco, R. L., ed. American Revolution, 1783
Blaug, M., ed. Who's who in economics, 548
Blazek, R., and E. Aversa. Humanities, 10
Bleiler, E. F., ed. Supernatural fiction writers, 1698
Bleiler, R., ed. Science fiction writers, 1697
Blevins, W. Dictionary of the American West, 1795
Bloomsbury guide to women's literature, C. Buck, ed., 1653
Bluebook, Harvard Law Review, 771
Blunden, C., and M. Elvin. Cultural atlas of China, 1894
Boatner, M. M., III. Civil War dictionary, 1790
Bob Vila's toolbox, B. Vila, 1189
Boger, L. A. Complete guide to furniture styles, 1291
Bohlander, R., ed. World explorers and discoverers, 1853
Bollard, J. K., ed. Pronouncing dictionary of proper names, 744, 1968
Bond, M. E., and M. M. Caron, comps. Canadian reference sources, 3
Bonk, M., ed. Alternative medicine yellow pages, 1082
Book of costume, M. Davenport, 1282
Book of food, F. Bissell, 1141
Book of old silver, English, American, foreign, S. B. Wyler, 1289
Book of the musical theatre, K. Ganzl and A. Lamb, 1368
Book of the states, 581
Book of the world, Kartographisches Institut Bertelsmann, 1885
Book of world-famous music, J. J. Fuld, 1384
Book review digest, 128
Book review index, 129, 130n
Booklist, 24, 147n
Books for adult new readers, F. J. Pursell, 36
Books for college libraries, 37
Books for public libraries, C. Koehn, ed., 38
Books for secondary school libraries, 39
Books in print, 47, 53n, 93n
Books in series, 61
Books on-demand author fiche guides, 48
Booth, C. J. *See* Kurpis, G. P.

Bopp, R. E., and L. C. Smith, eds. Reference and information services, 16
Bordman, G. American musical theatre, 1367; Oxford companion to American theatre, 1373
Borgatta, E. F., ed. Encyclopedia of sociology, 332
Borklund, E. Contemporary literary critics, 1638
Boston Women's Health Collective. Our bodies, ourselves for the new century, 1122
Boutell's heraldry, J. P. Brooke-Little, ed., 1957
Bowden, H. W. Dictionary of American religious biography, 211
Bowder, D., ed. Who was who in the Greek world, 1927; Who was who in the Roman world, 1927
Bowes, A. D., and H. N. Church. Bowe's and Church's food values of portions commonly used, 1108
Bowe's and Church's food values of portions commonly used, A. D. Bowes and H. N. Church, 1108
Bowker annual of library and book trade almanac, 86
Bowker, J., ed. Oxford dictionary of world religions, 175
Bowker staff, ed. American book trade directory, 89
Bowker's complete video directory, 1335, 1338n
Bowring, R., and P. Kornicki. Cambridge encyclopedia of Japan, 1855
Boyd, M. A. Craft supply sourcebook, 1450
Bracken, J. K. Reference works in British and American literature, 1601
Brackman, B., comp. Encyclopedia of pieced quilt patterns, 1463
Bradford, J. *See* Oakes, E. H.
Bradley, D., and S. F. Fishkin. Encyclopedia of civil rights in America, 566
Brand, J. R. Handbook of electronic formulas, symbols, and definitions, 946
Brands and their companies, D. Wood, ed., 458
Brassey's battles, J. Laffin, 1785
Brawer, M. Atlas of South America, 1891
Breakthroughs, C. L. Parkinson, 843
Breed, P. F., and F. M. Sniderman, comps. and eds. Dramatic criticism index, 1678; *see also* de Charms, D.
Breen, W. Walter Breen's complete encyclopedia of U.S. and colonial coins, 1486
Bremser, M., ed. International dictionary of ballet, 1320
Brennan, A. H. Consumer sourcebook, 1153
Brennan, S., ed. Women's information directory, 426
Brennan, S. J. *See* Krause, J. V.
Brett-Surman, M. K. *See* O'Farlow, J.
Brewer's dictionary of phrase and fable, A. Room, ed., 1608
Brickell, C., et al., eds. American Horticultural Society encyclopedia of gardening, 859
———, and J. D. Zuk, eds. American Horticulture Society: A-Z encyclopedia of garden plants, 858
Bridge, F., and J. Tibbets. Well-tooled kitchen, 1138
Briggs, G., and F. Taylor. Cambridge photographic atlas of the planets, 871
Briggs, K. M. Encyclopedia of fairies, 269
Bright, W., ed. International encyclopedia of linguistics, 710
Brimer, J. B. Homeowners' complete outdoor building book, 1163
Bristow, M. J. *See* Reed, W. L.
British writers, I. Scott-Kilvert, ed., 1731
Britt, S. *See* Case, B.
Broadcast communications dictionary, L. Diamant, ed., 1344
Broadcasting and cable yearbook, 1355
Brockman, N. C. African biographical dictionary, 1915
Broecker, W. L., ed. International Center of Photography encyclopedia of photography, 1304
Bromley, G. W., ed. International standard Bible encyclopedia, 192
Brooke-Little, J. P., ed. Boutell's heraldry, 1957
Brooklyn Public Library, Business Library staff, comp. Business rankings annual, 460
Brooks, T., and E. Marsh. Complete directory to prime time network and cable TV shows, 1346
Broude, G. J. Marriage, family, and relationships, 437
Brough, S., and H. Messinger, eds. Langenscheidt's new college German dictionary, 792
Broun, J. Encyclopedia of woodworking techniques, 1474
Brown, A., et al., eds. Cambridge encyclopedia of Russia and the former Soviet Union, 1855
Brown, L. Les Brown's encyclopedia of television, 1350
Brown, L., ed. New shorter Oxford English dictionary, 720
Brown, M., and R. S. Foudray, comps. Newbery and Caldecott medalists and honor book winners, 1676
Brown, R. E., et al., eds. New Jerome biblical commentary, 187
Brown, S., et al., eds., Biographical dictionary of twentieth-century philosophers, 168
Brown, S. W., ed. Contemporary novelists, 1685
Brown, T. Historical first patents, 845
Bruce, C., ed. Standard catalog of world paper money, v.3, 1484
Bruce, C. R. *See* Krause, C. L.; Mishler, C.
Bruce, F. F., ed. International Bible commentary, 185
Bruning, N. P. *See* Katz, J.
Brunnings, F. E. Folk song index, 1424
Brunvand, J. H., ed. American folklore, 264

Bruwelheide, J. H. Copyright primer for librarians and educators, 104
Buck, C., ed. Bloomsbury guide to women's literature, 1653
Bud Collins' modern encyclopedia of tennis, B. Collins and Z. Hollander, eds., 1595
Bud, R., and D. J. Warner, eds. Instruments of science, 846
Budavari, S., et al., eds. Merck index, 890
Buddhist handbook, J. Snelling, 250
Budget information for states, 606
Budget of the United States government, U.S. Office of Management and Budget, 606
Budget system and concepts, 606
Building a multi-use barn, J. Wagner, 1161
Bullfinch illustrated encyclopedia of antiques, P. Atterbury and L. Tharp, eds., 1290
Bunch, B., and A. Hellemans. Timetables of technology, 850
Bunson, M. Encyclopedia of the Middle Ages, 1808; Encyclopedia of the Roman Empire, 1810
Burak, S. *See* Zakalik, J.
Burchfield, R. W., ed. New Fowler's modern English usage, 742
Bureau of Public Affairs, U.S. Dept. of State. Background notes, 1874
Bureau of the Census. 1990 census of population and housing, 407; Bureau of the census catalog and guide, 407n; County and city data book, 404, 410n; Historical statistics of the United States, 1829; Population and housing characteristics for congressional districts of the 103rd congress, 409; State and metropolitan area data book, 410; USA counties on CD-ROM, 416
Bureau of the Census catalog and guide, Bureau of the Census, 407n
Burgess, M. Reference guide to science fiction, fantasy, and horror, 1695
Burgess, S. M., et al., eds. Dictionary of pentecostal and charismatic movements, 214
Burgess, W., et al. Dr. Burgess's atlas of marine aquarium fishes, 1214
———, and H. R. Axelrod. Dr. Burgess's mini-atlas of marine aquarium fishes, 1215
Burke, J. H. *See* Hackett, A. P.
Burn, B. Practical guide to impractical pets, 1227
Burnham, W. D. Presidential ballots, 614n
Burns, R. D., ed. Encyclopedia of arms control and disarmament, 565
Burton Goldberg Group staff. Alternative medicine, 1081
Business index, 449
Business information, M. R. Lavin, 440
Business information sources, L. M. Daniells, 441
Business organizations, agencies, and publications directory, J. Mast, ed., 459
Business periodicals index, 450
Business profitability data, J. B. Walton, 485
Business publication rates and data, 480
Business rankings annual, Brooklyn Public Library, Business Library staff, comp., 460
Butler, A., H. Thurston, and D. Attwater. Lives of the saints, 226
Butler, J. T. Field guide to American antique furniture, 1295
Buttlar, L J. Education, 642
Butz, R. How to carve wood, 1476
Buy wholesale by mail, 1150
Byers, P. K., ed. African American genealogical sourcebook, 1944
Bynagle, H. E. Philosophy, 158
Bynum, W. F., et al., eds. Dictionary of the history of science, 844
Byrne, R. Byrne's new standard book of pool and billiards, 1543
Byrne's new standard book of pool and billiards, R. Byrne, 1543

Cable, G. *See* Macho, J.
Cahill, M., ed. Everything you need to know about diseases, 1065; Everything you need to know about medical treatment, 1065
Calabi, S. Illustrated encyclopedia of fly-fishing, 1554
Calasibetta, C. M., ed. Fairchild's dictionary of fashion, 1469
Calvert, S. J. *See* Weber, O. S.
Calvocoressi, P., ed. Who's who in the Bible, 198
Cambridge air and space dictionary, P. M. B. Walker et al., eds., 936
Cambridge ancient history, 1786
Cambridge atlas of astronomy, J. Audouze and G. Israel, eds., 870, 876n
Cambridge dictionary of philosophy, R. Audi, ed., 160
Cambridge dictionary of science and technology, 936n
Cambridge encyclopedia, D. Crystal, ed., 149
Cambridge encyclopedia of Africa, R. Oliver and M. Crowder, eds., 1855
Cambridge encyclopedia of archaeology, A. Sherratt, ed., 431
Cambridge encyclopedia of Australia, S. Bambric, ed., 1855
Cambridge encyclopedia of China, B. Hook, ed., 1855
Cambridge encyclopedia of India, Pakistan, Bangladesh, Sri Lanka, Nepal, Bhutan, and the Maldives, F. Robinson, ed., 1855

Cambridge encyclopedia of Japan, R. Bowring and P. Kornicki, 1855
Cambridge encyclopedia of language, D. Crystal, 708
Cambridge encyclopedia of Latin America and the Caribbean, S. Collier et al., eds., 1855
Cambridge encyclopedia of Russia and the former Soviet Union, A. Brown et al., eds., 1855
Cambridge encyclopedia of the English language, D. Crystal, 713
Cambridge encyclopedia of the Middle East and North Africa, T. Mostyn and A. Hourani, eds., 1855
Cambridge gazetteer of the United States and Canada, A. Hobson, ed., 1856
Cambridge guide to American theatre, D. B. Wilmeth and T. L. Miller, eds., 1369
Cambridge guide to English literature, 1598n
Cambridge guide to literature in English, I. Ousby, ed., 1598
Cambridge guide to theatre, M. Banham, ed., 1370
Cambridge guide to world theatre, 1369n, 1370n
Cambridge historical encyclopedia of Great Britain and Ireland, C. Haigh, ed., 1787
Cambridge history of Latin America, L. Bethell, ed., 1788
Cambridge Italian dictionary, B. Reynolds, ed., 799
Cambridge medieval history, 1789
Cambridge paperback encyclopedia, D. Crystal, ed., 150
Cambridge photographic atlas of the planets, G. Briggs and F. Taylor, 871
Cameron, E. Encyclopedia of pottery and porcelain, 1280
Campbell, O. J., and E. G. Quinn, eds. Reader's encyclopedia of Shakespeare, 1739
Campbell, R. J. Psychiatric dictionary, 299
Can you name that team, D. B. Biesel, 1493
Canada gazetteer atlas, 1893
Canada's postal code directory, 71
Canadian almanac and directory, 103
Canadian encyclopedia, J. H. Marsh, ed., 1857
Canadian reference sources, D. Ryder, 3n
Canadian reference sources, M. E. Bond and M. M. Caron, comps., 3
Cancer, R. M. McAllister et al., 1094
Cancer sourcebook, F. E. Bair, ed., 1093
Cantor, G. North American Indian landmarks, 1907
———, ed. Historic landmarks of Black America, 1903
Cappon, L. J. ed. Atlas of early American history, 1839
Caring for the mind, D. Hales and R. E. Hales, 300
Carley, R. Visual dictionary of American domestic architecture, 1278
Carlson, B. W. *See* Thompson, S. E.
Carlson, D. G., and J. M. Giffin. Dog owner's home veterinary handbook, 1210
Carlson, K. J., et al. Harvard guide to women's health, 1119
Carmichael, D. R., S. B. Lilien, and M. Mellman, eds. Accountants' handbook, 499
Carnegie Library of Pittsburgh Science and Technology Department staff. Science and technology desk reference, 832
Carnes, M. C. *See* Garraty, J. A.
Carney, F., and C. Nimmo. Grand dictionnaire francais-anglais, anglais-francais/Larousse French-English, English-French dictionary, 787; Larousse French-English, English-French dictionary, 787
Caron, M. M. *See* Bond, M. E.
Carpenter, H., and M. Prichard. Oxford companion to children's literature, 1666
Carpenter, K. H. Sourcebook on parenting and child care, 1197
Carpenter's manifesto, J. Ehrlich and M. Mannheimer, 1181
Carroll, B. Sports video resource guide, 1514
Carroll's state directory, 596
Carruth, G., ed. Encyclopedia of American facts and dates, 1826
Carter, C., ed. Official NBA rules, 1537
Carwardine, M. Whales, dolphins, and porpoises, 997
Caschnitz, K. M. Professional sports statistics, 1506
Case, B., S. Britt, and C. Murray. Harmony illustrated encyclopedia of jazz, 1442
Cashman, N. D., ed. Slide buyers' guide, 1240
Cass, J., and M. Birnbaum. Comparative guide to American colleges, 678, 682n
Cassell's French dictionary, D. Girard et al., eds., 785
Cassell's German-English, English-German dictionary, H. T. Betteridge, comp., 790
Cassell's Latin dictionary, D. P. Simpson, ed., 804
Cassutt, M. Who's who in space, 941
Castillo, C., et al. University of Chicago Spanish dictionary, 813
Castleman, M. Healing herbs, 1085
Catalog of catalogs, E. L. Palder, 1151
Catalog of federal domestic assistance, Executive Office of the President, 394
Catalogue of crime, J. Barzun and W. H. Taylor, 1687
Catalogue of reproductions of paintings, 1233
Catholic almanac, 221
Catholic encyclopedia, 218n
Cator, M. *See* Commager, H. S.
Cats, D. Alderton, 1202
Cavendish, R., ed. Encyclopedia of the unexplained, 314; Man, myth, and magic, 316
CD-ROMs in print, E. E. Holmberg, ed., 49

Cecil textbook of medicine, J. Wyngarden, ed., 1035
Central Intelligence Agency. World factbook, 1880
Cerny, J. *See* Eakle, A.
Cerrito, J., ed. Contemporary artists, 1266
Chadwick, B. A., and T. B. Heaton, eds. Statistical handbook of the American family, 412
Chadwick, H., and G. R. Evans, eds. Atlas of the Christian church, 212
Chadwick, R., ed. Encyclopedia of applied ethics, 282
Challinor, J., and A. Wyatt, eds. Challinor's dictionary of geology, 917
Challinor's dictionary of geology, J. Challinor and A. Wyatt, eds., 917
Chalmers, I. Food professional's guide, 1135
Chambers dictionary of biology, P. M. B. Walker, ed., 974
Chambers nuclear energy and radiation dictionary, P. M. B. Walker, ed., 927
Chapman, A. J. *See* Sheehy, N.
Chapman, R. L., ed. Dictionary of American slang, 754; Roget's international thesaurus, 767
Charted knitting designs, B. G. Walker, 1460
Charton, B., ed. Facts on File dictionary of marine science, 925
Chase's calendar of events, 1144
Chemical exposure and human health, C. Wilson, 886
Chemical information management, W. Warr and C. Suhr, 879
Cheney, F. N., and W. J. Williams. Fundamental reference sources, 5
Chernow, B. A., and G. A. Vallasi, eds. Columbia encyclopedia., 152
Chess: an annotated bibliography, 1969–1988, A. S. Lusis, 1550
Chess: an annotated bibliography of works published in the English language, 1850–1968, D. A. Betts, 1550
Chesterman, C. W. Audubon Society field guide to North American rocks and minerals, 916
Chevalier, T., ed. Encyclopedia of the essay, 1716
Chevannes, B. Rastafari roots and ideology, 258
Chicago manual of style, 772, 777n
Chicano literature, J. A. Martinez and F. A. Lomeli, eds., 1724
Child, G., comp. Climbing, 1581
Childhood information resources, M. Woodbury, 344
Children's book prizes, R. Allen, 1672
Children's book review index, 130
Children's books, 1673
Children's books and their creators, A. Silvy, ed., 1660
Children's books in print, 50
Children's catalog, 40
Children's literature: a guide to information sources, M. W. Denman-West, 1661
Children's literature: a guide to the criticism, L. Hendrickson, 1662
Children's literature review, G. J. Senick, ed., 1663
Children's magazine guide, 65n
Children's song index, K. Laughlin et al., comps., 1422, 1426n
Children's television, J. Davis, 1345
Childress, J. F., and J. Macquarrie, eds. Westminster dictionary of Christian ethics, 286
Childwise catalog, J. Gillis and M. Fise, 1194
Chilton staff. Chilton's truck and van repair manual, 1022
Chilton's auto repair manual, K. A. Freeman et al., eds., 1018, 1022n
Chilton's easy car care, K. A. Freeman, ed., 1019
Chilton's import car repair manual, 1020, 1022n
Chilton's motorcycle and ATV repair manual, 1021
Chilton's truck and van repair manual, Chilton staff, 1022
Chilvers, I., and H. Osborne, eds. Oxford dictionary of art, 1256
Ching, F. D. K. Visual dictionary of architecture, 1279
Choice, 25
Choose to reuse, N. Goldbeck and D. Goldbeck, 958
Christenson, K. *See* Levinson, D.
Christian Science Monitor, 118n
Chronicle of the twentieth century, C. Daniel et al., eds., 1778
Chronology of women's history, K. Olsen, 418
Church, H. N. *See* Bowes, A. D.
Churches and church membership in the United States, 209
Cirker, B. *See* Cirker, H.
Cirker, H., and B. Cirker. Dictionary of American portraits, 1235
CIS annual, 558n
CIS catalog and price list, 558n
CIS index to publications of the United States Congress, 558
Citizen's guide to the federal budget, 606
Civil War dictionary, M. M. Boatner III, 1790
Civilizations of the ancient Near East, J. M. Sasson, ed., 1791
Claire Shaeffer's fabric sewing guide, C. B. Shaeffer, 1466
Clapham, C. Concise Oxford dictionary of mathematics, 1001
Clapp, J. J., and R. A. Kennedy, eds. American bench, 601
Clark, A. N. Longman dictionary of geography, 1863
Clark, Amy. *See* Clark, Andy
Clark, Andy, and Amy Clark. Athletic scholarships, 656

Clark, D. Negro leagues book, 1526
Clark, John. *See* Darton, M.
Clark, Judith. *See* Clark, R. E.
Clark, R. E., and J. Clark. Encyclopedia of child abuse, 345
Clarke, D., ed. Penguin encyclopedia of popular music, 1419
Classical and medieval literature criticism, 1746
Classical epic, T. J. Sienkewicz, 1747
Classical Greek and Roman drama, R. J. Forman, ed., 1748
Classical studies, F. W. Jenkins, 1749
Clayman, C., ed. Human body, 1089
Clayman, C. B., ed. American Medical Association family medical guide, 1060
Clewis, B. Index to illustrations of animals and plants, 982
Clifford, M. Master handbook of electronic tables and formulas, 948
Clifford, M., ed. Harmony illustrated encyclopedia of rock, 1444
Clift, V. A. *See* Low, W. A.
Climbing, G. Child, comp., 1581
Clute, J., and J. Grant, eds. Encyclopedia of fantasy, 1693
Clute, J., and P. Nicholls. Encyclopedia of science fiction, 1694
Coborn, J. Proper care of reptiles, 1222
Code of federal regulations, Office of the Federal Register, National Archives and Records Administration, 607
Coffin, T. P. *See* Cohen, H.
Cohen, H., and T. P. Coffin, eds. Folklore of American holidays, 1146
Cohen, M. L., et al. How to find the law, 555
———, and K. C. Olson. Legal research in a nutshell, 556
Cohen, P. T., and P. A. Volberding. AIDS knowledge base, 1079
Cohen, R. M. *See* Neft, D. S.
Cohen, S. B., ed. Columbia gazetteer of the world, 1858
Cohen-Stratyner, B. N. Biographical dictionary of dance, 1315
Coin atlas, J. Cribb et al., 1481
Coin world almanac, B. Deisher, ed., 1482
Coleman, A. M., ed. Companion encyclopedia of psychology, 291
Collcutt, M., et al. Cultural atlas of Japan, 1894
Collecting coins for pleasure and profit, B. Krause, 1483
Collecting paper money for pleasure and profit, B. Krause, 1483
College and research libraries, 26
College blue book, 675
College catalog collection on microfiche, 676
College costs and financial aid handbook, 696
College football bibliography, M. J. Smith Jr., comp., 1555
College handbook, 677
Collier, S., et al., eds. Cambridge encyclopedia of Latin America and the Caribbean, 1855
Collier's encyclopedia, L. S. Bahr and B. Johnson, eds., 151
Collins, B., and Z. Hollander, eds. Bud Collins' modern encyclopedia of tennis, 1595
Collins biographical dictionary of scientists, T. Williams, ed., 838
Collins dictionary of sociology, D. Jary and J. Jary, 330
Collins English-Italian, Italian-English dictionary, V. Macchi, ed., 800
Collins German-English, English-German dictionary, P. Terrell, ed., 791
Collins-Robert French-English, English-French dictionary, B. T. Atkins et al., 786
Collins Spanish-English, English-Spanish dictionary, C. Smith et al., eds., 809
Color encyclopedia of gemstones, J. E. Arem, 918
Columbia encyclopedia., B. A. Chernow and G. A. Vallasi, eds., 152
Columbia gazetteer of the world, S. B. Cohen, ed., 1858
Columbia Granger's index to poetry in anthologies, E. P. Hazen, ed., 1704
Columbia Granger's index to poetry in collected and selected works, N. Frankovich, ed., 1705
Columbia Granger's world of poetry, 1706
Columbia Granger's world of quotations on CD-ROM, R. Andrews, M. Biggs, and M. Seider, eds., 1618
Columbia guide to online style, J. Walker and T. Tyler, 773
Columbia guide to standard American English, K. G. Wilson, 739
Columbia Lippincott gazetteer of the world, 1858n, 1868n
Columbia University College of Physicians and Surgeons complete guide to early child care, 1096
Columbia University College of Physicians and Surgeons complete home medical guide, D. Tapley et al., eds., 1061
Commager, H. S., and M. Cator, eds. Documents of American history, 1834
Commire, A. Something about the author: facts and pictures about contemporary authors and illustrators of books for young people, 1669
Commodity year book, 514
Communications standard dictionary, M. H. Weik, 943
Community publication rates and data, 480

Compact D/SEC, 461
Compact disclosure, 461
Companies and their brands, 458n
Companion encyclopedia of psychology, A. M. Coleman, ed., 291
Comparative guide to American colleges, J. Cass and M. Birnbaum, 678, 682n
Complement to Genealogies in the Library of Congress, M. J. Kaminkow, 1934
Complete and systematic concordance to Shakespeare, M. Spevack, 1737n
Complete beverage dictionary, R. A. Lipinski and K. A. Lipinski, 1124
Complete bird owner's handbook, G. Gallerstein, 1200
Complete book of herbs, spices, and condiments, C. A. Rinzler, 1132
Complete book of Jewish observance, L. Trepp, 231
Complete book of pet care, P. Roach, 1199
Complete book of sewing, 1467
Complete book of U.S. presidents, W. A. DeGregorio, 620
Complete book of Winter Olympics, D. Wallechinsky, 1576
Complete cat book, R. Gebhardt, 1203
Complete catalogue of plays, 1359
Complete dinosaur, J. O'Farlow and M. K. Brett-Surman, eds., 985
Complete directory of large print books and serials, 51
Complete directory to prime time network and cable TV shows, T. Brooks and E. Marsh, 1346
Complete dog book, AKC staff, 1209
Complete drug reference, U.S. Pharmacopeia, 1099
Complete encyclopedia of hockey, Z. Hollander, ed., 1571
Complete encyclopedia of needlework, T. de Dillmont, 1454
Complete encyclopedia of stitchery, 1455
Complete film dictionary, I. Konigsberg, 1325
Complete guide to furniture styles, L. A. Boger, 1291
Complete guide to sewing, 1467
Complete home decorating book, N. Barnard, 1175
Complete home renovation manual, 1167
Complete illustrated guide to everything sold in hardware stores, S. R. Ettlinger, 1190
Complete quilting course, G. Lawther, 1462
Complete rhyming dictionary and poet's craft book, C. Wood, 745
Complete secretary's handbook, L. Doris, B. M. Miller, and M. A. De Vries, eds. 539
Complete step-by-step guide to home sewing, J. Argent, 1468
Complete stitch encyclopedia, J. Eaton, 1456
Complete wilderness training book, H. McManners, 1597
Complete world bartender guide, B. Sennett, ed., 1125
Completely illustrated atlas of reptiles and amphibians for the terrarium, F. J. Obst, 1221
Composers since 1900, D. Ewen, ed., 1400
Comprehensive catalog of U.S. paper money, G. Hessler, 1484
Comprehensive country music encyclopedia, Editors of Country Music magazine, 1437
Comprehensive etymological dictionary of the English language, E. Klein, 731
Compton's encyclopedia, D. Good, ed., 153
Computer glossary, A. Freedman, 896
Comrie, B., ed. World's major languages, 711
Conception, pregnancy, and birth, M. Stoppard, 1117
Concise Cambridge Italian dictionary, B. Reynolds, ed., 799n
Concise chemical and technical dictionary, H. Bennett, ed., 880
Concise Columbia encyclopedia, P. G. Lagasse, ed., 154
Concise dictionary of American biography, 1919n
Concise dictionary of American history, 1793n
Concise dictionary of American literary biography, 1641n
Concise dictionary of British literary biography, 1641n
Concise dictionary of classical mythology, B. Blackwell, 265
Concise dictionary of national biography, 1920
Concise dictionary of physics, 1010
Concise dictionary of slang and unconventional English, E. Partridge. P. Beale, ed., 756n
Concise dictionary of world history, 1824n,
Concise edition of Baker's biographical dictionary of musicians, N. Slonimsky, 1398n
Concise encyclopedia biochemistry, T. Scott and M. Eagleson, eds., 975
Concise encyclopedia of foods and nutrition, A. H. Ensmonger et al., 1109
Concise encyclopedia of Islam, A. Glasse, 251
Concise encyclopedia of special education, 653n
Concise Oxford companion to the theatre, P. Hartnoll and P. Found, eds., 1374
Concise Oxford dictionary of ballet, H. Koegler, 1316
Concise Oxford dictionary of botany, M. Allaby, ed., 959n, 984
Concise Oxford dictionary of earth sciences, A. Allaby and M. Allaby, eds., 912, 959n
Concise Oxford dictionary of ecology, M. Allaby, ed., 959
Concise Oxford dictionary of English etymology, T. F. Hoad, ed., 734n
Concise Oxford dictionary of mathematics, C. Clapham, 1001

Concise Oxford dictionary of zoology, 959n
Concise Oxford dictionary of zoology, M. Allaby, ed., 989
Concise science dictionary, 820, 1010n
Condition of education, U.S. Dept. of Education, 700
Congress A to Z, 635n
Congress and the nation, 582
Congressional district atlas, Bureau of the Census, 632
Congressional districts in the 1990s, 633
Congressional Quarterly almanac, 617n, 634
Congressional Quarterly's desk reference on American government, B. Wetterau, 583
Congressional Quarterly's guide to Congress, 635, 636n
Congressional Quarterly's guide to the presidency, M. Nelson, ed., 621
Congressional Quarterly's guide to the U.S. Supreme Court, E. Witt, 625
Congressional Quarterly's guide to U.S. elections, 615
Congressional staff directory, 638n
Congressional yearbook, 634n
Congressional yellow book, 72
Connolly, M. J. *See* Nolan, J. R.
Connor, B. M., and H. G. Machedlover. Ottemiller's index to plays in collections, 1364
Conn's current therapy, R. J. Rakel, ed., 1062
Conroy, W. *See* Sheehy, N.
Considine, D. M., and G. D. Considine, eds. Encyclopedia of chemistry, 881; Van Nostrand's scientific encyclopedia, 828
Considine, G. D. *See* Considine, D. M.
Constitutions of the world, 594n
Construction glossary, J. S. Stein, 953
Consultants and consulting organizations directory, J. McLean, ed., 462
Consumer Guide editors. Basketball almanac, 1531
Consumer health information source book, A. M. Rees, 1029
Consumer health USA, A. M. Rees, ed., 1030
Consumer magazine and agri-media rates and data, 480
Consumer Reports Books editors. How to clean practically anything, 1173
Consumer Reports buying guide issue, 1152
Consumer Reports editors and M. Schultz. Fix it yourself for less, 1184
Consumer Reports editors and T. Philbin. Illustrated hardware book, 1192
Consumer sourcebook, A. H. Brennan, 1153
Consumer Union editors. Home improvement cost guide, 1168
Consumer's directory of continuing care retirement communities, 333
Consumer's good chemical guide, J. Emsley, 960
Consumers' guide to product grades and terms, S. B. Gall and T. L. Gall, eds., 1154
Contemporary architects, M. Emanuel, ed., 1271
Contemporary art and artists, P. J. Parry, comp., 1234
Contemporary artists, J. Cerrito, ed., 1266
Contemporary authors, 1635
Contemporary authors autobiography series, 1636
Contemporary Black American playwrights and their plays, B. L. Peterson Jr., 1646
Contemporary composers, B. Morton, ed., 1409
Contemporary designers, S. Pendergast, ed., 1292
Contemporary dramatists, K. A. Berney, ed., 1677
Contemporary fashion, R. Martin, ed., 1283
Contemporary foreign language writers, J. Vinson and D. Kirkpatrick, eds., 1637
Contemporary literary criticism, 1631
Contemporary literary critics, E. Borklund, 1638
Contemporary novel, I. Adelman and R. Dworkin, 1684
Contemporary novelists, S. W. Brown, ed., 1685
Contemporary photographers, M. M. Evans, ed., 1300
Contemporary poets, T. Riggs, ed., 1707
Contemporary popular writers, D. Mote, ed., 1639
Contemporary theatre, film, and television, 1312
Contraceptive technology, R. A. Hatcher et al., 1118
Converse, P. E., et al. American social attitudes data sourcebook, 323
Coogans, M. D. *See* Metzger, B. M.
Cook, D. E., and I. S. Monro, comps. Short story index, 1900–1949, 1702
Cooke, Jacob E., ed. Encyclopedia of the North American colonies, 1809
Cooper, John E. *See* Benyon, P. H.
Cooper, R., and Charles Morris. Mr. Boston, 1125
Cooper, W. W., and Y. Ijiri, eds. Kohler's dictionary for accountants, 500
Copyright primer for librarians and educators, J. H. Bruwelheide, 104
Corcoran, J., E. Farkas, and S. Sobel. Original martial arts encyclopedia, 1575
Cordasco, F., ed. Dictionary of American immigration history, 1794
Cordy, H. V. Multicultural dictionary of proverbs, 1629
Core list of books and journals in education, N. P. O'Brien and E. Fabiano, 641
Cornell book of cats, S. Mordecai, ed., 1204
Corporate finance sourcebook, National Register staff, 486
Correard, M., and V. Grundy, eds. Oxford-Hachette French dictionary, 789
Corrigan, M. *See* Winks, R. W.
Corsini, R. J., ed. Encyclopedia of psychology, 295

Cosgrove, H., ed. Encyclopedia of careers and vocational guidance, 552
Cosley, S. *See* Steinberg, M. L.
Costa, B., and M. Costa. Micro handbook for small libraries and media centers, 12
Costa, M. *See* Costa, B.
Costello, E., and L. Lenderman. Random House American sign language dictionary, 750
Coulmas, F. Blackwell encyclopedia of writing systems, 707
Countries of the world, 1874n
Country study series, Foreign Area Studies, American University, 1875
County and city data book, Bureau of the Census, 404, 410n
County and city extra, 405, 408n
County courthouse book, E. Bently, 1942
Couper, A., ed. Times atlas and encyclopedia of the sea, 926
Cowan, T., and J. Maguire. Timelines of African-American history, 372
Cowboy encyclopedia, R. W. Slatta, 1859
CQ weekly report, 617n, 634
Craft supply sourcebook, M. A. Boyd, 1450
Craig, E., ed. Routledge encyclopedia of philosophy, 166
Craighead's international business, travel, and relocation guide to eighty-one countries, 487
Crandall, R. Shaking your family tree, 1952
Crane, N. B. *See* Li, X.
CRC handbook of chemistry and physics, D. R. Lide, ed., 887, 1002n
CRC handbook of chemistry and physics, student ed., R. C. Weast, ed., 887n
CRC standard mathematical tables and formulae, D. Willinger, ed., 1002
Creating your own woodshop, C. Self, 1472
Cribb, J., et al. Coin atlas, 1481
Crim, K., et al., eds. Perennnial dictionary of world religions, 176
Crime fiction II, A. J. Hubin, 1688
Crime in the United States, 351n
Crisfield, D. Pick-up games, 1580
Cross index title guide to classical music, S. G. Pallay, comp., 1403
Cross index title guide to opera and operetta, S. G. Pallay, comp., 1403
Cross, M. Reader's Digest complete book of embroidery, 1458
Crossword puzzle dictionary, A. Swanfeldt, 727
Crowder, M. *See* Oliver, R.
Crystal, D. Cambridge encyclopedia of language, 708; Cambridge encyclopedia of the English language, 713
———, ed. Cambridge encyclopedia, 149; Cambridge paperback encyclopedia, 150
Cultural atlas of Africa, J. Murray, 1894
Cultural atlas of China, C. Blunden and M. Elvin, 1894
Cultural atlas of France, J. Ardagh and C. Jones, 1894
Cultural atlas of Japan, M. Collcutt et al., 1894
Cultural atlas of Russia and the Soviet Union, R. Milner-Gulland and N. Dejevsky, 1894
Cultural atlas of Spain and Portugal, M. Vincent, 1894
Cultural encyclopedia of baseball, J. F. Light, 1523
Cummings, M. *See* Lorimer, L. T.
Cummings, P. Dictionary of contemporary American artists, 1267
Cumulative book index, 62
Cumulative index to The biographical dictionary of American sports, D. L. Porter, ed., 1510
Cumulative personal author indexes to the monthly catalog of U.S. government publications, 1941–1975, E. Przebienda, ed., 138
Cumulative subject index guide to United States government bibliographies, 1924–1973, E. A. Kanely, comp., 138
Cumulative subject index to the monthly catalog of United States government publications 1900 to 1971, 138
Cunningham, M. Fannie Farmer cookbook, 1134
Cunningham, S. Wicca, 262
Cunningham, W. P., et al., eds. Environmental encyclopedia, 964
Current biography, 1918
Current index to journals in education, 647
Current medical diagnosis and treatment, 1063
Current obstetric and gynecological diagnosis and treatment, 1063
Current pediatric diagnosis and treatment, 1063
Current, R. N., and P. D. Escott, eds. Encyclopedia of the Confederacy, 1806
Current surgical diagnosis and treatment, 1063
Currie, P. J., and K. Padlan, eds. Encyclopedia of dinosaurs, 988
Cushman, C., ed. Supreme Court justices: illustrated biographies, 627n
Cushman, R. F., and S. P. Koniak. Leading constitutional decisions, 628
Cyclopedia of literary characters, F. N. Magill and A. J. Sobczak, eds., 1614
Cyclopedia of literary characters II, F. N. Magill, ed., 1615
Cyclopedia of world authors, F. N. Magill, ed., 1640

Daintith, J., ed. Facts on File dictionary of chemistry, 883
———, et al., eds. Biographical encyclopedia of scientists, 836; Facts on File dictionary of physics, 1013

Dakin, N. Macmillan book of the marine aquarium, 1217
Dalal-Clayton, D. B. Black's agricultural dictionary, 853
Dalby, A., ed. Guide to world language dictionaries, 781
Dalley, A. F. *See* Netter, F. H.
Dance classics, N. Reynolds and S. Reimer-Torn, 1317
Dance film and video guide, D. Towers, comp., 1318
Dance handbook, A. Robertson and D. Hutera, 1319
Daniel, C., et al., eds. Chronicle of the twentieth century, 1778
Daniells, L. M. Business information sources, 441
Darley, G. *See* Lewis, P.
Darnay, A. J., ed. Statistical record of older Americans, 338
Darnton, M. *See* Bishop, P. D.
Dartnell direct mail and mail order handbook, R. S. Hodgson, 488
Dartnell office administration handbook, R. S. Minor and C. W. Fetridge, eds., 526
Dartnell sales manager's handbook, 533
Darton, M., and J. Clark. Macmillan dictionary of measurement, 1006
Dasch, E. J., ed. Encyclopedia of earth sciences, 914
Data sources: the comprehensive guide to the information processing industry, 903
Datapro directory of micro-computer software, 904
Davenport, M. Book of costume, 1282
Davies, J. G., ed. New Westminster dictionary of liturgy and worship, 219
Davis, E., ed. Basic music library, 1379
Davis, J. Children's television, 1345
Davis, M. B., ed. Native America in the twentieth century, 389, 1819
Davis, N., comp. and ed. Afro-American reference, 359
Day, A., and J. M. Harvey, eds. Walford's guide to reference material, v.2, 23
Day, A. C. Roget's thesaurus of the Bible, 197
Day by day: the eighties, E. Meltzer and M. Aronson, 1779
Day by day: the fifties, J. Merritt, 1779
Day by day: the forties, T. M. Leonard, 1779
Day by day: the seventies, T. M. Leonard et al., 1779
Day by day: the sixties, D. Nelson and T. Parker, 1779
de Charms, D., and P. F. Breed, Songs in collections, 1432
de Dillmont, T. Complete encyclopedia of needlework, 1454
de Prisco, A. Mini-atlas of dog breeds, 1208
De Sola, R., D. Stahl, and K. Kerchelich. Abbreviations dictionary, 722
De Vries, M. A. *See* Doris, L.
DeConde, A., ed. Encyclopedia of American foreign policy, 563
DeCurtis, A., et al., eds. Rolling Stone album guide, 1416
Definitive country, B. McCloud, 1438
Definitive Kobbe's opera book, Earl of Harewood, ed., 1407n
DeFrancis, B. Parents' resource almanac, 1196
DeGregorio, W. A. Complete book of U.S. presidents, 620
Deisher, B., ed. Coin world almanac, 1482
Dejevsky, N. *See* Milner-Gulland, R.
Delaney, J. J. Dictionary of saints, 225
DeMiller, A. L. Linguistics, 705
Demographic yearbook, UN Statistical Office, 406
Denman-West, M. W. Children's literature: a guide to information sources, 1661
Deserts, T. Allan and A. Warren, eds., 961
Deutsch, B. Poetry handbook, 1714
Dewey, D., and N. Acocello. Encyclopedia of major league baseball teams, 1525
Dewey, P. R. 303 CD-ROMs to use in your library, 21
Diagnostic and statistical manual of mental disorders, 301
Diagram Group staff. Family fun and games, 1578; Human body on file, 1087; Musical instruments of the world, 1388; Rules of the game, 1499
Diamant, L., ed. Broadcast communications dictionary, 1344
Diamond, M. American vegetarian cookbook from the Fit for Life kitchen, 1140
Dickinson's American historical fiction, V. B. Gerhardstein, 1725
Dictionary of advertising terms, L. Urdang, ed., 531n
Dictionary of American biography, 1917n, 1919, 1924n
Dictionary of American children's fiction, A. K. Helbig and A. R. Perkins, 1664
Dictionary of American diplomatic history, J. E. Findling, 1792
Dictionary of American food and drink, J. F. Mariani, 1142
Dictionary of American history, L. B. Ketz, ed., 1793
Dictionary of American idioms, A. Makkai, ed., 740
Dictionary of American immigration history, F. Cordasco, ed., 1794
Dictionary of American Negro biography, R. W. Logan and M. R. Winston, eds., 363
Dictionary of American portraits, H. Cirker and B. Cirker, 1235
Dictionary of American proverbs, W. Mieder, ed., 1626
Dictionary of American religious biography, H. W. Bowden, 211

Dictionary of American slang, R. L. Chapman, ed., 754
Dictionary of American slang, 2d supplemented ed., H. Wentworth and S. B. Flexner, comps. and eds., 754n
Dictionary of antiques, G. Savage, 1293
Dictionary of architecture and construction, C. M. Harris, ed., 1272
Dictionary of art, J. Turner, ed., 1243
Dictionary of Asian American history, H. Kim, ed., 377
Dictionary of banking, J. M. Rosenberg, 501
Dictionary of battles, 1802n
Dictionary of behavioral science, B. B. Wolman, comp. and ed., 292
Dictionary of bias-free usage, R. Maggio, 741
Dictionary of Bible and religion, W. M. Genz, ed., 190
Dictionary of biology, E. Martin, M. Ruse, and E. Holmes, eds., 976
Dictionary of British and American women writers, J. Todd, ed., 1654
Dictionary of business and management, J. M. Rosenberg, 451
Dictionary of card games, D. Parlatt, 1547
Dictionary of ceramic science and engineering, I. J. McColm, 954
Dictionary of Christianity in America, D. G. Reid, 199
Dictionary of classical mythology, P. Grimal and A. R. Maxwell-Hyslop, trans., 265
Dictionary of classical mythology: symbols, attributes, and associations, R. E. Bell, 266
Dictionary of clichés, E. Partridge, 751n
Dictionary of contemporary American artists, P. Cummings, 1267
Dictionary of contemporary photography, L. Stroebel and H. N. Todd, 1301
Dictionary of costume, R. T. Wilcox, 1284
Dictionary of ecology and environmental science, H. W. Art et al., eds., 962
Dictionary of eponyms, C. L. Beeching, 1962
Dictionary of euphemisms, R. W. Holder, 755
Dictionary of fictional characters, W. Freeman, 1616
Dictionary of first names, P. Hanks and F. Hodges, 1963
Dictionary of foreign phrases and abbreviations, K. Guinagh, trans. and comp., 735
Dictionary of foreign terms, C. O. S. Mawson, 736n
Dictionary of global climate change, W. J. Maunder, comp., 919
Dictionary of heraldry, S. Friar, 1956n
Dictionary of heraldry and related subjects, 1956n
Dictionary of human geography, R. J. Johnston et al., eds., 1860
Dictionary of Irish literature, R. Hogan, ed., 1765
Dictionary of Italian literature, P. Bondanella and J. C. Bondanella, eds., 1768
Dictionary of Jewish lore and legend, A. Unterman, 232
Dictionary of literary biography, 1641, 1643n
Dictionary of literary biography documentary series, 1641n
Dictionary of literary biography yearbook, 1641n
Dictionary of manufacturing terms, R. F. Veilleux, ed., 998
Dictionary of materials and manufacturing, V. John, ed., 999
Dictionary of Mexican American history, M. S. Meier and F. Rivera, 379
Dictionary of military terms, U.S. Department of Defense, comp., 1025
Dictionary of modern medicine, J. C. Segen, comp. and ed., 1036
Dictionary of modern war, E. Luttwak and S. Koehl, 562
Dictionary of national biography, 1919
Dictionary of occupational titles, U.S. Dept. of Labor, 551
Dictionary of ornament, P. Lewis and G. Darley, 1244
Dictionary of pentecostal and charismatic movements, S. M. Burgess et al., eds., 214
Dictionary of philosophy and psychology, J. M. Baldwin, ed., 293
Dictionary of saints, J. J. Delaney, 225
Dictionary of science, P. Lafferty and J. Rowe, eds., 821
Dictionary of scientific biography, 837n
Dictionary of scientific units, H. G. Jerrard and D. B. McNeill, 822
Dictionary of slang and unconventional English, E. Partridge, 756
Dictionary of superstitions, I. Opie and M. Tatem, 268
Dictionary of superstitions, S. Lasne and A. P. Gaultier, 267
Dictionary of surnames, P. Hanks and F. Hodges, 1964
Dictionary of the American West, W. Blevins, 1795
Dictionary of the history of ideas, P. P. Wiener, ed., 161
Dictionary of the history of science, W. F. Bynum et al., eds., 844
Dictionary of the liturgy, J. P. Lang, 215
Dictionary of the Middle Ages, J. R. Strayer, ed., 1796, 1808n
Dictionary of the natural environment, 1863n
Dictionary of the social sciences, J. Gould and W. L. Kolb, eds., 319
Dictionary of twentieth-century design, J. Pile, 1294

Dietrich, M., et al. Quilter's companion, 1462
Dietz, M. J., ed. 10,000 garden questions answered by twenty experts, 867
Digest of education statistics, U.S. Dept. of Education, 701
Dimmitt, R. B. Actor's guide to the talkies, 1949 through 1964, 1334; Title guide to the talkies, 1927 through 1963, 1334
Dinosaur Society's dinosaur encyclopedia, D. Lessem et al., eds., 987
Dinosaurs: the encyclopedia, D. F. Glut, 986
Direct mail list rates and data, 480
Directories in print, 69
Directory for exceptional children, 658
Directory of African American religious bodies, W. J. Payne, ed., 205
Directory of American scholars, 703
Directory of business and financial information services, 463
Directory of business periodical special issues, T. Wyckoff, ed., 442
Directory of corporate affiliations, 464
Directory of executive recruiters, 465
Directory of financial aids for minorities, G. A. Schlachter, 659
Directory of financial aids for women, G. A. Schlachter, 659
Directory of foreign manufacturers in the United States, J. S. Arpan and D. Ricks, eds., 466
Directory of historical agencies in the United States and Canada, 1944n
Directory of historical organizations in the United States and Canada, 1825
Directory of historical societies and agencies in the United States and Canada, 1825
Directory of nursing homes, 1053
Directory of physicians in the United States, 1054
Directory of religious organizations in the United States, 206
Directory of U.S. military bases worldwide, W. R. Evinger, ed., 597, 1026
Directory: juvenile and adult correctional departments, institutions, agencies and paroling authorities, American Correctional Assn., 348
Divining the future, E. Shaw, 311
Doane, G. H., and J. B. Bell. Searching for your ancestors, 1951
Doctor's book of home remedies, D. Tkac, 1083
Doctor's book of home remedies II, S. Kricheimer, 1083
Doctor's book of home remedies for children, Prevention Magazine editors, 1097
Documents of American history, H. S. Commager and M. Cator, eds., 1834
Dodge, R. W., D. A. Gaquin, and M. S. Littman. Places, towns, and townships, 408
Dog owner's home veterinary handbook, D. G. Carlson and J. M. Giffin, 1210
Dogra, R. C., and G. S. Mansukhani. Encyclopedia of the Sikh religion and culture, 252
Dogs, D. Alderton, 1211
Dollinger, M., et al. Everyone's guide to cancer therapy, 1095
Donin, H. H. To pray as a Jew, 247
Dorgan, C. A., ed. Statistical record of health and medicine, 1075
Doris, L., B. M. Miller, and M. A. De Vries, eds. Complete secretary's handbook, 539
Dorland's illustrated medical dictionary, 1037
Dorland's pocket medical dictionary, 1037
Dorling Kindersley encyclopedia of fishing, 1553
Douchant, M. Encyclopedia of college basketball, 1534
Dow Jones commodities handbook, 492n
Dow Jones investor's handbook, 492n, 515n
Dow Jones-Irwin business almanac, 492n
Dr. Axelrod's atlas of freshwater aquarium fishes, H. R. Axelrod, 1212
Dr. Axelrod's mini-atlas of freshwater aquarium fishes, H. R. Axelrod et al., 1213
Dr. Burgess's atlas of marine aquarium fishes, W. Burgess et al., 1214
Dr. Burgess's mini-atlas of marine aquarium fishes, W. Burgess and H. R. Axelrod, 1215
Dramatic criticism index, P. F. Breed and F. M. Sniderman, comps. and eds., 1678
Dresser, P. Nuclear power plants worldwide, 930
DSM-IV casebook, R. L. Spiter et al., 301
Duckles, V. H., and I. Reed, eds. Music reference and research materials, 1381
Dun & Bradstreet reference book of corporate managements, 476n
Dun & Bradstreet's guide to your investments, 515
Dunbar, G. S. Modern geography, 1864
Dunkling, L., and W. Gosling. Facts on File dictionary of first names, 1966
Dunnan, N. *See* Tuckerman, N.
Dupuy, R. E., and T. N. Dupuy. Harper encyclopedia of military history from 3500 B.C. to the present, 1815
Dupuy, T. N., et al., eds. International military and defense encyclopedia, 1027; *see also* Dupuy, R. E.
Dworkin, R. *See* Adelman, I.
Dynes, W. R., ed. Encyclopedia of homosexuality, 331

Eagleson, M. *See* Scott, T.
Eakle, A., and J. Cerny, eds. Source, 1953
Earl of Harewood, ed. Definitive Kobbe's opera book, 1407n
Earth sciences reference, M. McNeil, 913

Eastman, M. H. Index to fairy tales, myths and legends, 1665
Eaton, J. Complete stitch encyclopedia, 1456
Eatwell, J., et al., eds. New Palgrave, 455
Ebert, R. Roger Ebert's video companion, 1337
Eddleman, F. E., comp. American drama criticism, 1718
Editor and publisher international year book, 91
Editor and publisher market guide, 528
Editorials on file, 117
Editors of Country Music magazine. Comprehensive country music encyclopedia, 1437
Editors of Vegetarian Times and L. Moll. Vegetarian Times complete cookbook, 1140
Edney, A. ASPCA complete cat care manual, 1201
Education, L. J. Buttlar, 642
Education index, 648
Educational media and technology yearbook, 644
Educators grade guide to free teaching aids, 645
Educators guide to free films, filmstrips and slides, 645
Educators guide to free guidance materials, 645
Educators guide to free health, physical education, and recreation materials, 645
Educators guide to free home economics and consumer education materials, 645
Educators guide to free science materials, 645
Educators guide to free social studies materials, 645
Educators index of free materials, 645
Edwards, E. H. Horses, 1220
———, and B. Langris. Encyclopedia of the horse, 1218
Edwards, J., and M. Lufty, eds. Automotive dictionary, 1016
Edwards, P., ed. Encyclopedia of philosophy, 163, 166n
Edwards, R. L., ed. Encyclopedia of social work, 395
Eerdmans' handbook to the world's religions, 172
Eggenberger, D. Encyclopedia of battles, 1802
Ehrlich, E., and R. Hand Jr. NBC handbook of pronunciation, 743
———. *See also* Mawson, C. O. S.
Ehrlich, J., and M. Mannheimer. Carpenter's manifesto, 1181
Eicholz, A., ed. Ancestry's red book, 1946
Eighty years of best sellers, A. P. Hackett and J. H. Burke, 1681
Elder, J., ed. American nature writers, 1719
Electronic styles, X. Li and N. B. Crane, 774
Electronic university, 679
Electronics dictionary for technicians, T. Adamson, 944
Elementary school library collection, L. L. Homa, ed., 41
Elementary teachers guide to free curriculum materials, 645
Eliade, M., ed. Encyclopedia of religion, 173
Elliott, C. A., comp. Biographical index to American science, 837
Ellis, J., and J. Henderson. Running injury-free, 1588
Ellis, J. C. Index to illustrations, 1237
Ellmore, R. T. NTC's mass media dictionary, 1351
Elvin, M. *See* Blunden, C.
Emanoil, M., ed. Encyclopedia of endangered species, 990
Emanuel, M., ed. Contemporary architects, 1271
Ember, M. *See* Levinson, D.
Embree, A., ed. Encyclopedia of Asian history, 1801
Emerton, B. *See* Sparks, L.
Emily Post's etiquette, E. L. Post, 1157
Emsley, J. Consumer's good chemical guide, 960
Encyclopaedia of religion and ethics, J. Hastings et al., 281
Encyclopaedia of the musical film, S. Green, 1326
Encyclopaedia of the social sciences, E. R. A. Seligman and A. Johnson, eds., 320
Encyclopedia Americana, L. T. Lorimer and M. Cummings, eds., 155
Encyclopedia Judaica, 233
Encyclopedia of aesthetics, M. Kelly, 1245
Encyclopedia of Africa south of the Sahara, J. Middleton, ed., 1797
Encyclopedia of African American religions, L. G. Murphy, ed., 200
Encyclopedia of African-American culture and history, J. Salzman, D. L. Smith, and C. West, eds., 364, 1798
Encyclopedia of aging, G. L. Maddox, ed., 334
Encyclopedia of agricultural science, C. J. Arntzen and E. M. Ritter, eds., 854
Encyclopedia of alcoholism, G. Evans et al., 339
Encyclopedia of American architecture, R. T. Packard and B. Korab, 1273
Encyclopedia of American comics, R. Goulart, ed., 1246
Encyclopedia of American economic history, G. Porter, ed., 1799
Encyclopedia of American education, H. G. Unger, 651
Encyclopedia of American facts and dates, G. Carruth, ed., 1826
Encyclopedia of American foreign policy, A. DeConde, ed., 563
Encyclopedia of American history, R. B. Morris and J. B. Morris, eds., 1800
Encyclopedia of American political history, J. P. Greene, ed., 564
Encyclopedia of American religions, J. G. Melton, 201
Encyclopedia of anthropology, D. E. Hunter and P. Whitten, eds., 432

Encyclopedia of applied ethics, R. Chadwick, ed., 282
Encyclopedia of Arabic literature, J. S. Meisami and P. Starkey, eds., 1730
Encyclopedia of architecture, J. A. Wilkes, ed., 1274
Encyclopedia of arms control and disarmament, R. D. Burns, ed., 565
Encyclopedia of Asian history, A. Embree, ed., 1801
Encyclopedia of associations, S. Jaszcak, ed., 73
Encyclopedia of astronomy and astrophysics, R. A. Meyers, ed., 872
Encyclopedia of battles, D. Eggenberger, 1802
Encyclopedia of beer, C. P. Rhodes, ed., 1126
Encyclopedia of bioethics, W. T. Reich, ed., 283
Encyclopedia of Black America, W. A. Low and V. A. Clift, eds., 365
Encyclopedia of blindness and vision impairment, J. Sardegna and T. O. Paul, 1113
Encyclopedia of business information sources, J. Woy, ed., 443
Encyclopedia of careers and vocational guidance, H. Cosgrove, ed., 552
Encyclopedia of chemistry, D. M. Considine and G. D. Considine, eds., 881
Encyclopedia of child abuse, R. E. Clark and J. Clark, 345
Encyclopedia of civil rights in America, D. Bradley and S. F. Fishkin, 566
Encyclopedia of classical philosophy, D. J. Zeyl, ed., 162
Encyclopedia of climate and weather, S. H. Schneider, 920
Encyclopedia of college basketball, M. Douchant, 1534
Encyclopedia of computer science, A. Ralston et al., eds., 897
Encyclopedia of crime and justice, S. H. Kadish, ed., 349
Encyclopedia of cultural anthropology, D. Levinson and M. Ember, eds., 433
Encyclopedia of deafness and hearing disorders, C. Turkington and A. E. Sussman, 1114
Encyclopedia of democracy, S. M. Lipset, ed., 567
Encyclopedia of dinosaurs, P. J. Currie and K. Padlan, eds., 988
Encyclopedia of drug abuse, G. Evans et al., 340
Encyclopedia of drugs and alcohol, J. H. Jaffe, ed., 341, 1100
Encyclopedia of early Christianity, E. Ferguson, ed., 216
Encyclopedia of earth sciences, E. J. Dasch, ed., 914
Encyclopedia of educational research, M. C. Alkin, ed., 652
Encyclopedia of electronics, S. Gibilisco and N. Sclater, eds., 945
Encyclopedia of endangered species, M. Emanoil, ed., 990
Encyclopedia of environmental information services, S. Balachandran, ed., 963
Encyclopedia of ethics, L. C. Becker, ed., 284
Encyclopedia of fairies, K. M. Briggs, 269
Encyclopedia of fantasy, J. Clute and J. Grant, eds., 1693
Encyclopedia of feminism, L. Tuttle, 419
Encyclopedia of feminist literary theory, E. Kowaleski-Wallace, 1655
Encyclopedia of folk, country, and western music, I. Stambler and G. Landon, 1439
Encyclopedia of golf techniques, P. Foston, ed., 1564
Encyclopedia of health information sources, A. M. Rees, ed., 1031
Encyclopedia of herbs, spices, and flavorings, E. L. Ortiz, 1133
Encyclopedia of homosexuality, W. R. Dynes, ed., 331
Encyclopedia of human behavior, V. S. Ramachandran, ed., 294
Encyclopedia of human rights, E. Lawson, 568
Encyclopedia of jazz, L. Feather, 1442n
Encyclopedia of jazz in the seventies, L. Feather and I. Gitler, 1442n
Encyclopedia of jazz in the sixties, L. Feather, 1442n
Encyclopedia of Jewish history, J. Alpher, ed., 1803
Encyclopedia of language and linguistics, R. E. Asher and J. M. Y. Simpson, eds., 709
Encyclopedia of Latin American history and culture, B. A. Tenenbaum, 1804
Encyclopedia of Latin American literature, V. Smith, ed., 1754
Encyclopedia of literary epics, G. M. Jackson, 1604
Encyclopedia of major league baseball team histories: American League, P. C. Bjarkman, ed., 1524
Encyclopedia of major league baseball team histories: National League, P. C. Bjarkman, ed., 1524
Encyclopedia of major league baseball teams, D. Dewey and N. Acocello, 1525
Encyclopedia of mathematics, 1003n
Encyclopedia of medical devices and instrumentation, J. J. Webster, ed. in chief, 1038
Encyclopedia of microbiology, J. Lederberg, ed., 977
Encyclopedia of modern physics, R. A. Meyers and S. N. Shore, eds., 1011
Encyclopedia of Mormonism, D. H. Ludlow, ed., 217
Encyclopedia of Native American religions, A. Hirschfleder, 202
Encyclopedia of natural medicine, M. Murray and J. Pizzorno, 1084
Encyclopedia of North American sports history, R. Hickok, 1495
Encyclopedia of occultism and parapsychology, L. Shepherd, ed., 312

Encyclopedia of perennials, C. Woods, 860
Encyclopedia of philosophy, P. Edwards, ed., 163, 166n
Encyclopedia of physics, R. G. Lerner and G. L. Trigg, eds., 1012
Encyclopedia of pieced quilt patterns, B. Brackman, comp., 1463
Encyclopedia of popular music, C. Larkin, ed., 1417
Encyclopedia of pottery and porcelain, E. Cameron, 1280
Encyclopedia of practical photography, 1302
Encyclopedia of pro basketball team histories, P. C. Bjarkman, 1535
Encyclopedia of psychology, R. J. Corsini, ed., 295
Encyclopedia of religion, M. Eliade, ed., 173
Encyclopedia of rhetoric and composition, T. Enos, 1715
Encyclopedia of science fiction, J. Clute and P. Nicholls, 1694
Encyclopedia of snakes, C. Mattison, 991
Encyclopedia of social work, R. L. Edwards, ed., 395
Encyclopedia of sociology, E. F. Borgatta, ed., 332
Encyclopedia of southern culture, C. R. Wilson and W. Ferris, eds., 1861
Encyclopedia of special education, C. R. Reynolds and L. Mann, eds., 653
Encyclopedia of sports science, J. Zumerchick, ed., 1501
Encyclopedia of tarot, S R. Kaplan, 313
Encyclopedia of television, H. Necomb, ed., 1347
Encyclopedia of television: series, pilots and specials, V. Terrace, 1348
Encyclopedia of textiles, J. Jerde, 1000
Encyclopedia of the American constitution, L. W. Levy et al., eds., 569
Encyclopedia of the American constitution supplement, L. W. Levy et al., eds., 569
Encyclopedia of the American legislative system, J. H. Silbey, ed., 570
Encyclopedia of the American military, J. Jessup and L. Ketz, eds., 571
Encyclopedia of the American presidency, L. Levy and L. Fisher, eds., 622
Encyclopedia of the American religious experience, C. H. Lippy and P. W. Williams, eds., 203
Encyclopedia of the American West, C. Phillips and A. Axelrod, eds., 1805
Encyclopedia of the blues, G. Herzhaft, 1435
Encyclopedia of the cat, B. Fogle, 1205
Encyclopedia of the Confederacy, R. N. Current and P. D. Escott, eds., 1806
Encyclopedia of the Democratic Party, G. Kurian and J. D. Schultz, eds., 616
Encyclopedia of the essay, T. Chevalier, ed., 1716
Encyclopedia of the gods, M. Jordan, 270
Encyclopedia of the holocaust, I. Gutman, ed., 1807
Encyclopedia of the horse, E. H. Edwards and B. Langris, 1218
Encyclopedia of the Jewish religion, R. J. Z. Werblowsky and G. Wigoder, eds., 234
Encyclopedia of the Middle Ages, M. Bunson, 1808
Encyclopedia of the musical theatre, K. Ganzl, 1371
Encyclopedia of the North American colonies, J. E. Cooke, ed., 1809
Encyclopedia of the peoples of the world, A. Gonen, ed., 434
Encyclopedia of the Republican Party, G. Kurian and J. D. Schultz, eds., 616
Encyclopedia of the Roman Empire, M. Bunson, 1810
Encyclopedia of the Sikh religion and culture, R. C. Dogra and G. S. Mansukhani, 252
Encyclopedia of the solar system, P. Weissman, L. McFadden, and T. Johnson, eds., 873
Encyclopedia of the solid earth sciences, P. Keareyed, 915
Encyclopedia of the Third Reich, C. Zentner and F. Bedurftig, eds., 1811
Encyclopedia of the Third World, G. T. Kurian, 1862
Encyclopedia of the unexplained, R. Cavendish, ed., 314
Encyclopedia of the United Nations and international agreements, E. J. Osmanczyk, 572
Encyclopedia of the United States Congress, D. C. Bacon et al., 636
Encyclopedia of traditional epics, G. M. Jackson-Laufer, 1605
Encyclopedia of unbelief, G. Stein, ed., 164
Encyclopedia of urban planning, A. Whittick, ed., 417
Encyclopedia of utopian literature, M. E. Snodgrass, 1606
Encyclopedia of values and ethics, J. P. Hester, 285
Encyclopedia of visual art, L. Gowing, ed., 1247
Encyclopedia of western gunfighters, B. O'Neal, 1849, 1859n
Encyclopedia of witchcraft and demonology, R. H. Robbins, 271
Encyclopedia of witches and witchcraft, R. E. Guiley, 272
Encyclopedia of wood joints, W. Graubner, 1473
Encyclopedia of woodworking techniques, J. Broun, 1474
Encyclopedia of world art, 1248
Encyclopedia of world biography, 1921
Encyclopedia of world costume, D. Yarwood, 1285
Encyclopedia of world cultures, D. Levinson, ed., 435
Encyclopedia of world faiths, P. D. Bishop and M. Darnton, eds., 174.
Encyclopedia of world history, W. L. Langer, ed., 1812

Encyclopedia of world literature in the twentieth century, L. S. Klein, ed., 1607
Encyclopedia of world sport, D. Levinson and K. Christenson, eds., 1496
Encyclopedias, atlases, and dictionaries, M. Sader and A. Lewis, eds., 4
Encyclopedic dictionary of mathematics, Mathematical Society of Japan staff and K. Ito, eds., 1003
Encyclopedic dictionary of psychology, T. Pettijohn, ed., 296
Encyclopedic handbook of cults in America, J. G. Melton, 204
Endangered wildlife of the world, 992
Energy and American society, E. Willard Miller and R. M. Miller, 928
Energy supply A-Z, A. Godman, 929
English novel 1578–1956, I. F. Bell and D. Baird, 1733
English novel explication: criticisms to 1972, H. H. Palmer and A. J. Dyson, comps., 1732
English novel explication: supplement I, P. L. Abernethey et al., comps., 1732
English novel explication: supplement II, C. J. W. Kloesel and J. R. Smitten, comps., 1732
English novel explication: supplement III, C. J. W. Kloesel, comp., 1732
English novel explication: supplement IV, C. J. W. Kloesel, comp., 1732
English novel explication: supplement V, C. J. W. Kloesel, comp., 1732
English novel explication: supplement VI, C. J. W. Kloesel, comp., 1732
English-Russian, Russian-English dictionary, K. Katzner, 806
Enos, T. Encyclopedia of rhetoric and composition, 1715
Ensmonger, A. H., et al. Concise encyclopedia of foods and nutrition, 1109
Entertainment awards, D. Franks, 1313
Environmental encyclopedia, W. P. Cunningham et al., eds., 964
Environmentalists, A. Axelrod and C. Phillips, 965
Environmentalist's bookshelf, R. Merideth, 966
Eponyms dictionaries index, 1965
Epps, R. P., and S. C. Stewart, eds. Women's complete healthbook, 1122
Equipment directory of video, computer, and audio-visual products, 660
Erickson, H. Television cartoon shows, 1353
Erlewine, M., ed. All music guide, 1414n; All music guide to rock, 1414
Ernst, C. H. Venomous reptiles of North America, 996
Escott, P. D. *See* Current, R. N.
Espenshade, E. B., ed. Rand McNally Goode's world atlas, 1889
ESPN Information Please sports almanac, J. Hassan, 1504
Esposito, J. L., ed. Oxford encyclopedia of the modern Islamic world, 1865
Espy, W. R. Words to rhyme with, 747
Essay and general literature index, 114
Essential guide to psychiatric drugs, J. M. Gorman, 1101
Essential Kabbalah, D. C. Matt, 235
Essential runner, J. Hanc, 1586
Essential Shakespeare, L. S. Champion, 1735
Estell, K., ed. African-American almanac, 357
Esteva-Fabregat, C. *See* Kanellos, N.
Ettlinger, S. Kitchenware book, 1138
Ettlinger, S. R. Complete illustrated guide to everything sold in hardware stores, 1190
Europa world yearbook, 1876
Europa yearbook, 1876
European drama criticism, H. H. Palmer, comp., 1679
European writers, W. T. H. Jackson and G. Stade, eds., 1642
European writers: selected authors, 1642n
Evans, G., Encyclopedia of drug abuse, 340
———, et al. Encyclopedia of alcoholism, 339
Evans, G. R. *See* Chadwick, H.
Evans, M. M., ed. Contemporary photographers, 1300
Evans, W. J. *See* Robert, H. M., III
Evenings with the orchestra, D. K. Holoman, 1408
Everyman's United Nations, 584n
Everyone's guide to cancer therapy, M. Dollinger et al., 1095
Everyone's guide to outpatient surgery, J. Macho and G. Cable, 1064
Everyone's United Nations, 584
Everything you need to know about diseases, M. Cahill, ed., 1065
Everything you need to know about medical tests, SPC staff, 1065
Everything you need to know about medical treatment, M. Cahill, ed., 1065
Evinger, W. R., ed. Directory of U.S. military bases worldwide, 597, 1026
Ewen, D. American songwriters, 1420; Composers since 1900, 1400; Great composers, 1300–1900, 1401
———, comp. and ed. Musicians since 1900, 1410
———, ed. American popular songs from the Revolutionary War to the present, 1421
Executive Office of the President. Catalog of federal domestic assistance, 394
Exotic pets, A. Rosenfeld, 1223
Exotic pets, S. Messonnier, 1224

Exotica series 4 international, A. B. Graf, 861
Explorers and discoverers of the world, D. B. Baker, 1850
Exploring chemical elements and their compounds, D. L. Heiserman, 882
Exporters' encyclopaedia, 467

Fabiano, E. *See* O'Brien, N. P.
Facts about the presidents, J. N. Kane, 620n, 623
Facts on file, 105
Facts on File dictionary of astronomy, V. Illingworth, ed., 874
Facts on File dictionary of biology, E. Tootill, ed., 978
Facts on File dictionary of biotechnology and genetic engineering, M. L. Steinberg and S. Cosley, eds., 979
Facts on File dictionary of chemistry, J. Daintith, ed., 883
Facts on File dictionary of education, J. M. Shafritz et al., 654
Facts on File dictionary of environmental science, L. H. Stevenson and B. Wyman, 967
Facts on File dictionary of first names, L. Dunkling and W. Gosling, 1966
Facts on File dictionary of marine science, B. Charton, ed., 925
Facts on File dictionary of mathematics, C. Gibson, ed., 1004
Facts on File dictionary of physics, J. Daintith et al., eds., 1013
Facts on File dictionary of television, cable, and video, R. M. Reed and M. K. Reed, 1349
Facts on File encyclopedia of word and phrase origins, R. Hendrickson, 732
Facts on File encyclopedia of world mythology and legend, A. S. Mercatante, 273
Fairbanks, J. L., and E. B. Bates. American furniture, 1288
Fairchild's dictionary of fashion, C. M. Calasibetta, ed., 1469
Fairchild's dictionary of textiles, P. G. Tortora and R. S. Merkel, eds., 1470
Familiar quotations, J. Kaplan, ed., 1619
Family fun and games, Diagram Group, 1578
Family handyman easy repair, Reader's Digest editors, 1182
Famous first facts, J. N. Kane, ed., 106
Fannie Farmer cookbook, M. Cunningham, 1134
Farkas, E. *See* Corcoran, J.
Farm chemicals handbook, 855
Farmer, D. H., ed. Oxford dictionary of saints, 228
Farnham, M. M. Sailing for beginners, 1589
Fast, C. C. *See* Fast, T. H.
Fast, T. H., and C. C. Fast. Women's atlas of the United States, 424
Fauci, A. S., et al. Harrison's principles of internal medicine, 1035
Favorite hobbies and pastimes, R. S. Munson, 1451
Feather, L. Encyclopedia of jazz, 1442n; Encyclopedia of jazz in the sixties, 1442n
———, and I. Gitler. Encyclopedia of jazz in the seventies, 1442n
Federal register, Office of the Federal Register, National Archives and Records Administration, 607n
Federal regulatory directory, 598
Federal yellow book, 74
Federation Internationale de Football Association staff. Official rules of soccer, 1590
Feminist companion to literature in English, V. Blain et al., 1656
Feminist writers, P. Kester-Shelton, 1657
Fenton, A. D. *See* Peterson, C. S.
Ferguson, E., ed. Encyclopedia of early Christianity, 216
Ferguson, G. L., ed. Song finder, 1429
Ferguson, J. *See* Friar, S.
Ferris, W. *See* Wilson, C. R.
Fetridge, C. W. *See* Minor, R. S.
Fetzer, M. *See* Morehead, J.
Fiction catalog, 1682
Field guide to American antique furniture, J. T. Butler, 1295
Fifty southern writers after 1900, J. M. Flora and R. Bain, eds., 1726
Fifty southern writers before 1900, R. Bain and J. M. Flora, eds., 1726
Filby, P. W. Bibliography of American county histories, 1931, 1940n
———, ed. Passenger and immigration lists index, 1938
Film and video finder, National Information Center for Educational Media, 643
Film encyclopedia, E. Katz, ed., 1327
Film review index, P. K. Hanson and S. L. Hanson, 1323
Financial aid for the disabled and their families, G. A. Schlachter and R. D. Weber, 659
Financial aids for higher education, J. K. Santamaria, ed., 661
Find that tune, W. Gargan and S. Sharma, eds., 1423
Finders, C. *See* Robertson, L.
Findling, J. E. Dictionary of American diplomatic history, 1792
Fink, G. M., ed. Labor unions, 453
———, et al. Biographical dictionary of American labor, 453n
———, et al., eds. Biographical dictionary of American labor, 547

Finkelman, P., and J. C. Miller. Macmillan encyclopedia of world slavery, 1816
Finniston, M., ed. Oxford illustrated encyclopedia of invention and technology, 849
Firestone, M., and A. Scherer. Bead directory, 1453
Firkins, I. T., comp. Index to plays, 1362
Fise, M. *See* Gillis, J.
Fisher, L. *See* Levy, L.
Fishkin, S. F. *See* Bradley, D.
Fiske, E. B., et al. Fiske guide to colleges, 680
Fiske guide to colleges, E. B. Fiske et al., 680
Fitzroy Dearborn encyclopedia of banking and finance, C. J. Woelfel, ed., 502
Five centuries of American costume, R. T. Wilcox, 1286
Five kingdoms, A. Margulis and K. V. Schwartz, 980
Fix it fast, fix it right, G. Hamilton and K. Hamilton, 1183
Fix it yourself for less, Consumer Reports editors and M. Schultz, 1184
Flags of the world, E. M. Barraclough, ed., 1958
Fleming, J., and H. Honour. Penguin dictionary of decorative arts, 1299
Fletcher, B. F., and J. Musgrove. History of architecture, 1275
Flexner, S. B. *See* Stein, J.; *see also* Wentworth, H.
Flight and flying, D. Baker, 937
Flora, J. M., and R. Bain, eds. Fifty southern writers after 1900, 1726
———. *See also* Bain, R.
Focal encyclopedia of photography, L. Stroebel and R. Zakia, eds., 1303
Fogle, B. ASPCA complete dog care manual, 1207; Encyclopedia of the cat, 1205
Folcarelli, R. J. *See* Gillespie, J. T.
Folger book of Shakespeare quotations, B. Stevenson, 1736
Folk music sourcebook, L. Sandberg and D. Weissman, 1440
Folk song index, F. E. Brunnings, 1424
Folklore, T. A. Green, ed., 274
Folklore and folklife, S. Steinfirst, 275
Folklore of American holidays, H. Cohen and T. P. Coffin, eds., 1146
Folklore of world holidays, R. Griffin and A. H. Shurgin, eds., 1147
Folsom, F., and M. E. Folsom. America's ancient treasures, 439
Folsom, M. E. *See* Folsom, F.
Fons, M., and L. Porter. Quilter's complete guide, 1462
Food professional's guide, I. Chalmers, 1135
Football encyclopedia, D. S. Neft et al., 1556
Foreign Area Studies, American University. Country study series, 1875
Forthcoming books, 52
Fortune double 500 directory, 468
Fortune's directory of the 500 largest U.S. industrial corporations, 468
Foster, F. S. *See* Andrews, W. L.
Foudray, R. S. *See* Brown, M.
Foulkes, C., ed. Larousse encyclopedia of wine, 1128, 1130n
Found, P. *See* Hartnoll, P.
Foundation Center. Foundation directory, 75, 396
Foundation directory, Foundation Center, 75, 396
Foundation for Public Affairs. Public interest profiles, 590
Fox, J., and R. Hildebrand. Ortho's basic home building, 1165
Fox, K. *See* Grant, E.
Franchise annual, 469
Franchise opportunities handbook, Industrial Trade Administration and Minority Business Development Agency of U.S. Dept. of Commerce, 470
Frankel, L. *See* Bart, P.
Frankovich, N., ed. Columbia Granger's index to poetry in collected and selected works, 1705
Franks, D. Entertainment awards, 1313
Fraternal organizations, A. J. Schmidt, 324
Free magazines for libraries, D. J. Langston and A. M. Smith, 122
Freedman, A. Computer glossary, 896
Freedman, D. N. Anchor Bible dictionary, 189
Freeman, G. *See* Glassborow, J.
Freeman, K. A. Chilton's easy car care, 1019
———, et al., eds. Chilton's auto repair manual, 1018
Freeman, W. Dictionary of fictional characters, 1616
Freidel, F., and R. K. Showman. Harvard guide to American history, 1774
French, S. Basic catalogue of plays and musicals, 1359
Friar, S. Dictionary of heraldry, 1956n
———, and J. Ferguson. Basic heraldry, 1956
Friedman, L., and F. L. Israel, eds. Justices of the United States Supreme Court, 627
Friendly guide to the universe, N. Hathaway, 875
From radical left to extreme right, G. Skidmore and T. J. Spahn, 64
Frumkin, N. Guide to economic indicators, 489
Fuld, J. J. Book of world-famous music, 1384
Fulton, L., and E. Furber, eds. International directory of little magazines and small presses, 96
Fundamental reference sources, F. N. Cheney and W. J. Williams, 5
Furber, E. *See* Fulton, L.
Fyffe, A., and I. Peter. Handbook of climbing, 1582

Gale directory of databases, K. Nolan, ed., 905
Gale directory of publications and broadcast media, 95
Gale encyclopedia of medicine, 1039
Gale encyclopedia of multicultural America, J. Galens et al., 353
Gale encyclopedia of Native American tribes, S. Malinowski and A. Sheets, eds., 388, 1814n
Gale guide to Internet databases, J. Zakalik and S. Burak, eds., 909
Galens, J., et al. Gale encyclopedia of multicultural America, 353
Gall, S., and I. Natividad, eds. Asian American almanac, 374
Gall, S. B., and T. L. Gall, eds. Consumers' guide to product grades and terms, 1154
———. *See also* Zia, H.
Gall, T. L. *See* Gall, S. B.
Gallaudet encyclopedia of deaf people and deafness, J. V. Van Cleve, ed., 1115
Gallerstein, G. Complete bird owner's handbook, 1200
Gallup, G. H. Gallup poll, 325
Gallup poll, G. H. Gallup, 325
Gammond, P. Oxford companion to popular music, 1418
Ganly, J. V., and D. M. Sciattara, eds. Serials for libraries, 68
Ganzl, K. Encyclopedia of the musical theatre, 1371
———, and A. Lamb. Book of the musical theatre, 1368
Gaquin, D. A. *See* Dodge, R. W.
Garcia-Pelayo y Gross, R., ed. Larousse Spanish-English, English-Spanish dictionary, 810
Garden literature, 862
Gardening by mail, B. J. Barton, 863
Gardner, P. Simplest game, 1591
Garee, B., ed. Accent on living buyer's guide, 1112
Gargan, W., and S. Sharma, eds. Find that tune, 1423
Garland encyclopedia of world music, B. Nettl and R. Stone, eds., 1385
Garland recipe index, K. W. Torgeson and S. Weinstein, 1136
Garraty, J. A., and M. C. Carnes. American national biography, 1917
Garret, H. S., ed. HMO/PPO directory from Medical Device Register, 1055
Garrison, P. Illustrated encyclopedia of general aviation, 938
Garwood, A. N., ed. Weather America, 923
Gates, J. K. Guide to the use of libraries and information sources, 10
Gatland, K., et al. Illustrated encyclopedia of space technology, 939
Gaultier, A. P. *See* Lasne, S.
Gay and lesbian literary heritage, C. J. Summers, ed., 1650
Gay and lesbian literature, S. Malinowski, ed., 1651
Geary, D. How to sharpen every blade in your woodshop, 1191
Gebhardt, R. Complete cat book, 1203
Geiss, T. Random House crossword puzzle dictionary, 729
Gelbert, D. Sports halls of fame, 1503
Genealogical and biographical research, National Archives and Records Administration, 1933n
Genealogical and local history books in print, M. Hoffman, ed., 1932
Genealogical microfilm catalogs, National Archives and Records Administration, 1933
Genealogical periodical annual index, 1941
Genealogies in the Library of Congress, M. J. Kaminkow, 1934
Genealogist's address book, E. P. Bently, 1943
Genealogist's handbook, R. S. Wright III, 1947
General information concerning patents, U.S. Department of the Interior, U.S. Patent and Trademark Office, 831
General reference books for adults, 4n
General science index, 818
Genreflecting, D. T. Herald, ed., 1683
Genz, W. M., ed. Dictionary of Bible and religion, 190
George, L. Alternative realities, 308
George-Warren, H. *See* Romanowski, P.
Gettings, F. Arkana dictionary of astrology, 309
Gibaldi, J. MLA handbook for writers of research papers, 776
Gibilisco, S. Illustrated dictionary of electronics, 947
———, ed. McGraw-Hill encyclopedia of personal computing, 900
———, and N. Sclater, eds. Encyclopedia of electronics, 945
Gibson, C., ed. Facts on File dictionary of mathematics, 1004
Giffin, J. M. *See* Carlson, D. G.
Gilbar, A. Recipex, 1139
Gillespie, J. T. Best books for senior high readers, 35
———, and C. J. Naden, eds. Best books for children, 33
———, and R. J. Folcarelli. Guide to library collection development, 42
Gillis, J., and M. Fise. Childwise catalog, 1194
Ginsberg, L. H. Social work almanac, 401
Girard, D., et al., eds. Cassell's French dictionary, 785
Gladfetter, T. *See* Ross, C.
Glare, P. G. W., ed. Greek-English lexicon: a supplement, 796; Oxford Latin dictionary, 805
Glassborow, J., and G. Freeman, eds. Atlas of the United States, 1897

Glasse, A. Concise encyclopedia of Islam, 251
Glazier, S. Random House word menu, 766
Glossary of literary terms, M. H. Abrams, 1609
Glut, D. F. Dinosaurs: the encyclopedia, 986
Godman, A. Energy supply A-Z, 929
Goldbeck, D. *See* Goldbeck, N.
Goldbeck, N., and D. Goldbeck. Choose to reuse, 958
Goldstein, J. F. *See* Makinson, L.
Goldstein, N., ed. Associated Press stylebook and libel manual, 770
Golf Digest almanac, 1565
Golf Digest's best places to play, 1566
Golf Magazine's encyclopedia of golf, 1567
Gombrich, R. F. *See* Bechert, H.
Gonen, A., ed. Encyclopedia of the peoples of the world, 434
Gonzalez-Wippler, M. Santeria, 259
Good, D., ed. Compton's encyclopedia, 153
Good Housekeeping household encyclopedia, 1172
Gordon, A. *See* Gordon, L.
Gordon, L., and A. Gordon. American chronicle, 1777
Goren, C. H. Goren's new bridge complete, 1548
Goren's new bridge complete, C. H. Goren, 1548
Gorman, J. M. Essential guide to psychiatric drugs, 1101
Gosling, W. *See* Dunkling, L.
Gottlieb, B., et al., eds. New choices in natural healing, 1086
Goulart, R., ed. Encyclopedia of American comics, 1246
Gould, J., and W. L. Kolb, eds. Dictionary of the social sciences, 319
Gove, P. B., ed. Webster's third new international dictionary of the English language, 717, 761n
Government agencies, D. R. Whitnah, ed., 585
Government reference books 94/96, J. A. Schuler, ed., 6
Gowing, L., ed. Biographical dictionary of artists, 1247; Encyclopedia of visual art, 1247
GPO sales publications reference file, 53
GPO sales publications reference file magnetic tapes, 53
Graedon, J., and T. Graedon. People's guide to deadly drug interactions, 1104
Graedon, T. *See* Graedon, J.
Graf, A. B. Exotica series 4 international, 861
Grand dictionnaire francais-anglais, anglais-francais/Larousse French-English, English-French dictionary, F. Carney and C. Nimmo, 787
Granger's index to poetry, 1704n
Grant, E., and K. Fox, eds. Motion picture guide annual, 1332
Grant, J. *See* Clute, J.
Grant, J. C. B., and J. E. Anderson. Grant's atlas of anatomy, 1087
Grant, R. *See* Ballantine, R.
Grant's atlas of anatomy, J. C. B. Grant and J. E. Anderson, 1087
Graphic arts encyclopedia, G. A. Stevenson and W. A. Pakan, 1249
Graubner, W. Encyclopedia of wood joints, 1473
Gray's anatomy, P. L. Williams et al., eds., 1088
Graydon, D., and Mountaineers Books staff, eds. Mountaineering, the freedom of the hills, 1583
Great American trials, E. W. Knappman, ed., 573
Great book of the sea, F. Guerrini, 993
Great composers, 1300–1900, D. Ewen, 1401
Great foreign language writers, J. Vinson and D. Kirkpatrick, eds., 1637
Great song thesaurus, R. Lax and F. Smith, 1425
Greek and Latin authors, M. Grant, 1750
Greek and Roman authors, T. Gwinup and F. Dickinson, 1751
Greek-English lexicon, H. G. Liddell and R. Scott, eds., 796
Greek-English lexicon: a supplement, P. G. W. Glare, ed., 796
Green, D. H. Parent's choice, 1195
Green, S. Encyclopaedia of the musical film, 1326
Green, T. A., ed. Folklore, 274
Greenberg, B. How to run a traditional Jewish household, 236
Greenberg, I. Jewish way, 240
Greenberg, M. *See* Plano, J. C.
Greene, J. P., ed. Encyclopedia of American political history, 564
Greene, S. A. *See* Pohanish, R. P.
Greenwald, D., ed. McGraw-Hill encyclopedia of economics, 454
Greenwood, V. D. Researcher's guide to American genealogy, 1950
Greer, R. C. Illustration index, 3d ed., 1236
Gregory, R. L., and O. L. Zangwill. Oxford companion to the mind, 303
Grenville, J. A. S. Major international treaties, 609
———, and B. Wasserstein. Major international treaties since 1945, 609
Griffin, R., and A. H. Shurgin, eds. Folklore of world holidays, 1147
Grimal, P., and A. R. Maxwell-Hyslop, trans. Dictionary of classical mythology, 265
Grinstein, L. S., et al., eds. Women in chemistry and physics, 893
Groden, M., and M. Kreiswirth, eds. Johns Hopkins guide to literary theory and criticism, 1611
Grolier multimedia encyclopedia, 148n
Gross, E. American years, 1777
Grossman, J. *See* Turabian, K. L.
Grun, B. Timetables of history, 1782

Grundman, C. *See* Pulliam, T.
Grundy, V. *See* Correard, M.
Grzimek's encyclopedia of mammals, 994
Guenther, N. A. United States Supreme Court decisions, 630
Guerrini, F. Great book of the sea, 993
Guide to American directories, B. J. Klein, ed., 70
Guide to American law, 578n
Guide to American law yearbook, 578n
Guide to American poetry explication: colonial and nineteenth century, J. Ruppert, 1708
Guide to American poetry explication: modern and contemporary, J. R. Leo, 1708
Guide to British poetry explication, N. Martinez and J. G. R. Martinez, 1709
Guide to cooking schools, 1137
Guide to critical reviews, J. M. Salem, 1309
Guide to economic indicators, N. Frumkin, 489
Guide to foreign language courses and dictionaries, A. J. Walford and J. E. O. Screen, eds., 780
Guide to free computer materials, 645
Guide to French literature, A. Levi, 1762
Guide to genealogical research in the National Archives, 1935
Guide to heraldry, 1956n
Guide to historical literature, M. B. Norton, ed., 1772
Guide to independent study through correspondence instruction, 662
Guide to library collection development, J. T. Gillespie and R. J. Folcarelli, 42
Guide to literary agents and art/photo reps, 1261n
Guide to microforms in print, 54
Guide to monastic guest houses, R. J. Regalbuto, 222
Guide to popular U.S. government publications, F. W. Hoffmann and R. J. Ward, 133
Guide to publications of the executive branch, F. J. O'Hara, 134
Guide to reference books, R. Balay, ed., 7
Guide to reference materials for school library media centers, M. I. Nichols, ed., 8
Guide to special issues and indexes of periodicals, M. Uhlan and D. B. Katz, eds., 444
Guide to summer camps and summer schools, 681
Guide to the best wineries of North America, A. Guyot, 1127
Guide to the gods, M. Leach, 276
Guide to the literature of art history, E. Arntzen and R. Rainwater, 1230
Guide to the study of the United States of America, U.S. Library of Congress, General Reference and Bibliography Div., 1773
Guide to the use of libraries and information sources, J. K. Gates, 10
Guide to world language dictionaries, A. Dalby, ed., 781
Guiley, R. E. Encyclopedia of witches and witchcraft, 272; Harper's encyclopedia of mystical and paranormal experience, 315
Guinagh, K., trans. and comp. Dictionary of foreign phrases and abbreviations, 735
Guinness book of records, 107
Guinness book of sports records, M. Young, ed., 1505
Gutman, I., ed. Encyclopedia of the holocaust, 1807
Guyot, A. Guide to the best wineries of North America, 1127
Guyton, A. C., and J. E. Hall. Textbook of medical physiology, 1091
Gwinup, T., and F. Dickinson. Greek and Roman authors, 1751

H & R Block income tax guide, 542
Hackett, A. P., and J. H. Burke. Eighty years of best sellers, 1681
Hahn, H. Harley Hahn's Internet and web yellow pages, 910
Haigh, C., ed. Cambridge historical encyclopedia of Great Britain and Ireland, 1787
Hale, W. A., and J. P. Margham. HarperCollins dictionary of biology, 981
Hales, D., and R. E. Hales. Caring for the mind, 300
Hales, R. E. *See* Hales, D.
Hall, J. E. *See* Guyton, A. C.
Hall, K. L., ed. Oxford companion to the Supreme Court of the United States, 629
Hall, R. M. *See* Lovell, E. C.
Halliwell, L., and John Walker, ed. Halliwell's filmgoer's companion, 1328, 1336n
Halliwell's film and video guide, 1328n, 1336
Halliwell's filmgoer's companion, L. Halliwell and J. Walker, ed., 1328, 1336n
Halperin, M. *See* Pagell, R. A.
Hamilton, G., and K. Hamilton. Fix it fast, fix it right, 1183
Hamilton, K. *See* Hamilton, G.
Hammond atlas, 154n
Hampton, J. J., ed. AMA management handbook, 525
Hamstra, B. How therapists diagnose, 302
Hanc, J. Essential runner, 1586
Hand, R., Jr. *See* Ehrlich, E.
Hand tools, A. A. Watson, 1475
Handbook of American Indians north of Mexico, F. W. Hodge, 1813
Handbook of American popular culture, T. M. Inge, ed., 326
Handbook of American popular literature, T. M. Inge, ed., 326n
Handbook of American women's history, A. H. Zophy, ed., 1827

Handbook of climbing, A. Fyffe and I. Peter, 1582
Handbook of corporate finance, E. I. Altman, ed., 503
Handbook of denominations in the United States, F. S. Mead, 207
Handbook of electronic formulas, symbols, and definitions, J. R. Brand, 946
Handbook of financial markets and institutions, E. I. Altman, ed., 503
Handbook of Hispanic cultures in the United States, N. Kanellos and C. Esteva-Fabregat, eds., 380
Handbook of Latin American literature, D. W. Foster, ed., 1755
Handbook of mathematical, scientific, and engineering formulas, tables, functions, graphs, transforms, Research and Education Association staff, 1005
Handbook of North American Indians, 1814
Handbook of ornament, F. S. Meyer, 1296
Handbook of over-the-counter drugs and pharmacy products, M. Leber et al., 1102
Handbook of pseudonyms and personal nicknames, H. S. Sharp, 1967
Handbook of Russian literature, V. Terras, ed., 1770
Handbook of United States economic and financial indicators, F. M. O'Hara Jr. and R. Sicignano, 490
Handbook to literature, C. H. Holman and W. Harmon, 1610
Hanks, P., and F. Hodges. Dictionary of first names, 1963; Dictionary of surnames, 1964
Hanson, P. K., and S. L. Hanson. Film review index, 1323
Hanson, S. L. *See* Hanson, P. K.
Harley Hahn's Internet and web yellow pages, H. Hahn, 910
Harmon, W. *See* Holman, C. H.
Harmony illustrated encyclopedia of jazz, B. Case, S. Britt, and C. Murray, 1442
Harmony illustrated encyclopedia of rock, M. Clifford, ed., 1444
Harner, J. L. Literary research guide, 1599
Harper atlas of the Bible, J. B. Prichard, ed., 182
Harper dictionary of foreign terms, C. O. S. Mawson. E. Ehrlich, ed., 736
Harper encyclopedia of military history from 3500 B.C. to the present, R. E. Dupuy and T. N. Dupuy, 1815
Harper's Bible commentary, J. L. Mays, ed., 184
Harper's encyclopedia of mystical and paranormal experience, R. E. Guiley, 315
HarperCollins Bible dictionary, P. Achtemeier, ed., 184n, 191
HarperCollins dictionary of art terms and techniques, R. Mayer and S. Sheehan, 1250
HarperCollins dictionary of biology, W. A. Hale and J. P. Margham, 981
Harrap's new standard French and English dictionary, J. E. Mansion, R. P. L. Ledesert, and M. Ledesert, eds., 788
Harrap's shorter French and English dictionary, 788n
Harrap's standard German and English dictionary, 795n
Harris, C. M., ed. Dictionary of architecture and construction, 1272
Harris, T. *See* Andrews, W. L.
Harrison, C. H. Public schools USA, 698
Harrison's principles of internal medicine, A. S. Fauci et al., 1035
Hart, J. D., and P. Leininger. Oxford companion to American literature, 1727
Harte, J. Toxics A to Z, 970, 1076
Hartnoll, P., ed. Oxford companion to the theatre, 1370n, 1374
———, and P. Found, eds. Concise Oxford companion to the theatre, 1374
Hartt, F. Art, 1242
Harvard concise dictionary of music, D. M. Randel, comp., 1393
Harvard concordance to Shakespeare, M. Spevack, 1737
Harvard dictionary of music, W. Apel, 1393n
Harvard encyclopedia of American ethnic groups, S. Thernstrom et al., eds., 354
Harvard guide to American history, F. Freidel and R. K. Showman, 1774
Harvard guide to women's health, K. J. Carlson et al., 1119
Harvey, J. M. *See* Day, A.
Hassan, J. ESPN Information Please sports almanac, 1504
Hastings, J., et al. Encyclopaedia of religion and ethics, 281
Hatcher, R. A., et al. Contraceptive technology, 1118
Hathaway, N. Friendly guide to the universe, 875
Have a nice day—no problem, C. Ammer, 751
Havlice, P. P. Popular song index, 1428; World painting index, 1241
Hawkes, J. Atlas of early man, 427
Hawley's condensed chemical dictionary, R. J. Lewis Sr., 884
Hazardous chemicals desk reference, R. J. Lewis Sr., 888
Hazardous substances resource guide, R. P. Pohanish and S. A. Greene, eds., 889
Hazen, E. P., ed. Columbia Granger's index to poetry in anthologies, 1704
Heads of states and governments, H. M. Lentz, 603
Healing herbs, M. Castleman, 1085
Health United States, U.S. Department of Health and Human Resources, 1075
Heaton, T. B. *See* Chadwick, B. A.

Heim, M. E. Make it II, 1447
Heiserman, D. L. Exploring chemical elements and their compounds, 882
Helbig, A. K., and A. R. Perkins. Dictionary of American children's fiction, 1664
Hellebust, L., ed. State reference publications, 141
Hellemans, A. *See* Bunch, B.
Henderson, H., and B. Puckett, eds. Holidays and festivals index, 1148
Henderson, J. *See* Ellis, J.
Henderson, L., ed. Twentieth-century crime and mystery writers, 1690; Twentieth-century romance and historical writers, 1691
Hendrickson, L. Children's literature: a guide to the criticism, 1662
Hendrickson, R. Facts on File encyclopedia of word and phrase origins, 732
Henshaw, R. *See* LaBlanc, M. L.
Herald, D. T., ed. Genreflecting, 1683
Herbal drugs and phytopharmaceuticals, M. Wichtl, 1103
Herbert, M. C., and B. McNeil, eds. Biography and genealogy master index, 1912
Herbert, V., et al. Mount Sinai School of Medicine complete book of nutrition, 1110
Heritage of music, M. Raeburn and A. Kendall, eds., 1404
Heriteau, J. National Arboretum book of outstanding garden plants, 865
Herron, N. L., ed. Social sciences, 20
Herzhaft, G. Encyclopedia of the blues, 1435
Hessler, G. Comprehensive catalog of U.S. paper money, 1484
Hester, J. P. Encyclopedia of values and ethics, 285
Hewitt, J. Keeping unusual animals as pets, 1225
Hickok, R. Encyclopedia of North American sports history, 1495; Who's who of sports champions, 1512
Hiker's companion, C. Ross and T. Gladfetter, 1570
Hildebrand, R. *See* Fox, J.
Hill, L., ed. Black American colleges and universities, 673
Hindu world, B. Walker, 253
Hine, D. C., et al., eds. Black women in America, 362
Hinrichsen, D. *See* Lean, G.
Hirschfleder, A. Encyclopedia of Native American religions, 202
Hirschhorn, C. Hollywood musical, 1329
Hischak, T. S. Stage it with music, 1375
Hispanic-American almanac, N. Kanellos, ed., 381, 1828
Hispanic American genealogical sourcebook, 1944
Hispanic Americans information directory, C. B. Montney, ed., 382
Historic documents, 608
Historic landmarks of Black America, G. Cantor, ed., 1903
Historic U.S. court cases, J. W. Johnson, 626
Historical abstracts, 1775
Historical atlas of Africa, 1837n
Historical atlas of political parties in the United States Congress, K. C. Martis, 637
Historical atlas of United States congressional districts, K. C. Martis, 632
Historical atlas of World War I, A. Livesey, 1843
Historical atlas of World War II, J. Pimlott, 1844
Historical encyclopedia of world slavery, J. P. Rodriguez, ed., 1816
Historical first patents, T. Brown, 845
Historical statistics of Black America, J. C. Smith and C. P. Horton, 366
Historical statistics of the United States, Bureau of the Census, 1829
Historical tables, 606
Historical tables, J. Paxton, ed., 1830
History of architecture, B. F. Fletcher. J. Musgrove, ed., 1275
History of art, H. W. Janson and A. F. Janson, 1251
History of costume, B. Payne et al., 1287
Hitchcock, H. W., and S. Sadie, eds. New Grove dictionary of American music, 1390
HMO/PPO directory from Medical Device Register, H. S. Garret, ed., 1055
Hoad, T. F., ed. Concise Oxford dictionary of English etymology, 734n
Hobbs, J. B., comp. Homophones and homographs, 761
Hobbyist's sourcebook, 1452
Hobson, A., ed. Cambridge gazetteer of the United States and Canada, 1856
Hochman, S., ed. McGraw-Hill encyclopedia of world drama, 1680
Hodge, F. W. Handbook of American Indians north of Mexico, 1813
Hodges, F. *See* Hanks, P.
Hodgson, R. S. Dartnell direct mail and mail order handbook, 488
Hoffman, H. H., and R. L. Hoffman, comps. International index to recorded poetry, 1710
Hoffman, M., ed. Genealogical and local history books in print, 1932
Hoffman, R. L. *See* Hoffman, H. H.
Hoffmann, F. W., and R. J. Ward. Guide to popular U.S. government publications, 133
Hogan, R., ed. Dictionary of Irish literature, 1765
Holden, A., ed. Viking opera guide on CD-ROM, 1407n
———, et al., eds. Viking opera guide, 1407
Holder, R. W. Dictionary of euphemisms, 755
Holidays and anniversaries of the world, B. A. Baker, ed., 1145

Holidays and festivals index, H. Henderson and B. Puckett, eds., 1148
Holidays, festivals, and celebrations of the world dictionary, S. E. Thompson and B. W. Carlson, eds., 1149
Hollander, Z., ed. Complete encyclopedia of hockey, 1571; *see also* Collins, B.
Holleb, A. I., ed. American Cancer Society's complete book of cancer, 1092
Holler, F. L. Information sources of political science, p. 86
Hollywood musical, C. Hirschhorn, 1329
Holman, C. H., and W. Harmon. Handbook to literature, 1610
Holmberg, E. E., ed. CD-ROMs in print, 49
Holmes, E. *See* Martin, E.
Holoman, D. K. Evenings with the orchestra, 1408
Holy Qur'an = al-Qur'an al-hakim, M. H. Shakir, ed., 254
Homa, L. L., ed. Elementary school library collection, 41
Home book of proverbs, maxims, and famous phrases, 1627n
Home book of quotations, classical and modern, B. Stevenson, 1620, 1627n
Home design handbook, J. C. Myrvang and S. Myrvang, 1162
Home health guide to poisons and antidotes, C. Turkington, 1066
Home improvement cost guide, Consumer Union editors, 1168
Home improvements manual, Reader's Digest editors, 1180
Home Magazine's how your house works, D. Vandervoort, 1185
Home repair emergency handbook, G. Schnaser, 1186
Homeowners' complete outdoor building book, J. B. Brimer, 1163
Homophones and homographs, J. B. Hobbs, comp., 761
Honour, H. *See* Fleming, J.
Hook, B., ed. Cambridge encyclopedia of China, 1855
Hooper, D., and K. Whyld. Oxford companion to chess, 1551
Hoover, G., et al., eds. Hoover's handbook of world business, 472
Hoover's handbook of emerging companies, P. J. Spain and J. R. Talbot, eds., 471
Hoover's handbook of world business, G. Hoover et al., eds., 472
Horn, D. Literature of American music in books and folk music collections, 1380
———, and R. Jackson. Literature of American music in books and folk music collections: supplement 1, 1380
Horn, M., ed. World encyclopedia of comics, 1258
Hornblower, S., and A. Spawforth, eds. Oxford classical dictionary, 1752
Horse industry directory, 1219
Horses, E. H. Edwards, 1220
Horton, C. P. *See* Smith, J. C.
Hortus third, Liberty Hyde Bailey Hortorium staff, 864
Hospital statistics, 1051n
Hotel and travel index, 1904
Hourani, A. *See* Mostyn, T.
How therapists diagnose, B. Hamstra, 302
How things work in your home, Time-Life Books editors, 1187
How to carve wood, R. Butz, 1476
How to clean practically anything, Consumer Reports Books editors, 1173
How to find information about companies, 445
How to find the law, M. L. Cohen et al., 555
How to run a traditional Jewish household, B. Greenberg, 236
How to sharpen every blade in your woodshop, D. Geary, 1191
Howatson, M. C., ed. Oxford companion to classical literature, 1753
Hubin, A. J. Crime fiction II, 1688
Hudgeons, M. Official 1998 blackbook price guide of U.S. paper money, 1484; Official 1998 blackbook price guide of U.S. postage stamps, 1489; Official blackbook price guide to U.S. coins, 1485
Human body, C. Clayman, ed., 1089
Human body explained, P. Whitefield, ed., 1090
Human body on file, Diagram Group staff, 1087
Human relations area file, 433n, 435n
Humanities, R. Blazek and E. Aversa, 10
Humanities index, 123
Hunter, D. E., and P. Whitten, eds. Encyclopedia of anthropology, 432
Hurt, C. D. Information sources in science and technology, 814
Husband, J. F. *See* Husband, J.
Husband, J., and J. F. Husband. Sequels, 1686
Husen, T., and T. N. Postlethwaite, eds. International encyclopedia of education, 655
Hutera, D. *See* Robertson, A.
Huxley, A., et al. New Royal Horticultural Society dictionary of gardening, 866
Hyman, P. E., and D. D. Moore, eds. Jewish women in America, 241

IBM dictionary of computing, G. McDaniel, comp., 898
Ijiri, Y. *See* Cooper, W. W.
Illingworth, V., ed. Facts on File dictionary of astronomy, 874

Illustrated dictionary of ceramics, G. Savage and H. Newman, 1281
Illustrated dictionary of electronics, S. Gibilisco, 947
Illustrated dictionary of jewelry, H. Newman, 1297
Illustrated dictionary of ornament, M. Stafford and D. Ware, 1244n
Illustrated dictionary of science, M. Allaby, ed., 823
Illustrated encyclopedia of active new religions, sects, and cults, B. Beit-Hallahmi, 255
Illustrated encyclopedia of aquarium fish, G. Sandford, 1216
Illustrated encyclopedia of billiards, M. L. Shamos, 1544
Illustrated encyclopedia of fly-fishing, S. Calabi, 1554
Illustrated encyclopedia of general aviation, P. Garrison, 938
Illustrated encyclopedia of space technology, K. Gatland et al., 939
Illustrated hardware book, Consumer Reports editors and T. Philbin, 1192
Illustrated who's who in mythology, M. Senior, 277
Illustration index, 2d ed., L. E. Vance and E. M. Tracey, 1236
Illustration index, 3d ed., R. C. Greer, 1236
Illustration index, 4th ed., M. C. Appel, 1236
Illustration index, V–VIII, M. C. Appel, 1236
Immigrant and passenger arrivals, National Archives and Records Administration, 1933n
In search of your European roots, A. Baxter, 1936
Independent study catalog, 662
Index and directory of industry standards, 931
Index medicus, 1032
Index of majors and graduate degrees, 677
Index to America, 1776
Index to American reference books annual, 1990–94, 2n
Index to children's plays in collections, 2d ed., B. Kreider, 1360
Index to children's plays in collections, 3d ed., B. R. Trefny and E. C. Palmer, 1360
Index to children's songs, C. S. Peterson and A. D. Fenton, comps., 1426
Index to current urban documents, 135
Index to fairy tales, 1949–1972, N. O. Ireland, 1665
Index to fairy tales, 1973–1977, N. O. Ireland, 1665
Index to fairy tales, 1978–1986, N. O. Ireland and J. W. Sprug, comps., 1665
Index to fairy tales, 1987–1992, J. W. Sprug, comp., 1665
Index to fairy tales, myths and legends, M. H. Eastman, 1665
Index to handicraft books, 1447
Index to handicrafts, modelmaking, and workshop projects, E. C. Lovell and R. M. Hall, 1447
Index to how to do it information, N. M. Lathrop, comp., 1448
Index to illustrations, J. C. Ellis, 1237
Index to illustrations of animals and plants, B. Clewis, 982
Index to one-act plays for stage, radio and television, H. Logasa and W. Ver Nooy, comps., 1361
Index to plays, I. T. Firkins, comp., 1362
Index to plays in periodicals, D. H. Keller, 1363
Index to religious periodical literature, 171n
Index to reproductions of American paintings, I. S. Monro and K. M. Monro, 1238
Index to reproductions of European paintings, I. S. Monro and K. M. Monro, 1239
Index to The Sporting News, N. Kehde, ed., 1494
Indiana companion to traditional Chinese literature, W. H. Nienhauser Jr., ed., 1761
Industrial Trade Administration and Minority Business Development Agency of U.S. Dept. of Commerce. Franchise opportunities handbook, 470
Industry norms and key business ratios, 491
Information America, F. Malin and R. Stanzi, eds., 55
Information industry directory, 76
Information please almanac, 108
Information please environmental almanac, 968
Information sources in science and technology, C. D. Hurt, 814
Information sources of political science, F. L. Holler, p. 86
Informing the nation, F. J. O'Hara, ed., 136
Inge, T. M., ed. Handbook of American popular culture, 326; Handbook of American popular literature, 326n
Inlander, C. B., and the People's Medical Society staff. People's Medical Society health desk reference, 1072
Insecticide, herbicide, fungicide quick guide, 856
Insider's guide to the colleges, Yale Daily News staff, eds., 678n, 682
Instruments of science, R. Bud and D. J. Warner, eds., 846
International acronyms, initialisms, and abbreviations dictionary, 725
International Bible commentary, F. F. Bruce, ed., 185
International book trade directory, K. G. Saur staff, eds., 89n
International business information, R. A. Pagell and M. Halperin, 446
International Center of Photography encyclopedia of photography, W. L. Broecker, ed., 1304
International cookery index, R. H. Kleiman and A. M. Kleiman, 1136
International dictionary of architects and architecture, R. J. Van Vynckt, ed., 1276

International dictionary of ballet, M. Bremser, ed., 1320
International dictionary of films and filmmakers, 1330
International dictionary of management, H. Johannsen and G. T. Page, 527
International dictionary of medicine and biology, S. I. Landau, ed., 1040
International dictionary of opera, C. S. Larue, ed., 1405n
International directory of company histories, 452
International directory of engineering societies and related organizations, 932
International directory of little magazines and small presses, L. Fulton and E. Furber, eds., 96
International encyclopedia of dance, 1321
International encyclopedia of education, T. Husen and T. N. Postlethwaite, eds., 655
International encyclopedia of linguistics, W. Bright, ed., 710
International encyclopedia of population, J. A. Ross, ed., 321
International encyclopedia of psychiatry, psychology, psychoanalysis and neurology, B. B. Wolman, ed., 297
International encyclopedia of the social sciences, D. L. Sills, ed., 322
International financial statistics, 504
International index, 123
International index to recorded poetry, H. H. Hoffman and R. L. Hoffman, comps., 1710
International Institute for Strategic Studies. Military balance, 586
International literary market place, 92n
International military and defense encyclopedia, T. N. Dupuy et al., eds., 1027
International motion picture almanac, 1340
International relations dictionary, L. Ziring et al., 574
International standard Bible encyclopedia, G. W. Bromley, ed., 192
International television and video almanac, 1357
International vital records handbook, T. J. Kemp, 1948
International who's who, 1922
Introduction to reference work, W. A. Katz, 11
Introduction to United States government information sources, J. Morehead and M. Fetzer, 138
Inverted medical dictionary, M. J. Stanaszek et al., eds., 1041
Investment companies, 516
Investment statistics locator, L. H. Bentley and J. J. Kiesl, 517
Ireland, N. O. Index to fairy tales, 1949–1972, 1665; Index to fairy tales, 1973–1977, 1665
———, and J. W. Sprug, comps. Index to fairy tales, 1978–1986, 1665
Irwin business and investment almanac, 492
Irwin, R., ed. McGraw-Hill real estate handbook, 538
Israel, F. L. *See* Friedman, L.
Israel, G. *See* Audouze, J.
Ito, K. *See* Mathematical Society of Japan staff
Iverson, C., ed. American Medical Association manual of style, 769

J. K. Lasser's your income tax, 543
Jackson, G. M. Encyclopedia of literary epics, 1604
Jackson, K. T., ed. Atlas of American history, revised, 1838
Jackson, R. *See* Horn, D.
Jackson, W. T. H., and G. Stade, eds. European writers, 1642
Jackson-Laufer, G. M. Encyclopedia of traditional epics, 1605
Jacobs, D. W., ed. World book encyclopedia, 157
Jacobstein, B. *See* Willis, A.
Jacquet, C. H., ed. Yearbook of American and Canadian churches, 224
Jaffe, J. H., ed. Encyclopedia of drugs and alcohol, 341, 1100
James, L. K., ed. Nobel laureates in chemistry, 892
James, P., and N. Thorpe. Ancient inventions, 842
James, R. C., et al., eds. Mathematics dictionary, 1007
Jane's space directory, 940
Janson, A. F. *See* Janson, H. W.
Janson, H. W., and A. F. Janson. History of art, 1251
Japan, 1817
Japanese American history, B. Niiya, ed., 1831
Jarman, B., and R. Russell, eds. Oxford Spanish dictionary, 812
Jary, D., and J. Jary. Collins dictionary of sociology, 330
Jary, J. *See* Jary, D.
Jaszcak, S., ed. Encyclopedia of associations, 73
Jenkins, F. W. Classical studies, 1749
Jennings, L., et al. Best games, 1577
Jerde, J. Encyclopedia of textiles, 1000
Jerrard, H. G., and D. B. McNeill. Dictionary of scientific units, 822
Jessup, J., and L. Ketz, eds. Encyclopedia of the American military, 571
Jewish book of why, A. J. Kolatch, 237
Jewish holidays, M. Strassfield, 238
Jewish literacy, J. Telushkin, 239
Jewish way, I. Greenberg, 240
Jewish wisdom, J. Telushkin, 239
Jewish women in America, P. E. Hyman and D. D. Moore, eds., 241

Jingrong, W., ed. Pinyin Chinese-English dictionary, 784
Johannsen, H., and G. T. Page. International dictionary of management, 527
Johanson, C. J. *See* Sellen, B. C.
John, V., ed. Dictionary of materials and manufacturing, 999
Johns Hopkins guide to literary theory and criticism, M. Groden and M. Kreiswirth, eds., 1611
Johns Hopkins symptoms and remedies, S. Margolis, ed., 1067
Johnson, A. *See* Seligman, E. R. A.
Johnson, B. *See* Bahr, L. S.
Johnson, D. B., comp. National party platforms, 617
Johnson, J. W. Historic U.S. court cases, 626
Johnson, T. Rock climbing basics, 1584; *see also* Weissman, P.
Johnson, T. H., ed. Oxford companion to American history, 1822
Johnston, R. J., et al., eds. Dictionary of human geography, 1860
Johnston, W. M. Recent reference books in religion, 169
Jones, A. Larousse dictionary of world folklore, 436
Jones, C. *See* Ardagh, J.
Jones, J. Sports and recreation for the disabled, 1507
Jones, L. S. Art information, 1228
Jones, T., ed. Oxford-Harrap standard German-English dictionary, 795
Jordan, M. Encyclopedia of the gods, 270
Journal literature of the physical sciences, A. L. Primack, 815
Joy of cooking, I. S. Rombauer, 1134
Judaica reference sources, 242
Junior high school library catalog, 43n
Justices of the United States Supreme Court, L. Friedman and F. L. Israel, eds., 627

K. G. Saur staff, eds. International book trade directory, 89n
Kadish, S. H., ed. Encyclopedia of crime and justice, 349
Kaiser index to Black resources, 367
Kaminkow, M. J. Complement to Genealogies in the Library of Congress, 1934; Genealogies in the Library of Congress, 1934
———, ed. United States local histories in the Library of Congress, 1940
Kamp, J. Reference guide to American literature, 1728; *see also* Telgen, D.
Kane, J., and G. L. Alexander. Nicknames and sobriquets of U.S. cities, states, and counties, 1866
Kane, J. N. American counties, 1873; Facts about the presidents, 620n, 623; Famous first facts, 106
Kanellos, N., ed. Hispanic-American almanac, 381, 1828
———, and C. Esteva-Fabregat, eds. Handbook of Hispanic cultures in the United States, 380
Kanely, E. A., comp. Cumulative subject index guide to United States government bibliographies, 1924–1973, 138
Kapel, D. E., et al. American educators' encyclopedia, 650
Kaplan, J., ed. Familiar quotations, 1619
Kaplan, M., ed. Variety's directory of major U.S. show business awards, 1314
Kaplan, S. R. Encyclopedia of tarot, 313
Karp, R. S., and J. H. Schlessinger. Plays for children and young adults, 1366
Karpel, B., ed. Arts in America, 1229
Kartographisches Institut Bertelsmann. Book of the world, 1885
Katz, B. A., and L. S. Katz. Magazines for libraries, 66
Katz, D. B. *See* Uhlan, M.
Katz, E., ed. Film encyclopedia, 1327
Katz, J., and N. P. Bruning. Swimming for total fitness, 1594
Katz, L. S. *See* Katz, B. A.
Katz, W. A. Introduction to reference work, 11
Katzner, K. English-Russian, Russian-English dictionary, 806
Keareyed, P. Encyclopedia of the solid earth sciences, 915
Keegan, J., ed. Times atlas of the Second World War, 1846
Keeping unusual animals as pets, J. Hewitt, 1225
Kehde, N., ed. Index to The Sporting News, 1494
Keller, D. H. Index to plays in periodicals, 1363
Kelly, J. N. D. Oxford dictionary of popes, 227
Kelly, M. Encyclopedia of aesthetics, 1245
Kemp, T. J. International vital records handbook, 1948
Kendall, A. *See* Raeburn, M.
Kenkyusha's new English-Japanese dictionary, Y. Koine, ed., 801
Kenkyusha's new Japanese-English dictionary, K. Masuda, ed., 801
Kennedy, R. A. *See* Clapp, J. J.
Kennedy, S. E., ed. Reference sources for small and medium-sized libraries, 18
Kent, M., ed. Oxford dictionary of sports science and medicine, 1046
Kerchelich, K. *See* De Sola, R.
Kernfeld, B., ed. New Grove dictionary of jazz, 1443
Kerrigan, E. E. American badges and insignia, 1954; American war medals and decorations, 1955

Kester-Shelton, P. Feminist writers, 1657
Ketz, L. *See* Jessup, J.
Ketz, L. B., ed. Dictionary of American history, 1793
Keyser, D., and R. Sweetland, eds. Test critiques, 305
Keyser, D. J. *See* Sweetland, R. C.
Kies, C. Occult in the western world, 317
Kiesl, J. J. *See* Bentley, L. H.
Kim, H., ed. Dictionary of Asian American history, 377
King, A., ed. and comp. Quotations in black, 1625
Kirkpatrick, D. *See* Vinson, J.
Kister, K. F. Kister's atlas buying guide, 1881; Kister's best dictionaries for adults and young people, 712; Kister's best encyclopedias, 146
Kister's atlas buying guide, K. F. Kister, 1881
Kister's best dictionaries for adults and young people, K. F. Kister, 712
Kister's best encyclopedias, K. F. Kister, 146
Kitchenware book, S. Ettlinger, 1138
Klatell, J., et al. Mount Sinai Medical Center family health guide to dental health, 1071
Kleiman, A. M. *See* Kleiman, R. H.
Kleiman, R. H. American regional cookery index, 1136
———, and A. M. Kleiman. International cookery index, 1136
Klein, B. J., ed. Guide to American directories, 70
Klein, B. T., ed. Reference encyclopedia of the American Indian, 392
Klein, E. Comprehensive etymological dictionary of the English language, 731
Klein, L. S., ed. Encyclopedia of world literature in the twentieth century, 1607
Kline, V. Last lines, 1711
Klosesel, C. J. W., comp. English novel explication: supplement III, 1732; English novel explication: supplement IV, 1732; English novel explication: supplement V, 1732; English novel explication: supplement VI, 1732
———, and J. R. Smitten, comps. English novel explication: supplement II, 1732
Knappman, E. W., ed. Great American trials, 573
Kodansha's romanized Japanese-English dictionary, M. Yoshida, 802
Koegler, H. Concise Oxford dictionary of ballet, 1316
Koehl, S. *See* Luttwak, E.
Koehn, C., ed. Books for public libraries, 38
Kohler's dictionary for accountants, W. W. Cooper and Y. Ijiri, eds., 500
Koine, Y., ed. Kenkyusha's new English-Japanese dictionary, 801
Kolatch, A. J. Jewish book of why, 237; Second Jewish book of why, 237
Kolb, W. L. *See* Gould, J.
Koniak, S. P. *See* Cushman, R. F.
Konigsberg, I. Complete film dictionary, 1325
Korab, B. *See* Packard, R. T.
Korch, R. *See* Neft, D. S.
Korean War almanac, 1823n
Korn, P. Working with wood, 1477
Kornicki, P. *See* Bowring, R.
Kostelanetz, R. *See* Slonimsky, N.
Koszegi, M. A. *See* Melton, J. G.
Kovel, R. *See* Kovel, R. M.
Kovel, R. M., R. Kovel, and T. H. Kovel. Kovels' antiques and collectibles price list, 1478
Kovel, T. H. *See* Kovel, R. M.
Kovels' antiques and collectibles price list, R. M. Kovel, R. Kovel, and T. H. Kovel, 1478
Kowaleski-Wallace, E. Encyclopedia of feminist literary theory, 1655
Koykka, A. S. Project remember, 1939
Krasilovsky, M. W., and S. Shemel. This business of music, 1397
Krause, B. Collecting coins for pleasure and profit, 1483; Collecting paper money for pleasure and profit, 1483; Stamp collecting, 1491
Krause, C., et al., eds. Standard catalog of U.S. paper money, 1484
Krause, C. L., and C. Mishler. Standard catalog of world coins: eighteenth century, 1485
———, ———, and C. R. Bruce. Standard catalog of world coins, 1485; Standard catalog of world coins: seventeenth century, 1485; *see also* Mishler, C.
Krause, J. V., and S. J. Brennan. Basketball resource guide, 1533
Kreider, B. Index to children's plays in collections, 2d ed., 1360
Kreiswirth, M. *See* Groden, M.
Kricheimer, S. Doctor's book of home remedies II, 1083
Krieger, J., et al. Oxford companion to the politics of the world, 588
Krol, E. Whole Internet user's guide and catalog, 911
Kruzas, A. T., ed. Social service organizations and agencies directory, 400
Kurian, G., and J. D. Schultz, eds. Encyclopedia of the Democratic Party, 616; Encyclopedia of the Republican Party, 616
Kurian, G. T. Encyclopedia of the Third World, 1862
———, ed. World encyclopedia of parliaments and legislatures, 594; World press encyclopedia, 101
Kurpis, G. P., and C. J. Booth, eds. New IEEE standard dictionary of electrical and electronics terms, 952
Kusnet, J. *See* Arnold, A. L.

LaBlanc, M. L., ed. Professional sports team histories, 1497
———, and R. Henshaw. World encyclopedia of soccer, 1593
Labor unions, G. M. Fink, ed., 453
Lackmann, R. Same time . . . same station, 1352
Lafferty, P., and J. Rowe, eds. Dictionary of science, 821
Laffin, J. Brassey's battles, 1785
Lagasse, P. G., ed. Concise Columbia encyclopedia, 154
Lagowski, J. J., ed. Macmillan encyclopedia of chemistry, 885
Lamar, H. R., ed. New encyclopedia of the American West, 1821
Lamb, A. *See* Ganzl, K.
Landau, S. I., ed. International dictionary of medicine and biology, 1040
Landon, G. *See* Stambler, I.
Lane, M. T. State publications and depository libraries, 140
Lang, J. H. *See* Montague, P.
Lang, J. P. Dictionary of the liturgy, 215
Langenscheidt editorial staff. *See* Messinger, H.
Langenscheidt's condensed Muret-Sanders German dictionary, H. Messinger and the Langenscheidt editorial staff, 793n
Langenscheidt's new college German dictionary, S. Brough and H. Messinger, eds., 792
Langenscheidt's new Muret-Sanders encyclopedic dictionary of the English and German languages, O. Springer, ed., 793
Langer, W. L., ed. Encyclopedia of world history, 1812
Langley, B. C. Major appliances, 1188
Langris, B. *See* Edwards, E. H.
Langston, D. J., and A. M. Smith. Free magazines for libraries, 122
Language of real estate, J. W. Reilly, 537
Larkin, C., ed. Encyclopedia of popular music, 1417
Larousse dictionary of scientists, H. Muir, ed., 839
Larousse dictionary of world folklore, A. Jones, 436
Larousse encyclopedia of wine, C. Foulkes, ed., 1128, 1130n
Larousse French-English, English-French dictionary, F. Carney and C. Nimmo, 787
Larousse gastronomique, P. Montague and J. H. Lang, 1143
Larousse Spanish-English, English-Spanish dictionary, R. Garcia-Pelayo y Gross, ed., 810
Larson, D. E., ed. Mayo Clinic family health book, 1068
Larue, C. S., ed. International dictionary of opera, 1405n
Lasne, S., and A. P. Gaultier. Dictionary of superstitions, 267
Last lines, V. Kline, 1711
Lathrop, N. M., comp. Index to how to do it information, 1448
Latin American writers, C. A. Sole and M. I. Abreu, eds., 1756
Laughlin, K., et al., comps. Children's song index, 1422
Lavin, M. R. Business information, 440
Lawson, E. Encyclopedia of human rights, 568
Lawson, J. R., ed. Pocket billiard guidebook for pool players, tournament directors, and spectators, 1545
Lawther, G. Complete quilting course, 1462
Lax, R., and F. Smith. Great song thesaurus, 1425
Leach, M. Guide to the gods, 276
Leading constitutional decisions, R. F. Cushman and S. P. Koniak, 628
Lean, G., and D. Hinrichsen. Atlas of the environment, 957
Leary, L., comp. Articles on American literature, 1900–1950, 1722
———, C. Bartholet, and C. Roth. Articles on American literature, 1950–1967, 1722
———, and J. Auchard. Articles on American literature, 1968–1975, 1722
Leber, M., et al. Handbook of over-the-counter drugs and pharmacy products, 1102
Lederberg, J., ed. Encyclopedia of microbiology, 977
Lederman, E. Making life more liveable, 1116
Ledesert, M. *See* Mansion, J. E.
Ledesert, R. P. L. *See* Mansion, J. E.
Left index, J. Nordquist, ed., 124
Legal problem solver, 575
Legal research in a nutshell, M. L. Cohen and K. C. Olson, 556
Leininger, P. *See* Hart, J. D.; *see also* Perkins, G.
Lend me your ears, W. Safire, ed., 1835
Lenderman, L. *See* Costello, E.
Lentz, H. M. Heads of states and governments, 603
Leo, J. R. Guide to American poetry explication: modern and contemporary, 1708
Leonard Maltin's movie and video guide, L. Maltin, ed., 1337
Leonard, T. M. Day by day: the forties, 1779
———, et al. Day by day: the seventies, 1779
Lerner, R. G., and G. L. Trigg, eds. Encyclopedia of physics, 1012
Les Brown's encyclopedia of television, L. Brown, 1350
Lesly, P. Lesly's handbook of public relations and communications, 529
Lesly's handbook of public relations and communications, P. Lesly, 529
Lessem, D., et al., eds. Dinosaur Society's dinosaur encyclopedia, 987

Letitia Baldridge's new complete guide to executive manners, L. Baldridge, 1158
Levernier, J. A., and D. R. Wilmes, eds. American writers before 1800, 1721
Levi, A. Guide to French literature, 1762
Levinson, D., ed. Encyclopedia of world cultures, 435
———, and K. Christenson, eds. Encyclopedia of world sport, 1496
———, and M. Ember, eds. American immigrant cultures, 352; Encyclopedia of cultural anthropology, 433
Levy, L., and L. Fisher, eds. Encyclopedia of the American presidency, 622
Levy, L. W., et al., eds. Encyclopedia of the American constitution, 569; Encyclopedia of the American constitution supplement, 569
Levy, P. B., ed. 100 key documents in American democracy, 1836
Lewin, A. E. *See* Lewin, E.
Lewin, E., and A. E. Lewin, eds. Thesaurus of slang, 760
Lewine, R., and A. Simon. Songs of the theater, 1433
Lewis, A. *See* Sader, M.
Lewis, C. S. *See* Pisano, D. A.
Lewis, J. R. Astrology encyclopedia, 310
Lewis, P., and G. Darley. Dictionary of ornament, 1244
Lewis, R. J., Sr. Hawley's condensed chemical dictionary, 884; Hazardous chemicals desk reference, 888
Leyser, B. J., comp. Rock stars/pop stars, 1446
Li, X., and N. B. Crane. Electronic styles, 774
Li, Z. Y., et al., eds. New English-Chinese dictionary. 2d rev. ed., 783
Liberty Hyde Bailey Hortorium staff. Hortus third, 864
Librarian's companion, V. F. Wertsman, 87
Library journal, 27, 66n
Library literature, 115
Library of Congress: a guide to genealogical and historical research, J. Neagles, 1949
Liddell, H. G., and R. Scott, eds. Greek-English lexicon, 796
Lide, D. R., ed. CRC handbook of chemistry and physics, 887
Life insurance fact book, 511
Light, J. F. Cultural encyclopedia of baseball, 1523
Lilien, S. B. *See* Carmichael, D. R.
Lilley, W., III, et al. Almanac of state legislatures, 580
Limbacher, J. L., ed. Song list, 1431
Linguistics, A. L. DeMiller, 705
Linn's world stamp almanac, 1487
Lipinski, K. A. *See* Lipinski, R. A.
Lipinski, R. A., and K. A. Lipinski. Complete beverage dictionary, 1124
Lippy, C. H., and P. W. Williams, eds. Encyclopedia of the American religious experience, 203
Lipset, S. M., ed. Encyclopedia of democracy, 567
List, B. A. *See* Mount, E.
List of subject headings, B. M. Westby, ed., 1306n
Litchfield, M. W. Renovation, 1170
Literary agents of North America, A. Orrmont and L. Rosentiel, eds., 77
Literary and library prizes, O. S. Weber and S. J. Calvert, eds., 1617
Literary market place, 92
Literary research guide, J. L. Harner, 1599
Literary research guide, M. Patterson, 1599n
Literature analysis of microcomputer publications, M. Wasserman, ed., 895
Literature criticism from 1400 to 1800, 1632
Literature of American music in books and folk music collections, D. Horn, 1380
Literature of American music in books and folk music collections, 1983–1993, G. A. Marco, 1380
Literature of American music in books and folk music collections: supplement 1, D. Horn and R. Jackson, 1380
Littman, M. S., ed. Statistical portrait of the United States, 413; *see also* Dodge, R. W.
Litz, A. W. *See* Baechler, L.
Lives of the saints, A. Butler, H. Thurston, and D. Attwater, 226
Livesey, A. Historical atlas of World War I, 1843
Livingstone, E. A., ed. Oxford dictionary of the Christian church, 220
Loftus, G. *See* Savageau, D.
Logan, R. W., and M. R. Winston, eds. Dictionary of American Negro biography, 363
Logasa, H., and W. Ver Nooy, comps. Index to one-act plays for stage, radio and television, 1361
Lomeli, F. A. *See* Martinez, J. A.
Longman dictionary of geography, A. N. Clark, 1863
Lorimer, L. T., and K. A. Ranson, eds. Academic American encyclopedia, p. 24, 148
———, and M. Cummings, eds. Encyclopedia Americana, 155
Los Angeles Times, 118n
Louis L. Snyder's historical guide to World War II, L. L. Snyder, 1818
Louw, B. Atlas of languages, 706
Lovejoy's college guide, 683
Lovell, E. C., and R. M. Hall. Index to handicrafts, modelmaking, and workshop projects, 1447
Low, W. A., and V. A. Clift, eds. Encyclopedia of Black America, 365
Lowe, D. W., et al., eds. Official World Wildlife Fund guide to endangered species of North America, 983
Luce, T. J., ed. Ancient writers, 1745

Ludlow, D. H., ed. Encyclopedia of Mormonism, 217
Lufty, M. *See* Edwards, J.
Luongo, A. M. Soccer handbook for players, coaches, and parents, 1592
Lusis, A. S. Chess: an annotated bibliography, 1969–1988, 1550
Luttwak, E., and S. Koehl. Dictionary of modern war, 562

M. E. Snodgrass. Encyclopedia of utopian literature, 1606
Macchi, V., ed. Collins English-Italian, Italian-English dictionary, 800
Machedlover, H. G. *See* Connor, B. M.
Macho, J., and G. Cable. Everyone's guide to outpatient surgery, 1064
Macmillan Bible atlas, Y. Aharoni, ed., 183
Macmillan book of proverbs, maxims, and famous phrases, B. Stevenson, 1627
Macmillan book of the marine aquarium, N. Dakin, 1217
Macmillan centennial atlas of the world, 1886
Macmillan compendium, 173n
Macmillan dictionary of measurement, M. Darton and J. Clark, 1006
Macmillan encyclopedia of architects, A. K. Placzek, ed., 1277
Macmillan encyclopedia of chemistry, J. J. Lagowski, ed., 885
Macmillan encyclopedia of computers, M. G. Bitter, ed., 899
Macmillan encyclopedia of health, 1042
Macmillan encyclopedia of physics, 1014
Macmillan encyclopedia of world slavery, P. Finkelman and J. C. Miller, 1816
Macmillan guide to correspondence study, 663
Macquarrie, J. *See* Childress, J. F.
Maddox, G. L., ed. Encyclopedia of aging, 334
Magazine index, 125
Magazine index, abridged, 125
Magazines for children, S. K. Richardson, 65
Magazines for libraries, B. A. Katz and L. S. Katz, 66
Magazines for young adults, S. K. Richardson, 67
Maggio, R. Dictionary of bias-free usage, 741
Magill, F. N. Masterpieces of African-American literature, 1647; Masterpieces of Latino literature, 1757; Masterpieces of women's literature, 1658
———, ed. Cyclopedia of literary characters II, 1615; Cyclopedia of world authors, 1640; Magill's literary annual, 1612; Magill's survey of cinema, 1331; Masterpieces of world philosophy, 165; Masterplots, 1613; World philosophy, 167
———, and A. J. Sobczak, eds. Cyclopedia of literary characters, 1614
———, and T. F. Tilghman, eds. Magill's quotations in context, 1621
Magill's American film guide, 1331n
Magill's cinema annual, 1331
Magill's literary annual, F. N. Magill, ed., 1612
Magill's quotations in context, F. N. Magill and T. F. Tilghman, eds., 1621
Magill's quotations in context, second series, F. N. Magill and T. F. Tilghman, eds., 1621
Magill's survey of cinema, F. N. Magill, ed., 1331
Maguire, J. *See* Cowan, T.
Maillard, R., ed. New dictionary of modern sculpture, 1253
Mainiero, L., ed. American women writers, 1652
Maisel, L. S., ed. Political parties and elections in the United States, 618
Major appliances, B. C. Langley, 1188
Major international treaties, J. A. S. Grenville, 609
Major international treaties since 1945, J. A. S. Grenville and B. Wasserstein, 609
Major League Baseball staff. Official rules of major league baseball, 1528
Make it, J. F. Shields, 1447
Make it II, M. E. Heim, 1447
Making life more liveable, E. Lederman, 1116
Makinson, L., and J. F. Goldstein. Open secrets, 639
Makkai, A., ed. Dictionary of American idioms, 740
Makower, J., ed. Map catalog, 1882
Malin, F., and R. Stanzi, eds. Information America, 55
Malinowski, S., ed. Gay and lesbian literature, 1651; Notable Native Americans, 391
———, and A. Sheets, eds. Gale encyclopedia of Native American tribes, 388
Malinowsky, H. R., ed. Reference sources in science, engineering, medicine, and agriculture, 816
———, and G. J. Perry, AIDS information sourcebook, 1078
Maltin, L., ed. Leonard Maltin's movie and video guide, 1337
Man, myth, and magic, R. Cavendish, ed., 316
Mangrum, C. T., and S. S. Strichart, eds. Peterson's colleges with programs for students with learning disabilities, 689
Manheimer, R. J., ed. Older Americans almanac, 335
Mann, L. *See* Reynolds, C. R.
Mannheimer, M. *See* Ehrlich, J.
Mansion, J. E., R. P. L. Ledesert, and M. Ledesert, eds. Harrap's new standard French and English dictionary, 788
Mansukhani, G. S. *See* Dogra, R. C.
Mantle Fielding's dictionary of American painters, sculptors and engravers, G. B. Opitz, ed., 1268
Manual for writers of term papers, theses, and dissertations, K. L. Turabian, 775

Manual of exotic pets, P. H. Benyon and J. E. Cooper, eds., 1223
Map catalog, J. Makower, ed., 1882
Maps for America, M. M. Thompson and U.S. Geological Survey, 1883
March, A. L. Recommended reference books in paperback, 15
March, I., ed. Penguin guide to compact discs and cassettes, 1402
Marchesani, R. F. *See* Anson, J. L.
Marco, G. A. Literature of American music in books and folk music collections, 1983–1993, 1380
Marcuse, M. J. Reference guide for English studies, 1600
Margham, J. P. *See* Hale, W. A.
Margolis, S., ed. Johns Hopkins symptoms and remedies, 1067
Margulis, A., and K. V. Schwartz. Five kingdoms, 980
Mariani, J. F. Dictionary of American food and drink, 1142
Markel, R., S. Waggonere, and M. Smith, eds. Women's sports encyclopedia, 1498
Marketing information, H. C. Barksdale, ed., 530
Markus, J., and N. Sclater. McGraw-Hill electronics dictionary, 949
Marley, D. F. Pirates and privateers of the Americas, 1851
Marriage, family, and relationships, G. J. Broude, 437
Marsh, E. *See* Brooks, T.
Marsh, J. H., ed. Canadian encyclopedia, 1857
Marshall Cavendish encyclopedia of family health, 1042
Marti, J. Alternative health and medicine encyclopedia, 1081
Martin, E., M. Ruse, and E. Holmes, eds. Dictionary of biology, 976
Martin, J. Miss Manners' guide for the turn of the millennium, 1159; Miss Manners' guide to excruciatingly correct behavior, 1159; Miss Manners rescues civilization, 1159
Martin, M., and M. Porter. Video movie guide, 1337
Martin, R., ed. Contemporary fashion, 1283
Martindale-Hubbell law directory, 599
Martinez, J. A., and F. A. Lomeli, eds. Chicano literature, 1724
Martinez, J. G. R. *See* Martinez, N.
Martinez, N., and J. G. R. Martinez. Guide to British poetry explication, 1709
Martis, K. C. Historical atlas of political parties in the United States Congress, 637; Historical atlas of United States congressional districts, 632
Mary Ellen's clean house, M. E. Pinkham, 1174
Mason, F. *See* Balanchine, G.
Massey, H. C. Basic plumbing with illustrations, 1178
Mast, J., ed. Business organizations, agencies, and publications directory, 459
Master handbook of electronic tables and formulas, M. Clifford, 948
Masterpieces of African-American literature, F. N. Magill, 1647
Masterpieces of Latino literature, F. N. Magill, 1757
Masterpieces of women's literature, F. N. Magill, 1658
Masterpieces of world philosophy, F. N. Magill, ed., 165
Masterplots, F. N. Magill, ed., 1613
Masuda, K., ed. Kenkyusha's new Japanese-English dictionary, 801
Mathematical Society of Japan staff and K. Ito, eds. Encyclopedic dictionary of mathematics, 1003
Mathematics dictionary, R. C. James et al., eds., 1007
Mathematics illustrated dictionary, J. Bendick, 1008
Matt, D. C. Essential Kabbalah, 235
Matthews, J. L., and D. M. Berman. Social security, medicare and pensions, 337
Mattison, C. Encyclopedia of snakes, 991; Practical guide to exotic pets, 1226
Mattson, M. T. Atlas of the 1990 census, 403
Maunder, W. J., comp. Dictionary of global climate change, 919
Mawson, C. O. S. Dictionary of foreign terms, 736n
———, and E. Ehrlich. Harper dictionary of foreign terms, 736
Maxwell-Hyslop, A. R. *See* Grimal, P.
Mayer, R. Artist's handbook of materials and techniques, 1250n, 1265
———, and S. Sheehan. HarperCollins dictionary of art terms and techniques, 1250
Mayo Clinic book of pregnancy and baby's first year, 1117
Mayo Clinic family health book, D. E. Larson, ed. in chief, 1068
Mays, J. L., ed. Harper's Bible commentary, 184
McAllister, R. M., et al. Cancer, 1094
McArthur, T., ed. Oxford companion to the English language, 714
McCloud, B. Definitive country, 1438
McColm, I. J. Dictionary of ceramic science and engineering, 954
McDaniel, G., comp. IBM dictionary of computing, 898
McEvedy, C. Atlas of African history, 1837
McFadden, L. *See* Weissman, P.
McGillvray, A. V., and R. M. Scammon, eds. America at the polls, 614
McGinnis, T. Well cat book, 1204
McGrath, A., ed. Blackwell encyclopedia of modern Christian thought, 213
McGraw-Hill dictionary of scientific and technical terms, S. P. Parker, ed., 824

McGraw-Hill electronics dictionary, J. Markus and N. Sclater, 949
McGraw-Hill encyclopedia of economics, D. Greenwald, ed., 454
McGraw-Hill encyclopedia of personal computing, S. Gibilisco, ed., 900
McGraw-Hill encyclopedia of science and technology, 825
McGraw-Hill encyclopedia of world biography, 1921
McGraw-Hill encyclopedia of world drama, S. Hochman, ed., 1680
McGraw-Hill handbook of business letters, R. W. Poe, 493
McGraw-Hill handbook of more business letters, A. Poe, 493
McGraw-Hill real estate handbook, R. Irwin, ed., 538
McGraw-Hill recycling handbook, 969
McHenry, R., ed. New encyclopaedia britannica, 156
McLean, J., ed. Consultants and consulting organizations directory, 462
McManners, H. Backpacker's handbook, 1515; Complete wilderness training book, 1597
McMullin, T. A., and D. Walker. Biographical directory of American territorial governors, 602n
McNeil, M. Earth sciences reference, 913
McNeill, D. B. *See* Jerrard, H. G.
McPherson, J., ed. Atlas of the Civil War, 1841
Mead, F. S. Handbook of denominations in the United States, 207
Means illustrated construction dictionary, R. S. Means, 1164
Means, R. S. Means illustrated construction dictionary, 1164
Media review digest, 131, 1323n
Medical and health information directory, K. Backus, ed., 1056
Medical school admission requirements, 684
Medical tests and diagnostic procedures, P. Shtasel, 1069
Meier, M. S., and F. Rivera. Dictionary of Mexican American history, 379
Meisami, J. S., and P. Starkey, eds. Encyclopedia of Arabic literature, 1730
Mellman, M. *See* Carmichael, D. R.
Mellone, M. A. U.S. first day cover catalogue and checklist, 1492
Melloni, B. J., et al., eds. Melloni's illustrated medical dictionary, 1043
Melloni's illustrated medical dictionary, B. J. Melloni et al., eds., 1043
Melton, J. G. Biographical dictionary of American cult and sect leaders, 210; Directory of religious bodies in the United States, 208n; Encyclopedia of American religions, 201; Encyclopedic handbook of cults in America, 204; Religious bodies in the United States, 208
———, et al. New age encyclopedia, 257
———, and M. A. Koszegi. Religious information sources, 170
Meltzer, E., and M. Aronson. Day by day: the eighties, 1779
Melzer, A. H. *See* Rothwell, K. S.
Menopause and midlife health, M. Notelovitz and D. Tonnesson, 1120
Mental measurements yearbook, 304, 307n
Mercatante, A. S. Facts on File encyclopedia of world mythology and legend, 273
Mercer dictionary of the Bible, W. E. Mills et al., eds., 193
Merck index, S. Budavari et al., eds., 890
Merck manual of diagnosis and therapy, R. Berkow, ed., 1070
Merck veterinary manual, 995
Merideth, R. Environmentalist's bookshelf, 966
Merkel, R. S. *See* Tortora, P. G.
Merriam-Webster's biographical dictionary, 1922
Merriam-Webster's collegiate dictionary, 719
Merriam-Webster's collegiate thesaurus, 762
Merriam-Webster's dictionary of synonyms, 763
Merritt, J. Day by day: the fifties, 1779
Meserole, H. T., comp. MLA international bibliography of books and articles on modern language and literature, 1602
Messinger, H., and the Langenscheidt editorial staff. Langenscheidt's condensed Muret-Sanders German dictionary, 793n; *see also* Brough, S.
Messonnier, S. Exotic pets, 1224
Metaphors dictionary, E. Sommer and D. Weiss, eds., 752
Metraux, A. Voodoo in Haiti, 261
Metzger, B. M., and M. D. Coogans, eds. Oxford companion to the Bible, 196
Meyer, F. S. Handbook of ornament, 1296
Meyer's directory of genealogical societies in the USA and Canada, 1944
Meyers, R. A., ed. Encyclopedia of astronomy and astrophysics, 872
———, and S. N. Shore, eds. Encyclopedia of modern physics, 1011
Micarelli, C. Micarelli identification guide to U.S. stamps, 1488
Micarelli identification guide to U.S. stamps, C. Micarelli, 1488
Micro handbook for small libraries and media centers, B. Costa and M. Costa, 12
Microcomputer index, 906
Microsoft Press computer dictionary, 901
Middle Ages, 1808n
Middle and junior high school library catalog, 43

Middleton, J., ed. Encyclopedia of Africa south of the Sahara, 1797
Mieder, W., ed. Dictionary of American proverbs, 1626
Milestones in science and technology, E. Mount and B. A. List, 847
Military balance, International Institute for Strategic Studies, 586
Military service records, National Archives and Records Administration, 1933n
Miller, B. M. *See* Doris, L.
Miller, E. Willard, and R. M. Miller. Energy and American society, 928
Miller, Elizabeth W. Negro in America, 368
Miller, J. C. *See* Finkelman, P.
Miller, R. M. *See* Miller, E. Willard
Miller, T. L. *See* Wilmeth, D. B.
Miller, W. G. *See* Ash, L.
Million dollar directory, 473
Mills, W. E., et al., eds. Mercer dictionary of the Bible, 193
Milner-Gulland, R., and N. Dejevsky. Cultural atlas of Russia and the Soviet Union, 1894
Miner, E., H. Odagiri, and R. E. Morrell. Princeton companion to classical Japanese literature, 1769
Mini-atlas of dog breeds, A. de Prisco, 1208
Minor, R. S., and C. W. Fetridge, eds. Dartnell office administration handbook, 526
Minority organizations, E. H. Oakes, ed., 355
Minority Rights Group. World directory of minorities, 438
Mishler, C., C. Bruce, and C. L. Krause. Standard directory of world coins, 1485
———. *See also* Krause, C. L.
Miss Manners' guide for the turn of the millennium, J. Martin, 1159
Miss Manners' guide to excruciatingly correct behavior, J. Martin, 1159
Miss Manners rescues civilization, J. Martin, 1159
Mitchell, C. Speech index, supplement, 1717
MLA handbook for writers of research papers, J. Gibaldi, 776
MLA international bibliography of books and articles on modern language and literature, H. T. Meserole, comp., 1602
Mobil travel guide: major cities, 1905
Mobil travel guides, 1906
Modern American women writers, L. Baechler and A. W. Litz, 1659
Modern geography, G. S. Dunbar, 1864
Modern Irish writers, A. G. Gonzalez, ed., 1766
Modern proverbs and proverbial sayings, B. J. Whiting, comp., 1628
Modern reader's Japanese-English character dictionary, A. N. Nelson, 803
Moll, L. *See* Editors of Vegetarian Times
Monro, I. S., and K. M. Monro. Index to reproductions of American paintings, 1238; Index to reproductions of European paintings, 1239
———. *See also* Cook, D. E.
Monro, K. M. *See* Monro, I. S.
Montague, P., and J. H. Lang. Larousse gastronomique, 1143
Monthly catalog of United States government publications, 138
Montney, C. B., ed. Asian Americans information directory, 376; Hispanic Americans information directory, 382
Moody, M. K. *See* Sears, J. L.
Moody's bank and finance manual, 519
Moody's handbook of common stocks, 518
Moody's industrial manual, 519
Moody's international manual, 519
Moody's manuals, 519
Moody's municipal and government manual, 519
Moody's OTC [over-the-counter] industrial manual, 519
Moody's OTC unlisted manual, 519
Moody's public utilities manual, 519
Moody's transportation manual, 519
Moore, D. D. *See* Hyman, P. E.
Moore, P. Patrick Moore's A-Z of astronomy, 878
Mordecai, S., ed. Cornell book of cats, 1204
Morehead, A. H. New complete Hoyle, 1549
Morehead, J., and M. Fetzer. Introduction to United States government information sources, 138
Morningstar mutual funds, 520
Morrell, R. E. *See* Miner, E.
Morris, C., ed. Academic Press dictionary of science and technology, 819
Morris, Charles. *See* Cooper, R.
Morris dictionary of word and phrase origins, W. Morris and M. Morris, 733
Morris, J. B. *See* Morris, R. B.
Morris, M. *See* Morris, W.
Morris, R. B., and J. B. Morris, eds. Encyclopedia of American history, 1800
Morris, W., and M. Morris. Morris dictionary of word and phrase origins, 733
Morton, B., ed. Contemporary composers, 1409
Mosby staff. Mosby's medical, nursing, and allied health dictionary, 1044
Mosby's medical, nursing, and allied health dictionary, Mosby staff, 1044
Moss, M. Photography books index, 1306
Mossman, J., ed. Pseudonyms and nicknames dictionary, 1969
Mostyn, T., and A. Hourani, eds. Cambridge encyclopedia of the Middle East and North Africa, 1855
Mote, D., ed. Contemporary popular writers, 1639

Mothers of invention, E. A. Vare and G. Ptacek, 848
Motion picture guide, J. R. Nash and S. R. Ross, 1332
Motion picture guide annual, E. Grant and K. Fox, eds., 1332
Motor auto repair manual, [yr.], 1023
Motor light truck and van repair manual, 1024
Mount, E., and B. A. List. Milestones in science and technology, 847
Mount Sinai Medical Center family health guide to dental health, J. Klatell et al., 1071
Mount Sinai School of Medicine complete book of nutrition, V. Herbert et al., 1110
Mountaineering, the freedom of the hills, D. Graydon and Mountaineers Books staff, eds., 1583
Mountaineers Books staff. *See* Graydon, D.
Mr. Boston, R. Cooper and Charles Morris, 1125
Muhr, J. *See* Travers, B.
Muir, H., ed. Larousse dictionary of scientists, 839
Muirden, J. Amateur astronomer's hand-book, 868
Mullaney, M. M. Biographical directory of the governors of the United States, 1983–1988, 602; Biographical directory of the governors of the United States, 1988–1994, 602
Mullay, M. *See* Walford, A. J.
Multicultural dictionary of proverbs, H. V. Cordy, 1629
Municipal year book, 587
Munson, R. S. Favorite hobbies and pastimes, 1451
Murdock, G. P. Atlas of world cultures, 428n
Muret, E., D. Sanders, and O. Springer. Langenscheidt's new Muret-Sanders encyclopedic dictionary of the English and German languages, 793
Murphy, B., ed. Benét's reader's encyclopedia, 1603
Murphy, L. G., ed. Encyclopedia of African American religions, 200
Murphy, L. L., et al., eds. Tests in print, 307
Murray, C. *See* Case, B.
Murray, J. Cultural atlas of Africa, 1894
Murray, M., and J. Pizzorno. Encyclopedia of natural medicine, 1084
Museum of American Folk Art encyclopedia of twentieth-century folk art and artists, C. Rosenak and J. Rosenak, 1252
Museums of the world, 1262
Musgrove, J. *See* Fletcher, B. F.
Music: an illustrated encyclopedia, N. Ardley, 1386
Music index, H. Park, 1383
Music reference and research materials, V. H. Duckles and I. Reed, eds., 1381
Music since 1900, N. Slonimsky, 1387
Musical America, 1310
Musical instruments of the world, Diagram Group, 1388
Musicians since 1900, D. Ewen, comp. and ed., 1410
Muslim almanac, A. A. Nanji, ed., 256
Muslim peoples, R. V. Weekes, ed., 1865
Mutual fund sourcebook, 520n
Myrvang, J. C., and S. Myrvang. Home design handbook, 1162
Myrvang, S. *See* Myrvang, J. C.
Mystery and suspense writers, R. W. Winks and M. Corrigan, eds., 1689
Mythical and fabulous creatures, M. South, ed., 278

NADA official used car guide, 1017
Naden, C. J. *See* Gillespie, J. T.
Nanji, A. A., ed. Muslim almanac, 256
Nash, J. R., and S. R. Ross. Motion picture guide, 1332
National anthems of the world, W. L. Reed and M. J. Bristow, eds., 1389
National Arboretum book of outstanding garden plants, J. Heriteau, 865
National Archives and Records Administration. American Indians, 1933n; Black studies, 1933n; Genealogical and biographical research, 1933n; Genealogical microfilm catalogs, 1933; Immigrant and passenger arrivals, 1933n; Military service records, 1933n; National Archives microfilm resources for research, 1933n
National Archives microfilm resources for research, National Archives and Records Administration, 1933n
National atlas of Canada, 1893n, 1895
National atlas of the United States, U.S. Geological Survey, 1898
National directory of addresses and telephone numbers, 78
National directory of children, youth, and families services, P. Spencer, 346
National directory of chiropractic, 1057
National directory of drug abuse and alcoholism treatment and prevention programs, U.S. Department of Health and Human Services, 342
National electrical code, 950
National electrical safety code handbook, 951
National faculty directory, 664
National fax directory, 79
National five digit zip code and post office directory, 80
National Geographic atlas of the world, 1887
National Hockey League official guide and record book, NHL staff, 1572
National Information Center for Educational Media. Audiocassette and compact disc finder, 643; Film and video finder, 643

National jail and adult detention directory, 348n
National newspaper index, 118
National party platforms, D. B. Johnson, comp., 617
National Register staff. Corporate finance sourcebook, 486; Official Catholic directory, 223
National Safety Council staff, comp. Accident facts, Statistics Department, 1059
National trade and professional associations of the United States, 474
Native America in the twentieth century, M. B. Davis, ed., 389, 1819
Native American genealogical sourcebook, 1944
Native American women, G. M. Bataille, ed., 390
Natividad, I. *See* Gall, S.
Nautical almanac and astronomical ephemeris, 869n
NBC handbook of pronunciation, E. Ehrlich and R. Hand Jr., eds., 743
NCAA football, NCAA staff, 1557
NCAA staff. NCAA football, 1557; Official rules of basketball (NCAA), 1538
Neagles, J. Library of Congress: a guide to genealogical and historical research, 1949
Necomb, H., ed. Encyclopedia of television, 1347
Neft, D. S., et al. Football encyclopedia, 1556
———, R. M. Cohen, and R. Korch. Sports encyclopedia: pro football, 1561
Negro in America, Elizabeth W. Miller, 368
Negro leagues book, D. Clark, 1526
Nelson, A. N. Modern reader's Japanese-English character dictionary, 803
Nelson, D., and T. Parker. Day by day: the sixties, 1779
Nelson, M., ed. Congressional Quarterly's guide to the presidency, 621
Nemic, D. Rules of baseball, 1529
Netter, F. H., and A. F. Dalley, eds. Atlas of human anatomy, 1087
Nettl, B., and R. Stone, eds. Garland encyclopedia of world music, 1385
New A to Z of women's health, C. Ammer, 1121
New age encyclopedia, J. G. Melton et al., 257
New atlas of the universe, P. Moore, 876
New book of popular science, 826
New Cambridge modern history, 1820
New Catholic encyclopedia, 218
New century cyclopedia of names, p. 303
New choices in natural healing, B. Gottlieb et al., eds., 1086
New Columbia encyclopedia, 152n
New complete Hoyle, A. H. Morehead, 1549
New comprehensive American rhyming dictionary, S. Young, 746
New consultants, 462n
New dictionary of modern sculpture, R. Maillard, ed., 1253
New encyclopaedia britannica, R. McHenry, ed., 156
New encyclopedia of the American West, H. R. Lamar, ed., 1821
New English-Chinese dictionary, 782
New English-Chinese dictionary, 2d rev. ed., Z. Y. Li et al., eds., 783
New Fowler's modern English usage, R. W. Burchfield, ed., 742
New Grove dictionary of American music, H. W. Hitchcock and S. Sadie, eds., 1390
New Grove dictionary of jazz, B. Kernfeld, ed., 1443
New Grove dictionary of music and musicians, S. Sadie, ed., 1391, 1392n, 1405n, 1411n
New Grove dictionary of musical instruments, S. Sadie, ed., 1392
New Grove dictionary of opera, S. Sadie, ed., 1405
New Harvard dictionary of music, D. M. Randel, ed., 1393
New IEEE standard dictionary of electrical and electronics terms, G. P. Kurpis and C. J. Booth, eds., 952
New international atlas, 1888
New interpreter's Bible, 186
New Jerome biblical commentary, R. E. Brown et al., eds., 187
New Laurel's kitchen, L. Robertson, C. Finders, and B. Ruppenthal, 1140
New Oxford companion to literature in French, P. France, ed., 1763
New Oxford companion to music, D. Arnold, ed., 1388n, 1394
New Palgrave, J. Eatwell et al., eds., 455
New Palgrave dictionary of economics and the law, P. Newman, ed., 455n
New Princeton encyclopedia of poetry and poetics, 1712
New products from the U.S. government, U.S. Superintendent of Documents, 139
New pseudonyms and nicknames, 1969
New quotable woman, E. Partnow, ed., 1622
New Rolling Stone encyclopedia of rock and roll, P. Romanowski and H. George-Warren, eds., 1445
New Royal Horticultural Society dictionary of gardening, A. Huxley et al., 866
New rules for classic games, R. W. Schmittberger, 1579
New shorter Oxford English dictionary, L. Brown, ed., 720
New Sotheby's wine encyclopedia, T. Stevenson, 1129
New standard Jewish encyclopedia, G. Wigoder, ed., 243
New Strong's exhaustive concordance of the Bible, 188
New Testament abstracts, 180
New Westminster dictionary of liturgy and worship, J. G. Davies, ed., 219

New world Spanish/English, English/Spanish dictionary, S. Ramondino, ed., 811
New York Public Library writer's guide to style and usage, 777
New York Road Runners Club complete book of running and fitness, 1587
New York Times, 118n, 119n, 449n, 1309n
New York Times crossword puzzle dictionary, T. Pulliam and C. Grundman, 728
New York Times film reviews, 1333
New York Times index, 119
New York Times obituary index, 1914
New York Times theater reviews, 1372
Newbery and Caldecott awards, 1674
Newbery and Caldecott medal and honor books, L. K. Peterson and M. L. Solt, 1675
Newbery and Caldecott medalists and honor book winners, M. Brown and R. S. Foudray, comps., 1676
Newby, J. E. Black authors, 1645
Newman, H. Illustrated dictionary of jewelry, 1297; *see also* Savage, G.
Newman, P., ed. New Palgrave dictionary of economics and the law, 455n
Newspaper abstracts ondisc, 120
Newspaper rates and data, 480
NFL staff. Official [yr.] National Football League record and fact book, 1558; Official rules of the NFL, 1559
Ng, F., ed. Asian American encyclopedia, 375
NHL staff. National Hockey League official guide and record book, 1572; Official rules of the National Hockey League, 1573
Nicholls, P. *See* Clute, J.
Nicknames and sobriquets of U.S. cities, states, and counties, J. Kane and G. L. Alexander, 1866
Nienhauser, W. H., Jr., ed. Indiana companion to traditional Chinese literature, 1761
Niiya, B., ed. Japanese American history, 1831
Nineteenth-century literature criticism, 1633
Nineteenth century readers' guide to periodical literature, 126n
NIOSH pocket guide to chemical hazards, 891
Nobel laureates in chemistry, L. K. James, ed., 892
Nolan, J. R., and M. J. Connolly. Black's law dictionary, 561
Nolan, K., ed. Gale directory of databases, 905
Nordquist, J., ed. Left index, 124
North American Indian landmarks, G. Cantor, 1907
North American industry classification system (NAICS), Office of Management and Budget Staff, 494
Norton/Grove dictionary of women composers, J. A. Sadie and R. Samuel, eds., 1411
Norton, M. B., ed. Guide to historical literature, 1772
Norton's 2000.0: star atlas and reference handbook, I. Ridpath, ed., 877
Notable American women, 1924
Notable Americans, 1925
Notable Asian Americans, H. Zia and S. B. Gall, eds., 378
Notable Black American men, J. C. Smith, ed., 369
Notable Black American women, J. C. Smith, ed., 370
Notable Black American women, book II, J. C. Smith, ed., 370
Notable Hispanic American women, D. Telgen and J. Kamp, eds., 383
Notable Native Americans, S. Malinowski, ed., 391
Notelovitz, M., and D. Tonnesson. Menopause and midlife health, 1120
NTC's dictionary of advertising, J. C. Wiechmann, ed., 531
NTC's mass media dictionary, R. T. Ellmore, 1351
Nuclear power plants worldwide, P. Dresser, 930

OAG business travel planner, 1908
OAG desktop flight guide, 1909
Oakes, E. H., ed. Minority organizations, 355
———, and J. Bradford, eds. Resources for people with disabilities, 1112
O'Brien, G. Reader's catalog, 14
O'Brien, J. W., and S. R. Wasserman, eds. Statistics sources, 415
O'Brien, N. P., and E. Fabiano. Core list of books and journals in education, 641
Obst, F. J. Completely illustrated atlas of reptiles and amphibians for the terrarium, 1221
Occult in the western world, C. Kies, 317
Occupational outlook handbook, U.S. Bureau of Labor Statistics, 553
Occupational outlook quarterly, 553n
Odagiri, H. *See* Miner, E.
O'Farlow, J., and M. K. Brett-Surman, eds. Complete dinosaur, 985
Office of Information Resources Management, U.S. Environmental Protection Agency. Access EPA, 956
Office of Management and Budget Staff. North American industry classification system (NAICS), 494
Office of the Federal Register, National Archives and Records Administration. Code of federal regulations, 607; Federal register, 607n
Office of the Law Revision Counsel of the House of Representatives. United States Code, containing the general and permanent laws of the U.S., 613
Official ABMS directory of board certified medical specialists, 1058
Official airline guide, 1909

Official airline guide travel planner and hotel/motel redbook, 1908
Official baseball register, Sporting News staff, 1527
Official blackbook price guide to U.S. coins, M. Hudgeons, 1485
Official Catholic directory, National Register staff, 223
Official congressional directory, U.S. Congress, 631n, 638
Official GRE/CGS directory of graduate programs, 685
Official guide to U.S. law schools, 686
Official museum directory, 1263
Official NBA basketball encyclopedia, A. Sachane, ed., 1536
Official NBA rules, C. Carter, ed., 1537
Official 1998 blackbook price guide of U.S. paper money, M. Hudgeons, 1484
Official 1998 blackbook price guide of U.S. postage stamps, M. Hudgeons, 1489
Official [yr.] National Football League record and fact book, 1558
Official price guide to antiques and collectibles, 1479
Official railway guide, 1910
Official rules of basketball (NCAA), NCAA staff, 1538
Official rules of golf, USGA staff and Ancient Golf Club of St. Andrews, 1568
Official rules of major league baseball, Major League Baseball staff, 1528
Official rules of soccer, Federation Internationale de Football Association staff, 1590
Official rules of the National Hockey League, NHL staff, 1573
Official rules of the NFL, NFL staff, 1559
Official World Wildlife Fund guide to endangered species of North America, D. W. Lowe et al., eds., 983
Ogden, T. Two hundred years of the American circus, 1376
Ogilvie, M. B. Women in science, 841
O'Hara, F. J. Guide to publications of the executive branch, 134
———, ed. Informing the nation, 136
O'Hara, F. M., Jr., and R. Sicignano. Handbook of United States economic and financial indicators, 490
Ohles, J. F., and S. M. Ohles. Private colleges and universities, 697; Public colleges and universities, 697
———, ed. Biographical dictionary of American educators, 702
Old Testament abstracts, 180
Older Americans almanac, R. J. Manheimer, ed., 335
Olitzky, K. M. American synagogue, 230
Oliver, R., and M. Crowder, eds. Cambridge encyclopedia of Africa, 1855
Olsen, K. Chronology of women's history, 418
Olson, A. *See* Seager, J.
Olson, K. C. *See* Cohen, M. L.
One hundred one stories of the great ballets, G. Balanchine and F. Mason, 1322
O'Neal, B. Encyclopedia of western gunfighters, 1849
O'Neill, L. D. Women's book of world records and achievements, 425
Onions, C. T. Shakespeare glossary, 1741
———, et al., eds. Oxford dictionary of English etymology, 734
Open secrets, L. Makinson and J. F. Goldstein, 639
Opie, I., and M. Tatem. Dictionary of superstitions, 268
Opie, I. A., and P. Opie, eds. Oxford dictionary of nursery rhymes, 1667
Opie, P. *See* Opie, I. A.
Opitz, G. B., ed. Mantle Fielding's dictionary of American painters, sculptors and engravers, 1268
Original martial arts encyclopedia, J. Corcoran and E. Farkas. S. Sobel, ed., 1575
Ornstein, N. J., et al. Vital statistics on Congress, 640
Orrmont, A., and L. Rosentiel, eds. Literary agents of North America, 77
Ortho's basic home building, J. Fox and R. Hildebrand, 1165
Ortho's home improvement encyclopedia, A. Ahlstrand, ed., 1169
Ortiz, E. L. Encyclopedia of herbs, spices, and flavorings, 1133
Osborne, H., ed. Oxford companion to art, 1254; Oxford companion to the decorative arts, 1298; Oxford companion to twentieth-century art, 1255; *see also* Chilvers, I.
Osmanczyk, E. J. Encyclopedia of the United Nations and international agreements, 572
Ottemiller's index to plays in collections, B. M. Connor and H. G. Machedlover, 1364
Our bodies, ourselves for the new century, Boston Women's Health Collective, 1122
Ousby, I., ed. Cambridge guide to literature in English, 1598
Out-of-print GPO sales publications reference file, 53
Outlook, 518n
Over-the-counter and regional exchange reports, 522
Oxford classical dictionary, S. Hornblower and A. Spawforth, eds., 1752
Oxford companion to African American literature, W. L. Andrews, F. S. Foster, and T. Harris, eds., 1648

Oxford companion to American history, T. H. Johnson, ed., 1822
Oxford companion to American literature, J. D. Hart and P. Leininger, 1727
Oxford companion to American theatre, G. Bordman, 1373
Oxford companion to art, H. Osborne, ed., 1254
Oxford companion to Australian literature, W. H. Wilde et al., 1759
Oxford companion to Canadian history and literature, 1760n
Oxford companion to Canadian literature, W. Toye, ed., 1760
Oxford companion to chess, D. Hooper and K. Whyld, 1551
Oxford companion to children's literature, H. Carpenter and M. Prichard, 1666
Oxford companion to classical literature, M. C. Howatson, ed., 1753
Oxford companion to English literature, M. Drabble, ed., 1734
Oxford companion to German literature, M. Garland and H. Garland, 1764
Oxford companion to Irish literature, R. Welch and B. Stewart, 1767
Oxford companion to medicine, J. Walton et al., eds., 1045
Oxford companion to music, P. A. Scholes, 1394n
Oxford companion to musical instruments, A. Baines, 1388n
Oxford companion to popular music, P. Gammond, 1418
Oxford companion to Spanish literature, P. Ward, ed., 1771
Oxford companion to the Bible, B. M. Metzger and M. D. Coogans, eds., 196
Oxford companion to the decorative arts, H. Osborne, ed., 1298
Oxford companion to the English language, T. McArthur, ed., 714
Oxford companion to the mind, R. L. Gregory and O. L. Zangwill, 303
Oxford companion to the politics of the world, J. Krieger et al., 588
Oxford companion to the Supreme Court of the United States, K. L. Hall, ed., 629
Oxford companion to the theatre, P. Hartnoll, ed., 1370n, 1374
Oxford companion to twentieth-century art, H. Osborne, ed., 1255
Oxford companion to wine, J. Robinson, ed., 1130
Oxford dictionary of art, I. Chilvers and H. Osborne, eds., 1256
Oxford dictionary of English etymology, C. T. Onions et al., eds., 734
Oxford dictionary of English proverbs, F. P. Wilson, ed., 1630
Oxford dictionary of foreign words and phrases, J. Speake, 737
Oxford dictionary of modern Greek, J. T. Pring, ed., 797
Oxford dictionary of modern quotations, T. Augarde, ed., 1623
Oxford dictionary of nursery rhymes, I. A. Opie and P. Opie, eds., 1667
Oxford dictionary of opera, J. Warrack and E. West, 1406
Oxford dictionary of popes, J. N. D. Kelly, 227
Oxford dictionary of quotations, A. Partington, ed., 1624
Oxford dictionary of saints, D. H. Farmer, ed., 228
Oxford dictionary of sports science and medicine, M. Kent, ed., 1046
Oxford dictionary of the Christian church, E. A. Livingstone, ed., 220
Oxford dictionary of the Jewish religion, R. J. Z. Werblowsky and G. Wigoder, 244
Oxford dictionary of world religions, J. Bowker, ed., 175
Oxford-Duden German dictionary, W. Scholze-Stubenrecht and J. B. Sykes, eds., 794
Oxford encyclopedia of the modern Islamic world, J. L. Esposito, ed., 1865
Oxford English dictionary, J. A. Simpson and E. S. C. Weiner, 715, 720n, 734n
Oxford English dictionary additions series, J. Simpson and E. Weiner, eds., 715
Oxford-Hachette French dictionary, M. Correard and V. Grundy, eds., 789
Oxford-Harrap standard German-English dictionary, T. Jones, ed., 795
Oxford illustrated encyclopedia of invention and technology, M. Finniston, ed., 849
Oxford Latin dictionary, P. G. W. Glare, ed., 805
Oxford Russian dictionary, M. Wheeler et al., eds., 807
Oxford Spanish dictionary, B. Jarman and R. Russell, eds., 812
Oxford thesaurus, L. Urdang, 764

Packard, R. T., and B. Korab. Encyclopedia of American architecture, 1273
Padroli, H., and M. Tiegreen, eds. American golfer's guide, 1563
Pagell, R. A., and M. Halperin. International business information, 446
PAIS bulletin, 559n
PAIS foreign language, 559n
PAIS international, 559
Pakan, W. A. *See* Stevenson, G. A.

Palder, E. L. Catalog of catalogs, 1151
Pallay, S. G., comp. Cross index title guide to classical music, 1403; Cross index title guide to opera and operetta, 1403
Palmer, E. C. *See* Trefny, B. R.
Palmer, H. H., comp. European drama criticism, 1679
———, and A. J. Dyson, comps. English novel explication: criticisms to 1972, 1732
Palmer, P. *See* Thorn, J.
Panati, C. Panati's extraordinary origins, 109
Panati's extraordinary origins, C. Panati, 109
Pare, M. A. Sports stars, 1511
Parent's choice, D. H. Green, 1195
Parents' resource almanac, B. DeFrancis, 1196
Park, A. L., ed. Small business sourcebook, 447
Park, H. Music index, 1383
Parker, S. P., ed. McGraw-Hill dictionary of scientific and technical terms, 824
Parker, T. *See* Nelson, D.
Parkinson, C. L. Breakthroughs, 843
Parlatt, D. Dictionary of card games, 1547
Parrinder, G., ed. World religions from ancient history to the present, 179
Parry, P. J., comp. Contemporary art and artists, 1234; Photography index: a guide to reproductions, 1307
Partington, A., ed. Oxford dictionary of quotations, 1624
Partnow, E., ed. New quotable woman, 1622
Partridge, E. Concise dictionary of slang and unconventional English, 756n; Dictionary of clichés, 751n; Dictionary of slang and unconventional English, 756
Passenger and immigration lists bibliography, 1937
Passenger and immigration lists index, P. W. Filby, ed., 1938
Past worlds, 429
Patrick Moore's A-Z of astronomy, P. Moore, 878
Patterson, M. Literary research guide, 1599n
Patterson's American education, 687
Patterson's elementary education, 687
Paul, E., ed. Adoption directory, 343
Paul, T. O. *See* Sardegna, J.
Paxton, J., ed. Historical tables, 1830
Payne, B., et al. History of costume, 1287
Payne, W. J., ed. Directory of African American religious bodies, 205
PDR generics, 1105
Pearce, E. A., and C. G. Smith. Times Books world weather guide, 921
Pendergast, S., ed. Contemporary designers, 1292
Penguin dictionary of decorative arts, J. Fleming and H. Honour, 1299
Penguin dictionary of musical performers, 1412
Penguin dictionary of psychology, A. S. Reber, 298
Penguin dictionary of saints, D. Attwater, 226n
Penguin encyclopedia of popular music, D. Clarke, ed., 1419
Penguin guide to compact discs and cassettes, I. March, ed., 1402
Penguin guide to compact discs yearbook, 1402n
People's chronology, J. Trager, ed., 1780
People's guide to deadly drug interactions, J. Graedon and T. Graedon, 1104
People's Medical Society health desk reference, C. B. Inlander and the People's Medical Society staff, 1072
People's Medical Society staff. *See* Inlander, C. B.
Pequeño Larousse ilustrado, 808n
Perennnial dictionary of world religions, K. Crim et al., eds., 176
Performing arts, L. K. Simons, 1308
Periodical source index, 1941n
Periodical title abbreviations, 97
Periodicals for school media programs, S. K. Richardson, 67n
Perkins, A. R. *See* Helbig, A. K.
Perkins, B. *See* G. Perkins
Perkins, G., B. Perkins, and P. Leininger. Benét's reader's encyclopedia of American literature, 1723
Perry, G. J. *See* Malinowsky, H. R.
Pesticide manual, C. Tomlin, ed., 857
Peter, I. *See* Fyffe, A.
Peterson, B. L., Jr. Contemporary Black American playwrights and their plays, 1646
Peterson, C. S., and A. D. Fenton. Reference books for children, 17
———, ———, comps. Index to children's songs, 1426
Peterson, L. K., and M. L. Solt. Newbery and Caldecott medal and honor books, 1675
Peterson's annual guides to graduate study, 688
Peterson's colleges with programs for students with learning disabilities, C. T. Mangrum and S. S. Strichart, eds., 689
Peterson's guide to four-year colleges, 690
Peterson's guide to graduate and professional programs, an overview, 688
Peterson's guide to graduate programs in business, education, health, and law, 688
Peterson's guide to graduate programs in engineering and applied sciences, 688
Peterson's guide to graduate programs in the biological, agricultural and health sciences, 688
Peterson's guide to graduate programs in the humanities and social sciences, 688
Peterson's guide to graduate programs in the physical sciences and mathematics, 688
Peterson's guide to private secondary schools, 691

Peterson's guide to two-year colleges, 690
Peterson's internships, 554, 665
Peterson's register of higher education, 692
Peterson's study abroad, 666
Peterson's vocational and technical schools and programs, 693
Pettijohn, T., ed. Encyclopedic dictionary of psychology, 296
PGA manual of golf, PGA staff and G. Wiren, 1569
PGA staff and G. Wiren. PGA manual of golf, 1569
Philbin, T. *See* Consumer Reports editors
Phillips, C., and A. Axelrod, eds. Encyclopedia of the American West, 1805
———. *See also* Axelrod, A.
Phillips, D. J. Tennis sourcebook, 1596
Philosopher's index, 159
Philosophy, H. E. Bynagle, 158
Phonefiche, 81
Photographer's market, 1305
Photography books index, M. Moss, 1306
Photography index: a guide to reproductions, P. J. Parry, comp., 1307
Physician's desk reference, 1105
Physician's desk reference for non-prescription drugs, 1105
Physician's GenRx, 1105
Physician's guide to rare diseases, J. G. Thoene, ed., 1073
Pick, A., ed. Standard catalog of world paper money, 1484
Pick-up games, D. Crisfield, 1580
Pile, J. Dictionary of twentieth-century design, 1294
Pimlott, J. Historical atlas of World War II, 1844
Pinkham, M. E. Mary Ellen's clean house, 1174
Pinyin Chinese-English dictionary, W. Jingrong, ed., 784
Pirates and privateers of the Americas, D. F. Marley, 1851
Pisano, D. A., and C. S. Lewis, eds. Air and space history, 934
Pizzorno, J. *See* Murray, M.
Places rated almanac, D. Savageau and G. Loftus, 336n, 1877
Places, towns, and townships, R. W. Dodge, D. A. Gaquin, and M. S. Littman, 408
Placzek, A. K., ed. Macmillan encyclopedia of architects, 1277
Plano, J. C., and M. Greenberg. American political dictionary, 560
Plaut, W. G., and B. J. Bamberger, eds. Torah, 248
Play index, 1365
Plays for children and young adults, R. S. Karp and J. H. Schlessinger, 1366
Pocket billiard guidebook for pool players, tournament directors, and spectators, J. R. Lawson, ed., 1545
Poe, A. McGraw-Hill handbook of more business letters, 493
Poe, R. W. McGraw-Hill handbook of business letters, 493
Poetry criticism, 1713
Poetry explication, 1708n, 1709n
Poetry handbook, B. Deutsch, 1714
Pohanish, R. P., and S. A. Greene, eds. Hazardous substances resource guide, 889
Political handbook of the world, 589
Political parties and civic action groups, E. L. Schapsmeier and F. H. Schapsmeier, 576
Political parties and elections in the United States, L. S. Maisel, ed., 618
Political science, H. E. York, 557
Polk's financial institutions directory, 505
Pollard, E. B. Visual arts research, 1231
Pollock, B. *See* Shapiro, N.
Popular music, 1427
Popular music 1920–1979, N. Shapiro and B. Pollock, eds., 1427
Popular music 1980–1989, 1427
Popular song index, P. P. Havlice, 1428
Population and housing characteristics for congressional districts of the 103rd congress, Bureau of the Census, 409
Portable Baker's biographical dictionary of musicians, N. Slonimsky and R. Kostelanetz, 1398n
Porter, D. L., ed. Biographical dictionary of American sports, 1510; Cumulative index to The Biographical dictionary of American sports, 1510
Porter, G., ed. Encyclopedia of American economic history, 1799
Porter, L. *See* Fons, M.
Porter, M. *See* Martin, M.
Porter, R., ed. Biographical dictionary of scientists, 835
Post, E. L. Emily Post's etiquette, 1157
Postlethwaite, T. N. *See* Husen, T.
Practical guide to exotic pets, C. Mattison, 1226
Practical guide to impractical pets, B. Burn, 1227
Pratt's guide to venture capital sources, Venture Economics staff, eds., 506
Presidency A to Z, 621n
Presidential also-rans and running mates, L. H. Southwick, comp., 624
Presidential ballots, W. D. Burnham, 614n
Presidential vote, E. E. Robinson, 614n
Prevention Magazine editors. Doctor's book of home remedies for children, 1097
Price, D. H. Atlas of world cultures: a geographical guide to ethnographic literature, 428
Prichard, J. B., ed. Harper atlas of the Bible, 182
Prichard, M. *See* Carpenter, H.

Primack, A. L. Journal literature of the physical sciences, 815
Prince, M. M. Bieber's dictionary of legal citations, 771
Princeton companion to classical Japanese literature, E. Miner, H. Odagiri, and R. E. Morrell, 1769
Principal international businesses, 475
Pring, J. T., ed. Oxford dictionary of modern Greek, 797
Pringle, D., ed. St. James guide to horror, ghost, and gothic writers, 1696
Private colleges and universities, J. F. Ohles and S. M. Ohles, 697
Professional football, M. J. Smith Jr., 1560
Professional guide to diseases, 1074
Professional sports statistics, K. M. Caschnitz, 1506
Professional sports team histories, M. L. LaBlanc, ed., 1497
Project remember, A. S. Koykka, 1939
Pronouncing dictionary of proper names, J. K. Bollard, ed., 744, 1968
Proper care of reptiles, J. Coborn, 1222
Protocol, 1160
Przebienda, E., ed. Cumulative personal author indexes to the monthly catalog of U.S. government publications, 1941–1975, 138
Pseudonyms and nicknames dictionary, J. Mossman, ed., 1969
Psychedelics encyclopedia, P. Stafford, 1106
Psychiatric dictionary, R. J. Campbell, 299
Psychological abstracts, 288
Psychology, P. M. Baxter, 287
Ptacek, G. *See* Vare, E. A.
Public affairs information service bulletin, 634n
Public colleges and universities, J. F. Ohles and S. M. Ohles, 697
Public interest profiles, Foundation for Public Affairs, 590
Public library catalog, 44
Public papers of the presidents of the United States, U.S. Office of the Federal Register, 610
Public schools USA, C. H. Harrison, 698
Public welfare directory, American Public Welfare Assn., 397
Publication manual of the American Psychological Association, 778
Publishers, distributors, and wholesalers, 93
Publishers' trade list annual, 56
Publishers weekly, 63
Puckett, B. *See* Henderson, H.
Pulliam, T., and C. Grundman. New York Times crossword puzzle dictionary, 728
Purcell, G. R., and G. A. Schlachter. Reference sources in library and information services, 19
Purchasing an encyclopedia, S. Whiteley, ed., 147
Pursell, F. J. Books for adult new readers, 36
Quilt groups today, American Quilter's Society staff, 1464
Quilt I.D. book, 1465
Quilter's companion, M. Dietrich et al., 1462
Quilter's complete guide, M. Fons and L. Porter, 1462
Quinn, E. G. *See* Campbell, O. J.
Quotable Shakespeare, C. DeLoach, comp., 1738
Quotations in black, A. King, ed. and comp., 1625

Raeburn, M., and A. Kendall, eds. Heritage of music, 1404
Raimo, J. *See* Sobel, R.
Raimo, J. W. Biographical directory of American colonial and revolutionary governors, 1607–1789, 602n
———, ed. Biographical directory of the governors of the United States, 1978–1983, 602
Raintree Steck-Vaughn illustrated science encyclopedia, 827
Rainwater, R. *See* Arntzen, E.
Rakel, R. J., ed. Conn's current therapy, 1062
Ralston, A., et al., eds. Encyclopedia of computer science, 897
Ramachandran, V. S., ed. Encyclopedia of human behavior, 294
Ramondino, S., ed. New world Spanish/English, English/Spanish dictionary, 811
Rand, B. Bibliography of philosophy, psychology, and cognate subjects, 293n
Rand McNally commercial atlas and marketing guide, 532, 1899
Rand McNally encyclopedia of world rivers, 1867n
Rand McNally Goode's world atlas, E. B. Espenshade, ed., 1889
Rand McNally road atlas, 1900
Rand McNally road atlas and city guide of Europe, 1896
Rand McNally standard highway and mileage guide, 1901
Randel, D. M., comp. Harvard concise dictionary of music, 1393
———, ed. New Harvard dictionary of music, 1393
Random House American sign language dictionary, E. Costello and L. Lenderman, 750
Random House college thesaurus, J. Stein and S. B. Flexner, eds., 765
Random House crossword puzzle dictionary, T. Geiss, 729
Random House historical dictionary of American slang, 757
Random House unabridged dictionary, 716
Random House Webster's college dictionary, 721
Random House word menu, S. Glazier, 766
Ranson, K. A. *See* Lorimer, L. T.

Rastafari roots and ideology, B. Chevannes, 258
Rawson, H., and B. Aymar, eds. Rawson's dictionary of euphemisms and other doubletalk, 758
Rawson's dictionary of euphemisms and other doubletalk, H. Rawson and B. Aymar, eds., 758
Reader's adviser, M. Sader, 13
Reader's catalog, G. O'Brien, 14
Reader's Digest book of skills and tools, 1193
Reader's Digest complete book of cross stitch and counted thread techniques, E. Van Zandt, 1457
Reader's Digest complete book of embroidery, M. Cross, 1458
Reader's Digest editors. Family handyman easy repair, 1182; Home improvements manual, 1180
Reader's Digest family word finder, 765n
Reader's Digest illustrated book of cats, 1206
Reader's Digest knitter's handbook, M. Stanley, 1459
Reader's encyclopedia, 1603n
Reader's encyclopedia of Shakespeare, O. J. Campbell and E. G. Quinn, eds., 1739
Reader's encyclopedia of the American West, 1821n
Readers' guide to periodical literature, 126, 1323n
Reader's guide to the great religions, C. J. Adams, ed., 177
Reber, A. S. Penguin dictionary of psychology, 298
Recent reference books in religion, W. M. Johnston, 169
Recipex, A. Gilbar, 1139
Recommended reference books in paperback, A. L. March, 15
Reddy, M. A., ed. Statistical record of Native North Americans, 393
Reed, I. *See* Duckles, V. H.
Reed, M. K. *See* Reed, R. M.
Reed, R. M., and M. K. Reed. Facts on File dictionary of television, cable, and video, 1349
Reed, W. L., and M. J. Bristow, eds. National anthems of the world, 1389
Rees, A. M. Consumer health information source book, 1029
———, ed. Consumer health USA, 1030; Encyclopedia of health information sources, 1031
Reference and information services, R. E. Bopp and L. C. Smith, eds., 16
Reference and user services quarterly, 28
Reference book of corporate managements, 476
Reference books bulletin, 24n
Reference books for children, C. S. Peterson and A. D. Fenton, 17
Reference books for young readers, 5n
Reference encyclopedia of the American Indian, B. T. Klein, ed., 392
Reference guide for English studies, M. J. Marcuse, 1600
Reference guide to American literature, J. Kamp, 1728
Reference guide to science fiction, fantasy, and horror, M. Burgess, 1695
Reference guide to short fiction, T. Riggs, 1700
Reference handbook on the deserts of North America, G. L. Bender, ed., 1867
Reference services review, 29
Reference sources for small and medium-sized libraries, S. E. Kennedy, ed., 18
Reference sources in library and information services, G. R. Purcell with G. A. Schlachter, 19
Reference sources in science, engineering, medicine, and agriculture, H. R. Malinowsky, ed., 816
Reference works in British and American literature, J. K. Bracken, 1601
Refugee and immigrant resource directory, A. E. Schorr, ed., 398
Regalbuto, R. J. Guide to monastic guest houses, 222
Reich, W. T., ed. Encyclopedia of bioethics, 283
Reid, D. G. Dictionary of Christianity in America, 199
Reilly, J. W. Language of real estate, 537
Reimer-Torn, S. *See* Reynolds, N.
Reithmaier, L. Aviation/space dictionary, 935
Religion index one, 171
Religious bodies in the United States, J. G. Melton, 208
Religious information sources, J. G. Melton and M. A. Koszegi, 170
Renegger, N. J., comp. Treaties and alliances of the world, 609n, 611
Renovation, M. W. Litchfield, 1170
Reproducible federal tax forms for use in libraries, U.S. Internal Revenue Service, 544
Requirements for certification of teachers, counselors, librarians, administrators for elementary schools, and secondary schools, 699
Research and Education Association staff. Handbook of mathematical, scientific, and engineering formulas, tables, functions, graphs, transforms, 1005
Research guide for undergraduate students, N. L. Baker, 1599n
Research guide to biography and criticism, W. Beacham, ed., 1643
Research in education, 649
Researcher's guide to American genealogy, V. D. Greenwood, 1950
Resources for people with disabilities, E. H. Oakes and J. Bradford, eds., 1112
Resources in education, 649
Retirement places rated, D. Savageau, 336
Reverse acronyms, initialisms & abbreviations dictionary, 723

Reynolds, B., ed. Cambridge Italian dictionary, 799; Concise Cambridge Italian dictionary, 799n
Reynolds, C. R., and L. Mann, eds. Encyclopedia of special education, 653
Reynolds, N., and S. Reimer-Torn. Dance classics, 1317
Rhodes, C. P., ed. Encyclopedia of beer, 1126
RIA Federal tax handbook, 545
Richards' ultimate bicycle repair manual, R. Ballantine and R. Grant, 1542
Richardson, S. K. Magazines for children, 65; Magazines for young adults, 67; Periodicals for school media programs, 67n
Ricks, D. *See* Arpan, J. S.
Ridpath, I., ed. Norton's 2000.0: star atlas and reference handbook, 877
Riggs, T. Reference guide to short fiction, 1700
———, ed. Contemporary poets, 1707
Riley, J. Biographical encyclopedia of the Negro baseball leagues, 1522
Rinzler, C. A. Complete book of herbs, spices, and condiments, 1132
Ritter, E. M. *See* Arntzen, C. J.
Rivera, F. *See* Meier, M. S.
RMA annual statement studies, Robert Morris Associates, 491n, 495
Roach, P. Complete book of pet care, 1199
Robbins, R. H. Encyclopedia of witchcraft and demonology, 271
Robert, H. M., III, and W. J. Evans, eds. Robert's rules of order, 591
Robert Morris Associates. RMA annual statement studies, 495
Robert's rules of order, H. M. Robert III and W. J. Evans, eds., 591
Robertson, A., and D. Hutera. Dance handbook, 1319
Robertson, L., C. Finders, and B. Ruppenthal. New Laurel's kitchen, 1140
Robinson, E. E. Presidential vote, 614n
Robinson, F. Atlas of the Islamic world since 1500, 1842
———, ed. Cambridge encyclopedia of India, Pakistan, Bangladesh, Sri Lanka, Nepal, Bhutan, and the Maldives, 1855
Robinson, J., ed. Oxford companion to wine, 1130
Robinson, J. S. Tapping the government grapevine, 143
Rock climbing basics, T. Johnson, 1584
Rock 'n road, T. Toula, 1585
Rock stars/pop stars, B. J. Leyser, comp., 1446
Rodriguez, J. P., ed. Historical encyclopedia of world slavery, 1816
Roger Ebert's video companion, R. Ebert, 1337
Rogerson, J. W. Atlas of the Bible, 181
Roget's II, P. Strupp, ed., 768
Roget's international thesaurus, R. L. Chapman, ed., 767
Roget's thesaurus of the Bible, A. C. Day, 197
Rogoff, H. *See* Sternberg, M. L. A.
Rolling rivers, 1867n
Rolling Stone album guide, A. DeCurtis et al., eds., 1416
Rolling Stone encyclopedia of rock and roll, 1445n
Romanofsky, P., ed. Social service organizations, 399
Romanowski, P., and H. George-Warren, eds. New Rolling Stone encyclopedia of rock and roll, 1445
Rombauer, I. S. Joy of cooking, 1134
Room, A., ed. Brewer's dictionary of phrase and fable, 1608
Rosenak, C., and J. Rosenak. Museum of American Folk Art encyclopedia of twentieth-century folk art and artists, 1252
Rosenak, J. *See* Rosenak, C.
Rosenberg, J. M. Dictionary of banking, 501; Dictionary of business and management, 451
Rosenfeld, A. Exotic pets, 1223
Rosentiel, L. *See* Orrmont, A.
Ross, C., and T. Gladfetter. Hiker's companion, 1570
Ross, J. A., ed. International encyclopedia of population, 321
Ross, S. R. *See* Nash, J. R.
Rossel, M. Artist's complete health and safety guide, 1449
Roth, C. *See* Leary, L.
Rothwell, K. S., and A. H. Melzer. Shakespeare on screen, 1742
Routledge encyclopedia of philosophy, E. Craig, ed., 166
Rowe, J. *See* Lafferty, P.
Rules of baseball, D. Nemic, 1529
Rules of the game, Diagram Group, 1499
Running injury-free, J. Ellis and J. Henderson, 1588
Ruoff, A. L. B. American Indian literatures, 387
Ruppenthal, B. *See* Robertson, L.
Ruppert, J. Guide to American poetry explication: colonial and nineteenth century, 1708
Ruse, M. *See* Martin, E.
Russell, R. *See* Jarman, B.
Ryder, D. Canadian reference sources, 3n

Sachane, A., ed. Official NBA basketball encyclopedia, 1536
Sader, M. Reader's adviser, 13
———, ed. Topical reference books, 22
———, and A. Lewis, eds. Encyclopedias, atlases, and dictionaries, 4
Sadie, J. A., and R. Samuel, eds. Norton/Grove dictionary of women composers, 1411

Sadie, S., ed. New Grove dictionary of music and musicians, 1391, 1392n; New Grove dictionary of musical instruments, 1392; New Grove dictionary of opera, 1405; *see also* Hitchcock, H. W.
Safford, B. R., ed. Guide to reference materials for school library media centers, 8
Safire, W. Safire's new political dictionary, 577
———, ed. Lend me your ears, 1835
Safire's new political dictionary, W. Safire, 577
Sailing for beginners, M. M. Farnham, 1589
Salem, J. M. Guide to critical reviews, 1309
Sales manager's handbook, 533
Sales promotion handbook, 534
Salzman, J., D. L. Smith, and C. West, eds. Encyclopedia of African-American culture and history, 364
Same time . . . same station, R. Lackmann, 1352
Samuel, R. *See* Sadie, J. A.
Sandberg, L., and D. Weissman. Folk music sourcebook, 1440
Sanders, D. *See* Muret, E.
Sandford, G. Illustrated encyclopedia of aquarium fish, 1216
Santamaria, J. K., ed. Financial aids for higher education, 661
Santelli, R. Big book of blues, 1434
Santeria, M. Gonzalez-Wippler, 259
Sardegna, J., and T. O. Paul. Encyclopedia of blindness and vision impairment, 1113
Sasson, J. M., ed. Civilizations of the ancient Near East, 1791
Savage, B. L., ed. African American historic places, 358
Savage, G. Dictionary of antiques, 1293
———, and H. Newman. Illustrated dictionary of ceramics, 1281
Savageau, D. Retirement places rated, 336
———, and G. Loftus. Places rated almanac, 1877
Scammon, R. M. *See* McGillvray, A. V.
Scarne, J. Scarne's new complete guide to gambling, 1562
Scarne's new complete guide to gambling, J. Scarne, 1562
Scarre, C. Smithsonian timelines of the ancient world, 1781
Schapsmeier, E. L., and F. H. Schapsmeier. Political parties and civic action groups, 576
Schapsmeier, F. H. *See* Schapsmeier, E. L.
Scherer, A. *See* Firestone, M.
Schick, F. L., and R. Schick. Statistical handbook on U.S. Hispanics, 384
Schick, R. *See* Schick, F. L.
Schirmer biographical dictionary of dance, 1315n
Schlachter, G. A. Directory of financial aids for minorities, 659; Directory of financial aids for women, 659; *see also* Purcell, G. R.
———, and R. D. Weber. Financial aid for the disabled and their families, 659
Schlager, N. St. James Press gay and lesbian almanac, 327
———, ed. When technology fails, 829
Schlessinger, J. H. *See* Karp, R. S.
Schlicke, P. *See* Walford, A. J.
Schmidt, A. J. Fraternal organizations, 324
Schmittberger, R. W. New rules for classic games, 1579
Schmittroth, L., ed. Statistical record of children, 347; Statistical record of women worldwide, 421
Schnaser, G. Home repair emergency handbook, 1186
Schneider, S. H. Encyclopedia of climate and weather, 920
Scholarships, fellowships and loans, 667
Scholes, P. A. Oxford companion to music, 1394n
Scholze-Stubenrecht, W., and J. B. Sykes, eds. Oxford-Duden German dictionary, 794
Schomburg Center guide to Black literature from the eighteenth century to the present, R. M. Valade, ed., 1649
School library journal, 30
Schorr, A. E., ed. Refugee and immigrant resource directory, 398
Schroy, E. T., ed. Warman's antiques and collectibles price guide, 1480
Schuler, J. A., ed. Government reference books 94/96, 6
Schultz, J. D. *See* Kurian, G.
Schultz, M. *See* Consumer Reports editors
Schwann opus, 1382
Schwann spectrum, 1382
Schwartz, K. V. *See* Margulis, A.
Schwartzman, S. Words of mathematics, 1009
Sciattara, D. M. *See* Ganly, J. V.
Science and technology desk reference, Carnegie Library of Pittsburgh Science and Technology Department staff, 832
Science fiction writers, R. Bleiler, ed., 1697
Scientific style and format, 779
Sclater, N. *See* Gibilisco, S.; *see also* Markus, J.
Scott, J. S. VNR dictionary of civil engineering, 955
Scott, R. *See* Liddell, H. G.
Scott, T., and M. Eagleson, eds. Concise encyclopedia biochemistry, 975
Scott-Kilvert, I., ed. British writers, 1731
Scott's specialized catalogue of United States stamps, 1490
Scott's standard postage stamp catalogue, 1490
Screen, J. E. O. *See* Walford, A. J.
Screen world, J. Willis, 1341

Seager, J., and A. Olson. Women in the world, 423
Searching for your ancestors, G. H. Doane and J. B. Bell, 1951
Sears, J. L., and M. K. Moody, eds. Using government information sources, 144
Sears, M. E., ed. List of subject headings, 1306n; Song index, 1430, 1432n
Seasons of our joy, A. I. Waskow, 238
Second Jewish book of why, A. J. Kolatch, 237
Second treasury of knitting patterns, B. G. Walker, 1460
Segen, J. C., comp. and ed. Dictionary of modern medicine, 1036
Seider, M. *See* Andrews, R.
Selected characteristics of occupations defined in the revised Dictionary of occupational titles, U.S. Dept. of Labor, 551
Selection of U.S. Internal Revenue Service tax information publications, U.S. Internal Revenue Service, 546
Self, C. Creating your own woodshop, 1472
Seligman, E. R. A., and A. Johnson, eds. Encyclopaedia of the social sciences, 320
Sellen, B. C., and C. J. Johanson. Twentieth century American folk, self-taught, and outsider art, 1257
Senick, G. J., ed. Children's literature review, 1663
Senior high school library catalog, 39n, 45
Senior, M. Illustrated who's who in mythology, 277
Sennett, B., ed. Complete world bartender guide, 1125
Sequels, J. Husband and J. F. Husband, 1686
Serials directory, 98
Serials for libraries, J. V. Ganly and D. M. Sciattara, eds., 68
Shaeffer, C. B. Claire Shaeffer's fabric sewing guide, 1466
Shafritz, J. M., et al. Facts on File dictionary of education, 654
Shakespeare A to Z, C. Boyce, 1740
Shakespeare glossary, C. T. Onions, 1741
Shakespeare on screen, K. S. Rothwell and A. H. Melzer, 1742
Shakespearean criticism, 1743
Shaking your family tree, R. Crandall, 1952
Shakir, M. H., ed. Holy Qur'an = al-Qur'an al-hakim, 254
Shamos, M. L. Illustrated encyclopedia of billiards, 1544
Shankle, G. E. American nicknames, 1961, 1970n
Shapiro, N., and B. Pollock, eds. Popular music 1920–1979, 1427
Sharma, S. *See* Gargan, W.
Sharp, H. S. Handbook of pseudonyms and personal nicknames, 1967
———, comp. Advertising slogans of America, 456
Shatzkin, M., ed. Ballplayers, 1516
Shaw, E. Divining the future, 311
Shea, P., et al. Access America, 1902
Shearer, B. F., and B. S. Shearer. State names, seals, flags, and symbols, 1959
Shearer, B. S. *See* Shearer, B. F.
Sheehan, S. *See* Mayer, R.
Sheehy, N., A. J. Chapman, and W. Conroy, eds. Biographical dictionary of psychology, 290
Sheets, A. *See* Malinowski, S.
Shemel, S. *See* Krasilovsky, M. W.
Shepherd, L., ed. Encyclopedia of occultism and parapsychology, 312
Shepherd, W. R. Shepherd's historical atlas, 1845
Shepherd's historical atlas, W. R. Shepherd, 1845
Sherratt, A., ed. Cambridge encyclopedia of archaeology, 431
Shields, J. F. Make it, 1447
Shore, S. N. *See* Meyers, R. A.
Short story criticism, 1701
Short story index: collections indexed, 1900–1978, J. Yaakov, ed., 1702
Short story index, 1900–1949, D. E. Cook and I. S. Monro, comps., 1702
Showman, R. K. *See* Freidel, F.
Shtasel, P. Medical tests and diagnostic procedures, 1069
Shurgin, A. H. *See* Griffin, R.
Sicignano, R. *See* O'Hara, F. M., Jr.
Sienkewicz, T. J. Classical epic, 1747
Silbey, J. H., ed. Encyclopedia of the American legislative system, 570
Sills, D. L., ed. International encyclopedia of the social sciences, 322
Silvy, A., ed. Children's books and their creators, 1660
Similes dictionary, E. Sommer and M. Sommer, eds., 753
Simon, A. *See* Lewine, R.
Simons, L. K. Performing arts, 1308
Simplest game, P. Gardner, 1591
Simpson, D. P., ed. Cassell's Latin dictionary, 804
Simpson, J., and E. Weiner, eds. Oxford English dictionary additions series, 715
Simpson, J. A., and E. S. C. Weiner. Oxford English dictionary, 715, 720n, 734n
Simpson, J. M. Y. *See* Asher, R. E.
Singer, R., et al., eds. Atlas of American sport, 1508
Skidmore, G., and T. J. Spahn. From radical left to extreme right, 64
Slang and euphemism, R. A. Spears, 759
Slatta, R. W. Cowboy encyclopedia, 1859
Slide, A. American film industry, 1324

Slide buyers' guide, N. D. Cashman, ed., 1240
Slonimsky, N. Baker's biographical dictionary of musicians, 1398; Concise edition of Baker's biographical dictionary of musicians, 1398n; Music since 1900, 1387
———, and R. Kostelanetz. Portable Baker's biographical dictionary of musicians, 1398n
Small business sourcebook, A. L. Park, ed., 447
Smart consumer's directory, 1155
Smart medicine for a healthier child, J. Zand et al., 1098
Smith, A. M. *See* Langston, D. J.
Smith, C., et al., eds. Collins Spanish-English, English-Spanish dictionary, 809
Smith, C. C., ed. Twentieth-century science-fiction writers, 1699
Smith, C. G. *See* Pearce, E. A.
Smith, D. L., ed. Toll-free phone book USA 1998, 83; *see also* Salzman, J.
Smith, F. *See* Lax, R.
Smith, J. C. Black firsts, 361
———, ed. Notable Black American men, 369; Notable Black American women, 370; Notable Black American women, book II, 370
———, and C. P. Horton. Historical statistics of Black America, 366; Statistical record of Black America, 371
Smith, L. C. *See* Bopp, R. E.
Smith, M. *See* Markel, R.
Smith, M. J. Baseball: supplement 1, 1517
———, comp. Baseball, 1517
Smith, M. J., Jr. Professional football, 1560
———, comp. College football bibliography, 1555
Smith, V., ed. Encyclopedia of Latin American literature, 1754
Smithsonian timelines of the ancient world, C. Scarre, 1781
Smitten, J. R. *See* Kloesel, C. J. W.
Snelling, J. Buddhist handbook, 250
Sniderman, F. M. *See* Breed, P. F.
Snyder, L. L. Louis L. Snyder's historical guide to World War II, 1818
Sobel, R., ed. Biographical directory of the United States executive branch, 619
———, and J. Raimo, eds. Biographical directory of the governors of the United States, 1789–1978, 602
Sobel, S. *See* Corcoran, J.
Soccer handbook for players, coaches, and parents, A. M. Luongo, 1592
Social sciences, N. L. Herron, ed., 20
Social sciences index, 127, 318, 1775n
Social Security Administration. Social security handbook, 512
Social security handbook, Social Security Administration, 512
Social security, medicare and pensions, J. L. Matthews and D. M. Berman, 337
Social service organizations, P. Romanofsky, ed., 399
Social service organizations and agencies directory, A. T. Kruzas, ed., 400
Social work almanac, L. H. Ginsberg, 401
Social work dictionary, R. L. Barker, 402
Social work year book, 395
Sociology, S. H. Aby, 328
Software and CD-ROM reviews on file, 908
Software encyclopedia, 907
Software reviews on file, 908
Sole, C. A., and M. I. Abreu, eds. Latin American writers, 1756
Solt, M. L. *See* Peterson, L. K.
Something about the author: autobiography series, 1668
Something about the author: facts and pictures about contemporary authors and illustrators of books for young people, A. Commire, 1669
Sommer, E., and D. Weiss, eds. Metaphors dictionary, 752
———, and M. Sommer, eds. Similes dictionary, 753
Sommer, M. *See* Sommer, E.
Song finder, G. L. Ferguson, ed., 1429
Song index, M. E. Sears, ed., 1430, 1432n
Song list, J. L. Limbacher, ed., 1431
Songs in collections, D. de Charms and P. F. Breed, 1432
Songs of the theater, R. Lewine and A. Simon, 1433
Songwriter's market, 1396
Source, A. Eakle and J. Cerny, eds., 1953
Source book of health insurance data, 513
Sourcebook of criminal justice statistics, U.S. Department of Justice, Bureau of Justice Statistics, 350
Sourcebook on parenting and child care, K. H. Carpenter, 1197
South American handbook, 1878
South, M., ed. Mythical and fabulous creatures, 278
Southern, E. Biographical dictionary of Afro-American and African musicians, 1399
Southwick, L. H., comp. Presidential also-rans and running mates, 624
Spahn, T. J. *See* Skidmore, G.
Spain, P. J., and J. R. Talbot, eds. Hoover's handbook of emerging companies, 471
Sparks, L., and B. Emerton, comps. American college regalia, 694
Spawforth, A. *See* Hornblower, S.
SPC staff. Everything you need to know about medical tests, 1065
Speake, J. Oxford dictionary of foreign words and phrases, 737
Spears, R. A. Slang and euphemism, 759
Speech index, R. B. Sutton, 1717

Speech index, supplement, C. Mitchell, 1717
Spencer, D. D. Webster's new world dictionary of computer terms, 902
Spencer, P. National directory of children, youth, and families services, 346
Spevack, M. Complete and systematic concordance to Shakespeare, 1737n; Harvard concordance to Shakespeare, 1737
Spiritual community guide, 260
Spiter, R. L., et al. DSM-IV casebook, 301
Sport on film and video, D. Alder, ed., 1513
Sporting News official NBA guide, 1539
Sporting News official NBA register, 1540
Sporting News staff. Baseball guide, 1521; Official baseball register, 1527
Sports and recreation for the disabled, J. Jones, 1507
Sports encyclopedia: pro football, D. S. Neft, R. M. Cohen, and R. Korch, 1561
Sports fan's connection, 1502
Sports halls of fame, D. Gelbert, 1503
Sports Illustrated 1998 sports almanac, 1505
Sports Illustrated presents the complete book of the Summer Olympics, D. Wallechinsky, 1576
Sports rules encyclopedia, J. R. White, ed., 1500
Sports stars, M. A. Pare, 1511
Sports video resource guide, B. Carroll, 1514
Spot radio rates and data, 480
Spot television rates and data, 480
Springer, O. *See* Muret, E.
Sprug, J. W., comp. Index to fairy tales, 1987–1992, 1665; *see also* Ireland, N. O.
St. James guide to horror, ghost, and gothic writers, D. Pringle, ed., 1696
St. James Press gay and lesbian almanac, N. Schlager, 327
Stade, G. *See* Jackson, W. T. H.
Stafford, M., and D. Ware. Illustrated dictionary of ornament, 1244n
Stafford, P. Psychedelics encyclopedia, 1106
Stage it with music, T. S. Hischak, 1375
Stahl, D. *See* De Sola, R.
Stambler, I., and G. Landon. Encyclopedia of folk, country, and western music, 1439
Stamp collecting, B. Krause, 1491
Stanaszek, M. J., et al., eds. Inverted medical dictionary, 1041
Standard & Poor's industry surveys, 521
Standard & Poor's OTC profiles, 522n
Standard & Poor's register of corporations, directors and executives, 477
Standard & Poor's statistical service, 496
Standard & Poor's stock and bond guide, 522
Standard & Poor's stock market encyclopedia, 518
Standard & Poor's stock reports, 522
Standard ASE stock reports, 522
Standard book of Shakespeare quotations, 1736n
Standard catalog of U.S. paper money, C. Krause et al., eds., 1484
Standard catalog of world coins, C. L. Krause and C. Mischler. C. R. Bruce, ed., 1485
Standard catalog of world paper money, A. Pick, ed., 1484
Standard catalog of world paper money, v.3, C. Bruce, ed., 1484
Standard code of parliamentary procedure, A. Sturgis, 592
Standard corporation descriptions, 523
Standard directory of advertisers, 478
Standard directory of advertising agencies, 479
Standard directory of world coins, C. L. Krause, C. Mischler, and C. R. Bruce, 1485
Standard encyclopedia of the world's mountains, 1867n
Standard industrial classification manual, 497
Standard periodical directory [yr.], 99
Standard rate and data service directories, 480
Stanley, M. Reader's Digest knitter's handbook, 1459
Stanzi, R. *See* Malin, F.
Starer, D. Who to call: the parent's source book, 1198
Starkey, P. *See* Meisami, J. S.
State administrative officials classified by function, 581n
State and metropolitan area data book, Bureau of the Census, 410
State blue books, legislative manuals, and reference publications, 141
State elective officials and the legislatures, 581n
State legislative leadership, committees and staff, 581n
State names, seals, flags, and symbols, B. F. Shearer and B. S. Shearer, 1959
State publications and depository libraries, M. T. Lane, 140
State reference publications, L. Hellebust, ed., 141
State tax handbook, 541
Statesman's year-book, 1879
Statistical abstract of the United States, 404n, 410n, 411, 1829n
Statistical handbook of the American family, B. A. Chadwick and T. B. Heaton, eds., 412
Statistical handbook on U.S. Hispanics, F. L. Schick and R. Schick, 384
Statistical handbook on women in America, C. M. Taeuber, ed., 420
Statistical portrait of the United States, M. S. Littman, ed., 413
Statistical record of Black America, J. C. Smith and C. P. Horton, eds., 371
Statistical record of children, L. Schmittroth, ed., 347
Statistical record of health and medicine, C. A. Dorgan, ed., 1075

Statistical record of Hispanic Americans, 385
Statistical record of Native North Americans, M. A. Reddy, ed., 393
Statistical record of older Americans, A. J. Darnay, ed., 338
Statistical record of women worldwide, L. Schmittroth, ed., 421
Statistical yearbook, UN Statistical Office, 414
Statistics sources, J. W. O'Brien and S. R. Wasserman, eds., 415
Stedman's abbreviations, acronyms, and symbols, 1047
Stedman's medical dictionary, 1048
Stein, G., ed. Encyclopedia of unbelief, 164
Stein, J., and S. B. Flexner, eds. Random House college thesaurus, 765
Stein, J. S. Construction glossary, 953
Steinberg, M. L., and S. Cosley, eds. Facts on File dictionary of biotechnology and genetic engineering, 979
Steinfirst, S. Folklore and folklife, 275
Steinsaltz, A. Talmud, 245
Stern's performing arts directory, 1311
Sternberg, M. L. A. American sign language, 748
———, and H. Rogoff. American sign language dictionary, 749
Stetler, S. L., ed. Almanac of famous people, 1916
Stevenson, B. Folger book of Shakespeare quotations, 1736; Home book of quotations, classical and modern, 1620, 1627n; Macmillan book of proverbs, maxims, and famous phrases, 1627
Stevenson, G. A., and W. A. Pakan. Graphic arts encyclopedia, 1249
Stevenson, L. H., and B. Wyman. Facts on File dictionary of environmental science, 967
Stevenson, T. New Sotheby's wine encyclopedia, 1129
Stewart, B. *See* Welch, R.
Stewart, G. R. American given names, 1960; American place names, 1854
Stewart, S. C. *See* Epps, R. P.
Stone, R. *See* Nettl, B.
Stoppard, M. Conception, pregnancy, and birth, 1117
———, ed. Woman's body, 1122
Strassfield, M. Jewish holidays, 238
Strayer, J. R., ed. Dictionary of the Middle Ages, 1796
Strichart, S. S. *See* Mangrum, C. T.
Stroebel, L., and H. N. Todd. Dictionary of contemporary photography, 1301
Stroebel, L., and R. Zakia, eds. Focal encyclopedia of photography, 1303
Strupp, P., ed., Roget's II, 768
Student sociologist's handbook, P. Bart and L. Frankel, 329
Sturgis, A. Standard code of parliamentary procedure, 592
Subject bibliographies, U.S. Superintendent of Documents, 142
Subject collections, L. Ash and W. G. Miller, eds., 88
Subject guide to books in print, 57
Subject guide to children's books in print, 58
Suhr, C. *See* Warr, W.
Summers, C. J., ed. Gay and lesbian literary heritage, 1650
Summers, H. G., Jr. Vietnam War almanac, 1823
Sunset Books editors. Basic home repairs, 1176; Basic plumbing, 1177; Basic wiring, 1179
Sunshine, L. *See* Wright, J. W.
Supernatural fiction writers, E. F. Bleiler, ed., 1698
Supreme Court A to Z, 625n
Supreme Court justices: a biographical dictionary, M. I. Urofsky, ed., 627n
Supreme Court justices: illustrated biographies, C. Cushman, ed., 627n
Surgery book, 1064
Survey of buying power, 535
Sussman, A. E. *See* Turkington, C.
Sutton, R. B. Speech index, 1717
Sutton, W., ed. Adventuring with books, 32
Swanfeldt, A. Crossword puzzle dictionary, 727
Sweetland, R. *See* Keyser, D.
Sweetland, R. C., and D. J. Keyser, eds. Tests, 306
Swimming for total fitness, J. Katz and N. P. Bruning, 1594
Sykes, J. B. *See* Scholze-Stubenrecht, W.
Symptoms and early warning signs, M. Apple et al., 1067

T.E.S.S.: the educational software selector, 646
Taeuber, C. M., ed. Statistical handbook on women in America, 420
Talbot, J. R. *See* Spain, P. J.
Talmud, A. Steinsaltz, 245
Tanakh, 246
Tapley, D., et al., eds. Columbia University College of Physicians and Surgeons complete home medical guide, 1061
Tapping the government grapevine, J. S. Robinson, 143
Taragno, M. Basketball biographies, 1532
Tatem, M. *See* Opie, I.
Taylor, F. *See* Briggs, G.
Taylor, W. H. *See* Barzun, J.
Television and cable factbook, 1356
Television cartoon shows, H. Erickson, 1353
Telgen, D., and J. Kamp, eds. Notable Hispanic American women, 383
Telushkin, J. Jewish literacy, 239; Jewish wisdom, 239

Tenenbaum, B. A. Encyclopedia of Latin American history and culture, 1804
Tenney, M. C., and S. Barabas, eds. Zondervan pictorial encyclopedia of the Bible, 194
Tennis sourcebook, D. J. Phillips, 1596
Terrace, V. Encyclopedia of television: series, pilots and specials, 1348
Terras, V., ed. Handbook of Russian literature, 1770
Terrell, P., ed. Collins German-English, English-German dictionary, 791
Test critiques, D. Keyser and R. Sweetland, eds., 305
Tests, R. C. Sweetland and D. J. Keyser, eds., 306
Tests in print, L. L. Murphy et al., eds., 307
Textbook of medical physiology, A. C. Guyton and J. E. Hall, 1091
Tharp, L. *See* Atterbury, P.
Theatre world, J. Willis, ed., 1378
Thernstrom, S., et al., eds. Harvard encyclopedia of American ethnic groups, 354
Thesaurus of ERIC descriptors, 647, 649n
Thesaurus of slang, E. Lewin and A. E. Lewin, eds., 760
This business of music, M. W. Krasilovsky and S. Shemel, 1397
Thoene, J. G., ed. Physician's guide to rare diseases, 1073
Thomas register of American manufacturers and Thomas register catalog file, 481
Thompson, M. M., and U.S. Geological Survey. Maps for America, 1883
Thompson, S. E., and B. W. Carlson, eds. Holidays, festivals, and celebrations of the world dictionary, 1149
Thomson, D. Biographical dictionary of film, 1342
Thorn, J., and P. Palmer, eds. Total baseball, 1530
Thorndike, D., ed. Thorndike encyclopedia of banking and financial tables, 507
Thorndike encyclopedia of banking and financial tables, D. Thorndike, ed., 507
Thorpe, N. *See* James, P.
Thurston, H. *See* Butler, A.
Tibbets, J. *See* Bridge, F.
Tiegreen, M. Encyclopedia of golf techniques, P. Foston, ed., 1564
Tilghman, T. F. *See* Magill, F. N.
Time-Life Books editors. How things work in your home, 1187
Timelines of African-American history, T. Cowan and J. Maguire, 372
Times atlas and encyclopedia of the sea, A. Couper, ed., 926
Times atlas of the Second World War, J. Keegan, ed., 1846
Times atlas of the world, 1890
Times atlas of world history, G. Barraclough, ed., 1847
Times Books world weather guide, E. A. Pearce and C. G. Smith, 921
Timetables of history, B. Grun, 1782
Timetables of technology, B. Bunch and A. Hellemans, 850
Title guide to the talkies, 1927 through 1963, R. B. Dimmitt, 1334
Title guide to the talkies, 1964 through 1974, A. A. Aros, 1334
Title guide to the talkies, 1975 through 1984, A. A. Aros, 1334
Tkac, D. Doctor's book of home remedies, 1083
To pray as a Jew, H. H. Donin, 247
Todd, H. N. *See* Stroebel, L.
Todd, J., ed. Dictionary of British and American women writers, 1654
Toll-free phone book USA 1998, D. L. Smith, ed., 83
Tomlin, C., ed. Pesticide manual, 857
Tonnesson, D. *See* Notelovitz, M.
Tootill, E., ed. Facts on File dictionary of biology, 978
Topical reference books, M. Sader, ed., 22
Torah, W. G. Plaut and B. J. Bamberger, eds., 248
Torgeson, K. W., and S. Weinstein. Garland recipe index, 1136
Tortora, P. G., and R. S. Merkel, eds. Fairchild's dictionary of textiles, 1470
Total baseball, J. Thorn and P. Palmer, eds., 1530
Toula, T. Rock 'n road, 1585
Towers, D., comp. Dance film and video guide, 1318
Toxics A to Z, J. Harte, 970, 1076
Toye, W., ed. Oxford companion to Canadian literature, 1760
Tracey, E. M. *See* Vance, L. E.
Trade names dictionary, 458
Trager, J., ed. People's chronology, 1780
Travers, B., and J. Muhr, eds. World of invention, 830; World of scientific discovery, 851
Treasury of knitting patterns, B. G. Walker, 1460
Treaties and alliances of the world, N. J. Renegger, comp., 609n, 611
Treaties in force, U.S. Dept. of State, 612
Treese, J. D., ed. Biographical directory of the American Congress, 631
Trefny, B. R., and E. C. Palmer. Index to children's plays in collections, 3d ed., 1360
Trends and projections bulletin, 521n
Trepp, L. Complete book of Jewish observance, 231
Trigg, G. L. *See* Lerner, R. G.
Troy, L., ed. Almanac of business and industrial financial ratios, 484
Truitt, E. M. Who was who on screen, 1343

Tuckerman, N., and N. Dunnan. Amy Vanderbilt complete book of etiquette, 1156
Turabian, K. L., J. Grossman, and A. Bennet. Manual for writers of term papers, theses, and dissertations, 775
Turkington, C. Home health guide to poisons and antidotes, 1066
———, and A. E. Sussman. Encyclopedia of deafness and hearing disorders, 1114
Turner, E. J. *See* Allen, J. P.
Turner, J., ed. Dictionary of art, 1243
Tuttle, L. Encyclopedia of feminism, 419
Twentieth century American folk, self-taught, and outsider art, B. C. Sellen and C. J. Johanson, 1257
Twentieth-century American nicknames, L. Urdang, ed., 1970
Twentieth-century children's writers, L. S. Berger, ed., 1670
Twentieth-century crime and mystery writers, L. Henderson, ed., 1690
Twentieth century hockey chronicle, D. Barrett et al., 1574
Twentieth-century literary criticism, 1634
Twentieth-century romance and historical writers, L. Henderson, ed., 1691
Twentieth-century science-fiction writers, C. C. Smith, ed., 1699
Twentieth-century short story explication, W. S. Walker and B. K. Walker, 1703
Twentieth-century short story explication: interpretations, 1900–1975, W. S. Walker, comp., 1703
Twentieth-century short story explication, new series, 1703
Twentieth-century western writers, J. Vinson, ed., 1729
Two hundred years of the American circus, T. Ogden, 1376
Tyler, T. *See* Walker, J.

U.S. Bureau of Labor Statistics. Occupational outlook handbook, 553
U.S. Congress. Biographical directory of the United States Congress, 631; Official congressional directory, 638
U.S. Department of Agriculture. Agricultural statistics, 852
U.S. Department of Defense, comp. Dictionary of military terms, 1025
U.S. Department of Health and Human Resources. Health United States, 1075
U.S. Department of Health and Human Services. National directory of drug abuse and alcoholism treatment and prevention programs, 342
U.S. Department of Justice, Bureau of Justice Statistics. Sourcebook of criminal justice statistics, 350
U.S. Department of Justice, Federal Bureau of Investigation. Uniform crime reports for the United States, 351
U.S. Department of the Interior, U.S. Patent and Trademark Office. General information concerning patents, 831
U.S. Dept. of Commerce, Bureau of Industrial Economics. U.S. industrial outlook, 498
U.S. Dept. of Education. Condition of education, 700; Digest of education statistics, 701
U.S. Dept. of Labor. Dictionary of occupational titles, 551; Selected characteristics of occupations defined in the revised Dictionary of occupational titles, 551
U.S. Dept. of State. Treaties in force, 612
U.S. first day cover catalogue and checklist, M. A. Mellone, 1492
U.S. Geological Survey. National atlas of the United States, 1898; *see also* Thompson, M. M.
U.S. industrial outlook, U.S. Dept. of Commerce, Bureau of Industrial Economics, 498
U.S. Internal Revenue Service. Reproducible federal tax forms for use in libraries, 544; Selection of U.S. Internal Revenue Service tax information publications, 546
U.S. Library of Congress, General Reference and Bibliography Div. Guide to the study of the United States of America, 1773
U.S. master tax guide, 545
U.S. Office of Management and Budget. Budget of the United States government, 606
U.S. Office of the Federal Register. Public papers of the presidents of the United States, 610
U.S. Pharmacopeia. Complete drug reference, 1099
U.S. Superintendent of Documents. New products from the U.S. government, 139; Subject bibliographies, 142
Uhlan, M., and D. B. Katz, eds. Guide to special issues and indexes of periodicals, 444
Ulrich's international periodicals directory, 100
UN Statistical Office. Demographic yearbook, 406; Statistical yearbook, 414
Unger, H. G. Encyclopedia of American education, 651
Unger, L. ed. American writers, 1720
Uniform crime reports for the United States, U.S. Department of Justice, Federal Bureau of Investigation, 351
United States Code, containing the general and permanent laws of the U.S., Office of the Law Revision Counsel of the House of Representatives, 613
United States government manual, 585n, 593

United States local histories in the Library of Congress, M. J. Kaminkow, ed., 1940
United States Supreme Court decisions, N. A. Guenther, 630
Universal almanac, J. W. Wright, ed., 110
University of Chicago Spanish dictionary, C. Castillo et al., 813
Unterberger, A., ed. Who's who in technology, 840
Unterman, A. Dictionary of Jewish lore and legend, 232
Urdang, L. Oxford thesaurus, 764
———, ed. Dictionary of advertising terms, 531n; Twentieth-century American nicknames, 1970
Urofsky, M. I., ed. Supreme Court justices: a biographical dictionary, 627n
USA counties on CD-ROM, Bureau of the Census, 416
USA Today sports atlas, W. Balliett, ed., 1509
USGA staff and Ancient Golf Club of St. Andrews. Official rules of golf, 1568
Using government information sources, J. L. Sears and M. K. Moody, eds., 144

Valade, R. M., ed. Schomburg Center guide to Black literature from the eighteenth century to the present, 1649
Vallasi, G. A. *See* Chernow, B. A.
Value Line investment survey, A. Bernhard, 524
Van Cleve, J. V., ed. Gallaudet encyclopedia of deaf people and deafness, 1115
Van de Sande, W. S., ed. Black Americans information directory, 360
Van Nostrand's scientific encyclopedia, D. M. Considine and G. D. Considine, eds., 828
Van Vynckt, R. J., ed. International dictionary of architects and architecture, 1276
Van Zandt, E. Reader's Digest complete book of cross stitch and counted thread techniques, 1457
Vance, L. E., and E. M. Tracey. Illustration index, 2d ed., 1236
Vandervoort, D. Home Magazine's how your house works, 1185
Vare, E. A., and G. Ptacek. Mothers of invention, 848
Variety's directory of major U.S. show business awards, M. Kaplan, ed., 1314
Vegetarian Times complete cookbook, Editors of Vegetarian Times and L. Moll, 1140
Veilleux, R. F., ed. Dictionary of manufacturing terms, 998
Venomous reptiles of North America, C. H. Ernst, 996
Venture Economics staff, eds. Pratt's guide to venture capital sources, 506
Ver Nooy, W. *See* Logasa, H.
Vertical file index, 116
Video movie guide, M. Martin and M. Porter, 1337
Video source book, 1338
VideoHound's family video retriever, 1339
VideoHound's golden movie retriever, 1337, 1338n
Vietnam War almanac, H. G. Summers Jr., 1823
Viking opera guide, A. Holden et al., eds., 1407
Viking opera guide on CD-ROM, A. Holden, ed., 1407n
Vila, B. Bob Vila's toolbox, 1189
Vincent, M. Cultural atlas of Spain and Portugal, 1894
Vinson, J., ed. Twentieth-century western writers, 1729
———, and D. Kirkpatrick, eds. Contemporary foreign language writers, 1637; Great foreign language writers, 1637
Visual arts research, E. B. Pollard, 1231
Visual dictionary of American domestic architecture, R. Carley, 1278
Visual dictionary of architecture, F. D. K. Ching, 1279
Vital statistics on Congress, N. J. Ornstein et al., 640
VNR dictionary of civil engineering, J. S. Scott, 955
Vogue/Butterick step-by-step guide to sewing techniques, 1471
Vogue knitting, 1461
Voice of youth advocates, 31
Volberding, P. A. *See* Cohen, P. T.
Voodoo in Haiti, A. Metraux, 261

Waggonere, S. *See* Markel, R.
Wagner, J. Building a multi-use barn, 1161
Wakelyn, J. L. Biographical dictionary of the Confederacy, 1848
Waldman, C. Atlas of the North American Indian, 1784
———, and A. Wexler. Who was who in world exploration, 1852
Walford, A. J., and J. E. O. Screen, eds. Guide to foreign language courses and dictionaries, 780
———, M. Mullay, and P. Schlicke, eds. Walford's guide to reference material, v.1, 23
Walford's guide to reference material, v.1, A. J. Walford, M. Mullay, and P. Schlicke, eds., 23
Walford's guide to reference material, v.2, A. Day and J. M. Harvey, eds., 23
Walker, B. Hindu world, 253
Walker, B. G. Charted knitting designs, 1460; Second treasury of knitting patterns, 1460; Treasury of knitting patterns, 1460
Walker, B. K. *See* Walker, W. S.
Walker, D. *See* McMullin, T. A.

Walker, J., and T. Tyler. Columbia guide to online style, 773
Walker, John. *See* Halliwell, L.
Walker, L. American shelter, 1270, 1278n
Walker, P. M. B., ed. Chambers dictionary of biology, 974; Chambers nuclear energy and radiation dictionary, 927
———, et al., eds. Cambridge air and space dictionary, 936
Walker, W. S., comp. Twentieth-century short story explication: interpretations, 1900–1975, 1703
———, and B. K. Walker. Twentieth-century short story explication, 1703
Walkowicz, C. *See* Wilcox, B.
Wall Street Journal, 118n, 449n
Wallechinsky, D. Complete book of Winter Olympics, 1576; Sports Illustrated presents the complete book of the Summer Olympics, 1576
Walter Breen's complete encyclopedia of U.S. and colonial coins, W. Breen, 1486
Walters, L., ed. Bibliography of bioethics, 280
Walton, J., et al., eds. Oxford companion to medicine, 1045
Walton, J. B. Business profitability data, 485
Ward, P., ed. Oxford companion to Spanish literature, 1771
Ward, R. J. *See* Hoffmann, F. W.
Ward's business directory of U.S. private and public companies, 482
Ware, D. *See* Stafford, M.
Warman's antiques and collectibles price guide, E. T. Schroy, ed., 1480
Warner, D. J. *See* Bud, R.
Warr, W., and C. Suhr. Chemical information management, 879
Warrack, J., and E. West. Oxford dictionary of opera, 1406
Warren, A. *See* Allan, T.
Washington information directory, 598n, 600
Washington Post, 118n
Waskow, A. I. Seasons of our joy, 238
Wasserman, M., ed. Literature analysis of microcomputer publications, 895
Wasserman, S. R. *See* O'Brien, J. W.
Wasserstein, B. *See* Grenville, J. A. S.
Watson, A. A. Hand tools, 1475
We the people, J. P. Allen and E. J. Turner, 356
Weapons, 1028
Weast, R. C., ed. CRC handbook of chemistry and physics, student ed., 887n
Weather almanac, F. Bair, ed., 922
Weather America, A. N. Garwood, ed., 923
Weather of U.S. cities, F. E. Bair, ed., 924
Weber, O. S., and S. J. Calvert, eds. Literary and library prizes, 1617
Weber, R. D. *See* Schlachter, G. A.
Webster, J. J., ed. Encyclopedia of medical devices and instrumentation, 1038
Webster's new biographical dictionary, 1923n
Webster's new geographical dictionary, 1868
Webster's new world dictionary and thesaurus, 153n
Webster's new world dictionary of computer terms, D. D. Spencer, 902
Webster's new world dictionary of media and communications, R. Weiner, 1354
Webster's new world Hebrew dictionary, H. Baltsan, ed., 798
Webster's new world secretarial handbook, 540
Webster's third new international dictionary of the English language, P. B. Gove, ed., 717, 761n
Weekes, R. V., ed. Muslim peoples, 1865
Weekly compilation of presidential documents, 610n
Weight Watchers complete exercise book, J. Zimmer, 1552
Weik, M. H. Communications standard dictionary, 943
Weiner, E. *See* Simpson, J.
Weiner, E. S. C. *See* Simpson, J. A.
Weiner, R. Webster's new world dictionary of media and communications, 1354
Weinstein, S. *See* Torgeson, K. W.
Weiss, D. *See* Sommer, E.
Weissman, D. *See* Sandberg, L.
Weissman, P., L. McFadden, and T. Johnson, eds. Encyclopedia of the solar system, 873
Welch, R., and B. Stewart. Oxford companion to Irish literature, 1767
Well cat book, T. McGinnis, 1204
Wellness encyclopedia, Editors of the Univ. of California Wellness Letter, 1049
Wellness encyclopedia of food and nutrition, 1111
Well-tooled kitchen, F. Bridge and J. Tibbets, 1138
Wentworth, H., and S. B. Flexner, comps. and eds. Dictionary of American slang, 2d supplemented ed., 754n
Werblowsky, R. J. Z., and G. Wigoder. Oxford dictionary of the Jewish religion, 244
———, ———, eds. Encyclopedia of the Jewish religion, 234
Wertsman, V. F. Librarian's companion, 87
West, C. *See* Salzman, J.
West, E. *See* Warrack, J.
Westby, B. M., ed. List of subject headings, 1306n
Westminster dictionary of Christian ethics, J. F. Childress and J. Macquarrie, eds., 286
West's encyclopedia of American law, 569n, 578
Wetterau, B. Congressional Quarterly's desk reference on American government, 583
Wexler, A. *See* Waldman, C.
Whales, dolphins, and porpoises, M. Carwardine, 997

Wheeler M., et al., eds. Oxford Russian dictionary, 807
When technology fails, N. Schlager, ed., 829
Whitaker, C. S., ed. Alternative publications, 46
Whitaker, J. Whitaker's almanack, 111
Whitaker's almanack, J. Whitaker, 111
Whitburn, J. Billboard book of top forty hits, 1415
White, J. R., ed. Sports rules encyclopedia, 1500
Whitefield, P., ed. Human body explained, 1090
Whiteley, S., ed. American Library Association guide to information access, 1; Purchasing an encyclopedia, 147
Whiting, B. J., comp. Modern proverbs and proverbial sayings, 1628
Whitnah, D. R., ed. Government agencies, 585
Whitten, P. *See* Hunter, D. E.
Whittick, A., ed. Encyclopedia of urban planning, 417
Who to call: the parent's source book, D. Starer, 1198
Who was who in America, 1926
Who was who in the Greek world, D. Bowder, ed., 1927
Who was who in the Roman world, D. Bowder, ed., 1927
Who was who in the theatre, 1312n
Who was who in world exploration, C. Waldman and A. Wexler, 1852
Who was who on screen, E. M. Truitt, 1343
Whole Internet user's guide and catalog, E. Krol, 911
Who's who, 1928
Who's who among African Americans, 373
Who's who among Hispanic Americans, 386
Who's who in America, 1926n, 1929
Who's who in American art, 1269
Who's who in American education, 704
Who's who in American law, 604
Who's who in American music, 1413
Who's who in American politics, 605
Who's who in economics, M. Blaug, ed., 548
Who's who in finance and industry, 549
Who's who in space, M. Cassutt, 941
Who's who in technology, A. Unterberger, ed., 840
Who's who in the Bible, P. Calvocoressi, ed., 198
Who's who in the theatre, 1312n
Who's who in the world, 1930
Who's who of American women, 422
Who's who of religions, 178
Who's who of sports champions, R. Hickok, 1512
Whyld, K. *See* Hooper, D.
Wicca, S. Cunningham, 262
Wichtl, M. Herbal drugs and phytopharmaceuticals, 1103
Wiechmann, J. C., ed. NTC's dictionary of advertising, 531
Wiener, P. P., ed. Dictionary of the history of ideas, 161
Wigoder, G., ed. New standard Jewish encyclopedia, 243; *see also* Werblowsky, R. J. Z.
Wilcox, B., and C. Walkowicz. Atlas of dog breeds of the world, 1208
Wilcox, R. T. Dictionary of costume, 1284; Five centuries of American costume, 1286
Wilde, W. H., et al. Oxford companion to Australian literature, 1759
Wilkes, J. A., ed. Encyclopedia of architecture, 1274
William Shakespeare, J. F. Andrews, ed., 1744
Williams, P. L., et al., eds. Gray's anatomy, 1088
Williams, P. W. *See* Lippy, C. H.
Williams, T., ed. Collins biographical dictionary of scientists, 838
Williams, W. J. *See* Cheney, F. N.
Willinger, D., ed. CRC standard mathematical tables and formulae, 1002
Willis, A., and B. Jacobstein. America suburbs rating guide and fact book, 1872
Willis, J. Screen world, 1341
———, ed. Theatre world, 1378
Willis, R., ed. World mythology, 279
Wilmes, D. R. *See* Levernier, J. A.
Wilmeth, D. B., and T. L. Miller, eds. Cambridge guide to American theatre, 1369
Wilson, C. Chemical exposure and human health, 886
Wilson, C. R., and W. Ferris, eds. Encyclopedia of southern culture, 1861
Wilson, F. P., ed. Oxford dictionary of English proverbs, 1630
Wilson, K. G. Columbia guide to standard American English, 739
Winks, R. W., and M. Corrigan, eds. Mystery and suspense writers, 1689
Winston, M. R. *See* Logan, R. W.
Wiren, G. *See* PGA staff
Witt, E. Congressional Quarterly's guide to the U.S. Supreme Court, 625
Woelfel, C. J., ed. Fitzroy Dearborn encyclopedia of banking and finance, 502
Wolman, B. B., comp. and ed. Dictionary of behavioral science, 292
———, ed. International encyclopedia of psychiatry, psychology, psychoanalysis and neurology, 297
Woman's body, M. Stoppard, ed., 1122
Woman's guide to coping with disability, 1123
Women in chemistry and physics, L. S. Grinstein et al., eds., 893
Women in science, M. B. Ogilvie, 841
Women in the world, J. Seager and A. Olson, 423
Women's atlas of the United States, T. H. Fast and C. C. Fast, 424

Women's book of world records and achievements, L. D. O'Neill, 425
Women's complete healthbook, R. P. Epps and S. C. Stewart, eds., 1122
Women's information directory, S. Brennan, ed., 426
Women's sports encyclopedia, R. Markel, S. Waggonere, and M. Smith, eds., 1498
Wood, C. Complete rhyming dictionary and poet's craft book, 745
Wood, D., ed. Brands and their companies, 458
Woodall's campground directory, 1911
Woodbury, M. Childhood information resources, 344
Woods, C. Encyclopedia of perennials, 860
Words of mathematics, S. Schwartzman, 1009
Words on cassette, 59
Words to rhyme with, W. R. Espy, 747
Working with wood, P. Korn, 1477
World almanac and book of facts, 112
World atlas of archaeology, 430
World atlas of geomorphic features, 1867n
World book encyclopedia, D. W. Jacobs, ed., 157
World chamber of commerce directory, 483
World directory of minorities, Minority Rights Group, 438
World encyclopedia of cities, 1869
World encyclopedia of comics, M. Horn, ed., 1246n, 1258
World encyclopedia of parliaments and legislatures, G. T. Kurian, ed., 594
World encyclopedia of soccer, M. L. LaBlanc and R. Henshaw, 1593
World explorers and discoverers, R. Bohlander, ed., 1853
World factbook, Central Intelligence Agency, 1880
World guide to abbreviations of organizations, 726
World history, 1824
World motor vehicle data, 1015n
World mythology, R. Willis, ed., 279
World of Buddhism, H. Bechert and R. F. Gombrich, 263
World of invention, B. Travers and J. Muhr, eds., 830
World of learning, 84, 668
World of scientific discovery, B. Travers and J. Muhr, eds., 851
World painting index, P. P. Havlice, 1241
World philosophy, F. N. Magill, ed., 167
World press encyclopedia, G. T. Kurian, ed., 101
World radio TV handbook, 1358
World religions from ancient history to the present, G. Parrinder, ed., 179
World resources 1996–97, World Resources Institute staff, 971
World Resources Institute staff. World resources 1996–97, 971
Worldmark encyclopedia of the nations, 1870
Worldmark encyclopedia of the states, 1871
World's major languages, B. Comrie, ed., 711
World's master paintings, C. Wright, comp., 1264
Woy, J., ed. Encyclopedia of business information sources, 443
Wright, C., comp. World's master paintings, 1264
Wright, J. American almanac of jobs and salaries, 550
Wright, J. W., ed. Universal almanac, 110
———, and L. Sunshine. Best hospitals in America, 1052
Wright, R. S., III. Genealogist's handbook, 1947
Writers for children, J. M. Bingham, ed., 1671
Writer's market, 94
Wyatt, A. *See* Challinor, J.
Wyckoff, T., ed. Directory of business periodical special issues, 442
Wyler, S. B. Book of old silver, English, American, foreign, 1289
Wyman, B. *See* Stevenson, L. H.
Wynar, B. S., ed. American reference books annual, 2; Best reference books 1986–1990, 2
Wyngarden, J., ed. Cecil textbook of medicine, 1035
Wynn, R., ed. All music guide to jazz, 1441

Yaakov, J., ed. Short story index: collections indexed, 1900–1978, 1702
Yale Daily News staff, eds. Insider's guide to the colleges, 678n, 682
Yale University School of Medicine patient's guide to medical tests, B. L. Zaret, ed., 1077
Yarwood, D. Encyclopedia of world costume, 1285
Yearbook of American and Canadian churches, C. H. Jacquet, ed., 224
Yearbook of the United Nations, M. Nijhoff, 595
Year-round house care, G. Blackburn, 1171
Yepsen, R., ed. Adding on, 1166
York, H. E. Political science, 557
Young, M., ed. Guinness book of sports records, 1505
Young, S. New comprehensive American rhyming dictionary, 746
Your investments, 515n

Zakalik, J., and S. Burak, eds. Gale guide to Internet databases, 909
Zand, J., et al. Smart medicine for a healthier child, 1098
Zangwill, O. L. *See* Gregory, R. L.
Zaret, B. L., ed. Yale University School of Medicine patient's guide to medical tests, 1077
Zentner, C., and F. Bedurftig, eds. Encyclopedia of the Third Reich, 1811

Zeyl, D. J., ed. Encyclopedia of classical philosophy, 162
Zia, H., and S. B. Gall, eds. Notable Asian Americans, 378
Zimmer, J. Weight Watchers complete exercise book, 1552
Zimmerman, D. R. Zimmerman's complete guide to nonprescription drugs, 1107
Zimmerman's complete guide to nonprescription drugs, D. R. Zimmerman, 1107
Ziring, L., et al. International relations dictionary, 574
Zondervan pictorial encyclopedia of the Bible, M. C. Tenney and S. Barabas, eds., 194
Zophy, A. H., ed. Handbook of American women's history, 1827
Zumerchick, J., ed. Encyclopedia of sports science, 1501
Zwirn, J., comp. Accessing U.S. government information, 132